THE
CIVIL WAR
ALMANAC

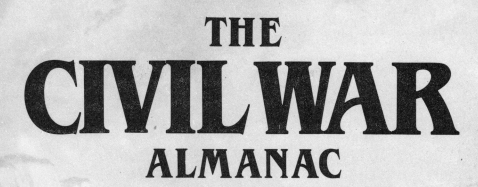

THE
CIVIL WAR
ALMANAC

Introduction by Henry Steele Commager

EXECUTIVE EDITOR: *John S Bowman*

TECHNICAL CONSULTANTS
Naval: Antony Preston / *Weapons:* Ian Hogg

WORLD ALMANAC PUBLICATIONS
NEW YORK, NEW YORK

A Bison Book

First published in 1983

Distributed by St. Martin's Press.

Library of Congress Catalog Card
Number: 82-61819

Newspaper Enterprise Association
ISBN: 0-88687-401-7
        0-88687-400-9 (Canada)

Printed in the United States of America
World Almanac
An Imprint of Pharos Books
A Scripps Howard Company
200 Park Avenue
New York, New York 10166

CONTENTS

INTRODUCTION

How do we explain the perennial interest in the American Civil War? It has been more than a century now since that war ended in the farmhouse at Appomattox. But the fires of interest, if not of hostility, still burn and the stories of battles and leaders, and of the suffering and heroism of Johnny Reb and Billy Yank still have the power to elicit fascination and passion.

There are many explanations for this. The Civil War was, in many ways, the last of the old wars and the first of the new. It was General Sherman who said that 'war is hell', and none will dispute that judgment. Yet to most Americans General Sherman's war has been, and still is, almost irresistibly romantic. The very names of this conflict, whether Civil War, or War Between the States or War for Southern Independence, conjure up a hundred images: Jackson standing like a 'stone wall' at 1st Bull Run (First Manassas); U S Grant becoming 'unconditional surrender' Grant; Lee upon Traveller saying, 'It is well that war is so terrible, or we should get too fond of it'; A P Hill, after a 30-mile march, breaking through the wheatfields at Antietam to save the day; Thomas standing like a rock at Chickamauga; Pickett's men streaming up the long slope of Cemetery Ridge, only to be mowed down by Union cannon; Farragut lashed to the mast at Mobile Bay, shouting 'Damn the torpedoes, full steam ahead'; Colonel Shaw leading his black regiment, the 54th Massachusetts, in a desperate charge against Fort Wagner, and dying on the ramparts; Sheridan pounding down the Winchester Pike; Lincoln pardoning the sleeping sentinels, reading Artemus Ward to his Cabinet, dedicating the cemetery at Gettysburg, greeted by thousands of frantic blacks as he walks the streets of conquered Richmond, and, in the end, invoking 'with malice toward none with Charity for all.' It is romantic because of the youthfulness of so many of its officers and soldiers, and the desperate devotion of so many of them who seemed to have no real stake in the issues.

The plain farmers of the South fighting for slavery, the German and Irish and Norwegian regiments fighting for their adopted country, and, by contrast, the

The bombardment of Port Royal, South Carolina, August 1861.

blacks (200 thousand of them, no less) enlisting in the struggle for freedom.

It was almost the last war which was fought on foot, where soldiers marched, and marched to songs that have become part of our heritage: 'John Brown's Body', 'Lorena', 'Dixieland', 'Marching Through Georgia'; and it still boasts a body of literature which no other war has produced, from Whitman's *Drum-Taps*, and Timrod's 'Ode to the Confederate Dead' and Lowell's noble 'Harvard Commemmoration Ode' to 20th century poetry and novels such as Benet's *John Brown's Body*, Margaret Mitchell's *Gone With The Wind*, Stark Young's *So Red The Rose* and MacKinlay Kantor's *Long Remember*. In Douglas Freeman's *Lee* and Carl Sandburg's *Lincoln*, it inspired the greatest scholarly and the most poetic of American biographies, and in Allan Nevin's *Ordeal Of The Union* one of the masterpieces of historical literature.

The Civil War was, too, almost the last war where combatants, on both sides, cherished notions of chivalry. That came readily enough to southern planters who thought of themselves as descendents of the Normans and played at being knights in armor. It was to be found equally in the soldiers in blue. Listen to General Joshua Chamberlain of the 20th Maine describing the Confederate surrender:

Before us in proud humiliation stood the embodiment of manhood: men whom neither toils and suffering nor the fact of death, nor disaster, nor hopelessness could bend from their resolve; standing before us now thin, worn, and famished, but erect, and with eyes looking level into ours, waking memories that bound us together as no other bond: was not such manhood to be welcomed back into a union so tested and assured? How could we help falling on our knees, all of us together, and praying God to pity and forgive us all?

Yet, too, the Civil War has some claim to being the first modern war, the first to approach—certainly in the South—what we now call 'Total War'; the first in which ironclad warships and submarines fought; the first where soldiers dug trenches and

put up wire entanglements; the first in which reconnaissance of enemy positions from balloons was made; the first to depend on railroads—and the destruction of which witnessed an even partial (and not very successful) attempt to control the national economy; the first in which blockades proved effective; the first where information and orders could be transmitted by telegraph. And if the Civil War produced in Lee a romantic commander who would himself lead a battlefield charge against the enemy, it produced also in Sherman and Grant modern generals whose tactics and strategy rested on continuous hammer-blows and on the destruction of enemy economy.

There is, too, a deeper explanation of our persistent interest in the Civil War: that it concerned issues not only of national, but of global importance, and that it settled these issues and settled them—as far as we now know—correctly. The first of these was the survival of the most interesting of all experiments in modern history—a nation which made, or contrived, itself. Could a nation 'so conceived and so dedicated . . . long endure'? No other nation had ever been created (Lincoln's phrase 'brought forth' is accurate); all others had grown over the centuries. And no other nation at that time had been created from below rather than organized from above—created, too, by an enlightened people, and 'dedicated to the proposition that all men are created equal'. No wonder that, in the 1860's, the whole of the Western World anxiously awaited the answer to that question of survival.

The second issue was, like the first, put most eloquently by Lincoln: could the nation endure 'half slave and half free'? Would a nation, dedicated in theory to freedom and equality, but still mired in slavery, be able to emancipate, not only the slaves, but itself from thralldom?

Not many wars can plead such persuasive justification. What, after all, was the Spanish-American war about; what was the War of the Philippines about; what was the Vietnam War about? Were any of these necessary, or even justifiable? But we know, without doubt, what the Civil War was about: it was about union and freedom. And we know that the war settled (dare we say once and for all) the question of union. We know too that it settled, at least legally, the question of slavery. Here, too, the whole world was an interested party: would the people who had pioneered freedom and equality at last vindicate their commitment to these noble goals? We are still working out an answer to that question, but we can be certain that, thanks to the Union Victory, the answer will eventually be that it can, and will.

This Almanac does not purport to be either a narrative or an interpretation of the Civil War. We have enough of these in battle histories, biographies, monographs and dramas. What the Almanac provides is something at once practical and—shall we say—disciplined: a combination of a chronology, a statistical record, a biographical dictionary, and an atlas. It is an encyclopedia which strives for accuracy, thoroughness and succinctness. Every student will, I think, be impressed by how much is condensed into such limited space. No previous chapter of our history has been quite so elaborately recorded as the Civil War: 70 volumes of *The Official Record of the War of the Rebellion*, plus 30 volumes of naval records and voluminous state records, joined by a hundred regimental histories. Yet even with all this we are still baffled by the inadequacy of documentation. We do not, for example, know just how many soldiers fought in the Union or Confederate Armies. We do not have accurate figures on casualties (in this area Confederate figures are mostly guesswork), nor do we know how many soldiers deserted. Historians still quarrel over the effectiveness of the blockade; and the history of finances—particularly Confederate —is all but chaotic. Here and elsewhere we must settle for what we have.

Meanwhile the editors of this Almanac have done a heroic job of assembling whatever statistics are available, organizing them logically, and providing us with such factual background as seems relevant. They have done an equally impressive job in both the narrative and the biographical portions of the almanac, and in such special studies as weapons. For all this we must be grateful.

Henry Steele Commager
AMHERST, MASSACHUSETTS

JUNE, 1982

A Lincoln-Douglas Debate—1858.

A cotton plantation on the Mississippi.

CHRONOLOGY

CHRONOLOGY

The approach to war

AUGUST 1619

ENGLISH SETTLERS in Jamestown, Virginia, purchase 20 black Africans from a Dutch frigate. Although these particular Africans are treated as indentured servants, it is not long before European colonists in North America are treating black Africans as slaves: they are imported, bought, and sold as though material property, and their children are condemned to a life of slavery. Most of these black Africans are held in the Southern colonies, but many thousands are also held by Northerners—and many Northerners profit directly and indirectly from the slave trade. In the ensuing decades, as the number of slaves increases to hundreds of thousands, slavery itself evolves into a legally sanctioned system.

JULY 1776

THE DECLARATION OF INDEPENDENCE—with its resounding 'self-evident' truth 'that all men are created equal'—is adopted 4 July. It is largely the work of Thomas Jefferson, himself a slaveowner, and it will be signed by many men who are also slaveowners.

1780-1804

IN THE Northern states, various laws are passed and court decisions handed down that effectively abolish slavery. In the South, however, where slavery has become inextricably involved in the economy and total way of life, slavery remains legally sanctioned and sustained.

MAY-SEPTEMBER 1787

IN PHILADELPHIA, 55 delegates from 12 states (Rhode Island refuses to participate) meet to draw up a federal constitution for a United States. The resultant document is in many ways a compromise among various conflicting views—sectional, economic, social, philosophical, and otherwise. One of the major splits is between the Southern states and the Northern states over the issue of allowing slavery to continue. But several Southern states refuse to join in any union if slavery is not allowed, so despite the warning of George Mason, a delegate from Virginia, that slaves 'bring the judgment of Heaven on a country', the Constitution includes three clauses that effectively sanction the continuation of slavery: (1) Fugitive slaves are to be returned to their owners; (2) Slave trade (that is, new Africans from abroad) is to be permitted until 1808 and (3) For the purpose of apportioning Congressional representatives on the basis of population, a slave is to be counted as 3/5 of a white person. In the debate that ensues in the states, most of the Northerners as well as Southerners who are opposed to ratifying the Constitution are simply against placing so much power in a national government and denying powers to the states.

JULY 1787

MEETING in New York City as the fading government under the Articles of Confederation, the Congress passes its last major act, the Territorial, or Northwest, Ordinance. One of its clauses states that 'there shall be neither slavery nor involuntary servitude in said territory'. Although immediately applicable only to the territory that will eventually be subdivided into the states of Ohio, Indiana, Illinois, Michigan and Wisconsin, the ordinance comes to suggest a national policy of designating all new territories and states as 'free soil'—that is, as off limits to slavery.

DECEMBER 1791

THE FIRST ten amendments to the constitution—known as the Bill of Rights—are put into effect. They guarantee many individual rights but say nothing about slavery or the rights of black Americans.

OCTOBER 1793

ELI WHITNEY applies for a patent on a cotton gin, a device that greatly increases the speed and ease with which cotton fibers are separated from the seeds. This machine will soon increase the need for labor to produce more cotton, and since most of the cotton is grown in the Southern states, this will lead to the need for more slaves.

NOVEMBER-DECEMBER 1798

THE LEGISLATURES of Kentucky and Virginia adopt resolutions contending that the Alien and Sedition Acts are unconstitutional and that individual states retain the right to determine this. These Acts are passed in June and July by a Congress controlled by the Federalist Party desirous of restricting the growth and freedoms of the Jeffersonian Republicans. What is particularly significant is that these resolutions, defiant expressions of states' rights, were written by Thomas Jefferson and James Madison, both of whom would become President of the United States.

NOVEMBER 1799

THE KENTUCKY legislature passes another resolution reaffirming that of 1798 but adding that 'the remedy for [what states consider] infractions of the constitution' is 'nullification'.

AUGUST 1800

GABRIEL PROSSER, a black slave coachman, plans a revolt to liberate thousands of slaves in the Richmond, Virginia, area. On the day when the uprising is scheduled, a heavy thunderstorm washes away the bridge over which about a thousand armed slaves were to pass. Meanwhile, the state authorities have been following events thanks to an informer and they move in and arrest Prosser and many of his followers. Prosser and at least 37 others are executed. Although this is but one of more than 250 rebellions by slaves during some two centuries up to 1861, it is one of the more ambitious ones and convinces many Southerners that only strict measures can maintain the institution of slavery.

JANUARY 1808

FROM THE FIRST DAY of the new year, the importation of slaves from abroad into the United States is legally ended, as called for by the Constitution. But the buying and selling of slaves within the United States continues, and in practice many new slaves continue to be smuggled into the states. The enabling legislation itself provides that these smuggled slaves, when apprehended, are to be turned over to the state authorities and that the states may then sell the slaves.

DECEMBER 1814-JANUARY 1815

A NUMBER of prominent New Englanders, strongly opposed to the war that the United States has been fighting against England since 1812, gather for secret meetings in Hartford, Connecticut. Various propositions are considered, including seceding from the union, but by the end the only course those attending can agree on is to propose certain amendments to the Constitution. Meanwhile, on 14 December, the Treaty of Ghent is signed, ending the war, so the Hartford Convention's recommendations become moot. What is not moot, however, is the notion that representatives from a section of the United States might see their states' rights taking precedence over the union and its constitution.

DECEMBER 1816-JANUARY 1817

THE AMERICAN COLONIZATION SOCIETY is founded in Washington, DC to aid in settling freed slaves in Africa. Although it will eventually obtain indirect aid from the United States government and will aid in moving 11,000 blacks to the new African country of Liberia, the Society is by no means endorsed by either black Americans or white abolitionists. Many from both these groups see the goals of this Society as merely avoiding the issue of slavery and the

The first cotton gin.

rights of blacks in America.

JANUARY-MARCH 1820

THE HOUSE OF REPRESENTATIVES passes a bill calling for the admission of Maine to the United States. Since there are II free (that is, non-slave) states and II slave states, the admission of Maine as a free state would upset the balance that is jealously guarded by all parties in the union. Therefore, the Senate adopts a bill that combines the admission of Maine with the admission of Missouri as a slave state. In addition, the Senate adopts a further compromise, an amendment that would bar slavery in the rest of the Louisiana Purchase north of 36° 30' latitude. The House of Representatives then votes to accept the Senate bill with its amendment, and this becomes known as the Missouri Compromise.

MAY 1822

DENMARK VESEY, a former slave who had purchased his own freedom in 1800, is arrested, convicted and executed for planning an uprising of slaves in the area around Charleston, South Carolina. Vesey's original plan called for an attack on Charleston on a Sunday in July, a time when many white people would be out of the city. But Vesey is betrayed by a black slave and is apprehended before he and his followers can do much more than make a few weapons. Vesey is hanged along with 34 other blacks. As word of the planned revolt spreads, various slave states and border states pass 'black codes', laws greatly restricting the freedom of movement and general conduct of slaves.

MAY 1824

CONGRESS passes another Protective Tariff Law, but it still leaves the South feeling discriminated against even while Northern manufacturers are unsatisfied with it. By 1827, this law will have prompted such protests as the anti-tariff meeting in Columbia, South Carolina, where Thomas Cooper, president of South Carolina College, will ask: 'Is it worth while to continue this Union of States, where the North demands to be our masters and we are required to be their tributaries?'

APRIL-MAY 1828

CONGRESS passes another Tariff Law, one calling for relatively high duties on a variety of goods but affecting raw materials more than manufactured goods. The promoters of the bill are motivated at least in part by a desire to embarrass President John Quincy Adams, but he ends up signing it. Very soon it becomes known to Southerners as the 'tariff of abominations' and leads to widespread protests and demands by some that the Southern states separate from the union.

DECEMBER 1828

THE SOUTH CAROLINA legislature adopts a series of resolutions condemning the Tariff Act of 1828 and questioning its constitutionality. Appended to the formal resolutions is an unsigned essay, 'South Carolina Exposition and Protest', which argues that any federal laws considered unconstitutional may be 'nullified' by a state convention. What makes this Exposition of 1828 so significant, aside from its support for the absolute sovereignty of the individual states, is the fact that its author is John C Calhoun, previously a strong nationalist, and now the Vice-President of the United States. The Georgia legislature also adopts resolutions against the Tariff Act of 1828.

JANUARY 1830

THE SENATE is debating the issue of the sale of the vast lands of the American West, but it soon becomes apparent that the real subject under discussion is that of states' rights versus federal power. This sets Southern Senators against Northern Senators, and in his ringing climax to his defense of the latter, Daniel Webster concludes, 'Liberty and Union, now and forever, one and inseparable!'

JANUARY 1831

WILLIAM LLOYD GARRISON, among the more radical of the abolitionists, begins publishing in Boston *The Liberator*, a newspaper dedicated to the abolition of slavery.

AUGUST 1831

NAT TURNER, a pious but radical slave preacher, leads an uprising of slaves in Southampton County, Virginia. At least 60 whites are killed before soldiers put down the rebellion. Turner and 12 of his followers are executed, while about 100 blacks are killed during the search for the rebels.

The discovery of Nat Turner.

JULY 1832

ANOTHER TARIFF ACT is adopted by Congress. Although more moderate than that of 1828, it still leaves the South dissatisfied.

NOVEMBER 1832

A SPECIAL STATE CONVENTION meets in South Carolina, one of the most outspoken of the Southern states, and adopts an ordinance that nullifies the Tariff Acts of 1828 and 1832. The South Carolina legislature then adopts measures to enforce this ordinance—even allowing for military preparations and secession if the Federal government resorts to force.

DECEMBER 1832

PRESIDENT JACKSON issues a proclamation —after reinforcing the Federal forts off Charleston—warning the people of South Carolina that no state can secede from the union 'because each secession . . . destroys the unity of a nation'.

JANUARY-MARCH 1833

IN THE UPROAR that follows President Jackson's proclamation, the South Carolina legislature defies 'King Jackson' and even raises a volunteer unit to repel any 'invasion'. Jackson then asks Congress to adopt a 'force bill' to enable him to enforce the provisions of the Tariff Acts of 1828 and 1832. But Henry Clay, always anxious to work out a compromise that will save the union, draws up a new tariff bill that is presented to the House of Representatives. The bill includes a gradual cutback in tariffs, and when word of its probable acceptance is passed to South Carolina, the legislature suspends its nullification ordinance. Congress then adopts both the tariff compromise and the force bill, and President Jackson signs them within 24 hours. The confrontation is averted.

DECEMBER 1833

THE AMERICAN ANTI-SLAVERY SOCIETY is organized due primarily to the efforts of

CHRONOLOGY

Arthur and Lewis Tappan, wealthy New York City merchants, and Theodore Weld, a prominent abolitionist minister. Weld, through his writings and speeches, will continue to play a major role in convincing many Americans of the necessity and justice of abolishing slavery.

OCTOBER 1835

IN BOSTON, a mob parades William Lloyd Garrison through the streets with a rope around his neck to express their disgust with his extreme views on slavery. And in Utica, New York, people meeting to organize an anti-slavery society are attacked by a mob (said to be led by a judge and a congressman).

DECEMBER 1835

SANTA ANNA, President of Mexico, proclaims a unified constitution for all territories of Mexico. The North American settlers in Texas announce that they intend to secede from Mexico rather than give up their 'right' to slavery, which Mexico had abolished.

FEBRUARY-MARCH 1836

SANTA ANNA leads the siege of the Alamo, where 182 Texans are finally killed when the Mexicans overwhelm the fort. The heroic defense, however, inspires the North American settlers to meet in a convention, declare their independence, and draft a constitution.

APRIL 1836

UNDER GENERAL SAM HOUSTON, Texans defeat the Mexicans and capture Santa Anna at the battle of San Jacinto. The Texans ratify their own constitution, elect Sam Houston as President, and send an envoy to Washington to demand annexation to the United States or recognition of the independent Republic of Texas. Since they intend to legalize slavery in any case, the debate that follows in Congress once again pits pro-slavery Southerners against anti-slavery Northerners.

MAY 1836

SOUTHERN MEMBERS of the House of Representatives get a majority to vote for a 'gag' resolution, one that declares that all petitions or papers that in any way involve the issue of slavery should be 'laid on the table'—that is, there should be no discussion. The House of Representatives will continue to vote such a 'gag rule' at the outset of every session until 1844, but instead of burying the issue of slavery it only sharpens the differences between the two sides.

MARCH 1837

ON HIS LAST DAY IN OFFICE, President Jackson recognizes the independent Lone Star Republic of Texas. Jackson has been avoiding this decision for many months, not wanting to aggravate the problems that already separate the South and the North.

The death of Captain Ferrer of the Amistad.

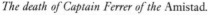

Union signal tower, 1861.

Torch signaling at Fredericksburg.

The Union forces charge.

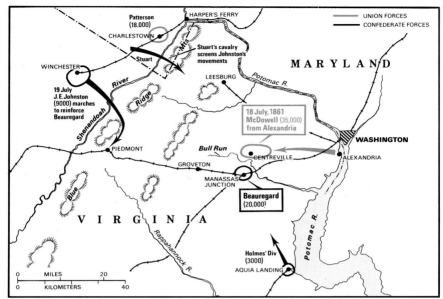

Bull Run (Manassas) 18 July 1861.

Beardslee magneto telegraph used by the Union.

Zouave troopers on picket guard, November 1861.

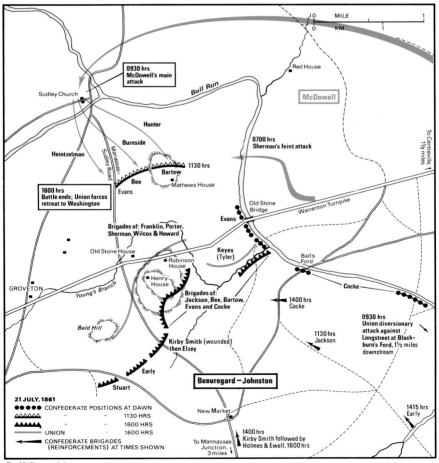

MILE

KM

Red House

McDowell

**0930 hrs
McDowell's main
attack**

Bull Run

Sudley Church

**0700 hrs
Sherman's feint attack**

Hunter

Burnside

To Centreville,
1½ miles

Heintzelman

Sudley Road

Manassas-

1130 hrs
Bartow

Bee

Mathews House

Evans

**1600 hrs
Battle ends; Union forces
retreat to Washington**

Old Stone
Bridge

Warrenton Turnpike

Evans

Brigades of: Franklin, Porter,
Sherman, Wilcox & Howard

Keyes
(Tyler)

Ball's
Ford

Old Stone House

Robinson
House

Cocke

GROVETON

Young's Branch

Henry
House

Brigades of:
Jackson, Bee, Bartow,
Evans and Cocke

**1400 hrs
Cocke**

**0930 hrs
Union diversionary
attack against
Longstreet at Black-
burn's Ford, 1½ miles
downstream**

Bald Hill

**1130 hrs
Jackson**

Kirby Smith (wounded)
then Elzey

Early

Beauregard – Johnston

Stuart

**1415 hrs
Early**

21 JULY, 1861

●●●●● CONFEDERATE POSITIONS AT DAWN
△△△△△ "   "   " 1130 HRS
▲▲▲▲▲ "   "   " 1600 HRS
——— UNION   1600 HRS
◢ CONFEDERATE BRIGADES
(REINFORCEMENTS) AT TIMES SHOWN

New Market

1400 hrs
Kirby Smith followed by
Holmes & Ewell, 1600 hrs

To Mannassas
Junction,
3 miles

Bull Run (Manassas) 21 July 1861.

Zouave troopers rest, November 1861.

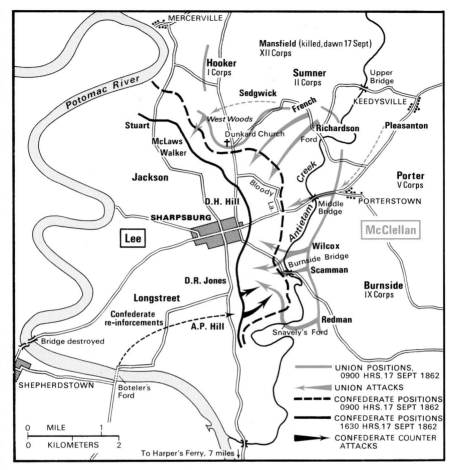

Sharpsburg, 17 September 1862.

A blockade runner ashore on the beach (1864).

21

General Sheridan on his famous ride.

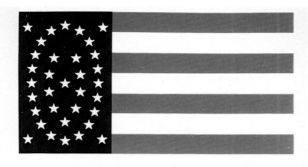

Chancellorsville, Gettysburg, 34-star flag.

Blockade runners on the move.

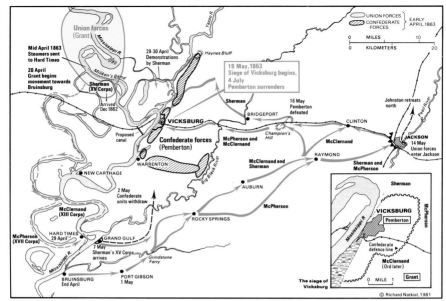

Map labels:

UNION FORCES
CONFEDERATE FORCES
EARLY APRIL, 1863

MILES
KILOMETERS

Yazoo R.

Union forces (Grant)

Mississippi R.

Mid April 1863
Steamers sent to Hard Times

20 April
Grant begins movement towards Bruinsburg

Milliken's Bend

29-30 April
Demonstrations by Sherman

Haynes Bluff

Sherman (XV Corps)

Arrived Dec 1862

19 May, 1863
Siege of Vicksburg begins, 4 July Pemberton surrenders

Sherman

BRIDGEPORT

16 May
Pemberton defeated

CLINTON

Johnston retreats north

Pearl River

JACKSON
14 May
Union forces enter Jackson

VICKSBURG

Proposed canal

Confederate forces (Pemberton)

McPherson and McClernand

Champion's Hill

McClernand

WARRENTON

Big Black River

McClernand and Sherman

RAYMOND

Sherman and McPherson

NEW CARTHAGE

2 May
Confederate units withdraw

AUBURN

McClernand (XIII Corps)

McPherson

ROCKY SPRINGS

McPherson (XVII Corps)

HARD TIMES
29 April

GRAND GULF

7 May
Sherman's XV Corps arrives

Grindstone Ferry

Mississippi R.

BRUINSBURG
End April

PORT GIBSON
1 May

Inset:
Sherman
VICKSBURG
Pemberton
Mississippi R.
McPherson
Confederate defence line
McClernand (Ord later)
Grant
The siege of Vicksburg
MILE

© Richard Natkiel, 1981

Vicksburg and its seige.

The Union assault at Vicksburg 19 May 1863.

A Union recruiting poster, 1863.

David Glasgow Farragut.

Farragut at the Battle of Mobile Bay, 5 August 1864.

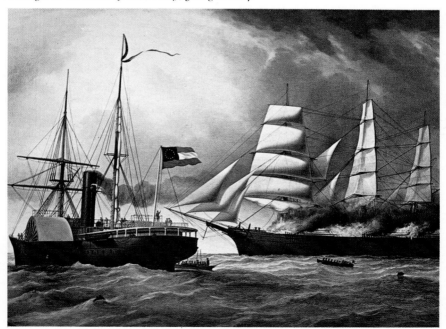

The Nashville *burning the merchant* Harvey Birch.

Yorktown 1864.

The third day of Gettysburg.

The Union Signal Corps using semaphore.

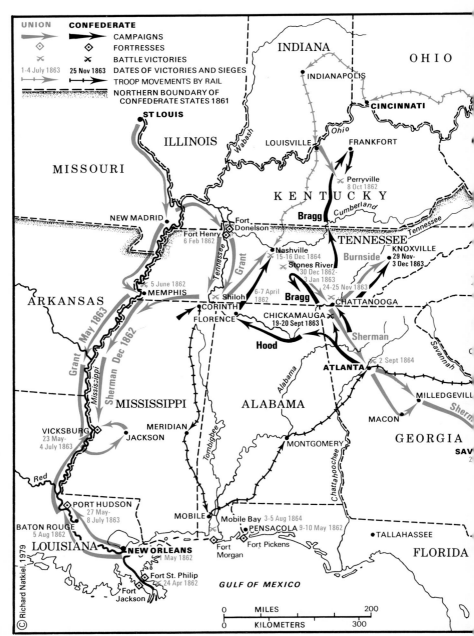

Left: The major campaigns of the Civil War.

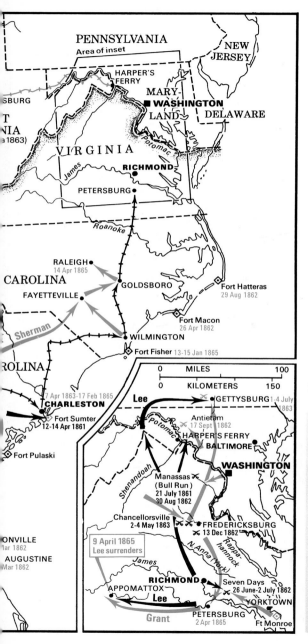

PENNSYLVANIA
Area of inset

NEW JERSEY

HARPER'S FERRY

MARY-
■ WASHINGTON
LAND
DELAWARE

...SBURG

...T
...NIA
(...a 1863)

VIRGINIA

Potomac

RICHMOND

PETERSBURG ●

Roanoke

James

RALEIGH ●
14 Apr 1865

CAROLINA

FAYETTEVILLE ●

GOLDSBORO

Fort Hatteras
29 Aug 1862

Sherman

Fort Macon
26 Apr 1862

●WILMINGTON

...ROLINA

◇ Fort Fisher 13-15 Jan 1865

0	MILES			100
0	KILOMETERS			150

...7 Apr 1863-17 Feb 1865
CHARLESTON

Lee

✕●GETTYSBURG 1-4 July
...863

◇ Fort Sumter
12-14 Apr 1861

Antietam
✕ 17 Sept 1862

HARPER'S FERRY

Potomac

BALTIMORE

◇ Fort Pulaski

WASHINGTON

Shenandoah

Manassas ✕
(Bull Run)
21 July 1861
30 Aug 1862

Chancellorsville
2-4 May 1863 ✕● FREDERICKSBURG
✕ 13 Dec 1862

...ONVILLE
...1ar 1862

9 April 1865
Lee surrenders

James

N.Anna (York)

Rappa
hannock

...AUGUSTINE
...Mar 1862

RICHMOND ●

APPOMATTOX
Lee

Seven Days
✕ 26 June-2 July 1862

YORKTOWN

Grant

PETERSBURG
2 Apr 1865

Ft Monroe

Below: A Civil War Campaign Medal.

31

A Union recruiting poster.

This leaves a union of 13 free states and 13 slave states, but of the large territories that remain to be converted into states, only one—Florida—is controlled by slave-holders, while three non-slave territories still exist. A movement to admit Texas as a 'slave territory' to balance out these free territories is defeated.

AUGUST 1839

THE SPANISH SLAVE-SHIP *Amistad*, carrying 53 African slaves between two Cuban ports, is taken over in a mutiny led by Cinque, one of the slaves. They kill the captain and the crew except for two who are forced to navigate the ship to North American waters, where a United States warship brings the *Amistad* into a Connecticut port. Spain immediately demands that the slaves be turned back to the Spaniards, but Americans force the case into the courts. Eventually it will be taken all the way to the Supreme Court, where John Quincy Adams argues for their right to be freed. In March 1841 the Supreme Court rules this way, and Cinque and the others are returned to Africa.

APRIL 1841

WILLIAM HENRY HARRISON, ninth President of the United States, dies after one month in office and is succeeded by his Vice-President, John Tyler. When Tyler declares a Sunday as a 'day of national prayer', various speakers use the occasion to speak out on the issue of slavery. One minister in the South is reported as taking the occasion to preach on 'current wild notions of equality'.

JANUARY 1842

THE UNITED STATES SUPREME COURT rules, in *Prigg v. Commonwealth of Pennsylvania*, that a Pennsylvania law forbidding the seizure of fugitive slaves in that state is unconstitutional. But the opinion goes on to state that the enforcement of fugitive slave laws is entirely a Federal responsibility, so various Northern states use this as a

Anti-abolitionist tract—1831.

loophole and adopt personal liberty laws.

APRIL 1844

A TREATY AGREEING to the annexation of Texas to the United States, negotiated by John C Calhoun, now Secretary of State, is signed and President Tyler submits it to the Senate.

JUNE 1844

THE TEXAS ANNEXATION TREATY is rejected by the Senate, where antislavery forces convince a majority that admitting a slave state will simply lead to another confrontation between the South and the North.

NOVEMBER 1844

JAMES K. POLK defeats Henry Clay for the Presidency. Polk is virtually an unknown politician, but his somewhat aggressive-expansionist views on acquiring Texas, Oregon and California strike a receptive chord among Americans. He owes his very nomination, in part, to the fact that the more obvious Democratic candidate, Martin Van Buren, had earlier in the year published a letter opposing the annexation of Texas. Clay had published a similar letter, and it is agreed that this contributed to his defeat.

FEBRUARY-MARCH 1845

THE HOUSE OF REPRESENTATIVES and the Senate, acting on the proposal of President-elect Polk, adopt a joint resolution for the annexation of Texas. This is essentially a procedure to bypass the requirement of a 2/3 vote of the Senate alone, traditionally used to ratify a treaty. The resolution also authorizes the President to negotiate a new treaty with Texas that could be approved by either procedure, but the President does not immediately exercise this choice. Mexico, however, severs diplomatic relations with the United States as soon as the resolution is adopted.

JULY 1845

TEXAS FORMALLY AGREES to annexation, so President Polk simply decides to treat it as a state, even though it remains Mexican territory under international law. Polk sends a detachment of the United States army, led by General Zachary Taylor, to the southwestern border of Texas to guard the state against an 'invasion' from Mexico.

MARCH-APRIL 1846

GENERAL TAYLOR takes his troops onto the left bank of the Rio Grande, always recognized as Mexican territory, on the orders of President Polk. Despite Mexico's evident desire to find some face-saving way of negotiating its way out of an armed conflict, President Polk persists in seeking an excuse for a war. It comes in late April when a small Mexican cavalry unit inflicts a few casualties on United States troops blockading a Mexican town.

MAY 1846

AT THE REQUEST of President Polk, Congress approves a declaration stating that 'By the act of the Republic of Mexico, a state of war exists between that Government and the United States'. But in the debate leading up to this declaration, and in the months to follow, it is clear that this war with Mexico is yet another divisive issue between the North and the South: Southerners tend to support the war as they see it leading to more territory to be worked by slaves, while Northerners oppose the war for that very reason.

JUNE 1846

NORTH AMERICAN SETTLERS in California, long seeking to break away from the rule of Mexico, proclaim the existence of the Republic of California. Meanwhile, there has long been simmering a dispute between the United States and Great Britain over the border between the Oregon Territory and Canada. President Polk, anxious to gain support for the widening war with Mexico, submits to the Senate a treaty that extends the international boundary along latitude 49° to Puget Sound and then to the ocean through the Juan de Fuca Strait. In return for Southern support for the treaty, President Polk agrees to reduce certain tariffs. The Senate ratifies the treaty.

AUGUST 1846

PRESIDENT POLK asks Congress to appropriate $2 million to help purchase territory from Mexico in negotiations that he assumes will follow any fighting. The appropriation bill comes to the House where it is amended to include what is known as the Wilmot Proviso, so named after an otherwise obscure Pennsylvania Representative, David Wilmot, who introduces the amendment. Using words taken verbatim from the Northwest Ordinance of 1787, the Wilmot Proviso states that 'neither slavery nor involuntary servitude shall ever exist in any part of' the territories that might be acquired from Mexico. The House passes the appropriation with this amendment, but the lines between Northerners and Southerners are once more sharply drawn.

FEBRUARY-MARCH 1847

THE SENATE takes up the appropriation bill with the Wilmot Proviso, and ends up passing the former without the latter. The House then approves the Senate version of the appropriation bill, so that the question of slavery within the territories remains open. But during the Senate's debate on the Wilmot Proviso, John Calhoun introduces four resolutions that attempt to provide justification for the Southern position.

Essentially Calhoun argues that Congress has no right to limit existent or prospective states in matters of laws pertaining to slavery. Furthermore, since slaves are like any property that might be taken into a territory, Congress has the obligation to protect slavery. Calhoun's doctrine effectively sets aside the Missouri Compromise of 1820, and although the Senate in no way endorses it, the doctrine is in the air.

SEPTEMBER 1847

GENERAL WINFIELD SCOTT marches victorious into Mexico City after a whirlwind campaign since landing at Vera Cruz in May.

DECEMBER 1847

SENATOR LEWIS CASS of Michigan, in a letter to A P Nicholson, a Tennessee politician, sets forth the doctrine that slavery should be left to the decision of the territorial government. Because Cass is an influential politician—he will run for President in 1848—his proposal is given serious consideration. It will become known as the doctrine of 'popular sovereignty' and will attract many supporters anxious to sidestep either the constitutional or the moral issues of slavery.

FEBRUARY 1848

THE UNITED STATES signs the Treaty of Guadalupe Hidalgo, ending the war with Mexico. The United States gets over 500,000 square miles that include what will become the states of California, Nevada, Utah, most of New Mexico and Arizona, and parts of Wyoming and Colorado. Texas is also conceded to the United States, with the boundary at the Rio Grande. This makes the United States a transcontinental republic, but it also opens up new land to be disputed by pro- and anti-slavery forces.

MARCH 1848

THE SENATE ratifies the treaty, and President Polk gets an appropriation bill to pay Mexico—but without the Wilmot Proviso.

AUGUST 1848

PRESIDENT POLK signs the bill organizing the Oregon Territory without slavery. The bill has passed with the support of Southern Senators, who clearly are willing to concede Oregon to the 'free-soilers' with the understanding that other territory belongs to the slaveholders.

NOVEMBER 1848

ZACHARY TAYLOR, hero of the Mexican War, is elected President. Taylor is a slaveholder but is not especially committed to the principle of slavery.

SEPTEMBER-OCTOBER 1849

CALIFORNIANS GATHER at a convention in Monterey and adopt a constitution that establishes a state forbidding slavery. They then ask for admission into the Union.

DECEMBER 1849

PRESIDENT TAYLOR asks Congress to admit California as a state. Southerners object because as another free state, this will leave the slave states in a minority. There is talk again among some, such as Calhoun, of secession, but Taylor says he will crush secession even if he himself has to take to the field again.

JANUARY 1850

THE AGING SENATOR HENRY CLAY, who has dedicated his career to preserving the Union, is annoyed at the extremists from both the South and North who threaten to resort to force. He offers to the Senate a series of resolutions that he hopes all sides can agree to. The resolutions involve admitting California as a free state on the grounds that this is its people's own wish; meanwhile, no decision will be made at this time in regard to slavery in the other territory gained from Mexico—but the clear implication is that it will later be made according to the settlers' wishes. Other topics in Clay's resolutions include a strict new fugitive slave law and the barring of trade in slaves—but not slavery itself—from Washington, DC.

FEBRUARY-MARCH 1850

IN OPENING THE SENATE DEBATE on his resolutions, Clay pleads for a compromise by both sides. But the strongest advocates of both sides oppose compromise—Senator William Seward of New York arguing that 'there is a higher law than the Constitution which regulates our authority' while Senator John Calhoun of South Carolina argues that not only must the North concede the right of extending slavery but must also 'cease the agitation of the slave question'. (Calhoun is so ill that his speech is read for him by Senator James Mason of Virginia.) But the decisive speech is made by the Senator from Massachusetts, Daniel Webster, long a political opponent of Clay and a moral opponent of slavery. 'I speak today for the preservation of the union', he begins, and he proceeds to argue that the North must be ready to accept even slavery for this cause. Webster does not convert everyone immediately, but the spirit of compromise is now abroad.

JUNE 1850

LEADERS from nine Southern states convene in Nashville, Tennessee to discuss the issues of slavery and states' rights. Although some delegates openly advocate secession, the moderates prevail. The convention ends when they adopt several modest resolutions, but one calls for extending the Missouri Compromise line of 36° 30′ all the way across the new territories to the Pacific coast.

JULY 1850

PRESIDENT TAYLOR, who has opposed the compromise measures of Clay, dies and Vice-President Millard Fillmore assumes the office.

SEPTEMBER 1850

CONGRESS ADOPTS five bills based on the original resolutions of Henry Clay, and they come to be known as the Compromise of 1850. The one that continues to give Northerners the most trouble is the strict Fugitive Slave Act. President Fillmore signs all the acts.

NOVEMBER 1850

SOUTHERN LEADERS reconvene in Nashville, and since the more extreme delegates hold the majority there is much talk of the South's right to secede.

DECEMBER 1850

A STATE CONVENTION in Georgia votes its desire to remain in the Union—but declares that the state will secede if the compromise of 1850 is not observed by the North.

JUNE 1851

UNCLE TOM'S CABIN, by Harriet Beecher Stowe, begins to appear as a serial in the

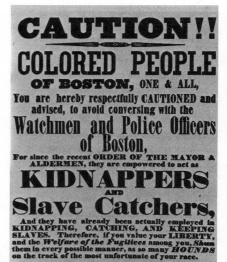

A poster from 1851.

National Era, an anti-slavery paper published in Washington, DC.

MARCH 1852

THE COMPLETE NOVEL,, *Uncle Tom's Cabin*, or *Life Among the Lowly*, is published in Boston. Within a year it will sell over one million copies and its portrayal of slave life serves to arouse both Northerners and Southerners.

NOVEMBER 1852

FRANKLIN PIERCE defeats General Winfield Scott for the Presidency on a Democratic Party platform that supports the Compromise of 1850.

JANUARY 1854

A NATIONAL COMPETITION for the lucrative transcontinental railroad route has been underway for some time. Senator Stephen A Douglas of Illinois, hoping to have the route pass through the Great Plains region, supports a bill that he hopes will win over proponents of the southern route (promoted, among others, by Jefferson Davis, now Secretary of War under President Pierce). Douglas agrees to divide the central territory into two, Kansas Territory and Nebraska Territory; the assumption is that one will be settled by pro-slavery people and the other by anti-slavery people; since Douglas endorses the concept of 'popular sovereignty', which means that the settlers will be able to decide for themselves, the bill effectively repeals the Missouri Compromise of 1820, as both Kansas and Nebraska lie above latitude 36° 30′. The debate that follows once again pits pro-slavery Southerners against anti-slavery Northerners.

FEBRUARY 1854

AT RIPON, WISCONSIN, anti-slavery opponents of the Kansas-Nebraska bill meet and recommend forming a new political party, the Republican Party. In the months that follow, others meeting in various Northern states join in the formation of the new party.

APRIL 1854

THE EMIGRANT AID SOCIETY is formed in Massachusetts to encourage anti-slavery supporters to settle in Kansas and thus 'save' it as a free state. Relatively soon, about 2,000 people go under the auspices of this project.

MAY 1854

THE KANSAS-NEBRASKA ACT, creating the two new territories, is adopted by Congress with a clear majority, and President Pierce signs it. But many Northerners, even those who had previously advocated moderation, denounce this new development. In particular, Northerners threaten to stop obeying the Fugitive Slave Law of 1850.

JULY 1854

IN MICHIGAN, antislavery men meeting to join the new Republican Party, demand that both the Kansas-Nebraska Act and the Fugitive Slave Law be repealed. In the Kansas Territory, the Federal government opens a land office to supervise the distribution of land, but pro-slavery and anti-slavery settlers are staking claims and fighting each other with little regard for any laws.

MARCH 1855

ELECTIONS for a territorial legislature are held in Kansas. Several thousand pro-slavery Missourians cross into Kansas and vote, thus electing a pro-slavery legislature. The election is recognized by the Federal governor of the territory.

JULY 1855

THE KANSAS LEGISLATURE meets and not only adopts an extremely strict series of pro-slavery laws but also expels the anti-slavery legislators.

OCTOBER-NOVEMBER 1855

FREE-SOIL KANSANS hold a convention of

their own in Topeka and adopt a constitution that outlaws slavery. (But they will also adopt a law that bars all blacks from Kansas.) A virtual civil war now exists, with frequent clashes between the pro- and anti-slavery elements in Kansas.

DECEMBER 1855

THE FREE-SOIL PEOPLE of Kansas approve the Topeka constitution (and the law banning blacks).

MAY, 1856

CHARLES SUMNER, the Senator from Massachusetts and an outspoken anti-slavery man, gives a vituperative speech against the pro-slavery elements in the Senate. Three days later, as Sumner is sitting at his Senate desk, a South Carolina Representative, Preston Brooks, beats Sumner with a stick. It will be three years before Sumner fully recovers, but he is regarded as a martyr by Northern abolitionists—while many Southerners praise Congressman Brooks. In Kansas, late in May, pro-slavery men attack Lawrence, center of the anti-slavery settlers, and kill one man. In retaliation, a band of anti-slavery men, led by the fiery abolitionist John Brown, kill five pro-slavery men at Pottawotamie Creek.

JULY 1856

THE HOUSE OF REPRESENTATIVES votes to

The attack on Senator Sumner.

admit Kansas as a state with its anti-slavery Topeka Constitution, but the Senate rejects this, so the issue is left open when Congress adjourns.

NOVEMBER 1856

JAMES BUCHANAN, the Democratic candidate, defeats John Frémont, the Republican candidate, for the Presidency in a contest that is fought quite openly along the lines of South versus North, pro-slavery versus anti-slavery.

MARCH 1857

THE SUPREME COURT hands down its decision in the Dred Scott case, and a majority declare that the Missouri Compromise of 1820 is unconstitutional. Scott is a black slave whose owner took him from the slave state of Missouri into the free state of Illinois and territory north of the latitude 36° 30′, and then back to Missouri. Scott sued for his freedom, but the Court rules that he had never ceased to be a slave and so could not be considered a citizen with the right to sue in a federal court. But the most far-reaching impact of the decision comes from the claim that Congress has no right to deprive citizens of their property—such as slaves—anywhere within the United States. An outburst of protest from Northerners and Republicans greets the decision.

DECEMBER 1857

A PRO-SLAVERY CONSTITUTION for Kansas is approved by the territorial legislature meeting at Lecompton, Kansas.

JANUARY-APRIL 1858

KANSANS REJECT the pro-slavery Lecompton constitution, but President Buchanan proceeds to ask Congress to admit Kansas as a state under this constitution. After considerable opposition by individual Congressmen and several revisions, a bill is passed by both houses that allows for another popular vote by Kansans on their constitution.

JUNE 1858

THE REPUBLICAN PARTY of Illinois nominates a former one-term Representative, Abraham Lincoln, to challenge the incumbent Senator, Stephen A Douglas. Although personally opposed to slavery, Douglas has tried to straddle the issue in order to hold the Democratic Party together, but his promotion of popular sovereignty—that is, allowing each territory or state to decide the issue for itself—has only antagonized many staunch pro-slavery Democrats from the South. Lincoln, however, chooses to meet the issue head on, and in his acceptance speech at the convention he asserts, 'I believe this government cannot endure permanently half slave and half free.'

AUGUST-OCTOBER 1858

LINCOLN AND DOUGLAS meet in towns across Illinois in a series of seven debates. Although Lincoln is little known outside Illinois and Douglas is a national figure desperately trying to placate his own party, the debates help to define the most pressing issue confronting the nation. Lincoln takes a strong stand against slavery, on moral, social, and political grounds, while Douglas defends not slavery as such but the right of Americans to vote their preference. Douglas will be elected Senator by the Democratic majority in the Illinois legislature, but Lincoln emerges on the national stage as an articulate and respected spokesman for the anti-slavery position.

MARCH 1859

THE SUPREME COURT reverses a decision of the Wisconsin Supreme Court in *Ableman v. Booth* and rules that state courts may not free federal prisoners. Booth had been convicted in a federal court for having rescued a fugitive slave, and in upholding this conviction, the United States Supreme Court confirmed the constitutionality of the Fugitive Slave Act of 1850. The Wisconsin legislature declares that 'this assumption of jurisdiction by the federal judiciary . . . is an act of undelegated

A cartoon of Lincoln and Douglas.

power, void, and of no force.' Although in this instance it is an anti-slavery state defying the federal authority, this is yet another case of a state asserting its rights. In any case, the federal government rearrests and imprisons Booth.

MAY 1859

THE annual SOUTHERN COMMERCIAL CONVENTION, an organization designed to promote economic development, after many years of considering the issue of reopening the African slave trade, votes to approve the following: 'In the opinion of this Convention, all laws, State or Federal, prohibiting the African Slave Trade, ought to be repealed.'

OCTOBER 1859

KANSANS VOTE to ratify an anti-slavery constitution. At Harper's Ferry, Virginia (now West Virginia) John Brown, one of the most radical of the abolitionists, leads an armed group (five black, 13 white men) that seizes the federal arsenal. Although this is the first action in his vague plan to establish a 'country' for fugitive slaves in the Appalachians, there is no support from outside people. Within 24 hours he and four other survivors are captured by a force of United States Marines led by Colonel Robert E Lee. Within six weeks he is tried for criminal conspiracy and treason, convicted and hanged. Although most Northerners condemn the way that Brown went about his plan, Southerners note that many Northerners admire Brown and his goals. They see Brown's raid as confirming their worst fears about the violence and upheaval that would prevail if the blacks are not held down firmly.

FEBRUARY 1860

JEFFERSON DAVIS, the Senator from Mississippi, presents a set of resolutions to the Senate to affirm that the federal government cannot prohibit slavery in the territories but must actually protect slaveholders there. But Davis is less interested in getting the whole Senate's approval than that of the Democratic members, for he is anticipating the forthcoming Democratic Party convention and Presidential election. Davis wants to commit the Democratic Party against Stephen Douglas and his concept of popular sovereignty.

APRIL-MAY 1860

THE DEMOCRATIC PARTY holds its convention in Charleston, South Carolina. When the pro-slavery platform is rejected, delegates from eight Southern states depart. But the remaining delegates are unable to agree on a candidate, so the convention adjourns.

MAY 1860

IN CHICAGO, the Republican Party, on its

John Brown holds at Harper's Ferry.

Separating a slave mother and child.

third ballot, nominates Abraham Lincoln as its Presidential candidate. To gain the nomination, Lincoln has had to present himself as fairly moderate on the question of slavery, and the party's platform declares that it is for prohibiting it in the territories only but against interfering with slavery in the states.

JUNE 1860

THE DEMOCRATIC Party reconvenes, this time in Baltimore, and after another walkout by the anti-Douglas forces, he is nominated for the Presidency. Later, the Southern Democrats convene in Baltimore and nominate the then Vice-President, John C Breckinridge, to run for President on a platform that calls for the protection of the right to own slaves.

JULY-OCTOBER 1860

IN THE CAMPAIGN the issues are reduced to slavery and sectionalism. Extremists on both sides do little except to fan the fears of people, North and South. Only Stephen Douglas of the candidates even bothers to travel to all sections in an attempt to broaden his appeal, but even he soon realizes that his cause is lost because of the split within his own party. Various Southern spokesmen make it clear that secession will follow if Lincoln is elected.

NOVEMBER 1860

ABRAHAM LINCOLN is elected President with a clear majority of the electoral college votes but only a plurality of the popular votes. Although Lincoln had deliberately muffled his message of attacking slavery, there is no mistaking the fact that for the first time in its history the United States has a President of a party that declares that 'the normal condition of all the territory of the United States is that of freedom'. Within days of Lincoln's election Southern leaders are speaking of secession as an inevitable necessity.

DECEMBER 1860

SOUTH CAROLINA, long a leader in threatening secession, holds a state convention that votes to secede from the union. Meanwhile, Congress convenes and in an effort to work out some compromise each house appoints a special committee. A member of the Senate's committee, John J Crittenden of Kentucky, introduces a series of proposals, the chief of which calls for a constitutional amendment that restores the Missouri Compromise line across the continent and for all time. Although Crittenden's proposals and various others will eventually be brought before both houses, they will prove to be ineffectual in the face of events. Members of President Buchanan's cabinet are quitting in December to protest either his actions or inaction. And Major Robert A Anderson, in command of the federal forts in the harbor of Charleston, South Carolina, moves his entire force to the larger and more defensible of the two, Fort Sumter. A delegation from South Carolina comes to Washington and demands that President Buchanan remove all federal troops from Charleston. Buchanan, who has always been sympathetic to the Southern position on slavery and states' rights, cannot accede to such a demand. He announces that Fort Sumter will be defended 'against hostile attacks, from whatever quarter', and authorizes preparation of a relief expedition by sea. In Illinois, President-elect Lincoln tries to avoid taking any position that will exacerbate the situation, but at the same time he has made himself clear: 'Let there be no compromise on the question of *extending* slavery.'

2 JANUARY 1861

WASHINGTON After South Carolina's vote to secede and Charleston's initiating war preparations, President Buchanan refuses to acknowledge officially a letter received from South Carolina commissioners. This letter, concerning Major Anderson's decision to hold Fort Sumter with a garrison of Federal troops, prompts the Cabinet to order reinforcement of the fort.

MILITARY The USS Brooklyn is readied at Norfolk, Virginia despite General Winfield Scott's preference for a non-naval vessel to aid Fort Sumter. That same day, South Carolina seizes the inactive Fort Johnson in Charleston Harbor. Defense of the capital is placed in the hands of Colonel Charles Stone, who is charged with organizing the District of Columbia militia.

3 JANUARY 1861

WASHINGTON The compromise plan authored by Senator John J Crittenden is considered for submission to public referendum, an idea receiving only lukewarm support in Congress.

MILITARY Former Secretary of War Floyd's orders to remove guns from Pitts-

Expulsion of blacks in Boston, 1860.

burgh, Pennsylvania, on down through forts in the South are reversed by the War Department. With future defense in mind, Georgia state troops take over Fort Pulaski on the Savannah River.

5 JANUARY 1861

WASHINGTON in the nation's capital, senators from seven Southern states meet, afterwards advising secession for their states—Alabama, Arkansas, Florida, Georgia, Louisiana, Mississippi, and Texas.

MILITARY Alabama further commits herself to the Southern course by seizing Forts Morgan and Gaines in order to defend Mobile. Meanwhile, 250 troops are on their way to Fort Sumter. The use of the *Brooklyn* having been vetoed by General Scott, the merchant ship *Star of the West* is called into service and sails from New York with those Federal troops.

6 JANUARY 1861

MILITARY Florida troops seize the Federal arsenal at Apalachicola.

7 JANUARY 1861

WASHINGTON Senator Crittenden speaks for conciliation and moderation, although he is against secession. He addresses the Senate, saying 'I am for the Union; but, my friends, I must also be for the equal rights of my State under the great Constitution and in this great Union.'

MILITARY The takeover of Fort Marion at St Augustine, Florida is accomplished by state troops. Like all such actions, this meets with little, if any, opposition; most of the arsenals and forts are unmanned, and the Federal government is loath to provoke confrontation by making outright defense preparations.

8 JANUARY 1861

WASHINGTON President Buchanan urges adoption of the Crittenden Compromise, which would use the Missouri Compromise line to divide the proposed slave and non-slave territories. Jacob Thompson of Mississippi, Buchanan's Secretary of the Interior, resigns and is replaced by Chief Clerk Moses Kelley as Acting Secretary.

MILITARY In Florida, Federal troops at Fort Barrancas open fire on a handful of men who advance on the Pensacola site.

9 JANUARY 1861

SECESSION Despite Buchanan's pleas, Southern sentiment runs high in favor of secession; Mississippi votes 84-15 to leave the Union, a move greeted with public celebration.

MILITARY The *Star of the West* approaches Charleston Harbor but is fired upon prior to reaching Fort Sumter. No damage is done to the ship but it quickly retreats, heading back to New York. Although some officers at Fort Sumter are anxious to return the fire opened on the relief vessel, Major Anderson forbids this action. He complains to Governor Pickens about volleys fired on a ship bearing the United States flag. The South Carolina governor replies that a United States ship represents a hostile presence that the now-independent state cannot tolerate. Anderson soon appeals to Washington, but there is little change in the situation, although Charleston reacts excitedly to this near outbreak of war. Fort Sumter remains under United States control.

10 JANUARY 1861

WASHINGTON Jefferson Davis addresses the Senate, calling for a decisive reponse to Southern demands. He decries the use of 'physical force' to settle those demands, asking instead that United States authority be maintained 'by constitutional agreement between the States'.

MILITARY Lieutenant A G Slemmer transfers Federal troops from Fort Barrancas to Fort Pickens on Santa Rosa Island after Florida votes 62-7 to secede. Orders to Major Anderson at Fort Sumter emphasize defensive preparations, despite the continual seizure, elsewhere, of

Federal properties. Forts Jackson and St Philip in Louisiana are taken over by state troops, as is the arsenal at Baton Rouge.

11 *JANUARY* 1861

SECESSION Furthering the Southern cause, Alabama's State Convention votes 61-39 to secede. Conversely, the New York legislature votes for pro-Union resolutions.

MILITARY Louisiana's troops occupy the United States Marine Hospital near New Orleans. President-elect Lincoln writes to James T Hale of Pennsylvania that 'if we surrender, it is the end of us, and of the government'.

12 *JANUARY* 1861

WASHINGTON Mississippi representatives leave the House. In an appeal to the Senate, New York's Senator Seward states, 'I do not know what the Union would be worth if saved by the use of the sword'.

MILITARY In Florida, state troops demand the surrender of Fort Pickens after having seized Fort Barrancas and its barracks, Fort McRee and the naval yard at Pensacola. Fort Pickens remains in Federal hands, however.

13 *JANAUARY* 1861

WASHINGTON Buchanan receives envoys from both Major Anderson and Governor

The Underground Railroad.

Pickens concerning the disposition of Fort Sumter. The President emphasizes that the fort will not be turned over to South Carolina authorities.

14 *JANUARY* 1861

MILITARY Fort Taylor at Key West, Florida, is garrisoned by United States troops. This effectively prevents its future takeover by the South. Fort Taylor represents a major Gulf Coast base of Union operation and will become an important coaling station for blockaders during the war. Fort Pike, near New Orleans, Louisiana falls into state hands.

16 *JANUARY* 1861

WASHINGTON The Senate, resolving that the Constitution should not be amended, virtually kills the Crittenden Compromise.

19 *JANUARY* 1861

SECESSION Georgia secedes on a vote of 208–89 despite indications of Union support. Moderate leaders in that state include Alexander Stephens, later to be Vice-President of the Southern Confederacy. This type of moderate not withstanding, the move to secede is a strong one, prompted by the earlier election of Lincoln to the presidency.

20 *JANUARY* 1861

MILITARY Mississippi troops take Fort Massachusetts on Ship Island in the Mississippi Gulf after several previously unsuccessful attempts at seizure of this military installation.

21 *JANUARY* 1861

WASHINGTON Five senators representing the states of Alabama, Florida and Mississippi withdraw from the chamber. All make farewell speeches, Jefferson Davis among them, who asserts 'I concur in the action of the people of Mississippi believing it to be necessary and proper'. Davis is severely downcast by this exigency, that night praying for peace, according to his wife.

SLAVERY Boston, Massachusetts is the site of an address by Wendell Phillips, an ardent abolitionist. His message hails the secession of slave states, for which he had little use or respect since they seemed to be only disruptive forces in the Federal union.

24 JANUARY 1861

MILITARY The arsenal at Augusta, Georgia falls into state hands. Federal troops from Fort Monroe, Virginia, are sent to reinforce Fort Pickens in Florida.

26 JANUARY 1861

SECESSION An ordinance of secession passes the Louisiana State Convention 114-17.

MILITARY In Savannah, Georgia, both Fort Jackson and the Oglethorpe Barracks are taken by state troops.

29 JANUARY 1861

WASHINGTON Kansas, with a constitution that prohibits slavery, receives the necessary congressional approval to become the Union's 34th state. This action is the outcome of several years of bitter fighting between pro- and anti-slavery people in that former territory.

31 JANUARY 1861

MILITARY New Orleans, Louisiana is the scene of further takeovers. The United States Branch Mint and Customs House and the schooner *Washington* are seized by the state, ending a month of similar events throughout the South. The defiance of secessionists continues unabated and Washington seems unable, or unwilling, to still the confusion and unrest engendered by Southern actions.

1 FEBRUARY 1861

WASHINGTON William H Seward, Secretary of State-designate, is the recipient of a letter from Lincoln in which the latter states, 'I am inflexible' in reference to extending slavery in the territories.

SECESSION With a vote of 166-7 at the State Convention, Texas secedes from the Union, the seventh state to do so.

4 FEBRUARY 1861

WASHINGTON The Peace Convention meets at the nation's capital, with 131 members from 21 states, although none of the seceded states send any delegates to this assembly. The Convention is headed by former President John Tyler, who joins with others of like mind in a last desperate effort to compromise and save the Union.

SECESSION At Montgomery, Alabama, a convention of representatives assembles. This is the initial meeting of the Provisional Congress of the Confederate States of America, attended by many former United States senators, among them Louisiana's Judah Benjamin and John Slidell. Benjamin is later to become Attorney General, then Secretary of War, in Jefferson Davis' Cabinet. He and Slidell have been law partners together in New Orleans. Slidell later becomes famous for his involvement in an international incident, the *Trent* affair.

5 FEBRUARY 1861

WASHINGTON Fort Sumter is again the subject of attention as the President sum-

A slave auction in the South.

marily dismisses any notions held by South Carolina that the United States will give up its jurisdiction over the fort. Meanwhile, the Peace Convention attempts to arrange a settlement of differences between the secessionists and those who wish to uphold the Union. Speaking to the delegates, John Tyler indicates that 'the eyes of the whole country are turned to this assembly, in expectation and hope'.

SECESSION At Montgomery, Alabama, plans proceed for the establishment of 'a Confederacy of the States which have seceded from the Federal Union', according to Christopher Memminger of South Carolina.

8 *FEBRUARY* 1861

SECESSION A Constitution is provisionally adopted by the Montgomery convention. With several significant changes, the document closely resembles the United States Constitution, those changes having to do with the right to own slaves, the treatment of fugitive slaves, and the power of sovereign states.

9 *FEBRUARY* 1861

SECESSION In a unanimous decision, Jefferson Davis of Mississippi is elected Provisional President of the Confederate States of America. Alexander Stephens joins him as Provisional Vice-President. These two are moderate enough in their public views to please the border states and it is hoped that those states not yet seceded will soon do so now that the Confederacy has chosen able, and not fanatic, leaders. In a further move to preserve order and prevent a radical break, the Provisional Congress at Montgomery states that the laws of the United States of America are to remain valid unless they interfere with stated laws of the Confederacy. Tennessee declines the opportunity to hold a state convention which would rule on secession; the popular vote on this decision is 68,282 to 59,449.

MILITARY Fort Pickens, Florida does not receive the reinforcements that arrive on the USS *Brooklyn* because of the desire of both Federal and state authorities that the balance of power not be disturbed.

10 *FEBRUARY* 1861

SECESSION The arrival of a telegram announcing his election to the Presidency of the newly-formed Confederacy catches Jefferson Davis by surprise in Mississippi. He is immediately involved in plans for a trip to the capital at Montgomery, Alabama in order to take part in his inauguration, which the Confederacy clearly hopes to hold before Lincoln can take over the Federal government.

11 *FEBRUARY* 1861

WASHINGTON Preparations are made for the inauguration as President-elect Lincoln leaves Springfield, Illinois, for his journey to the Federal capital.

SECESSION Jefferson Davis leaves his Mississippi plantation, Brierfield, and at Montgomery, Alabama Vice-President Alexander Stephens is sworn in but does not take advantage of the occasion to make any official statements.

12 *FEBRUARY* 1861

SECESSION As Lincoln travels to his inauguration in Washington, DC, he makes numerous stops along the way. Speaking before various groups, the President-elect is cautious in expressing his opinions. To German-Americans at Cinncinnati, Ohio, he states his earlier intention of remaining silent about 'national difficulties'. Earlier, in that same city he asked the citizenry to remain loyal to the Constitution. Jefferson Davis is making his way to the Confederate capital and, like Lincoln, speaks to the crowds gathering along the way. He observes that a possible outcome of secession is war.

MILITARY State troops take possession of United States munitions stored at Napoleon, Arkansas.

15 *FEBRUARY* 1861

WASHINGTON The Peace Conference

45

CHRONOLOGY

Lincoln's First Inauguration, 1861.

drags on, attending to each detail with discussion and debate. Many Federal military officers, such as Raphael Semmes of the Navy, are resigning their posts to become part of Southern military and naval forces.
SECESSION   Again, Lincoln makes a cryptic observation, this time at Pittsburgh, Pennsylvania that 'there is really no crisis except an *artificial* one!' Similar comments accompanied his address earlier to a crowd in Cleveland, Ohio.

18 *FEBRUARY* 1861

SECESSION   At his inauguration, Jefferson Davis points out 'the American idea that governments rest on the consent of the governed'. It is clear that he would like to avoid armed conflict, but it is also apparent that he holds the Southern position to be sacred. His words—'obstacles may retard, but they cannot long prevent, the progress of a movement sanctified by its justice'—leave little doubt as to his dedication. Elsewhere, Lincoln progresses from Buffalo eastward to Albany, New York.

19 *FEBRUARY* 1861

SECESSION   A Confederate Cabinet takes shape in Montgomery, Alabama. Secretaries of State, War and the Treasury, Toombs, Walker and Memminger, are joined by Judah Benjamin as Attorney General, Stephen Mallory as Secretary of the Navy, and John Reagan as Postmaster General. At New York City, an estimated 500,000 persons greet Lincoln as he arrives in that Northern city.
MILITARY   Louisiana obtains control of the United States paymaster's office located at New Orleans.

20 *FEBRUARY* 1861

MILITARY   The Department of the Navy of the Confederacy is established. In addition, the Provisional Congress empowers President Davis to contract for the manufacture and purchase of war goods.

22 *FEBRUARY* 1861

SECESSION   At a Washington's Birthday celebration in Philadelphia, Pennsylvania, Lincoln points out that 'there is no need of bloodshed and war'. After having received an assassination threat the previous day, Lincoln leaves with a bodyguard for the nation's capital. It is arranged that he, detective Allan Pinkerton and a friend will travel by a revised schedule and route.

23 *FEBRUARY* 1861

WASHINGTON   The President-elect arrives safely in the city at 6:00 am. Various delegations greet him throughout the day, including members of the Peace Convention.
SECESSION   In Texas, voters respond favorably to appeals for secession in a public referendum.

27 *FEBRUARY* 1861

WASHINGTON   At the Peace Conference, deliberations result in six proposed Constitutional amendments. Although the proposals have no chance of acceptance, they are sincerely conceived. Meanwhile, United States Representatives strike down plans for a constitutional convention, vote against amendments to interfere with slavery and against the Crittenden Compromise.

SECESSION Jefferson Davis, now head of the Confederacy, appoints three men to approach officials in the Federal capital with offers of peaceful negotiation of differences. Davis also receives missives from Governor Pickens in Charleston, South Carolina; the head of that state observes the need for Confederate takeover of Fort Sumter to preserve 'honor and safety'.

28 FEBRUARY 1861

SECESSION Missouri holds a State Convention: its purpose is to debate secession. North Carolina comes out in favor of the Union at its election concerning the possibility of a State Convention; secessionists garner 46,409 votes in favor of holding such a convention, those against the assembly tally 46,603 votes.

MILITARY The stalemate at Fort Sumter continues, Major Robert Anderson staying in nearly constant communication with Washington. States that have seceded and formed the Confederacy grow increasingly more willing to confirm their independent status. With the inauguration only days away, the mood in Washington is expectant but subdued; there is little real action as the incoming administration awaits the beginning of its tenure.

2 MARCH 1861

WASHINGTON Senator John J Crittenden of Kentucky attempts to push a Constitutional amendment through the Senate, but fails. This amendment, a culmination of Peace Convention efforts, is the final compromise issue supported by Crittenden, who now directs his energies at monitoring the inevitable conflict between North and South.

3 MARCH 1861

MILITARY General Winfield Scott, head of the United States Army, indicates in a letter to Secretary of State Seward that relief of Fort Sumter is not practical.

4 MARCH 1861

WASHINGTON Abraham Lincoln is inaugurated as the 16th President of the United States of America at the nation's capital where some 30,000 people are assembled. Because of threats against the President's life, troops are everywhere. In his address to the nation on this momentous occasion, Lincoln emphasizes his position on slavery, stating that he is not opposed to the institution where it is already established. He further points out that the states voting for secession are in error, since 'the Union of these States is perpetual'. Taking the stance that acts against the Federal government are 'insurrectionary or revolutionary', Lincoln vows to uphold the Union, saying to refractory Southerners, 'in *your* hands, my dissatisfied fellow countrymen, and not in *mine*, is the momentous issue of civil war'.

5 MARCH 1861

MILITARY Fort Sumter, again the subject of concern on both Northern and Southern sides, becomes a point of intense discussion between Lincoln and General Scott. It appears from Major Anderson's messages that the fort cannot be maintained without replacements and reinforcements, and the estimated number of troops needed at the South Carolina site hovers around 20,000.

Davis's inauguration in Montgomery.

Both Scott and Lincoln agree that the disposition of Fort Sumter should be confronted soon.

6 *MARCH* 1861

WASHINGTON Despite Lincoln's refusal to deal with them, the Confederate commissioners appointed by Jefferson Davis try to establish negotiations with the Republicans now in office.

7 *MARCH* 1861

WASHINGTON Martin J Crawford, John Forsyth, and A B Roman, the men Davis has sent to represent the Confederacy in the United States capital, continue to press for an appointment with Lincoln's administration. In addition, they contact influential individuals in Washington who express some support for the Southern position, or who are known to be on the side of peaceful negotiation rather than armed conflict.

11 *MARCH* 1861

MILITARY Lincoln is told by General Scott that the Army can no longer be responsible for the immediate reinforcement of Fort Sumter. He tells the President that the situation at Charleston is reaching crisis proportions which the Army alone cannot effectively handle.

13 *MARCH* 1861

WASHINGTON Since Lincoln is averse to validating the Confederate nation in any respect, he counsels Secretary of State Seward to refuse meetings with Confederate ambassadors on any grounds. In avoiding such a conference, the President hopes to sidestep the question of whether or not those Southern states forming the Confederacy have actually left the Union.

15 *MARCH* 1861

MILITARY In the hopes of avoiding armed conflict, Seward does not support the reinforcement of Fort Sumter since that move would, he feels, most definitely precipitate a response from the Confederacy. Lincoln, in the midst of the varying opinions of his Cabinet, delays any final word concerning the issue in South Carolina.

16 *MARCH* 1861

SECESSION Another state, Arizona, votes to leave the Union and join the Confederacy, in a convention at Mesilla. The Confederate government later establishes a territorial government for Arizona.

INTERNATIONAL The Confederacy, knowing that its future depends greatly on recognition by other governments, appoints commissioners to Britain.

18 *MARCH* 1861

SECESSION A State Convention having turned down a move to secede 39-35, Arkansas agrees to an election later in the summer which will allow for public voting on the secession question.

MILITARY While Confederate President Jefferson Davis hopes that Federal troops under Major Robert Anderson will withdraw, the president nevertheless communicates with Governor Pickens concerning the fortification of the area around Charleston, South Carolina. Davis points out that it is unlikely that 'the enemy would retire peacefully from your harbor'.

25 *MARCH* 1861

WASHINGTON The capital is alive with rumors from Charleston, South Carolina, but there is little reliable information about the situation there. The next day, President Lincoln and his Cabinet meet to discuss Fort Sumter and how to best deal with the mounting crisis.

29 *MARCH* 1861

WASHINGTON The President finally announces his plan for Fort Sumter. An evacuation of that installation would not be attempted, but instead, a force would be sent to supply and support the troops already stationed there. It is Lincoln's preference that this force should be in readiness 'as early as the 6th of April'. The Cabinet's support of President Lincoln's decision to keep Fort Sumter in Federal hands is three to two in favor, Secretary of War Simon Cameron keeping silent about his wishes in this matter.

31 *MARCH* 1861

WASHINGTON   President Lincoln, having taken a stance on Fort Sumter, now prepares to act on Fort Pickens' dilemma. A force is ordered to Florida to relieve the latter military post, while rumors fly in the capital that Fort Sumter is to be abandoned; there is no truth to these rumors, as Lincoln's orders of 29 March prove.

MILITARY   Yet another Federal outpost, Fort Bliss in Texas, surrenders its jurisdiction to state troops. The toll of Federal property lost to Southern hands continues to mount, and the mood in both the Union and the Confederacy is pessimistic as to the outcome of the current problems. The Lincoln administration has taken steps which it feels are both emphatic yet non-provoking.

1 *APRIL* 1861

WASHINGTON   President Lincoln receives a message from Secretary of State Seward in which the latter speaks of relations between the United States and France, Britain, Spain and Russia. Seward indicates his willingness to assume responsibility for dealing with the Confederacy. In addition, the Secretary of State tells the President that the issue with the Confederacy ought to center around union or disunion rather than slavery, and advises that Fort Sumter be abandoned while Federal occupation of other forts should continue. Lincoln's tactful yet firm response proves that he, and not Seward, will continue to make policy decisions. In a separate action, the President orders the USS *Powhatan* to proceed to Florida where it can then aid Fort Pickens. This effectively removes the *Powhatan* from the Fort Sumter rescue efforts. Secretary of State

Seward has advised this course of action but it is not made clear to the Department of the Navy, introducing some later confusion when the Fort Sumter expedition is finally underway.

3 *APRIL* 1861

WASHINGTON   The President meets with his Cabinet concerning Fort Sumter and issues related to the relief and reinforcement of that Federal installation.

MILITARY   In Charleston Harbor, the Federal schooner *Rhoda H Shannon* is fired on by Confederate batteries.

4 *APRIL* 1861

WASHINGTON   Lincoln writes to Major Anderson, informing him of the upcoming relief of Fort Sumter, saying 'the expedition will go forward'. Anderson is told to maintain the situation as it now stands, if possible, but he has been given the freedom to decide what the response would be to an attack by the Confederates.

SECESSION   At its State Convention, Virginia votes 89-45 against holding a referendum on the most important secession question.

5 *APRIL* 1861

WASHINGTON   Formal orders are given by Secretary of the Navy concerning the Fort Sumter expedition. Four vessels are told to provision the fort, but among these is the *Powhatan* which is already on its way to Fort Pickens, Florida under orders from the President.

6 *APRIL* 1861

WASHINGTON   State Department Clerk Robert S Chew carries a message to South Carolina Governor Pickens regarding Fort Sumter: the Federal action will be one of provisioning rather than reinforcing on the condition that there be no resistance to or interference with the supply efforts. Lincoln directs Seward to reverse former orders concerning the USS *Powhatan* but it is too late to do so.

CHRONOLOGY

7 *APRIL* 1861

SECESSION   General Beauregard conveys the message to Major Anderson that no further communication between Fort Sumter and Charleston will be permitted by Confederate authorities.

8 *APRIL* 1861

SECESSION   In response to Lincoln's 6 April message concerning the supply of Fort Sumter, the Confederacy readies its forces in the vicinity of Charleston Harbor.
MILITARY   The Federal cutter *Harriet Lane* leaves New York for Ft Sumter.

9 *APRIL* 1861

MILITARY   From New York, two more vessels sail for Charleston Harbor; one, the steamer *Baltic,* carries naval agent Gustavus Fox, a former naval officer who later becomes President Lincoln's Assistant Secretary of the Navy.

10 *APRIL* 1861

MILITARY   Beauregard receives word from Confederate Secretary of War Leroy Pope Walker that he is to require the surrender of Fort Sumter from the Federals. All around the fort, Confederate troops prepare for the expected conflict; a floating battery is stationed by rebels off Sullivan's Island in Charleston Harbor.

11 *APRIL* 1861

WASHINGTON   Three Confederate commissioners sent to the Federal capital leave for the South and carry with them the conviction that their government will not be recognized by Lincoln.
MILITARY   Major Anderson receives messengers from General Beauregard— Confederate Colonel James Chesnut, formerly a United States Senator; Colonel A R Chisolm, Governor Pickens' representative, and Captain Stephen D. Lee, formerly of the United States Army. These three men convey to Anderson that Beauregard is 'ordered by the Government of the Confederate States of America to demand the evacuation of Fort Sumter'. Anderson's refusal prompts Beauregard to contact War Secretary Walker; the latter encourages the Confederate general to wait and see whether Anderson evacuates so as to 'avoid the effusion of blood'. The Confederacy appears willing to hold its fire on Fort Sumter if the Federal garrison does nothing to further precipitate armed conflict.

THE CIVIL WAR

12 *APRIL* 1861

MILITARY   The three Confederate messengers to Fort Sumter, Chesnut, Chisolm and Lee, return to Major Anderson once more after speaking with General Beauregard. They try once more to ask for a time of probable evacuation of the fort by Federal troops. The major indicates 12:00 PM 15 April as a target time in the event that he receives no supplies or orders from Washington. The Confederacy, knowing that help is undoubtedly on its way, refuses to accept this statement from Major Anderson and gives the Federal commander written notification of an attack to commence in one hour's time. At Fort Johnson, Captain George S James signals the other harbor batteries to open fire. At 4:30 AM, a rotation of fire proceeds against Fort Sumter, continuing through the day and at intervals through the night. The city of Charleston reacts with excitement, many people watching the bombardment from rooftops. The Federal vessels sent by Washington are visible at sea, prompting further anticipation as to the outcome of the Southern attack. At Fort Pickens on Santa Rosa Island in Florida, the United States Navy lands troops to reinforce the existing garrison. This action prevents the Confederacy from gaining control of this important Gulf Coast fortification, providing Union forces with a critically positioned base in the South.

13 *APRIL* 1861

WASHINGTON The President, as yet unaware of the battle at Fort Sumter, states that 'I shall hold myself at liberty to repossess, if I can, places like Fort Sumter if taken from Federal control'.

MILITARY The Federal garrison at Fort Sumter is left with no option but to surrender to Confederate officers. This action is declared at 2:30 PM. Major Robert Anderson, with no remaining food and an insufficient number of men, concludes that further conflict is purposeless and that his troops have done their best under difficult conditions. No lives have been lost and the wounded are few on both sides, despite the firing of some 40,000 shells during the battle.

14 *APRIL* 1861

WASHINGTON The Cabinet and President Lincoln meet after receiving official notice of the surrender at Fort Sumter. The chief executive calls for 75,000 volunteers, and also for a session of Congress to meet on 4 July 1861.

MILITARY Major Anderson and his men leave Fort Sumter and proceed northward, by sea, after a ceremony of surrender. On this occasion, an accidental blast kills two and injures four Union soldiers as a stockpile of ammunition is inadvertently detonated.

The attack on Fort Sumter.

15 *APRIL* 1861

WASHINGTON Lincoln issues a public proclamation calling for 75,000 militia to still the insurrection in South Carolina, eliciting an instant supportive response from Northern states. Border states such as Kentucky, Maryland, Missouri, North Carolina and Virginia, are areas of discontent and uncertainty. Kentucky and North Carolina ultimately refuse to respond to Lincoln's appeal while the New York legislature commits $3 million in aid for the Northern cause.

17 *APRIL* 1861

SECESSION Baltimore, Maryland is the setting for a meeting held by secessionists. Missouri and Tennessee decide against meeting Lincoln's requests for volunteers, and at Richmond, Virginia the State Convention passes 88-55 a secession ordinance. A public referendum is to be held in that state on 23 May for a final decision on the secession question. For all intents and purposes, Virginia is now viewed by the rest of the nation as a part of the Confederacy.

THE CONFEDERACY Jefferson Davis announces that the Confederate government will accept applications for letters of marque, a move which will permit privateering, a practice that to many seems little better than legalized piracy.

NAVAL At Indianola, Texas, the steamer *Star of the West* is taken in Gulf waters by Confederate troops under General Van Dorn; the ship will later become a receiving vessel in the Confederate Navy.

18 *APRIL* 1861

WASHINGTON At the capital, the President is informed by eyewitnesses as to the events at Fort Sumter. It is alleged that Lincoln has approached Colonel Robert E Lee and has asked him to command the Union Army; Lee has purportedly declined the offer. It is clear that while there are staunch supporters for both the Union and the Confederacy, there are also those who prefer to avoid further conflict.

19 *APRIL* 1861

WASHINGTON The President makes one of his strongest moves up to this time, ordering the blockade of all ports in the Confederate states. This order immediately causes the Federal Department of the Navy to place its ships at all critical ports, and the blockade is soon extended to include North Carolina and Virginia. It is one effort which proves effective, though in varying degrees, throughout the war.

THE NORTH In New York, the Sixth Massachusetts Regiment travels toward Washington, pausing at Baltimore, Maryland. A vital railroad nexus, this city is important for both the supply and defense of the Federal capital. As the Massachusetts troops move through Baltimore on their way to the Washington depot, they are attacked by rioters carrying Confederate flags. Nine civilians and four soldiers are killed in the melee. The troops reach the capital and are ultimately quartered in the Senate Chamber. It appears that Washington will lose a railroad link with the North as a result of this Baltimore riot, causing the Federal Navy to carry troops to Washington via Philadelphia and Annapolis.

20 *APRIL* 1861

THE NORTH A move later censured by

The attack at Baltimore, 19 April 1861.

Union officials is that of Commandant Charles S McCauley giving orders to burn the Federal Gosport Naval Yard near Norfolk, Virginia. Calculated to prevent the property from falling into Confederate hands, the base has been an important Federal military installation and its loss creates difficulty for Union operations along the coast. The Fourth Massachusetts Regiment arrives to support Fort Monroe.

THE CONFEDERACY Robert E Lee resigns his post with the Federal Army, choosing to side with the South. Many Confederate merchants are now repudiating debts to the North.

21 *APRIL* 1861

THE NORTH In Baltimore, Maryland rioting continues while the President meets with that city's mayor to discuss ways of ending the violence.

SECESSION Monongahela County in the western part of Virginia hosts meetings of anti-secessionists, who resolve to support the Union despite the stand taken by the remainder of the state.

22 *APRIL* 1861

WASHINGTON The difficulties in Baltimore have continued to threaten the Federal capital because troops heading for Washington must go through Maryland. Lincoln's words to the Baltimore YMCA —'you . . . would not lay a straw in the way of those who are organizing . . . to capture this city'—indicate his concern for the defense of Washington.

THE CONFEDERACY Jefferson Davis is in communication with Virginia's Governor John Letcher and hopes that the latter will be able to 'sustain Baltimore if practicable'.

WESTERN THEATER Cairo, Illinois is garrisoned by state troops.

TRANS-MISSISSIPPI Arkansas Governor H M Rector refuses to send troops to support the Union. The Federal arsenal at Fayetteville, Arkansas is taken by North Carolina state troops.

24 *APRIL* 1861

WASHINGTON The President continues

to worry about the security of the capital city as invasion from the South looms in the horizon. In writing to Reverdy Johnson, a Maryland political leader, Lincoln says, 'I do not mean to let them invade us without striking back'.

25 *APRIL* 1861

WASHINGTON The Seventh New York Regiment arrives in Washington, much to President Lincoln's relief.

TRANS-MISSISSIPPI In a secret action against the pro-secessionists in Missouri, Captain James H Stokes of Chicago, Illinois goes to St Louis from Alton, Illinois. Upon arrival, he and his men remove 10,000 muskets from the arsenal, returning to Alton the next morning with munitions for Illinois troops.

27 *APRIL* 1861

WASHINGTON In a bold action, Lincoln suspends the writ of habeas corpus in an area stretching from Philadelphia, Pennsylvania to Washington, DC, and then leaves General Scott in charge of supervising any incidents arising out of that suspension. Lincoln does this in part to provide for a cessation of the turmoil that has been plaguing Baltimore, Maryland and causing troop transport to be severely disrupted because of it. In addition, the President extends the Federal blockade of Southern ports to include Virginia and North Carolina.

THE CONFEDERACY Richmond, Virginia is offered by the Virginia Convention as a capital for the Confederacy, to replace Montgomery, Alabama.

29 *APRIL* 1861

SECESSION The State legislature of Maryland repudiates secession with a vote of 53-13.

THE CONFEDERACY Jefferson Davis speaks at the second session of the Confederate Provisional Congress. Explaining reasons for secession, the Confederate leader says, 'we protest solemnly in the face of mankind that we desire peace at any sacrifice save that of honor and independence'.

30 *APRIL* 1861

WASHINGTON Complying with orders from the President, Federal troops evacuate Indian Territory forts, leaving the Five Civilized Nations—Cherokees, Chickasaws, Choctaws, Creeks and Seminoles—virtually under Confederate jurisdiction and control.

1 *MAY* 1861

THE NORTH Soldiers killed in the Baltimore riots are honored at ceremonies in Boston, Massachusetts. A call for volunteers to support the Union is publicized in the Nebraska Territory.

EASTERN THEATER Confederate troops under Colonel T J Jackson are sent to Harper's Ferry, Virginia by General Robert E Lee.

NAVAL Federals seize two Confederate ships in Atlantic waters, and the United States Navy blockades the mouth of the James River.

3 *MAY* 1861

WASHINGTON Making preparations for the war which now appears inevitable, Lincoln sends out a call for 42,000 Army volunteers and another 18,000 seamen. He also forms the Department of the Ohio, to be commanded by George Brinton McClellan. General Winfield Scott, the General-in-Chief of the Federal Army, explains that, with the aid of a powerful blockade, it is possible to 'envelop' the states along the entire length of the Mississippi River and provide for subjugation of insurgents in this way. The arrangement is known as the Anaconda Plan.

INTERNATIONAL The Confederacy has sent commissioners to London, England to meet with the British Foreign Minister in the attempt to gain recognition for their government in the South. The United States complains to the British Ministry about this meeting although it is an unofficial one, according to the British, who are not interested in upsetting their relations with the United States.

5 *MAY* 1861

THE CONFEDERACY State troops abandon, temporarily, the city of Alexandria, Virginia, which lies across the Potomac River from the Federal capital.

6 *MAY* 1861

SECESSION At Little Rock, Arkansas, the state legislature votes 69-1 in favor of secession. Elsewhere, Tennessee votes to set a public referendum on secession; while the 8 June deadline for this election is one month away, the state legislature's 66-25 vote in favor of secession confirms the direction that Tennessee will take in the upcoming conflict.

THE CONFEDERACY Jefferson Davis gives approval to the Confederate Congressional bill declaring a state of war between the United States and the Confederate States.

7 *MAY* 1861

WASHINGTON Major Robert Anderson, who had gained national recognition as the commander in charge of Union forces at Fort Sumter, South Carolina, is assigned to recruit troops for the Federal cause. President Lincoln asks Anderson to obtain Union volunteers from Kentucky and western Virginia.

BORDER STATES Conflicting sentiments cause a riot at Knoxville, Tennessee; pro-secessionists clash with Union supporters, resulting in injuries and one fatality.

9 *MAY* 1861

THE NORTH At Newport, Rhode Island, the USS *Constitution* and the steamer *Baltic* are preparing to set up the United States Naval Academy since it can no longer be based in Annapolis, Maryland, due to the uncertain nature of that area's political sentiments. It seems important to locate the Academy in an area which is solidly pr-Union.

THE CONFEDERACY James D Bullock is charged with purchasing arms and vessels from the British for the Confederate cause.

NAVAL The Virginia blockade precipitates gunfire between Confederate batteries on shore at Gloucester Point and the Federal vessel *Yankee*.

10 *MAY* 1861

THE CONFEDERACY President Jefferson Davis orders the purchase of warships and munitions for the Confederacy. Naval Secretary Mallory suggests ironclads as logical additions to the small Confederate Navy, hoping that this will favor the Southerners, for their Union opponents have a much larger and more diverse fleet.

SECESSION A riot in St Louis, Missouri results when United States troops clash with pro-secessionist state militia. While Federal forces do not provoke the attack, under the leadership of Captain Nathaniel Lyon they march to the state militia barracks at Camp Jackson where armaments for secessionists are allegedly stored. The state forces led by General D M Frost surrender peacefully, but during the ensuing march, curious crowds trigger further violence. In the fracas, a reported 29 are killed or fatally injured.

11 *MAY* 1861

THE NORTH Both Wheeling, in western Virginia, and San Francisco, California are scenes of pro-Union demonstrations, even though a strong secessionist element remains in the latter area.

SECESSION At St Louis, the unrest continues. Fights between civilians and the Fifth Reserve Regiment result in seven more deaths. Eventually, Federal control is resumed and the secessionists slowly back down.

13 *MAY* 1861

THE NORTH General Benjamin F Butler moves Federal troops into Baltimore without official authorization. Butler has received notice of possible riots in that Maryland city.

INTERNATIONAL Britain's Queen Victoria announces her nation's position of neutrality. She further states that the British will assist neither side, but will give each the rights accorded belligerents.

14 MAY 1861

THE NORTH General Butler continues his occupation of the city of Baltimore, Maryland.

WESTERN THEATER Major Robert Anderson receives word from President Lincoln that Kentucky Unionists are to be given aid, despite their state's neutral position.

16 MAY 1861

WASHINGTON Orders go out to Commander John Rodgers to take charge of the United States naval operations on rivers in the West.

SECESSION In Kentucky, the legislature proposes its intention that the state retain its neutral status.

18 MAY 1861

EASTERN THEATER In its first offensive against the South, the Union engages rebel batteries at Sewall's Point, Virginia.

NAVAL The blockade of Virginia is complete with the sealing off of the Rappahannock River.

20 MAY 1861

SECESSION North Carolina assembles a convention at Raleigh, voting for secession.

THE NORTH In order to reveal pro-secessionist evidence, United States marshals in the North appropriate the previous year's telegraph dispatches.

THE CONFEDERACY Confederate Provisional Congressmen vote to relocate their nation's capital at Richmond, Virginia.

23 MAY 1861

SECESSION In a vote of 97,000 to 32,000, Virginia moves in favor of secession. The western portion of the state, however, is clearly pro-Union and has been for some time contemplating a formal break with the rest of the state.

24 MAY 1861

EASTERN THEATER Alexandria, Virginia is occupied by Federal troops moving quietly across the Potomac River. In this way the Union begins to defend Washington. Virginia troops display little resistance. The first Union combat fatality of the Civil War occurs during this move: 24-year-old Elmer Ellsworth, head of the Eleventh New York Regiment, dies in an attempt to remove a Confederate flag from a hotel roof. The man who shot Ellsworth, the hotel keeper James Jackson, is then shot by a Union soldier. Both the North and the South have martyrs for their respective causes. Newspapers give full play to the emotions in reporting the events—'Jackson perished amid the pack of wolves' was the way one Southern newspaper chose to describe the killing.

SLAVERY In an action provoking questions as to the disposition of slaves by the North, General Benjamin F Butler holds three slaves at Fort Monroe. The issue is quickly interpreted as one of whether slaves are to be regarded as contraband. This will become an increasingly difficult controversy, ultimately ruled on by Secretary of War Cameron in July 1861.

26 MAY 1861

WASHINGTON Lincoln's Postmaster General Blair announces the cutting of postal connections with the Confederate States as of 31 May 1861.

NAVAL Additional blockades are established: one at Mobile, Alabama and one at New Orleans, Louisiana.

27 MAY 1861

WASHINGTON In a case concerning the legality of Lincoln's suspension of the writ of habeas corpus, Chief Justice Roger B Taney decrees the arrest of John Merryman illegal. Merryman was imprisoned for recruiting Confederate soldiers, an arrest made by General Cadwalader, who argued that Lincoln's proclamation allowed such action. It is Lincoln's view that in time of rebellion such moves are required in order to preserve public safety.

29 MAY 1861

WASHINGTON Dorothea Dix is received by Secretary of War Cameron, who accepts her offer of help in setting up hospitals for the Union Army.

30 MAY 1861

THE NORTH Grafton, Virginia, in the western part of the state, is occupied by Union troops who are sent to protect citizens and to guard the Baltimore & Ohio Railroad line.

31 MAY 1861

THE NORTH Union troops, which have evacuated forts in Indian territory, reach Fort Leavenworth, Kansas. The path they travel is later known as the Chisholm Trail after one of their guides, Jesse Chisholm. THE CONFEDERACY General Beauregard is given command of the Confederate Army of the Potomac in northern Virginia, otherwise known as the Alexandria Line.

1 JUNE 1861

EASTERN THEATER Northern Virginia is the scene of fighting at Arlington Mills and Fairfax County Courthouse. A Confederate captain, John Q Marr, is killed in this minor skirmish, one of the early Southern fatalities. INTERNATIONAL British territorial waters and ports are proclaimed off-limits to belligerents carrying spoils of war.

3 JUNE 1861

THE NORTH Forty-eight-year old Stephen A Douglas dies, probably of typhoid fever. The Democrats lose a staunch, committed leader, and the Union, a strong supporter. In the nation's capital,

President Lincoln mourns the 'Little Giant' who defeated him in the race for a Senate seat, but who lost his bid for the presidency. EASTERN THEATER Western Virginia is again the focus of conflict, Union forces surprising Confederates at Phillippi. The rebels, under Colonel G A Porterfield, flee. This Northern triumph, so easily accomplished, came to be known as the 'Phillippi Races' due to the Confederates' rapid retreat under fire. It was in some ways responsible for western Virginia's later break with the main part of the state. With Confederate troops no longer in the vicinity, the majority of western Virginians, who were pro-Union, could more easily express their support for the North.

5 JUNE 1861

THE NORTH Arms and gunpowder are seized by Federal marshals at the Du Pont works in Delaware and at Merrill & Thomas, a gun factory in Baltimore, Maryland.

6 JUNE 1861

WASHINGTON Lincoln's Cabinet declares that the Union government will pay for all war expenses that are incurred once the states have mobilized their volunteers.

8 JUNE 1861

WASHINGTON The United States Sanitary Commission is given executive approval. This board will help maintain healthful conditions for Union troops. SECESSION In a public referendum, Tennessee favors secession 104,913 to 47,238. This popular action serves to formalize the course already chosen for the state by its legislature.

10 JUNE 1861

EASTERN THEATER At Bethel Church, Virginia, Federal troops are forced into retreat by aggressive Confederates. Union fatalities total 18, with 53 wounded. The Southerners lose only one man and sustain

The charge at Fairfax Courthouse.

seven injured. Colonel Charles Stone and his forces head out on an expedition which is part of the planned defense of the Federal capital.

11 *JUNE* 1861

TRANS-MISSISSIPPI Troubles in St Louis, Missouri continue as General Nathaniel Lyon meets with a pro-Southern state government. Lyon is angered over what he feels is local intervention in orders given to Federal troops.

12 *JUNE* 1861

TRANS-MISSISSIPPI In a further effort to promote the Confederacy in his state, Governor Claiborne Jackson of Missouri puts out a call for 50,000 volunteers. He hopes to repel what he perceives as attempts by Federals to take over the state.

14 *JUNE* 1861

EASTERN THEATER Harper's Ferry, Virginia is abandoned by rebels hoping to avoid being cut off by McClellan and Patterson who are advancing from the west and the north.

17 *JUNE* 1861

WASHINGTON The President observes Professor Thaddeus S C Lowe demonstrate the use of a hot-air balloon. Some military advisors hope to employ balloons for observation of enemy movements

during the war.

TRANS-MISSISSIPPI In Missouri, Union troops establish themselves at the state capital at Jefferson City. Elsewhere, pro-Confederate troops are defeated at Boonville, thus providing Federals with further control of the Missouri River.

19 *JUNE* 1861

THE NORTH A meeting of Virginians loyal to the Union elects Francis H Pierpont as provisional governor of what will soon be West Virginia.

24 *JUNE* 1861

EASTERN THEATER At Mathias Point, Virginia Confederate batteries are attacked by Federal gunboats. Three days later, Confederates repel Union attempts to land troops at this point

27 *JUNE* 1861

WASHINGTON In order to plan military strategies for the Southern coast, delegates from the Army, Navy and Coast Survey, convene in the Federal capital. This body was later to make valuable recommendations throughout the war.

29 *JUNE* 1861

WASHINGTON President Lincoln and his Cabinet meet with key military leaders to examine the future course to be taken by Union forces. Generals McDowell and Scott describe their plans, recognizing the importance of maintaining public support and enthusiasm.

30 *JUNE* 1861

NAVAL The CSS *Sumter* successfully slips past the Union blockade, despite efforts by the USS *Brooklyn* to prevent it.

1 *JULY* 1861

WASHINGTON In order to fill the need for Federal troops, the War Department decrees that both Kentucky and Tennessee are to be canvassed for volunteers. This despite the fact that Tennessee has joined the Confederacy, having voted to secede at the 6 May state convention, a vote confirmed by public referendum in June. Kentucky has, at this point in time, voted to remain neutral.

2 JULY 1861

WASHINGTON General John Frémont meets with President Lincoln. The two discuss Frémont's upcoming command of the Missouri forces in an area of violent unrest.

THE NORTH At Wheeling, West Virginia the new legislature convenes, having been recognized by the United States.

EASTERN THEATER Federal troops under General Robert Patterson head for the Shenandoah Valley where they intend to curtail the movement of Confederates toward Mannassas, Virginia. At Hoke's Run, in West Virginia, Union forces clash with rebel troops resulting in a Federal victory.

3 JULY 1861

EASTERN THEATER Patterson's soldiers march to Martinsburg, Virginia, causing the Confederates, who are commanded by General Joseph E Johnston, to pull back.

4 JULY 1861

WASHINGTON It is the Fourth of July, Independence Day, and in the Federal capital a special session of the Twenty-Seventh Congress meets. Called by the president, this session is to handle war measures partially sketched out by Lincoln in a message directed to the assembled body. According to the President, the North has done everything in its power to maintain peace and has attempted to solve problems precipitated by the South without resorting to war. Blaming Southerners for the Fort Sumter affair, the chief executive emphasizes that the questions facing the nation have to do with the United States' maintaining 'its territorial integrity, against its own domestic foes'. Lincoln reiterates his position concerning the indivisibility of the Federal Union, once again making

clear his stance on declaring war against the Confederacy. He makes a request for an additional 400,000 men to aid the Union.

EASTERN THEATER Harper's Ferry, Virginia is the site of a brief engagement between Confederates and Northern troops as the latter stream into the Shenandoah Valley.

5 JULY 1861

TRANS-MISSISSIPPI Carthage, Missouri witnesses an attack by Federal forces on pro-secessionist Missouri troops under the command of Governor Claiborne Jackson, a staunch Confederate. While the Missouri troops are less well organized than the Union forces, they outnumber the latter three to one. As the Southern cavalry attacks both sides of the Union line, the Northern troops under Franz Sigel fall back. Total losses are tallied at 40 to 50 Confederates killed and 120 wounded, while the Union reports 13 deaths and 31 wounded. In spite of this, the battle is considered a Confederate victory. It slows considerably the Federal push into southwest Missouri and provides the South with a sense of triumph so important to Confederate morale.

8 JULY 1861

TRANS-MISSISSIPPI The Confederacy, anxious to remove all Federal presence from the New Mexico Territory, places General Henry Hopkins Sibley in command of rebel troops in that area. In Florida, Missouri an encampment of Confederates is attacked and dispersed.

10 JULY 1861

WASHINGTON President Lincoln, in a letter to the Inspector General of Kentucky's militia, Simon B Buckner, indicates that the Union forces will not enter that neutral state.

EASTERN THEATER General McClellan in West Virginia sends troops forward to meet Confederates at Rich Mountain. This force of four regiments and a cavalry unit is under the command of General William S Rosecrans. In addition to this movement, General T A Morris is sent by McClellan to meet rebels at Laurel Hill, Virginia.

11 *JULY* 1861

EESTERN THEATER   The road to Beverly, Virginia is opened by General Rosecrans' troops. Attacking Colonel John Pegram's Confederates, Rosecrans forces the rebels to surrender at Rich Mountain. At Laurel Mountain, General Garnett's forces have evacuated their posts, heading for the Cheat River Valley after General Morris attacks the Laurel Mountain position. Altogether the Union fatalities for these two engagements are listed at 12, with 49 wounded. The Confederate estimates are not available.

12 *JULY* 1861

WESTERN THEATER   As McClellan occupies Beverly, in West Virginia, the Confederate troops retreat from Laurel Hill. In the west and south of this position, another group of Union soldiers, under the command of Jacob Cox, is moving in to meet with rebels in the Great Kanawah Valley. These Southern troops are under the command of former Virginia Governor General Henry Wise.

13 *JULY* 1861

WASHINGTON   Missouri Representative John Clark is expelled from the House by a vote of 94 to 45.
WESTERN THEATER   At Carrickford, Virginia, Union troops crush the Confederate forces of General Robert S Garnett who is killed in the ensuing battle. McClellan has now enabled Federals to take control of the entire area in West Virginia, an important move forward for the Union due to the communications links, including railroad lines, found there. It also provides Union troops with a base of operation from which to launch raids into Virginia proper. The number of rebels killed at Carrickford totals 20 compared to 53 Union lost.

14 *JULY* 1861

WESTERN THEATER   After the Rich Mountain and Laurel Hill battles, the North is anxious to press further into Virginia. Toward this end, General McDowell advances on Fairfax Courthouse, Virginia with 40,000 Union troops.
NAVAL   In the harbor at Wilmington, North Carolina, the USS *Daylight* establishes a blockade. This effort is only partially effective and soon demands additional ships to make it successful.

17 *JULY* 1861

WESTERN THEATER   General Beauregard requests aid in repulsing the Federal advance into Virginia. Beauregard is stationed near Manassas, Virginia, with a force of about 22,000 men. Confederate President Jefferson Davis orders General Joseph Johnston to Manassas so as to meet Beauregard's request for more troops.

18 *JULY* 1861

EASTERN THEATER   Blackburn's Ford, Virginia, proves to be a test for the upcoming battle at Manassas, Virginia. McDowell's Union forces are encamped at nearby Centreville, and a small party of soldiers is sent forward to examine the area around Blackburn's Ford. The men meet Confederates under the command of James Longstreet and a strong skirmish ensues during which the Federals lose 19 men and sustain 38 wounded. The rebels have 15 fatalities and 53 injured but succeed in pushing the Union troops back. In addition, a small clash occurs at Mitchell's Ford. Jefferson Davis, upon hearing of the Confederate success at Blackburn's Ford, says to Beauregard, 'God be praised for your successful beginning'.

20 *JULY* 1861

EASTERN THEATER   Both Union and Confederate forces prepare for the imminent battle, Johnston's 1400 troops having joined those 2500 of Jackson at Manassas. McDowell is situated with around 1300 men near Sudley Ford on Bull Run, a creek running by Manassas; this creek will make the battle known as First Bull Run to Northerners, while Southerners know it as First Manassas—a second battle at this locale being fought in August 1862. Other Union troops are to travel by the Stone Bridge over Bull Run. There is little time left—one Union soldier comments on the 'ominous stillness'.

21 JULY 1861

EASTERN THEATER Unknown to McDowell's troops, which are situated at Sudley Ford on Bull Run, Johnston has combined forces with Jackson. McDowell hopes to surprise the rebels by striking them on the left flank of their stance at the Stone Bridge, but after Northern artillery begins at about 5 o'clock in the morning, the Confederates learn of the Union advance. Accordingly, General N G Evans meets McDowell's troops as the latter approach from Sudley Ford, holding the southern position until around noon. The Confederates then fall back to Henry House Hill where Evans and others, Jackson among them, make a strong stand. (It is because of his unit's stout defense that Jackson will thereafter be known as 'Stonewall'.) McDowell's forces advance on this Confederate position at Henry House Hill around 2 o'clock, Beauregard and Johnston aiding Evans' beleaguered troops. Despite Union attempts to charge this position, the rebels hold fast and are successful in driving Federals back in defeat. As McDowell's men pull away, panic strikes when a shell destroys a wagon; the main road of retreat is blocked and the Union troops scatter. The Confederate victory is observed by Jefferson Davis from Manassas, Virginia. It is a costly triumph: the rebels list 387 dead, 1582 wounded, 13 missing; Union troops lose 460 men, sustain 1124 injuries and list 1312 as missing. Lincoln, learning of the defeat, immediately closets himself with his Cabinet, and throughout the North runs the conviction that the war has begun in earnest.

Bull Run, 21 July 1861.

22 JULY 1861

SECESSION Confusion continues in Missouri as the State Convention meets at Jefferson City, voting to uphold the Union and providing for a new government to be established at St Louis. Pro-South Governor Claiborne Jackson continues to claim that his administration is the only legal body in the state.

24 JULY 1861

EASTERN THEATER In West Virginia, Union General Jacob Cox attacks Confederates who are commanded by General Henry Wise. This action at Tyler Mountain causes Wise to evacuate the area around Charleston and to pull back to Gauley Bridge.

25 JULY 1861

WASHINGTON The Crittenden Resolution passes, 30-5. This bill states that the war is to be fought to preserve the Union and uphold the Constitution, not to alter slavery in its established form.

TRANS-MISSISSIPPI Missouri remains an area of unrest. Fighting breaks out at Harrisville and at Dug Springs. Confederates in the New Mexico Territory clash with Union troops from Fort Fillmore; the rebels, under Captain John Baylor, hope to press the Federals to leave the Southwest, which would open the area to Confederate control. The Union soldiers are able to push the rebels back, however. The following day, the same Union troops, under the command of Major Isaac Lynde, are confronted at Fort Fillmore by Baylor's troops and Lynde abandons the position. This despite the fact that Lynde's forces outnumber Baylor's, the rebels having but 250 men to the Federal's 500. Lynde is subsequently discharged from the Army for this action, but after the war was placed on the retirement list.

27 JULY 1861

WASHINGTON At the Northern capital, President Lincoln hands over command of the Federal Division of the Potomac to General George McClellan. The latter replaces McDowell, whose forces had been so badly beaten at Bull Run. Lincoln indicates that Union forces should push toward Tennessee by seizing Manassas Junction, Virginia and Strasburg, Kentucky, in the Shenandoah Valley.

30 JULY 1861

WASHINGTON Secretary of War Simon Cameron is pressed by General Benjamin Butler at Fort Monroe, Virginia to make a determined policy concerning former slaves now in Federal hands. Butler by now has about 900 former slaves and is unclear as to their status as property. He asks Cameron, 'What shall be done with them?' SECESSION In Missouri, the State Convention votes 56-25 to declare the Governor's office open. In addition, the Secretary of State and Lieutenant Governor's offices are now vacant, as are the seats in the legislature. Most of those holding office in Missouri were pro-Confederate. The following day, Hamilton Gamble is elected Governor of pro-Union Missouri.

31 JULY 1861

WASHINGTON President Lincoln names Ulysses S Grant, stationed in Illinois, as a General of Volunteers. The month has seen a variety of military activity at Bull Run and elsewhere. The Federal blockade is fairly successful, although Confederate

privateers are still quite active. Throughout the North and the South civilians and soldiers alike prepare for further action as it becomes clear that the war will not be over in a short time but is likely to proceed for some months.

1 AUGUST 1861

THE CONFEDERACY Captain John Baylor, who successfully routed Union troops at Fort Fillmore, decrees that all territory in Arizona and New Mexico south of the 34th parallel belongs to the Confederate States of America. There is some dissent among pro-Unionists in New Mexico who object to the wholesale takeover of their Territory. Advising General Johnston to take advantage of 'the weakness' which would be felt by the Union forces after their defeat at Bull Run, Confederate President Jefferson Davis urges further action in Virginia. He sends General Robert E Lee to take top command of forces in the area of West Virginia after General Garnett's defeat at Carrickford.

2 AUGUST 1861

WASHINGTON For the first time in United States history, the Congress passes a national income tax bill which provides also for tariffs to aid in the war effort. These Congressional measures are to raise $500 million for Union support. The income tax of three percent is applicable to incomes exceeding $800 per year, but is never actually put into effect. TRANS-MISSISSIPPI Another fort in the southwest, Fort Stanton, in the New Mexico Territory, is evacuated by Federal troops as a result of Baylor's Confederates. Further disturbances occur in Missouri; Dug Springs is the site of a small clash between Federals, led by Nathaniel Lyon, and pro-secessionists under General McCulloch's command. General Frémont sends reinforcements to General Lyon who anticipates continued unrest in southwestern Missouri.

CHRONOLOGY

5 *AUGUST* 1861

TRANS-MISSISSIPPI In Missouri, General Nathaniel Lyon pulls his troops out of Dug Springs as reports indicate that Confederates are advancing in large numbers.

NAVAL The USS *Vincennes* captures a rebel blockade runner, the *Alvarado*, and burns it off the coast of Florida near Fernandina.

6 *AUGUST* 1861

WASHINGTON Lincoln is empowered by Congress to pass measures concerning Army and Navy actions. The President decides that slaves used by the South against the North will be freed. Since there is some dispute as to Kentucky's neutral position, a Union military camp is established near Lexington in a show of Federal force.

7 *AUGUST* 1861

EASTERN THEATER In Virginia, where General Benjamin Butler is in command at Fort Monroe, the town of Hampton is burned by Confederates. The commander General John Bankhead Magruder, indicates that the action is partially in response to Butler's quartering of runaway slaves.

NAVAL In a further attempt to improve Union naval operations, a new version of ironclads are put into production and later prove to be a vital part of Union operations.

8 *AUGUST* 1861

WASHINGTON In further reply to General Butler's queries, Secretary of War Simon Cameron points out the need for Union troops to adhere to fugitive slave laws, but only in Union territory. Those states in insurrection were exempt from this protection. Further, Cameron tells Butler that escaped slaves cannot be returned to owners in the Confederate states.

10 *AUGUST* 1861

TRANS-MISSISSIPPI General Nathaniel Lyon is killed at Wilson's Creek, Missouri, where he has led 5200 men to meet rebel troops under the command of General Benjamin McCulloch. The Confederates are joined in this encounter by pro-southern Missouri militia under the command of Sterling Price. While Union troops are defeated at Wilson's Creek, they put up a valiant fight, pushing back two rebel charges on Bloody Ridge, the spot where Lyon falls. After this fatality, the Federals pull back, commanded now by Major Samuel Sturgis, and march to Rolla, Missouri, to the southwest of St Louis. The Confederate's force of 15,000 was depleted by 421 deaths and 1300 wounded as compared to Federal losses of 263 fatalities and 721 injuries. The battle of Wilson's Creek is the second important clash between the two enemies and gives the South another significant victory following that of Bull Run in Virginia.

12 *AUGUST* 1861

TRANS-MISSISSIPPI In Texas, Confederates are attacked by Apache Indians who kill 15 rebels. It is not Confederate practice to make war with the Indians, engaged as they are in efforts to gain control of the southwest for the Confederacy.

14 *AUGUST* 1861

EASTERN THEATER Grievances among the troops of the 79th New York Regiment provoke mutiny by these volunteers. Among other things, the men requested, and had been denied, a furlough, precipitating an action that results in several arrests and places the entire unit under armed guard.

TRANS-MISSISSIPPI Due to the unsettled conditions in St Louis, Missouri, General John Frémont issues a declaration of martial law in that city.

15 *AUGUST* 1861

EASTERN THEATER Another group of soldiers disrupts its regiment, the Second Maine Volunteers. Altogether 60 men are assigned to duty on Dry Tortugas, off Key West, Florida as a disciplinary measure.

TRANS-MISSISSIPPI General Frémont

fears continuing conflict in Missouri, so he requests aid from Washington. Lincoln recognizes threats posed by McCulloch and Price, who can easily invade with Confederate forces. The President therefore directs the War Department to arrange reinforcements for Frémont.

16 *AUGUST* 1861

THE NORTH In several separate cases, certain newspapers in the Union states are brought to court for alleged pro-Confederate leanings, among them the Brooklyn *Eagle*, the New York *Journal of Commerce* and the New York *Daily News*.
TRANS-MISSISSIPPI Missouri continues to experience clashes between Northern and Southern forces, this time near Fredericktown and Kirkville.

19 *AUGUST* 1861

THE NORTH Seizure of pro-South newspapers continues as offices in West Chester and Easton, Pennsylvania are attacked by loyal Unionists. An *Essex County Democrat* editor in Haverhill, Massachusetts, is tarred and feathered for similar Southern sympathies expressed in the newspaper.
THE CONFEDERACY In an action which does little to settle the discord in Missouri, the Congress of the Confederacy allies with that state, essentially providing for the establishment of a Confederate state government.

20 *AUGUST* 1861

THE CONFEDERACY President Jefferson Davis approves the addition of more commissioners to represent the Confederacy in Europe. It is hoped that supplies and armaments so necessary to Southern victory will be obtained from France, Britain and Spain.
TRANS-MISSISSIPPI Skirmishing continues in Missouri: Jonesboro is the site of fighting which follows clashes between Union and Confederate forces at Klapsford several days earlier.

24 *AUGUST* 1861

THE CONFEDERACY At Richmond, Virginia, three new Confederate commissioners to Europe are appointed: John Slidell to France; James Mason to Britain; and Pierre Rost to Spain.

26 *AUGUST* 1861

EASTERN THEATER Virginia is a scene of much action as skirmishing breaks out at Wayne Court House and Blue's House in the western regions of the estate.
NAVAL At Hampton Roads, Virginia, Union vessels move out toward Cape Hatteras, North Carolina in preparation for a Federal assault on Confederate fortifications there. This operation is under the command of Commodore Silas Stringham and General Benjamin Butler who have eight vessels and 900 men at their disposal.

27 *AUGUST* 1861

EASTERN THEATER The Union expeditionary force at Cape Hatteras, North Carolina lands troops under fire. Confederate batteries attempt to prevent a Federal takeover of the area, without success. The rebels had established two positions, Fort Clark and Fort Hatteras, but abandon the former, enabling the Union to occupy with no resistance. The following day sees the surrender of Fort Hatteras, which sustains considerable damage from Federal batteries. There are few casualties among Union or Confederate troops. The successful takeover by Federals of this strategic point on Hatteras Inlet gives the North an important advantage in its efforts to crush the blockade-runners, since the area commands control of an important route used by those Confederate vessels.

30 *AUGUST* 1861

TRANS-MISSISSIPPI General John Frémont, in an action which Lincoln later terms 'dictatorial', declares martial law throughout Missouri. In an unauthorized act, Frémont allowed for the confiscation of property belonging to 'those who shall take up arms against the United States', and also makes an emancipation proclamation concerning slaves of pro-Southerners: 'their slaves . . . are hereby declared free men'. In defense of this extremely unpopular move, Frémont explains that Missouri suffers from 'helplessness of civil authority and total insecurity of life'.

1 *SEPTEMBER* 1861

EASTERN THEATER   Western Virginia is again an area of light military activity, Blue Creek, Boone Court House, and Burlington all witnessing their share of brief skirmishing.

TRANS-MISSISSIPPI   Jefferson County, Missouri is the focus of action in the west. At Cape Girardeau in Missouri, General Ulysses S Grant assumes command of Federal forces.

2 *SEPTEMBER* 1861

WASHINGTON   In response to General Frémont's proclamations concerning martial law and emancipation of slaves, President Lincoln communicates to the General his concerns that the actions are precipitate. The President feels that there is a danger of alienating Southern Federal sympathizers and 'perhaps ruin our rather fair prospect for Kentucky'.

3 *SEPTEMBER* 1861

WESTERN THEATER   General Polk orders Southern troops into Kentucky in order to hold Confederate positions there. These forces are under the command of Gideon Pillow, and the move effectively terminates Kentucky's neutral status. General Polk's orders result in part from the belief held by Confederates that the Union would soon attempt to take military control of Kentucky.

5 *SEPTEMBER* 1861

WASHINGTON   The President and the Cabinet confer with General Scott, discussing General Frémont's conduct and future position in the Army.

WESTERN THEATER   General Grant, upon hearing of Polk's move into Columbus, Kentucky, begins preparations for an expedition to Paducah, Kentucky, which is near the mouth of the Cumberland River.

6 *SEPTEMBER* 1861

WESTERN THEATER   General Grant's forces move into Paducah, Kentucky in order to prevent Confederates from seizing the city. The action, provoking no fighting or bloodshed, proves to be strategically critical as it allows Federals an important foothold in an area that will be central to the western river campaign in the upcoming year. General Charles F Smith is given command of forces in western Kentucky as General Grant leaves for his headquarters at Cairo, Illinois.

9 *SEPTEMBER* 1861

WASHINGTON   General Frémont's conduct in Missouri continues to worry President Lincoln, who is advised by some military officials to relieve Frémont of his command there. The President directs General David Hunter to go to Missouri to provide Frémont with aid.

EASTERN THEATER   General Rosecrans' troops advance on Confederates near Carnifex Ferry, Virginia, where skirmishing has been continuing, indicating the probability of a battle in that area in the future.

10 *SEPTEMBER* 1861

WASHINGTON   The President receives Mrs John Frémont, wife of the general; she has traveled to the Union capital to provide support for her husband's position in Missouri. She is concerned about Lincoln's being influenced against General Frémont, and the interview, by some accounts, is not a calm one.

EASTERN THEATER   Confederates at Carnifex Ferry, Virginia, fall back after being attacked by General Rosecrans. The Union troops outnumber the Southerners, and the Northern victory is instrumental in helping to preserve western Virginia for the Union.

11 *SEPTEMBER* 1861

WASHINGTON The proclamations issued by General Frémont concerning property confiscation and the emancipation of slaves in Missouri, issued on 30 August 1861, prompt President Lincoln to write to the General. Lincoln tells Frémont that the proclamations must be altered in order to align them with Federal Acts of Congress, otherwise they remain unacceptable.

EASTERN THEATER Fighting breaks out at Cheat Mountain, western Virginia, between General Lee's forces and those of General John Reynolds. Although Lee has planned a surprise attack on Reynold's Union forces at Cheat Mountain Summit and at Elkwater, severe precipitation and the difficult terrain prevent Confederates from carrying out the assault as designed. Federal troops hold their ground as the rebels pull back, and this Union victory at Cheat Mountain secures the area of West Virginia for the North. Estimates of Confederate casualties total near 100; Federals killed and wounded tally only around 21 men.

12 *SEPTEMBER* 1861

WASHINGTON Lincoln communicates with Mrs Frémont about her husband, assuring her that he, the President, is not 'acting in any hostility' toward the general. Accordingly, he dispatches Judge Joseph Holt to St Louis, Missouri with instructions to urge moderation and modification of Frémont's proclamation of 30 August.

16 *SEPTEMBER* 1861

WESTERN THEATER In Kentucky, the Cumberland River is the scene of intensified action as the USS *Conestoga* takes two Confederate vessels. Ship Island, Mississippi is vacuated by rebel forces, leaving the area open to subsequent occupation by Union troops. The North is to use Ship Island as an operating base for action along the Gulf Coast.

TRANS-MISSISSIPPI In Missouri, Confederate General Price continues to press Colonel Mulligan's troops at Lexington; the latter is waiting for help from General Frémont.

18 *SEPTEMBER* 1861

WASHINGTON The President meets with his Cabinet; General Frémont is once again the topic of discussion as reports concerning his command in the West are presented. The Secretary of the Navy receives word that Federal expeditions to the Southern coast are to commence within the month.

THE NORTH Another publication, the Louisville, Kentucky, *Courier*, is prevented from using the postal service. The newspaper has indicated an alleged hostility to the Union cause and several employees are arrested by Federal officials when the headquarters of the *Courier* are seized.

19 *SEPTEMBER* 1861

WESTERN THEATER In Kentucky, the Confederates are making a strong defense along a line including the area around Cumberland Gap, Bowling Green and Columbus. Pro-Union Kentucky troops are driven out of the vicinity of Barboursville, Kentucky by General Felix Zollicoffer's rebel forces.

TRANS-MISSISSIPPI Beleagured Union troops at Lexington, Missouri are acutely aware of their precarious position as Price's forces continue to lay siege to the city. Unless reinforcements appear, surrender is inevitable.

20 *SEPTEMBER* 1861

TRANS-MISSISSIPPI General John Frémont's inaction in bringing relief to Colonel Mulligan's troops at Lexington, Missouri leads to the enforced surrender of those forces after more than a week of siege. General Sterling Price, the Confederate officer who led the offensive, lost

25 men out of 18,000 troops, while Mulligan's force of 3600 Federals was reduced by 39 fatalities. Because of Frémont's failure to send reinforcements, the general receives further criticism of his already questionable behavior in handling matters.

23 *SEPTEMBER* 1861

TRANS-MISSISSIPPI General Frémont's sensitivity to criticism provokes him to close the offices of the St Louis *Evening News* and to arrest the editor of that publication. The latter raised some questions about Frémont's inaction during the siege of Lexington, Missouri.

25 *SEPTEMBER* 1861

EASTERN THEATER Forces led by General Lee and General Rosecrans continue to converge on the Kanawha Valley of western Virginia.

WESTERN THEATER Minor clashes occur between Union and Confederate troops near the Cumberland River in Kentucky and also near Lewinsville, Virginia; Chapmansville, western Virginia; and at Canada Alamosa, New Mexico Territory.

27 *SEPTEMBER* 1861

WASHINGTON In a meeting with the Cabinet, President Lincoln and General McClellan confer over plans for an offensive in Virginia. There is much public pressure for increased action in this area.

30 *SEPTEMBER* 1861

WASHINGTON After four weeks of brief engagements but no major battles between Union and Confederate forces, President Lincoln is left anxious to establish firm control in Kentucky and settle matters with General Frémont in Missouri. In addition, the lack of military action in Virginia continues to draw criticism from both civilian and military observers.

1 *OCTOBER* 1861

WASHINGTON President Lincoln

appoints General Benjamin Butler to the post of commander of the Department of New England; this branch of the Army is used largely to recruit and train soldiers for upcoming campaigns. The Cabinet confers with Generals Scott and McClellan. In addition, the chief executive directs his Cabinet to make preparations for the implementation of an East coast expedition to commence in November. This eventually is known as the Port Royal, South Carolina operation under the command of General Thomas S Sherman.

THE CONFEDERACY Centreville, Virginia is the site of a strategy planning session between Confederate President Jefferson Davis and Generals Johnston, Beauregard and Smith. They meet to discuss a possible solution to problems posed by the Southern offensive in Virginia which is what the citizenry of the Confederate nation are currently demanding. An assessment of the army's capabilities leads to the conclusion that such a move to attack the North at this time would be foolhardy. Southern troops are neither sufficiently provisioned nor available in the numbers necessary for an offensive; the consensus is to wait until spring and watch further developments on all fronts, not just in Virginia.

NAVAL Confederates seize the Federal supply steamer *Fanny* at Pamlico sound, North Carolina. In this capture, 31 Union soldiers are taken, along with a large number of military supplies.

2 *OCTOBER* 1861

EASTERN THEATER Confederates are defeated at Chapmansville, Virginia; there is also skirmishing at Springfield Station, in that same state.

TRANS-MISSISSIPPI Union troops succeed in disrupting a rebel camp at Charleston, Missouri, where clashes between pro-Union and secession groups have been occurring for several days.

3 *OCTOBER* 1861

THE CONFEDERACY The governor of Louisiana, Thomas O Moore, bans the shipment of cotton to Europe in order to place pressure on European nations. It is hoped that this may sway opinion in favour of recognition of the Confederacy.

EASTERN THEATER Greenbriar, Virginia sees the rout of Confederate troops. This victory enables the Northern forces, which have made this reconnaissance from their Cheat Mountain encampment, to take possession of valuable cattle and horses. The Pohick Church, Virginia area is occupied by Federal forces.

4 OCTOBER 1861

WASHINGTON The President observes another balloon ascension by Thaddeus Lowe. The Chief executive also meets with military and government officials concerning General Frémont's duties in the Department of the West. John Ericsson of New York submits a contract, which is approved by the Cabinet, to build ironclad warships for the Union Navy. The vessels ultimately constructed include the *Monitor*, which is later to take part in a decisive naval battle.

THE CONFEDERACY Treaties are signed by the Confederates with the Cherokee, Shawnee and Seneca Indian tribes; this enables the rebels to utilize willing Indians in their confrontations with Union troops.

NAVAL Two more Confederate vessels fail in an attempt to slip by the Federal blockade. The USS *South Carolina* seizes the rebel ships off Southwest Pass near New Orleans, Louisiana. The Southern forces attack Federal troops near the Hatteras Inlet forts, but with no success in their attempt to retake those critically positioned bases now in Union hands.

5 OCTOBER 1861

TRANS-MISSISSIPPI In California, Federal troops carry out an expedition to Oak Grove and Temecula Ranch; their objective is to reveal the position of alleged pro-Confederates.

INTERNATIONAL Disputes about whether the British should or should not support the Confederacy's claim are in evidence as the London *Times* shows sympathy with the Union; the London *Post* speaks out in favor of recognizing the Confederacy.

7 OCTOBER 1861

WASHINGTON After discussion with his Cabinet and military advisors, President Lincoln has sent Secretary of War Simon Cameron to investigate conditions in the West. Cameron carries a letter to General Samuel R Curtis from the President in which the latter asks for an assessment of General Frémont's command.

TRANS-MISSISSIPPI In Missouri, General Frémont has gathered troops and set out on a mission to intercept Confederate General Sterling Price. This belated action ultimately does little to redeem Frémont in the eyes of the President and his advisors.

8 OCTOBER 1861

EASTERN THEATER General Robert Anderson, the former hero of Fort Sumter and currently in command of the Union Department of the Cumberland, is relieved of his post and replaced by General Sherman. Anderson has for a period of time been suffering from nervous strain and is unable to continue his military duties; after his departure from this last post, he never again resumes military active duty. Soon, General Sherman experiences similar exhaustion in the demanding position of head of the Cumberland troops, although Sherman remains in command at Louisville, Kentucky.

9 OCTOBER 1861

WESTERN THEATER Santa Rosa Island in Pensacola Bay, Florida is the scene of a Confederate assault on Union batteries. A force of 1000 troops under the command of General Richard Heron Anderson tries unsuccessfully to destroy the Federal shore batteries and is obliged to withdraw. Troops from Fort Pickens on Santa Rosa Island are instrumental in the rebuff of this Southern force.

CHRONOLOGY

10 *OCTOBER* 1861

THE CONFEDERACY Confederate President Jefferson Davis expresses his concerns about troop organization, railroad transportation in the South and the use of blacks as laborers for the Confederate Army, in a letter to General G W Smith. Later to come out in favor of their employment by the military, Davis at this early date is unable to speak with conviction for the use of slaves in the Army as regular soldiers.

12 *OCTOBER* 1861

TRANS-MISSISSIPPI Minor clashes take place in Missouri which continues to be in an uproar, partly as a result of Frémont's orders. Fighting goes on for two days near Clintonville and Pomme de Terre, Missouri, and southern raiders under former Virginian and now partisan fighter, Jeff Thompson, push into the Ironton area of that state from Stoddard County.

NAVAL At the mouth of the Mississippi River the Confederate ironclad *Manassas* confronts the USS *Richmond* as well as the USS *Vincennes*. Despite the fact that both the *Richmond* and the *Vincennes* are run aground, they manage to pull back. The Federal blockade resumes after a short time, but the clash is one that puts the Union at a psychological disadvantage.

INTERNATIONAL John Slidell, Confederate commissioner to France, and James Mason, Commissioner to Britain,

Union Fleet under attack, 12 October 1861.

successfully slip past the Union blockade of Charleston, South Carolina on the *Theodora*. Their next stop is Cuba, but they are en route to Europe in order to help their government buy armaments and to work for recognition of the Confederacy by European powers.

14 *OCTOBER* 1861

WASHINGTON President Lincoln once again places himself in a vulnerable position, although one that he feels is defensible, when he orders General Winfield Scott to suspend the writ of habeas corpus. Scott is given the authority to implement suspension from points in Maine to the Federal capital.

TRANS-MISSISSIPPI Jeff Thompson, one-time mayor of St Louis and now a pro-secessionist in the Missouri State Militia, establishes southeastern Missouri as an area which he and his troops are determined to rid of Federal 'invaders'.

15 *OCTOBER* 1861

TRANS-MISSISSIPPI In Missouri, Thompson's raiders again strike a party of Union soldiers near Potosi, capture 50 and burn the Big River Bridge.

NAVAL In order to overtake the vessel that allegedly carries John Slidell and James Mason, three Union gunboats leave New York in search of the *Nashville*, despite the fact that the commissioners are sailing to Cuba on the *Theodora*.

16 *OCTOBER* 1861

THE CONFEDERACY Jefferson Davis encounters difficulties with Confederate Army sodiers who are concerned with their states' defenses. The Confederate president is besieged with requests from regular soldiers who want to return home to aid state militia. Davis feels it a matter of principle and public interest to deny granting these requests.

EASTERN THEATER Near Harper's Ferry, Virginia there is a clash between Federals and rebels.

TRANS-MISSISSIPPI Lexington, Missouri

is taken over by Union forces. The town had been under the control of a rebel garrison, although most of the Confederates have already evacuated the area.

18 OCTOBER 1861

WASHINGTON The President meets with his Cabinet to discuss General Winfield Scott's future military service. The aging commander of the Army is now being considered for retirement of a voluntary nature, although it is clear that there are those who would be glad to see Scott leave active military duty, General McClellan among them. Lincoln is called upon to settle disagreements between McClellan and General Sherman; a coastal expedition to the south is being planned and McClellan is reluctant to furnish Sherman with the necessary troops for such a foray.

WESTERN THEATER Federals make a gunboat expedition down the Mississippi River, and minor fighting breaks out in Kentucky near Rockcastle Hills.

TRANS-MISSISSIPPI Jeff Thompson's forces in Missouri clash with Northern troops from Cape Girardeau as the Ironton area continues to experience a great deal of action and unrest.

20 OCTOBER 1861

EASTERN THEATER The Potomac River area, under the command of Union General Nathaniel Banks, contains several important points, among them Edward's Ferry and Conrad's Ferry. Both of these are situated near Leesburg, Virginia, where Confederate General Nathan Evans is positioned. Federal activity in the area includes the occupation of Drainesville, Virginia by General George McCall's troops. General Charles Stone is ordered by General McClellan to engage in a 'slight demonstration' so as to provoke the Confederates at Leesburg to some action. Although Stone complies, taking troops into the area, he pulls back after no conclusive engagement.

21 OCTOBER 1861

EASTERN THEATER Leesburg, Virginia witnesses battling between rebels and Federal troops, the latter under General Charles Stone's command. Stone is pushing toward Leesburg on orders from Washington and is assisted by Colonel Edward Baker, who is shuttling troops across the Potomac River from Ball's Bluff and Edward's Ferry. When fire from Confederate troops succeeds in pushing the Union troops back at Ball's Bluff and a retreat is in order, Colonel Baker is killed. The men attempt to withdraw but panic and confusion, as well as steep and hilly terrain along the river bank, prevent an orderly retreat. Men are drowned and shot as boats swamp and as the Union troops attempt to escape via the steep cliffs. Losses are severe: 49 killed, 158 wounded, 714 missing and presumed drowned; Confederates tally their casualties at 36 dead, 117 wounded, 12 missing. The disorderly and costly defeat of the Union troops causes a public outcry against General Stone who was charged by the press as being an inept commander, friendly toward the enemy and a traitor to the Northern cause. Colonel Baker, a former Senator from Oregon and a friend of President Lincoln, is considered a martyr. There is little criticism aimed at General McClellan, under whose orders the entire operation was carried out. The South is overjoyed at the victory and General Nathan Evans is given wide public acclaim as the hero of this battle of Leesburg, or Ball's Bluff, Virginia.

22 OCTOBER 1861

WASHINGTON The Cabinet and President Lincoln meet to confer about General Frémont's situation in the west, and also to discuss the defeat at Balls' Bluff. In addition, it is learned that the Confederates are in control of all important points on the Potomac River south of Alexandria.

23 OCTOBER 1861

WASHINGTON The writ of habeas corpus is suspended in the District of Columbia in all military-related cases.

CHRONOLOGY

WESTERN THEATER Skirmishing breaks out in Kentucky near West Liberty and at Hodgenville. This line of Confederate troops in Kentucky is a matter of grave concern to the Union and to General Sherman in particular as he does not want Confederates to advance further into Kentucky.

24 OCTOBER 1861

WASHINGTON President Lincoln reaches a decision concerning the termination of General John Frémont's command in the Western Department. Via General S R Curtis, he sends orders that relieve Frémont of his position and hand over control of the Western troops to General David Hunter. Lincoln advises Curtis to withhold delivery of these orders if Frémont should 'be in the immediate presence of the enemy, in expectation of a battle'. Lincoln attends the funeral of Colonel Baker who was killed at Ball's Bluff, Virginia.

25 OCTOBER 1861

TRANS-MISSISSIPPI In Missouri, General Frémont's forces are on an expedition to rout Confederates under Sterling Price and are occupying Springfield, far from Price's location near Lexington. Frémont is aware that orders are on their way from Washington which will remove him from his command, and he is anxious to prevent or delay their delivery.

NAVAL An important project begins at Greenpoint, Long Island, with the laying of the keel of the USS *Monitor*. Although it is not the first ironclad vessel for either side, the *Monitor* will later earn a role in naval history because of its crucial battle with the Confederate ironclad, *Merrimack* (9 March 1862).

26 OCTOBER 1861

EASTERN THEATER South Branch Bridge in western Virginia is an area of some minor skirmishing between Union and rebel soldiers. Romney, in the northern reaches of western Virginia, is the scene of Union action against Confederate forces, which are cleaned out with few casualties.

27 OCTOBER 1861

TRANS-MISSISSIPPI General Frémont is now in pursuit of Confederate General Sterling Price, whom Frémont believes to be moving toward Springfield, Missouri. In actuality, Price is not in that area, and Frémont's intended confrontation is not an immediate possibility.

29 OCTOBER 1861

EASTERN THEATER An expedition to the Confederate coast leaves Hampton Roads, Virginia, under the command of Federal General Thomas W Sherman and Flag Officer Samuel Du Pont. This fleet of 77 vessels carries one of the largest forces yet assembled by the United States, consisting of about 12,000 men. The ships soon experience difficult weather in storms off Cape Hatteras, North Carolina.

31 OCTOBER 1861

WASHINGTON General Winfield Scott makes a formal petition to President Lincoln concerning resignation from his position as General-in-Chief of the Union Army. Despite his experience—he is a veteran of both the War of 1812 and the Mexican War—Scott is prompted to this action by his advancing age and personality clashes with younger, ambitious military personnel. Scott convinces Lincoln to grant his retirement request and is succeeded by General McClellan.

WESTERN THEATER Fighting of a minor nature breaks out in Morgantown, Kentucky with an attack on a Federal encampment by rebel soldiers. The Union troops are able to withstand this attack although the Confederates suffer moderate losses. The month ends with no major realignment on the part of either the North or the South; both sides are waiting for spring weather. Frémont continues to pursue Price's Confederates in Missouri.

Scott's last meeting with the Cabinet.

1 *NOVEMBER* 1861

WASHINGTON General Winfield Scott voluntarily relinquishes his post as General-in-Chief of the United States Army. Scott's decision allows 34-year-old General George Brinton McClellan to assume control of the Army; President Lincoln and the Cabinet bid General Scott farewell as the aging war hero makes his way to retirement at West Point. There is a great deal of enthusiasm for the younger McClellan, who appears to be eminently suited for the position he now assumes.

EASTERN THEATER In western Virginia, near Gaulery Bridge and Cotton Hill, Confederates attack General Rosecrans' troops. The rebel force, under the command of General John B Floyd, clashes with Federals for three days but ultimately withdraws without success.

TRANS-MISSISSIPPI General Frémont, in Missouri, communicates with General Price's messengers, agreeing to exchange prisoners. This decision is made without Lincoln's authorization and the President later abrogates the arrangement.

NAVAL Off Cape Hatteras, North Carolina, a storm has scattered the Port Royal expedition ships, leaving a badly damaged fleet to make its way to its destination as best it can. The USS *Sabine* is lost in this heavy weather, the Marines aboard escaping to safety before the vessel goes down.

4 *NOVEMBER* 1861

THE CONFEDERACY President Davis and General Beauregard continue to disagree over what was appropriate at Manassas, or Bull Run, Virginia. Davis contacts Generals Lee, and Cooper, in order to gain their support for his position as the president is aware of rumors circulating about his administration's ineptitude.

6 *NOVEMBER* 1861

THE CONFEDERACY The South holds elections, and the results of these prove that Jefferson Davis is a popular and respected a leader as when first chosen provisional president. He is elected to a six-year term of office as President of the Confederacy and is once again joined by Alexander Stephens as Vice-President.

7 *NOVEMBER* 1861

WESTERN THEATER Cairo, Illinois sees the departure of a force of 3500 Union soldiers, under the command of General Ulysses S Grant, which departs for a point near Columbus, Kentucky, on the Mississippi. The troops travel in two gunboats and four other vessels, disembarking at Belmont, Missouri, opposite Confederate defenses at Columbus. Rebel General Leonidas Polk quickly crosses the river with a force of Confederates and pushes the Union troops back into their boats which carry them northward again. This inconclusive raid was accompanied by another, similar, reconnaissance from Paducah, Kentucky to Columbus, but neither of these two actions results in gain for the North. There are casualties, however; Federal losses tally at 120 killed and 383 wounded. The rebels lose 105, with 494 wounded. The strategic value of this operation at Belmont, Missouri is insignificant but it does allow General Grant to exercise his military capabilities without having to deal with the stress and danger of a major battle with Confederates.

NAVAL The Port Royal operation under Flag Officer S F Du Pont is underway, the

Fort Walker under bombardment, 7 November 1861.

The landing of troops at Fort Walker.

Port Royal bombardment, 7 November 1861.

Union squadron easily evading the relatively weak Confederate defenses as it sails into Port Royal Sound between Forts Beauregard and Walker. The ensuing exchange of fire between the Federal vessels and the shore batteries sees the rebels retreat from the two fortifications to take up positions further inland. The North loses eight men in the battle, with 23 wounded and Confederate losses are similarly light —11 killed, 48 wounded, 3 captured, 4 missing. The Port Royal expedition is considered a success as it places Union troops in a strategically critical area between Savannah and Charleston, and Port Royal proves to be important as a refueling depot for the Federal blockaders operating in the area.

8 *NOVEMBER* 1861

WESTERN THEATER In Kentucky, pro-Unionists rise up against rebel troops in the eastern region of the state. The Confederate commander in charge there, General Felix Zollicoffer, is obliged to request reinforcements due to the disruption caused by these ardent mountaineer Unionists.

THE CONFEDERACY The Port Royal operation causes telegraph offices in the South to be beseiged with people wanting information about the Union invasion. Newspapers seize the opportunity to promote unity for the Cause. The Charleston *Mercury* states, 'Our Yankee enemies will, sooner or later, learn to their cost the difference between invaders for spoils and power'. Despite this bravado, many civilians fear the possible outcome of this recent military action and hundreds prepare to evacuate the south Atlantic coastal area.

INTERNATIONAL The USS *San Jacinto*, under the command of Captain Charles Wilkes, stops at Havana, Cuba and finds the two Confederate commissioners, James Mason and John Slidell, awaiting passage to Europe on the British packet *Trent*. As the *Trent* sails into open waters in the Old Bahama Channel, the *San Jacinto* forces the British vessel to stop. Wilkes demands that Mason and Slidell be turned over to him. This accomplished, the *San Jacinto* sails to Hampton Roads, Virginia with the two commissioners under armed guard. The British captain and crew make their way back to Britain with the families of Mason and Slidell still aboard the *Trent*. More immediately it becomes an international *cause célèbre* of such magnitude as to provoke the possibility of armed conflict between the United States and Britain, and it also creates an incident which the Confederacy can use against the Federals.

11 *NOVEMBER* 1861

WASHINGTON A celebration in honor of the new General-in-Chief of the United States Army, General George Brinton McClellan, includes a torchlight parade in the nation's capital. On the Potomac, further balloon ascents take place under the direction of Professor Thaddeus Lowe.

13 *NOVEMBER* 1861

WASHINGTON President Lincoln calls on General McClellan at his home, waiting to speak with the new commander of the Union Army. McClellan retires without acknowledging the President.

15 *NOVEMBER* 1861

WASHINGTON The war effort on the home front receives aid from the Young Men's Christian Association. A committee known as the US Christian Commission will help provide nurses for war hospitals, supplies, and various services to the Union forces.

INTERNATIONAL The larger ramifications of the *Trent* affair become apparent to both the North and South as the USS *San Jacinto* arrives at Fort Monroe, Virginia. Slidell and Mason are to be transferred to a prison at Fort Warren, in Boston Harbor, Massachusetts. Captain Wilkes, the hero of the hour for his courageous and daring action in seizing the Confederate commissioners, is soon to receive more subdued acclaim as the Cabinet and other advisors to the President recognize the seriousness of Wilkes' action. Not only does this *Trent*

affair provide the Confederacy with an incident which might garner foreign support, it also places relations between Britain, France and the United States in a precarious position.

16 *NOVEMBER* 1861

WASHINGTON Postmaster General Montgomery Blair speaks out against Wilkes' action in capturing James Mason and John Slidell. He is joined in this protest by Senator Charles Sumner of Massachusetts; both men urge the surrender of the Confederate commissioners.

18 *NOVEMBER* 1861

WASHINGTON In order to arrange for a Federal expedition to New Orleans, Commodore David Dixon Porter is charged with obtaining and provisioning gunboats for the Union.

SECESSION At Hatteras, North Carolina, a convention of pro-Union delegates from 42 counties meets and repudiates the order of 20 May 1861 concerning that state's secession from the Union. The convention appoints Marble Nash Taylor as Provisional Governor of North Carolina. In Kentucky, Confederate soldiers convene at Russellville and adopt a secession ordinance which results in Kentucky's having two state governments, on pro-North and the other pro-secession, just as in Missouri.

THE CONFEDERACY The Provisional Government of the Confederate States of America convenes in its fifth session at Richmond, Virginia.

20 *NOVEMBER* 1861

WASHINGTON General McClellan reviews some 60,000 troops in the nation's capital.

TRANS-MISSISSIPPI Brief confrontations break out at Butler, Missouri. In California, Federal forces begin pursuit of a Confederate group, the Showalter Party, and several days later the troops capture 18 men, including the leader, Daniel Showalter, southeast of Los Angeles, California. EASTERN THEATER Confederate General John B Floyd pulls his troops out of an encampment near Gauley River, Virginia, destroying tents and equipment in his quick withdrawal.

21 *NOVEMBER* 1861

THE CONFEDERACY Reorganization of the Confederate Cabinet places Judah Benjamin in the post of Secretary of War. Benjamin succeeds Leroy Pope Walker in this slot, the latter having encountered a fair amount of criticism for what was considered an ineffectual handling of some military issues. The Attorney General's position goes to Thomas Bragg. General Lloyd Tilighman is appointed commander of Forts Henry and Donelson on the Tennessee and Cumberland Rivers. These two positions are strategically located and are important to the Confederate defense against invasion of the South.

22 *NOVEMBER* 1861

NAVAL An engagement begins between Federal batteries at Fort Pickens, Florida and Confederates at Forts McRee and Barrancas as well as the Pensacola Naval Yard. The Union ground forces are aided by the USS *Niagara* and the USS *Richmond* on the first day of the barrage. There is damage to both sides but it proves to be an ultimately inconclusive exchange.

24 *NOVEMBER* 1861

WASHINGTON Lincoln and his Cabinet meet to discuss the *Trent* affair and its significance to the Northern war effort. The two Confederate commissioners, Slidell and Mason, arrive in Boston, Massachusetts at Fort Warren, on the USS *San Jacinto*.
WESTERN THEATER Federal troops achieve a foothold on Tybee Island, in Georgia. This location on the Savannah River is of great strategic importance as it controls the entrance to the harbor and access to Fort Pulaski, the main fortification protecting Savannah from attack.

25 *NOVEMBER* 1861

NAVAL The Confederate Naval Department prepares to convert the former USS *Merrimack*, now the CSS *Virginia*, to an ironclad vessel. The CSS *Sumter* seizes a Federal ship while the Union blockade succeeds in capturing a blockade runner off the coast of South Carolina.

26 *NOVEMBER* 1861

THE NORTH In Wheeling, in western Virginia a convention adopts a new state constitution calling for the formation of the state of West Virginia after that area's secession from the rest of the state. In Boston, Captain Wilkes, the instigator of the *Trent* affair, is honored for his accomplishments at a special banquet.
NAVAL The CSS *Sumter* seizes yet another Federal vessel in the Atlantic, while at Savannah, Georgia, rebels try without success to engage Union ships in fire from Fort Pulaski.

27 *NOVEMBER* 1861

WESTERN THEATER Ship Island, Mississippi is the destination of a Union expeditionary force to be leaving from Hampton Roads, Virginia. The intent is to set up a base of operations against New Orleans, Louisiana and the general Gulf Coast area.
INTERNATIONAL The *Trent* affair is becoming more serious as word of the unlawful seizure of Confederate diplomats reaches Great Britain. In London, signs reading 'Outrage on the British Flag' begin to appear.

28 *NOVEMBER* 1861

THE CONFEDERACY The Provisional Congress at Richmond formally admits Missouri to the Confederacy.
EASTERN THEATER Federal officials in the Port Royal, South Carolina vicinity are given authorization by Washington to seize agricultural products and slaves. The latter will work for the Federal defense of the area.

30 *NOVEMBER* 1861

INTERNATIONAL In a letter to Great Britain's Minister to the United States, Lord Lyons, the British Foreign Secretary, Lord John Russell, communicates Britain's displeasure at the seizure of Confederate diplomats John Slidell and James Mason. He further requests that the Union apologize for the seizure and release the two diplomats to Britain's jurisdiction. The British Navy is placed on alert but is told to avoid any hostilities. Lyons is directed to leave Washington, DC in one week's time if there is no satisfactory response to Britain's request for redress of the affair.

1 *DECEMBER* 1861

WASHINGTON In a communication to General McClellan, President Lincoln questions the new chief about the Army's movement. The President is somewhat concerned that little action has taken place. He asks of the Army of the Potomac, 'How *long* would it require to actually get it in motion?'

NAVAL Successfully preventing the blockade runner *Albion* from carrying supplies to the Confederates, the United States gunboat *Penguin* seizes the vessel and its cargo, which includes armaments, various foodstuffs, tin, copper and military equipment valued near $100,000.

2 *DECEMBER* 1861

WASHINGTON The Thirty-Seventh Congress meets in the nation's capital for its regularly scheduled session. The mood here is a less positive one than it had been in July when the Congress last met. There is continued concern over repercussions stemming from the *Trent* affair and there are some who feel that the Army in Virginia ought to have made an offensive prior to the coming of winter. In general, there are criticisms of Lincoln's current military plans which are made up of a three-fold strategy: the plans call basically for the re-accession of Tennessee to facilitate the position of the Army in the heart of the

Confederacy; taking control of the Mississippi River and focusing on the eastern theater of war, especially between Richmond, Virginia and Washington, DC.

WESTERN THEATER Federal General Henry Halleck is authorized to suspend the writ of habeas corpus in the area commanded by the Department of the Missouri.

NAVAL Newport News, Virginia is the setting for a naval skirmish between four Union gunboats and the Confederate vessel *Patrick Henry*. As a result of the exchange, the *Patrick Henry* sustains considerable damage.

3 *DECEMBER* 1861

WASHINGTON President Lincoln makes his State of the Union address to Congress. In this message the chief executive stresses that 'the Union must be preserved, and hence all indispensable means must be employed'.

WESTERN THEATER At Ship Island, Mississippi the first of the troops in General Butler's expedition to the Gulf Coast area are landed. The Federal steamship *Constitution* carries this initial offensive force, made up of the 26th Massachusetts regiment and the 9th Connecticut regiment.

4 *DECEMBER* 1861

WASHINGTON Another Federal office holder, Senator John Breckenridge of Kentucky, is expelled from his position, in this case by a vote of 36–0. Formerly Buchanan's Vice-President, Breckenridge had joined the rebel Army in November after exhausting all possibilities for the negotiation of peace between the two opposing forces.

TRANS-MISSISSIPPI General Henry Halleck authorizes the arrest of any persons found helping the pro-secessionist movement in St Louis, Missouri. Those arrested for aiding the enemy are to be executed by the military.

INTERNATIONAL Britain's Queen Victoria issues a statement prohibiting any exports to the United States including armaments or materials for their production.

5 DECEMBER 1861

WASHINGTON Congress considers several bills which would abolish slavery, particularly in territory 'in rebellion'. The Secretary of War reports that the regular army has 20,334 men, and volunteers total 640,637. Naval Secretary Gideon Welles shows that the Federal Navy tallies 22,000 sailors and marines.

7 DECEMBER 1861

EASTERN THEATER The Potomac River Dam Number Five is the site of a small clash between Federals and rebel soldiers. WESTERN THEATER Further military activity takes place as a group of Confederate troops takes Glasgow, Missouri. NAVAL In a move to prevent the Confederate evasion of the blockade, the USS *Santiago de Cuba* stops the English ship *Eugenia Smith*. The Union vessel, under the command of Daniel Ridgely, succeeds in seizing J W Zacharie of New Orleans, Louisiana. Zacharie is a known Confederate purchasing agent and this incident serves to increase the agitation engendered by the *Trent* affair.

8 DECEMBER 1861

NAVAL The Northern whaling industry is now affected by the conflict; the CSS *Sumter* seizes the whaler *Eben Dodge* in Atlantic waters.

9 DECEMBER 1861

WASHINGTON To replace John Breckenridge as Senator from Kentucky, Garret Davis is elected. As a result of criticism and debate over military defeats such as that at Ball's Bluff, the United States Senate calls for the establishment of the Joint Committee on the Conduct of the War. In a vote of 33–3, the approval of this committee paves the way for a series of investigations and interrogations which are uneven, though useful, in terms of resulting reports.

THE CONFEDERACY Along the southern Atlantic coast, plantation owners burn their cotton crops to prevent confiscation by the Union. Seizing every opportunity to enlarge upon the significance of such acts and the threats posed by the anticipated Union advance, the Charleston, North Carolina *Courier* asserts that by destroying the cotton, planters prevent the North from enjoying 'the extensive spoils with which they have feasted their imagination, and the obtainment of which was one of their chief objects'.

TRANS-MISSISSIPPI Missouri remains the scene of brief and minor encounters between the Union and the Confederacy. Union Mills, Missouri witnesses skirmishing and in the Indian Territory, pro-South forces made up largely of Indians, push pro-Union Creek Indians out of the vicinity of Chusto-Talasah, or Bird Creek, later to known as Tulsa, Oklahoma. The Confederate efforts are soon briefly discontinued however, due to a shortage of adequate provisions and to the tenacity of the Creeks.

10 DECEMBER 1861

WASHINGTON The proposal which will set up the Joint Committee on the Conduct of the War is approved by the Federal House of Representatives.

THE CONFEDERACY The Congress of the Confederacy admits Kentucky to the rebel's jurisdiction as their thirteenth state. This despite the sentiment of a majority of Kentucky's citizens against such a move. The tenure of Kentucky in the Confederacy is short-lived; barely one month later, the rebel forces have virtually relinquished claim on that state, preferring to try to hold Tennessee.

11 DECEMBER 1861

THE CONFEDERACY Charleston, South Carolina is ravaged by fire, and half of the city is destroyed, including much of the business district. Such an occurrence does psychological damage to the Confederacy, as Charleston is an important center of operations in the South. Combined with the Hilton Head Island occupation by Union troops and the relatively effective Federal blockade, the fire proves to be extremely fortuitous to the North.

13 *DECEMBER* 1861

EASTERN THEATER Heavy fighting breaks out at Camp Allegheny, Buffalo Mountain, in western Virginia. Union troops under General R H Milroy attack the rebel encampment. Casualties in the Federal camp total 137, causing the force to fall back to Cheat Mountain. The Confederates suffer heavy losses (146 casualties) and they, too, retreat to Staunton, Virginia in the Shenandoah Valley.

14 *DECEMBER* 1861

INTERNATIONAL Britain falls into mourning at the unexpected death of Queen Victoria's husband and consort, His Royal Highness Prince Albert. Two weeks previous the Prince had prepared correspondence relative to the *Trent* affair and the seizure of Confederate diplomats Mason and Slidell; he had recommended a moderate course of action and the avoidance of outright hostilities with the United States over the affair. Despite this, there remains great apprehension over possible war between the United States and Britain.

17 *DECEMBER* 1861

EASTERN THEATER Various military operations of a minor nature occur on this day. At Chisolm Island, South Carolina, there is skirmishing, and at Rockville in that state confrontations between Union soldiers and rebels take place. The Union garrison at Hilton Head poses such a threat to Confederates at Rockville that the Southerners leave the vicinity. Near Harper's Ferry, General 'Stonewall' Jackson carries out maneuvers along the Potomac River with his Confederate troops.
NAVAL Savannah Harbor is the scene of

efforts by Federals to prevent shipping access: seven stone-laden vessels are sunk in the harbor at its entrance. On Green River in Kentucky, there is a battle which leaves 10 Union soldiers dead and 17 wounded. Confederate losses in this exchange total 33 killed and 55 wounded.

18 *DECEMBER* 1861

WASHINGTON · President Lincoln and his Cabinet meet to discuss the *Trent* affair. Meanwhile, Lord Lyons, the British Minister in Washington, receives his orders from London concerning Britain's demands for Slidell and Mason's immediate release. General McClellan and the President confer at the General's house about upcoming military strategy concerning the Union Army.

19 *DECEMBER* 1861

INTERNATIONAL A meeting between United States Secretary of State Seward and the British Minister, Lord Lyons, results in an exchange of information and terms over the *Trent* affair. Lyons explains Britain's position and gives the United States seven days in which to respond to those demands.

20 *DECEMBER* 1861

NAVAL In the shipping lanes off Charleston, North Carolina, sixteen outmoded whaling vessels are sunk in order to prevent access to the city harbor by blockade runners. Although the Union efforts in this respect were often repeated, they were of only limited effectiveness overall.
INTERNATIONAL The British Navy sends two ships to Canada in order to have forces in readiness if the *Trent* affair should necessitate formal military action against the United States.

21 *DECEMBER* 1861

WASHINGTON Further meetings between Lord Lyons and Secretary of State Seward result in a communication several days later to Lord Russell, British Foreign

Minister. In this letter, Lyons asserts: 'I am so concerned that unless we give our friends here a good lesson this time, we shall have the same trouble with them again very soon . . . Surrender or war will have a very good effect on them'. It appears that there is, in fact, some sentiment in favor of a stepped-up confrontation between the two countries, although Britain continues to exhibit restraint in the matter. The Confederacy's attitude is one of hopeful anticipation, newspapers in the South promoting the possibility of armed conflict between the United States and Britain, and commenting on its favorable effects for the Confederacy.

23 *DECEMBER* 1861

WASHINGTON   Once again, Lord Lyons requests the surrender of Slidell and Mason in a communication with Seward. The Cabinet meets with President Lincoln to discuss the matter further. After the latter conference, Massachusetts Senator Charles Sumner counsels the President on the advisability of releasing the two Confederate commissioners.

24 DECEMBER 1861

WASHINGTON   In the Federal capital, Congress passes duties on such luxury items as coffee, tea, sugar and molasses. At the War Department orders are given which suspend enlistment of cavalry soldiers. The President prepares for a full Christmas day, with expected meetings between members of the Cabinet and himself over the *Trent* affair.

25 *DECEMBER* 1861

WASHINGTON   Although the President and Mrs. Lincoln entertain guests for Christmas dinner, a decision concerning the disposition of Mason and Slidell is the focus of the day. The decision is to be forthcoming within the next 24 hours.
EASTERN THEATER   The fighting continues at Cherry, in western Virginia, and near Fort Frederick, Maryland.

26 *DECEMBER* 1861

WASHINGTON   The United States agrees to surrender Confederate commissioners James Mason and John Slidell into the keeping of Great Britain. After many meetings the Cabinet acknowledges the seizure of the diplomats as illegal and terms the action a misunderstanding on the part of Captain Charles Wilkes. Lord Lyons receives the statement made by United States officials, and Secretary of State Seward orders the men released from their incarceration at Fort Warren, in Massachusetts.
TRANS-MISSISSIPPI   St Louis, Missouri is placed under martial law, a ruling which also extends to all railroads in that state. General Henry Halleck gives this order, which is unpopular at best. Clashes between pro-Union Creek Indians and Confederates occur at Christenahlah in Indian Territory. The retreating Creeks flee to Kansas after suffering extensive losses.
NAVAL   Union blockaders are attacked by a small group of Confederate vessels at the mouth of the Savannah River. Despite its intent, the rebel offensive succeeds in dislodging the blockade only temporarily.

27 *DECEMBER* 1861

TRANS-MISSISSIPPI   Skirmishes break out at Hallsville, Missouri and a clash between rebels and Union soldiers, under the command of General Benjamin Prentiss at Mount Sion, Missouri results in the dispersion of the 900 Confederates who had been stationed there.

29 *DECEMBER* 1861

TRANS-MISSISSIPPI   In Missouri, Jeff Thompson's rebels continue to be active against pro-Union forces in that state. The rebels there fight forces in Commerce and also attempt an attack against the steamer *City of Alton*.

30 *DECEMBER* 1861

INTERNATIONAL   James Mason and John Slidell are transferred to the custody of Lord Lyons, the British Minister to the United States.

31 *DECEMBER* 1861

WASHINGTON President Lincoln, due to the fact that General McClellan is ill, contacts General Halleck in Missouri. The chief executive is concerned that the Union Army seems to lack direction and focus. He asks Helleck, 'are General Buell and yourself in concert?' hoping that the Western Department will be pressed into action of some sort.

1862

1 *JANUARY* 1862

EASTERN THEATER At Fort Pickens, Florida, Union troops fire on Confederate batteries at Pensacola. At Fort Barrancas there is a similar exchange of fire. The Port Royal area in South Carolina witnesses skirmishing as Federals continue their move to establish a permanent base at this important South Atlantic Coastal location; this latter conflict results in rebel batteries being pushed out of their positions on Port Royal Island, South Carolina.

WESTERN THEATER While skirmishes at Dayton, Missouri, cause some extensive damage to that town, General Halleck receives communications from Washington concerning the Army's inactivity. Halleck is encouraged to advance with his own troops, as well as with forces under General Buell, on Nashville, Tennessee and Columbus, Kentucky.

INTERNATIONAL James Mason and John Slidell, the two Confederate commissioners seized on the *Trent* and now released by the Union government, board a British Schooner off Provincetown, Massachusetts in the first leg of their journey to England. The British vessel *Rinaldo* will take the two men to London where they will continue their interrupted attempt to gain recognition and support for the Confederacy. With their departure, the *Trent* affair, which caused so much consternation in Washington, DC and which carried with it the possibility of a serious conflict between the British and American governments, is effectively closed.

3 *JANUARY* 1861

THE CONFEDERACY The Confederate president, Jefferson Davis, expresses worry over the Union presence on Ship Island, Mississippi. In a letter to that state's governor, the president says that the troops stationed at Ship Island have planned an offensive which 'no doubt, is intended against Mobile or New Orleans'.

EASTERN THEATER There is some movement of Union troops in Virginia as General Jackson's forces leave Winchester. The object of this winter march, termed the Romney Campaign, is the destruction of the lines of the Baltimore and Ohio Railroad and the dams along the Chesapeake and Ohio Canal. There is skirmishing at Big Bethel, Virginia as the Union troops seize the town and Confederates fall back, evacuating the area.

5 *JANUARY* 1862

EASTERN THEATER The operations around Hancock, Maryland continue unabated as Confederate troops try to rout the Federals who have retreated to this position. The rebel batteries are located at positions along the Potomac River.

6 *JANUARY* 1862

WASHINGTON There is growing sentiment in official circles against General McClellan as he appears to be reluctant to commit troops to any concerted action. Accordingly, a group of senators approach President Lincoln with the suggestion that McClellan be replaced. Lincoln rejects this proposal, and in like concern over what seems to be a general lack of intent, the President communicates with General Buell, who is positioned in Kentucky. The President makes strong recommendations that the Union forces advance in order to

Pinkertons in Virginia, 1862.

provide support for 'our friends in East Tennessee'.

7 *JANUARY* 1862

EASTERN THEATER The troops which have been positioned at Hancock, Maryland are now directed away from the vicinity of the Potomac, moving toward Romney, Virginia. A result of this is skirmishing between Federals and rebel soldiers at Blue's Gap, Virginia, where Colonel Dunning's Northern troops rout Confederates and seize two of their cannon.

9 *JANUARY* 1862

WASHINGTON It is a matter of intense concern to the President that neither General Buell nor Halleck have responded to the administration's urging that the Western troops advance. Lincoln discusses the issue with General McClellan who continues to recuperate from probable typhoid fever. The United States Congress is absorbed by discussions of the slavery problem, petitions being submitted which would curtail or terminate that institution. Some measures suggested include the possible colonization of former slaves elsewhere in the world; reimbursing owners for the loss of their property; emancipation of slaves and various combinations of all these solutions.

10 *JANUARY* 1862

WESTERN THEATER At Cairo, Illinois, General Grant's troops make preparations for an expedition into Kentucky by way of the Mississippi River. Near Prestonburg, Kentucky Union forces under General Garfield clash with Humphrey Marshall's Confederates at the forks of Middle Creek. The result of this encounter is not completely decisive; both sides retreat and feel that they have defeated the other.
EASTERN THEATER Romney, Virginia is evacuated as General Jackson's troops push into the vicinity of western Virginia. The town is taken over by Confederates who will camp there during the cold weather.

11 *JANUARY* 1862

WASHINGTON After considerable difficulty with the War Department's administration, President Lincoln accepts the resignation of Simon Cameron as War Secretary. As a conciliatory gesture, Lincoln suggests appointing him to the post of Minister to Russia. While Cameron and his department have been under considerable criticism for fraudulent actions and general incompetence, there has been little actual evidence that Cameron himself is a corrupt individual.
EASTERN THEATER The Northern Navy carries 15,000 troops under the command of General Ambrose Burnside to the Atlantic coast near North Carolina. Commodore Louis Goldsborough is in charge of the naval squadron consisting of approximately 100 ships. These forces will augment the troops which have already established a firm hold in the Port Royal environs, causing further threat to Confederates in that area.

13 *JANUARY* 1862

WASHINGTON To fill the position in his Cabinet vacated by Simon Cameron, the President chooses Edwin Stanton. He was the Attorney General in Buchanan's administration and is now a lawyer in the nation's capital. In a continuing effort to spur General Buell and General Halleck to action in the West, President Lincoln writes to both men, stating his wish to press the Confederacy, 'menacing him with superior forces at *different* points, at the *same* time'.

15 *JANUARY* 1862

WASHINGTON Edwin Stanton receives the Senate's approval and becomes Lincoln's Secretary of War. Stanton is an anti-slavery man and is a personal friend of General McClellan.

WESTERN THEATER General Grant moves into the Kentucky-Tennessee area as gunboats on the Tennessee River reach toward Fort Henry. Both the naval and land forces work in tandem for a period of 10 days, pressing further into Confederate territory, gathering information about enemy positions.

16 *JANUARY* 1862

WESTERN THEATER Confederate troops under General Felix Zollicoffer are positioned north of the Cumberland River despite General Crittenden's orders to the contrary. This arrangement proves later to be an unsatisfactory one. Union troops are said to be pushing forward toward this rebel encampment.

NAVAL Cedar Keys, Florida sees the burning of blockade runners, as well as dockside property, by the Federal Navy.

17 *JANUARY* 1862

NAVAL General Charles Smith attacks the area around Fort Henry on the Tennessee River.

18 *JANUARY* 1862

WESTERN THEATER Union troops are beginning to close in on Confederate troops at Mill Springs and Somerset on the Cumberland River in Kentucky. General Crittenden's troops should be partially protected by Zollicoffer's soldiers, but they are not because of the latter's careless positioning of his men north of the Cumberland River.

19 *JANUARY* 1862

WESTERN THEATER Rebels are defeated at Mill Springs, Kentucky by Northern soldiers in a battle that claims 39 Union lives, wounds 207, and totals 15 Federals captured. The Southern forces indicate 125 killed, 309 wounded, and 99 missing. Due to Zollicoffer's poor strategy, the rebels are obliged to retreat across the Cumberland River when Union General Thomas' men force them to fall back. Zollicoffer is killed in this battle; Crittenden, as senior officer, is castigated for having lost control of the positioning of troops. This exchange is perhaps most significant because the rebel defeat means a gap in the Confederate line of defense in the Tennessee-Kentucky area. This clash proves invaluable to the North as it enables the capture of 10 cannon, 100 wagons, over 1000 horses and a large number of boats as well as munitions and provisions.

20 *JANUARY* 1862

NAVAL Federals attempt to disrupt rebel blockade running by sinking stone-laden vessels in the harbor at Charleston, South Carolina. Off the coast of Alabama, a Confederate ship trying to run the Union blockade is halted; running the *J W Wilder* ashore, Federals make an effort to board the vessel but are prevented from doing so by rebel troops in the area.

21 *JANUARY* 1862

WESTERN THEATER Union forces under General McClernand return to the Columbus, Kentucky vicinity. Although this group of about 5000 men had only minimal contact with the rebels, their presence served to alert the Confederacy as to the strength of the Federal army in the area; in this respect it was a significant operation.

22 *JANUARY* 1862

EASTERN THEATER The Port Royal force poses an important threat to Roanoke Island near Hatteras Inlet, South Carolina. The Union troops under General Burnside are gathering strength and it is thought that, by naming General Henry Wise to the rebel command on Roanoke, the Federals may be deterred from seizing yet another position in Confederate territory.

23 JANUARY 1862

TRANS-MISSISSIPPI Martial law in St Louis provides for seizure of pro-South property in the event that its owners have refused to support pro-Union fugitives. General Halleck, who has strengthened these martial law orders, allows for the arrest of persons attempting to subvert the law.

NAVAL Another group of stone-laden ships is sunk in Charleston Harbor to prevent Confederate shipping. A clash between Union blockades and the rebel vessel *Calhoun* near the mouth of the Mississippi River results in that vessel being taken by the North. The following day two more Confederate ships are run aground and burned as they try to slip away from Federals at this Mississippi point near the Southwest Pass.

27 JANUARY 1862

WASHINGTON After months of delay and frustration, President Lincoln issues *General War Order Number One*: 'that the 22nd of February 1862, be the day for a general movement of the Land and Naval forces of the United States against the

The St Louis riots.

insurgent forces'. The President does this only after exhortations by military and civilian advisors and in the hopes that the Union armies as well as the Gulf Naval forces will come to some conclusive action with Confederates.

30 JANUARY 1862

THE NORTH In a brief ceremony at Greenpoint, Long Island, the ironclad *Monitor* is launched. John Ericsson, the Swedish-born designer of this ship and others like it, states that such vessels are critical to the Northern efforts and 'will admonish the leaders of the Southern Rebellion that the batteries on the banks of their rivers will no longer present barriers to the entrance of the Union forces'.

INTERNATIONAL The two Confederate commissioners from the *Trent* affair, James Mason and John Slidell, arrive in England after their delayed voyage is completed.

31 JANUARY 1862

WASHINGTON Another statement, the President's *Special War Order Number One*, is issued in the Federal capital (this special order supplemented Lincoln's *General War Order Number One* of 27 January 1862). Lincoln hopes to press the Army of the Potomac to confront Confederates in Virginia as the Union troops are told to take possession of 'a point upon the Railroad South Westward of what is known as Manassas Junction'.

INTERNATIONAL In Britain, Queen Victoria makes known once more the position of neutrality being observed by her country in the matter of the United States Civil War. This statement does little to encourage the Confederacy, which hopes for support from European powers and which is now experiencing further doubts and diminished expectations as Federal forces seem to gather strength on all fronts.

1 FEBRUARY 1862

WESTERN THEATER Cairo, Illinois sees preparations for an expedition under General Grant. This campaign will aim for the seizure of Fort Henry, a Confederate position on the Tennessee River. General Halleck, in St Louis, Missouri has approved of this movement and Grant's troops are now readying for the upcoming action.

3 *FEBRUARY* 1862

WASHINGTON President Lincoln communicates with General McClellan, who continues to disagree, both in public and private, with the chief executive. The two men have different preferences for the disposition of the Virginia forces: Lincoln favors a direct overland movement, his General-in-Chief wishes to land troops on the coast and then march inland to the Confederate capital at Richmond, Virginia. WESTERN THEATER General Grant's operation to Fort Henry gets underway as a Federal fleet moves up the Tennessee River and transports head for Paducah, Kentucky from Cairo, Illinois. INTERNATIONAL At Southampton Harbor, in England, the Confederate steamer *Nashville* prepares to leave port for the United States. A Federal gunboat, the *Tuscarora*, sets off to capture the Southern vessel. Such an action is prevented, however, by the British ship HMS *Shannon*.

4 *FEBRUARY* 1862

THE CONFEDERACY Confederate House Delegates at the capital in Richmond, Virginia enter into a debate concerning free blacks' enlistment in the Southern Army. The *Examiner*, a Richmond newspaper, exhorts citizens to support the Cause by re-enrollment in the Army and a stronger commitment to the struggle between the North and South. Some observers are worried that Southerners are becoming tired and are 'not sufficiently alive to the necessity of exertion'.

5 *FEBRUARY* 1862

WESTERN THEATER General Grant's force is scheduled to open its attack on Fort Henry on the Tennessee River within 24 hours. General Charles Smith's men seize an evacuated Fort Heiman near Fort

Virginia Infantry in camp near Leesburg.

Henry, establishing Union troops there. Meanwhile, 3000 Confederates under General Lloyd Tilighman prepare as best they can for the upcoming attack on Fort Henry.

6 *FEBRUARY* 1862

WESTERN THEATER The Confederate position at Fort Henry is attacked by Federals. The Southern General Tilighman removes the bulk of his troops from the fort and remains behind with a handful of men to try to defend the post. At around 11 in the morning the Union forces strike, shelling the fort from gunboats. The troops at the fort respond with their artillery, striking both the *Essex* and the *Cincinnati*; by 2 that afternoon the battle is over as the Confederate guns are destroyed by Union fire. Tilighman surrenders 78 soldiers and 16 hospital patients to Flag Officer Andrew Foote. Southern losses tally at 5 killed, 11 wounded, and 5 missing; the Federals lose 11 men and sustain 31 injuries. The ground troops, some 15,000 strong, under General Grant, arrive too late to engage in the fighting. Having sent the major portion of his garrison to Fort Donelson on the

Confederate Army recruiting in Virginia.

Cumberland River, General Tilighman has at least prevented the Union force from easily taking immediate possession of the entire area. The Federals move from the vicinity to fortify their vessels as Confederate General Bushrod Johnson assumes command of Fort Donelson and puts out a request for reinforcements and provisions.

7 *FEBRUARY* 1862

WESTERN THEATER Federal Troops under General Grant himself make an expedition to Fort Donelson near Dover, Tennessee, in preparation for the upcoming attempt to seize that Confederate position. Confederate troops are ordered into the area as the Kentucky defenses further deteriorate. Meetings among Confederate Generals Johnston, Beauregard and Hardee attest to the severity of this most recent military development between North and South. Roanoke Island sees the advance of General Burnside's forces. Commodore Goldsborough succeeds in routing some minor Southern positions there, and later in the day Burnside's troops land. On the Tennessee River, Union guns destroy two Confederate transports.

8 *FEBRUARY* 1862

WASHINGTON Lincoln confers with General McClellan, asking for information about the Department of the West, and for reports on vessels sent toward Harper's Ferry on the Potomac River. The President, besieged with worry over the nation's military strength, is also filled with concern for his son, Willie, who lies ill with typhoid. WESTERN THEATER The Confederates at Roanoke Island are moved to the northern end of their position as General Burnside's 7500 Union soldiers attack. Colonel Shaw's Confederates are seriously outnumbered and their regular commander, General Henry Wise, is too ill to be in charge, necessitating the temporary command of Shaw. The latter makes an attempt to hold the Southern position, but it is an exercise in futility. He surrenders after 23 men are killed and 62 are

Zouaves in a charge at Roanoke.

wounded. The Confederates relinquish 30 guns in this takeover and lose an important position on the Atlantic coast, a severe blow to the Southern efforts. Union losses in this exchange are totalled at 37 killed, 214 wounded, 13 missing.

NAVAL Two Confederate vessels, the *Sallie Wood* and the *Muscle*, are taken by the Federals at Chickasaw, Mississippi. In a follow-up of Confederates fleeing the Roanoke Island battle, 13 Union gunboats traverse the Pasquotank River in the direction of Elizabeth City, North Carolina.

10 *FEBRUARY* 1862

WESTERN THEATER Clean-up operations at Roanoke Island, North Carolina are finished, and General Burnside, now firmly established at this position, prepares for further campaigning against the Confederates in the area of New Berne. General Grant completes preparations for his troops offensive against Fort Donelson. NAVAL Gunboats under Union control meet Confederates at Elizabeth City, North Carolina and demolish the remaining vessels in the Confederate fleet. On the Tennessee River, Union gunboats capture three Confederate vessels while six more are burned by secessionists to prevent their falling into Union hands.

11 *FEBRUARY* 1862

WESTERN THEATER The action against Fort Donelson commences as General Grant's troops begin to march and General

McClernand's Union forces move out from their position at Fort Henry. Federal gunboats begin to advance, traveling up the Cumberland River. This Union activity provokes the evacuation by Confederates of Bowling Green, Kentucky and renders the previously fortified Kentucky line defenseless; only Columbus, Kentucky remains relatively secure.

12 *FEBRUARY* 1862

WESTERN THEATER   As Grant's forces of 40,000 encircle the hills around Fort Donelson and the town of Dover, Tennessee, the Federal gunboats move into position to attack from the river. Confederates at the fort number about 18,000. Further action in the Roanoke Island vicinity results in the possession of Edenton, North Carolina by Union forces.

13 *FEBRUARY* 1862

WESTERN THEATER   The awaited attack on Fort Donelson occurs. The Confederate command has transferred to General John Floyd, whose arrival with Confederate reinforcements proves to be ultimately useless. The Federal attack from the right and left is led by General C F Smith and General McClernand, respectively, and Grant soon receives further aid from auxiliary troops by the end of the day. Fort Heiman nearby sees some brief action and portions of Bowling Green, Kentucky are burned as the Southern evacuation continues.

14 *FEBRUARY* 1862

WASHINGTON   The War Secretary, with the President's approval, issues orders releasing political prisoners who will take the oath of allegiance to the United States. A general amnesty is proclaimed for all those who comply with the oath and who agree to comply in no further aid of the rebellion.
WESTERN THEATER   The battle at Fort Donelson in the Cumberland River area is expanded by the arrival of four Union iron-clads and several wooden vessels although the easy victory which Grant anticipated is not forthcoming. The Union General sees a temporary withdrawal of this river fire as shore batteries threaten serious damage to the Federal vessels. The Union ironclads *St Louis* and *Louisville* are badly hit and rendered virtually useless. Flag Officer Andrew Foote, who so ably performed at Fort Henry, is wounded in this rain of Southern shelling. Bowling Green, Kentucky is taken by Federals. A meeting of Confederate commanders recommends that Gideon Pillow's forces attack the Federal right flank to the south of Fort Donelson.

15 *FEBRUARY* 1862

WESTERN THEATER   Fighting continues on the Cumberland River as Confederates under General Gideon Pillow attempt to break through Federal lines which surround the fort. The Southerners succeed in this effort, providing their troops with an escape route toward Nashville, Tennessee. Hesitation on the part of several commanders places the Confederates back at their posts, while Grant tries to close the line with the help of Generals Smith and McClernand. He is partially successful in this attempt. In Dover, Tennessee, Confederate generals discuss their options: surrender seems inevitable but there is resistance from General Floyd. In the end, Floyd does leave the battle area with General Pillow, placing General Buckner in the position of having to surrender the fort.

16 *FEBRUARY* 1862

WESTERN THEATER   In a statement which leaves the Southerners no room for negotiation, General Grant issues his terms for the disposition of Fort Donelson: 'No terms except unconditional and immediate surrender can be accepted. I propose to move immediately upon your works'. General Buckner is left with no alternative, and so relinquishes possession of the military position which had proved to be a costly one to hold. Estimates of Southern casualties hover around 1500, and it appears that somewhere near 1200 soldiers surrendered. Union troops under General Grant show losses of 500 killed, 2100 wounded, and 224 missing out of a total fighting force of 27,000. Needless to say, this victory of the North is of major importance and proves to be similarly significant a defeat in Southern eyes. Tennessee and Kentucky are lost and the Cumberland and Tennessee Rivers are in Union control now. The following day, news of the battle reaches Washington, DC, where there is rejoicing over the outcome. The battle proves to be important to General Grant's career—he is now promoted to Major General of Volunteers. The Confederacy sees disruption throughout Tennessee as civilians attempt to flee the area.

The capture of Fort Donelson.

18 FEBRUARY 1862

THE CONFEDERACY The dismissal on the previous day of the Provisional Congress of the Confederacy is followed by the initial meeting of the First Congress of the Confederate States of America. Structured now as a two-part government, the Congress is composed of representatives exclusively from slaveholding states in the South, with the exception of Delaware and Maryland.

20 FEBRUARY 1862

WASHINGTON President and Mrs Lincoln suffer the tragedy of losing their twelve-year-old son, Willie, to typhoid fever. This personal stress is compounded by news of fatalities at Fort Donelson; the President seems engulfed by sorrow.
WESTERN THEATER Further pullbacks of Confederate troops result in the evacuation of Columbus, Kentucky. In Tennessee, the Confederate Governor, Isham Harris, decrees that the state capital will be fixed at Memphis as Nashville is in the line of Union troop advances. At the latter location, the Southern army is commanded by General Albert Johnston to move to a position southeast of the city near Murfrees-

boro. A group of 1000 late arrivals to the Southern defense at Fort Donelson is captured by Union troops.

21 FEBRUARY 1862

THE NORTH The convicted slave trader Nathaniel Gordon is hanged at New York City, the first time the Union has ever imposed this punishment.
TRANS-MISSISSIPPI A Confederate victory results when the forces of General H H Sibley attack Union troops near Fort Craig, at Valvarde, New Mexico Territory. The Federals under the command of Colonel E R S Canby lose 68 men, with 160 wounded and 35 missing out of a total of 3810 men. Southerners numbering 2600 suffer 31 deaths, 154 wounded and 1 missing. The Confederates move toward Santa Fe after seizing six pieces of Union artillery.

22 FEBRUARY 1862

THE CONFEDERACY After his election to the presidency of the Confederacy (up to now he has been provisional president), Jefferson Davis' inauguration is held at Richmond, Virginia. In his address to the Confederate nation, Davis says, 'We are in arms to renew such sacrifices as our fathers made to the holy cause of constitutional liberty'.

24 FEBRUARY 1862

EASTERN THEATER Harper's Ferry is

taken over by General Banks' Union soldiers. Near Pohick Church, Virginia, there is minor skirmishing between Southern and Northern troops.

WESTERN THEATER At Nashville, Tennessee, Buell's Federals take over and the Confederate cavalry troops there under General Nathan Forrest are pressed to retreat.

27 FEBRUARY 1862

THE CONFEDERACY Jefferson Davis is given authorization by the Confederate Congress to suspend the privilege of habeas corpus. The Confederate president issues a call for martial law in both Norfolk and Portsmouth, Virginia.

NAVAL The Federal ironclad *Monitor* leaves its New York harbor under sealed orders.

28 FEBRUARY 1862

THE CONFEDERACY Southerners hold a day of fasting at the request of President Davis. In writing to his commander of the Army of Northern Virginia, General Joseph Johnston, Jefferson Davis observes that there is a need for thoughtful, planned defense. He tells Johnston that 'traitors show the tendencies heretofore concealed, and the selfish grow clamorous . . . at such an hour, the wisdom of the trained, and the steadiness of the brave, possess a double value'.

EASTERN THEATER Charleston, Virginia is occupied by Federal troops.

1 MARCH 1862

THE CONFEDERACY Richmond, Virginia witnesses the arrest of John Minor Botts for treason against the Confederacy. Botts, a former Virginian congressman and avowed neutral, is seized along with thirty others, among them the Reverend Alden Bosserman, a Universalist minister. The latter has prayed for an end to 'this unholy rebellion'. The Confederate capital is now under martial law, President Jefferson Davis placing General John Winder in control of the city.

WESTERN THEATER General Beaure-

gard positions troops along the Mississippi River while General Henry Halleck directs General Grant to take his forces toward Eastport, Mississippi. There are brief clashes between Union and Confederate soldiers at Pittsburg Landing, where gunboats have traveled up the Tennessee River. They destroy a Confederate battery positioned there by General Beauregard's troops.

3 MARCH 1862

WESTERN THEATER Accusations are leveled at General Ulysses Grant by General Henry Halleck concerning Grant's tardy appearance during the Fort Donelson takeover. Halleck is given permission by President Lincoln to transfer General C F Smith to command the troops going up the Tennessee River out of Fort Henry; it is felt that Grant's recent conduct does not warrant his taking responsibility for the upcoming action.

4 MARCH 1862

WASHINGTON General Andrew Johnson receives Senate approval as the military governor of Tennessee.

THE CONFEDERACY General Robert E Lee is replaced by General John Pemberton as commander of the Confederate Department of South Carolina, Georgia and East Florida. Lee has been called to Richmond by President Jefferson Davis to assume duties as a military advisor in Virginia. The Confederate president runs into problems with various congressmen dissatisfied with the defense of the Mississippi River. These congressmen demand additional batteries to cover the river despite the efforts of Davis' administration to provide the best defenses possible.

5 MARCH 1862

WESTERN THEATER At Jackson, Tennessee, General Beauregard takes charge of defenses of the Mississippi Valley. Federals begin to position themselves around Savannah, Tennessee as General Johnston's Confederates begin a move to prevent the further entrenchment of Union forces in the area. General C F Smith's Federals at Savannah are quickly joined by three gunboats and 80 troop transports.

TRANS-MISSISSIPPI Fighting continues in Arkansas as Sterling Price's Southerners combine with General Van Dorn's forces against Union General Samuel Curtis. An attack is imminent, Van Dorn positioning his troops just past Fayetteville and Elm Springs, Arkansas.

6 MARCH 1862

WASHINGTON President Lincoln, in part responding to suggestions from various senators, requests the states' cooperation in devising ways to abolish slavery. This message to Congress indicates the availability of Federal financial funding for aiding emancipation efforts in individual states.

THE CONFEDERACY A proclamation is issued by the Confederate Congress concerning the destruction of valuable cotton and tobacco crops in the event that Northern troops advance further into Virginia. Military authorities are charged with the responsibility for carrying out this disposal of Confederate property if the need arises.

TRANS-MISSISSIPPI In Arkansas, near Fayetteville, forces under Confederate General Earl Van Dorn clash with Union soldiers under General Samuel Curtis. While this fighting is limited, it presages an upcoming battle. Van Dorn is anxious to command an optimum position and therefore moves his troops to a situation at Pea Ridge, to the right of Curtis' encampment.

7 MARCH 1862

EASTERN THEATER McClellan takes the Federal Army of the Potomac toward the southwestern region of Virginia where General Joseph Johnston's Confederates are encamped at Manassas. The Union soldiers are well positioned and are prepared to do battle with the Confederates whom they expect to vanquish easily. In Winchester, Virginia, there is skirmishing.

The Battle of Pea Ridge, 6-8 March 1862.

TRANS-MISSISSIPPI The Federal forces at Pea Ridge, or Elkhorn Tavern, Arkansas, are surprised by General Van Dorn's Confederate troops in an attack from the latter's northern position. About 17,000 Confederates, including some Indian troops, make valiant attempts to rout the Union soldiers, but the North is ultimately victorious. Van Dorn's forces are made up of Missouri state guards under Sterling Price, as well as General McCulloch's division and General Pike's troops which are comprised of three Indian regiments.

8 MARCH 1862

WASHINGTON The President and General McClellan discuss plans for the Army of the Potomac, and other military advisors concur with McClellan's desire to enter Virginia by way of the peninsula southeast of Richmond. In *General War Order Number Two*, the chief executive provides for certain of the Union troops to be positioned as defenses for the Federal capital during the upcoming campaign, despite the fact that this will draw off troop strength from the offensive.

TRANS-MISSISSIPPI The battle at Pea Ridge, Arkansas, the most significant of Civil War battles in the trans-Mississippi west, sees the deaths of both Generals McCulloch and McIntosh, depriving the Confederacy of two able commanders. Federals under General Curtis continue to hold out for a second day of fighting, whch ends as Van Dorn and his men retreat to the Arkansas River with orders to leave the state and remove to the Mississippi River to aid in the defense of Confederate positions there. The tally of casualties for Southerners shows that the Confederacy has lost around 800 men, while the North suffers 1384 dead and wounded.

NAVAL   In Virginia, at Hampton Roads, the ironclad *Merrimack* approaches a squadron of Federal vessels, all much less well defended and ill-equipped to battle with the heavily armored Confederate ship. In the ensuing encounter, two Union vessels are put out of commission—the USS *Cumberland* and the USS *Roanoke*—the USS *Minnesota* is heavily damaged. Flag Officer Franklin Buchanan of the *Merrimack* is slightly wounded during the fight, though in general, few Confederates suffer serious injury. The Union forces suffer a greater number of casualties and damage to their ships is especially severe. A Confederate military observer notes, 'Pains, death, wounds, glory—that was the sum of it'. Late in the day of the battle between the *Merrimack* and these various Federal vessels, the USS *Monitor* appears in the harbor at Hampton Roads after a difficult journey south from New York.

The Monitor *vs the* Merrimack *(CSS* Virginia*)*.

A drawing of the 9 March 1862 fight.

9 *MARCH* 1862

EASTERN THEATER   The Confederate army in Virginia under General Joseph Johnston moves near a position at Rappahannock Station close to the Rappahannock River. Union soldiers under McClellan move out, but do not engage rebels in any fighting. They soon return to Alexandria after finding only empty camps left behind by Confederates.

NAVAL   In a battle of special significance to naval warfare, the CSS *Merrimack* and the USS *Monitor* clash in the harbor at Hampton Roads. Beginning around 9 in the morning, fighting continues for nearly two hours until injuries force both commanders to pull back. While the exchange of fire is impressive, there is relatively little damage done to either vessel and the battle has no real victor. Federals are considered to have a stronger position as the *Merrimack* is unable to easily maneuver elsewhere due

The ironclads at Hampton Roads.

The sinking of the Cumberland, *8 March 1862.*

89

to unwieldy construction. There is concern that the Confederate vessel may make its way to Washington, DC or New York City, but this worry is soon dispelled.

11 *MARCH* 1862

WASHINGTON   In issuing another major military order, *War Order Number Three*, President Lincoln removes General George McClellan from his command as General-in-Chief of the Union Armies. McClellan is given the Army of the Potomac, and he, along with other generals, will be under the direction of the Secretary of War; no General-in-Chief is to be yet appointed.

THE CONFEDERACY   After their flight from the military action at Fort Donelson, Generals Floyd and Pillow submit reports to Confederate President Jefferson Davis. The president does not accept these reports and removes both Pillow and Floyd from their commands.

EASTERN THEATER   Manassas Junction, Virginia is investigated by Union troops, who find little of value left in the wake of retreating Confederate soldiers. At Winchester, Virginia, 4600 Confederates are under the command of General Jackson who takes his troops southward.

Manassas Junction, after the Confederate evacuation.

Confederate Naval battery at Manassas.

13 *MARCH* 1862

THE CONFEDERACY   General Robert E Lee is given the responsibility of overseeing Confederate military positions. Confederate president Jefferson Davis does not define the specific nature of this advisory post held by Lee.

EASTERN THEATER   Meetings between General McClellan and his staff provide a clearing house for plans concerning placement of the Army of the Potomac. General Johnston is situated near the Rappahannock and there is great concern in avoiding direct confrontation there as Federals march on Richmond, Virginia. McClellan intends to bring troops to the Confederate capital via the York and James Rivers. McClellan, intent on moving via the Peninsula, is warned by Prsident Lincoln's Secretary of War that Washington, DC must remain protected, as must Manassas Junction, Virginia. General McClellan is told to 'at all events, move such remainder of the army at once in pursuit of the enemy'.

WESTERN THEATER   General Burnside's troops disembark at New Berne, North Carolina, on the western branch of the Neuse River.

TRANS-MISSISSIPPI   Skirmishing occurs at Point Pleasant, Missouri, leading to the area's capture by General Pope who also provoked the evacuation of New Madrid by his military actions. In this move, the Confederates abandon large quantities of arms and provisions estimated at a value of $1 million.

14 MARCH 1862

WASHINGTON   In a continuing discussion of his position concerning slavery, President Lincoln attempts to justify the proposed financial compensation to slaveholders. Lincoln feels that such recompense 'would not be half as onerous as would be an equal sum, raised *now*, for the indefinite prosecution of the war'.

WESTERN THEATER   In North Carolina, the town of New Berne is taken by General Burnside's 11,000 men, who push General Branch's 14,000 Confederates out. This position is maintained by Federals for the duration of the war, proving an effective point of departure for inland expeditions. There are some 600 Confederate casualties after this battle, including 64 deaths. Union troops tally 90 killed with 380 wounded.

TRANS-MISSISSIPPI   The capture of New Madrid, Missouri by General John Pope's Federals places the Northern forces in a position which will enable them to make an assault on Island Number Ten in the Mississippi River. This latter Confederate post defends east Tennessee.

15 MARCH 1862

WESTERN THEATER   General Grant resumes command of field forces in Tennessee after General Halleck absolves Grant of charges of misconduct at Fort Donelson.

17 MARCH 1862

EASTERN THEATER   General McClellan and the Army of the Potomac move out on the Peninsular Campaign, heading for the James and York Rivers.

18 MARCH 1862

THE CONFEDERACY   Jefferson Davis names Judah Benjamin Secretary of State. Benjamin has up until now served as War Secretary and has been under considerable criticism in that position.

EASTERN THEATER   At Aquia Creek, Virginia, Confederates occupy the town.

WESTERN THEATER   General Albert Johnston's Confederates begin arriving in Corinth, Kentucky, from Murfreesboro.

20 MARCH 1862

EASTERN THEATER, PENINSULAR CAMPAIGN   At Strasburg, Virginia, where the day before had seen some action, there is a general pullback of Federals as General Jackson's forces advance. At Phillippi, western Virginia, there is light skirmishing.

22 MARCH 1862

EASTERN THEATER, PENINSULAR CAMPAIGN   Light fighting takes pace at Kernstown, Virginia between General Shields' Union soldiers and General Jackson's advancing Confederates.

23 MARCH 1862

EASTERN THEATER, PENINSULAR CAMPAIGN   About 9000 Union troops clash with 4200 Confederates at Kernstown, Virginia. Skirmishing of the previous day has led the Confederates to assume a smaller enemy force, but, although outnumbered, Jackson's troops perform admirably. They retreat, ultimately, after suffering 80 killed, 375 wounded, 263 missing, compared to Union losses of 118 killed, 450 injured and 22 missing. This battle is the preliminary to the Shenandoah Valley Campaign. Strategically important, the battle provides a diversion important to the Southern forces: Lincoln, now fearing an offensive on the Federal capital, issues orders that General McDowell's troops remain as part of Washington's defense. This means fewer troops for the Peninsular Campaign. In addition, this assault at Kernstown suggests the possibility of a threat on Harper's Ferry, and General Banks' troops are ordered to return to that vicinity rather than join McClellan.

WESTERN THEATER   Fort Macon, at Beaufort, North Carolina, is the object of the next move by Burnside's Federals. The following day sees General John Parke's

CHRONOLOGY

soldiers approach Fort Macon and request its surrender. The subsequent refusal results in a Union siege of that Confederate position.

24 MARCH 1862

SLAVERY The emancipation issue continues to be one fraught with emotion. In Cincinnati, Ohio, the abolitionist Wendell Phillips speaks and is greeted with a barrage of eggs and rocks. Lincoln, commenting on the prospect of compensated emancipation, notes in a letter to newspaperman Horace Greeley that 'we should urge it persuasively, and not menacingly, upon the South'.

26 MARCH 1862

TRANS-MISSISSIPPI State militia in Missouri clash at Hammondsville with Confederate forces; at Warrensburg pro-Unionists confront Confederates; the latter are repelled in both cases. In Colorado Territory there is an encounter between Southern cavalry and Union forces near Denver City resulting in the capture of 50 Confederate cavalrymen. In New Mexico Territory, Confederates meet a troop of Union soldiers coming toward Santa Fe from Fort Union. There is a fight between the two forces at Apache Canyon, resulting in a victory for Union troops who fall back to an area near Glorietta.

28 MARCH 1862

EASTERN THEATER, PENINSULAR CAMPAIGN Brief fighting occurs on the Orange and Alexandria Railroad in Virginia over a period of several days. Shipping Point, Virginia is occupied by Federal troops.
TRANS-MISSISSIPPI The New Mexico Territory sees a major battle between North and South at La Glorietta Pass. Union troops under Colonel John Slough clash with Confederates under Colonel W R Scurry, pushing the Federals back. Confederate supply wagons at nearby Johnson's Ranch are attacked by Major John

Chivington's men, causing the Confederates to fall back to Santa Fe and effectively stopping the Southern invasion. Of 1100 Confederates, 36 are killed, 60 wounded; Union troops totalling 1324 lose 31, with over 50 wounded.

29 MARCH 1862

EASTERN THEATER, PENINSULAR CAMPAIGN In western Virginia, William Rosecrans' command of the Mountain Department is given over to General Frémont. Middlebury, Virginia witnesses a cavalry charge by Union troops in pursuit of a fleeing Confederate detachment.
WESTERN THEATER General Albert Johnston pulls the Confederate forces together at Corinth, Mississippi; General Beauregard is his next in command. Generals Polk, Bragg, Hardee, and Crittenden are also there with their troops.

1 APRIL 1862

EASTERN THEATER, PENINSULAR CAMPAIGN General John Wool's force of 12,000 men at Fort Monroe, in Virginia, is supplemented by General McClellan's movement of 12 divisions of the Northern Army of the Potomac. In addition, the Federal Shenandoah forces are pushing toward General Jackson's position near Woodstock and Edenburg, Virginia.
NAVAL Northern troops move, via gunboats, up the Tennessee River and Federal forces are able to complete a mission at Island Number Ten on the Mississippi River.

2 APRIL 1862

WASHINGTON Persident Lincoln's suggestions about compensated emancipation receive favorable attention in the United States Senate. This plan—which would allow Federal financial support to Northern states willing to provide compensation—is intended as a means by which to encourage the freeing of slaves. Although proposed by Lincoln it is a plan which will never be implemented.

WESTERN THEATER Shiloh, or Pittsburgh Landing, in Tennessee, is the goal that General A S Johnston's Confederates have in mind as they are ordered to move out of the Federal position from Corinth, Mississippi. Confederate troops succeed in encircling a portion of the 2nd Illinois Cavalry at Farmington, Mississippi. The Northern troops are able, however, to break through the enemy lines and escape.

TRANS-MISSISSIPPI In Missouri, various military actions continue as Confederates and Northern soldiers skirmish at Walkersville, and as a Union reconnaissance sets out for Jackson, Whitewater and Dallas, from Cape Girardeau. Along the Mississippi River, from Cairo, Illinois to New Madrid, Missouri, there is a great deal of damage done to various installations as a result of severe tornadoes.

3 APRIL 1862

WASHINGTON The United States Senate passes a bill, 29–14, to abolish slavery in the District of Columbia. President Lincoln is gravely concerned about the defense of the nation's capital. He finds that General McClellan has arranged for the distribution of troops so as to provide for less than 20,000 men in the Washington, DC area. Accordingly, the chief executive orders the retention of an additional corps to ensure the safety of the Northern capital; the impact on McClellan's troop strength for the Peninsular Campaign is negligible, as McClellan has nearly 112,000 men for his siege of Yorktown, to begin the following day.

WESTERN THEATER General A S Johnston's Confederates move to attack Shiloh, on the Tennessee River, where General Grant's Northern troops are encamped. Apalachicola, Florida surrenders to Federal troops.

4 APRIL 1862

EASTERN THEATER, PENINSULAR CAMPAIGN The campaign continues to take shape as General McClellan proceeds to bear down on Yorktown. The Southern forces are greatly outnumbered; General Johnston's troops total around 17,000 as compared to McClellan's enormous Army of the Potomac consisting of over 100,000 troops. Much of the Confederate Army of Northern Virginia has been shifted into position on the Peninsula to afford some increased defense of the Southern position there. The Confederate line of defense stretches along an eight-mile front; the prospects for the South are not good.

5 APRIL 1862

THE NORTH Difficulties over the oath of allegiance to the Union occur between the military governor of Tennessee, Andrew Johnson, and city officials of Nashville. The result is the suspension of the mayor, aldermen, and councilmen of that occupied area.

EASTERN THEATER, PENINSULAR CAMPAIGN In a valiant, but seemingly futile effort, General Joseph Johnston's troops continue to gather reinforcements for the imminent conflict at Yorktown, Virginia. The Confederates are outnumbered by McClellan's stronger and larger Army of the Potomac.

WESTERN THEATER General Grant's forces continue to be relatively unaware of the Confederate troops bearing down on their position at Shiloh, in Tennessee.

6 APRIL 1862

WESTERN THEATER The battle of Shiloh, or Pittsburgh Landing, in Tennessee, comes after several days of Confederate preparations which have gone largely unnoticed by Federals. General Grant's troops fall back after several hours, despite the fierce defense of their position at the Hornet's Nest, a defense orchestrated by General Prentiss' division. While the initial force of Confederates under General Johnston presses General William Nelson's Federals to the breaking point, the day ends without any conclusive victory for either the North or the South. The following day sees the destruction of Prentiss'

The Battle of Shiloh, 7 April 1862.

The Charge of General Grant at Shiloh.

division and the concurrent wearing down of Beauregard's troops. The Confederate command has been assumed by Beauregard after General Johnston is killed on the previous day. Fresh troops from Union General Wallace's division and from Generals Nelson and Crittenden, give Grant's forces the necessary reinforcement and bolstering. In like manner, General Beauregard is waiting for 20,000 men under General Van Dorn, hoping to make another offensive for the Confederates; without Van Dorn's forces this is clearly impossible. Unfortunately for the Confederates, Van Dorn's men do not arrive; Beauregard orders a retreat to Corinth, Mississippi, leaving Northern troops to remain in much the same position they had occupied prior to the battle of Shiloh. While it is unclear whether or not the Union has gained a great deal from the two-day clash, the Federals have main-tained a firm hold on positions that they had previously taken, and they also achieve a splitting of the rebel forces along the Mississippi River and an evacuation of much of the Confederate force in Tennessee. Losses at the battle of Shiloh total 13,047 for the North; 10,694 for the Confederates.

7 *APRIL* 1862

NAVAL The Federal gunboats *Carandolet* and *Pittsburgh* run the Confederate installations at Island Number Ten in the Mississippi River near New Madrid, Missouri. Under the direction of General John Pope, troops succeed in cutting a canal through the marshy area near the island, thus allowing the Federal vessels to go southward around the island and land four regiments in Tennessee below the Confederate position on Island Number Ten.

10 *APRIL* 1862

WESTERN THEATER Skirmishing occurs at Fernandina, Florida and in Illinois. Union General W H L Wallace succumbs to injuries he received at the battle of Shiloh. In the harbor of Savannah, Georgia, Fort Pulaski readies itself for an attack by Federals. Commanded by General Quincy Adams Gillmore, the Northern assault takes place from a position opposite the fort on Tybee Island. The Confederates have about 40 guns but the Federals' long range guns and penetrating shells are no match for the masonry fort, which sustains heavy damage. The bombardment at Fort Pulaski begins at 8 in the morning and continues throughout the night, the Federal guns at Tybee Island being stilled the following day at around 2 in the afternoon. Three hundred and sixty Confederates are taken prisoner; one Union soldier is killed, as is one Southerner.

11 *APRIL* 1862

WASHINGTON In a vote of 93–39, the House of Representatives passes a bill which calls for the gradual abolition of slavery in the District of Columbia.

WESTERN THEATER   In Tennessee, several hundred Confederates are captured when the town of Huntsville is occupied by Federals. The Memphis and Charleston Railroad is close by this site and this is another example of how the South is slowly losing its grip on Tennessee. The Union begins to marshall its forces for a push toward Confederate positions at Corinth, Mississippi. General Henry Halleck has assumed command of these troops with Generals Buell, Grant and Pope directly beneath him.

NAVAL   At Newport News, Virginia the *Merrimack*, the South's ironclad, seizes three small merchant ships but does not engage in conflict with the Federal vessel *Monitor*, as anticipated. The *Monitor* has been awaiting the approach of the Confederate vessel, but then gives no indication of desiring an actual encounter.

12 *APRIL* 1862

THE NORTH   James Andrews, a spy for the Union, had led a group of 21 men through the Confederate lines in order to seize a train on the Western and Atlantic Railroad. Taking the locomotive, the *General*, Andrews and his men head northward, followed by Confederates in the locomotive *Texas*. Andrews and his men are caught by the Southern forces and are eventually executed, with the exception of 14 who are imprisoned.

EASTERN THEATER, PENINSULAR CAMPAIGN   General Joseph Johnston sends troops to support besieged Yorktown, Virginia. The situation of the Peninsular Campaign is still one which bodes ill for the vastly outnumbered Confederates.

13 *APRIL* 1862

WESTERN THEATER   Fort Pulaski, Georgia is termed a free area by General David Hunter, providing for the confiscation and setting free of all slaves in the vicinity.

TRANS-MISSISSIPPI   The evacuation of New Mexico Territory by Confederates continues, with Union soldiers pressing Southern troops back as far as El Paso,

16 *APRIL* 1862

WASHINGTON   President Lincoln signs into law a bill which will prohibit slavery in the District of Columbia.

THE CONFEDERACY   In a culmination of several weeks' preparations, President Jefferson Davis gives his approval to a Congressional proposal that will require a military draft in the Confederate states. This law states that 'all persons residing within the Confederate states, between the ages of 18 and 35 years . . . shall be held to be in the military service'. This action, while believed to be necessary by many due to the critical need to upgrade the military strength of the Confederacy, is nevertheless a move which is at variance with the generally accepted traditions embracing states' rights and rugged individualism endorsed by many in the Confederacy.

17 *APRIL* 1862

WESTERN THEATER   Confederate attention is focused on the increase in military strength of Federal troops at Ship Island, Mississippi, which is now supplemented by Union vessels on the Mississippi River. The latter include a fleet under Flag Officer David Farragut and Commander David Porter with a mortar fleet. The intention of these Union forces is the takeover of New Orleans, Louisiana, which is situated in what is rapidly becoming a vulnerable and defenseless position upriver.

18 *APRIL* 1862

EASTERN THEATER, PENINSULAR CAMPAIGN   Northern troops under General McDowell occupy Falmouth, Virginia, and at Yorktown, a Confederate attack on Union troops is unsuccessful, the latter forces pushing the Southern troops back.

NAVAL   As they had feared, the Confederates are subject to a barrage of mortar fire from Federal gunboats.

20 *APRIL* 1862

NAVAL   In a continuing bombardment of

the Fort Jackson and Fort St Philip area, Federal troops attempt to open the river further by removing obstructions placed there by Confederates.

23 APRIL 1862

NAVAL Flag Officer David Farragut orders the Federal fleet on the Mississippi River to move past Forts Jackson and St Philip. Due to the inconclusive nature of the recent attacks on these two fortifications, it seems appropriate that the North push onward to its ultimate goal of New Orleans, Louisiana.

24 APRIL 1862

NAVAL Farragut's fleet is able to slip past the Confederate forts on the Mississippi despite valiant attempts on the part of Southern forces to prevent this. The Union force makes its way up-river towards New Orleans. Encountering further Confederate resistance in the form of a ram, *Manassas*, Federals counter with their own fire, ultimately losing only the ship *Varuna* and 36 men. The Confederates lose 8 ships and 61 men.

25 APRIL 1862

WESTERN THEATER North Carolina's Fort Macon under Confederate Colonel Moses White surrenders to the Federal forces which have been besieging it for nearly a month. The next day, formal ceremonies relinquish Southern jurisdiction of Fort Macon to Union General John Parke, and 400 Confederate soldiers become Northern prisoners-of-war.
NAVAL Farragut's forces seize the city of New Orleans, Louisiana, which has been left defenseless after Confederate General Mansfield Lovell and his 4000 troops withdraw. There is little resistance to the Union takeover by the civilian populations, and 4 days later, on 29 April, New Orleans is formally surrendered to Federal forces.

27 APRIL 1862

WESTERN THEATER As a result of the

capture several days earlier of New Orleans, four Confederate forts—Livingston, Quitman, Pike and Wood—surrender to the North. At Fort Jackson, to the south, Confederate troops mutiny against their own officers and many flee in the face of their impending imprisonment. The following day both Forts Jackson and St Philip surrender, totally removing any Confederate resistance to Northern action on the Mississippi River as far up as New Orleans. General Benjamin Butler arrives with troops, landing just north of Fort St Philip. Butler will see to the management of the captured city which is, according to his written observation of several days later, a 'city under the dominion of the mob'.

28 APRIL 1862

WESTERN THEATER In Mississippi, General Halleck is preparing to move on General Beauregard's position at Corinth.

29 APRIL 1862

WESTERN THEATER General Halleck continues to ready his force of over 100,000 troops so as to attack Beauregard, whose forces are considerably smaller. Skirmishing breaks out at Cumberland Gap, Kentucky and near Bridgeport, Alabama. The conquering Federals at New Orleans post a United States flag on the New Orleans Custom House and on the City Hall, much to the sorrow and anger of the citizenry.

1 MAY 1862

EASTERN THEATER, PENINSULAR CAMPAIGN The siege of Yorktown, Virginia continues as Federals under McClellan prepare to attack. Guns are readied for the assault scheduled to begin in several days.

3 MAY 1862

EASTERN THEATER, PENINSULAR CAMPAIGN Yorktown, Virginia is evacuated by General Joseph Johnston's troops. The enormous force of the Army of the Potomac has overwhelmed the Confederates without a major battle, and the Southern troops now move toward Richmond. McClellan's forces have been successful with their siege tactics, and they enter Yorktown the following day.

WESTERN THEATER Near Corinth, Mississippi, where General Beauregard's troops are stationed, there is minor skirmishing at Farmington. General Halleck's Federals are moving now in the direction of Corinth, hoping to arrive there on the following day.

5 *MAY* 1862

WASHINGTON President Lincoln and his Secretaries of War and the Treasury, Stanton and Chase, leave the capital. They travel by ship to Fort Monroe where they will observe the Federal troops' advance into Virginia.

EASTERN THEATER, PENINSULAR CAMPAIGN As a result of the Confederate evacuation of Yorktown, there is serious fighting between advancing Federals and retreating Confederates at Williamsburg. In all, 1703 Southern soldiers are lost during the encounter which claims 456 Union troops, with 373 listed as missing.

7 *MAY* 1862

EASTERN THEATER, PENINSULAR CAMPAIGN Further clashes occur in the Shenondoah Valley; General Franklin's Federals are attacked by General G W Smith's Confederates who hope to keep the road from Williamsburg to Yorktown, Virginia protected. This clash at Eltham's Landing, Virginia foreshadows the events of the upcoming week. In order to boost morale and to help encourage General McClellan to move on to Richmond, President Lincoln visits the *Monitor* and meets with various military officials.

8 *MAY* 1862

EASTERN THEATER The Battle of McDowell, a major battle of the Shenandoah Valley Campaign, sees General Stonewall Jackson's Confederates repulse

an attack by Federals under the command of General Robert Schenk. The Southern troops, numbering around 10,000, fight the 6000 Union troops. Jackson's forces pursue the fleeing Federals toward Franklin, West Virginia, but continue only for several days, returning to the Shenandoah.

9 *MAY* 1862

EASTERN THEATER, PENINSULAR CAMPAIGN President Lincoln meets with General McClellan, who is advancing slowly toward Richmond, Virginia. The chief executive admonishes McClellan for his difficulties in maintaining cooperation between himself and corps leaders. Norfolk, Virginia is evacuated by Confederates in a costly move. While they destroy much of their supplies and equipment, they still leave a large amount of valuable material to the Federals pushing into the area the following day.

WESTERN THEATER At Hilton Head, South Carolina General David Hunter, commander of the Department of the South, frees slaves in South Carolina, Florida and Georgia. This move, not given Congressional authorization nor approval by President Lincoln, is later repudiated by the chief executive. Mississippi is the scene of clashes between Confederates and advancing Federals near Corinth. Pensacola, Florida is evacuated by Confederates and within three days the Union Army has taken hold of the area.

10 *MAY* 1862

EASTERN THEATER The Federal push to gain further control in Virginia continues unabated. Jackson moves in on Franklin, West Virginia; Norfolk and Portsmouth are occupied by 5000 Union troops. This operation began by troops landing at Willoughby Point and involved, among other things, the burning of the naval yard at Gosport, Virginia. President Lincoln is personally involved in this action in that he superintends the movement of this Federal expeditionary force.

NAVAL At Fort Pillow, Tennessee, on the

Mississippi River, a Confederate force of eight gunboats attacks seven Union vessels, the latter made up of sturdy ironclads. The Confederate flotilla is singularly ill-equipped to make this offensive at Plum Run Bend a successful one, but Captain James Montgomery commands the Confederates in a valiant manner and under his direction the Southern boats succeed in sinking the Union ironclads *Cincinnati* and *Mound City*. Despite this, the Confederate gunboats are forced, ultimately, to retreat to Memphis, Tennessee after the Union guns disable their ships.

11 *MAY* 1862

NAVAL   The Confederate ironclad *Merrimack*, after having confronted the Union ironclad *Monitor* in a spectacular stand-off on 9 March 1862, is destroyed by the Confederate navy: The Union troops advancing on Virginia have placed the Confederates in a situation requiring destruction of a valuable naval vessel, which would otherwise revert to enemy hands.

12 *MAY* 1862

WASHINGTON   In a reversal of his blockade order, President Lincoln issues a proclamation which opens the ports of Beaufort, North Carolina; Port Royal, South Carolina; and New Orleans, Louisiana. This order will take effect on 1 June 1862 and will provide for the resumption of commercial operations at these formerly Confederate-held ports.

13 *MAY* 1862

THE CONFEDERACY   The situation at the Confederate capital of Richmond, Virginia assumes crisis proportions in the face of advancing Federal troops. As McClellan's Army of the Potomac presses the Southerners, President Davis' wife, Varina, joins many others who decide to leave the threatened city.
EASTERN THEATER   General Jackson prepares to confront Confederate General Nathaniel Banks and his troops at Strasburg, Kentucky, as part of the Shenandoah Valley Campaign.
NAVAL   The Confederate steamer *Planter* is seized in Charleston Harbor by eight blacks. They pilot the vessel, which has seven guns, out of the harbor. At Natchez, Mississippi Union gunboats under David Farragut, take over jurisdiction of the city.

15 *MAY* 1862

EASTERN THEATER, PENINSULAR CAMPAIGN   Land forces pressing in on Richmond, Virginia move closer to the Confederate capital. Nearby, General Joseph Johnston's troops are moving back across the Chickahominy River. In west Virginia, at Ravenswood and Princeton, minor skirmishing occupies Confederate and Federal troops. Major fighting breaks out at Drewry's Bluff in Virginia, where Federals invading near the Confederate capital deal with gunfire from Fort Darling.
NAVAL   The battle at Drewry's Bluff involves the Northern ironclad *Monitor* and the gunboat *Galena*. The Union force is eventually forced to retreat as the Confederate defenses at Fort Darling prove adequate.

16 *MAY* 1862

WESTERN THEATER   In one of his most controversial actions to date, General Benjamin Butler at New Orleans, Louisiana issues what is known as the 'Woman Order'. The full text of this *General Order Number 28* is indicative of Butler's complete disregard for convention and his, at times, tyrannical attitude toward the citizens of this vanquished city. The order reads, in part, 'As the officers and soldiers of the United States have been subjected to repeated insults from the women (calling themselves ladies) of New Orleans . . . when any female shall . . . show contempt for the United States, she shall be regarded as a woman of the town plying her avocation'. The Woman Order, while not revoked by the Lincoln administration, helped to set the stage for Butler's removal from the military governorship of New Orleans on 16 December 1862. The day after the issuance of the Woman Order, Butler stops the New Orleans newspapers, *Bee* and *Delta* under the control of Federal authorities.

17 *MAY* 1862

EASTERN THEATER, PENINSULAR CAMPAIGN   General McDowell is at Fredericksburg, Virginia and receives orders to advance toward the Confederate capital at Richmond in order to be in concert with McClellan's forces.

18 *MAY* 1862

EASTERN THEATER, PENINSULAR CAMPAIGN   In Virginia, Union troops press closer to Richmond, taking Suffolk and occupying that town 17 miles south of Norfolk. In the Shenandoah Valley, Confederate General Stonewall Jackson continues to push the Federals, clashing with General Nathaniel Banks.

NAVAL   Vicksburg, on the Mississippi River, is the object of David Farragut's advance with a Federal fleet, the city being under the protection of Confederate General M L Smith who will not surrender jurisdiction to the North. It is important to the Federals to take possession of this Confederate city since it commands an important position on the Mississippi.

19 *MAY* 1862

WASHINGTON   In an action reversing an earlier decision made by General David Hunter, President Lincoln countermands the order of 9 May 1862 which liberated slaves in the Department of the South. Lincoln's position is that General Hunter had exceeded his official authority in issuing such a liberation order, and that such decisions are to be made only by the chief executive.

THE CONFEDERACY   President Jefferson Davis, in continued communication with his wife, indicates the Confederate position concerning preparation for the Federal offensive on Richmond, Virginia: 'We are uncertain of everything except that a battle must be near at hand'.

EASTERN THEATER, PENINSULAR CAMPAIGN   There is little change in the continuing buildup of Union troop strength in the area surrounding Richmond, Virginia.

20 *MAY* 1862

WASHINGTON   President Lincoln signs into law a bill authorizing the Homestead Act. Designed to aid both the private citizen who wishes to obtain quality land at affordable rates, the Homestead Act makes 160-acre quarter sections available for a nominal fee to those who can improve the parcel of land for five years. This is later to be considered a critical instrument in the settlement of the West and the development of western agricultural lands.

EASTERN THEATER, PENINSULAR CAMPAIGN   The Army of the Potomac under General McClellan is now only eight miles from Richmond, Virginia, the Confederate capital. In an attempt to prevent Union General Nathaniel Banks from moving troops to meet and support McClellan, Confederate General Stonewall Jackson and General Richard Ewell take their 16,000 men into the Luray Valley area of the Shenandoah. By moving north Jackson hopes to block Banks' path out of the western reaches of the Shenandoah. The Virginia Central railroad is attacked by Union troops at Jackson's River Depot.

21 *MAY* 1862

EASTERN THEATER, PENINSULAR CAMPAIGN   General McClellan continues to ask President Lincoln for more troops to augment the Army of the Potomac; this time he requests help from McDowell's forces which are enroute to Richmond, Virginia.

22 *MAY* 1862

EASTERN THEATER, PENINSULAR CAMPAIGN   General Stonewall Jackson pushes further toward Front Royal, West Virginia, in preparation for a major engagement with Federals on the following day.

CHRONOLOGY

WESTERN THEATER General Henry Halleck continues to direct his troops in the skirmishing which occurs at Corinth, Mississippi between the Federals and the Confederate forces under General Beauregard.

23 MAY 1862

EASTERN THEATER After having journeyed to Fredericksburg, Virginia, President Lincoln confers with General McDowell who is positioned at Aquia Creek and Fredericksburg. The following day, Lincoln sends orders to McDowell, telling the general to direct 20,000 troops into the Shenandoah area in order to prevent Confederates from moving their forces any closer to Banks' troops of the Army of the Potomac. Lincoln tells McDowell, 'Your object will be to capture the forces of Jackson and Ewell'. At Front Royal, West Virginia, General Jackson's troops encounter 8000 Union soldiers and take the area from Federal control. This victory is a relatively easy one, and does little to improve Banks' position, which is now seriously threatened.

24 MAY 1862

WASHINGTON President Lincoln confers with his Cabinet; the result of this discussion is the issuance of new military orders to General Frémont. The general is instructed to advance against General Jackson's forces in the Shenandoah Valley. Because of Lincoln's new orders to General McDowell, also concerning Jackson, the President communicates the information to General McClellan that an increase in his troop strength is at this time impossible.

25 MAY 1862

WASHINGTON Communications between the President and General McClellan continue as Lincoln presses his General-in-Chief to 'either attack Richmond or give up the job and come to the defence of Washington'. The Union Secretary of War, Edwin Stanton, puts out a call for additional men to be supplied by any state that can spare more troops. Orders go out to give military transport top priority on railroad lines in the North.

EASTERN THEATER In the Shenandoah Valley, at Winchester, Virginia, General Stonewall Jackson attacks Federal positions. While the Federals maintain their stance for a time, the offensive on the right, by troops under the command of Jackson, and on the left by Ewell's troops, eventually compel General Nathaniel Banks' forces to pull back in a retreat toward Harper's Ferry, Virginia. This encounter at Winchester claims 400 Confederate casualties—68 dead, 329 wounded, 3 missing. General Banks' troops had totaled nearly 8000 at the start of this clash; he lost 62 men, with 243 wounded and 1714 either missing or captured.

26 MAY 1862

WASHINGTON The discussion over allocation of troop strength and troop movement continues as President Lincoln asks General McClellan, 'Can you get near enough to throw shells into the city?'

EASTERN THEATER There is little that Union General Nathaniel Banks can do but continue to move back away from Jackson's Confederates after the defeat at Winchester, Virginia. Banks moves the following day across the Potomac River into Federal territory near Williamsport.

29 MAY 1862

EASTERN THEATER, PENINSULAR CAMPAIGN · Various actions occur to consolidate the Federal position near Richmond, Virginia. Approximately 40,000 Union troops gather near Jackson's Confederates at Harper's Ferry. There is skirmishing at the South Anna River in Virginia, where Federals burn a 500 foot bridge and ultimately capture the nearby town of Ashland.

WESTERN THEATER The pressure that General Halleck's Federals have put on General Beauregard's troops at Corinth, Mississippi has finally caused the Confederate general to give orders to retreat toward Tupelo, Mississippi.

30 *MAY* 1862

EASTERN THEATER, PENINSULAR CAMPAIGN   At Front Royal, in West Virginia, Union troops under General Shields occupy the town after a minor clash with General Jackson's retreating Confederates. Jackson is pulling away from the Harper's Ferry area so as to avoid being cut off by Frémont and McDowell.

WESTERN THEATER   At Corinth, Mississippi, over 2000 prisoners are taken by Federal troops moving into the city. General Beauregard's Confederates have destroyed much of value that could not be taken out of Corinth; General Halleck's success in occupying the city is a real one but it is a success which lacks some degree of triumph simply because the campaign has taken over one month to reach fruition.

31 *MAY* 1862

EASTERN THEATER, PENINSULAR CAMPAIGN   Movements by Confederate General Joseph Johnston and McClellan's Army of the Potomac result in a major operation at the battle of Fair Oaks and Seven Pines. This somewhat delayed offensive by Johnston is only marginally effective strategically, causing the Federal troops to pull back on the following day, but doing little to lessen the threat posed to the Confederate capital at Richmond, Virginia. In all, Confederate losses are tallied at

The Battle of Fair Oaks, 31 May 1862.

6134 while Union troops lose 5031. General Johnston is wounded in this battle, causing Confederate President Jefferson Davis to name General Robert E Lee as commander of the Army of Northern Virginia.

1 *JUNE* 1862

WASHINGTON   President Lincoln sends a telegram to General McClellan concerning the situation at Richmond, Virginia. He tells the general: 'Hold all your ground, or yield any only inch by inch and in good order'.

EASTERN THEATER, PENINSULAR CAMPAIGN   General Jackson's Confederate troops meet those of Union General McDowell as Jackson continues to retreat to a position near Harrisonburg, Virginia.

3 *JUNE* 1862

WESTERN THEATER   The Confederate garrison at Fort Pillow, near Memphis, Tennessee, evacuates its position, leaving the city helpless in the face of advancing Union troops which have already taken Corinth, Mississippi. McClellan's forces meet and skirmish with Confederates on James Island, South Carolina. This is a position near Charleston, which is the object of the Federal advance in that area.

4 *JUNE* 1862

EASTERN THEATER, PENINSULAR CAMPAIGN   Richmond, Virginia remains threatened by the Union Army of the Potomac which is resting after the Fair Oaks and Seven Pines battle earlier in the week. Some skirmishing does occur, however, mainly in West Virginia, near Big Bend. General Stonewall Jackson and his Confederate troops continue to pull back into the Shenandoah Valley.

5 *JUNE* 1862

EASTERN THEATER, PENINSULAR CAMPAIGN   Inclement weather prevents General McClellan's forces from pushing further toward Richmond, Virginia, where the Confederates anticipate attack from the Union Army and where Confederate General Robert E Lee is preparing a defensive operation with the Army of Northern Virginia.

TRANS-MISSISSIPPI Skirmishing breaks out at various locations—Sedalia, Missouri, Round Grove, in Indian Territory and near the Little Red River in Arkansas.

NAVAL The Federal fleet which is moving toward Memphis, Tennessee passes Fort Wright and Fort Randolph unharrassed. The five ironclads and four rams making up the Union flotilla are under the direction of Commodore Charles Davis. They come to rest at anchor two miles above Memphis.

6 JUNE 1862

NAVAL Confederate Captain James Montgomery, with an inadequate force of gunboats, engages the Union flotilla at a point near Memphis, Tennessee. Commodore Davis' resources far exceed those of the Confederates, who have only 28 guns compared to the Union strength of 68 guns. As crowds gather in the pre-dawn hours, the Federals and Confederates clash, and within two hours the latter force has been almost completely disabled. The one vessel, *Van Dorn*, left to the Confederates after the river battle, escapes. Triumphant Federals accept the surrender of Memphis shortly before noon. This battle is significant in that it opens the Mississippi, the target of future Union operations against Confederates in the area.

The gunboats at Memphis, 6 June 1862.

7 JUNE 1862

EASTERN THEATER, PENINSULAR CAMPAIGN As Confederates retreat, coming closer to Harrisburg, skirmishing breaks out at Union Church, Virginia when they meet advancing Northern troops. Reconnaissance efforts on the part of Federals at Chickahominy Creek bring those troops close to the Confederate capital of Richmond, where General Lee is readying his Confederates for an offensive, as well as for the defense of the city.

WESTERN THEATER The difficult relations engendered by Union General Benjamin Butler's treatment of New Orleans citizens are made even more uncomfortable when Butler orders William Mumford hanged. Mumford, having removed and destroyed the United States flag on display over the New Orleans Mint, was seized, imprisoned, tried, and found guilty of treason against the Federal government.

8 JUNE 1862

EASTERN THEATER, PENINSULAR CAMPAIGN Near Port Republic, Virginia, the battle of Cross Keys nearly causes the retreat of Confederate forces. While Jackson's troops are advancing against General Frémont's Federals, Confederate General R S Ewell was the commander of forces which are able to hold off the Union troops and defend General Jackson's men. The Federals, numbering 10,500, were held off by 6500 of Ewell's troops.

9 JUNE 1862

EASTERN THEATER, PENINSULAR CAMPAIGN Fighting continues in the area of Cross Keys, Virginia, but the battle today between Jackson's troops and those of Frémont and Shields takes place at Port Republic. The Confederates make a strong stand and eventually push the Northern troops back. General Ewell's Confederates are an important resource in this offensive as they hold Frémont's men away from Jackson's main force. The battle here at Port Royal and the previous day's encounter at Cross Keys signal the end of Jackson's current campaign in the Shenandoah.

12 *JUNE* 1862

EASTERN THEATER, PENINSULAR CAMPAIGN In one of the more flamboyant moves of the war, Confederate General J E B Stuart takes a force of cavalry and artillery out on a reconnaissance of the Federal positions on the Peninsula. This action, which covers a period of several days, is an important one as it disturbs supply and communication networks. Riding completely around McClellan's Union Army force, General Stuart seriously disrupts the morale of the Federals who feel threatened by what is a seemingly larger enemy force than actually exists. This move (which comes to be known as Stuart's First Ride Around McClellan), is responsible for encouraging Southerners who have been suffering from numerous defeats and invasions over the past months. Stuart's move is buttressed by Jackson's forces who are reinforced at Lee's command, and who add to the threat posed by a mobile cavalry under General Stuart.

16 *JUNE* 1862

WESTERN THEATER At James Island, South Carolina, Federal troops engage in a battle at Secessionville. The losses are significant, Union General H W Benham's forces losing 107 men, with 487 wounded and 89 missing. The Confederates under General N G Evans lose 52, with 144 injured and 8 missing. The Union force is repulsed despite its vigorous assault on a position which is critical to the control of Charleston Harbor. In Winchester, Tennessee, skirmishes break out.

17 *JUNE* 1862

WASHINGTON President Lincoln oversees the reorganization of commands in the East. Resentful at being placed under General John Pope, General John Frémont resigns from the new Army of Virginia.

General Franz Sigel steps into the vacancy created by Frémont's resignation. This move by Frémont places him in a position of ambiguity and he spends the remainder of the war in New York, hoping for further orders.

NAVAL In Arkansas, on the White River, Union gunboats draw fire from Confederate batteries positioned at St Charles. The Federal steamer *Mound City* is severely damaged when her boiler explodes, killing and wounding 125 men.

19 *JUNE* 1862

WASHINGTON President Lincoln outlines his controversial Emancipation Proclamation which outlaws slavery in all the states which continue to be in rebellion against the Federal government.

20 *JUNE* 1862

WESTERN THEATER The Federal advance against Vicksburg, Mississippi has begun under the command of General Thomas Williams. Admiral David Farragut aids in the attempt by providing gunboat protection. Confederates under General Van Dorn, who commands the Department of Southern Mississippi and Louisiana, attempt to further fortify the city.

21 *JUNE* 1862

EASTERN THEATER, PENINSULAR CAMPAIGN While the Richmond, Virginia area remains calm and quiet as a whole, there is some minor skirmishing between Federals and Confederates at the Chickahominy Creek. The Northern and Confederate armies are both awaiting the inevitable battle; as the President of the Confederacy, Jefferson Davis, points out in a latter, 'A total defeat of McClellan will relieve the Confederacy of its embarassments in the East'.

23 *JUNE* 1862

WASHINGTON President Lincoln leaves the Federal capital on a trip to New York and West Point. The President intends to discuss current and future military strategies with the retired General Winfield Scott.

24 *JUNE* 1862

EASTERN THEATER, PENINSULAR CAMPAIGN White House, Virginia is evacuated as McClellan's troops press forward, and at Mechanicsville there is minor skirmishing between Confederate and Union soldiers.

WESTERN THEATER General Van Dorn's troops are at beleagured Vicksburg, Mississippi where 3000 Federals are encamped closeby.

25 *JUNE* 1862

EASTERN THEATER, PENINSUAR CAMPAIGN An effort by Confederates to deflect what they fear will be a crippling blow to Richmond, the Confederate capital, begins with the Seven Days' Campaign. The first of a series of engagements, the Oak Grove Battle, sees Confederate General John Magruder conduct operations calculated to confuse Federals into assuming a larger Confederate force than is actually assembled. While Magruder attempts this, General Lee attacks McClellan's forces gathered east of Richmond; despite a relatively ineffective assault on the Union troops, General McClellan is considerably more concerned than he had previously been about his army's safety. A total of 51 killed, 401 wounded, and 64 missing on the Federal side results from this engagement; Confederates lose 40 men with 263 injuries and 13 missing.

27 *JUNE* 1862

EASTERN THEATER, PENINSULAR CAMPAIGN The battle of Gaines' Mills, the third in a series in the Seven Days' Campaign, sees General Lee's troops break through Federal lines and follow the Northern force as it heads for Harrison's Landing, Virginia. The Federals are undaunted however, and the Confederate command is not able to take advantage of the weaknesses in the Union lines. General Porter takes his Federal troops back across the Chickahominy to rejoin McClellan's main army. General Magruder, south of the Chickahominy, continues to press the Union troops there with a greatly outnumbered force of Confederates. The results of the Gaines' Mills battle is a total of 6837 casualties for the North as compared to 8750 for the South. As McClellan pulls his army back, the Confederates see some relief in the strain placed on their defenses at Richmond.

28 *JUNE* 1862

EASTERN THEATER, PENINSULAR CAMPAIGN At Garnett's and Golding's Farms, fighting between Confederate and Union troops continued in Virginia. The Northern forces are pulling away from Richmond in the direction of the Potomac River. At White House Landing, Northern troops destroy supplies and equipment as they complete their evacuation of the area.

NAVAL Admiral David Farragut takes his fleet past Confederate shore batteries at Vicksburg, Mississippi, losing 15 men and sustaining injuries to 30 others. All but three Federal vessels succeed in slipping past the Confederate fortifications but this in no way indicates an easy victory over the Confederates at Vicksburg. The Northern offensive will continue for over a year.

Union mortarboats firing on Vicksburg.

29 JUNE 1862

EASTERN THEATER, PENINSULAR CAMPAIGN The Seven Days Campaign continues as Southern troops clash with Union forces at Savage's Station. This battle sees Federals withdraw east of Richmond, Virginia, toward the James River, leaving behind over 2000 injured and ailing soldiers. It is a battle that can only be considered inconclusive.

30 JUNE 1862

EASTERN THEATER, PENINSULAR CAMPAIGN At White Oak Swamp, Virginia, the sixth in a series of battles occurs as Union soldiers under General McClellan attempt to consolidate forces, succeeding to a certain degree in comparison to Longstreet's and Jackson's troops which seem plagued with confusion. It is in part this confusion and lack of coordination which allows McClellan to assume a safely entrenched position on Malvern Hill to the north of the James River.

1 JULY 1862

WASHINGTON President Lincoln signs into law a Federal income tax which levies a three percent tax on annual incomes of $600 to $10,000 and five percent on incomes above $10,000. Unlike a similar act passed in the previous year, this one actually goes into effect.

EASTERN THEATER, PENINSULAR CAMPAIGN The defeat of Confederate troops after a short battle at Malvern Hill spells the end of the Seven Days' Campaign in Virginia. Confederate troops under General Lee attack McClellan's Army of the Potomac at a point north of Richmond, Malvern Hill. In this battle, the Confederate forces appear disorganized and make only minimal impact on Union troops which are equipped with better guns. Despite this final assault which goes badly for the South, the Northern army is prevented from taking the Southern capital of Richmond, Virginia. And despite the ability of Lee's forces to hold the Federals at bay, the Union Army of the Potomac is

not destroyed or even seriously disabled. Throughout the Seven Days' Campaign there are thousands of casualties—the North tallying nearly 16,000 dead, injured and missing. Confederates estimate over 20,000 casualties.

2 JULY 1862

WASHINGTON In a move which is later to become important to the further development of vast agricultural lands in the west, President Lincoln signs the Morrill Land Grant Act into law. This law will give states apportionments of public land on which to build agricultural colleges. This act is introduced in Congress by Senator Justin Morrill of Vermont.

EASTERN THEATER, PENINSULAR CAMPAIGN Harrison's Landing, Virginia is the goal of McClellan's army which is retreating from its recent battle at Malvern Hill. Some minor skirmishing breaks out as the Union forces pull away.

4 JULY 1862

WASHINGTON This eighty-sixth celebration of Independence Day is observed with more than the usual enthusiasm.

WESTERN THEATER In Kentucky, Confederate Colonel John Hunt Morgan begins a series of raids which later earn him recognition from the Confederate Congress for his 'varied, heroic, and invaluable services in Tennessee and Kentucky'.

7 JULY 1862

THE NORTH General McClellan, having reached Harrison's Landing on the James River, is visited by President Lincoln. In view of the recent difficulties faced by the Army of the Potomac which were, in McClellan's opinion, exacerbated by Lincoln's refusal to send more troops to aid in the Peninsular Campaign, the general delivers a letter to the President. In this letter, General McClellan points out what he perceives as weaknesses in Lincoln's current military and political strategies. He attempts to persuade the President to maintain a more conservative approach in

CHRONOLOGY

conducting the war, urging that the war 'should not be at all a war upon population, but against armed forces and political organizations.'

9 JULY 1862

WESTERN THEATER Confederate John Hunt Morgan seizes Tompkinsville, Kentucky. The Confederate Colonel and his cavalry unit are continuing to carry out a series of raids against Federal positions.

NAVAL At Hamilton, North Carolina, Confederate positions on the banks of the Roanoke River fall into Federal hands. Several Confederate vessels are taken by the North, and about 35 Southerners are killed. The Federals lose two men and sustain 10 injuries.

10 JULY 1862

EASTERN THEATER The Northern Army of Virginia, commanded by General John Pope, is positioned in the Shenandoah Valley. General Pope makes clear that civilians in the area are obligated to give aid to and prevent disruption of the Federal military efforts there. Pope prescribes harsh treatment in response to any resistance from the people in the Shenandoah Valley.

WESTERN THEATER Colonel Morgan and his raiders press Federals in Kentucky, and the Southern commander urges the people of the area to 'rise and arm, and drive the Hessian invaders from their soil'.

11 JULY 1862

WASHINGTON President Lincoln appoints General Henry Halleck to the position of General-in-Chief of the Federal Army. Halleck has proven to be an able and far-sighted leader, and his most recent actions at the successful seizure of Corinth, Mississippi, suggest that he will continue to exhibit sound judgement in military matters.

13 JULY 1862

WASHINGTON President Lincoln is in correspondence with General McClellan over the allotment of soldiers for the attempted seizure of Richmond, Virginia. It is becoming increasingly difficult for Lincoln to ignore the fact that McClellan has yet to launch an effective offensive against Confederates on the Peninsula.

EASTERN THEATER Movement of General Lee's Confederates away from Richmond, Virginia suggests the beginning of another campaign against the threatening Northern forces. A bridge near Rapidan Station, Virginia is destroyed by Northern troops as they skirmish with Confederates at this point on the Rapidan River.

WESTERN THEATER At Murfreesboro, Tennessee, Federal forces are defeated by General Nathan Bedford Forrest's 1000 troops. Northern General Thomas Crittenden and his men make a valiant defense but are overpowered and nearly all are captured by the Confederates. The North loses a large amount of valuable military equipment and supplies in this raid on their position at Murfreesboro.

14 JULY 1862

WASHINGTON President Lincoln asks Congress to approve a law which will compensate 'any state which may abolish slavery within its limits'. The congressional approval that Lincoln seeks is not forthcoming, however, as 20 border states disagree with the President's plan. In a separate action, Congress passes a law creating the state of West Virginia which has seceded from the state of Virginia as a result of the split between North and South.

EASTERN THEATER The Union Army of Virginia under General John Pope's command receives orders from him concerning its conduct towards the enemy. In this famous address to the Northern troops, General Pope makes clear his stance and that which he expects his army to take: 'The strongest position a soldier should desire to occupy is one from which he can most easily advance against the enemy.'

15 JULY 1862

NAVAL In a spectacular battle on the

Mississippi, the Southern ironclad *Arkansas* engages three Federal vessels, and proceeds downriver. Near the city of Vicksburg, Admiral David Farragut attacks the *Arkansas* with the Federal fleet but to no avail. The Union loses 18 men, sustains 50 injuries and lists 10 men as missing. Confederates tally 10 killed and 15 wounded.

17 JULY 1862

WASHINGTON The Second Confiscation Act is signed into law by President Lincoln. This act provides for the freedom of those slaves coming into Federal jurisdiction from outside the Union, and also gives the president certain powers to grant amnesty and pardon in cases where he deems such actions appropriate. (This act supplements, in many ways, the Emancipation Proclamation as it deals with slaves outside the Confederacy. The Emancipation Proclamation is concerned with the disposition of those slaves who are in the territories in rebellion.)

WESTERN THEATER Confederate raiders under Colonel John Hunt Morgan make a surprise attack on Northern troops at Cynthiana, Kentucky. After several hours of fighting to defend their positions there, the Federals are overcome and Southern troops occupy the town. At this engagement, 17 Federal soldiers and 24 Confederates are killed. Skirmishing occurs at Columbia, Tennessee.

20 JULY 1862

WESTERN THEATER Colonel Morgan's Confederate raiders are surprised by Union cavalry near Owensville, Kentucky, with the result that the Southern soldiers are dispersed, the Federals taking horses and equipment from them.

22 JULY 1862

WASHINGTON President Lincoln presents his Emancipation Proclamation to his Cabinet. This action produces surprise in most quarters. The War Department announces that the military is empowered to employ as paid laborers any persons of African descent.

23 JULY 1862

EASTERN THEATER Confederates near Carmel Church, Virginia are attacked by Federal cavalry. In Northern Virginia, General John Pope announces that all disloyal citizens within his jurisdiction are to be arrested.

WESTERN THEATER Confederate troops under General Braxton Bragg are advancing on Chattanooga, Tennessee from their base at Tupelo, Mississippi.

27 JULY 1862

TRANS-MISSISSIPPI There is skirmishing at various points between Federals and Confederates: near Brown's Spring, Missouri; in Carroll, Ray and Livingston counties in that state; and near Fort Gibson in Indian Territory.

28 JULY 1862

TRANS-MISSISSIPPI Confederates lose 10 men at Bollinger's Mills, Missouri, as Federal forces make a successful assault on the Southern position there.

29 JULY 1862

TRANS-MISSISSIPPI At Moore's Mills in Missouri, Confederates are routed by Union guerillas. Southern losses tally at 62 dead, 100 wounded. Federals lose 16 men and sustain 30 injuries.

INTERNATIONAL Union officials in England are unsuccessful in an attempt to prevent the Confederate vessel *Alabama* from sailing out of Liverpool. Commanded by Captain Raphael Semmes, the *Alabama* will inflict much damage to Federal vessels in Atlantic waters, and is the ship responsible for a series of claims against the British government brought by United States ambassador Charles F Adams.

1 AUGUST 1862

EASTERN THEATER Federal troops under General McClellan, stationed at Harrison's Landing, Virginia are bombarded by Confederate batteries. The Federals return the fire and are able, after losing six

CHRONOLOGY

men, to silence the Confederate guns.
TRANS-MISSISSIPPI Skirmishing breaks out in Missouri at Ozark, Grand River and Carrolton. In addition, at Newark, Missouri, Northern soldiers battle unsuccessfully with Southern troops resulting in surrender after several hours. About 70 Federals surrender to the Confederates in this action, while Southern casualties tally over 100 dead and injured.

2 AUGUST 1862

WASHINGTON Secretary of State Seward communicates the Federal government's position on mediation offers from Britain. Seward counsels United States Ambassador to Britain, Charles F Adams, to decline any suggested mediation of the ongoing civil conflict in the United States
EASTERN THEATER Orange Court House, Virginia, having been occupied by several Southern cavalry regiments, is seized by troops from General John Pope's Army of Virginia. These forces cross the Rapidan River, clashing with Confederates who lose 11 men and see 52 taken as prisoners; the Federals sustain five casualties in this encounter. Malvern Hill, Virginia is retaken by troops from General McClellan's Army of the Potomac.

3 AUGUST 1862

WASHINGTON General-in-Chief Henry Halleck sends orders to General McClellan that the Army of the Potomac is to be relocated. In order to better provide for the defense of the Federal capital, McClellan's troops are to be stationed at Alexandria and at Aquia Landing, in Virginia. This conflicts with McClellan's views of the military needs of the Peninsula, and the general clashes bitterly with Halleck over this order.

4 AUGUST 1862

WASHINGTON The President issues military orders which are to provide for a draft of upwards of 300,000 men. This order never goes into effect, but in a separate action Lincoln makes provision for the recognition and promotion of competent military personnel. President Lincoln also declines the opportunity to enlist two black regiments from Indiana.

5 AUGUST 1862

THE WESTERN THEATER At Baton Rouge, Louisiana, Confederate forces attack Union troops stationed there. General John Breckenridge and about 2600 Southerners fight with 2500 Union soldiers under the command of General Thomas Williams, who is subsequently killed. The Confederates are eventually pushed back to a point some 10 miles out of the city, due in part to the inability of the Southern gunboat *Arkansas* to relieve the land forces. At this battle, Federals lose 383 men, the South tallies 453 dead. In Tennessee, Fort Donelson is attacked and the Union troops garrisoned there push the Southerners back after a fierce fight.

7 AUGUST 1862

EASTERN THEATER Confederate troops in Virginia push toward Union positions at Culpepper Court House and Madison Court House. Federals pull back from their recently recovered position at Malvern Hill, and there is skirmishing between Federals and southern troops at Wolftown, Virginia.
TRANS-MISSISSIPPI Fort Fillmore, in the New Mexico Territory, witnesses the routing of Confederate troops in the area by Federal forces under Colonel E R S Canby. Montevallo, Missouri is the site of skirmishing.

8 AUGUST 1862

WASHINGTON Secretary of War Stanton orders that anyone attempting to evade military service shall be subject to arrest.
WESTERN THEATER At Cumberland Gap in Tennessee, Confederates and Federals engage each other in fighting which ultimately leaves the Southern troops the losers—they tally 125 killed and injured as compared to Union casualties of 3 dead and 15 wounded.

9 *AUGUST* 1862

EASTERN THEATER, SECOND BULL RUN CAMPAIGN   At Cedar Mountain, Virginia, General Jackson's Confederates are positioned near Culpepper, and intend to strike the Union forces under General John Pope. In what is ultimately an unsuccessful action, General Banks and his Federals attack Jackson. This attack is foiled by General A P Hill's arrival; the Confederate troops under Hill manage to push Bank's forces back. It is by now clear to General Jackson that McClellan's Army of the Potomac will be moving into the region with reinforcements for Pope's troops. At this battle of Cedar Mountain, the beginning of the Second Bull Run Campaign (also known as Second Manassas) that lasts until September 1862, Union losses tally at 314 dead, 1445 injured, 622 missing Southern forces report 1341 casualties.

11 *AUGUST* 1862

WESTERN THEATER   Various actions occur—near Columbia, Tennessee there is minor fighting between Southern troops and Northern forces while similar clashes occur near Williamsport, also in Tennessee. In Corinth, Mississippi, an announcement by Union General Ulyssess Grant states that those fugitive slaves in the area under his jurisdiction shall be employed by the military.

12 *AUGUST* 1862

WESTERN THEATER   Confederate Colonel John Hunt Morgan carries out a raid on Gallatin, Tennessee, the result of which is the capture of the town where a Federal garrison, composed of four companies, is stationed. This takeover is short-lived, however, as Gallatin falls back into Union hands within 24 hours.

13 *AUGUST* 1862

EASTERN THEATER, SECOND BULL RUN CAMPAIGN   Various minor skirmishes occur between Southerners and Northern troops in Virginia near Orange Court House. General Robert E Lee's forces begin to advance on Gordonsville, where this Army of Northern Virginia will soon be immersed in the Second Battle of Bull Run.

TRANS-MISSISSIPPI   Confederates clash with, and are defeated by, Northern forces at Yellow Creek, in Missouri. Around 60 Southern soldiers fall into Union hands after this engagement.

NAVAL   The Potomac River is the site of a collision between two Federal steamers, the *George Peabody* and the *West Point*. A total of 83 lives are lost in this accident.

16 *AUGUST* 1862

EASTERN THEATER, SECOND BULL RUN CAMPAIGN   Following orders, General McClellan moves out of Harrison's Landing, in Virginia, with his Army of the Potomac. He proceeds northward to meet General Pope's Federals near Alexandria. Skirmishing breaks out in West Virginia at Wire Bridge.

17 *AUGUST* 1862

TRANS-MISSISSIPPI   Minnesota sees the beginning of a six-week uprising of Sioux Indians, who are in revolt because of living conditions on their reservations. After nearly 300 whites are massacred by the Indians, Federal forces, led by General H H Sibley, are able to quell the uprising which continues until 23 September 1862.

18 *AUGUST* 1862

EASTERN THEATER, SECOND BULL RUN CAMPAIGN   In order to protect his troops from Lee's advancing forces while waiting for the arrival of McClellan's army, General John Pope retreats to the north. At this time, information regarding Lee's movements have been captured by the Federals. Pope is now situated across the Rappahannock River from Lee's Army of Northern Virginia. Skirmishing breaks out at Rapidan Station and Clark's Mountain, in Virginia.

THE CONFEDERACY   At Richmond, Virginia, the Second Session of the Confeder-

CHRONOLOGY

ate Congress assembles. President Jefferson Davis makes a statement concerning the Southern nation's progress. While railing against the Union Army's treatment of Southerners, Davis also speaks encouragingly about 'our final triumph in the pending struggle against despotic usurpation'.

WESTERN THEATER In Tennessee, Clarksville is surrendered to Confederate forces. The Union commander there, Colonel R Mason, puts up no resistance to Southern troops prior to surrendering the city; he is later to be removed from military duty 'for repeated acts of cowardice'.

19 *AUGUST* 1862

THE NORTH Editor of the *New York Tribune* Horace Greeley speaks out on the slavery issue, criticizing President Lincoln's stance. In his letter to the *Tribune*, titled 'The Prayer of Twenty Millions', Greeley says, 'All attempts to put down the Rebellion and at the same time uphold its inciting cause are preposterous and futile.'

TRANS-MISSISSIPPI The Sioux Indians continue in their uprising, creating major difficulties in Minnesota; the following day, Fort Ridgely is attacked by Indians but manages to withstand the assault.

20 *AUGUST* 1862

EASTERN THEATER, SECOND BULL RUN CAMPAIGN General McClellan's Army of the Potomac continues to advance toward a position near Alexandria, Virginia in order to reinforce General Pope's troops. The latter have encountered Jackson's men at various points between Culpeper and the Rappahannock.

21 *AUGUST* 1862

EASTERN THEATER, SECOND BULL RUN CAMPAIGN Confederate troops crossing the Rappahannock encounter strong resistance from Federals; over 700 Southern soldiers lose their lives in this operation and nearly 2000 are captured by Union troops.

WESTERN THEATER In Tennessee, Confederate General Braxton Bragg moves his forces to a position above Chattanooga, and Gallatin is surrendered to the South by Union troops.

22 *AUGUST* 1862

WASHINGTON Responding to Horace Greeley's *New York Tribune* letter, 'The Prayer of Twenty Millions', President Lincoln speaks in defense of his strategy. He points out his main objective, which is to preserve the Union, and that any and all efforts to achieve this preservation are, in his eyes, appropriate: 'I would save the Union. I would save it the shortest way under the Constitution ... If I could save the Union without freeing *any* slave I would do it, and if I could save it by freeing *all* the slaves I would do it.'

23 *AUGUST* 1862

EASTERN THEATER A heavy barrage of Federal artillery opens along the Rappahannock, fire which is returned promptly by Southern batteries. After about five hours, this firing stops. Skirmishing occurs at Beverly Ford, Fant's Ford and at Smithfield Springs, all in Virginia.

25 *AUGUST* 1862

WASHINGTON Orders go out from Edwin Stanton, Secretary of War, to the Southern Department. These orders provide for the enlistment of black soldiers, 'up to five thousand in number and to train them as guards for plantations and settlements'.

EASTERN THEATER, SECOND BULL RUN CAMPAIGN At Waterloo Bridge, Virginia, there is heavy skirmishing between Confederates and Federals. The Southern forces under General Stonewall Jackson proceed out from their position on the Rappahannock, camping at Salem the following day and preparing for the impending battle with Union troops.

26 *AUGUST* 1862

EASTERN THEATER, SECOND BULL RUN

CAMPAIGN Also known as the Second Manassas, the campaign takes full shape as Confederates under General Jackson move in on Union General John Pope's troops. Manassas Junction and the railroad line there are seized by Southern forces. As Jackson divides his troops and encircles Pope's position, it becomes apparent to the latter that despite twice as many men, he may be forced to withdraw. Jackson's attempts to 'always mystify, mislead, and surprise the enemy if possible' appear to be proving successful. General Pope does little while Jackson's men move into position near Sudley Mountain, on Stony Ridge. McClellan continues to move in to provide support for Pope's forces.

TRANS-MISSISSIPPI In an effort which combines both land and naval forces, Union troops seize the Southern steamer *Fair Play* which is laden with arms and ammunition. This takeover occurs on the Yazoo River in Arkansas and is the result of an expedition led jointly by General Samuel Curtis and Commodore Charles Davis. In this venture, the Federals are rewarded with the acquisition of 1200 Enfield rifles, 4000 muskets, and nearly 7000 pounds of powder.

27 *AUGUST* 1862

EASTERN THEATER, SECOND BULL RUN CAMPAIGN Kettle Run, Virginia is one of several places which sees heavy skirmishing. General Hooker and his Federal troops are able to rout the Confederates at this point. Other sites of fighting in Virginia include Bull Run Bridge, Buckland Bridge and Waterford. The Confederates have now been able to interrupt communications between President Lincoln and General Pope. The latter is exhibiting some confusion as he pulls back from the formerly held poitions along the Rappahannock and moves slightly northward.

28 *AUGUST* 1862

EASTERN THEATER, SECOND BULL RUN CAMPAIGN General Jackson's forces prepare to proceed to a point near Groveton, Virginia and they engage Federals there who are commanded by General Rufus King. The fighting is extremely fierce at this battle of Groveton, and many casualties are sustained by both North and South. General John Pope, operating under the mistaken assumption that Jackson is retreating toward the Shenandoah Valley, directs his troops to Groveton in order to rout the Confederates who remain there after the battle. Fredericksburg, Virginia is evacuated by Union troops.

29 *AUGUST* 1862

EASTERN THEATER, SECOND BULL RUN CAMPAIGN In a strategic error, General Pope allows his men to attack Jackson's Confederates so as to cut off the latter's retreat. Pope is unaware that the Southern forces have no intention of withdrawing, even though there are 20,000 Confederates to repel 62,000 Federals. This imbalance is soon minimized by the arrival of additional Southern troops under General Longstreet. Pope's somewhat disorganized troops are no match for the Confederates who have been anticipating and preparing for this, the Second Battle of Bull Run, or Manassas, for several days. Union General John Pope, oblivious to the fact that Longstreet has arrived with reinforcements, intends to pursue the fight further the following day. Unfortunately for the Northern troops, this gives Longstreet an opportunity to crush a portion of Pope's left flank, causing a retreat over the Bull Run and saving a large number of Federal soldiers.

31 *AUGUST* 1862

EASTERN THEATER, SECOND BULL RUN CAMPAIGN There is minor skirmishing in the aftermath of the Union defeat at the Second Battle of Bull Run. General Pope consolidates his forces near Centreville, Virginia. Weldon, Virginia sees fighting— 110 Confederates left dead and 5 Union soldiers killed at this engagement.

WESTERN THEATER Minor fighting occurs in Alabama and Kentucky.

CHRONOLOGY

1 *SEPTEMBER* 1862

EASTERN THEATER, SECOND BULL RUN CAMPAIGN A battle at Chantilly, or Ox Hill, Virginia proves to be the final clash between North and South in the Second Battle of Bull Run. The day-long engagement between 1300 Federals and 800 Confederates results in victory for the South. The defeat of the North is compounded by the deaths of Union Generals J J Stevens and Philip Kearney. General Pope finally retreats toward Washington, DC.

WESTERN THEATER In Kentucky, General E Kirby Smith and his Southern troops cause apprehension at Lexington since it is expected that the Confederates will try to take the city. The state legislature in Kentucky adjourns and moves to a more secure location at Louisville.

2 *SEPTEMBER* 1862

WASHINGTON In an important command change, President Lincoln orders General McClellan to take over the Union Army of Virginia and the forces now defending Washington, DC. This is a move made without the full support of Lincoln's Cabinet; notably, Secretary of War Edwin Stanton withholds his approval.

3 *SEPTEMBER* 1862

WASHINGTON General Halleck is the recipient of a report made by General John Pope concerning the action of various officers at the Second Battle of Bull Run. Pope charges McClellan with lack of support, pointing out the need for reinforcements at the time Jackson was attacking and the tardiness with which McClellan's men arrived.

WESTERN THEATER Frankfort, Kentucky is occupied by General E Kirby Smith's Confederates, and in the Geiger's Lake area there is minor skirmishing.

4 *SEPTEMBER* 1862

EASTERN THEATER Various minor engagements occur as the Confederate Army of Northern Virginia under General Robert E Lee moves towards Maryland. General A G Jenkins conducts raids in West Virginia near Point Pleasant.

NAVAL The Federal blockade off Mobile Bay, Alabama is unsuccessful in preventing the Confederate steamer *Oreto* from making it safely to port, despite the valiant efforts of the Union *Oneida*.

7 *SEPTEMBER* 1862

WASHINGTON Due to the Confederate Army's positioning itself at Frederick, Maryland, the Union capital at Washington, DC is in turmoil. Many fear an immediate invasion there and citizens of other nearby cities—Baltimore and Hagerstown, Maryland and Harrisburg, Pennsylvania—make various arrangements to arm themselves against the alleged invaders. Many people evacuate their homes.

WESTERN THEATER Minor skirmishing breaks out at Murfreesboro and Pine Mountain Gap, Tennessee. General Bragg advances with his Confederates. Kentucky being their goal; Bowling Green is occupied by Union forces.

8 *SEPTEMBER* 1862

EASTERN THEATER The Confederate Army of Northern Virginia under General Lee creates fear and confusion among the citizens of Maryland where Lee and his forces are encamped. In response to these feelings, Lee makes an attempt to explain the Southern position: 'We know no enemies among you, and will protect all, of every opinion. It is for you to decide your destiny freely, and without constraint. This army will respect your choice, whatever it may be.' Close to the Federal capital, General Nathaniel Banks takes charge of defense forces.

9 *SEPTEMBER* 1862

EASTERN THEATER, ANTIETAM CAMPAIGN Williamsburg, Virginia is attacked by Confederates but Union troops there successfully repel the advance. General Longstreet receives orders to approach Boonesboro, Maryland with his Confederates.

Confederate artillery at Antietam

Skirmishing occurs at Monocacy Church and Barnesville, both in Maryland.

10 *SEPTEMBER* 1862

EASTERN THEATER, ANTIETAM CAMPAIGN
Gauley, Virginia witnesses an attack on Union forces by Confederates posted in the area. Fayetteville, West Virginia sees military action which results in a Southern victory. General McClellan continues to advance on Lee's Army which is positioned near Frederick, Maryland.

WESTERN THEATER Cincinnati, Ohio anticipates an invasion by Confederates and prepares to make defense of the city. Militia is called out to repel the imminent invasion.

12 *SEPTEMBER* 1862

EASTERN THEATER, ANTIETAM CAMPAIGN
General McClellan pushes towards Frederick, Maryland with the Army of the Potomac which has absorbed the Army of Virginia. Skirmishing continues in the vicinity.

13 *SEPTEMBER* 1862

EASTERN THEATER, ANTIETAM CAMPAIGN
In what proves to be a stroke of luck for the Union forces, General Lee's orders for the Maryland invasion are discovered by Union soldiers. Due to this, General McClellan is able to approach with more accuracy the Confederate positions near Harper's Ferry, where Jackson has been posted; Hagerstown, where General Longstreet is to be stationed and South Mountain, the location of Jeb Stuart's cavalry. It is now clear that McClellan can take advantage of the divided strength of Lee's army.

14 *SEPTEMBER* 1862

EASTERN THEATER, ANTIETAM CAMPAIGN
The battle of Crampton's Gap, the first of several engagements making up the Antietam Campaign, occurs. As Confederate troops under the command of General LaFayette McLaws prepare to attack Harper's Ferry, Virginia, Union troops move in on them. Under General William Franklin this Union force is able, after a day of fighting, to cause the Confederates to pull back. The Union general is over-cautious in his judgement of the Southern Forces's abilities, even after their retreat. This results in the eventual capture of Harper's Ferry by the Confederates since Franklin's reluctance to engage McLaws again permits the latter to regroup and support Lee's assault on Harper's Ferry the following day. In a separate battle, that of South Mountain, Federals under General Alfred Pleasonton attack Confederates at Turner's Gap, Virginia. The engagement results in the Southern forces being pushed out of the higher ground. At this battle, the Union troops lose 325 men and sustain 1403 injuries. Likewise, the South sees 325 soldiers killed and 1561 wounded. The latter forces report 800 missing while Northern soldiers missing tally only 85.

Carrying off the wounded at Antietam.

The Battle of Antietam, 17 September 1862.

Soldiers killed in 'Bloody Lane' – Antietam.

15 SEPTEMBER 1862

EASTERN THEATER, ANTIETAM CAMPAIGN
The fighting in Northern Virginia continues as General Lee's Confederates, under General Stonewall Jackson's leadership, attack Harper's Ferry. This episode in the Antietam Campaign sees Federal troops unable to withstand the fierce assault and nearly 12,000 Union soldiers are captured after attempts at relatively brief defenses. The Federal commander at Harper's Ferry, General Dixon S Miles, is killed during this battle. At Sharpsburg, Southern forces arrive after having been pushed out of their position at South Mountain, Virginia. The Confederate Army under General Lee is now preparing to confront the Northern forces at the Sharpsburg location.

17 SEPTEMBER 1862

EASTERN THEATER, ANTIETAM CAMPAIGN
Despite the fact that the Southern forces are greatly outnumbered by General McClellan's Army of the Potomac, General Lee positions his troops for an attack along Antietam Creek. The Northern assault coming early in the day is disorganized and it allows the Confederates to rally somewhat. Union General Burnside attacks the southern right flank, pushing the Southern troops aside, crossing Burnside Bridge, and advancing on Antietam, a movement which is halted by General A P Hill's arrival. The latter has been dealing with the surrender of Harper's Ferry and

has only been able to join the rest of Lee's forces late in the day. Hill's advent on the battle scene prevents any further movements by the Federals and saves the Confederate right. At this battle of Antietam, or Sharpsburg, the Confederates suffer heavy losses, as do the Union forces. However threatened General Lee's troops are in terms of manpower or positioning, they continue to hold their ground, a withdrawal not being considered until the following day. Casualties for the North are tallied at 2108 killed, 9549 wounded, 753 missing; for the South, estimates list 2700 killed, 9024 wounded, and 2000 missing. The Battle of Antietam is considered by many to be 'the bloodiest single day of the war'.
WESTERN THEATER   In the west, General Braxton Bragg accepts the surrender of Mumfordsville, Kentucky as the Union commander, Colonel John Wilder, relinquishes control of that city.

18 SEPTEMBER 1862

EASTERN THEATER, ANTIETAM CAMPAIGN
Late in the day, General Robert E Lee and his Army of Northern Virginia move out of Maryland after the engagement at Antietam the previous day. With this invasion of the North via Maryland in a shambles, the Confederates once more find themselves in a defensive position.

19 SEPTEMBER 1862

EASTERN THEATER   Portions of Harper's Ferry, Virginia, are burned by retreating Confederates. Skirmishing occurs near

Sharpsburg and Williamsport, Maryland. WESTERN THEATER In a battle which claims 782 Federal casualties, Southern troops attack Union forces at Iuka, Mississippi. The Confederates, under General Sterling Price, number nearly 17,000. The Federals have around 9000 and are attacked as Union General Rosecrans leads a movement into the town. After several hours the Northerners have overwhelmed Price's forces and the latter retreat toward the south.

21 *SEPTEMBER* 1862

EASTERN THEATER In Virginia, Federals crossing the Potomac engage in skirmishing with Southern troops at Shepherdstown. This results ultimately in a retreat by Union forces, who lose about 150 men.

WESTERN THEATER In Kentucky, General Braxton Bragg takes his Southern troops to Bardstown. The purpose of this is to enable Bragg's men to join with General E Kirby Smith's troops, but it allows Union General Buell to push forward to Louisville, Kentucky. At Mumfordsville, Kentucky, Union troops retake the town which had previously fallen to Confederates.

22 *SEPTEMBER* 1862

WASHINGTON President Lincoln makes a move which is to help terminate slavery as a United States institution. In presenting the Emancipation Proclamation to his Cabinet, Lincoln has chosen a time, after the Union success at Antietam, which he hopes will prove most advantageous.

24 *SEPTEMBER* 1862

WASHINGTON President Lincoln suspends the writ of habeas corpus for any individuals who are deemed guilty of 'discouraging volunteer enlistments, resisting militia drafts, or guilty of any disloyal practice, affording comfort to Rebels.'

1 *OCTOBER* 1862

WASHINGTON President Lincoln travels to Harper's Ferry to discuss the future of the Army of the Potomac with General McClellan.

THE CONFEDERACY At the Confederate capital of Richmond, Virginia, the newspaper *Whig* voices an opinion concerning Lincoln's recent Emancipation Proclamation, 'It is a dash of the pen to destroy four thousand millions of our property, and is as much a bid for . . . insurrection, with the assurance of aid from the . . . United States.'

2 *OCTOBER* 1862

WESTERN THEATER Columbia, Mississippi is the scene of a major battle between Federals and Confederates. The latter forces, under the command of Generals Van Dorn and Sterling Price, press Northern troops northwest of Corinth. On this first day of fighting, the Federals are forced into a defensive position.

4 *OCTOBER* 1862

WESTERN THEATER The second day of intense fighting at Corinth, Mississippi sees Federals under General Rosecrans hit hard by Van Dorn's Confederate troops. Despite this intense offensive, the Southerners are forced to withdraw before nightfall. Van Dorn's men are positioned, after this retreat, at Chewalla, Mississippi. Casualties at the close of the battle tally as follows: Union soldiers killed, 355; wounded, 1841; missing, 324. The Confederates estimate that they have lost 473 men here, have 1997 injured, and 1763 missing. The result of this battle at Corinth, Mississippi does not give the South the satisfaction of securing the railroad center there, nor does it cause General Rosecrans to pull back towards Ohio. There is minor fighting in Kentucky at Bardstown and at Clay Village. Middleton, Tennessee also sees a brief engagement between Federals and Confederates.

5 *OCTOBER* 1862

WESTERN THEATER Outside of Corinth,

Mississippi, Federals under General Rosecrans' command follow retreating Confederates, although Van Dorn's men are able to slip away from this Northern force. They are apprehended, however, by Federal General E O C Ord's men near the Hatchie River in Tennessee. This results in fighting of an intense, albeit brief, nature. The fighting associated with Corinth, Mississippi ends as Confederates break free of Ord's troops and head for Holly Springs. In Kentucky, General Braxton Bragg and his Southern troops move away from Bardstown and are followed by General Buell's Federals.

6 *OCTOBER* 1862

WESTERN THEATER General Braxton Bragg and his Confederates pull back toward Harrodsburg, Kentucky, pursued by General Buell's Northern troops. The latter occupy Bardstown, Kentucky.

8 *OCTOBER* 1862

EASTERN THEATER Minor fighting breaks out Virginia near Fairfax.
WESTERN THEATER The battle of Perryville, Kentucky occurs, involving General Braxton Bragg's Confederates and General Don Carlos Buell's Northern troops. The result of this encounter, the most significant of the battles fought in Kentucky, is that Bragg is compelled to retreat southeastward. Casualties are listed, for the Federals, at 845 dead, 2851 wounded, 515 missing, out of a total of 36,940 men. Confederates tally 510 killed, 2635 injured, 251 missing out of a total troops strength of 16,000.

9 *OCTOBER* 1862

EASTERN THEATER At Chambersburg, Pennsylvania, Confederate General J E B Stuart begins several days of raiding which he carries as far as Cashtown, Pennsylvania. Stuart has crossed Federal lines in order to accomplish this and has ridden his 1800 troops in a circle around General McClellan's inactive Army of the Potomac.

10 *OCTOBER* 1862

THE CONFEDERACY A request is made by Confederate President Jefferson Davis to draft 4500 blacks. The purpose of this is to further aid the Confederate army in its construction of fortifications around Richmond, Virginia.

11 *OCTOBER* 1862

THE CONFEDERACY In Richmond, Virginia, the Confederate Congress passes a bill, approved by President Jefferson Davis, which amends the military draft law. According to the new regulations, anyone owning 20 or more slaves is exempt from service in the Confederate Army. This law is publicized amid much controversy due to its selective nature, and serves to heighten a sense of class conflict in the Confederacy, some viewing the military situation as a 'rich man's war and a poor man's fight'.
EASTERN THEATER Chambersburg, Pennsylvania witnesses the continued raiding by J E B Stuart's Confederates. They seize around 500 horses and destroy several trains before crossing the Potomac and returning to Virginia near Poolesville, several days later.

12 *OCTOBER* 1862

TRANS-MISSISSIPPI Ozark, Missouri is the jumping-off point for a Northern expeditionary force headed for Yellville, Arkansas. This mission lasts for seven days. There is light fighting near Arrow Rock in Missouri.

15 *OCTOBER* 1862

EASTERN THEATER Part of the Army of the Potomac under General McClellan is involved in an expedition from Sharpsburg, Maryland to Smithfield, West Virginia. They also take part in a reconnaissance beginning at Harper's Ferry and ending in Charlestown, West Virginia.

18 *OCTOBER* 1862

WESTERN THEATER Confederate John Hunt Morgan, with 1500 men, routs Federal cavalry forces outside Lexington, Kentucky. The Southerners enter the city and seize 125 prisoners.

20 *OCTOBER* 1862

WESTERN THEATER There are various episodes of minor skirmishing. Hermitage Ford, Tennessee sees light action as does Wild Cat, Kentucky. Near Nashville, Tennessee, Union troops push back troops of Confederates under the command of General Nathan Bedford Forrest. Near Bardstown, Kentucky, Southern forces manage to attack and destroy a line of 81 Federal wagons. The Confederates are subsequently able to seize yet another train of wagons several hours later in Bardstown itself.

21 *OCTOBER* 1862

WASHINGTON An announcement by President Lincoln urges support, in Tennessee, for state elections. Lincoln entreats both civilian and military personnel to move to elect state government officials, a legislature and members of Congress.

22 *OCTOBER* 1862

WESTERN THEATER Confederate General Braxton Bragg is successful in withdrawing Southern troops from Kentucky where Federals under General Buell continue to make their presence felt following the battle of Perryville on 8-9 October 1862. There is a Union reconnaissance to Waverly, Tennessee leaving from Fort Donelson. This expedition encounters Confederate forces, skirmishing several times during the next three days. Loudon, Kentucky is seized by a force of Confederate cavalry under the command of Southern General Joseph Wheeler.

TRANS-MISSISSIPPI At Maysville, Arkansas, what is known by some as the second battle of Pea Ridge is fought. Union forces are successful in pushing 5000 Confederates out of the area into the Valley of the Arkansas. Southerners suffer losses of artillery and horses at this encounter.

Ulysses S Grant

24 *OCTOBER* 1862

WASHINGTON Because of his failure to prevent Bragg's Confederates from escaping from Kentucky, General Don Carlos Buell is relieved of command of Federal troops in Kentucky and Tennessee. President Lincoln authorizes General William Rosecrans to take over the responsibility for these troops as well as Federal forces in the Department of the Cumberland.

WESTERN THEATER In Brownsville, Tennessee, Confederate forces are routed by Federals. At Morgantown, Kentucky, Union troops seize 16 Southern soldiers. On St Helena Island, in South Carolina, there is a brief skirmish between Union and Confederate troops.

TRANS-MISSISSIPPI Fayetteville, Arkansas sees light fighting and there is a Federal expedition from Independence, Missouri, which, in the course of its three-day maneuver, encounters several guerilla forces around Greenton, Chapel Hill and Hopewell.

25 *OCTOBER* 1862

WASHINGTON President Lincoln is again in communication with General McClellan over the Army of the Potomac. The chief executive is becoming increasingly annoyed with the general's seeming inability to launch any major assault against Confederates in Virginia. As a telegram to McClellan indicates, Lincoln is not above venting his anger at the general's delays:

'Will you pardon me for asking what the horses of your army have done since the battle of Antietam that fatigue anything?' This is in response to a communication from McClellan about 'sore tongued and fatigued horses'.

26 OCTOBER 1862

EASTERN THEATER General McClellan moves the Federal Army of the Potomac across the river into Virginia, causing the President to write from Washington, DC that he 'rejoiced' in this overdue action.

27 OCTOBER 1862

WESTERN THEATER In Louisiana, the battle of Labadieville takes place on Bayou Lafourche. Confederates are routed at this battle, losing 6 men, sustaining 15 wounded and reporting 208 taken prisoner. Federals report 18 dead and 74 wounded.

NAVAL Federal blockaders on Bull's Bay in South Carolina successfully seize the British steamer *Anglia.*

28 OCTOBER 1862

EASTERN THEATER General McClellan is moving his Potomac Army troops toward Warrenton, Virginia and this causes Confederate General Robert E Lee to push his troops slightly to the south. Lee wishes to prevent his forces from being encircled by McClellan's men. Union forces occupy Halltown, Virginia, and there is light skirmishing at Snicker's Gap.

TRANS-MISSISSIPPI At Fayetteville, Arkansas, there is a clash between 1000 Union soldiers and about 3000 Confederates encamped there. The Federal forces follow the retreating Southerners into the area around the Boston Mountains.

31 OCTOBER 1862

WESTERN THEATER The upcoming Federal action against Vicksburg, Mississippi is foreshadowed by the gathering of Northern troops at Grand Junction, Tennessee. These troops are moving in from Corinth, Mississippi and Bolivar, Tennes-

see. Union forces scheduled to act as relief for the garrison at Nashville, Tennessee move through Bowling Green, Kentucky.

1 NOVEMBER 1862

WESTERN THEATER In New Orleans, Louisiana, military governor General Benjamin Butler tightens restrictions on movement to and from the city. In addition, Butler allows for the freeing of all imprisoned 'slaves not known to be the slaves of loyal owners'. Vicksburg, Mississippi is the target of a campaign being planned by General Ulysses Grant.

4 NOVEMBER 1862

THE NORTH Congressional elections in Northern states prove advantageous to Democrats in New York, New Jersey, Illinois and Wisconsin. New York elects a Democrat as Governor, Horatio Seymour. There are some Republican victories in border states, in California, Michigan and New England, however, which help the Republicans maintain control of the House of Representatives.

WESTERN THEATER In Mississippi, General Grant's Federals successfully occupy La Grange. This occupation, as well as a similar one at Grand Junction, Tennessee, is in preparation for the upcoming Vicksburg campaign. Union troops in Georgia destroy the southern saltworks at Kingsbury.

5 NOVEMBER 1862

WASHINGTON In one of the more significant command changes of the war, President Lincoln removes General George Brinton McClellan from his post as head of the Army of the Potomac. After months of attempting to support McClellan, Lincoln is alleged to have said, 'sending reinforcements to McClellan is like shovelling flies across a barn.' The general has been extremely reluctant to make any offensives against Lee'a army in Virginia, and any of his efforts in that direction are so minimal as to be virtually unnoticed. The official orders read: 'By direction of the President, it is ordered that Major General McClellan be relieved from the command of the Army of the Potomac; and that Major General Burnside take the command of that Army.' In another shift in command, General Fitz John Porter is replaced by General John Hooker.

7 *NOVEMBER* 1862

EASTERN THEATER General George McClellan is notified of his removal from the command of the Army of the Potomac. Completely surprised by this turn of events, he makes an extreme effort to prevent those around him from seeing how amazed he is to receive this news: 'I am sure that not the slightest expression of feeling was visible on my face.'

8 *NOVEMBER* 1862

WASHINGTON Further command changes see General Benjamin Butler replaced as head of the Department of the Gulf. Butler is succeeded by General Natheniel Banks, whose orders include the directive that 'The President regards the opening of the Mississippi River as the first and most important of our military and naval operations.'

9 *NOVEMBER* 1862

EASTERN THEATER Virginia witnesses some light action in Greenbrier County, and at Warrenton, Virginia General Burnside officially takes over command of the Army of the Potomac. A Union cavalry charge into Fredericksburg results in the taking of 34 Confederates as prisoners of war. Federals lose only one man out of a force of 54.

10 *NOVEMBER* 1862

EASTERN THEATER At Warrenton, Virginia, General George Brinton McClellan says his farewell respects to the Army of the Potomac there. Well-liked and respected by the troops, McClellan's departure was an occasion marked by near-idolization of 'Little Mac'.

13 *NOVEMBER* 1862

WESTERN THEATER Military actions of a minor, inconclusive nature continue. At Nashville, Tennessee, Union and Confederate soldiers engage in skirmishing. A railroad depot near Holly Springs, Mississippi is taken by Federals. General Braxton Bragg, intent on joining forces with General Breckenridge, pushes his Army of Tennessee toward Murfreesboro from Chattanooga, Tennessee.

14 *NOVEMBER* 1862

EASTERN THEATER The newly-appointed chief of the Army of the Potomac, General Burnside, reorganizes his troops placing Generals Sumner, Hooker and Franklin in charge of three main divisions of the Army. This is in preparation for an assault on the confederate capital at Richmond, Virginia.
WESTERN THEATER General Braxton Bragg has positioned his Confederate troops near Nashville, at Tullahoma, Tennessee.

15 *NOVEMBER* 1862

EASTERN THEATER General Burnside moves his Potomac Army troops out of Warrenton, Virginia and advances on Fredericksburg. There is an exchange of artillery fire between Union and Southern forces at Fayetteville, Virginia.

17 *NOVEMBER* 1862

NAVAL The Southern steamer *Alabama*, under the command of Captain Rapheal Semmes, sails into the harbor at Martinique, followed by the USS *San Jacinto* although the latter vessel quickly leaves the harbor in order to better lie in wait for the Confederate ship.

18 *NOVEMBER* 1862

EASTERN THEATER, FREDERICKSBURG CAMPAIGN General Burnside and his

Army of the Potomac arrive in Falmouth, Virginia, on the banks of the Rappahannock River across from Fredericksburg, Virginia. Skirmishing breaks out between Union and Confederate soldiers at Rural Hill, Virginia.

NAVAL Despite the efforts of the *San Jacinto*, the confederate *Alabama* manages to leave Martinique.

19 *NOVEMBER* 1862

EASTERN THEATER Both Union and Confederate forces are taking positions in the vicinity of Fredericksburg, Virginia. General Longstreet is established near Culpeper; General Burnside, near Falmouth. The Confederate cavalry under J E B Stuart is positioned at Warrenton Junction, in Virginia.

WESTERN THEATER General Ulysses Grant sends out reconnaissance forces to ascertain the strength of Confederate troops defending Vicksburg, Mississippi. Federal forces leave Grand Junction, Tennessee on a two day expedition to Ripley, Mississippi.

20 *NOVEMBER* 1862

EASTERN THEATER The Confederates in Virginia stationed near Fredericksburg are heartened by the arrival of General Robert E Lee. Charlestown, Virginia sees some minor skirmishing.

21 *NOVEMBER* 1862

EASTERN THEATER As military strength builds in the vicinity, the mayor of Fredericksburg, Virginia is issued a request for surrender by General Burnside. Refusing to give in, the mayor is told to evacuate women, children and injured or infirm persons from the town.

22 *NOVEMBER* 1862

WASHINGTON In the Federal capital, orders go out from Secretary of War Stanton to release all those imprisoned for political reasons—those who had been found guilty of draft evasion, of discouraging

others to enlist in the armed service, and for other similar actions.

EASTERN THEATER In a reversal of Burnside's orders of the previous day, General Sumner tells the mayor of Fredericksburg, Virginia that he will not fire on the town. This agreement is made in exchange for a promise of 'no hostile demonstrations' from the townspeople.

26 *NOVEMBER* 1862

WASHINGTON In order to meet with his recently-appointed general of the Potomac Army, President Lincoln leaves the Federal capital for Aquia Creek, Virginia.

27 *NOVEMBER* 1862

EASTERN THEATER President Lincoln confers with General Burnside. The two are not in total agreement about the proper strategy to employ in the current situation along the Rappahannock. The General ultimately decides not to defer to the President's wishes and instead follows his own plan for an assault on Fredericksburg where most of Lee's forces are concentrated.

28 *NOVEMBER* 1862

EASTERN THEATER At Frankfort, Virginia, Confederate troops are routed by Union forces and 110 Southerners are taken prisoner.

TRANS-MISSISSIPPI General James Blunt and his Federals stage an attack on Confederate positions at Cane Hill, Arkansas. The 8000 southern troops there are under the command of General John Marmaduke. Blunt's 5000 men pursue Marmaduke into the Boston Mountains after beating them back, but this chase is called off due to the strategic danger it creates for the Union forces. At this encounter, Federals tally losses at 40 men while the Southern total is considerably higher at 435.

30 *NOVEMBER* 1862

NAVAL The Confederate steamer *Alaba-*

Humphrey's charge at Fredericksburg.

ma continues to be elusive as it sails Atlantic waters and threatens Northern shipping. The Federal vessel *Vanderbilt* makes an attempt to capture the Southern vessel, but is unsuccessful.

1 DECEMBER 1862

WASHINGTON Congress meets in the Federal capital; President Lincoln addresses this, the third session of the 37th Congress, giving his State of the Union message. In addition to remarks made about the North's progress in the war and the positive condition of the Federal economy, the chief executive discusses several constitutional amendments. These proposed amendments center around slavery, suggesting plans for colonization, for financial compensation to previous slave owners as well as to cooperating states. Lincoln points out that '. . . *we* cannot escape history, . . . In *giving* freedom to the *slave*, we *assure* freedom to the free.'

3 DECEMBER 1862

WESTERN THEATER Near Nashville, Tennessee Confederates attack Northern soldiers along the Hardin Pike. Grenada, Mississippi is seized by General Hovey's Federals, who number about 20,000. This takeover occurs after Southerners have destroyed 15 locomotives and approximately 100 railroad cars in the face of advancing Northern troops.

4 DECEMBER 1862

EASTERN THEATER FREDERICKSBURG CAMPAIGN Winchester, Virginia falls into Union hands, resulting in the capture of 145 Southern soldiers. Near Fredericksburg, Virginia Northern troops clash with Confederates on the Rappahannock River and also on Stone's River, near Stewart's Ferry.

6 DECEMBER 1862

WASHINGTON As a result of the Indian uprisings in Minnesota during September, President Lincoln orders the execution of 39 Indians, the hangings to take place on 19 December 1862.
TRANS-MISSISSIPPI There is an attack on Federal troops at Cane Hill, Arkansas.

CHRONOLOGY

7 DECEMBER 1862

THE CONFEDERACY Confederate General John Pemberton receives a communication from President Jefferson Davis concerning the defense of Vicksburg, Mississippi. The Confederate President is worried about Pemberton's ability to hold out against an attack by Grant's men. Davis asks Pemberton: 'Are you in communication with General J E Johnston? Hope you will be reinforced in time.

WESTERN THEATER Hartville, Tennessee is the scene of yet another raid by John Hunt Morgan and his men. Federal forces, under Colonel A B Moore, suffer losses tallied at 2096, 1800 being taken prisoner by the Southern raiders.

TRANS-MISSISSIPPI In Arkansas, the battle of Prairie Grove takes place as Confederate General Thomas Hindman surprises 10,000 Northern troops. The latter, commanded by Generals James Blunt and Francis Herron, are unable, despite their combined forces, to repel the Confederates, who also number 10,000. The South suffers 164 fatalities, 817 injuries, and reports 336 missing at this battle, whereas Federals report 175 dead, 813 wounded, 263 missing.

10 DECEMBER 1862

WASHINGTON A bill creating the state of West Virginia passes the United States House of Representatives on a vote of 96-55. This follows a similar action by the Senate on 14 July 1862.

EASTERN THEATER FREDERICKSBURG CAMPAIGN The Union troops under General Burnside's command around Fredericksburg, Virginia increased their preparation for an advance on that city. Port Royal, Virginia is bombarded by Federal gunboats in retaliation for an attack on the latter by Confederate shore batteries.

11 DECEMBER 1862

EASTERN THEATER FREDERICKSBURG CAMPAIGN Fredericksburg, Virginia is occupied by Union forces under General Burnside. The Confederates in the vicinity are poised in readiness for the upcoming attack.

WESTERN THEATER More skirmishing breaks out near Nashville, Tennessee. At Columbia, Tennessee Confederate General Nathan Bedford Forrest moves out with nearly 2500 men in an attempt to disrupt General Grant's lines of communication.

13 DECEMBER 1862

EASTERN THEATER FREDERICKSBURG CAMPAIGN Approximately 72,000 Confederates under General Stonewall Jackson's command are attacked at Fredericksburg, Virginia by Union troops totalling about 106,000. The forces under General William Franklin attack Southern positions just across the Rappahannock to the south of the city. Meanwhile, General Sumner advances on positions north of the city and is able initially to break through the Confederate defenses, but the result is that Union soldiers are now forced to attack Southern troops placed at the foot of Marye's Heights. The Confederates are firmly entrenched and it is impossible for Federals to do more than struggle along the base of the ridge where the South is positioned. The attempt by Northern troops is a genuine but futile one. One Union soldier comments: 'It was a great slaughter pen . . . they might as well have tried to take Hell.' The casualties are high—12,700 killed and wounded among the Federals. The Confederates report 5300 dead or injured, among them, Generals Cobb and Gregg. General Robert E Lee remarks of this day's fight; 'I wish these people would go away and let us alone.'

WESTERN THEATER At Tuscumbia, Alabama there is a clash between Federal and Southern troops as Union soldiers attack and rout Confederates there. Mississippi sees a six-day offensive staged by Federal forces on the Mobile and Ohio Railroad which runs between Tupelo and Corinth.

14 DECEMBER 1862

EASTERN THEATER FREDERICKSBURG

CAMPAIGN   The Northern Army of the Potomac in and around Fredericksburg, Virginia makes preparations to move back across the Rappahannock River. Despite the Union Army's vulnerable position after the battle of Fredericksburg, the Southern forces under the command of General Lee do not attack Burnside's troops prior to their withdrawal.

15 *DECEMBER* 1862

WESTERN THEATER   In Tennessee, General Grant's forces, which are on their way to Vicksburg, Mississippi experience difficulties with Confederate forces under General Nathan Bedford Forrest. The latter has, with approximately 2500 soldiers, started towards Vicksburg intending to interfere with the Federal troops' communications along the way. New Orleans, Louisiana, sees the departure of General Benjamin Butler, who has been forced to step down as military governor. Few of the citizens of New Orleans are sorry to see the General leave.

16 *DECEMBER* 1862

WASHINGTON   The execution of Sioux Indians, slated for 19 December 1862, has been delayed by President Lincoln. A new date of 26 December 1862 has been set.
EASTERN THEATER   West Virginia witnesses an outbreak of skirmishing at Wardensville. General Burnside and the Army of the Potomac occupy Falmouth, Virginia. The General has made a statement concerning his part in the failure at Fredericksburg, a failure for which he assumes total responsibility.
WESTERN THEATER   After General Butler's departure from New Orleans, Louisiana, General Nathaniel Banks takes command there, assuming responsibility for the Federal Department of the Gulf. Tennessee is the site of Confederate General N B Forrest's march against Grant. North Carolina sees skirmishing in various places, among them White Hall and Goshen Swamp.

17 *DECEMBER* 1862

WASHINGTON   President Lincoln experiences difficulties with the Federal Cabinet. Secretary of the Treasury Salmon Chase is in conflict with Secretary of State Seward and also with Seward's son who is the latter's assistant. The result is that both Sewards submit their resignations to the chief executive although Lincoln will not accept them.
WESTERN THEATER   General Grant makes public *General Order Number Eleven* concerning speculation but specifically singling out Jews as the object of the declaration against illegal trade: 'The Jews, as a class violating every regulation of trade established by the Treasury Department and also department orders, are hereby expelled from the department within twenty-four hours from the receipt of this order.' While the order is rescinded several weeks later, on 4 January 1863, Grant's reputation is damaged by the adverse publicity surrounding the controversial statement.

18 *DECEMBER* 1862

WESTERN THEATER   Lexington, Tennessee is the site of a skirmish between cavalry under the command of Confederate Nathan Bedford Forrest and Union cavalry troops. The Confederates report 35 casualties compared to 17 listed by the Federals as killed or wounded. New Berne, North Carolina sees the return of Northern expeditionary forces after eight days of minor skirmishing and raids.

19 *DECEMBER* 1862

WASHINGTON   President Lincoln convenes his Cabinet to discuss the tendered resignation of Secretary of State Seward. Also at this meeting are members of the Senate Republican caucus committee.
WESTERN THEATER   At Spring Creek in Tennessee there is an encounter between Northern and Southern troops and another at Jackson, in that same state.

20 *DECEMBER* 1862

WASHINGTON   Compounding the crisis

in Lincoln's Cabinet triggered by Seward's abruptly proferred resignation, Secretary of the Treasury Salmon Chase also submits a request to be permitted to step down from his post. After discussing the situation at length with his advisors, and with the remaining Cabinet members, Lincoln makes a decision not to accept the resignations. This effectively prevents any further upheaval but does little to alleviate the pressures stemming mainly from political differences experienced by the Cabinet as a whole.

WESTERN THEATER   Grand Junction, Tennessee is attacked by Confederates with the results that Federals tally 50 casualties. In Mississippi, at Holly Springs, Northern troops under General Grant are surprised by General Earl Van Dorn's Southerners. The latter capture an enormous supply of stores worth over $1 million and take about 1500 Northern soldiers prisoner. To prevent such a valuable commodity from falling into enemy hands, Confederates burn over 4000 bales of cotton. This attack on Holly Springs, Mississippi seriously hampers Union General Grant's efforts to move on Vicksburg.

23 DECEMBER 1862

THE CONFEDERACY   Due to Union General Benjamin Butler's military governorship of New Orleans, Louisiana and the intensely bitter feelings resulting from his tenure there, Confederate President Jefferson Davis brands the general a felon and an enemy of mankind. The chief executive suggests immediate execution of Butler if he should be seized by Confederates, and further states that any Federal Army officers imprisoned by the Confederacy shall not be released prior to Butler's punishment.

25 DECEMBER 1862

WASHINGTON   As part of their observation of the Christmas holiday, the President and Mrs Lincoln pay visits to several hospitals in the Federal capital where injured soldiers convalesce.

WESTERN THEATER   In Tennessee, near Brentwood, there is some inconclusive fighting and similar activity along the Edmondson Pike. John Hunt Morgan's raiders clash with Union troops near Bear Wallow in Kentucky. Glasgow, Kentucky is seized and occupied by Confederate troops. In Mississippi, north of Vicksburg, Sherman's forces conduct operations.

26 DECEMBER 1862

WESTERN THEATER   Vicksburg, Mississippi is the goal of advancing Federal forces. These troops, under the command of General William Sherman, are positioned on the Yazoo River to the north of Vicksburg. In Tennessee, General William Rosecrans pushes toward the Confederate encampment at Murfreesboro. There is some minor fighting along the way, near La Vergne, Franklin and Knob Gap.

TRANS-MISSISSIPPI   As a result of the Sioux Indian uprising in Minnesota, causing the death of over 450 white settlers, 38 Indian participants in the uprising are executed at Mankato, Minnesota.

27 DECEMBER 1862

WESTERN THEATER   Near Vicksburg, the Federal advance troops of General Sherman clash with Confederates. In addition, Northern gunboats fire on Southern shore batteries positioned at Haine's Bluff, Mississippi. Efforts to disrupt communication between the Vicksburg troops and reinforcements include the destruction of the Vicksburg and Shreveport Railroad. In Kentucky, there is an attack on Confederate forces resulting in 17 dead or wounded, and 57 taken prisoner by the Federals. John Hunt Morgan's Confederate raiders complete a successful attack on Elizabethtown, Kentucky, which results in the capture of a Federal garrison there.

28 DECEMBER 1862

WESTERN THEATER   Mississippi witnesses minor fighting near Vicksburg, as General William T Sherman pushes closer to the city. In Kentucky, Confederate John

Burning of the Capitol at Baton Rouge.

Hunt Morgan and his men blow up a bridge at Muldraugh's Hill. Baton Rouge, Louisiana is heavily damaged by fire.

TRANS-MISSISSIPPI In Van Buren, Arkansas, there is an outbreak of fighting between Confederates and Federals. The latter are under the command of General James Blunt. The Union troops are successful in seizing 100 prisoners as well as many supplies and some equipment. In Missouri, Federal troops evacuate New Madrid.

29 *DECEMBER* 1862

WESTERN THEATER The Federal forces gathering north of Vicksburgh, Mississippi clash with Confederates at Chickasaw Bayou. While Northern troops make a concerted effort to break through the Confederate defenses there at Chickasaw Bluffs, it is an operation that meets with no success. General Sherman, whose men are outnumbered by the Southern troops, says later: 'I reached Vicksburg at the time appointed, landed, assaulted and failed.' The Federal forces of 31,000 are reduced by 208 fatalities, 1005 wounded and 563 missing at this battle. Southern losses tally 63 dead, 134 injured, 10 missing out of a total fighting force of 14,000.

30 *DECEMBER* 1862

WASHINGTON President Lincoln makes final preparations for the announcement of his Emancipation Proclamation. He submits drafts of the document to his Cabinet in the hopes that he will be given practical advice as to the final wording.

WESTERN THEATER Confederate raider John Hunt Morgan and his men clash with Union troops as they pull out of New Haven, Kentucky. Bridges are destroyed by Union General Samuel Carter as his troops conduct a raid on Union, Tennessee. In that same state, Federal General William Rosecrans and his men close in on the Confederate positions at Murfreesboro.

NAVAL In stormy waters off Cape Hatteras, the USS *Monitor* is lost after severe difficulties; this results in the death of 16 men and officers. The USS *Rhode Island* manages to rescue another 47 men.

31 *DECEMBER* 1862

WASHINGTON President Lincoln meets with General Burnside to discuss the latter's role in the Union defeat of Fredericksburg, Virginia. In addition to this meeting, the President confers once again with his cabinet about the Emancipation Proclamation and signs a bill establishing West Virginia as the nation's 35th state.

WESTERN THEATER The battle of Stone's River, or Murfreesboro, Tennessee, commences on the last day of the year as General Rosecrans' Federals face General Bragg's Confederates. The Southern attack on the Federal position comes at dawn and by noon, despite several vigorous counterattacks by the Union forces, the latter are on the defensive. By night time, General Rosecrans' troops are battered but not defeated and awaiting a resumption of fighting on the following day.

1863

1 *JANUARY* 1863

WASHINGTON President Lincoln signs the Emancipation Proclamation, stating that 'all persons held as slaves within said designated States, and parts of States, are, and henceforward shall be free.' Reactions are, for the most part, enthusiastic. The provisions for freed slaves include assurances that former slaves are to be permitted to serve in the military service. Continued difficulties with General Burnside over the after effects of the Fredericksburg defeat still plague the President. After meeting with the chief executive, Burnside states in an open letter that he has felt little support from fellow officers and that he considers retirement in order to 'promote the public good'. Lincoln persuades Burnside to reconsider.

WESTERN THEATER Murfreesboro, Tennessee is relatively stable after the previous day's fighting. Both Generals Bragg and Rosecrans position their troops and there is some minor skirmishing as the troops assume a more advantageous stance. In Mississippi, Union General Sherman makes preparations to pull troops out of the vicinity north of Vicksburg, and elsewhere in that state there is a minor clash between Federals and Confederates at Bath Springs.

2 JANUARY 1863

WESTERN THEATER The second day of major fighting in the battle of Stone's River, or Murfreesboro, Tennessee, sees General Breckenridge's Confederates badly defeated after their attempt to establish a hold on high ground. Both of the armies pause once again, each anticipating a withdrawal by the other. General Sherman pulls away from the Yazoo River in Mississippi, putting aside any further attempts to seize the area north of Vicksburg.

3 JANUARY 1863

WESTERN THEATER General Braxton Bragg moves his Confederate Army of Tennessee away from Murfreesboro. This is in spite of the fact that the South remained in relative control of positions after the battle of Stone's River, or Murfreesboro, on 31 December 1862. This move is

later to garner Bragg considerable criticism from military advisors.

4 JANUARY 1863

WESTERN THEATER Fort Hindman, Arkansas is the goal of 30,000 Federal troops which, under the command of General McClernand, are transported north on the Mississippi in an unauthorized movement intended to implement seizure of the Confederate post. Skirmishing occurs in Tennessee in the wake of General Bragg's withdrawal from the area around Murfreesboro.

NAVAL The Union blockade continues to reap gains as the USS *Quaker City* seizes yet another Confederate blockade runner off the coast of Charleston, South Carolina.

7 JANUARY 1863

TRANS-MISSISSIPPI There is a major attack on Springfield, Missouri by Confederate troops under the command of Generals Marmaduke and Price. They move on and capture, Ozark, Missouri.

8 JANUARY 1863

WESTERN THEATER Ripley, Tennessee, witnesses the capture of 46 Southern soldiers by Captain Moore's Union troops. In the skirmish there, the Union suffers three wounded. The Confederates, under Colonel Dawson's command, tally eight dead, and 20 injured plus those taken prisoner. In a separate action, a six-day expedition and raid under Confederate General Joseph Wheeler places Mill Creek, Harpeth Shoals and Ashland under attack.

9 JANUARY 1863

EASTERN THEATER Suffolk, Virginia sees the defeat of Confederate forces under the command of General Pryor. Federals, under General Corcoran's command, lose 104 during this encounter. At Fairfax Court House, Virginia, there is minor skirmishing.

INTERNATIONAL The French Minister to the United States confers with the Minister of Foreign Affairs in France in order to clarify their country's role in a possible mediation attempt between the Confederacy and the Union.

10 JANUARY 1863

WASHINGTON President Lincoln writes to General Curtis in Missouri about the various ways to handle the slave problem in St Louis. In a separate action General Fitz John Porter is court marshalled and cashiered from the Federal Army. This is due to Porter's failure to follow orders at the battle of Second Manassas on 29 August 1862.

TRANS-MISSISSIPPI At Galveston, Texas, Union gunboats positioned there bombard the city. An important operation under General McClernand proceeds as Fort Hindman, Arkansas, on the Arkansas River, is surrounded by Union troops and Federal gunboats effectively silence any Confederate artillery from the fort. Southern forces there are under the command of General T J Churchill. Elsewhere there is skirmishing of a minor variety of Carrollton, Arkansas.

11 JANUARY 1863

TRANS-MISSISSIPPI Fort Hindman, Arkansas is seized by Federal troops under General McClernand and Admiral David Porter. During this battle, the Union loses 134 men, suffers 898 wounded and 29 missing while Confederates tally 28 killed, 81 wounded and 4720 prisoners taken. In Missouri, Union Colonel Merrill engages Confederates under General Marmaduke in battle with a resulting 35-man loss for the Federals who defeat the Southern troops. The latter lose 150 men.

NAVAL In three separate operations, the Confederacy is involved in confrontations with the Union. Off the coast of Memphis, Tennessee, the South sinks the USS *Grampers Number Two*. At Bayou Teche, Louisiana, the Confederate gunboat *Cotton* is seized and destroyed by General Weitzel. Again, proving its superiority, the Confederate cruiser *Alabama* attacks and sinks the Federal vessel *Hatteras* in waters off the coast of Texas.

12 JANUARY 1863

THE CONFEDERACY At the Confederate capital in Richmond, Virginia, the third session of the First Confederate Congress meets. President Jefferson Davis addresses the assembly, emphasizing his hopes for European recognition of the Southern nation.

15 JANUARY 1863

THE CONFEDERACY In a letter to General Braxton Bragg concerning the Confederate position in the Murfreesboro-Tullahoma vicinity of Tennessee, President Jefferson Davis advises that the general should seek to 'select a strong position and fortifying it, to wait for an attack'.

16 JANUARY 1863

WESTERN THEATER In Alabama, the Confederate privateer *Florida* slips through the Union blockade and makes its way safely out of Mobile Bay. The vessel subsequently is responsible for the capture and destruction of 15 Federal ships before its own capture in waters off Bahia, Brazil.

19 JANUARY 1863

EASTERN THEATER The Federal Army of the Potomac is about to engage in its second attempt to gain control of Fredericksburg, Virginia. General Burnside makes preparations to cross the Rappahannock River with his troops and is aided by division commanders Hooker and Franklin. There is some minor skirmishing elsewhere in Virginia, near Williamsburg and Burnt Ordinary.

20 JANUARY 1863

EASTERN THEATER The Army of the Potomac continues its plans to sweep down on Fredericksburg, Virginia. A change in the weather conditions from snow to rain creates transportation difficulties. Reflecting on this change, General Burnside reports, 'From that moment we felt that the winter campaign had ended'. It becomes increasingly more difficult for the Federal forces to make any significant progress on this front.

CHRONOLOGY

21 JANUARY 1863

WASHINGTON President Lincoln communicates with General Halleck concerning orders given by General Grant. These orders, which are being revoked, concerned the expulsion of Jews from the Department of the Mississippi. Lincoln's position in this controversy is that revocation of such orders is necessary since 'as it in terms proscribed an entire religious class, some of whom are fighting in our ranks'. The President, in a separate order, formally dismisses General Fitz John Porter from miitary service. (This presidential order will later be revoked after an 1879 review, and Porter subsequently is reinstated as a colonel in the Federal Army.)

EASTERN THEATER The Federal Army of the Potomac is still stalled along the banks of the Rappahannock River in Virginia. General Burnside is soon to be faced with a decision concerning effective withdrawal from the area, since the rain has been steadily falling for 30 hours. It is only a short time before Burnside realizes that crossing the river is impossible.

22 JANUARY 1863

EASTERN THEATER General Burnside, faced with extremely bad weather and mud everywhere, prepares to pull the Army of the Potomac back from its position—an admission that the Fredericksburg, Virginia campaign was not to be fruitful. Known as the 'mud march', this withdrawal is described by a private in the 118th Pennsylvania Volunteers: 'Further progress was impracticable . . . It was some twelve miles back to the nearest camp. Pontoons, artillery trains could not be moved.

WESTERN THEATER General Grant takes overall responsibility for Union troops in the region of Arkansas and its general vicinity. The upcoming push to take Vicksburg, Mississippi is the goal of General Grant and he begins the preparations by resuming Federal efforts to dig a canal through the marshy area across from Vicksburg.

23 JANUARY 1863

EASTERN THEATER In an abrupt and stinging move, General Burnside issues orders which will take Generals Hooker, Franklin, Newton and Brooks out of command in the Army of the Potomac. Motivated in part by the frustration at the difficulties encountered because of poor weather, Burnside has not evidenced a total commitment to the command forced on him three months prior to now. The orders he has served on the generals are never actually approved by President Lincoln.

25 JANUARY 1863

WASHINGTON In a meeting with General Burnside, President Lincoln discusses the General's plans for the dismissal of Generals Hooker, Franklin, Newton and Brooks. Later, the President confers with his Cabinet and with General Halleck. The outcome is the removal of General Burnside from the command of the Army of the Potomac. In his place, General Joseph Hooker is appointed as General in Chief of the Potomac Army. Burnside is apparently not displeased with this change, and will assume military responsibilities in the Western Theater.

26 JANUARY 1863

EASTERN THEATER General Joseph Hooker, 48 years old and a West Point graduate, officially assumes command of the Union Army of the Potomac. It is hoped by the President as well as by the soldiers themselves, that 'Fighting Joe' will prove to be both able and assertive, qualities which seemed lacking in the sincere but militarily inept General Burnside. In a letter to General Hooker, the President offers encouragement and cautions the general to avoid mixing 'politics with your profession'. Lincoln praises Hooker's confidence, 'which is a valuable, if not an indispensable quality'.

27 JANUARY 1863

THE NORTH A Philadelphia newspaperman, A D Boileau, is arrested on charges that his *Journal* is publishing anti-Union matter.

THE CONFEDERACY In a message to Georgia Governor Brown, President Jefferson Davis makes note of the urgent need to step up the cultivation of cotton and produce. 'A short supply of provisions presents the greatest danger to a successful . . . war'.

NAVAL In a fierce bombardment from the ironclad USS *Montauk*, the Confederate Fort McAllister in Georgia sustains some damage. Firing from the Federal vessel in the Ogeechee River lasts for a better portion of the day.

29 JANUARY 1863

THE CONFEDERACY Defense of Vicksburg, Mississippi is uppermost in President Jefferson Davis's mind, since this city is critical to the control of an important stretch of the Mississippi River. Accordingly, the President sends a cable to General Pemberton at Vicksburg, asking, 'Has anything or can anything be done to obstruct the navigation from Yazoo Pass down?' The Confederate president is well aware that General Grant means to press his Union troops on the city as soon as possible.

EASTERN THEATER Near Suffolk, Virginia, Union troops engage in minor skirmishing with Confederate forces. There is similar light fighting at Turner's Mills, also in Virginia.

NAVAL The Stono River in South Carolina is the site of an exchange between Confederate shore batteries and the Union gunboat *Isaac Smith*. The result is that the vessel first runs aground during the encounter and is then captured by the Confederates.

31 JANUARY 1863

WESTERN THEATER Despite the Confederate pullback from Murfreesboro, Tennessee earlier in the months, there continues to be a series of minor confronta-

tions between Union and Confederate soldiers in that vicinity. While on a reconnaissance mission from Murfreesboro to Franklin, Federals engage Southern troops at Unionville, Middleton and Dover. At the latter location, the North sustains five injuries while Confederates report 12 dead and 300 taken prisoner.

NAVAL At Charleston, South Carolina, there is a spectacular battle between Southern gunboats and Northern blockaders. The Confederate vessels *Chicora* and *Palmetto State*, both ironclads, succeed in damaging the Federal *Mercedita* and *Keystone State* extensively. The former vessel's crew suffer four killed and three injured, many of these casualties being the result of steam explosions from broken boilers. Despite this action, which does no damage to the Confederate ironclads, the harbor remains under the Federal blockade—although the South declares otherwise.

1 FEBRUARY 1863

THE CONFEDERACY Wartime inflation had made a serious impact on the Confederate currency so that it is estimated that the Confederate dollar has a buying power of only 20 cents.

WESTERN THEATER In Tennessee, Franklin is taken and occupied by Union troops. The Federal forces in New Berne, North Carolina set off on an expedition which will last for ten days and will take them to Plymouth.

2 FEBRUARY 1863

EASTERN THEATER The Union Army of the Potomac under the command of General Joseph Hooker encounters hostile fire as it gathers information about the area surrounding the Rappahannock River. There is skirmishing at Rappahannock Station.

NAVAL Vicksburg, Mississippi is again the focus of action taken by the Union. The Federal vessel *Queen of the West* makes its way past Vicksburg, although the ram was fired on by Confederate shore batteries and sustained minor damage. The commanding officer of the vessel, Colonel Charles Ellet, was hoping to destroy the Southern ship *City of Vicksburg* and to put Confederate shipping in jeopardy. While unable to do this, Ellet succeeds in slipping by the shore batteries without losing his ship.

3 *FEBRUARY* 1863

WASHINGTON The Federal Congress recognizes naval Commander John Worden's contribution to the Union war effort. Worden was the officer in charge of the USS *Monitor* at the time it battled the CSS *Merrimack* in March 1862. Worden was also in command of the *Monitor* when it foundered and was lost off Cape Hatteras, North Carolina in December 1862. Secretary of State Seward confers with the French Minister about the latter's handling of possible mediation. These mediation proposals are ultimately declined.

WESTERN THEATER In Tennessee, Fort Donelson is once again under attack, this time by Confederates under Generals Wheeler and Forrest. The Union troops garrisoned at the fort, under Colonel Harding, are able to hold out against the Southerners. Losses after the battle there indicate Northern dead at 12, with 30 injured. The Southern reports list 100 killed and 400 wounded, with 300 prisoners. Vicksburg, Mississippi sees the *Queen of the West* attack and seize three Southern vessels. More Federal troops move out of Murfreesboro on a reconnaissance mission.

TRANS-MISSISSIPPI In Missouri, Federal troops under Major Reeder engage in skirmishing with Southern forces at Mingo Swamp. The casualties reported by Confederates indicate nine dead and 20 wounded. At Yazoo Pass in Arkansas, Union soldiers are able to break through the levee, providing a passage for troops along the Yazoo River north of Vicksburg, Mississippi. It is intended that this channel will facilitate the Northern force's taking of the city at a date in the near future.

4 *FEBRUARY* 1863

WESTERN THEATER Union troops at Lake Providence, Louisiana are routed by the forces of the Confederate Third Louisiana division. The latter, however successful in this, sustains 30 casualties.

5 *FEBRUARY* 1863

INTERNATIONAL Queen Victoria makes an official statement concerning Great Britain's refusal to enter into mediation attempts between the Union and the Confederacy at this time. The reasons given include the observation that such matters cannot be 'attended with a probability of success'.

EASTERN THEATER General Joseph Hooker, newly appointed commander of the Union Army of the Potomac, reorganizes the force and makes a variety of command changes. There continues to be reconnaissance efforts around Rappahannock Bridge and Grove Church, Virginia. In West Virginia, Union troops embark on a four-day mission to Wyoming County from Camp Piatt.

6 *FEBRUARY* 1863

WASHINGTON After the re-establishment of the Federal Department of Washington, the command of said department is given to General S F Heintzelman. Secretary of State Seward makes official the Federal government's refusal of mediation offers from Napoleon III's government in France. Seward conveys this information to the French minister, M Mercier.

7 *FEBRUARY* 1863

EASTERN THEATER At Williamsburg, Virginia, Confederates ambush a Federal cavalry unit, resulting in the death and injury of 11 Union soldiers.

NAVAL Despite its secure hold on Southern ports, the Federal blockade fails in preventing three Confederate raiders from slipping through its cordon. The three vessels make it safely to port at Charleston,

South Carolina. At Galveston, Texas, the South manages to remove the threat of the blockade, announcing the port there and at Sabine Pass to be open.

10 *FEBRUARY* 1863

EASTERN THEATER   At Chantilly, Virginia, there is minor fighting between Union and Southern soldiers. In West Virginia, Northern troops embark on a three-day reconnaissance, leaving from Beverly and heading for Pocahontas County. There is continued reconnaissance and exploration along the Rappahannock River as the Army of the Potomac reorganizes and assesses its position.

WESTERN THEATER   Camp Sheldon, Mississippi is once again the site of desultory skirmishing. In Louisiana, at Old River, Federal troops under Captain Tucker are successful in pushing back a force of Confederates. The resulting casualty list indicate that the South has 11 killed and wounded, with 25 men taken prisoner. The North reports eight dead and wounded.

12 *FEBRUARY* 1863

WESTERN THEATER   Bolivar, Tennessee witnesses the defeat of Union forces, resulting in four dead and five injured. At Sandy Ridge, North Carolina, some Union troops skirmish with Confederates troops. NAVAL   Captain Ellet's *Queen of the West* manages to fire on and destroy a number of Confederate wagon trains carrying supplies and ammunition, this taking place on the Red River. In Arkansas, the USS *Conestoga* takes two Southern steamers on the White River. The blockade runner CSS *Florida* manages to seize and destroy the Yankee clipper *Jacob Bell* in the waters of the West Indies. The *Jacob Bell* was carrying a cargo of Chinese tea and other goods of an estimated value of $2 million; the entire cargo is lost. Off Vicksburg, Mississippi, the Union ironclad gunboat *Indianola* successfully runs past Confederate shore batteries.

Destruction of the Jacob Bell, *13 February 1863.*

14 *FEBRUARY* 1863

EASTERN THEATER   Annandale, Virginia sees the defeat of a Federal cavalry unit at the hands of Confederate troops. Skirmishing breaks out along the Hillsborough Road and at Union Mills.

TRANS-MISSISSIPPI   Cypress Bend, Arkansas is the site of light skirmishing between Federal and Confederate troops. NAVAL   Despite its recent success in avoiding serious damage or capture, the Union vessel *Queen of the West*, under the command of Capt Charles Ellet, finally suffers defeat. At first its operation on the Red River is successful and it manages to seize the Southern vessel *New Era Number Five*. Subsequently, however, the Federal ship runs aground and is abandoned by its crew when the boiler threatens to explode. The USS *De Soto* is in the vicinity and provides a safe escape vehicle for the *Queen of the West*'s crew who then transfer to the captured *New Era Number Five*. Ellet and his men take this vessel downstream where they connect with the ironclad *Indianola* on the following day, at a point just south of Natchez, Mississippi.

15 *FEBRUARY* 1863

WESTERN THEATER   Minor fighting breaks out in Tennessee near Nolensville. The Federal force there under the command of Sergeant Holmes manages to defeat Southern forces, killing eight, wounding 20 and taking four Southern prisoners. There is also skirmishing at Cainsville,

Tennessee, where Union Colonel Monroe is successful in holding off cavalry under Confederate General John Hunt Morgan. The tally of casualties shows two Federals killed, 12 injured; 20 Confederates dead, a large number wounded and six taken prisoner.

16 FEBRUARY 1863

WASHINGTON The Federal Senate passes the conscription act, which has yet to be signed unto law by President Lincoln but which has the chief executive's full support. This new draft law is intended to fill the ranks of the Union Army which is not adequately served by voluntary enlistment. In addition, desertion is found to be an increasingly serious problem. Late in 1862, Provost-Marshal General Simeon Draper estimated that around 100,000 soldiers had deserted their posts. This new draft law will, it is hoped, better provide for the interests of the Union than has the system in use until now.

WESTERN THEATER Skirmishing occurs at Yazoo Pass, Mississippi, as General Grant's men encounter Confederate opposition to the Federal preparation for a campaign on Vicksburg.

17 FEBRUARY 1863

WESTERN THEATER Lexington, Tennessee is the starting point for a Federal expedition which will last five days and will take troops to Clifton, Tennessee. In Memphis, there is skirmishing between Union forces and Confederates.

NAVAL The Federal vessel *Indianola* is now in position near Vicksburg at the juncture of the Red River and the Mississippi River. The *Indianola* will carry on a harassing campaign against the Southern vessels headed upriver to Vicksburg. The USS *Hercules* is attacked by Confederates which prompts the burning of nearby Hopefield, Arkansas in retaliation.

18 FEBRUARY 1863

EASTERN THEATER The Army of Northern Virginia sees several divisions of its Confederate troops removed from the vicinity of Fredericksburg, Virginia. These troops are to position themselves near Richmond, in order to protect the Southern capital from attack.

19 FEBRUARY 1863

THE NORTH In Iowa, Federal troops convalescing in a hospital in Keokuk become angry over the anti-Union sentiment expressed in the local newspaper *Constitution*. Accordingly, the soldiers break into and ransack the news office.

THE CONFEDERACY President Jefferson Davis sends a letter to General Joseph Johnston, and in it the Confederate chief executive comments on his reluctance to remove General Braxton Bragg from command. Davis says to Johnston, 'It is scarcely possible for him to possess the requisite confidence of the troops'. Bragg's officers have expressed extreme dissatisfaction in his manner of command.

WESTERN THEATER At Coldwater, Mississippi, Southern troops under the command of Colonel Wood lose a minor confrontation with Federals. The results are six Confederate dead, three wounded, 15 taken prisoner.

20 FEBRUARY 1863

WESTERN THEATER Yazoo Pass, Mississippi sees Union troops hold off an attack on their positions by Confederates. The casualty lists record five Northern soldiers wounded, six Confederates killed and 26 taken prisoner.

23 FEBRUARY 1863

WASHINGTON At the Federal capital, former War Department Secretary Simon Cameron hands in his resignation as Minister to Russia.

WESTERN THEATER Skirmishing occurs at Athens, Kentucky and in the vicinity of Fort Caswell, in North Carolina.

24 FEBRUARY 1863

WESTERN THEATER In an unlooked-for

blow to its river operations, the Federal Navy suffers from the capture of its ironclad gunboat *Indianola*. After repeated ramming from the Confederates, the *Indianola* is forced to surrender, its commander Commodore George Brown terming it 'a partially sunken vessel'.

25 *FEBRUARY* 1863

THE CONFEDERACY Inflated prices continue to plague the Confederate nation, and reports from Charleston, South Carolina indicate that a half-pound loaf of bread costs $25.00 and that flour is selling for $65.00 a barrel.

EASTERN THEATER There are repeated incidents of minor skirmishing in Virginia. These outbreaks between Federal and Confederate forces occur in Strasburg, Chantilly, near Winchester and also at Hartwood Church.

26 *FEBRUARY* 1863

THE NORTH In an affirmation of support for the Union, the Cherokee Indian National Council repeals its former ordinance of secession.

THE CONFEDERACY President Jefferson Davis informs General T H Holmes that he is concerned for the welfare of Confederate citizens in the Trans-Mississippi District. The chief executive feels that it is necessary to be diligent in both crop cultivation and military matters if the South wishes to maintain its hold on the area.

EASTERN THEATER Skirmishing occurs in Germantown, Virginia. At Woodstock, in that same state, Confederate forces clash with Union troops but are defeated, the latter suffering losses of 200 killed and wounded. General Longstreet takes command of Southern troops in the Confederate Department of Virginia and North Carolina.

28 *FEBRUARY* 1863

WESTERN THEATER On Georgia's Ogeechee River, the USS *Montauk* attacks and destroys the Confederate steamer

Nashville. The *Montauk* is under the command of Commodore J L Worden, who commanded the Union's ironclad *Monitor* during its famous encounter with the Southern vessel *Merrimack*.

1 *MARCH* 1863

WASHINGTON In order to discuss upcoming military appointments, some of which will be submitted for congressional approval within a few days, President Lincoln meets with Secretary of War Edwin Stanton and other advisors.

WESTERN THEATER In North Carolina, Union troops leave New Berne on a five-day reconnaissance to Swan Quarter. During the course of this expedition, there are numerous incidents of skirmishing.

2 *MARCH* 1863

WASHINGTON While Congress approves several hundred military promotions and appointments that the President has submitted, actions are also taken to dismiss 33 Army officers from the service as a result of their court-martials for a variety of charges.

EASTERN THEATER There is minor skirmishing in Virginia at Neosho and Aldie. The Army of the Potomac, under General Hooker, continues to make preparations to advance against General Robert E Lee's positions in Virginia.

WESTERN THEATER Tennessee sees skirmishing near Petersburg, the results of which are reports that Confederates suffer 12 dead and 20 wounded. Union troops set out on a three-week reconnaissance mission that begins in New Orleans, Louisiana and will take them to the Rio Grande in Texas.

3 *MARCH* 1863

WASHINGTON A number of comprehensive measures are passed by Congress, the most important of which is the new Enrollment Act, often called the Conscription Act, which calls for the enlistment in military service of all able-bodied male citizens between 20 and 45 years of age. This service will be for a three-year period, and the law also provides for these forces to be called up by Federal decree, without State intervention. On the whole, the Enrollment Act is well-received at least by the military. It passes both Houses of Congress. Generals Rosecrans, Sherman and Grant are particularly pleased about the prospect of receiving fresh troops as a result of this bill; the estimate of how many men would actually be drafted hovers around 3 million, but in reality, the first ten months of 1863 sees a total of only 21,331 new soldiers. The final tally of men enrolled during 1863-64 is about 170,000—falling far short of original estimates but clearly benefitting the military in a moderate way. The Financial Bill passed by Congress at this time is intended to aid the Federal economy in part by the issuance of Treasury notes. In addition, Congress authorizes suspension of the writ of habeas corpus throughout the entire Union. This measure is controversial and 36 Democratic Representatives express their desire to go on record as protesting such a sweeping move to deprive individual freedom, although this protest is not formally lodged. The Territory of Idaho is formed in the area which had previously been a portion of Washington.

4 *MARCH* 1863

WASHINGTON The Thirty-Seventh Congress of the United States adjourns after completing its legislative activities. Among the final measures passed is one establishing the National Academy of Sciences to be based in Washington, DC.
WESTERN THEATER In Tennessee, near Spring Hill, General Van Dorn succeeds in capturing several of General Rosecrans' regiments. At Unionville, there is minor skirmishing, and a ten-day reconnaissance sets out from Murfreesboro, encountering considerable hostile fire from Confederates in the area.

5 *MARCH* 1863

THE NORTH A newspaper office in Col-

umbus, Ohio, that of the *Crisis*, is ransacked by Union troops after the publication of anti-Union sentiments.
WESTERN THEATER Vicksburg, Mississippi continues to prepare and fortify against the inevitable battle looming ahead. Union forces are involved in constructing a canal across from the city, operations which are occasionally interrupted by fire from Confederate shore batteries. Near Franklin, Tennessee the Federal troops under Colonel Coburn's command are attacked and defeated by Confederates. The latter occupy the town, and Union losses are reported at 100 dead, 300 injured, 1306 taken prisoner. Southern casualties are tallied at 180 dead, 450 wounded.

7 *MARCH* 1863

WESTERN THEATER The preparations for a campaign against Vicksburg, Mississippi continue as Union General Banks advances toward Baton Rouge, Louisiana in order to connect with General Ulysses Grant's plans for Vicksburg.

8 *MARCH* 1863

EASTERN THEATER Fairfax County Court House, in Virginia, is the temporary headquarters of Union General E H Stoughton. The General and his men are captured there by Captain Mosby's Confederates. This proves to be a valuable takeover for the South; they seize a number of prisoners, 58 horses, and much equipment and ammunition.

9 *MARCH* 1863

WESTERN THEATER There are various incidents of minor skirmishing—at St Augustine, Florida and in Tennessee near Salem. In Louisiana, near Port Hudson, General Nathaniel Banks' troops encounter Confederates as the former continue to move toward General Grant's position.
TRANS-MISSISSIPPI Arkansas continues to see action near Chalk Bluff, and in Missouri, a Federal expedition moves out from

Bloomfield for a six-day reconnaissance mission which will take them to Kennett and Hornersville.

10 *MARCH* 1863

WASHINGTON   A proclamation of general amnesty is read by President Lincoln in order to encourage soldiers who are absent without leave to return to their regiments. This agreement is that if these men report back to their units and active duty by 1 April 1863, they will not suffer any adverse consequences. The alternative is that these soldiers would be charged with desertion and arrested.

WESTERN THEATER   Union forces commanded by Colonel Higginson and made up predominantly black regiments occupy Jacksonville, Florida. Skirmishing breaks out in Tennessee near Covington, where Federal Colonel Grierson is successful in defeating Colonel Richardson's Southern troops.

11 *MARCH* 1863

WESTERN THEATER   In an effective action against the Northern preparations to move against Vicksburg, Mississippi, Confederate troops construct a defensive outpost known as Fort Pemberton. Union forces attempting to move past this position on the Yalobusha River, find that their gunboats are unable to withstand the fire from shore batteries at Fort Pemberton, where Confederates are under the command of General W W Loring. After six days of exchanging fire, the Union troops under General Grant are obliged to give up this preparatory effort of the Vicksburg campaign.

13 *MARCH* 1863

THE CONFEDERACY   Due to the carelessness of a factory worker who accidentally detonated a device on which she is working, the Confederate Ordnance Laboratory at Brown's Island near Richmond, Virginia is the site of an explosion. As a result, 69 factory workers, of whom 62 are women, are either killed or injured. The fact that such a high proportion of casualties at an industrial site are women is a direct result of the Confederacy's response to wartime needs: not only are women taking the place of men on the farms, but when needed, they are taking over in both clerical and industrial roles to release men for military service.

14 *MARCH* 1863

NAVAL   Port Hudson, Lousiana, where Confederate troops are positioned north of Baton Rouge, is subject to bombardment from Union gunboats under Admiral David Farragut's command. This attempt by Federals to move past a Southern defense and head toward Vicksburg costs the Navy the USS *Mississippi* which runs aground and is eventually burned. The USS *Hartford* and the *Albatross* are successful in making it past Port Hudson, but two other vessels in the flotilla, the *Monongahela* and the *Richmond*, sustain considerable damage and are forced to turn back. During this bombardment and destruction of one Federal ship, 65 men are listed as killed or missing.

15 *MARCH* 1863

WESTERN THEATER   In Mississippi, where Vicksburg residents and troops garrisoned there brace themselves for the seemingly inevitable Northern attack, Federal forces attempt to pass by Haines' Bluff but are unsuccessful.

NAVAL   In the continuing blockade of Southern ports, the Federal Navy is foiled once more as the *Britannia*, a British vessel, slips through the cordon off Wilmington, North Carolina. The Union blockade has been much more successful during the opening months of 1863, however, and authorities are pleased with their record of captures.

17 *MARCH* 1863

EASTERN THEATER   The Army of the Potomac sends a cavalry corps, under the command of General William Wood Averell, to attack General Fitz Lee at Culpeper, Virginia. Taking 2100 men and six pieces of artillery, Averell engages 800 Southerners and four guns at the battle of Kelly's Ford. After a full day of fighting, the Federals pull back from the site. Losses are tallied at 78 Union casualties to 133 for the Confederates.

19 MARCH 1863

NAVAL Admiral Farragut has successfully maneuvered past Natchez, Mississippi and is now moving past Confederate batteries at Grand Gulf with his two vessels, the *Hartford* and the ironclad *Albatross*. Farragut is now positioned just below Vicksburg.

20 MARCH 1863

WESTERN THEATER In Florida there is some minor skirmishing at St Andrew's Bay. In Tennessee, near Milton, Confederates are attacked and defeated by Colonel Hall's Union troops who lose seven men and sustain three injuries. The South reports 40 dead, 140 wounded and 12 missing after this encounter. In Mississippi another Union attempt to reach Vicksburg, this time via Steele Bayou, proves unsuccessful as Admiral Porter takes 11 vessels along this water route, encountering Confederate fire at Rolling Fork. General Sherman has provided land reinforcements to help Porter's expedition and these reinforcements prove critical to the defense of Porter's fleet at Rolling Fork.

21 MARCH 1863

WESTERN THEATER Tennessee witnesses various outbreaks of skirmishing: Union troops headed for Saulsbury on a reconnaissance from La Grange encounter hostile fire from Confederate forces, and there is fighting at Salem. Southern troops attack a Federal railroad train between Bolivar and Grand Junction, Tennessee. In Kentucky, Mount Sterling is seized by Confederates under the command of Col-

onel Cluke. Several Federal expeditions begin—one from New Orleans headed to Ponchatoula, and one going from Bonnet Carre to the Amite river in Lousiana.

22 MARCH 1863

WESTERN THEATER The area around Murfreesboro, Tennessee continues to see much action between Federals and Confederate troops. In Kentucky there are several encounters between North and South as General John Hunt Morgan's cavalry attacks Federal positions there, and John Pegram's Confederates conduct operations against Union troops. These operations will continue throughout the rest of the month.

TRANS-MISSISSIPPI In Missouri Union forces are attacked and defeated by some irregular raiders near Blue Spring. In the sharp skirmishing, nine are killed, several are injured and five are taken prisoner.

23 MARCH 1863

WESTERN THEATER The Union vessels *Hartford* and *Albatross*, positioned in waters just south of Vicksburg, make an attack on Confederate shore batteries at Warrenton. In Kentucky Union troops attack Mount Sterling where two days previously Confederates had seized the area. After brief fighting, Northern forces are once again in control there. Jacksonville, Florida, is the sight of Federal reconnaissance efforts.

24 MARCH 1863

WESTERN THEATER Northern troops attempt to make progress in their move toward Vicksburg, Mississippi, this time using Black Bayou as a passageway. This attempt is fruitless, however, both the geography and the Confederate troops posted in the area causing interminable delays. General Grant decides to terminate these efforts, and orders General Sherman to withdraw from the area in the final expedition in the Steele's Bayou area, the last of several endeavors to reach Vicksburg.

25 MARCH 1863

WASHINGTON President Lincoln approves command changes as General Burnside assumes responsibility for the Department of the Ohio. Burnside, formerly chief commander of the Army of the Potomac in Virginia, takes this new command after it is vacated by General Horatio Wright, who is transferred to the Army of the Potomac as a division commander.

NAVAL The final Union expedition to Vicksburg, that via black Bayou, causes the North some difficulty as Confederates bombard the *Lancaster* and the *Switzerland*, two Northern rams, with artillery from shore. The *Lancaster* is destroyed and sinks; the *Switzerland* escapes, although it is badly damaged. Elsewhere, it is reported that Union ironclad vessels have left Hilton Head, North Carolina and are making their way towards the harbor at Charleston, South Carolina.

26 MARCH 1863

WASHINGTON In a letter which reveals some of Lincoln's private sentiments concerning the former slave population, the chief executive says to Governor Andrew Johnson of Tennessee: 'The colored population is the great *available* and yet unavailed of, force for restoring the Union. The bare sight of fifty thousand armed and drilled black soldiers on the banks of the Mississippi, would end the rebellion at once'.

THE NORTH In West Virginia the citizens vote on and approve a referendum which will provide for the emancipation of slaves, to be effected over a period of months.

27 MARCH 1863

WASHINGTON President Lincoln meets with members of several American Indian tribes, advising them to turn to 'the cultivation of the earth' in order to provide for economic stability for their people.

29 MARCH 1863

EASTERN THEATER At Point Pleasant, West Virginia there is some brief skirmishing which results in one Northern soldier dead, 12 Southerners killed and 14 wounded. There is also fighting at Williamsburg, and Kelly's Ford, Virginia, where Confederates and union troops clash.

WESTERN THEATER General Grant, anxious to establish a successful route to Vicksburg, Mississippi, directs General McClernand to open such a route from Milliken's Bend to an area just south of Vicksburg at New Carthage. McClernand is joined in this effort by Admiral Porter, who is to provide naval support—both troop transport and supply delivery.

30 MARCH 1863

WASHINGTON President Lincoln announces the establishment of a day of fasting and prayer throughout the Union. This is set for 30 April 1863.

WESTERN THEATER Kentucky sees an encounter between North and South at Dutton Hill, where Confederates fight valiantly for five hours, only to be defeated by a stronger Federal force. In North Carolina there is skirmishing at Rodman's Point on the Pamlico River.

31 MARCH 1863

EASTERN THEATER Drainesville, Virginia sees Union cavalry clash with Southerners under Colonel Mosby with the result that the Federals are defeated and lose 60 men.

WESTERN THEATER Union troops evacuate Jacksonville, Florida. At Eagleville, Tennessee there is skirmishing and at Lexington, in that state, Northern forces begin a four-day reconnaissance mission heading for the Duck River.

NAVAL The CSS *Nashville* attempts to run the Union blockade in waters of the Savannah River. The vessel is sunk by a Northern ironclad. On the Mississippi, Union Admiral David Farragut is successful in taking the *Hartford*, the *Switzerland* and the *Albatross* past Confederate shore batteries at Grant Gulf, Mississippi.

2 *APRIL* 1863

THE CONFEDERACY The Confederate capital of Richmond, Virginia is the site of a bread riot—instigated by various factors, chief among them the very real specter of hunger facing many in the city and other parts of the Southern nation. A mob of people initially demand bread from a bakery wagon but soon harass nearby shops, destroying property and necessitating the call-out of local police; one store reports losses of $13,000 in merchandise. President Jefferson Davis makes a brave move, placing himself in the middle of the gathered crowd and stating, 'We do not desire to injure anyone, but this lawlessness must stop. I will give you five minutes to disperse, otherwise you will be fired upon' (this, in reference to the assembled militia nearby). When the mob recognizes that the intent of the militia is to fire, the crowd disperses and the riot is over without bloodshed, although a number of arrests are made.

3 *APRIL* 1863

WASHINGTON The President makes preparations to visit the Army of the Potomac, where he will meet with General Hooker.
THE CONFEDERACY There are concerns on the part of President Jefferson Davis that the trans-Mississippi area will fall into Federal hands unless the Eastern bank of the Mississippi River can be adequately defended. In a letter to Arkansas Governor Harris Flanagin, Davis says, 'The defense of the fortified places on the Eastern bank is therefore regarded as the defense of Arkansas quite as much as that of Tennessee, Mississippi and Louisiana'.

4 *APRIL* 1863

WASHINGTON President Lincoln leaves the Federal capital of Fredericksburg, Virginia, where he will meet with generals of the Army of the Potomac.

5 *APRIL* 1863

INTERNATIONAL The British take action against several Confederate vessels, detaining them at Liverpool. One of these, the *Alexandria*, has been undergoing construction in preparation for its use as a blockade runner in Confederate waters. The indication by this action is that Great Britain is changing its views regarding active support of the Federals. While the *Alexandria* is ultimately released, its seizure and detention serve to notify the Confederacy that they can expect less and less from Palmerston's government in terms of recognition or support.

6 *APRIL* 1863

WASHINGTON After conferring with General Hooker at Potomac Army headquarters, President Lincoln notes, 'our prime object is the enemies [sic] army in front of us, and is not with, or about, Richmond'.
WESTERN THEATER As General Grant has ordered, General McClernand has proceeded to New Carthage, Mississippi. There is some brief fighting between Federals and Confederate troops as a result of this advance toward Vicksburg, Mississippi.

Fredericksburg, 3 April 1863.

7 *APRIL* 1863

WESTERN THEATER   There are various episodes of minor skirmishing as Southern forces under General Wheeler conduct raids on several railroads in Tennessee. The Louisville and Nashville line and the run between Nashville and Chattanooga are the targets of these surprise attacks occuring for four days.

NAVAL   The Union vessel *Barataria*, plying the waters of the Amitie River in Louisiana, is attacked and seized by Southern troops. At Charleston, South Carolina, Federal naval forces attack Fort Sumter with a fleet of nine ironclad vessels. These forces are led by Flag Officer Samuel DuPont, and the attack provokes both Fort Sumter and Fort Moultrie to retaliate. The USS *Weehawken* is hit, along with the *Passaic*, the *Montauk*, the *Nantucket* and the *Patapsco*. The Federals are unable to return the Confederate fire in any effective way, being too severely disabled. DuPont withdraws the remaining vessels, and both Confederates and Federals sustain extensive damage; the South reports seven dead, the North, two killed and 13 injured. The USS *Keokuk* is hit so badly as to be unsalvageable and it sinks the following day. This action indicates to Federals that, despite their hopes, the important Southern port of Charleston cannot be taken by naval action alone, but will require an operation of combined land and sea forces.

8 *APRIL* 1863

WESTERN THEATER   McClernand's Union troops in Mississippi engage in skirmishing in the vicinity of New Carthage, near Milliken's Bend. The troops were carrying supplies and preparing a route for General Grant's upcoming operations against Vicksburg. A particularly sharp skirmish occurs at James' Plantation between McClernand's men and Southern forces in the area.

10 *APRIL* 1863

WASHINGTON   President Lincoln, after spending the morning reviewing Potomac Army troops at Falmouth, Virginia, disembarks from Aquia Creek and returns to the Federal capital late in the day.

THE CONFEDERACY   In an emphatic statement concerning his beleagured nation's needs, President Jefferson Davis points out that 'We must not forget . . . that the war is not yet ended.' He advises Confederates to concentrate their agricultural efforts on crops other than tobacco and cotton; these cash crops are considered less critical now than 'corn, oats, peas, potatoes and other food for man and beast.' It has become obvious to Davis, to government authorities and to the general citizenry, that the Southern economy is nearly at the breaking point, that to purchase food and industrial products from abroad will be less and less feasible. The nation must redouble its efforts at self-sufficiency, as the recent bread riot in Richmond, Virginia points out. Several months prior to this, a newspaper in the Confederate capital, the *Dispatch*, indicated that the cost of feeding a family increased over the first two years of the war from $6.65 to $68.25 per week.

WESTERN THEATER   In Tennessee, near the town of Franklin, General Granger's troops attack Confederate forces under General Van Dorn, defeat the latter in a brief battle which leaves 100 Northern soldiers dead and injured. Confederate losses are tallied at 300 killed or wounded.

11 *APRIL* 1863

WASHINGTON   Having recently met with General Hooker and other Potomac Army officers in Virginia, President Lincoln now holds meetings with his Cabinet and with General Halleck. At these meetings, the President discusses strategies for both the Eastern and Western theaters with emphasis on the upcoming Vicksburg campaign under General Grant.

EASTERN THEATER   In Virginia there is skirmishing near Williamsburg and near the month-long Blackwater River. Confederate troops under Longstreet begin a mouth-long siege of Suffolk, Virginia.

WESTERN THEATER In Louisiana Federal General Nathaniel Banks takes 17,000 troops on an expedition toward the Red River, where Confederates are gathered at Fort de Russy.

12 APRIL 1863

WASHINGTON In a letter to President Lincoln, General Hooker indicates his desire to cross the Rappahannock River and outflank General Robert E Lee and his Confederates.

WESTERN THEATER The Amitie River in Louisiana is the site of a minor skirmish between Federals and Confederates. Stewartsborough, Tennessee is the scene of brief skirmishing as Federal reconnaissance efforts are conducted in the area.

13 APRIL 1863

WESTERN THEATER General Burnside, commander of the Department of the Ohio, issues a proclamation stating that Confederate sympathizers in the vicinity are to be deported to Southern lines. In addition, he states that the death penalty is to be meted out to those convicted of aiding the Southern cause.

14 APRIL 1863

WESTERN THEATER In Louisiana, at Bayou Teche, Union troops confront Confederates, resulting in 150 Northern casualties. The Southern tallies are not definitive, but in general it is agreed that their losses are much more substantial than Federal casualty figures. At this engagement, the *Queen of the West*, formerly a Union vessel but now in Confederate hands, is bombarded and destroyed by Northern fire.

15 APRIL 1863

EASTERN THEATER In an estimate of troop strength, General Hooker, head of the Army of the Potomac, reports that he has nearly 130,000 men at his disposal. This contrasts with General Lee's forces in the area which number about 60,000.

There is, once again, skirmishing near Suffolk, at Norfleet House, Virginia.

NAVAL Two Federal whaling ships are seized by the CSS *Alabama* which continues to ply Atlantic waters. The *Alabama* takes the two Union vessels off the coast of the Brazilian island of Fernando de Noronha.

16 APRIL 1863

THE CONFEDERACY President Jefferson Davis puts his signature on a bill passed by Congress which will allow soldiers below the age of majority to hold military commissions.

NAVAL In a successful venture involving 12 vessels, Admiral David Porter runs the Confederate batteries at Vicksburg, Mississippi. There is but one ship lost as Porter's fleet sails through a heavy bombardment of shelling from shore. The fleet comes to rest at Bruinsburg, Mississippi.

17 APRIL 1863

WESTERN THEATER Colonel Benjamin Grierson leads 1700 men on a 16-day raiding mission that leaves La Grange, Tennessee at dawn. Intended to divert Confederate strength and attention from the buildup of Federal forces near Vicksburg, Grierson's raid ultimately covers a 600-mile area of Mississippi.

TRANS-MISSISSIPPI A raiding party that sets out from Arkansas is led by Confeder-

Porter runs the blockade at Vicksburg

140

The Siege of Vicksburg.

ate General John Marmaduke. These forces harass Federal positions throughout Missouri for a 16-day period.

18 *APRIL* 1863

WESTERN THEATER There is minor activity near New Iberia, Louisiana, the location of a Southern salt works. Federal troops seize and destroy this operation. In Hartsville, Tennessee there is continued skirmishing. Grierson's Union raiders encounter the first disruption in their line of march near the town of New Albany, Mississippi, where light skirmishing breaks out.

TRANS-MISSISSIPPI Arkansas is the site of fighting as Southern troops attack Northern forces at Feyetteville, but with little success. In Missouri, Union troops conduct several reconnaissance efforts.

19 *APRIL* 1863

WASHINGTON In order to gather further information about the status of the Potomac Army, President Lincoln takes General Halleck and War Secretary Edwin Stanton to Aquia Creek, Virginia on a one-day fact-finding mission.

WESTERN THEATER There is continued skirmishing in Mississippi connected with Grierson's raid, Pontotoc seeing a brief encounter between Federals and Confederates. In Tennessee there is skirmishing at Coldwater, where Colonel Bryant's Union forces successfully subdue Southern troops there.

20 *APRIL* 1863

WASHINGTON After its approval by Congress, the bill allowing West Virginia to enter the Union is declared by President Lincoln as taking effect on 20 June 1863.

WESTERN THEATER In Louisiana, General Nathaniel Banks and his Northern troops successfully take Opelousas. During this ground operation, the Federal naval forces operating in the area take Butte-a-la-Rose. In Tennessee there is a Union reconnaissance from Murfreesboro to the area around McMinnville in an operation lasting for a ten-day period.

TRANS-MISSISSIPPI In Missouri, there is an encounter between Northern and Southern troops at Patterson. The result of this action is the defeat of Federals under Colonel Smart, with an approximate 50 casualties. Bloomfield, Missouri also sees minor skirmishing.

22 *APRIL* 1863

THE CONFEDERACY President Jefferson

General Meade and his staff.

The siege of Vicksburg, 1863.

Davis communicates with General John Pemberton at Vicksburg, Mississippi. The Confederate President advises the general to consider disrupting Federal naval operations by sending fire rafts down the Mississippi River.

EASTERN THEATER In Virginia, near the town of Strasburg, Confederate troops are defeated by Majors McGee and White. The results of this minor encounter are that Southerners lose five men, with nine injured and 25 taken prisoner. There are also outbreaks of fighting near Belle Plain, Virginia, as Union troops set out from there to Port Royal on a reconnaissance lasting three days.

NAVAL At Vicksburg, Mississippi, Federals make an attempt to send 18 vessels past Confederate shore batteries. There is some success in this venture; although the Union loses one transport and six barges, General Grant's troops receive the supplies carried by the 11 remaining vessels.

24 *APRIL* 1863

THE CONFEDERACY In a controversial move, the Confederate Congress approves a tax measure which places an eight percent tax on all agricultural products grown in the previous year. In addition, there is a 10 percent tax placed on profits made from the purchase or sale of most food, clothing and iron. Taxes on licenses are included in this tax bill, and a graduated income tax is instituted. Estimates of the revenues generated

from the 10 percent tax-in-kind levied on agricultural products grown or slaughtered in 1863 hover around $62 million. This last component of the tax law is considered to be particularly difficult, some terming it confiscatory.

WESTERN THEATER In Alabama, Confederate troops encounter Northern forces under General Grenville Dodge at Tuscumbia, and are defeated there. In Mississippi, Grierson's Federal raiders push further into Confederate territory and engage in fighting near Birmingham.

TRANS-MISSISSIPPI On the Iron Mountain Railroad in Missouri, the North successfully routs Southern troops near St Louis. In addition, Confederate General John Marmaduke and his forces skirmish at Mill Creek, in Missouri.

25 *APRIL* 1863

EASTERN THEATER Fighting in West Virginia at Greenland Gap see Federals clash with Southern forces. The former tally losses at 15 dead with 60 taken prisoner; the Confederates estimate close to 100 killed and a large but undetermined number of prisoners.

WESTERN THEATER In Mississippi the forces of General Grant, intent on taking possession of Vicksburg, engage in skirmishing near Hard Times Landing.

26 *APRIL* 1863

WESTERN THEATER General Streight sends troops on a raid, leaving from Tuscumbia, Alabama. In Kentucky a band of Southern troops known as the Texan Legion surrenders at Franklin. There is a raid on Deer Creek, Mississippi, staged by Union forces.

TRANS-MISSISSIPPI The Federal garrison at Cape Girardeau, Missouri is attacked by Confederate raiders under the command of General John Marmaduke. The Union troops there successfully repel the Southern forces, and the latter suffer 40 dead, 200 wounded. Union troops under the command of General John McNeil report six dead and six wounded at this encounter.

27 *APRIL* 1863

EASTERN THEATER CHANCELLORSVILLE CAMPAIGN   The Federal Army of the Potomac under General Hooker's command moves along the Rappahannock River, heading in the direction of Chancellorsville, Virginia. Hooker has approximately 70,000 men with him. Staying behind is General Sedgwick, with 30,000 men, in position near the Confederate camp at Fredericksburg.

28 *APRIL* 1863

EASTERN THEATER   The Army of the Potomac crosses the Rappahannock River. WESTERN THEATER   In Georgia, there is a clash between Union Confederate cavalry at Sand Mountain. The result of this is the defeat of Southern forces.

29 *APRIL* 1863

EASTERN THEATER, CHANCELLORSVILLE CAMPAIGN   There is a severe threat to General Robert E Lee's Confederates as the major portion of the Federal Army of the Potomac continues to cross the Rappahannock River. There is minor skirmishing near Fredericksburg and at Crook's Run, near Kellysville, Virginia.
WESTERN THEATER   Union troops conduct a reconnaissance that leaves La Grange, Tennessee and moves into Mississippi several days later. At Vicksburg, Mississippi Union troops under General Sherman stage an attack near Snyder's Mill in order to distract Confederate forces within the area.
NAVAL   Union gunboats fire on Southern positions at Grand Gulf, Mississippi, although the effort, headed by Admiral David Porter, is ultimately useless in providing a clear route for the passage of General Grant's forces to Vicksburg.

30 *APRIL* 1863

THE CONFEDERACY   In order to try to save Vicksburg, Mississippi from General Grant's imminent attack, President Jefferson Davis advises General Joseph E Johnston of General Pemberton's situation at the beleagured Mississippi city: 'General Pemberton telegraphs that unless he has more cavalry, the approaches to North Mississippi are almost unprotected.'
EASTERN THEATER, CHANCELLORSVILLE CAMPAIGN   General Stoneman and his detachment of Union cavalry lead a raid on the Confederate Army of Northern Virginia, destroying portions of the Virginia Central Railroad and cutting General Robert E Lee's communication lines. As a result of this operation, which lasts for seven days, the Union force, totalling about 10,000, suffers around 150 casualties. The South tallies its losses at about 100 killed and injured, with 500 soldiers taken prisoner. General Hooker, encamped near Chancellorsville with the Army of the Potomac, reports that 'the operations of the last three days have determined that our enemy must ingloriously fly, or come out from behind their defenses.'
WESTERN THEATER   In Mississippi, General McClernand's Union troops cross the Mississippi River near Bruinsburg. Near Vicksburg, General Grant prepares to push inland with his Federal forces stating, 'All the campaigns, labor, hardships . . . were for the accomplishment of this one object.'

1 *MAY* 1863

THE CONFEDERACY   The First Confederate Congress establishes a Provisional Navy and draws up a resolution that will provide for the punishment of Northern white Army officers captured while in command of Northern black military units.
EASTERN THEATER, CHANCELLORSVILLE CAMPAIGN   At Chancellorsville, Virginia General Hooker's Army of the Potomac engages General Lee's Confederates in the early part of the day. Later, in the afternoon, Hooker's force of nearly 70,000 men pull away from the Southern forces and all of General Lee's 47,000 troops to take an

offensive position. The Potomac Army gathers in an area of rather dense undergrowth known as Virginia Wilderness where a portion of Lee's Army, under the command of General Stonewall Jackson, will make a devastating attack on the Federal Army's right flank.

WESTERN THEATER, VICKSBURG CAMPAIGN After having crossed the Mississippi River the previous day, General McClernand's Union troops advance on the Southern position at Fort Gibson. Under the command of Confederate General John Bowen, Southern troops march from Grand Gulf, Mississippi to attempt to divert McClernand's advance but to no avail. The Federals push steadily forward, resulting in the Southern troops' evacuation of the town of Port Gibson. The way becomes steadily more clear for Grant's forces to march on Vicksburg. The losses at this encounter are tallied at 131 Federals killed, 719 wounded and 25 missing. Confederates report 1150 casualties and 500 taken prisoner.

2 MAY 1863

EASTERN THEATER, CHANCELLORSVILLE CAMPAIGN The Army of the Potomac continues to fight at Chancellorsville, Virginia. General Stonewall Jackson takes his Confederates past the Federal right flank to the west and attacks late in the day. This maneuver is aided by General Lee's fire on the Federal left, into Union General Meade's men. While regrouping, General Stonewall Jackson is wounded in the arm by one of his own men; General A P Hill, another Confederate officer, is also wounded—J E B Stuart is now to take command. The Federals are dispersed and pushed back towards Chancellorsville, largely due to General Stonewall Jackson's brilliant strategy.

WESTERN THEATER, VICKSBURG CAMPAIGN Bayou Pierre, Mississippi sees fighting as Grant's men push inland to Vicksburg. Colonel Grierson's men are completing their 600 mile raid, riding hard into Baton Rouge, Louisiana after having

skirmished at several points, including Robert's Ford on the Comite River. The total losses reported for this daring 16-day raid are three killed, seven wounded, nine missing, and five men left sick. Grierson estimates that Confederates suffered 100 dead, 500 prisoners taken as a result of his raiders' efforts, and that the South has lost over 50 miles of railroad line and approximately 3000 guns.

3 MAY 1863

THE NORTH In Iowa, Catholic members of the pro-Confederate Knights of the Golden Circle are told by their bishop that they will be excommunicated if they do not resign from this fraternal order.

EASTERN THEATER, CHANCELLORSVILLE CAMPAIGN Fighting at Chancellorsville, Virginia continues as the Confederates pound away at Northern positions. The latter are forced to pull back to the Chancellor's House as General Lee's troops steadily shell the area from a position known as Hazel Grove. Late in the evening, General Hooker orders General Sedgwick to fire on Confederate positions at Fredericksburg and the ensuing engagement becomes known as Second Fredericksburg. The Federals at first appear to gain the upper hand, but as they push through the weakened Confederate defense, General Lee opens a new attack on Sedgwick's men at Salem Church, Virginia, halting any further Union advance.

WESTERN THEATER, VICKSBURG CAMPAIGN The Confederate positions at Grand Gulf, Mississippi are evacuated as a result of General Grant's advance. There is continued skirmishing throughout the vicinity near Vicksburg as Northern troops encounter Confederates.

4 MAY 1863

WASHINGTON President Lincoln waits in the Federal capital for a word from General Hooker concerning the outcome of the battle at Chancellorsville, Virginia. The President fears the outcome and questions

Hooker about the Federal positions at Fredericksburg, Virginia.

EASTERN THEATER, CHANCELLORSVILLE CAMPAIGN The Federal army of the Potomac fails to gain the offensive at Chancellorsville, and General Lee's Confederates continue to push Sedgwick's troops back, forcing them to cross the Rappahannock during the late evening. Fredericksburg is once again out of the Union's grasp. General Hooker, unwilling to risk another attack, orders the entire Potomac Army force to withdraw across the river. At these Chancellorsville engagements, casualties are heavy—the North loses 1606 men, with 9762 injured and another 5919 counted as missing, all of these casualties occurring between 27 April and 4 May. The South reports 1665 dead, 9081 wounded and 2018 missing. Among the casualties is General Stonewall Jackson, whose arm has now been amputated as a result of the wound received on 2 May; Davis contacts General Lee by telegraph and tells the victorious general that the nation has 'reverently united with you in giving praise to God for the success with which He has crowned your arms.'

WESTERN THEATER, VICKSBURG CAMPAIGN General Grant pushes into the area south of Vicksburg and minor fighting occurs on the Big Black River.

NAVAL As part of the Vicksburg Campaign, the *Albatross* and several other Union gunboats attack Fort De Russy on Louisiana's Red River. This effort proves fruitless and results in damage only to the *Albatross*.

5 *MAY* 1863

THE NORTH In Dayton, Ohio Clement Vallandigham, former congressman and a leading Copperhead, or Peace Democrat, having termed the war 'wicked and cruel', is charged with treason and brought before a military commission by General Burnside, the arresting officer.

TRANS-MISSISSIPPI In the Utah Territory the Union forces stage an operation, leaving Camp Douglas and intent on subduing pro-South Indians in the vicinity. This expedition heads towards the Bear River in Indian Territory.

6 *MAY* 1863

THE NORTH Clement Vallandigham is sentenced to close confinement for the duration of the war as a result of his inflammatory statements earlier in the week.

EASTERN THEATER Despite the defeat of the Federal Army of the Potomac at Chancellorsville, Virginia, General Joseph Hooker makes a public statement of congratulation to the army: 'The men are to be commended on the ahievements of the past seven days.' President Lincoln and General Halleck visit Hooker to confer with him on military strategy. As Stonewall Jackson continues to suffer from his wounds, General A P Hill takes charge of the Second Corps of the Confederate Army of Northern Virginia.

WESTERN THEATER, VICKSBURG CAMPAIGN In Mississippi, Tupelo is the scene of a clash between Union forces under Colonel Corwyn and Southerners commanded by General Ruggles. The latter are defeated and 90 Confederates are taken prisoner.

7 *MAY* 1863

WASHINGTON Full of concern over the turn of events in Virginia, President Lincoln has returned to the Federal capital after conferring with General Hooker in Virginia. Lincoln writes a letter to Hooker in which he says, 'If possible I would be very glad of another movement early enough to give us some benefit from the fact of the enemies [sic] communications being broken, but neither for this reason or any other, do I wish anything done in desperation or rashness.'

THE CONFEDERACY With the victory at Chancellorsville behind them, the Southern leaders turn to Vicksburg, Mississippi with hope and concern. President Davis contacts the Confederate commander General John Pemberton, saying, 'To hold

CHRONOLOGY

both Vicksburg and Port Hudson is necessary to our connection with Trans-Mississippi. You may expect whatever it is in my power to do for your aid.'

9 *MAY* 1863

THE NORTH In a response to General Hooker's congratulatory words to his Army of the Potomac on 6 May 1863, a *New York World* editorial makes the following remarks: 'Whoever knows the facts of the last two weeks will shudder as he reads this order. Whoever does not, let him credit it and believe that his ignorance is bliss.'

WESTERN THEATER, VICKSBURG CAMPAIGN In Mississippi, where Vicksburg is threatened by General Grant's Federals, there is skirmishing near Utica, and also at Big Sandy Creek. In Louisiana, General Nathaniel Banks' Union troops arrive in Alexandria after having conducted a series of successful raids.

10 *MAY* 1863

THE CONFEDERACY Since the amputation of his arm, Confederte General Jackson has contracted pneumonia, living only for several days longer. His death today comes as a terrific blow to the Southern nation; psychologically as well as strategically, Jackson has been an important military figure. Beloved by his men, and relied on heavily by General Lee, Jackson dies at the age of 39 at Guinea's Station, Virginia. A note from General Lee to General Jackson dated 3 May 1863, and sent in reference to the latter's injured arm, indicates the depth of Lee's regard for General Stonewall Jackson: 'I cannot express my regret at this occurrence. Could I have directed events, I should have been disabled in your stead. I congratulate you upon the victory which is due to your skill and energy.'

11 *MAY* 1863

WASHINGTON In a continuing current of agitation and strained feelings, President Lincoln is once more caught between opposing political opinions, prompting Secretary of the Treasury Salmon Chase to present his resignation. The chief executive once more refuses to accept Chase's offer to step down.

THE NORTH Clement Vallandigham applies, in Cincinnati, Ohio for a writ of habeas corpus but is turned down by the United States Circuit Court there.

12 *MAY* 1863

WESTERN THEATER, VICKSBURG CAMPAIGN General Grant's Union troops move closer to Vicksburg, and a division under the command of General John Logan is positioned at Raymond. Logan's Federals are attacked at this point, 15 miles from Vicksburg, by Confederate forces under the command of General John Gregg. The fighting causes Southern troops to fall back towards Jackson, Mississippi, and each side reports upward of 500 casualties. This skirmish makes clear to General Grant that the South has sufficient troop strength to defend Vicksburg and causes the Union commander to plan preliminary assaults on Confederate positions outside the city.

13 *MAY* 1863

WESTERN THEATER, VICKSBURG CAMPAIGN General Pemberton, making preparations for the anticipated attack by Union forces, places Confederates in position at Edward's Station, or Edward's Depot, Mississippi. General Grant's men head toward this point and also toward Jackson, northeast of Vicksburg.

TRANS-MISSISSIPPI In Missouri there is a Union reconnaissance effort out of Newtonia headed to Centre Creek; this operation lasts until 18 May.

14 *MAY* 1863

EASTERN THEATER There is much concern over the command of the Federal Army of the Potomac. President Lincoln is in contact with General Joseph Hooker, who has done little with the Army since Chancellorsville. Lincoln writes to the General, saying, 'Some of your troops and

Division Commanders are not giving you their entire confidence.'

WESTERN THEATER Despite inclement weather, General Grant moves his troops nearer to Jackson, Mississippi, where Confederates have pulled back further north. This latter movement is deemed necessary by Confederate General Johnston since he knows his troops are vastly outnumbered. Grant strikes General Gregg's brigade first, and then that of General W H T Walker. By late afternoon, the Southern forces can no longer hold back the Union troops and the latter move in to occupy Jackson, Mississippi around 4:00 pm. To the south, Federal General Nathaniel Banks takes his forces out of Alexandria, Louisiana, heading for Port Hudson, north of Baton Rouge. Port Hudson is considered the second most critical Confederate position on the Mississippi River.

15 MAY 1863

THE NORTH Union troops break into the office of the *Jeffersonian* at Richmond, Indiana and wreck the facilities there. This action is precipitated by anti-Union sentiments published by the newspaper.

WESTERN THEATER, VICKSBURG CAMPAIGN Both Confederates and Federals take positions near Edward's Station, Mississippi. General Pemberton has concentrated most of his Southern force here, with a garrison remaining at Vicksburg for the defense of that city. Pemberton is attempting to locate and destroy the Federal lines of communication, an attempt which is fruitless since Grant's strategy of concentrating his troops precludes the necessity of such communications.

16 MAY 1863

WESTERN THEATER, VICKSBURG CAMPAIGN The battle of Champion Hill, or Baker's Creek, Mississippi occurs as Grant's Federals clash with Pemberton's Confederates. General McClernand leads his Union forces, attacking the Southern left flank, and McPherson advances on the right of Pemberton's troops. The position at Champion's Hill is held by about 20,000

Confederate soldiers but despite several occasions on which the 29,000 Federals are pushed back, the North ultimately gains possession of the hill. Pemberton's men retreat toward Vicksburg and the Big Black River in Mississippi. This battle at Champion's Hill, or Baker's Creek, is considered to be the most severe in the entire Vicksburg campaign. The reports of casualties are an indication of this: Union losses are tallied at 410 dead, 1884 wounded, 187 missing for a total of 2441 altogether out of the original 29,000 men. The Confederacy enters the battle with nearly 20,000 troops and reports 381 killed, approximately 1800 wounded and 1670 listed as missing. This is a total of 3851 casualties for the South.

17 MAY 1863

WESTERN THEATER, VICKSBURG CAMPAIGN As Pemberton's Confederates continue their retreat, General Grant pursues, and a fight at the Big Black River Bridge is the result. A short but fierce encounter, this battle sees Pemberton's men attempt to slow Grant's progress by burning the bridges spanning the river, succeeding partially but at a cost of 1700 Confederates taken prisoner by the North. Federals report losses of 39 dead, 237 wounded and 3 missing out of a fighting force of nearly 10,000. The South stages their defense at this position with about 4000 men. Elsewhere, Union General Nathaniel Banks pushes to a point directly across the Mississippi River from Port Hudson.

18 MAY 1863

THE CONFEDERACY Alarmed over the developments at Vicksburg, President Jefferson Davis exhorts civilians and militia in Mississippi to aid General Johnston's efforts and encourages the latter to join forces with Pemberton so as to make an effective attack on Federal forces threatening Vicksburg.

WESTERN THEATER, VICKSBURG CAMPAIGN As General Grant moves his Federals closer to Vicksburg, crossing the

CHRONOLOGY

Big Black River on re-constructed bridges, General John Pemberton decides to remain with his forces in the city. So begins the siege of Vicksburg, Mississippi by Federals.

19 *MAY* 1863

WASHINGTON The issues surrounding the arrest and imprisonment of Ohio congressman Clement Vallandigham have yet to be laid to rest. Secretary of War Edwin Stanton, carrying out President Lincoln's orders, directs that Vallandigham be sent outside of Federal military boundaries and not be allowed to return.

WESTERN THEATER, VICKSBURG CAMPAIGN Anticipating a relatively easy access to the city, General Grant advances to Confederate fortifications outside Vicksburg, Mississippi. General John Pemberton's troops are well-positioned, however, and the Federals are unable to cut through Southern fortifications. Generals Sherman, McClernand and McPherson all attack with their troops, the result of which is the loss of nearly 1000 Federals in this initial assault on Vicksburg.

20 *MAY* 1863

TRANS-MISSISSIPPI In Indian Territory there is minor skirmishing between Union and Confederate troops at Fort Gibson.

NAVAL The Confederacy continues to foil the Union blockade efforts as two Southern vessels make it safely to the harbor at Charleston, South Carolina from Nassau, in the Bahamas. Federal blockaders are able, however, to capture two other Confederate ships, one off the coast of Nassau and one off the mouth of the Neuse River in North Carolina.

21 *MAY* 1863

WESTERN THEATER, VICKSBURG CAMPAIGN Federal General Nathaniel Banks moves his troops into position in the area near Port Hudson, Louisiana. The bulk of this force is concentrated at Bayou Sara; other troops are moving along the Clinton

Road from Baton Rouge; still others encounter hostile fire from Confederates near Plains Store. These maneuvers of Banks' troops mark the beginning of the siege of Port Hudson.

NAVAL At Yazoo City, Mississippi the Confederates destroy a number of workshops in the navy yard and also destroy two steamboats and a gunboat. These actions are completed in the face of an advancing enemy flotilla heading toward the city on the Yazoo River.

22 *MAY* 1863

WASHINGTON President Lincoln meets with convalescing soldiers at the White House. At this meeting, the President points out that 'the men upon their crutches were orators; their very appearance spoke louder than tongues'.

WESTERN THEATER, VICKSBURG CAMPAIGN Vicksburg, Mississippi suffers a second attack from General Grant's Union forces. Despite the well-planned assault on Confederate positions there, Grant's men are unable to make any breakthrough. Generals Sherman and McClernand are each able to gain a brief hold at several points, one at Railroad Redoubt, but neither gains a permanent grasp. The Southern defenses are strong and are enhanced by the natural, deep ravines surrounding the city. A Northern soldier, R B Scott of the 67th Indiana Volunteers, recounts the severity of the attack: 'Every experienced soldier . . . awaited the signal. It came, and in a moment the troops sprang forward, clenching their guns as they started on the charge . . . Twenty thousand muskets and 150 cannon belched forth death and destruction . . . Our ranks were now becoming decimated . . . . The charge was a bloody failure'. This second attack on Vicksburg in three days results in heavy losses for the Union: 502 dead, 2550 injured, 147 missing out of a total troop strength of 45,000. Confederates report losses of less than 500 men. The number of casualties makes clear to Grant that direct attacks on the city are fruitless and he concludes that 'The work to be done was to make our position as strong against the enemy as his was against us'.

23 *MAY* 1863

WESTERN THEATER The Port Hudson, Louisiana area is the site of fighting as the bulk of General Banks' Federals cross the Mississippi and head toward their goal. Haines' Bluff, Mississippi sees minor skirmishing. At Vicksburg, the Southern forces continue to man their defenses as General Grant's Federals reinforce their positions.

24 *MAY* 1863

THE CONFEDERACY President Jefferson Davis is not in complete agreement with General Pemberton's decision to hold Vicksburg, Mississippi. The Confederate President telegraphs a message to General Johnston saying, 'the disparity of numbers renders prolonged defense dangerous'.

EASTERN THEATER At Fredericksburg, Virginia the Federal Army of the Potomac, under General Hooker's command, continues to wait, facing the prospect of a clash with General Lee's Army of Northern Virginia.

WESTERN THEATER There is some minor reorganization of Union forces in the Murfreesboro area where General William Rosecrans and his men oppose Confederates under General Braxton Bragg at this Tennessee location. In Mississippi, the siege against Southern positions continues to take shape at Vicksburg, as does the siege of Port Hudson, Louisiana. Both of these hold the potential for the defeat of the Confederates in their desire to maintain control of the Mississippi River.

25 *MAY* 1863

THE NORTH After his sentence of imprisonment had been rescinded by President Lincoln, Ohio congressman Clement Vallandigham is given over to Confederates by Federal military officials in Tennessee. This entire episode is one which pro-

vokes outrage from both supporters of Vallandigham in the North and those loyal to the Union who wish to see actions such as his dealt with severely.

WESTERN THEATER, VICKSBURG CAMPAIGN Federal attempts at direct attack being put aside, General Grant now devises a means by which to break through Confederate defenses at Vicksburg, Mississippi. The Union troops there dig a tunnel near the city into which they place, and detonate, 2200 pounds of gunpowder. This explosion is supposed to open up an access route to the city itself, but the Southern troops are waiting in another line of defense to prevent such entry. General Grant explains: 'The effect was to blow the top of the hill off and make a crater where it had stood. The breach, however, was not sufficient to enable us to pass a column through. In fact, the enemy had thrown up a line further back.'

NAVAL The Union Navy is successful in capturing two Southern steamboats, the *Red Chief* and the *Starlight*, on the Mississippi River. In another action, the CSS *Alabama* seizes two vessels off the coast of Bahia, Brazil.

27 *MAY* 1863

WESTERN THEATER, VICKSBURG CAMPAIGN The Federal siege of Port Hudson, Louisiana begins as troops under General Banks stage an initial attack on Confederate defenses there. The latter troops are under the command of General Franklin Gardner and number around 4500. The Union assault is made by approximately 13,000 men, but despite their hopes for an easy victory, Banks' forces are unable to overcome their rather disorganized offensive and the strong repulse made by Gardner's men. The Union reports losses at this action against Confederates at Port Hudson to be 1995—293 killed, 1545 wounded, 157 missing. The South tallies casualties to be around 235. Once more, the Union is unable to gain an easy foothold in the vicinity of Vicksburg and Port Hudson.

NAVAL In an attempt to seize Fort Hill, a Southern position on the Mississippi, Admiral David Porter attacks with the Union gunboat *Cincinnati*. This action, directed by General William Sherman, is unsuccessful as Confederate shore batteries destroy the Union vessel, sinking it and killing or wounding 40 men. There is an attack on Union gunboats at Greenwood, Mississippi. In Georgia on the Chattahoochie River, the CSS *Chattahoochie* explodes by accident, killing 18 men.

28 *MAY* 1863

THE NORTH In a first for the Union, a regiment of black soldiers leaves Boston. The 54th Massachusetts Volunteers will train at Hilton Head, South Carolina.

29 *MAY* 1863

WASHINGTON President Lincoln receives a letter from General Burnside in which the latter proffers his resignation as commander of the Department of the Ohio. Burnside takes this step because of the release of Ohio congressman Clement Vallandigham and Lincoln's action rescinding Burnside's imprisonment orders. President Lincoln refuses to accept Burnside's resignation.

30 *MAY* 1863

THE CONFEDERACY General Robert E Lee and President Jefferson Davis meet to discuss the situation at Vicksburg, Mississippi. The President recognizes that General Johnston's failure to attack Grant's positions has perhaps cost the Confederacy its hold on Vicksburg. He says to Lee, 'General Johnston did not . . .attack Grant promptly and I fear the result is that which you anticipated if time was given'.

1 *JUNE* 1863

THE NORTH There is heated opposition to an action taken by General Burnside in the Department of the Ohio. The General calls for the suppression of the *Chicago Times*. This because 'of the repeated expressions of disloyal and incendiary statements'. Citizens of Chicago, Illinois, and the city's mayor, F C Sherman, apeal to President Lincoln to strike down Burnside's orders.

2 *JUNE* 1863

WASHINGTON President Lincoln, reviewing the information that he has concerning Mississippi, wires a message to General Grant asking, 'Are you in communication with General Banks?' It is the opinion of military advisors in Washington that Banks and Grant should combine their forces, but the two generals continue their separate operations.

EASTERN THEATER In Virginia there is some minor skirmishing around Upperville and Strasburg. General Lee's troops make preparations to move out of their current position in the Fredericksburg, Virginia area. These Confederate troops of the Army of Northern Virginia number about 89,000 men organized into three corps plus a cavalry unit. The corps are under the command of Generals Longstreet, Ewell and Hill, with J E B Stuart in command of the cavalry's six brigades.

3 *JUNE* 1863

EASTERN THEATER, GETTYSBURG CAMPAIGN General Robert E Lee's Confederate Army of Northern Virginia moves out of the Fredericksburg vicinity at the start of a month-long campaign which will culminate in the battle of Gettysburg, Pennsylvania. Lee has come to the decision to stage an invasion of the North. As these Southern troops advance north, there is an incident of skirmishing near Fayetteville, Virginia. The Federal Army of the Potomac, under General Hooker's command, numbers approximately 122,000 men; it has conducted various reconnaissance efforts prior to this date and Hooker is aware of Lee's intentions.

WESTERN THEATER, VICKSBURG CAMPAIGN Various maneuvers take place; in

Louisiana, Union troops conduct a reconnaissance around Clinton. Minor fighting breaks out at Simsport, Louisiana. General Grant receives some reinforcements in the Vicksburg area from the Ninth Army Corps, stationed until now in Kentucky.

4 JUNE 1863

EASTERN THEATER, GETTYSBURG CAMPAIGN General Robert E Lee and his Confederates move toward Culpeper Court House with Generals Ewell and Longstreet and their two armies of Northern Virginia Corps I and II. General A P Hill and the III Corps remains in the Fredericksburg, Virginia area. Union troops conduct reconnaissance efforts for two days, leaving Yorktown Virginia and heading for Walkerton and Aylett's in that state.

WESTERN THEATER, VICKSBURG CAMPAIGN In Mississippi, Confederates prepare to endure the siege which has been implemented by General Grant's Union forces.

5 JUNE 1863

EASTERN THEATER, GETTYSBURG CAMPAIGN In the course of a reconnaissance effort in the Fredericksburg area by General Sedgwick's Federal VI Corps of the Potomac Army, there is severe fighting in Virginia. This encounter, known as the

Artillery on the Rappahannock, 4 June 1863.

Battle of Franklin's Crossing, or Deep Run, sees Union troops clash with Confederates positioned in trenches. The result of this fighting is that although the Federals take 35 prisoners and report 6 Confederates dead and 35 wounded, the Army of Northern Virginia is still very much in force at Fredericksburg. It is President Lincoln's advice to General Hooker that the Federal Army of the Potomac should concentrate on the portion of Lee's Confederates that is moving out away from Fredericksburg. It is apparent that to attack the Fredericksburg position would be less profitable.

6 JUNE 1863

EASTERN THEATER, GETTYSBURG CAMPAIGN General Hooker is still attempting to pinpoint General Lee's destination and intention in moving most of the Confederate Army out of Fredericksburg, Virginia. General J E B Stuart and his Confederate cavalry corps of 8000 men stage a reiew at Brandy Station, Virginia.

7 JUNE 1863

WESTERN THEATER, VICKSBURG CAMPAIGN A serious clash between Federals and Confederates occur as the latter attack the Union troops garrisoned at Milliken's Bend in Louisiana. While Confederates under General McCulloch are successful in pushing the Federals back to the Mississippi, the Union troops, under General Thomas, are aided in their defense of the area by the intervention of two gunboats, the *Lexington* and the *Choctaw*. After the intervention, the Confederates pull back. Losses at this encounter at Milliken's Bend are reported by the Federals at 652 dead and injured, by Confederates at 185 casualties. The plantation Brierfield in Mississippi is burned by Union troops; Brierfield is the home of Confederate President Jefferson Davis.

8 JUNE 1863

EASTERN THEATER, GETTYSBURG CAM-

CHRONOLOGY

PAIGN General Robert E Lee attends a cavalry review of General J E B Stuart's corps. This occurs at Culpeper Court House, Virginia.

WESTERN THEATER, VICKSBURG CAMPAIGN At Vicksburg, Mississippi General Grant's troops shell the city; this is a constant, 24-hour bombardment which causes residents to take cover in caves or remain hidden in their houses in order to avoid the destructive showers.

9 JUNE 1863

EASTERN THEATER, GETTYSBURG CAMPAIGN In order to gain further information about Confederate positions, General Hooker directs a portion of United States cavalry under the command of General Alfred Pleasonton to conduct a reconnaissance in the area of the Rappahannock River at a location known as Brandy Station, Fleetwood Hill, or Beverly Ford. The battle occurring here between Pleasonton's 11,000 troops and Confederate General J E B Stuart's cavalry forces is considered to be the most severe cavalry fight of the entire war. It results in little real gain for the Federals, although General Hooker obtains some information about Confederate troop strength, movement and positions. Stuart's cavalry manages to hold the location at a cost of some 523 casualties out of nearly 10,000 troops engaged. The Union reports 81 dead, 403 wounded and 382 missing.

10 JUNE 1863

WASHINGTON President Lincoln is in communication with General Hooker, advising him as to a course of action for the Federal Army of the Potomac in Virginia. According to Lincoln, the Army's best strategy is to 'Fight him when the opportunity offers. If he stays where he is, fret him.'

THE NORTH There is a beginning wave of alarm among communities north of the Potomac River as word of Lee's advancing Confederate Army becomes available.

EASTERN THEATER, GETTYSBURG CAM-

PAIGN The Army of Northern Virginia moves its II Corps under General Ewell out of Culpeper, Virginia on a northwestern course.

NAVAL The Federal vessel *Maple Leaf,* loaded with Confederates taken prisoner by Union troops, is forced ashore by its passengers near Cape Henry, Virginia. This group of prisoners is being transferred from Fort Monroe to Fort Delaware, but is successful in making its escape once the vessel reaches the coast.

11 JUNE 1863

THE NORTH In Ohio, Peace Democrats submit the name of former congressman Clement Vallandigham for nomination as governor. This despite the fact that Vallandigham, convicted of treason against the Union, has been banished to the Confederacy and has been subsequently transferred by the Southern government to Canada.

WESTERN THEATER Once more, Triune, Tennessee is the scene of skirmishing, this time as General Nathan Bedford Forrest's Confederates clash with Federals in that area of the state. Elsewhere, there is fighting in South Carolina at Little Folly Island and also in Mississippi, near Corinth.

12 JUNE 1863

THE NORTH Because of an anticipated invasion and attack on the citizens of Pennsylvania, the Governor of that state, Andrew Curtin, calls out the militia. He also requests aid from New York State to repel the assumed influx of Confederates under General Robert E Lee.

THE CONFEDERACY President Jefferson Davis receives an offer from his Vice President, Alexander Stephens, concerning a possible mediation between the Confederacy and the Union. Stephens' suggestion has to do with a diplomatic effort to promote 'a correct understanding and agreement between the two Governments'.

EASTERN THEATER, GETTYSBURG CAMPAIGN As General Lee's Army of Northern Virginia moves north, passing the Blue Ridge and going into the Shenandoah Valley, the Confederate troops clash with Federals at Newtown, Cedarville and Middletown, Virginia.

13 *JUNE* 1863

EASTERN THEATER, GETTYSBURG CAMPAIGN At Winchester, Virginia there is skirmishing as Confederates, under General Ewell, push into the area, causing the battle of Second Winchester, Virginia. Ewell takes over and occupies Berryville, Virginia. There is other fighting in the area near Bunker Hill and White Post, Virginia. At the battle of Second Winchester the Federals, under General Milroy, lose 300 men in their encounter with the Southern forces, who report losses of 850 dead or wounded.

14 *JUNE* 1863

WESTERN THEATER Northern General Nathaniel Banks tells Confederates at Port Hudson, Louisiana to surrender. Failing this capitulation, Banks plans an assault to commence at daybreak. This Federal attack by about 6000 troops is carried out against 3750 Confederates, who hold off the Federals.

TRANS-MISSISSIPPI In Arkansas there is an attack on the USS *Marmora*, near Eunice. The town is nearly destroyed by fire following this action as Federals retaliate the Confederate action against the vessel.

15 *JUNE* 1863

WASHINGTON In the Federal capital, President Lincoln seeks support from the state militia of Pennsylvania, Maryland, Ohio and West Virginia in the face of the northward advance of Lee's Confederates. The President asks the governors of these states to provide 100,000 troops. In addition there is an order, sent out by the Federal Department of the Navy, to disable the CSS *Tacony*, a Southern vessel which has been successful in interfering with Northern shipping along the Eastern coastline.

EASTERN THEATER, GETTYSBURG CAMPAIGN There is a fierce attack on Federal positions at Winchester, Virginia as General Milroy's 9000 Northern troops attempt to hold the area. General Ewell's Confederates are successful in pushing the Union force back in the direction of Harper's Ferry. In addition to the victory at Winchester, Southern troops also attack Federal positions at Berryville and Martinsburg. At the Winchester battle, Union losses are reported at 95 killed, 348 injured and over 4000 missing or captured; the losses Confederates indicate: 47 killed, 219 wounded, 3 missing. The Confederacy seizes a large quantity of supplies and ammunition: 23 guns, 300 wagons, 300 horses and much food. The Southern Army continues to press northward, arousing the inhabitants of Maryland and Pennsylvania, and achieving results which provoke Hooker's message to President Lincoln that indicates the Southern invasion is something 'it is not in my power to prevent'. There is a Confederate cavalry raid at Chambersburg, Pennsylvania; J E B Stuart's cavalry acts as a front-line unit for General Longstreet's corps that is heading out from Culpeper Court House.

16 *JUNE* 1863

EASTERN THEATER, GETTYSBURG CAMPAIGN General Hooker takes his Federal Army of the Potomac and positions it at Fairfax Court House, Virginia as General Lee and his Confederate Army of Northern Virginia cross the Potomac River.

17 *JUNE* 1863

EASTERN THEATER, GETTYSBURG CAMPAIGN Skirmishing continues as General Lee's Confederates push further north. The fighting on this day occurs at Point of Rocks, Maryland.

WESTERN THEATER, VICKSBURG CAMPAIGN The siege of Vicksburg continues unabated. Union forces clash with Confederates as the latter attack gunboats and land positions, the latter occurring today at a point near Commerce, Mississippi.

NAVAL On the Wilmington River, in Warsaw Sound, Georgia, Captain John Rodgers, commander of the Federal vessel *Weehawken*, is successful in forcing the surrender of the Confederate ironclad vessel, the *Atlanta*. Union naval forces on the *Weehawken* and the *Nahant*, commanded by Captain John Downes, clash with the *Atlanta*, resulting in several casualties on either side.

18 JUNE 1863

EASTERN THEATER, GETTYSBURG CAMPAIGN Further skirmishing breaks out at Aldie, Virginia as Lee's Confederates push further north. There is a Union reconnaissance in the Peninsular area of Virginia.

WESTERN THEATER, VICKSBURG CAMPAIGN General John McClernand is relieved of his command of the Thirteenth Army Corps by General Ulysses Grant. This is due to McClernand's repeated acts of insubordination and his apparent unwillingness to cooperate with the rest of the Army. He is replaced by General E O C Ord.

19 JUNE 1863

EASTERN THEATER, GETTYSBURG CAMPAIGN Generals Ewell, Hill and Longstreet probe further north as the Confederate Army of Northern Virginia continues its invasion. There are encounters between these Southern troops and Union forces, skirmishing breaking out at Middleburg, Virginia as the North attempts to slow the progress made by Lee's Army.

WESTERN THEATER, VICKSBURG CAMPAIGN There is continued skirmishing in the area of Vicksburg as the siege continues.

20 JUNE 1863

WASHINGTON President Lincoln issues a proclamation which declares the state of West Virginia as the 35th state of the Union. THE NORTH In an effort to provide some defense of the city, citizens in Baltimore, Maryland erect fortifications to the north and west in order to repel any Confederate raids on the city.

WESTERN THEATER, VICKSBURG CAMPAIGN Various incidents of skirmishing take place; in Louisiana, at La Forche Crossing there is minor fighting over a two-day period. The Federal batteries around Vicksburg, Mississippi shower that city with shells.

TRANS-MISSISSIPPI In Missouri, a Union reconnaissance leaves Waynesville. At Government Springs, in the Utah Territory, Union forces clash with Indians.

21 JUNE 1863

EASTERN THEATER, GETTYSBURG CAMPAIGN There is fierce, but minor fighting in Virginia as General Hooker's Potomac Army encounters Lee's advancing Confederates at Upperville and at Haymarket. In Maryland, where Union and Southern troops encounter each other, there are similar clashes near Frederick.

22 JUNE 1863

EASTERN THEATER, GETTYSBURG CAMPAIGN The fighting continues to be minor and fragmentary as Lee's Army of Northern Virginia pushes on and engages Federals near Aldie, Virginia. At Greencastle, Pennsylvania, Union and Confederate troops clash. As General Lee moves in to Chambersburg, Pennsylvania citizens in Philadelphia close down businesses and shops.

NAVAL The CSS *Tacony*, under the command of Lieutenant Charles Read, seizes five Federal fishing vessels in waters off the coast of New England, proving the fallability of the Union blockade once again.

23 JUNE 1863

EASTERN THEATER, GETTYSBURG CAMPAIGN General Joseph Hooker prepares his Federal Army of the Potomac to cross the river of the same name in. Virginia. In Yorktown, Union troops begin a reconnaissance that lasts for five days and heads for South Anna Bridge.

WESTERN THEATER, TULLAHOMA CAMPAIGN Under the command of General William Rosecrans, the Federal Army begins a major, and a successful, effort to harass Confederates in the Tullahoma, or Middle Tennessee, Campaign. By operating against General Braxton Bragg's Confederates in this effort, the Union General prevents Bragg from moving toward Vicksburg with reinforcements. In this way, Rosecrans is supporting General Grant's campaign at Vicksburg, Mississippi.

TRANS-MISSISSIPPI In the Nebraska Territory there is fighting at Pawnee Agency. In the Nevada Territory, Union soldiers engage Indians in combat near Canon Station. Sibley, Missouri is the site of minor skirmishing between Federals and Southern forces.

mained at Vicksburg to endure the constant attacks by General Grant's troops: 'Hardly any part of the city was outside the range of the enemy's artillery except the south- . . . Just across the Mississippi, seven 11-inch and 13-inch mortars were put in position and trained directly on the homes of the people . . . how people subsisted was another wonder . . . There were some stores that had supplies, and prices climbed steadily, but first nobody had the money, and then nobody had the supplies.' In Louisiana, there is a Confederate raid at Berwick Bay where injured Union soldiers are convalescing. General Taylor's Southern troops, numbering approximately 4000, are easily able to seize the post at Berwick Bay and gain access to much-needed supplies.

24 JUNE 1863

EASTERN THEATER, GETTYSBURG CAMPAIGN Sharpsburg, Maryland sees fighting as Hooker's Potomac Army clashes with troops under the command of Longstreet and Hill. The latter are moving to join forces with Confederate General Ewell, who has arrived in Maryland, and with whom they will advance on Pennsylvania.

WESTERN THEATER, TULLAHOMA CAMPAIGN General Braxton Bragg encounters Federals near Bradyville and Big Springs Ranch in Tennessee, where General William Rosecrans is advancing into the middle of the state. There is also skirmishing at Middleton, Tennessee and some brief, but fierce, action at Hoover's Gap. At the latter engagement, Southern forces report a large number of casualties while the Union lists 45 dead and injured.

WESTERN THEATER, VICKSBURG CAMPAIGN There is a slight increase in the pressure placed on Confederates at the besieged city of Vicksburg; food is becoming more scarce and the shelling from Federal batteries has been stepped up. A civilian observer, Edward Gregory, describes the hardships suffered by those who had re-

25 JUNE 1863

THE CONFEDERACY A worried President Jefferson Davis contacts General Braxton Bragg in Tennessee. The President points out the urgent need for reinforcements at Vicksburg, where General Johnston is intent on harassing General Grant's forces to prevent the continued siege of the city. Davis also appeals to General Beauregard, located at Charleston, South Carolina for additional troops for General Johnston. Davis fears that without these reinforcements, 'the Mississippi will be lost'.

EASTERN THEATER, GETTYSBURG CAMPAIGN This day marks the start of Confederate General J E B Stuart's Gettysburg raid (a maneuver that military historians would later criticize as it removed Stuart's Confederate cavalry from the vicinity of the upcoming battle at Gettysburg). Rather than follow strictly the directions provided by General Lee on 22 June 1863, Stuart takes a route around Hooker's rear and flank, avoiding the protection afforded by the Blue Ridge route to the west. Stuart, by this action, crosses the Potomac Army's main supply line and captures upward of 125 Federal wagons and takes more than 400 prisoners.

CHRONOLOGY

26 *JUNE* 1863

EASTERN THEATER, GETTYSBURG CAMPAIGN General Jubal Early and his Confederate forces move into Gettysburg, Pennsylvania, at first encountering some of Hooker's Potomac Army troops and skirmishing with them outside Gettysburg. Although General Hooker wires the President of his intention to move against Lee's Army of Northern Virginia, there is an indication that Lincoln is dubious about Hooker's abilities.

WESTERN THEATER, TULLAHOMA CAMPAIGN There is minor skirmishing at Beech Grove, Tennessee. There is a fight between Rosecrans' Federals and Bragg's Confederates at Shelbyville, where the Northern casualty lists show 45 dead, 463 injured, 13 missing. The South reports 1634 casualties, plus many taken prisoner by the North.

NAVAL After having successfully taken 21 Federal vessels in less than three weeks, Confederate Lieutenant Charles Read in command of the schooner *Archer* attempts to seize the Federal cutter *Caleb Cushing*, at anchor in the harbor at Portland, Maine. This attempt is foiled by Federal naval steamers; the *Archer* is destroyed and the Confederates taken prisoner.

27 *JUNE* 1863

WASHINGTON After conferring with General Henry Halleck, President Lincoln decides to remove General Joseph Hooker from his command of the Army of the Potomac. It is decided that General George Meade will replace Hooker; Halleck sends word to Meade of this change. Meanwhile, General Hooker has sent a message to the President concerning the evacuation of Harper's Ferry, Virginia, which Hooker feels is critical. Hooker points out that unless this action is taken he can no longer act as head of the Potomac Army. When Halleck countermands the orders concerning Harper's Ferry, it leads to Hooker's decision to resign from command of the Army of the Potomac.

EASTERN THEATER, GETTYSBURG CAMPAIGN General Robert E Lee's Army of Northern Virginia moves into Chambersburg, Pennsylvania after having forced the surrender of York. The Southern Army is headed for the state capital at Harrisburg. Elsewhere, J E B Stuart and his cavalry forces encounter Federals near Fairfax Court House, Virginia; in the fighting that ensues, all but 18 of the Union cavalry troops are captured by Stuart's Confederates.

WESTERN THEATER, TULLAHOMA CAMPAIGN At Guy's Gap and again at Shelbyville, Tennessee, there is skirmishing between Federal and Confederates. In that same vicinity General Rosecrans' Union forces occupy Manchester, forcing General Bragg to the decision to pull back with his Southern troops to Tullahoma.

28 *JUNE* 1863

WASHINGTON General George Meade is appointed to replace Hooker. President Lincoln and General Halleck learn that, while the newly-appointed Potomac Army chief is uninformed as to the 'exact condition of the troops and the position of the enemy', he is planning to move the Federal Forces toward the Susquehanna River. Both Lincoln and Halleck feel much confidence in Meade, and hope that he will mount an attack on Lee's invading Southern Army. There are, at this point, around 100,000 Federal troops concentrated in the area around Frederick, Maryland.

EASTERN THEATER, GETTYSBURG CAMPAIGN There is skirmishing at Chambersburg, Pennsylvania where the forces of Generals Longstreet and Hill are positioned. General Ewell is at Carlisle; General Early at York. After learning that the Federal Army is north of the Potomac River, General Lee makes a change in his original plan to march on Harrisburg. The new strategy requires that Hill and Longstreet join Ewell and move on Gettysburg and Cashtown.

WESTERN THEATER, VICKSBURG CAMPAIGN In Louisiana, at Donaldsville, the Southern forces under General Taylor

Destruction of the Columbia Railroad Bridge.

attack Federals. The latter garrison, under the command of Major J D Bulle, is able to withstand the assault with the help of Federal gunboats. Both Vicksburg, Mississippi and Port Hudson, Louisiana continue under siege.

29 JUNE 1863

EASTERN THEATER, GETTYSBURG CAMPAIGN At Winchester, Maryland there is a fierce cavalry skirmish between Confederates under J E B Stuart and Union forces under Major N B Knight. The Confederates are attacked by Knight's Federals, but because of Stuart's stronger force, the Southerners repel the assault. At this encounter, the North reports nine casualties, the South, 18 dead and wounded. General George Meade moves his Union Army of the Potomac toward Gettysburg. General Robert E Lee's forces push to this point in Pennsylvania also.

WESTERN THEATER, TULLAHOMA CAMPAIGN General Rosecrans continues to harass Southern forces in Tennessee, skirmishing breaking out at Hillsborough, Decherd and Lexington. Columbia, Kentucky, also sees fighting.

30 JUNE 1863

WASHINGTON Despite pressure from supporters of the former Potomac Army chief, President Lincoln refuses to place General George Brinton McClellan back in command of that critical force which is only hours away from battle at Gettysburg, Pennsylvania.

EASTERN THEATER, GETTYSBURG CAMPAIGN Confederate cavalry General J E B Stuart once more engages Federal cavalry forces, this time at Hanover, Pennsylvania. General Kilpatrick's Federals are able to mount a serious counterattack which nearly results in the capture of Stuart. At this cavalry skirmish, the Union reports 19 killed, 73 wounded, 123 missing. Confederates list 9 dead, 50 wounded, 58 missing. General Reynolds' Union troops are sent by General Meade to occupy Gettysburg.

WESTERN THEATER, TULLAHOMA CAMPAIGN Fighting continues in the mid-Tennessee area, as General Braxton Bragg pulls his Confederates across the Tennessee River in a retreat from Tullahoma. General Rosecrans establishes his Federals at Chattahoochee, Tennessee.

1 JULY 1863

EASTERN THEATER, GETTYSBURG CAMPAIGN A three-day battle begins at Gettysburg, Pennsylvania as cavalry forces under Union General Buford clash with General A P Hill's Confederate cavalry

Reinhart's drawing 'High Tide at Gettysburg.'

early in the day. This fighting occurs along the Chambersburg Road but moves closer to Gettysburg proper as the day wears on. Confederate General Ewell's troops join the battle by afternoon, with Longstreet and Hill's men, and make a strong push against the Union Eleventh Corps which is commanded by Federal General O O Howard. This latter force is driven back away from Gettysburg in a fierce clash of men and horses, toward the southeast, an area known as Cemetery Ridge and Cemetery Hill. The hard-fighting Federals, entrenched at this position by late in the day, are not harassed further by General Lee's army, however. This gives time for Union General Meade, commander of the Potomac Army, to reinforce Cemetery Hill with more Union troops. It is at this position that Generals Howard and Doubleday are strengthening their fortifications for the next attack by Confederates. General Robert E Lee wishes that General Ewell will make an attack on the Federals at Cemetery Hill immediately, prior to any further reinforcement. However, General Ewell chooses not to advance on the Union forces there on this first day of the battle of Gettysburg. The Southern Army of Northern Virginia now holds the town of Gettysburg and is waiting for the arrival of General Longstreet's Corps prior to making any more offensives against the Northern forces which outnumber them. Casualties at this engagement show that the Federals have suffered a great deal more than General Lee's forces: General O O Howard's Eleventh Corps sees over 4000 taken prisoner. In addition, Federal General John Reynolds is killed in the mid-morning fighting which takes place along the Chambersburg Road by McPherson's Ridge. Meanwhile, the Confederate General Archer is taken prisoner. Archer is the first general officer in the Army of Northern Virginia to be taken by the Federals since General Robert E Lee had assumed command of this Confederate force.

WESTERN THEATER, TULLAHOMA CAMPAIGN While fighting continues in Tennessee along the Elk River, near Bethpage Bridge and in the Tullahoma vicinity where Rosecrans' Union troops now are positioned, the major thrust of the Federal campaign against Confederates under General Braxton Bragg is over. The Southern forces are pulling southward toward Chattanooga.

WESTERN THEATER, VICKSBURG CAMPAIGN There is skirmishing near Edward's Station in the vicinity of Vicksburg, Mississippi as General Johnston's Confederates continue to fend off the harassing forces of General Grant's Union troops. Inside the city, General John Pemberton's men struggle, under increasingly poor conditions, to continue their defense of Vicksburg.

2 JULY 1863

EASTERN THEATER, GETTYSBURG CAMPAIGN The second day of fighting at this critical Civil War battle sees Federals positioned at Big Round Top and Little Round Top, along Cemetery Ridge. Lee's forces are placed along Seminary Ridge, below the Union lines. Fighting breaks out late in the day as General Longstreet's First Corps pushes against General Daniel Sickles' Federals at the Peach Orchard and

'Aftermath of Gettysburg,' 1863.

Union and Confederate dead at Gettysburg.

along the Emmitsburg Road. Meanwhile, General G K Warren successfully withstands a Confederate assault on Federal positions. Despite Confederate General Hood's forces pressing the Union troops at the Round Tops, the South is unable to do more than gain a slight foothold at the lower sections of those hills; the Federals hold fast to their superior vantage points at the summits. General Ewell's Confederate troops attack Union positions at Culp's Hill and Cemetery Hill, but only General Edward Johnson's Confederates make any appreciable progress, that at the lower portion of Culp's Hill where they seize some positions not adequately defended by the Twelfth Corps of the Federal Potomac Army. The latter has left this southeast section of Culp's Hill open while concentrating better Union defenses at the Round Tops.

WESTERN THEATER, TULLAHOMA CAMPAIGN While Bragg's Southern troops continue their line of retreat, there is minor skirmishing around Morris' Ford, at Elk River and near Rock Creek Ford, all in Tennessee.

WESTERN THEATER, VICKSBURG CAMPAIGN There is little change in the situation at besieged Vicksburg, Mississippi where General John Pemberton remains entrenched with his Confederates inside the defenses of the city. There is some exchange of artillery fire between Pemberton's and Grant's troops.

3 JULY 1863

WASHINGTON There is an anxious vigil at the Federal capital as the President awaits information about the battle of Gettysburg.

EASTERN THEATER, GETTYSBURG CAMPAIGN This final day of battle at Gettysburg, Pennsylvania opens with the Federal Army of the Potomac, under the command of General George Meade, preparing for an attack by General Robert E Lee's Army of Northern Virginia. Despite General Longstreet's feeling that a Confederate offensive is risky due to the larger Federal force, General Lee is firmly committed to making an assault on the Middle of Meade's forces. Accordingly, 15,000 troops are sent to make what will be the final Southern attempt against the Union at Gettysburg. In the early afternoon, Generals Pettigrew, Trimble and Pickett group their men and advance on Federals in the vicinity of the Emmitsburg Road. The Federals are strung out in a line, facing the advancing Confederates, from Culp's Hill to Big Round Top and Devil's Den. The famous Confederate maneuver (later to become known as Pickett's Charge, despite the fact that it is General Longstreet who is in command of this operation and General Pickett's men form only part of the attacking force) does little to save the South's Army at Gettysburg, however, and the hand-to-hand combat which ensues sees

Three Confederate prisoners at Gettysburg.

the death of Confederate General Armistead. The battle of Gettysburg ends with the Southern forces retreating and attempting to regroup as a counterattack is expected, although it never occurs. General Lee has ventured into a nearly untenable position on this final day of fighting; to send 15,000 men against what he knew to be a larger enemy force was a gamble, and Lee loses it.

WESTERN THEATER, VICKSBURG CAMPAIGN The situation in Mississippi mirrors that in Pennsylvania: after weeks of siege, the Confederate forces under the command of General John Pemberton display white truce flags. The decision to surrender has been made with understandable reluctance, but the Confederate General ventures forth to meet with Union General Ulysses Grant in order to work out terms of surrender, despite the fact that Grant has already dictated his terms: 'You will be allowed to march out, the officers taking with them their side arms and clothing, and the field, staff and cavalry officers one horse each. The rank and file will be allowed all their clothing but no other property.' After the six-week siege, there is clearly no alternative for the South; they have almost no food and a continued entrenchment is pointless. The following day, Independence Day, is chosen for a formal surrender, and both North and South are well aware of its significance.

4 JULY 1863

EASTERN THEATER, GETTYSBURG CAMPAIGN The Confederate Army of Northern Virginia now heads slowly back toward Virginia, aided by poor weather as rain engulfs the area making it difficult for Meade's army to follow in pursuit, although the Union commander of the Potomac Army is later criticized for failing to do so. The casualty lists for the three-day encounter at Gettysburg, Pennsylvania, show that both the North and the South suffered terrible losses. The Confederate Army reported 3903 dead, 18,735 injured and 5425 missing out of a total of 75,000

men—this means that 28,063, or more than one-third of the Confederates at Gettysburg, were listed as casualties. The North, having gone into battle with 88,289 men, sustained 3155 dead, 14,529 wounded, and 5365 missing, or a total of 23,049 casualties.

WESTERN THEATER, VICKSBURG CAMPAIGN The Confederates formally surrender Vicksburg, Mississippi, to the Union Army, and nearly 29,000 men under Pemberton's command march out of the city. It is hoped that news of this Union triumph will hasten the end of the Port Hudson, Louisiana siege, and that the entire region of the Mississippi will soon be under the control of the Federal Army.

5 JULY 1863

EASTERN THEATER, GETTYSBURG CAMPAIGN Lee's Army of Northern Virginia continues its retreat while Meade lags in pursuit. A few skirmishes, largely fought by cavalry, occur at towns in Pennsylvania and at Smithburg, Maryland.

WESTERN THEATER Grant begins to parole the Confederate defenders of Vicksburg, each prisoner signing a pledge not to fight again until duly exchanged for a Northern prisoner.

6 JULY 1863

EASTERN THEATER, GETTYSBURG CAMPAIGN Minor skirmishes continue along Lee's route of withdrawal, but the Federals still can put together no organized pursuit. In one action, Federal cavalry officer Buford is repulsed by Lee's advance guard at Williamsport, Maryland.

WESTERN THEATER Federal General Sherman moves troops toward Jackson, Mississippi

7 JULY 1863

WASHINGTON Lincoln is encouraged by news of the fall of Vicksburg but, worried that Lee will escape with his army, writes to Meade urging him to attack without delay.

EASTERN THEATER, GETTYSBURG CAM-

PAIGN Lee's army entrenches at Hagerstown, Maryland, ready to cross the storm-swollen Potomac as soon as the waters lower. Minor skirmishes continue in outlying towns, and Federal forces move into Maryland Heights.

WESTERN THEATER Confederate General Braxton Bragg, driven from West Tennessee by Rosecrans' Army of the Cumberland, gathers his troops around Chattanooga, Tennessee.

8 JULY 1863

EASTERN THEATER, GETTYSBURG CAMPAIGN Lee's forces remain at Hagerstown, Maryland and skirmishes occur at Boonsborough and Williamsport, Maryland. In spite of his recent defeat and present dangerous position, Lee writes to President Davis, 'I am not in the least discouraged.'

WESTERN THEATER Discouraged by the fall of Vicksburg, the besieged Confederate defenders of Port Hudson, Louisiana surrender, leaving the whole of the Mississippi River under Federal control. In his diary, one Port Hudson resident notes that during the six weeks of the siege he and his friends consumed 'all the beef, all the dogs, and all the rats that were obtainable.' The fall of Port Hudson gives the Union over 6000 Confederate prisoners along with large quantities of arms and ammunition. Elsewhere, Confederate raider John H Morgan and 2500 men, beginning a sweep through Indiana and toward Ohio, cross the Ohio River into Indiana with only light Federal resistance. Many in Ohio fear that this action will galvanize rising Copperhead sentiment in their state.

9 JULY 1863

EASTERN THEATER, GETTYSBURG CAMPAIGN There is a small skirmish at Beaver Creek, Maryland, but Lee continues to have no substantial opposition.

WESTERN THEATER The Confederate leader of Port Hudson, General Gardner, formally surrenders to Federal General Nathanial Banks. Though the Mississippi is now under Union control, Federal shipping will have continuing troubles with guerilla attacks. Near Jackson, Mississippi Sherman closes on General J E Johnston, commander of the Confederate Department of the West.

10 JULY 1863

EASTERN THEATER, GETTYSBURG CAMPAIGN Meade's army begins to move with more determination toward Lee's forces, now gathering in Williamsport, Maryland; skirmishes erupt in several nearby towns, including a serious encounter at Falling Waters.

WESTERN THEATER Federal forces prepare for an assault on Battery Wagner, a Confederate defensive position on Morris Island in Charleston Harbor, South Carolina.

11 JULY 1863

THE NORTH Pursuant to the Union Enrollment Act of March 3, the first names of draftees are drawn in New York.

EASTERN THEATER, GETTYSBURG CAMPAIGN Meade begins preparing for an attack on Lee's forces, which still await the lowering of the Potomac.

WESTERN THEATER Federal forces mount their first attack on Battery Wagner in Charleston Harbor, but are repulsed after gaining the parapets. In Mississippi, Sherman besieges some of Johnston's forces in West Jackson.

12 JULY 1863

EASTERN THEATER, GETTYSBURG CAMPAIGN Meade finally catches up to Lee's army, but engages only in light and ineffective reconnaissance. Lee, building campfires to give the illusion of a settled camp, begins to move his troops over the now subdued Potomac on boats and a new pontoon bridge. Meade contemplates an attack the next day, but is dissuaded by his staff.

WESTERN THEATER Fighting is seen in Canton, Mississippi, near Jackson, between Sherman's and Johnston's forces. Moving through Indiana, Morgan's raiders meet increased resistance.

13 *JULY* 1863

THE NORTH, DRAFT RIOTS As a result of the first drawing of names for the draft in New York, resentment that has been growing toward the Federal Enrollment Act of 3 March boils over into a violent four-day riot. A mob of over 50,000 people, most of them Irish working men, swarm into the New York draft office, setting it afire and nearly killing its superintendent. Over the next few days an evacuated black orphanage and the offices of Horace Greeley's *Tribune* are burned by the rioters. Increasingly, the violence is directed toward blacks, who are attacked, looted, and killed at random; but the rioters also loot businesses, beat to death a Union colonel, and assault the home of the mayor. At length, Federal troops just back from Gettysburg are called in and quell the mob, leaving over 1000 dead and wounded and ending what history will note as one of the darkest homefront episodes of the war and the worst race riot in American history.

New York anti-draft rioters, 25 July 1863.

Less serious draft riots break out in Boston, in Troy, New York and other towns in the East and Ohio.

EASTERN THEATER, GETTYSBURG CAMPAIGN During the night, Lee and his Army of Northern Virginia complete their evacuation from Williamsport over the Potomac, their withdrawal again lighted by the campfires that are also deceiving the Union army into thinking them encamped.

14 *JULY* 1863

EASTERN THEATER, GETTYSBURG CAMPAIGN Finally pressing toward an attack, Meade's Army of the Potomac moves into Southern positions at Williamsport and discovers them to be abandoned. Thus ends the North's best chance for a quick end to the war. This day Lincoln writes in an unsent letter to Meade, 'Your golden opportunity is gone, and I am distressed immeasurably because of it.' Nonetheless, Lee's last opportunity for an invasion of the North has been stopped.

WESTERN THEATER Confederate troops emerge on a sortie from Battery Wagner, near Charleston, South Carolina. Clashes are seen at Iuka, Mississippi and Elk River in Tennessee.

NAVAL Federal ships extend their control over the James River in Virginia by taking Fort Powhatan.

15 *JULY* 1863

THE CONFEDERACY Stricken by the defeats at Gettysburg, Vicksburg and Port Hudson, and the dangerous situations in Charleston and Jackson, President Davis writes to one of his generals, 'The clouds are truly dark over us.'

EASTERN THEATER, GETTYSBURG CAMPAIGN Lee's army moves southward along the Shanandoah Valley of Virginia, in good condition though short of shoes and supplies.

16 *JULY* 1863

THE NORTH The Draft Riots subside in New York.

EASTERN THEATER   Morgan's raiders continue their ill-defined exploits in Ohio, meeting with increasing Federal resistance.

WESTERN THEATER   J E Johnston, fearing Sherman's superior forces, pulls his forces out of Jackson, Mississippi and leaves the city to Union occupation.

18 JULY 1863

WESTERN THEATER   Federal forces mount a second unsuccessful attack on Battery Wagner, South Carolina. After an extensive naval bombardment, a frontal attack is attempted by Federal forces, but the troops are turned back. By the end of the day Federal casualties total 1515 to the defenders' 174. Losses to the Fifty-fourth Massachusetts Colored Infantry are especially severe, and their commander, Colonel R G Shaw, is killed. After this action shows that a direct attack against the Battery is inadvisable, a siege is commenced by Federal troops and ships. The Confederates begin moving guns from Fort Sumter to strategic positions within Charleston Harbor.

19 JULY 1863

EASTERN THEATER, GETTYSBURG CAMPAIGN   In pursuit of Lee, Meade's army crosses the Potomac at Harper's Ferry and Berlin, Maryland.

WESTERN THEATER   In Ohio, Morgan's raiders, now greatly reduced by skirmishes and desertions, are overwhelmed by Hobson and Shackelford, who kill and capture over 800 of his men. With only 300 men left, Morgan escapes toward Pennsylvania with Hobson in pursuit.

20 JULY 1863

THE NORTH   Merchants in New York meet to discuss relief of black victims of the Draft Riots.

EASTERN THEATER, GETTYSBURG CAMPAIGN   Moving away from the Potomac towards Lee's army, Meade sends parties to take over the passes of the Blue Ridge Mountains. Nearby, skirmishes erupt at Ashby's Gap and Berry's Ferry.

22 JULY 1863

EASTERN THEATER, GETTYSBURG CAMPAIGN   Meade prepares an assault on Manassas Gap in the Blue Ridge Mountains, Virginia, hoping to open a route for his men into the Shenandoah Valley; there they could intercept Lee's column as it moves south through the Valley.

23 JULY 1863

EASTERN THEATER, GETTYSBURG CAMPAIGN   Federal forces under General W H French push through Manassas Gap only to meet stiff resistance from Confederates; while French is delayed, the Southern Corps of Longstreet and Hill move south out of reach down the Shenandoah. Meade has thus failed to cut Lee's army in two.

24 JULY 1863

EASTERN THEATER, GETTYSBURG CAMPAIGN   Meade's forces enter the Shenandoah Valley, Virginia, to find, as they did at Williamsport, that the enemy has gone; Union troops then continue to Warrenton.

WESTERN THEATER   The Federal siege of Battery Wagner in Charleston Harbor continues with heavy shelling of the stronghold from Union ships. The remnants of Morgan's raiders continue to be harassed by Federal pursuers at Washington and Athens, Ohio.

26 JULY 1863

WESTERN THEATER   Confederate raider John Hunt Morgan and the last of his men are brought to bay at New Lisbon, Ohio. Since crossing the Ohio River they have averaged 21 hours a day in the saddle and have covered large distances on what was nonetheless a strategically pointless expedition, especially since hoped-for Copperhead support in Ohio and Indiana has failed to materialize. As one commentator later observes, 'This reckless adventure... deprived [Morgan] of his well-earned reputation.' Morgan and his officers are sent to Ohio State Penitentiary, from which he later escapes.

28 *JULY* 1863

EASTERN THEATER, GETTYSBURG CAMPAIGN Confederate Partisan Ranger J S Mosby begins a series of daring harassing maneuvers around Meade's army; his raiders strike quickly and disappear.

1 *AUGUST* 1863

THE CONFEDERACY The growing incidence of desertion in the Confederate army, balanced with the increasingly desperate need for manpower, leads President Davis to offer amnesty to those absent without leave. He then writes that the citizens of the South have no choice but 'victory, or subjugation, slavery and utter ruin of yourselves, your families, and your country.'

EASTERN THEATER, GETTYSBURG CAMPAIGN Brandy Station, scene of a June cavalry battle, sees another skirmish between the opposing cavalries of Lee and Meade, as minor encounters continue.

WESTERN THEATER Federals begin organizing further troop actions in Charleston Harbor, South Carolina.

NAVAL Confederate raids on Federal shipping increase on the Mississippi; D D Porter is given command of Union naval forces on the river.

4 *AUGUST* 1863

WESTERN THEATER Bombardment continues in Charleston Harbor, as Federals prepare for action the immense 'Swamp Angel,' a 200-pound Parrott gun which fires incendiary shells.

6 *AUGUST* 1863

NAVAL The British-built CSS *Alabama* captures the Federal bark *Sea Bride* near the Cape of Good Hope.

8 *AUGUST* 1863

THE CONFEDERACY Lee, dejected and in ill health, writes President Davis offering his resignation as commander of the Army of the Potomac. Davis refuses the request, writing, 'our country could not bear to lose you.'

10 *AUGUST* 1863

TRANS-MISSISSIPPI A Federal expedition to Little Rock, Arkansas begins as troops led by General Fredrick Steele leave Helena, Arkansas.

11 *AUGUST* 1863

WESTERN THEATER Federal preparations for an offensive in Charleston Harbor are stopped by heavy shelling from Fort Sumter and Battery Wagner.

12 *AUGUST* 1863

WESTERN THEATER Northern artillery, using their accurate Parrott guns, once again commence heavy shelling of the forts in Charleston Harbor, as a new offensive begins.

16 *AUGUST* 1863

WESTERN THEATER, CHICKAMAUGA CAMPAIGN After much delay and official prodding, the Federal Army of the Cumberland under Rosecrans moves eastward from Tullahoma toward the Tennessee River; the goal is Chattanooga and Braxton Bragg's Army of Tennessee. At the same time, Union General Burnside moves down from the Lexington, Kentucky area toward eastern Tennessee. Rosecrans plans to envelop the Confederates between himself and Burnside; anticipating this strategy, Bragg reorganizes his troops, requesting all available reinforcements. South of Chattanooga, Federal Generals Thomas and McCook are brought up to threaten Bragg's only railway link. The stage and the principal actors are now preparing for the complex, protracted, and bloody engagements of the Chickamauga and Chattanooga Campaigns in southern Tennessee.

17 *AUGUST* 1863

WESTERN THEATER Fort Sumter in Charleston receives its first major bombardment from Union land and naval batteries. Its brick walls begin to be demolished, but the 5009 shells rained on the fort in the next eight days cause few casualties among the defenders and no exploitable breaches in the walls.

18 *AUGUST* 1863

WASHINGTON President Lincoln fires a few test rounds of the Union's new Spencer Repeating Carbine, a rifle soon to give Federal soldiers an important advantage over the South's muzzle-loaders.

20 *AUGUST* 1863

TRANS-MISSISSIPPI In Arizona Territory Colonel 'Kit' Carson moves against the Navaho Indians, who have been engaged in actions against settlers since the United States occupied New Mexico in 1846.

21 *AUGUST* 1863

WESTERN THEATER, CHICKAMAUGA CAMPAIGN Rosecrans' forces reach the Tennessee River outside Chattanooga and begin preparations for the coming offensive. TRANS-MISSISSIPPI Around 450 irregular Confederate raiders under William Clarke Quantrill stage a dawn terrorist raid on Lawrence, Kansas, leaving 150 civilians dead, 30 wounded, and much of the town a smoking ruin. In 1862 Quantrill had been denied a commission by Confederate Secretary of War J A Seddon, who termed his notions of war 'barbarism.' For some time the town of Lawrence has been strongly Unionist and abolitionist, thus earning Quantrill's enmity. This strategically pointless raid demonstrates a certain Southern loss of faith in conventional military operations, and many in the South find this and later similar actions disturbing to their sense of divine approval for the Confederate cause: one raider has shouted into the window of a woman whose husband he

has just murdered, 'We are friends from Hell!'

22 *AUGUST* 1863

WESTERN THEATER In Charleston Harbor, the Swamp Angel, pride of the Federal battery, blows itself up on the 36th round. As one observer later noted, 'The [gun] turned out to have been more destructive to Union gun crews than to Rebel property.'

23 *AUGUST* 1863

WESTERN THEATER Union batteries cease their first bombardment of Fort Sumter, leaving it a mass of rubble but still unconquered.

25 *AUGUST* 1863

WESTERN THEATER A Union offensive fails to overrun Confederate rifle pits before Battery Wagner in Charleston Harbor. TRANS-MISSISSIPPI In the wake of Quantrill's terrorist raid on Lawrence, Kansas, the Federal commander in Kansas City issues a misguided and ineffective anti-guerrilla directive ordering many civilians in the area out of their homes; much property and crops are destroyed, and 20,000 are left homeless. Resentment over these measures is to last for years.

26 *AUGUST* 1863

WESTERN THEATER Confederate rifle pits before Battery Wagner are captured in a second Union effort.

29 *AUGUST* 1863

NAVAL In Charleston Harbor, South Carolina, the experimental Confederate submarine *H L Hunley* sinks on a test cruise, drowning five crewmen. The ship is soon raised and is later to see action.

30 *AUGUST* 1863

WESTERN THEATER Heavy Federal shelling resumes on Fort Sumter. Confederates within the fort, meanwhile, are

Field Headquarters of the New York Herald.

opposed, and begins to suspect that Bragg is fleeing him. Elsewhere, dwindling supplies of food and clothing result in protests and looting by women in Mobile, Alabama.

engaged in digging their cannon out of the rubble and moving them into Charleston for the anticipated defense of the city.

1 *SEPTEMBER* 1863

WESTERN THEATER Union batteries pour 627 rounds into Fort Sumter near Charleston, reducing its walls to still smaller fragments but not dislodging its defenders.

CHICKAMAUGA CAMPAIGN Moving toward Chattanooga, Rosecrans' Army of the Cumberland begins a four-day crossing of the Tennessee River largely unopposed by Bragg's Army of Tennessee. Bragg, meanwhile, receives two divisions of reinforcements.

2 *SEPTEMBER* 1863

WESTERN THEATER With no opposition, Federal General Burnside's troops occupy Knoxville, Tennessee to remain there as a resource for Union forces in Chattanooga.

4 *SEPTEMBER* 1863

WESTERN THEATER Union General Ulysses S Grant, in a perhaps inebriated mishap, is fallen on by his horse in New Orleans; the general, soon to be called to Chattanooga, will be partly lame for some weeks.

CHICKAMAUGA CAMPAIGN In Chattanooga, Rosecrans completes his army's crossing of the Tennessee, still nearly un-

5 *SEPTEMBER* 1863

WESTERN THEATER, CHICKAMAUGA CAMPAIGN Rosecrans, convinced that Bragg's Army of Tennessee is evacuating Chattanooga, moves into the Georgia mountains south of the city. Determined to pursue the supposed Confederate retreat, the Union commander takes the risky step of separating his army into three groups in order to go as quickly as possible through three widely-spaced gaps in the mountains.

INTERNATIONAL Despite Federal protests, British shipbuilders have for some time been constructing vessels for the Confederacy, the most successful of which is the CSS *Alabama*; this ship has been preying on Federal commerce since mid-1862 and has captured or destroyed over 60 Union ships. Finally responding to Washington's protests, the British government on this day seizes in Liverpool's Laird shipyards two newly-built ironclads with ramming spars that have been ordered by the Confederacy. This seizure of the so-called 'Laird Rams' halts the growth of the Confederate Navy and ends the last major diplomatic crisis between Washington and Britain during the war.

6 *SEPTEMBER* 1863

WESTERN THEATER, CHICKAMAUGA CAMPAIGN As Federal troops close around his city, General Bragg, perhaps fearing a repeat of the siege of Vicksburg, decides to evacuate Chattanooga. In Charleston, Confederate commander P G Beauregard decides that it would be too costly to fight the coming Union assault on Battery Wagner and Battery Gregg. He evacuates the forts. Fort Sumter, by now nearly a heap of brick dust, still holds out.

7 *SEPTEMBER* 1863

WESTERN THEATER The Federal infantry assault on Batteries Wagner and Gregg finds the enemy evacuated.

8 *SEPTEMBER* 1863

TRANS-MISSISSIPPI Federal transports and three gunboats from New Orleans enter the Sabine Pass in Texas to attack a small Confederate defensive fort. Within an hour two Union ships have been disabled and one forced to surrender with a loss of some 70 men. The operation is soon abandoned, with the North having sustained a minor but embarassing defeat that considerably boosts the spirits of Western Confederates.

WESTERN THEATER, CHICKAMAUGA CAMPAIGN Bragg's troops, now numbering some 65,000, march out of Chattanooga and withdraw toward Lafayette, Georgia.

9 *SEPTEMBER* 1863

WESTERN THEATER, CHICKAMAUGA CAMPAIGN The Federal Army of the Cumberland is now spread in three groups north to south across 40 miles of mountains. The northernmost group, under Crittenden (whose brother is a Southern general), advances through Chattanooga while the others, Thomas in the middle and McCook many miles to the south, pursue what Rosecrans believes to be a fleeing enemy. Indeed, by now the Federal commander is convinced he will chase Bragg to Atlanta if not to the sea. In fact, the Union army is racing into a very clever trap. Though some of Bragg's staff, who dislike their harsh and fractious commander and serve him badly, are later to insist he has not planned it, there is little doubt that Bragg has constructed his trap well, and that it has every chance of success: his army, now outnumbering Rosecrans', is gathering at Lafayette, Georgia, and preparing to defeat the widely-separated Federal forces one group at a time.

In Virginia, Longstreet's divisions have departed from Lee's army and are beginning a long railway journey to reinforce Bragg; they will arrive on 18 and 19 September.

10 *SEPTEMBER* 1863

WESTERN THEATER, CHICKAMAUGA CAMPAIGN Having created a brilliant trap, Bragg and his staff now proceed to spring it ineptly and too soon. Before the Federals are totally committed, Bragg orders an attack at McLemore's Cove, but it fails to be mounted. During the day both Crittenden and Thomas discover strong parties of the enemy in their paths, and both are able to fall back and regroup. It is soon to become clear to the whole Federal staff that Bragg is by no means retreating.

TRANS-MISSISSIPPI Federal forces occupy Little Rock, Arkansas, after Confederate forces evacuate; this development poses a serious threat to the Confederate Trans-Mississippi area.

11 *SEPTEMBER* 1863

WESTERN THEATER, CHICKAMAUGA CAMPAIGN Once again Bragg orders an attack on isolated Federal forces and once again it fails to materialize.

KNOXVILLE CAMPAIGN Burnside, still occupying the city, offers his resignation to Lincoln; the President refuses the resignation and asks Andrew Johnson to form a Union state government.

12 *SEPTEMBER* 1863

WESTERN THEATER, CHICKAMAUGA CAMPAIGN By this time Rosecrans has realized the perilous position of his armies, divided in the face of concentrated enemy

The Battle of Chickamauga.

167

forces. Urgent orders are issued to his wings to move toward the center. McCook's forces to the south begin after midnight an exhausting 57-mile journey through the mountains that will unite them with Thomas on the 17th. Meanwhile, Bragg has ordered General Polk to attack next day a part of Crittenden's forces at Lee and Gordon's Mill on Chickamauga Creek.

13 *SEPTEMBER* 1863

EASTERN THEATER Weakened by Longstreet's removal to Tennessee, Lee's forces withdraw across the Rapidan River. Meade's army moves from the Rapahannock to the Rapidan, occupying Culpeper Court House.

WESTERN THEATER, CHICKAMAUGA CAMPAIGN Bragg arrives at Lee and Gordon's Mill expecting to find Crittenden's XXI Corps annihilated by Polk, as planned in his orders; instead, he finds that Polk has made no move and that Crittenden has safely concentrated his forces. Yet again, Bragg's plans have been frustrated by subordinates. His trap has failed. He and his army now wait for reinforcements and for the arrival of the enemy from the west.

15 *SEPTEMBER* 1863

WASHINGTON As Meade's advance to the Rapidan is completed, Lincoln writes that the Union army should attack Lee at once.

17 *SEPTEMBER* 1863

WESTERN THEATER, CHICKAMAUGA CAMPAIGN Union troops move toward concentration around Lee and Gordon's Mill on Chickamauga Creek. By the end of the day the divided forces are within supporting distance of one another. Bragg, now on the east bank of the creek, begins to develop his battle plan: he will turn the Union left flank and get behind Rosecrans' army, cutting off the roads to Chattanooga. The stage is now set for the bloodiest battle of the war in the Western Theater. It is

prophetic that the ancient Cherokee Indian name for this creek is *Chickamauga*, meaning 'River of Death.'

18 *SEPTEMBER* 1863

WESTERN THEATER, CHICKAMAUGA CAMPAIGN Bragg has planned a major attack this day, but cannot get his forces to the west bank of Chickamauga Creek in time. Extensive cavalry skirmishes break out at various locations. The first of Longstreet's forces arrive from Virginia. All day and night Rosecrans is busy concentrating and placing his troops, anticipating Bragg's plan to attack his left and get behind him. Because of the dense woods in the area, broken only by a few small fields, neither commander can determine the strength and position of his enemy; moreover, it is difficult for commanders to observe their own positions, a factor which will be of serious consequence to the battle.

19 *SEPTEMBER* 1863

WESTERN THEATER, CHICKAMAUGA CAMPAIGN Dawn finds both fronts solidly facing one another along a six-mile line. A Northern captain describes the feelings of the soldiers before the battle: 'Through that forenoon we saw the constantly moving columns of the enemy's infantry and saw battery after battery as they moved before us like a great panorama. In such moments men grow pale and lose their nerve. They are hungry but they can not eat; they are tired, but they can not sit down. You speak to them, and they answer as if half asleep; they laugh, but the laugh has no joy in it.' The fighting begins almost by accident. Thomas sends one of his divisions to reconnoiter near the creek on the Union left; these troops suddenly encounter the dismounted cavalry of Nathan Bedford Forrest, who returns fire and calls for infantry help. Soon hostilities have erupted along most of the battle line. Throughout the ensuing day of intermittent but fierce fighting, Bragg throws his strongest efforts against the Union left, pursuing his plan to get behind the enemy and cut them off from Chattanooga. Rosecrans responds by moving division after division to his left, extending his battle line north. By the end of the day losses are enormous on both sides, but neither has gained any significant advantage. The battle sinks to a standstill: dead men blanket the thick woods, wounded men crawl toward the rear, stretchermen carry hundreds to the overworked field hospitals which are soon marked by bloody heaps of amputated limbs.

During the afternoon Longstreet has arrived with the bulk of his troops; it takes him until II o'clock at night to locate Bragg, who gets out of bed for a conference. The plan for the following day is decided upon: Polk will attack at dawn in the north, and the attack will be joined successively by companies down the line southward, to climax with an all-out assault by Longstreet on the Union right. Meanwhile, Rosecrans decides on a defensive strategy and his men begin building rough breastworks.

20 *SEPTEMBER* 1863

WESTERN THEATER, CHICKAMAUGA CAMPAIGN   At dawn, Bragg, unable in the dense forest and morning fog to see his troops, waits for the sound of Polk's attack. After over an hour of inactivity, he sends a messenger to Polk, who is discovered to be comfortably breakfasting in a farmhouse. To the query about his attack, Polk replies, 'Do tell General Bragg that my heart is overflowing with anxiety for the attack—overflowing with anxiety, sir.' This being reported back to Bragg, the commander swears 'in a manner that would have powerfully assisted a mule team in getting up a mountain,' and about 9.30 AM hours orders his right flank into attack against Thomas on the Union left. Once again the Confederates struggle determinedly to flank the Federals; but Thomas's men hold at the breastworks and, as it did the day previous, the fighting sways back and forth indecisively. Then about eleven o'clock that morning there occurs a strange and fatal error.

Union commander Rosecrans, mistaken as to the location of his divisions in the thick brush, orders T J Wood to close up on and 'support' J J Reynolds, whom he supposes to be immediately on Wood's left; Rosecrans' order is thus intended to tighten his battle line. But in fact, there is another whole division between Wood and Reynolds. Wood, taking the order literally, pulls back out of the line and moves left toward Reynolds, thereby leaving a gaping hole in the Union line. But before Wood has completed his withdrawal, Longstreet, whether because he has seen the withdrawal or whether through a coincidence fortuitous to say the least, charges in a solid column directly into this gap, with devastating effect.

The Union line has been cut in two, the right wing is in disorderly rout and Thomas's men are being pushed left toward Snodgrass Hill. Thousands of Federals are killed or captured, the rest are running. Along with McCook and Crittenden, a panicky and demoralized Rosecrans flees to Chattanooga, assuming his whole army is being destroyed. But Rosecrans is wrong. On the Federal left Thomas has maintained firm control of his troops, and assumes a virtually impregnable position on Snodgrass Hill. For the rest of the day, Thomas's men desperately turn back wave after wave of attacks, several of them hand-to-hand, as nearly the whole Confederate army swarms up the precipitous slopes. At three o'clock in the afternoon, when Thomas is nearly out of ammunition and is threatened from the rear, he is reinforced from the north by General Granger, who has fortunately violated his morning's orders to keep his Reserve Corps in place. With Granger's men and bullets, Thomas holds the position until nightfall and then withdraws in good order toward Chattanooga. His army's heroic defense has saved the Union forces from utter rout, and General George Henry Thomas will hereafter come to be known as the 'Rock of Chickamauga.'

The battle losses on both sides are staggering. In two days of fighting the Union has 1656 killed, 9756 wounded, and 4757 missing, totaling 16,169 casualties; the Confederates have 2132 dead, 14,674 wounded, 1468 missing, totaling 18,274. Both sides have lost about 28 percent of their strength. The battle is unusual in that the crucial decisions have been taken largely by subordinate officers, especially Longstreet for the South and Thomas for the North.

21 SEPTEMBER 1863

WESTERN THEATER, CHATTANOOGA CAMPAIGN As the ragged and demoralized Union army gathers in Chattanooga, Bragg is urged by Longstreet to move quickly against the retreating enemy; but he does not give the orders until four o'clock in the afternoon, too late to reach the city, thus giving the Federals time to organize their defenses. In Knoxville, Burnside receives a wire from Lincoln: 'Go to Rosecrans with your forces, without a moment's delay.' Burnside, pressed by enemy forces, stays put.

22 SEPTEMBER 1863

WASHINGTON Lincoln mourns the death at Chickamauga of his brother-in-law, Confederate General Ben Hardin Helm. WESTERN THEATER, CHATTANOOGA CAMPAIGN Bragg orders an attack on Federal positions below Missionary Ridge in Chattanooga; the troops reach the area to find the enemy 'ready to receive and entertain us . . . we expected to be flung against the forts to certain destruction.' Realizing the Federals have now firmly dug in, Bragg cancels the attack. By failing to pursue the Federal retreat before it can organize, Bragg has missed his second great opportunity to destroy the Union army. Now, as his forces occupy the commanding heights of Missionary Ridge and Lookout Mountain, his third and final opportunity takes shape. A few days after having thought they were chasing the Confederates to Atlanta, the Federals find themselves defeated and besieged.

23 SEPTEMBER 1863

WASHINGTON Lincoln and his cabinet hold an urgent meeting about the crisis in Chattanooga. It is decided to send by rail Hooker's two corps from the Army of the Potomac, still in Virginia, to Alabama in support of Rosecrans. By 25 September the troops are entrained and moving south with extraordinary speed. By 15 November, 17,000 of these and other reinforcements will have arrived at Bridgeport, Alabama, along with thousands of horses and mules.

25 SEPTEMBER 1863

WASHINGTON Lincoln, angry at Burnside's failure to aid Rosecrans, writes in an unsent letter that he has been 'struggling- . . . to get you to assist General Rosecrans in an extremity, and you have repeatedly declared you would do it, and yet you steadily move the contrary way.'

28 SEPTEMBER 1863

WESTERN THEATER, CHATTANOOGA CAMPAIGN Bragg is informed by President Davis that Union reinforcements are en route. Rosecrans, attempting to justify his handling of the battle—especially in regard to charges that he advanced recklessly and lost his nerve after Longstreet's attack—brings his own charges against subordinates McCook and Crittenden, who are ordered to Indianapolis for a court of inquiry. Eventually the two generals are exonerated, and history will tend to confirm the charges against Rosecrans, who is a hard-working and methodical leader but often excitable and ineffective on the battlefield.

30 SEPTEMBER 1863

WESTERN THEATER, CHATTANOOGA CAMPAIGN Bragg has thought that Rosecrans might evacuate Chattanooga, but seeing that the Federals show no signs of leaving, he orders cavalry raids by Wheeler on Union lines of communication; these raids continue into October.

2 OCTOBER 1863

WESTERN THEATER, CHATTANOOGA CAM-
PAIGN Hooker's men begin to arrive in
Bridgeport, Alabama, eventually to support
Union forces in Chattanooga. During the
next two days 20,000 men and 3000 horses
and mules will arrive, all having traveled
1159 miles by rail in just over a week. Meanwhile, Confederate cavalry troops continue
to raid vital Union supply lines, closing the
route between Bridgeport and Chattanooga and forcing Rosecrans to rely on a
long, muddy and mountainous wagon road
on the north side of the Tennessee River. A
later Southern raid on this route destroys in
one day 300 wagons and 1800 mules.
Though the Confederates cannot shut off
Union supplies entirely, the specter of
famine looms for the besieged Army of the
Cumberland.

3 OCTOBER 1863

WESTERN THEATER, CHATTANOOGA CAM-
PAIGN Wheeler's cavalry raids continue
on troops and supply routes around Chattanooga. A six-day bombardment of Fort
Sumter in Charleston Harbor ends with
560 rounds having been fired to no particular effect.

5 OCTOBER 1863

WESTERN THEATER, CHATTANOOGA CAM-
PAIGN Wheeler's cavalry breaks a vital
Union supply line by destroying a bridge at
Stone's River, near Murfreesboro. The
Confederate raiders will be very active in
the coming days all around eastern Tennessee. In Chattanooga the famine
deepens among Federal troops; draft
mules are dying by the hundreds, with
cavalry and artillery horses weakening.
Soldiers are seen searching in the dust for
grains of corn dropped by their animals.
NAVAL In an attempt to loosen the
Federal blockade of Charleston Harbor,
the Confederate semi-submersible
steamship *David* hits the Federal ironclad
New Ironsides with a spar torpedo. Damage
to the Union ship is extensive but not critical, and two of the *David*'s four crew are

captured; the other two crew take the near-
ly-swamped ship back to Charleston. This
is the first successful Southern semi-
submersible attack of the war; the only Union attempt at a submersible, the *Alligator*,
sank under tow in April 1863, after several
unsuccessful trials. In general, the experimental submarines of both sides
throughout the war cause more fatalities to
crews than to enemies.

9 OCTOBER 1863

EASTERN THEATER, BRISTOE CAMPAIGN
Lee, still outnumbered but wishing to capi-
talize on Meade's loss of Hooker's troops
sent to reinforce Alabama, moves his Army
from the Rapidan to the west and north. He
is trying to flank Meade's army and drive
them from the west. Over the next month
Lee forces Meade to retreat some 40 miles
for a time, but achieves little strategic gain
other than to destroy a railroad the Federals have been repairing.
WESTERN THEATER, CHATTANOOGA CAM-
PAIGN Wheeler's Confederate cavalry
raiders return to Chattanooga having
attacked Rosecran's supply and communication lines all around east Tennessee.

10 OCTOBER 1863

EASTERN THEATER, BRISTOE CAMPAIGN
Skirmishes break out around the Rapidan
in Virginia as Lee tries to get behind the
right flank of the Army of the Potomac.
WESTERN THEATER, CHATTANOOGA CAM-
PAIGN Confederate President Davis arrives on the scene near Chattanooga to
survey the siege and to attempt mediation
in the growing feud between Bragg and his
generals.

12 OCTOBER 1863

EASTERN THEATER, BRISTOE CAMPAIGN
Amid daily skirmishings, Lee's Army of
Northern Virginia continues moving west
and north toward Manassas and Washington. Meade slowly withdraws.

13 OCTOBER 1863

THE NORTH Republican Union candidates are successful in a number of state elections. In Ohio Vallandigham, the Canadian-exiled Copperhead candidate for governor, loses decisively but still receives a surprisingly large vote.

14 OCTOBER 1863

EASTERN THEATER, BRISTOE CAMPAIGN Lee attempts to cut off Meade's withdrawal with an attack under A P Hill on Union corps near Bristoe Station. There ensues a day of inconclusive but costly maneuvering which gains no clear results; though Meade is forced back near the Potomac, his column is not broken. Lee's forces lose 1900 captured and killed to Meade's 548.

15 OCTOBER 1863

WESTERN THEATER For the second time, the Confederate submarine *H L Hunley* sinks during a practice dive in Charleston Harbor, this time drowning its inventor along with seven crew. The ship will be raised yet again.

16 OCTOBER 1863

WASHINGTON The government announces sweeping changes in the organization of its army. The Departments of Ohio, Cumberland and Tennessee are combined into the Military Division of the Mississippi, the whole to be commanded by General Ulysses S Grant. The new commander, still limping from his horse accident, is ordered to leave his post at Vicksburg and go to Illinois; his eventual destination is Chattanooga. Meanwhile, Lincoln encourages Meade, through Halleck, to attack Lee immediately; Meade, however, is not to find during the Bristoe Campaign an opportunity that suits him.

17 OCTOBER 1863

EASTERN THEATER, BRISTOE CAMPAIGN Not wishing to give Meade a chance for an attack, Lee's forces withdraw amid skirmishing away from Bull Run and toward the Rappahannock.
WESTERN THEATER En route through Illinois to Louisville, Kentucky, Grant is given his instructions by Secretary of War Stanton. Grant has his choice of commanders for the Army of the Cumberland: retain Rosecrans, or replace him with Thomas. Without comment, Grant chooses Thomas; Rosecrans, as a result of his tarnished reputation after Chickamauga, has lost the most important command of his career.

18 OCTOBER 1863

WESTERN THEATER, CHATTANOOGA CAMPAIGN General Thomas, succeeding Rosecrans in Chattanooga, declares: 'We will hold this town till we starve.' His army is close to starving as he speaks. Meanwhile, U S Grant officially takes over command of the Military Division of the Mississippi, thus being in charge of the whole area between the Mississippi River and the eastern mountains.

20 OCTOBER 1863

EASTERN THEATER, BRISTOE CAMPAIGN The Army of Northern Virginia gathers on its old line across the Rappahannock, the Bristoe Campaign having accomplished little except to add to the war's casualty statistics; between 10 and 21 October the South has lost 1381 in killed and wounded, the Union 2292 killed, wounded, and captured.

23 OCTOBER 1863

THE CONFEDERACY President Davis removes another of Bragg's quarreling subordinates, General Leonidas Polk, sending him to Mississippi. Late in the day Grant arrives in Chattanooga after an exhausting ride from Bridgeport, during which he has experienced first-hand the difficulties of the Union supply line.

24 OCTOBER 1863

WASHINGTON Once again President Lincoln prods Meade: 'With all possible expedition . . . get ready to attack Lee.'
WESTERN THEATER, CHATTANOOGA CAM-

PAIGN   In his memoirs, General Grant will describe his first day in Chattanooga: 'The men had been on half rations for a considerable time. The beef was so poor that the soldiers were in the habit of saying that they were living on "half rations of hard bread and *beef dried on the hoof*." It looked, indeed, as if but two courses were open: the one to starve, the other to surrender or be captured. As soon as I reached Chattanooga, I started out to make a personal inspection, taking Thomas with me. We crossed to the north side and reached the Tennessee at Brown's Ferry, some three miles below Lookout Mountain, unobserved by the enemy. Here we left our horses and approached the water on foot. There was a picket station of the enemy on the opposite side, in full view, and we were within easy range, but they did not fire upon us. They must have seen that we were all commissioned officers but, I suppose, they already looked on the garrison at Chattanooga as their prisoners of war. That night I issued orders for opening the route to Bridgeport—a *cracker line*, as the soldiers appropriately termed it.' The plan for the 'cracker line' is partly Grant's and partly Rosecrans'—by various means a river route to Bridgeport is to be opened. Meanwhile, from his position on Missionary Ridge, Bragg has become confident about his advantage over the Union army. His advantage, though, is shortly to be lessened.

26 OCTOBER 1863

WESTERN THEATER, CHATTANOOGA CAMPAIGN   In the first step to opening the cracker line, Hooker's men from Virginia leave Bridgeport, Alabama, and move across the Tennessee toward Chattanooga. Elsewhere, another major Union bombardment commences in Charleston Harbor.

27 OCTOBER 1863

WESTERN THEATER, CHATTANOOGA CAMPAIGN   At three in the morning, 1500 Federals drift silently down the Tennessee River in pontoons to Brown's Ferry; the pontoons are destined to form a bridge for Hooker's men to enter Chattanooga. The plan works—with only light resistance Hazen's men are established on the far shore, the bridge is laid, and Hooker's forces move over it. The cracker line is now open and Chattanooga is reinforced; shortly, supplies will arrive from Bridgeport. Meanwhile, in Charleston Harbor, 625 shots are fired at Fort Sumter, which has now become more a symbol of Confederate resistance (as well as Federal persistance) than a military objective.

28 OCTOBER 1863

WESTERN THEATER, CHATTANOOGA CAMPAIGN   General Bragg, having failed to prevent the establishment of the Union bridgehead at Brown's Ferry, orders troops under Longstreet to attack on this night an isolated division of Hooker's army at Wauhatchie. This being one of the rare night attacks of the war, the fighting is extremely confused; on both sides the officers scarcely know where the enemy is. After intensive fighting, the Confederates are driven back; each side suffers over 400 casualties. The cracker line will not be seriously challenged again.

29 OCTOBER 1863

WESTERN THEATER   Federal batteries send 2691 shells into Fort Sumter, killing 33 of the defenders. The stepped-up firing will continue for days, but the fort will not surrender.

30 OCTOBER 1863

WESTERN THEATER, CHATTANOOGA CAMPAIGN   The little Federal steamship *Chattanooga*, built on the upper Tennessee River, arrives in Chattanooga with 40,000 rations and tons of feed. Union soldiers and animals are back on full rations and are no longer quite so firmly besieged. Although no men have starved during the siege, Chattanooga is covered with thousands of dead horses and mules, many of them having starved to death.

CHRONOLOGY

2 NOVEMBER 1863

WASHINGTON President Lincoln is invited to the dedication of a new cemetery at Gettysburg and asked to make 'a few appropriate remarks'; actually, his words are intended to be something of a benediction to the main address by orator and statesman Edward Everett. Lincoln, who rarely gets out of Washington these days, accepts the invitation.

4 NOVEMBER 1863

WESTERN THEATER, CHATTANOOGA CAMPAIGN In a move that dangerously weakens his forces around Chattanooga, Bragg sends Longstreet's corps, including Wheeler's cavalry, to reinforce Confederate troops around Knoxville, which is still occupied by Burnside's Union army. The decision to send these 20,000 men has in fact been made by President Davis, and is to some extent another response to friction among his generals—Bragg and Longstreet do not get along. This shifting of forces poses an immediate threat to Knoxville; Grant makes a tactical decision not to weaken his own army by reinforcing Burnside, but rather to attack the weakened Bragg as soon as possible and only then to mass his forces against Longstreet. Before he can attack, though, Grant must await the arrival by rail of Sherman's forces, now delayed by the necessity of repairing their own rail route.

6 NOVEMBER 1863

EASTERN THEATER Hostilities break out at Droop Mountain, West Virginia, where advancing Federal troops under Brigadier General W A Averell find a Confederate force holding the road. Averell manages to envelop the enemy and scatter them, after which he continues his expedition against remaining enemy troops and rail links in West Virginia.

7 NOVEMBER 1863

EASTERN THEATER, BRISTOE CAMPAIGN In a maneuver against Lee's Confederate forces, Meade sends troops across the Rapahannock near Kelly's Ford. The first Union attacks do not move the enemy, but at dusk an advance by two Union brigades, including one of the rare bayonet attacks of the war, succeeds in overrunning the Confederate positions and taking a bridgehead. Two Confederate divisions lose 2023 in dead and captured, a figure which shocks the Southern Army. Lee withdraws to the Rapidan, and the contending armies have thus returned to the positions they held at the beginning of the Bristoe Campaign.

9 NOVEMBER 1863

WASHINGTON Pursuing one of his favorite pastimes, President Lincoln attends the theater; he enjoys a play called *The Marble Heart*, starring John Wilkes Booth.

10 NOVEMBER 1863

WESTERN THEATER The unconquerable mound of rubble called Fort Sumter has received 1753 Federal rounds since 7 November. This bombardment has so far killed no defenders, but Union batteries keep firing.

12 NOVEMBER 1863

WESTERN THEATER, KNOXVILLE CAMPAIGN Confederate General Longstreet arrives at Loudon, Tennessee; he and Wheeler are directed to organize an assault on Burnside at Knoxville.

15 NOVEMBER 1863

WESTERN THEATER, CHATTANOOGA CAMPAIGN Federal General Sherman arrives, en route to Chattanooga, at Bridgeport, Alabama with 17,000 men; they have moved 675 miles by boat, rail, and foot. Sherman himself joins Grant in Chattanooga for briefings on the impending offensive. Wheeler's Confederate cavalrymen cross the Tennessee River and join Longstreet's infantry.

16 NOVEMBER 1863

WESTERN THEATER, KNOXVILLE CAM-

PAIGN   At Campbell's Station near Knoxville, Confederate General Longstreet tries and fails to cut off Burnside's retreat into Knoxville. The Federals are now driven back to the city, but Confederate forces lack the means of mounting a regular siege.

17 *NOVEMBER* 1863

WASHINGTON   President Lincoln begins to write his speech for the dedication of the military cemetery at Gettysburg. Contrary to the later tradition that the speech was written hastily on the train, his address is a carefully-considered and much-labored-over statement.

18 *NOVEMBER* 1863

WASHINGTON   A special train leaves the Capital for Gettysburg carrying President Lincoln, Secretary of State Seward, and other notables, including the French ambassador.

19 *NOVEMBER* 1863

THE NORTH, GETTYSBURG ADDRESS   A crowd of 15,000 people gathers for the dedication of the military cemetery at Gettysburg. Edward Everett, the main speaker, gives a brilliant two-hour historical discourse on the battle, using information furnished by Meade and other Union officers. After Everett concludes, Lincoln rises and in his high toneless voice gives his 'little speech'. When he has finished, the reception is polite but unenthusiastic; the President considers the address a 'flat failure'. Over the next few days it receives a few compliments, Everett assuring the President that the speech said more in two minutes than he said in two hours. It is perhaps natural that no one at the time can foresee that these ten sentences would come to be considered one of the most moving and exquisite utterances in the language.

20 *NOVEMBER* 1863

WESTERN THEATER, CHATTANOOGA CAMPAIGN   Grant's plans have called for an attack on Confederate positions on the day following, but as Sherman's forces begin to arrive at Brown's Ferry near the city, heavy rains delay preparations for the battle.

KNOXVILLE CAMPAIGN   Confederate General Longstreet prepares an attack on a salient of Fort Sanders in Knoxville but delays the attack for over a week to await further reinforcements from Chattanooga and to have his plans checked by Bragg's chief engineer.

21 *NOVEMBER* 1863

WASHINGTON   Lincoln has become ill with a mild form of smallpox. As he takes to his bed, the President comments, 'At last I have something I can give everybody.' This is a low point in his presidency.

WESTERN THEATER, CHATTANOOGA CAMPAIGN   Federal commander U S Grant has developed his plan of battle: Sherman's forces on the Union left wing will attempt to overrun the north end of Missionary Ridge; following this, Hooker will create a 'demonstration' on the right wing, moving part way up Lookout Mountain and diverting troops from the enemy center to meet his advance; after this, Thomas will commence the main attack in the center of the Confederate entrenchments on the ridge. Bragg remains sanguine about his position, regarding his army as impregnable: Even during the battle he will reassure an anxious bystander, 'Madam, are you mad? There are not enough Yankees in Chattanooga to come up here. Those are all my prisoners.' In accordance with Grant's plan, General Sherman's troops begin moving to the left flank.

22 *NOVEMBER* 1863

WESTERN THEATER, CHATTANOOGA CAMPAIGN   Changing plans on the eve of battle, Grant now orders Thomas's men to make a demonstration' in front of Missionary Ridge on the following day; the main engagement is to begin on 24 November.

CHRONOLOGY

23 NOVEMBER 1863

WESTERN THEATER, BATTLE OF CHATTA-NOOGA At dawn Union batteries open up on Missionary Ridge. Confederate cannon return the fire. Soon thereafter, Southern troops on the ridge are entertained by the appearance below their positions of 20,000 Union troops, clad in their best uniforms and marching in perfect ranks, bayonets gleaming, to the vigorous music of military bands. The Rebels watch calmly, assuming a grand parade is under way. Suddenly the parade wheels and charges furiously up the slopes: the Battle of Chattanooga has begun. In short order Federal troops overrun Orchard Knob, a hill between Chattanooga and Missionary Ridge. Grant orders reinforcements and entrenchments on the Knob, which will become his command post the following day. The Union has established a beachhead on Confederate positions.

24 NOVEMBER 1863

WESTERN THEATER, BATTLE OF CHATTA-NOOGA After midnight, Sherman's troops move across the Tennessee River. One of his men describes the operation: 'My regiment was in Sherman's corps. We had marched twenty miles a day. Now this corps was to form the left of Grant's forces, cross a deep river in the darkness and assault the nearly inaccessible position of Bragg's army. That night we lay in bivouac in the woods close by the Tennessee River. We knew that 116 rude pontoon boats had been built for us and were lying hidden in a creek near by. We had almost no rations for the army. As for the horses and mules, they had already starved to death by the thousands and were lying around everywhere. . . . At two o'clock we heard some splashing in the water . . . the boats had come for us. . . Quietly, two by two, we slipped down to the water's edge and stepped into the rude flatboats. "There's room for thirty in a boat," said a tall man . . . who stood on the bank near us in the darkness. Few of us had ever before heard the voice of our beloved commander. Sherman's personal presence, his sharing the danger we were about to undertake, gave us confidence. In a quarter of an hour a thousand of us were out in the middle of the river afloat in the darkness. Silently we sat there, our rifles and our spades across our knees . . . In half an hour we were out on the opposite bank and creeping through the thicket, a spade in one hand and a rifle in the other . . . we formed in line of battle and commenced digging holes for ourselves. We worked like beavers, turn about: no spade was idle for one moment. Daylight found us there, two thousand strong, with rifle pits a mile in length. Other brigades got over the river, pontoons soon were down . . . What a sight for General Bragg when he woke up that morning at his headquarters perch on top of Missionary Ridge!'

By one o'clock that afternoon Sherman's forces are across the new pontoon bridge and moving to attack the north end of Missionary Ridge. Meanwhile, Hooker is initiating his 'demonstration' on Lookout Mountain, which is in fact only lightly occupied by Confederates. A dense fog enshrouds the slopes, and Hooker's advance is not discovered until his troops are a few yards away from the enemy. Federals steadily push the few defenders back up the rough and cloud-covered slopes; by noon a Confederate stand at Craven's Farm has been driven back, and Hooker's troops entrench just below the summit. The remaining Confederates withdraw during the night. Hooker's advance, considerably exaggerated as to difficulty, is known to history as 'The Battle Above the Clouds', on account of the heavy fog that obscures the fighting. On the left wing, Sherman has by four o'clock in the afternoon encountered only enemy outposts as he seizes what his map tells him is the northern end of Missionary Ridge; he is surprised to discover that he has only occupied an outlying hill—a large and exposed ravine separates him from Missionary Ridge proper. Both he and the Confederates opposite on the ridge begin to strengthen their positions. By the end of the day Union efforts are victorious all down the line,

25 *NOVEMBER* 1863

WESTERN THEATER, BATTLE OF CHATTA-
NOOGA Before sunrise, Hooker sends
detachments up the slopes of Lookout
Mountain, from which the last defenders
have withdrawn during the night; dawn reveals to the Union army below the Stars
and Stripes flying at the summit, and soldiers cheer amid their preparations for battle. From his command post on Orchard
Knob, Grant orders his wings to advance,
Sherman in the north and Hooker in the
south, and holds his main attack on the
center until the flanks have gained some
ground and diverted enemy forces.
However, both these attacks soon bog
down. Sherman is repulsed on the left as
Bragg moves troops and cannon from the
Confederate center to resist the attack.

The fighting between Sherman's and
Bragg's forces sways back and forth until
midafternoon, with Grant moving reinforcements from his center and Bragg
moving troops and cannon from his center
to resist the attack. Fearing that his main
attack on the center is being fatally delayed,
around three o'clock in the afternoon
Grant signals Thomas's men to begin the
assault on the heavily entrenched enemy
center at the top of Missionary Ridge. Certain there will be fierce resistance, Grant
has ordered his troops to stop halfway up
the slope and reorganize. In his memoirs,
Grant will describe the attack: 'In an in-

credibly short time Generals Sheridan and
Wood were driving the enemy before them
toward Missionary Ridge . . . Our men
drove the troops in front of the lower line of
rifle pits so rapidly, and followed them so
closely, that Rebel and Union troops went
over the first line of works almost at the
same time . . . The retreating hordes being
between friends and pursuers caused the
enemy to fire high to avoid killing their own
men. In fact, on that occasion the Union
soldier nearest the enemy was in the safest
position.' This situation results in what
seems to observers at the time to be an
incomprehensible breach of orders. Rather
than stopping to reorganize as ordered,
Federal soldiers continue their charge up
the ridge without pause; to do otherwise
will leave them open to a murderous fire
from the crest. Not understanding this, a
furious Grant turns and asks Thomas,
'Who ordered those men up the hill?' Thomas speculates that they must have ordered
themselves. Grant replies, 'Someone will
suffer for it, if it turns out badly.' But the
attack, one of the most spectacular of its
kind in history, an advance up a heavily-
occupied slope into the teeth of the enemy
guns, turns out brilliantly for the Union.
Shouting 'Chickamauga' as they charge,
Federal soldiers overrun line after line of
defenses until the Rebels on the crest are
desperately hurling rocks at the onrushing
enemy.

The crest is, therefore, broached and
the Confederates are in panic-stricken rout
toward Chickamauga. Thousands are captured; Bragg himself barely escapes. Union
troops gather at the top, cheering wildly as
General Sheridan appears on his horse.
'What do you think at this, General?' someone shouts. 'I think you disobeyed orders,
you damned rascals,' Sheridan replies
happily. Meanwhile, Hooker is rolling up
the Confederate positions to the south;
Sherman is still meeting resistance in the
north, but those Confederate defenders retreat that night toward where the defeated
Army of Tennessee is gathering in Ringgold, Georgia. Grant later writes, 'The victory at Chattanooga was won more easily

Thomas's charge at Chattanooga.

The Battle of Missionary Ridge, 25 November 1863.

than expected by reason of Bragg's grave mistakes: first, in sending away Longstreet, his ablest corps commander, [in fact, this was President Davis's order, though perhaps requested by Bragg] . . . ; second, in placing so much of his force on the plain in front of his impregnable positions.' Casualties are comparatively low for such a major battle. Union forces lose 5824 from all causes, 10 percent of their 56,359 effectives; the South loses 6667 of 64,165, about the same proportion. While the Confederacy has been bested in yet another major conflict, their forces have not been vitally damaged.

26 *NOVEMBER* 1863

EASTERN THEATER   Skirmishing breaks out around the Rapidan in Virginia as Federal forces begin an offensive against the greatly outnumbered Lee. Meade hopes now to turn the Confederate right flank and force the Army of Northern Virginia back to Richmond.

WESTERN THEATER, CHATTANOOGA CAMPAIGN   Bragg's retreating Army of Tennessee moves toward Ringgold, Georgia, with Federal troops under Thomas and Sherman in pursuit. Several clashes break out before the Union forces halt.

KNOXVILLE CAMPAIGN   Outside Knoxville, Confederate General Longstreet prepares his assault on Fort Sanders.

27 *NOVEMBER* 1863

EASTERN THEATER   Parrying Meade's new initiative, Lee strengthens his right flank, as fighting breaks out near the Rapi-

dan. At Mine Run, Meade finds Lee's forces strongly posted, and his offensive falters; it will not regain momentum in the following days. At Ohio State Penitentiary in Columbus, Confederate raider John Hunt Morgan and some of his officers escape and head South; the future career of Morgan, however, will be of less usefulness to the Confederacy.

29 *NOVEMBER* 1863

WESTERN THEATER, KNOXVILLE CAMPAIGN   Longstreet finally launches his attack on Federal positions at Fort Sanders (called Fort Loudon by the Confederates), seeking to dislodge Burnside's army from nearby Knoxville. Rather than beginning with an artillery bombardment, which might have opened a breach in the steep sides of the parapet, Longstreet ill-advisedly commences with an infantry attack. The advance, made in bitter cold, is ineffective; the men are slowed by Union wire entanglements and then bog down in a ditch, lacking the scaling ladders needed to move onto the parapet. Unable to advance or retreat, Longstreet ends the attack, whereupon Federals capture 200 men in the ditch. It is a half-hearted and bungled operation, and the South's last chance to end the Union occupation of Knoxville. Chattanooga has fallen, and Union reinforcements are on the way.

30 *NOVEMBER* 1863

THE CONFEDERACY   President Davis accepts the resignation of Braxton Bragg, the defeated commander of the Army of Tennessee. The month ends with a further sinking of Confederate hopes in the wake of a series of crucial defeats. The Confederate victory of Chickamauga is now made worthless; of the Chattanooga Campaign only recriminations remain.

1 *DECEMBER* 1863

EASTERN THEATER   After the failure of their advance at Mine Run, Meade and the Army of the Potomac withdraw across the Rapidan and set up winter quarters.

2 DECEMBER 1863

WESTERN THEATER   Lieutenant General W H Hardee temporarily assumes command of the Army of Tennessee following Braxton Bragg's resignation. Bragg asks his army to support the new commander and suggests Davis consider a new offensive.

3 DECEMBER 1863

WESTERN THEATER, KNOXVILLE CAMPAIGN   In the face of advancing Union reinforcements, Longstreet abandons his siege of Knoxville and moves his troops toward winter quarters at Greeneville, Tennessee. Thus ends the Knoxville Campaign, a major Federal victory largely by default. Burnside, by failing now to pursue Longstreet, obliges Grant to keep a large force in Tennessee until spring.

6 DECEMBER 1863

NAVAL   In Charleston Harbor, South Carolina, a strong tide breaks over the Union blockade ironclad *Weehawken* and pours into an open hatch; the ship promptly sinks with two dozen of the crew.

7 DECEMBER 1863

THE CONFEDERACY   On the same day as the convening of the Union 38th Congress, the fourth session of the Confederate First Congress meets in Richmond. President Davis addresses the body, putting the most hopeful face he can on what has been a discouraging year.

8 DECEMBER 1863

WASHINGTON   At the end of his annual message to Congress, President Lincoln makes his first major statement of reconstruction in a Proclamation of Amnesty and Reconstruction: a full pardon will be given to all Confederates, excepting government officials, high-ranking army officers, those who resigned the US military for the Confederacy, and those who have mistreated white or black prisoners of war (such as by

enslaving the latter). All property except slaves will be restored to Rebels. Pardons will be conditional on an oath of allegiance to the United States. Federal statehood will be recognized in any seceded state if one-tenth of the citizens swear allegiance and forswear slavery. The President's statement is received with widespread approval in the North.

NAVAL   A Northern Copperhead band seizes the Union merchant ship *Chesapeake* near Cape Cod; the vessel is pursued by Federal ships and retaken off the coast of Canada near Nova Scotia on 17 December.

9 DECEMBER 1863

WESTERN THEATER   At his own request, General Burnside is relieved as Federal commander at Knoxville and is succeeded by Major General J G Foster. Burnside has been much criticized for failing to help Rosecrans at Chattanooga and for not pursuing the retreat of Longstreet. It will be said of Burnside that it is to his discredit that he is a poor commander and to his credit that he knows it. Meanwhile on this day, Longstreet, covering his political flank, dismisses several of his staff pending his charges against them (later dismissed) for alleged failures in the Knoxville Campaign.

11 DECEMBER 1863

WESTERN THEATER   In a day of comparatively light Federal bombardment of Fort Sumter, a chance shell blows up a powder magazine within the stronghold; 11 are killed and 41 wounded, but the defenders still do not give in.

14 DECEMBER 1863

WASHINGTON   The widow of Confederate general B H Helm, who was killed in action at Chickamauga, is given amnesty by President Lincoln after she swears allegiance to the Union. Mrs Helm is the half-sister of Lincoln's wife, Mary Todd Lincoln.

CHRONOLOGY

16 *DECEMBER* 1863

THE CONFEDERACY In spite of past differences between them regarding promotion, President Davis names General J E Johnston, formerly in Mississippi, as permanent successor to Bragg as commander of the Department of Tennessee. Bragg's former subordinate, General Leonidas Polk, is given charge of the Army of Mississippi.

25 *DECEMBER* 1863

WINTER QUARTERS Although minor hostilities continue in various theaters, all the military celebrate Christmas as best they can.

WESTERN THEATER In one of a continuing series of raids on Confederate salt works, Federal troops destroy a factory at Bear Inlet, North Carolina. Skirmishes break out at Fort Brooke, Florida.

TRANS-MISSISSIPPI Near Fort Gaston, California, Federal troops engage in skirmishes with Indians.

NAVAL Federal vessels see action at John's Island and Stone River, South Carolina, with the USS *Marblehead* being badly damaged by Confederate shore batteries.

31 *DECEMBER* 1863

THE CONFEDERACY After a year of setbacks for the Confederate cause, the Richmond (Virginia) *Examiner* observes, 'Today closes the gloomiest year of our struggle.' Few in the South would disagree. The superior manpower and material resources of the North have begun to tell, and the Union army is soon to prepare for the first time a unified strategy for the final conquest of the Confederacy.

1864

1 *JANUARY* 1864

WINTER QUARTERS Temperatures plunge below zero from the North well into the South and make for miserable conditions among the soldiers and sailors, but some minor actions are ordered on various fronts.

4 *JANUARY* 1864

THE CONFEDERACY In one of a series of increasingly stern orders that create new hardships for the citizens of the South, President Davis authorizes General Lee to commandeer food supplies in Virginia. The Confederate troops and animals in winter quarters are indeed seriously underfed, but the civilian population of the South has also suffered considerable deprivation. Such orders do not improve Davis's popularity.

6 *JANUARY* 1864

WESTERN THEATER In another Confederate guerrilla action against Federal shipping on the Mississippi River, the steamer *Delta* is attacked.

TRANS-MISSISSIPPI Federal Colonel 'Kit' Carson continues his operations against the Navajo in New Mexico Territory, trapping a number of Indians in the Canyon de Chelly. In an infamous action, these Navajo will be forced on the 300-mile 'Long Walk to Fort Sumner, New Mexico.

7 *JANUARY* 1864

WASHINGTON Desertion continues to be a serious problem in the North as well as in the South. Nonetheless, President Lincoln commutes the death sentence of an army deserter, commenting, 'I am trying to evade the butchering business lately.' He will commute a considerable number of such sentences.

8 *JANUARY* 1864

THE CONFEDERACY Confederate raider John Hunt Morgan, back from his escape from prison in Ohio, is feted by his government in Richmond.

13 *JANUARY* 1864

WASHINGTON Pursuant to his Proclamation of Amnesty and Reconstruction of 8 December, President Lincoln urges Federal officials in Florida and Louisiana to form Union governments 'with all possible dispatch.'

14 JANUARY 1864

THE CONFEDERACY   President Davis writes to General Johnston, now commander of the Department of Tennessee, observing that troops may need to be sent to Alabama or Mississippi. Davis is beginning to consider strategy for the coming year's struggle.

18 JANUARY 1864

THE CONFEDERACY   All white males between 18 and 45 (shortly to be changed to 17 and 50) have been conscripted for service in the Southern Army. Today there are protest meetings in North Carolina as opposition grows to the conscription law.

21 JANUARY 1864

WESTERN THEATER   In another response to Lincoln's Proclamation of Amnesty and Reconstruction, pro-Union leaders in Tennessee plan a constitutional convention to set up a government and abolish slavery.

23 JANUARY 1864

WASHINGTON   Lincoln gives his approval to a plan for dealing with freed slaves in which they will be hired for pay to work for their former masters.

25 JANUARY 1864

WESTERN THEATER   Shelling continues on Confederate Fort Sumter in Charleston Harbor, South Carolina, the bombardment having been nearly continuous since 12 August 1863.'

27 JANUARY 1864

THE CONFEDERACY   Braxton Bragg is called to Richmond to confer with President Davis, if 'health permits'. Bragg suf-

fers from serious headaches and has been accused of leading battles when both he and his troops would be better off if he were home in bed.

31 JANUARY 1864

WASHINGTON   Implying that he will loosen the requirements stated in his Proclamation of Amnesty and Reconstruction, Lincoln writes to General Banks in New Orleans that Banks is 'at liberty to adopt any rule which shall admit to vote any unquestionably loyal free state men and none others. And yet I do wish they would all take the oath.'

1 FEBRUARY 1864

WASHINGTON   The turmoil that followed the Enrollment Act of the previous year has to some extent subsided, so there is little resistance when President Lincoln calls for 500,000 additional draftees for the Union Army. A plan to colonize Île à Vache in San Domingo with American blacks is aborted, Lincoln sending a ship to bring back colonists wanting to return. Congress paves the way for Grant's promotion to General-in-Chief of United States armies by reviving the rank of lieutenant general; this action has been ferried through a somewhat reluctant Congress by Grant's patron, Elihu Washburne, who will also assure Lincoln that Grant has no presidential ambitions.

WESTERN THEATER   Hostilities break out along Batchelder's Creek, the beginning of Confederate General Pickett's attempt to recapture New Berne, North Carolina. The attack is called off when Federals draw back to the inner defenses.

2 FEBRUARY 1864

WESTERN THEATER   A group of Confederate soldiers under Pickett board the US gunboat *Underwriter* in the Neuse River near New Berne, North Carolina. The Rebels kill the commander and three of the crew, capturing the remainder. Finding the boilers cold, they set fire to the vessel and, after some skirmishing, abandon the operation on the following day. This and a few ensuing minor clashes mark the end of Confederate efforts to recapture New Berne.

3 FEBRUARY 1864

THE CONFEDERACY Declining Southern fortunes in the war inspire increasingly severe actions from the government in Richmond. This day President Davis recommends suspension of writs of habeas corpus for those guilty of dissent of various kinds, spying, desertion, and associating with the enemy.

WESTERN THEATER, MERIDIAN CAMPAIGN After Vicksburg fell, Lincoln turned his attention to Louisiana and Arkansas. In order to drive the Rebels entirely out of those states, a campaign is planned on the Red River; but this cannot be implemented until the rising of the river in March. General Sherman is ordered to commence preparations for this campaign. In the meantime, he decides to strengthen the Union position in Vicksburg by destroying the two primary railroads of central Mississippi. He leaves Vicksburg this day with 25,000 men. In conjunction with Sherman's move, a mounted column of 7000 is to leave Memphis, Tennessee under General W Sooy Smith and attempt to drive Confederate cavalry from northern Mississippi, after which they will sweep down the rail line toward Meridian, Mississippi, and join Sherman around 10 February. The commander of Confederate forces in the area is General Leonidas Polk, formerly under Bragg in Tennessee, with about 20,000 widely scattered forces including cavalry under Nathan Bedford Forrest.

5 FEBRUARY 1864

WESTERN THEATER, MERIDIAN CAMPAIGN Moving steadily toward Meridian, Mississippi, Sherman's men march into Jackson; minor skirmishes occur along the route to Jackson and at Clinton.

6 FEBRUARY 1864

THE CONFEDERACY The fourth session of the First Confederate Congress continues its work, banning imports of luxuries and circulation of US currency; it also decrees that half of various food and tobacco shipments must be given to the government before ships may leave ports.

EASTERN THEATER Federal forces under Meade meet unexpected Confederate resistance on a foray across the Rapidan River in Virginia; held down all day by enemy fire, they retreat during the night.

WESTERN THEATER, MERIDIAN CAMPAIGN Sherman's forces move out of Jackson, Mississippi toward Meridian.

7 FEBRUARY 1864

WESTERN THEATER, MERIDIAN CAMPAIGN General Polk continues his withdrawal before Sherman's advance toward Meridian; skirmishes break out at Brandon, Morton and Satartia, Mississippi. Elsewhere, Union troops take over Jacksonville, Florida, with little resistance from Confederates; over the next few days a Feceral expedition will move out from Jacksonville to destroy Southern supply bases.

9 FEBRUARY 1864

WASHINGTON President Lincoln sits for several photographs (one of which is later to be used for the US five-dollar bill).

WESTERN THEATER In the largest and most dramatic escape of the war, Union prisoners dig their way out of Libby Prison in Richmond, Virginia. Formerly the candle warehouse of Libby and Sons, the large building has been used as a prison for captured Federal officers. While conditions in the camps of both sides are largely poor and growing worse throughout the war, those in Libby Prison are to be exceeded in infamy only by Andersonville. Of the 109 Union officers who escape this day, 48 are recaptured (including their leader, Colonel Thomas E Rose), two drown, and 59 reach Federal lines.

11 FEBRUARY 1864

WESTERN THEATER One day after he was

originally ordered to have completed his advance in support of Sherman, General Sooy Smith begins his advance, moving out of Collierville, near Memphis, Tennessee. Heavy rains in the swampy countryside have delayed his preparations, and his progress is slow. He will encounter little enemy resistance until he reaches West Point on 20 February. In West Virginia another of the increasingly common incidents of Confederate guerrilla action is seen. Irregulars under Major H W Gilmore throw a train off its tracks, then proceed to rob the civilian crew and passengers.

12 *FEBRUARY* 1864

WESTERN THEATER, MERIDIAN CAMPAIGN   Now two Federal forces are closing in on Meridian, Mississippi, Sherman's from the west and Sooy Smith's from the north. Engagements break out at Decatur and Chunky Station along Sherman's route.

14 *FEBRUARY* 1864

WESTERN THEATER, MERIDIAN CAMPAIGN   With little opposition from General Polk, Sherman's army marches into Meridian, Mississippi. Sherman, in a preview of his tactics in Georgia, does considerably more than his announced plan of dismantling railroad lines. In his own words: 'For five days, 10,000 men worked hard and with a will in that work of destruction . . . Meridian, with its depots, storehouses, arsenals, hospitals, offices, hotels and cantonments no longer exists.' He will spend several days engaged in this rampage (which of course includes the railroads) while waiting for the arrival of Sooy Smith, who by now is much overdue. Meanwhile in Florida, a part of Gillmore's army occupies Gainesville.

15 *FEBRUARY* 1864

THE CONFEDERACY   President Jefferson Davis becomes increasingly concerned that Sherman will continue from Meridian to Montgomery, Alabama.

16 *FEBRUARY* 1864

WESTERN THEATER, MERIDIAN CAMPAIGN   Minor fighting occurs between Sherman's and Polk's men at Lauderdale Springs, near Meridian. President Davis's apprehensions about a Federal move on Mobile, Alabama are increased by Union forays around that city.

TRANS-MISSISSIPPI   A Union campaign against Indians is begun from Fort Walla Walla in Washington Federal Territory.

NAVAL   Federal actions against blockade-runners continue as the Confederate ships *Pet* and *Spunky* are taken near Wilmington, North Carolina.

17 *FEBRUARY* 1864

THE CONFEDERACY   The privilege of the writ of habeas corpus is suspended by the Confederate Congress, though this applies only to arrests made by authority of the President or the Secretary of War. The Congress also extends the limits of conscription to men between 17 and 50, prompting Vice-President Stephens to write: 'Far better that our country should be overrun by the enemy, our cities sacked and burned, and our land laid desolate, than that the people should suffer the citadel of their liberties to be entered and taken by professed friends.' In short, the Vice-President is accusing the President of betraying the most precious ideals of the nation. The hostility between these two men is an increasing handicap to the Confederacy. Within the whole South a desperate demand for peace is also simmering.

WESTERN THEATER   A watchman on the sloop USS *Housatonic*, one of the largest blockade ships in Charleston harbor, sees 'something in the water' making its way toward the ship. The 'something' is the Confederate semi-submersible ship *H L Hunley*, which is armed with a spar torpedo. On impact the torpedo blows a hole in the *Housatonic*, and both vessels sink, the sloop losing five men and the submarine seven. The tiny *H L Hunley* is long, slim, and cigar-shaped, and is hand-propelled by its crew, who lie down along its length; by the time of this, its final sinking, it has, during tests and its single action, drowned at least 33 sailors. Although this event sends trepidation through the Union blockading fleet, effective submarine warfare is still many years in the future.

18 *FEBRUARY* 1864

WESTERN THEATER, MERIDIAN CAMPAIGN In Meridian, Mississippi, Sherman's soldiers continue dismantling the railroads and the town while waiting for their originally intended cooperating group, the cavalry under Sooy Smith, who have just reached the prairie region of eastern Mississippi and are engaged in minor skirmishes around Okolona.

20 *FEBRUARY* 1864

WESTERN THEATER, MERIDIAN CAMPAIGN Giving up his wait for the arrival of Sooy Smith, Sherman begins a slow withdrawal from Meridian back to Vicksburg, Mississippi. His campaign has lost him only 21 killed, 68 wounded, and 81 missing. After he leaves, the Confederates begin repairing the railroad lines he has destroyed.

BATTLE OF OLUSTEE, FLORIDA In January, President Lincoln has written to Major General Gillmore urging him to bring Florida under Union control and form a state government, in time to be represented in the coming Republican presidential convention. After a series of forays from Jacksonville, the Federals have concentrated some 5500 troops near Olustee or Ocean Pond, while the Confederates have 5200 infantry and cavalry near Lake City. In the morning of this day a Union cavalry brigade opens battle at Olustee with a successful advance against Confederate outposts; but then two Federal regiments, after heavy fighting and serious casualties, break and flee in confusion. Other brigades replace the two that have run, holding ground with heavy losses until the Rebels have nearly exhausted their ammunition. After dark, Union troops withdraw. Losses are high,

Sherman's men destroying the railroad, 1864.

particularly to Union black soldiers: a total of 1861 killed, wounded, captured and missing for the Union to the Confederates' 934 casualties.

21 *FEBRUARY* 1864

WESTERN THEATER, MERIDIAN CAMPAIGN Sooy Smith's cavalry runs into the Confederate troops of Nathan Bedford Forrest at West Point, Mississippi; thinking the enemy is stronger than it actually is, Smith precipitously orders a retreat after only light skirmishing. His men withdraw reluctantly.

22 *FEBRUARY* 1864

WASHINGTON President Lincoln has increasingly run afoul of the extreme antislavery wing of his party, who are known as the Radical Republicans. Radical Horace Greeley, for example, will call for a new Republican presidential candidate. Secretary of the Treasury Chase has had a series of wrangles with Lincoln and has regularly offered to resign. On this day Chase is seriously compromised by what comes to be called the 'Pomeroy Circular' (named after the Kansas Senator who initiated the paper), a Radical paper proposing Chase for President. The Secretary admits to Lincoln that he knows of the proposal but denies having seen the circular. Later evidence suggests, however, that he did know of it.

WESTERN THEATER, MERIDIAN CAM-

PAIGN Overtaken by Forrest's pursuing cavalry near Okolona, Mississippi, Sooy Smith's retreating Federals attempt a stand against the enemy, but the 7th Indiana, believing themselves about to be overwhelmed by a superior force, breaks precipitously and runs, leaving behind five guns of its battery without firing a shot. A series of delaying actions over a nine-mile line covers the Union retreat until five o'clock in the evening, when a stand is mounted against Forrest's charging cavalry. The Union 4th Mississippi Cavalry mounts a charge against Forrest which succeeds in checking his advance, but not significantly turning it back. The Union forces then withdraw in great disorder to Memphis.

Meanwhile in Tennessee, Thomas's Army of the Cumberland begins a reconnaissance of Johnston's Army of Tennessee in their winter quarters in Dalton, Georgia. In what will be called the Federal Demonstration on Dalton, Thomas is trying to find out if Johnston has weakened his army by reinforcing Polk in Mississippi and Longstreet in Tennessee.

23 FEBRUARY 1864

WASHINGTON As Lincoln ponders his response to the Pomeroy Circular, the Cabinet meets without Chase.

24 FEBRUARY 1864

WASHINGTON Congress approves revival of the rank of lieutenant general, thus paving the way for U S Grant to become General-in-Chief of the Union army.

Lincoln reads the Emancipation Proclamation.

Among several other measures voted by Congress concerning enlistment and the draft, Lincoln approves a plan to free slaves who enlist, while paying their masters a $300 compensation.

THE CONFEDERACY In another unpopular move, President Davis appoints General Braxton Bragg to be in charge of 'the conduct of military operations in the army of the Confederacy'; in effect, Bragg is now chief of staff. Longstreet has accused Davis of approving failure and disparaging success; this accusation seems not exaggerated given Davis's continuing support of the inept Bragg and his disparagement of General Joe Johnston and other effective officers.

WESTERN THEATER The Demonstration on Dalton continues as Federals drive the enemy from outposts at Tunnel Hill, Georgia.

25 FEBRUARY 1864

WESTERN THEATER Thomas's forces near Dalton gather and attempt to force through Buzzard Roost Gap. Federals under Palmer try for an envelopment in the morning but are held off by a strong Confederate force. Union attempts are later made on the enemy right and center, but both fail and the latter incurs heavy casualties. It finally having become clear that Johnston's forces are by no means weakened, the Federals retreat and the reconnaissance is terminated. Union troops have lost 345 casualties to around 167 for the South.

26 FEBRUARY 1864

WESTERN THEATER In the wake of the Meridian Campaign, Sooy Smith's routed cavalry straggle back into Memphis while Sherman's men skirmish around Canton, Mississippi.

27 FEBRUARY 1864

THE CONFEDERACY At Andersonville, Georgia (near Americus) Federal enlisted men captured by the South begin to arrive at an unfinished prison compound called

CHRONOLOGY

Camp Sumter. Built hastily when the numbers of Union war prisoners became unmanageable in Richmond, the prison consists of a 16½-acre log stockade, later enlarged, divided by a stream. Over the next year conditions in the prison will deteriorate until disease and death resulting from poor sanitation, crowding, exposure, and inadequate diet become outrageous.

WESTERN THEATER The Federal Demonstration on Dalton, Georgia, finishes with a skirmish near Catoosa Station.

28 FEBRUARY 1864

EASTERN THEATER After reports of miserable conditions in war prisons in Richmond and light Confederate forces in the city, President Lincoln and Secretary of War Stanton have authorized a raid that will attempt to seize the Confederate capital by a surprise attack, free the prisoners, and distribute amnesty proclamations. Pursuant to this plan, 3500 mounted raiders under General Judson Kilpatrick drive off enemy outposts and cross the Rapidan at Ely's Ford this night. With Kilpatrick is one-legged (from a wound at Gettysburg) Colonel Ulric Dahlgren, a son of the Union Navy commander Admiral Dahlgren. Kilpatrick, who has originated the plan for the raid, is a controversial leader; one report states that his 'notorious immoralities set so demoralizing an example to his troops that . . . his surbordinates could only mitigate its influence.' At the same time, Kilpatrick is noted for 'a dare-devil recklessness that dismayed his opponents and imparted his own daring to his men.'

29 FEBRUARY 1864

EASTERN THEATER The Kilpatrick Dahlgren raid takes shape as the two leaders separate at Spotsylvania, Kilpatrick moving with the main body toward Richmond and Dahlgren heading for Goochland with 500 men. During the night the Confederate War Department in Rich-

mond learns of the raid and orders emergency measures.

TRANS-MISSISSIPPI In preparation for the impending Red River Campaign, Union vessels begin to scout the Black and Ouachita Rivers in Louisiana.

1 MARCH 1864

WASHINGTON Lincoln nominates U S Grant for lieutenant general, the rank recently revived for Grant by Congress.

EASTERN THEATER Federal raiders Kilpatrick and Dahlgren close in on Richmond. The Confederate capital is in fact lightly defended by regular forces but, word having arrived of the raiders' approach, a collection of Southern civilians, wounded soldiers, and veterans gathers to defend the city. Approaching Richmond, Kilpatrick runs into these defenders and takes them to be a major force of the enemy; he has, too, no idea of the whereabouts of Dahlgren, who is supposed to have joined him. After light skirmishing, Kilpatrick decides the Confederate forces are too much for him and withdraws across the Chickahominy River to await Dahlgren. Dahlgren, meanwhile, has had problems as well. In the morning he splits his force of 500 men, sending one group under Captain Mitchell down the north bank of the James River to destroy property and enter Richmond. Dahlgren, leading the other body of men, asks the assistance of a black youth to show him a place to ford the river. Deliberately or not, however, the youth leads Dahlgren to an unfordable stretch of the James, delaying the raiders' advance considerably. Outraged and suspecting treachery, Dahlgren summarily hangs the youth before proceeding down the north bank of the James to join his other force at Short Pump, eight miles from Richmond. The party then advances, meeting increasingly stiff resistance, until by nightfall they are within two and one-half miles of the Confederate capital. Despairing of continuing his advance after nightfall, Dahlgren at this point gives up the attempt on Richmond and orders a retreat.

2 *MARCH* 1864

WASHINGTON   The Senate confirms Grant's nomination as lieutenant general. Along with being the highest ranking officer, Grant will assume the title of General-in-Chief of the Army of the United States.

EASTERN THEATER   The forces of the failed Kilpatrick-Dahlgren raid continue their retreat, Kilpatrick's rearguard still being harassed as he moves away and Dahlgren's men split into two groups, both seeking to join with Kilpatrick. Late in the evening, Captain Mitchell and his men will rejoin Kilpatrick. All day, Confederate cavalry under Lieutenant J Pollard pursue Dahlgren and his group, who are moving north. Late in the day the Confederates circle ahead of Dahlgren and join Captain E C Fox at Mantapike Hill, near King and Queen Court House where they set up an ambush. Around 11 in the evening Dahlgren and his men ride unsuspectingly into the trap. In short order Dahlgren is killed and 92 of his soldiers captured.

Then something is discovered that is soon to make Dahlgren's name notorious. A thirteen-year-old boy named William Littlepage finds two documents on the Union commander's body. One, signed by Dahlgren and apparently written as an address to his raiders, reads: 'We hope to relieve the prisoners from Belle Isle first, and having seen them fairly started, we will cross the James River into Richmond, destroying the bridges after us, and exhorting the released prisoners to destroy and burn the hateful city; and do not allow the rebel leader, Davis, and his traitorous crew to escape.' The second document, unsigned, reads, 'once in the city it must be destroyed, and Jeff Davis and cabinet killed.' Lieutenant Pollard will forward these two documents to Robert E Lee, who will send photographic copies of them to Federal General Meade with an inquiry as to their origin. A subsequent Federal investigation into the matter leads nowhere, and Meade eventually replies to Lee: 'Neither the United States Government, myself, nor General Kilpatrick authorized, sanctioned, or approved the burning of the city of Richmond and the killing of Mr Davis and his cabinet, nor any other act not required by military necessity and in accordance with the usages of war.' Whether Meade's declaration is a fact or a cover-up will never quite be decided, but the affair does damage to the honor of the Union.

4 *MARCH* 1864

WASHINGTON   Andrew Johnson is confirmed by the Senate as Federal Military Governor of Tennessee.

EASTERN THEATER   Kilpatrick and his men raid around the area where Colonel Dahlgren was killed before they return to Meade's army. The Kilpatrick–Dahlgren raid has cost the Federals 340 men and 583 horses, as well as a large number of weapons including Spencer repeating rifles, a gun that has become increasingly important to the Northern army. The Confederates find they cannot use the captured repeaters, however, because they lack the proper cartridges.

WESTERN THEATER   Most of Federal General Sherman's men return to Vicksburg following their advance to Meridian, Mississippi. Fighting breaks out at Rodney, Mississippi, and Murfreesboro, Tennessee.

5 *MARCH* 1864

THE CONFEDERACY   Attempting to reduce excessive profiteering from its blockade-runners as well as to improve its desperately low supplies, the government in Richmond issues orders requiring all vessels to give half their cargo space to government shipments.

8 *MARCH* 1864

WASHINGTON   At a White House reception, President Lincoln steps uncertainly up to a short, disheveled-looking military man and inquires, 'This is General Grant, is it?' 'Yes,' Grant replies. The soon-to-be lieutenant general has met his commander-in-chief for the first time. After a few pleasantries with Lincoln, Grant joins Secretary Seward in the East Room, where the general is obliged to stand on a sofa to shake hands with the cheering crowd. Following the reception, Lincoln, Grant, and Secretary of War Stanton confer in the Blue Room, and the President makes some suggestions about Grant's remarks to be made on the morrow: 'Tomorrow, at such time as you may arrange with the Secretary of War, I desire to make you a formal presentation of your commission as Lieutenant-General. I shall then make a very short speech, to which I desire you to reply. . . . There are two points that I would like to have you make in your answer: first, to say something which shall prevent or obviate any jealousy of you from any of the other generals in the service, and secondly, something which shall put you on as good terms as possible with the Army of the Potomac.'

9 *MARCH* 1864

WASHINGTON In an early-afternoon ceremony attended by the Cabinet, U S Grant is officially given his commission as lieutenant general, thus becoming commander of all the Union Armies. In some embarrassment, Grant stumbles through a hastily-written speech which makes neither of the points Lincoln has asked him to. Soon afterward Grant and the President have their first private talk, which Grant recounts in his memoirs: 'He stated to me that he had never professed to be a military man or to know how campaigns should be conducted, and never wanted to interfere in them; but that procrastination on the part of commanders, and the pressure from the people at the North and from Congress, *which was always with him*, forced him into issuing his series of Military Orders. . . . He did not know that they were not all wrong, and did know that some of them

were. All he wanted, or had ever wanted, was some one who would take the responsibility and act, and call on him for all the assistance needed.' It is clear that Lincoln believed he had at last found a commander in whom he can have complete faith. He goes so far as to say to Grant he does not want to know what the general plans to do. After his interview with the President, Grant immediately leaves Washington for Brandy Station, Virginia, headquarters of the Army of the Potomac.

10 *MARCH* 1864

EASTERN THEATER Grant confers with General Meade, commander of the Army of the Potomac, at Brandy Station. This is the beginning of what will become a close and fruitful association.

TRANS-MISSISSIPPI, RED RIVER CAMPAIGN In the first move of the Federal Red River Campaign, General A J Smith's command leaves Vicksburg heading down the Mississippi River toward the Red River, which runs through northwestern Louisiana. Smith's troops are escorted by a formidable force including 13 ironclads and seven gunboats. This expedition has been planned for some months, and the intention is to establish more complete Union control in Louisiana and eastern Texas. The plans have been largely promoted and drawn by General-in-Chief Halleck (soon to be demoted), over the objections of Generals Grant, Sherman and Banks, who feel operations against the enemy in Mobile, Alabama, should be given priority. Nonetheless, Banks, as commander of the Department of the Gulf, is ordered to coordinate the expedition: he is to take 17,000 troops to link up with 10,000 of Sherman's men and 15,000 of Steele's in Alexandria, Louisiana, or thereabouts. (Steele, commander of the Department of Arkansas, will start so late and proceed so slowly as to miss the campaign.) Opposing the expedition are around 30,000 Confederate troops under Kirby Smith; other obstacles are low water, inhospitable country, and the depredations of snipers. From the beginning, Federal efforts will be further hampered by lack of cooperation among the forces and by an insatiable desire for the seizure of valuable cotton by naval and military personnel.

12 *MARCH* 1864
TRANS-MISSISSIPPI, RED River CAMPAIGN The Federal fleet and troop transports reach the mouth of the Red River and head upriver toward Alexandria, Louisiana.

14 *MARCH* 1864
TRANS-MISSISSIPPI, RED RIVER CAMPAIGN Moving up the river, Union forces easily overwhelm the partially-completed Confederate Fort de Russy, near Simsport, Louisiana, from the land side, capturing 210 prisoners and several guns. Meanwhile, the Federal fleet bursts through a dam nine miles below and proceeds up the river.

15 *MARCH* 1864
WASHINGTON Transferring power from the military to the new civil governor of Louisiana, Lincoln takes another step in his reconstruction of that state, a model for his reconstruction plans.

16 *MARCH* 1864
TRANS-MISSISSIPPI, RED RIVER CAMPAIGN Nine Union gunboats have arrived in Alexandria, Louisiana; Federal troops occupy the town and await the arrival of further land forces. Elsewhere, a ten-day Federal reconnaissance begins in Missouri.

17 *MARCH* 1864
WESTERN THEATER Grant and Sherman confer in Nashville, Tennessee, on their plan of attack on General Johnston and the Confederate army in Dalton, Georgia. Formally receiving command of the Union armies on this date, Grant announces, 'Headquarters will be in the field, and, until further orders, will be with the Army of the Potomac.' In short, Grant is turning his

primary attention to Lee and his Army of Northern Virginia.

18 *MARCH* 1864
TRANS-MISSISSIPPI A convention in Arkansas ratifies a pro-Union constitution and abolishes slavery.

19 *MARCH* 1864
THE CONFEDERACY In Georgia, the state legislature gives a vote of confidence to President Davis and suggests that after any significant Confederate military victory a peace proposal should be made to Washington, the proposal predicated on Southern independence.
TRANS-MISSISSIPPI, RED RIVER CAMPAIGN Federal cavalry under Banks begin to arrive at Alexandria, Louisiana, but the whole force will not be assembled until the 26th. The next few days see small-scale Confederate attacks on the Federal advance guard.

21 *MARCH* 1864
TRANS-MISSISSIPPI, RED RIVER CAMPAIGN Federal General J A Mower surprises Confederate General Richard Taylor near Henderson's Hill, Louisiana, capturing nearly 250 men, 200 horses, and four guns. This action deprives the Confederates for the time being of their means of scouting.

23 *MARCH* 1864
WASHINGTON Back in the capital after conferring with Sherman, Grant prepares for the simultaneous advance of all his armies.
TRANS-MISSISSIPPI, RED RIVER CAMPAIGN Continuing the planned massing of forces, Federal troops under Frederick Steele move south from Little Rock, Arkansas, to join Banks and his forces on the Red River.

24 *MARCH* 1864
WASHINGTON Grant and Lincoln confer

at the White House.

WESTERN THEATER   Confederate cavalry under Nathan Bedford Forrest capture Union City in West Tennessee.

TRANS-MISSISSIPPI, RED RIVER CAMPAIGN   Federal General Banks, commander of the Department of the Gulf and leader of the campaign, arrives in Alexandria, Louisiana, only to discover two new snags in the operation: first, he is ordered to return Sherman's troops—10,000 men under A J Smith—to that general by 15 April, for the Atlanta campaign; second, it becomes clear that the river is so low as to make it barely possible for his fleet to move away from Alexandria. Nonetheless, Banks issues orders for an advance to Shreveport.

25 MARCH 1864

WESTERN THEATER   Following his capture of Union City in Tennessee, Forrest attacks Paducah, Kentucky, on the banks of the Ohio, entering the city but not capturing the Federal garrison there.

26 MARCH 1864

WESTERN THEATER   Threatened by cavalry sent by Sherman, Forrest's Confederates withdraw from Paducah, Kentucky, toward Fort Pillow on the Mississippi River.

28 MARCH 1864

THE NORTH   A group of Copperheads attacks Federal soldiers in Charleston, Illinois. In the worst anti-war outbreak since the July 1863 Draft Riots of New York City, five are killed and 20 wounded as more Union troops are called out to quell the disturbance.

TRANS-MISSISSIPPI, RED RIVER CAMPAIGN   Confederate troops begin to mass under General Richard Taylor, preparing to resist the advance of Federal forces up the river.

29 MARCH 1864

WASHINGTON   Responding to press criticism of his handling of Gettysburg,

Meade has contemplated requesting a court of inquiry; Lincoln, wishing to avoid the potential divisiveness of such a move, dissuades Meade from the request.

TRANS-MISSISSIPPI, RED RIVER CAMPAIGN   Before the arrival of the Federal forces, who are advancing toward Shreveport, Confederates set fire to ten miles of cottonfields along the riverbank.

3 APRIL 1864

TRANS-MISSISSIPPI, RED RIVER CAMPAIGN   The river is rising slightly, but it is still so low that Federal ships have barely been able to pass through the rapids above Alexandria until today, when the last of the 13 gunboats and 30 transports make the passage. Seven gunboats and several large transports remain behind in Alexandria; the supplies largely have to be landed before the rapids, hauled around in wagons, and reshipped. The supply line for this expedition is becoming increasingly difficult and thin. During the day Federal forces concentrate near Natchitoches.

4 APRIL 1864

WASHINGTON   President Lincoln writes: 'I am naturally anti-slavery. If slavery is not wrong, nothing is wrong. . . . And yet I have never understood that the Presidency conferred upon me an unrestricted right to act officially upon this judgement and feeling.' Concerned about French interests in Mexico and their possible repercussions in Texas—one of the reasons for the Red River Campaign—the House of Representatives passes a resolution saying the United States will not tolerate a monarchy in Mexico. In fact, this monarchy is already decreed; it is to be a puppet regime of France's Napoleon III, who invaded Mexico in 1862. And this regime does in fact have its eye on Texas, though its army will be kept occupied by Juarez until that leader's final victory.

5 APRIL 1864

TRANS-MISSISSIPPI, RED RIVER CAMPAIGN   Confederate General Taylor and his army of 16,000 fall back from the Federal advance and group around Mansfield, Louisiana, placing themselves between Banks and his goal, Shreveport. The Federal land forces by this time are marching in a thin line on a single narrow road, encumbered by a wagon train of ammunition and provisions that stretches for 12 miles through the barren, enemy-held wilderness. The Union fighting ships and transports, meanwhile, continue to make poor headway up the low waters of the Red River.

6 *APRIL* 1864

WESTERN THEATER Meeting in New Orleans, a Union constitutional convention adopts a new state constitution and abolishes slavery.

7 *APRIL* 1864

THE CONFEDERACY The government orders General Longstreet to move northward and rejoin Lee's Army of Northern Virginia. Longstreet has been in Tennessee since last winter, where he participated in the Chattanooga and Knoxville Campaigns. Lee is beginning to prepare his response to Grant's anticipated next move.

8 *APRIL* 1864

WASHINGTON By a vote of 38 to 6, the Senate passes the Thirteenth Amendment to the Constitution, abolishing slavery in the United States and all areas under its jurisdiction. While this amendment would have been unlikely before the war, the vote shows that by now the North clearly perceives the importance and moral significance of the gesture.

TRANS-MISSISSIPPI, RED RIVER CAMPAIGN Confederate General Taylor moves his army from Mansfield, Louisiana, forward to Sabine Crossroads to meet the advance of Banks' ground forces, who are moving toward Shreveport. The armies face one another most of the afternoon, reluctant to enter battle. Union Colonel R B Irwin describes the action that ensues:

'About 4 o'clock, when the two lines had been skirmishing and looking at each other for a couple of hours, Taylor suddenly delivered his attack by a vigorous charge of Mouton's division on the left of the Pleasant Hill Road.... Walker followed astride and on the right of the road, with Bee's brigade of cavalry on his right. The Federal line formed on the cleared slope, about 4500 in all, met with spirit the fierce onset of more than double their numbers, but were soon overcome. The artillery was powerless in the woods.... Franklin received Banks' orders to move to the front at a quarter-past three. He at once sent for Emory and led forward Cameron, whose division, advancing at the double-quick, arrived on the field, five miles away, an hour later, just in time to witness and for a brief interval to check the disaster, but not to retrieve it. The whole Union line was again driven back. To complete the confusion, a wild panic ensued among the teamsters of the cavalry train, which was close behind. (This order of march has been severely criticized, but ... it did not cause but only aggravated a disaster really brought about by accepting battle at the head of a column twenty miles long, at the hands of an enemy formed in complete order of battle, in a position previously chosen by him, where our artillery could not be used.' Taylor's army pursues the retreating Federals, but Emory's division makes a successful stand and covers the retreat, saving the Union army from disaster.

After the Battle of Sabine Crossroads the Federal army withdraws and forms another defensive line at Pleasant Hill; one soldier writes of this withdrawal as 'our skedaddle from the rebs.' The Federals have lost 113 killed, 581 wounded, and 1541 missing, for a total of 2235 out of 12,000 engaged—a very high percentage; Southern losses are estimated at 1000 killed and wounded of 8800 engaged.

9 *APRIL* 1864

WASHINGTON General U S Grant begins

to issue orders pursuant to his grand strategy of advancing against Southern armies on all fronts: Banks is directed to advance on Alabama; Sherman will move against Johnston and the Army of Tennessee in Georgia; Sigel will move down the Shenandoah Valley in Virginia; Butler will turn toward Richmond; and the Army of the Potomac will advance inexorably against Lee and the Army of Northern Virginia. Grant tells Meade: 'Wherever Lee goes, there you will go also.'

TRANS-MISSISSIPPI, RED RIVER CAMPAIGN At daylight, Confederate General Taylor orders his whole army forward in pursuit of the retreating Federal forces. In the afternoon contact is made with the Union line at Pleasant Hill. The Confederates open their attack around five in the evening, at first driving back the Union left flank and killing Colonel Benedict, the brigade commander. But as the Confederates turn toward the center, a Federal counterattack repulses them, after which the Union army advances successfully, driving the enemy away in some confusion.

Banks at first wants to continue the advance toward Shreveport, but, in the absence of support from Steele (who is obstructed by enemy actions in Arkansas), finally decides to withdraw to Grand Ecore, Louisiana. While the day's battle has been technically a Northern victory, it has in fact halted the progress of the Red River Campaign, which has been plagued by problems and mistakes from the beginning. Moreover, General Banks has probably erred in withdrawing now. A report to President Davis from Confederate Trans-Mississippi commander Kirby Smith, who arrives late at night, states: 'Taylor's troops were repulsed and thrown into confusion . . . the Missouri and Arkansas troops . . . were broken and scattered. The enemy recovered artillery which we had taken, and two of our pieces were left in his hands . . . To my great relief I found in the morning that the enemy had fallen back in the night . . . Our troops were completely paralyzed.' But now the Union army faces great difficulties in withdrawing its large force. The end of Federal efforts on the Red River marks the last important operation by either side in Louisiana—Confederate forces will hold the state west of the Mississippi River until the end of the war. The failure of the expedition also means Banks will be delayed in his planned support of Sherman.

10 APRIL 1864

TRANS-MISSISSIPPI, RED RIVER CAMPAIGN The Union expedition under Steele, which had departed Little Rock to aid Banks in Louisiana, returns under Confederate fire to Little Rock. Taylor's Confederates move back from Pleasant Hill to Mansfield while the Federals gather at Grand Ecore.

11 APRIL 1864

TRANS-MISSISSIPPI, RED RIVER CAMPAIGN The gunboats and transports of the Federal flotilla now face the problem of retreat on the lowering waters of the river. They begin to withdraw to the accompaniment of shelling from Confederate shore batteries and rifle fire. Meanwhile, a pro-Union state government is inaugurated in Little Rock, Arkansas.

12 APRIL 1864

WESTERN THEATER Confederates under Nathan Bedford Forrest, on a raiding expedition against Federal operations in Tennessee and Kentucky, surround Union Fort Pillow on the Mississippi in Tennessee. The fort is held by about 557 troops, nearly half of them black. Forrest arrives at midmorning to take command, and deploys his men in positions from which they can attack the fort without exposing themselves to fire. This done, he sends an ultimatum to the fort's commander, Major W F Bradford, who at length declines to surrender. The ensuing Southern attack is swift and successful, with only 14 Confederates killed and 86 wounded. But what sends shockwaves through the country, shockwaves that will reverberate for years, are the Union casualties and the disputed reasons for those casualties. Southern accounts claim that the Federal losses—231 killed, 100 wounded, 168 whites and only 58 blacks captured—occur because the Federals refuse to surrender in the face of certain defeat and try to fight their way out of the fort. The Northern report, which history will in some degree vindicate, states that the fort surrendered almost immediately, and that what followed was a massacre by Confederates of defenseless Union troops, especially blacks. Grant, in his memoirs, quotes a portion of a letter by Forrest which states: 'The river was dyed with the blood of the slaughtered for two hundred yards. . . . It is hoped that these facts will demonstrate to the Northern people that Negro soldiers cannot cope with Southerners.' Whatever is the true extent of Southern atrocities in this action, the accusations will inflame the North.

TRANS-MISSISSIPPI, RED RIVER CAMPAIGN Retreating Union gunboats and troop transports are ambushed near Blair's Landing; after a brisk exchange, the Confederates are driven off, losing their commander but inflicting 57 casualties on Union soldiers.

15 *APRIL* 1864

WESTERN THEATER Andrew Johnson, head of the new pro-Union government of Tennessee, makes a speech (in Knoxville) supporting emancipation.

TRANS-MISSISSIPPI, RED RIVER CAMPAIGN Union ships gather along with land forces in Grand Ecore, Louisiana, whence they will depart under enemy fire toward Alexandria.

17 *APRIL* 1864

WASHINGTON In a move that puts increased pressure on the dwindling supply of manpower for the Southern army, Grant decides to exchange no more prisoners with the South until such releases are balanced equally, as they have not been previously. He also announces: 'No distinction whatever will be made in the exchange between white and colored

prisoners.' Currently the North holds about 146,634 Southern prisoners.

19 *APRIL* 1864

WASHINGTON Congress authorizes an act permitting the Nebraska Territory to join the Union.

WESTERN THEATER The USS *Smithfield*, principal support of the Federal garrison in Plymouth, North Carolina, is rammed and sunk by the CSS *Albemarle*, which then moves effectively against other Union ships in the area.

20 *APRIL* 1864

WESTERN THEATER The Confederate force under R F Hoke that has surrounded the Federal garrison at Plymouth, North Carolina, completes its capture of the city. Federals lose 2500 men and large quantities of supplies. This is the first Southern victory in the area in a while, and it raises Confederate spirits considerably; nonetheless, the city has little strategic significance, and Grant has already concluded it is not worth defending—if the major military moves of the summer succeed, Plymouth and nearby Washington, North Carolina, will revert to Federal control naturally. Thus, after Plymouth falls, Grant orders the abandonment of Washington but strengthens the strategically valuable port of New Berne.

21 *APRIL* 1864

TRANS-MISSISSIPPI, RED RIVER CAMPAIGN Continuing his withdrawal from the disastrous campaign, Federal General Banks moves his land forces out of Grand Ecore and marches 32 miles nonstop to Cloutiersville, Louisiana. Meanwhile, the Federal rear guard is driven from Natchitoches by Confederate cavalry commander J A Wharton, who continues pursuing the Federals as they move toward Cloutiersville. A Southern force under General H P Bee tries to block Banks' retreat near Cloutiersville, but this group is driven off by a Union frontal attack. Federals arrive at the town in good condition but still in serious danger. The Vessel *Eastport*, largest of the ironclads in the Federal fleet on the Red River, is afloat after having been sunk by a torpedo on 15 April.

22 *APRIL* 1864

WASHINGTON Following an act of Congress, the phrase 'In God We Trust' begins to be stamped on Federal coins.

THE CONFEDERACY Now that black troops are beginning to be used regularly by the Northern army—one example being the soldiers at Fort Pillow—the Confederacy turns its attention to dealing with black prisoners. President Davis writes: 'If the negro [prisoners] are escaped slaves, they should be held safely for recovery by their owners. If otherwise, inform me.'

25 *APRIL* 1864

TRANS-MISSISSIPPI, RED RIVER CAMPAIGN Banks' retreating army begins arriving at Alexandria, Louisiana. An order arrives from Grant officially terminating the operation, but these orders are to be suspended on 30 April.

26 *APRIL* 1864

WESTERN THEATER Pursuant to Grant's order after the fall of the Federal garrison at Plymouth, North Carolina, Union soldiers begin to pull out of nearby Washington.

TRANS-MISSISSIPPI, RED RIVER CAMPAIGN Federal troops and some of the fleet have arrived relatively unhurt in Alexandria, but the navy remains in an extremely hazardous situation, with several of the ships stuck above the rapids near Alexandria. Union Lieutenant Colonel Joseph Bailey proposes an extraordinary plan for freeing the ships from the river, which by now has fallen in places to three feet in depth: A series of dams will be built to raise the river; when the required seven feet of depth is reached, chutes will be opened for the ships to move through. Meanwhile this day, the ironclad *Eastport*, sunk on 15 April and raised on 21 April, runs aground several times and is finally blown up by its crew above the rapids leading to Alexandria. Immediately thereafter, the crew is attacked by Confederate infantry, who are at length driven off. As Union gunboats proceed down the river they run into Southern artillery, which hit the gunboat *Cricket* with 19 shells; the ship loses 31 of her crew of 50 before escaping. Two Federal pumpboats are also destroyed before the ships move out of range; one, the *Champion 3*, explodes from a hit in the boiler and scalds to death 200 black crewmen. (This type of tragedy is not uncommon in steamships during the war.)

27 *APRIL* 1864

WASHINGTON The plans are made, the armies poised, and Grant issues his orders. He would later describe this event in his memoirs: 'By the 27th of April spring had so far advanced as to justify me in fixing a day for the great move. On that day Burnside left Annapolis to occupy Meade's position between Bull Run and the Rappahannock. Meade was notified and directed to bring his troops forward to his advance; on the following day Butler was notified of my intended advance on the 4th of May, and he was directed to move, the night of the same day, and get as far up the James River as possible by daylight, and push on from there to accomplish the task given him. He was also notified that reinforcements were being collected in Washington, which would be forwarded to him should the enemy fall back into the trenches at Richmond. The same day Sherman was directed to get his forces up ready to advance on the 5th. Sigel, at Winchester, was notified to move in conjunction with the others.'

28 *APRIL* 1864

EASTERN THEATER As they have been since late 1863, Federal batteries continue their shelling of Fort Sumter in Charleston Harbor, sending 510 rounds into the fort over the next seven days in this one-sided battle.

30 *APRIL* 1864

THE CONFEDERACY President Davis reinforces his previous statement about black Federal prisoners: 'Captured slaves should be returned to their masters on proof and payment of charges.' On this same day, Davis's young son Joe dies from a fall off the Confederate White House.

TRANS-MISSISSIPPI, RED RIVER CAMPAIGN One of the most imaginative engineering feats in military history commences as work is begun on the dams that are intended to float the stranded Federal fleet over the rapids above Alexandria on the Red River. The work will be completed in the astonishing period of ten days.

1 *MAY* 1864

WASHINGTON Brigadier General John P Hatch replaces Major General Q A Gillmore as commander of the Federal Department of the South.

WESTERN THEATER Skirmishing breaks out between Sherman's and Johnston's troops at Stone Church, Georgia.

2 *MAY* 1864

THE CONFEDERACY In his speech at the opening session of the Second Confederate Congress, President Jefferson Davis accuses Federal troops of 'barbarism'.

TRANS-MISSISSIPPI, RED RIVER CAMPAIGN Confederates harass Banks' withdrawing army at Well's Plantation, Wilson's Landing and Bayou Pierre, as the Federals continue their retreat toward Alexandria, Louisiana. Work continues on the dams that are intended to float the Union fleet down the lowered river. Minor actions are seen at Kneelands Prairie in California, and at Bee Creek, Missouri.

3 *MAY* 1864

EASTERN THEATER, WILDERNESS CAMPAIGN The Army of the Potomac, still nominally under Meade but in fact directed by Grant, is on the eve of its long-awaited move against Lee's Army of Northern Virginia. A few days before, Grant has written

Chief of Staff Halleck: 'The Army of the Potomac is in splendid condition and evidently feels like whipping somebody.' How and where to do the whipping is a subject of contention within the Union staff. Grant wishes to move against the Confederate right flank, using the easy access to water transportation from the junction of the Rappahannock and Rapidan, while Meade wants to attack the Rebel left flank, which will avoid the risk of fighting in the Wilderness and cut off Lee from further northward excursions toward Washington. By attacking across the Wilderness—an area in northern Virginia that takes its name from the dense forest and underbrush that make it virtually uninhabitable—Grant hopes to cut Lee off from Richmond, and perhaps capture his whole army. Grant's view prevails, and the Army of the Potomac is ordered to cross the Rapidan the morning of 4 May.

TRANS-MISSISSIPPI Steele's forces finally arrive back in Little Rock, Arkansas, after their bungled attempt to aid the also bungled Red River Campaign.

4 *MAY* 1864

WASHINGTON The House of Representatives passes, over Lincoln's objections, the Wade-Davis Reconstruction Bill, which contains several stiffly punitive measures directed toward the South. If put into law, it will destroy Lincoln's more moderate reconstruction plans; nonetheless, the bill is opposed by extreme Radical Republicans like Thaddeus Stevens, for whom it is insufficiently severe.

EASTERN THEATER, WILDERNESS CAMPAIGN The Army of the Potomac crosses the Rapidan toward Lee, its forces 122,000 strong to Lee's contingent of 66,000 hungry and ill-clad men. The Union corps are under the direction of Generals Hancock, Warren, Sedgwick and Burnside. Grant has intended to march through the heavy forest of the Wilderness so as to gain open territory for battle, but he is forced to stop just on the edge of the Wilderness and wait for his supply train to catch up. Lee, who has anticipated Grant's move this time, as he will so often in the future, moves his army up quickly so as to catch the Federals in the Wilderness. This is familiar territory for the Confederates, and within the tangled trees and brush, uneven ground, and numberless pits and gullies, the superior numbers of the Federal troops will be ineffective and their artillery will be nearly useless. The Confederate forces are carefully positioned, General Ewell on the Orange Turnpike and General A P Hill on the Plank Road; Longstreet's corps and Stuart's cavalry are ordered to move in. During the day there is some fighting in front of the Union advance, but as both armies settle down for the night neither is quite sure of the other's position, and Grant does not yet understand that Lee is going to force him to fight in the Wilderness. Meanwhile, another element of Grant's master plan against the Confederacy is set in motion as troops under General Benjamin Butler assemble near the James River, preparing to move upriver toward Richmond.

WESTERN THEATER In Chattanooga, Sherman prepares his part of Grant's plan, readying his troops for their march to Atlanta. There is light skirmishing at Varnell's Station in Georgia.

TRANS-MISSISSIPPI, RED RIVER CAMPAIGN Harassment of the Union fleet on the river continues as Confederates destroy a steamer and capture two others at David's Ferry, Louisiana.

5 MAY 1864

EASTERN THEATER, BATTLE OF THE WILDERNESS Federal General Warren notifies Grant and Meade of an enemy force—Ewells'—on the Orange Turnpike; thinking that this is only a division. Grant orders Warren to attack. These forces quickly join in a fierce battle, and it becomes clear that Lee's army is opposing the Federals in force. Because of the thick woods, the men often grapple at almost point blank range; battlelines become confused in the smoke-filled forest, regiments

losing contact with one another. Soldiers and leaders follow the battle by the sound of firing, and often find themselves shooting at an enemy they can see only by the flashing of guns. Late in the afternoon Confederate General Hill's advance along the Plank Road is met by Hancock; a separate and equally desperate contest ensues. Again the fighting is at close quarters, often hand-to-hand with bayonets and clubbed muskets, the artillery silent for fear of doing harm to unseen friendly troops. All day the fighting surges back and forth, but as evening falls nothing significant has been gained by either side, and the forces retire to await the next day's battle. During the night, troops of both sides frequently wander into enemy lines.

Also on this day, General Butler and 40,000 men land at Bermuda Hundred, in the 'bottle' formed by the James and Appomattox Rivers. Though Butler's plan has been supervised by Grant, it is a poor one: Bermuda Hundred is excellent for a defensive position, but is not properly situated for an offensive.

WESTERN THEATER After the Confederates' occupation of Plymouth and Washington, North Carolina, they move against the port of New Berne, which Grant has ordered held at all costs. The attack on New Berne today is turned back by Federal defenders, but the Confederate ironclad ram CSS *Albemarle* roams threateningly on the Roanoke River, fighting to a draw with seven Federal blockading ships and disabling the USS *Sassacus*.

TRANS-MISSISSIPPI, RED RIVER CAMPAIGN Confederate shore batteries destroy two Federal wooden gunboats and a transport on the river near Dunns Bayou. The Union fleet is still marooned above Alexandria.

6 MAY 1864

THE CONFEDERACY President Davis writes anxiously to General Beauregard, instructing him to meet Butler's threat on Petersburg from the south.

EASTERN THEATER, BATTLE OF THE WIL-DERNESS During the night Grant orders a general attack by Sedgwick, Warren and Hancock, to commence at 5 o'clock in the morning. Reinforcements are moved up on both sides. Before the Union advance can be launched, however, Rebels attack Sedgwick on the Union right flank, and the firing gradually spreads along the line. Federal General Hancock moves against the weak positions of Hill, who has unwisely failed to entrench his forces. Hill's lines are soon enveloped on the Orange Plank Road and are in danger of being routed. But at the critical moment, Longstreet's reinforcements, awaited by Hill since the previous day, make a dramatic appearance, moving down the Orange Plank road at a trot. Soon the Union advance is checked and the Federals thrown back to their original breastworks; a further Confederate advance captures these works, but is not able to break the Union line.

About 10 o'clock in the morning, after turning back the Union advance, Longstreet decides to take the offensive against the Federal left flank. He finds an unfinished railroad cut that provides a clear route to the Federal flank and sends four brigades to the attack. Before noon the Federals are overwhelmed by these forces; the Union left is rolled up northward in confusion. But then disaster strikes the Confederate advance, as recounted by Southern General E M Law: 'General Longstreet rode forward and prepared to press his advantage. . . . Longstreet and Kershaw rode with General Jenkins at the head of his brigade as it pressed forward, when suddenly the quiet that had reigned for some moments was broken by a few scattering shots on the north of the road, which were answered by a volley from Mahone's line on the south side. The firing in their front, and the appearance of troops on the road whom they failed to recognize as friends through the intervening timber, had drawn a single volley, which lost to them all the fruits of the splendid work they had just done. General Jenkins was killed and Longstreet seriously wounded by our

own men.' (This occurs within five miles of where Stonewall Jackson was mortally wounded by his own men a year before.) As he is taken from the battlefield, Longstreet orders General Field to press the attack, but the Confederate forces are in confusion after the accident; Lee comes forward to organize the forces and prepare a new offensive, but the impetus has been lost and the Federals have time to regroup and fortify their positions. A Confederate attack later in the afternoon is halted at the Union breastworks.

Elsewhere during the day Sheridan's and Stuart's cavalry have clashed inconclusively at Todd's Tavern. Confederate General John B Gordon, having ascertained that the Federal right flank is close at hand and quite exposed, has spent all day seeking Ewell's permission for an attack. Permission is given by Lee late in the afternoon, and two brigades move out, overlapping the right of Sedgwick's corps. The surprised Federals are driven from a large portion of their works, losing six hundred in captured, including Generals Seymour and Shaler. The Union army is now in imminent danger of being cut off from its supply line on the Rapidan. Receiving the increasingly serious, and often exaggerated, reports of this crisis, Grant issues orders with his usual calm demeanor, but, as one of his generals reports: 'when all proper measures had been taken, Grant went into his tent, threw himself face down on his cot and gave way to the greatest emotion . . . [He] was stirred to the very depths of his soul . . . and not till it became apparent that the enemy was not pressing his advantage did he recover his perfect composure.' Had Gordon attacked earlier in the day he might have pressed his advantage home; but the Confederate move is halted by the arrival of darkness, and both armies entrench for the night.

Casualties in the two days of fighting have been staggering: the North has lost 2246 killed, 12,037 wounded, and 3383 missing, a total of 17,666 of 100,000 engaged; the Confederate losses, from the usual incomplete records kept on Southern casualties, are something over 7500 of 60,000 engaged; the Union losses are thus more than twice the Confederate, but the North has lost only a slightly larger percentage of its army than has the South. Although the troops do not yet know it as they entrench in the evening, the Battle of the Wilderness is over. But the tragedy is not quite over as darkness falls. Brush fires have broken out in the thick woods; several times during the day the fighting has stopped by mutual consent while soldiers of both armies work side by side to move their wounded out of the burning woods. During the night the forest fires rage, and while the entrenched armies listen to the screams of the trapped, 200 Federal wounded die in the flames.

Between the James and Appomattox Rivers, meanwhile, Butler's troops begin their entrenchment on a three-mile line north to south across the neck of the peninsula formed by the two rivers. The Federals are within sight of the steeples of Petersburg, seven miles away; Richmond lies fifteen miles to the north. At this point the Confederates have less than 10,000 men in the area around Petersburg and Richmond; the Federal force is four times that number. A small force of Confederates under Beauregard repel 1000 Union troops who, on Butler's orders, attempt to cut the Richmond and Petersburg railroad line. This is the first action in the comedy of errors that will constitute Butler's campaign on Richmond.

7 *MAY* 1864

EASTERN THEATER, WILDERNESS CAMPAIGN By dawn the weather around the Wilderness is rainy, the troops not moving out of their entrenchments. Early in the morning a reporter observes the following: 'Grant and Meade had retired a little from the crowd and stood by the roadside in earnest conversation—Grant, thoughtful, a cigar in his mouth, a knife in one hand and a stick in the other, which he was whittling to a point. He whittled slowly toward him. His thoughts were not yet crystallized. Suddenly he commenced on the other end of the stick, whittled energetically from him, and word was at once sent to General Warren and the other corps to move in the direction of Spotsylvania.' Grant, sure that Lee is retreating south, has decided on the bold stroke of attempting again to flank Lee on the Confederate left, moving round the Army of North Virginia toward Richmond. But Grant is doubly mistaken; Lee has not retreated, and the Federal flanking movement is no surprise. On this morning Lee observes to General Gordon: 'General Grant is not going to retreat. He will move his army to Spotsylvania . . . I am so sure of his next move that I have already made arrangements to march by the shortest practicable route, so that we may meet him there.' During the day marching orders are issued to both armies. The battle of the Wilderness has been a draw, and the race to the vital Confederate crossroad of Spotsylvania has begun.

To the south in Virginia, another effort by 8000 of Butler's men on the Richmond and Petersburg Railroad is rebuffed at Port Walthall Junction by a force of some 2700 Confederates. Federals are already beginning to refer to their campaign as a 'stationary advance.'

WESTERN THEATER, ATLANTA CAMPAIGN Since November of 1873 the two great armies of the West have been stationary, Sherman's Federals in Chattanooga and Johnston's Army of Tennessee in nearby Dalton, Georgia. As part of Grant's overall plan, Sherman has been ordered 'to move against Johnston's army, to break it up, and to get into the interior of the enemy's country as far as you can, inflicting all the damage you can against their war resources.' Sherman's success in his mission, surpassing all expectations, will leave him with a reputation as perhaps the greatest Federal commander of the war. Sherman's first goal in his disruption of the Confederacy is the vital supply, manufacturing, and communications center of Atlanta. He has assembled a conglomeration of several armies, including the stolid but effective General Thomas's Army of the Cumberland, McPherson's Army of the Tennessee and Schofield's Army of the Ohio, a total of over 100,000 men. His opponent, leader of the Confederate Army of Tennessee, is General J E Johnston, an erratic but effective leader whose fine strategic sense is often offset by poor administrative work and lack of attention to detail. Johnston is also liable to quarrels with superiors, and has never been liked by President Davis. His subordinates include corps commanders Hardee, Hood and, soon to arrive, Polk; including Wheeler's 2000 cavalry, Johnston's forces number about 62,000. This day Sherman begins his advance with a move toward Johnston's left flank, the enemy's defenses in Dalton, Georgia, being too strong to attack directly. Pursuing this strategy, a corps under Palmer drives Confederate outposts from Tunnel Hill, pushing them to Buzzard's Roost.

8 *MAY* 1864

EASTERN THEATER, SPOTSYLVANIA CAMPAIGN Warren's troops, exhausted from four days of fighting in the Wilderness, arrive at the end of their long forced march to find that, instead of being in retreat toward Richmond, the Rebels are in their path and ready to fight in force. The Confederates have won the race to Spotsylvania. Warren's Federal cavalry arrive at Spotsylvania about 8 o'clock in the morning and clash with Stuart's cavalry, who are

General Wild's troops liberating slaves.

blocking the Brock road. Stuart immediately calls for assistance from Anderson, whose men are resting nearby. Soon the head of Warren's column is thrown back. Frustrated by their unexpected collision with the enemy, Meade and Sheridan have a violent quarrel in the afternoon, Meade accusing Sheridan's cavalry of being in the way of Warren's forces and crucially impeding them. Sheridan replies that he did not order the cavalry into position, that Meade himself must have done it; the cavalry officer concludes by telling Meade to order the cavalry himself. Following this quarrel, Sheridan convinces Grant to let him make a raid around Lee's army that will disrupt supply lines, take on Jeb Stuart, and join Butler in moving on Richmond. Thus begins Sheridan's Richmond Raid.

It is clear to both armies that battle is about to be resumed. Meanwhile, Sedgwick arrives to reinforce Warren and in the late afternoon forces of the two generals assault Anderson's right wing, but the Confederates, aided by the arrival of Ewell's men, repulse this attack with heavy losses on the Union side. Both sides now begin building entrenchments and await the remainder of their forces.

WESTERN THEATER, ATLANTA CAMPAIGN Sherman's men probe the forces of the Army of Tennessee in several locations around Confederate positions on Rocky Face Ridge. Union troops move on the Confederates at Buzzard Gap, and a similar unsuccessful attempt is made along the Lafayette-Dalton road at Dug Gap.

9 *MAY* 1864

EASTERN THEATER, SPOTSYLVANIA CAMPAIGN The armies continue their entrenching operations in a day of light fighting. Lee has laid his lines out to utilize the brows of the slopes in the open fields. In the middle of his east-to-west lines is a curved salient of breastworks that looks somewhat like a horseshoe. It will be known to history as the 'Bloody Angle.' During this day the Union loses one of its finest leaders when corps commander General John Sedgwick is felled by a Southern sharpshooter. (Sedgwick's last words, addressed to a dodging soldier, are, 'They couldn't hit an elephant at this distance.') Also during the day, Sheridan's cavalry leaves on their Richmond Raid, pursued by Stuart's cavalry. Sheridan's men damage Southern supply lines at Beaver Dam Station.

Elsewhere, Butler again lumbers into action in the direction of Petersburg, sending his whole army against communication lines and the railroad, some of which are destroyed. Finding the enemy strongly entrenched at Swift Creek, Generals Smith and Gillmore suggest to Butler that they place a pontoon bridge across the Appomattox. This plan could bring considerable Union strength against Petersburg, but it is summarily rejected by Butler, whose criticism of the plan is such as to check advice from his staff for the rest of the campaign. WESTERN THEATER, ATLANTA CAMPAIGN Five Federal assaults are repulsed from the crest of Dug Gap by Johnston's men. Federal cavalry are also driven back from Poplar Place with heavy losses. Sherman's General McPherson routs a small Confederate force at Snake Creek Gap and presses on nearly to Resaca, bringing his men behind Johnston's lines. However, finding strong defenses at Resaca, McPherson pulls back to Snake Creek Gap, for which he is severely criticized by Sherman. While he has failed to cut Johnston's line of retreat, McPherson's effort will convince the Army of Tennessee to abandon Dalton. TRANS-MISSISSIPPI, RED RIVER CAMPAIGN The Union gunboat *Lexington* passes through a gap in a Union-built dam above Alexandria, the first ship of the flotilla to make it through the rapids. During the next few days the rest of the fleet will follow.

10 *MAY* 1864

EASTERN THEATER, SPOTSYLVANIA CAMPAIGN Lee has directed solid breastworks

and entrenchments to be made all along his line, but he faces battle with two of his three corps commanders out of action—Longstreet is wounded, replaced by Anderson, and an ailing A P Hill is replaced by Jubal Early. During the day the Union corps of Warren, Hancock and Wright (who has replaced Sedgwick) are thrown against the Confederate left and left-center; all of these attacks are repulsed with heavy Federal losses. Meanwhile, Sheridan finishes his work at Beaver Dam Station, having destroyed two locomotives, over 100 railroad cars, 10 miles of track, medical stores, and a large quantity of rations. Sheridan's subordinate, General George Custer, recaptures 378 Union prisoners who had been taken in the Battle of the Wilderness. Sheridan's men move on toward Richmond; Confederate cavalry commander Jeb Stuart rides to intercept them.

In southeast Virginia, Federal General Butler's men destroy a few more railroad tracks before being ordered back into their 'bottle,' the defenses on the peninsula at Bermuda Hundred. The withdrawal allows Beauregard time to send six brigades to defend nearby Drewry's Bluff. WESTERN THEATER, ATLANTA CAMPAIGN Polk's corps from Mississippi is en route to reinforce Johnston's Confederates as the commander learns of McPherson's penetration of his defenses at Snake Creek Gap. Sherman, meanwhile, decides to move his whole army through the vulnerable gap.

11 *MAY* 1864

EASTERN THEATER, SPOTSYLVANIA CAMPAIGN On a day of heavy rain there is no fighting. Movements along Federal lines lead General Lee to wonder if Grant is not beginning yet another flanking movement. To prepare his response to that possibility, Lee orders artillery moved from his left and center, including the horseshoe salient; thus his potentially strongest defensive position is left without artillery. It is on that position that Grant orders Hancock to move at dawn tomorrow. During the day Grant also writes to Chief of Staff Halleck, 'I . . . propose to fight it out on this line if it takes all summer.' In Blacksburg, in southwest Virginia, Federals skirmish during a raid on Confederate railroads. But there is fighting elsewhere today. Jeb Stuart and his cavalry reach Yellow Tavern in the morning and position themselves to block Sheridan's way to Richmond. Sheridan's cavalry arrive before noon and mount a few probing attacks on the Confederate line. In the late afternoon the Federals attack in force. During this attack General Jeb Stuart, at the age of 31 one of the most colorful and effective of Southern cavalry leaders, is mortally wounded while firing at the enemy from his horse; he dies in Richmond the following day. Federals also mortally wound General James B Gordon and drive the Rebel cavalry back. But the engagement gives the Confederates time to strengthen Richmond, and Sheridan, realizing that it would be unwise to move on the Confederate capital, begins to ride south toward the James, to link up with Butler.

12 *MAY* 1864

EASTERN THEATER, SPOTSYLVANIA CAMPAIGN At 4 o'clock in the morning on what is to become one of the bloodiest days of the war, Confederates within the horseshoe salient hear the sound of commands and jumbled voices from the Federal lines. Suddenly through the torrential rain a wave of 20,000 Federals charges directly at the front of the salient; the defenders see only a solid wall of blue pouring toward and then over their breastworks, which are taken with little resistance. Federals capture over 2000 enemy, including many from the Stonewall Brigade, several officers, and 20 cannon, which have been moved up this morning only to be captured. The remaining Confederates fall back to a second line of breastworks on the neck of the salient, and, regrouping there, begin to pour a murderous fire into the advancing Federals while Lee, realizing

the imminent danger to his whole army, quickly moves up reinforcements under General Gordon.

By 10 o'clock in the morning the Confederates have moved into place every man that can be spared from the entire army, and the Federals are driven back to a stand on the north side of the horseshoe salient. There follows a truly terrible day of fighting, with both sides making a series of fruitless and costly attempts to advance.

During the night, Lee orders his forces out of the salient. In the fighting for this small piece of territory the Union has suffered 6800 casualties to the South's 5000, and the salient has earned its historic name of 'Bloody Angle.' At the end of the day a Yankee soldier says simply, 'This has been the most terrible day I have ever lived.'

To the southeast, Sheridan, riding to join Butler, is attacked by troops moved out from Richmond to trap him against the Chickahominy River. Below Richmond, Federal General Butler begins advancing toward Confederate positions at Drewry's Bluff, which is being steadily strengthened by General Beauregard.

WESTERN THEATER, ATLANTA CAMPAIGN During the night General Johnston moves the Army of Tennessee out of Dalton, establishing new defenses north and west of Resaca, Georgia, just in front of Sherman's advancing forces. The two generals have established the pattern of the whole campaign; as if in a formal dance, Sherman will move his superior forces to one flank or the other of his enemy, and Johnston will execute a graceful retreat.

13 *MAY* 1864

THE NORTH Horace Greeley, reflecting the feelings of many Northern Republicans dissatisfied with Lincoln, writes in his New York *Tribune*: 'Our own conviction is . . . that it is advisable for the Union Party to nominate for President some other among its able and true men than Mr. Lincoln.' EASTERN THEATER, SPOTSYLVANIA CAMPAIGN Union troops shift to the south and east, again sidling toward Richmond around the right flank of the enemy. There is no fighting, but both sides deal with their wounded and dead.

Along the Chickahominy, Sheridan escapes from Southern attackers and moves toward Butler, who is this day engaged in slowly moving his forces into position at Drewry's Bluff.

WESTERN THEATER Skirmishes break out as the armies of Sherman and Johnston move into position around Resaca, Georgia. In Charleston Harbor, South Carolina, yet another major Federal bombardment begins on Fort Sumter.

TRANS-MISSISSIPPI, RED RIVER CAMPAIGN The last Federal gunboats move past the dams erected on the river, heading toward the Mississippi while Banks' troops march out of Alexandria toward Simsport. It has been a notable recovery from what has otherwise been a humiliating failure for the North. Meanwhile, Confederates under Jo Shelby begin a series of raids north of the Arkansas River that will go on through the month.

14 *MAY* 1864

EASTERN THEATER, SPOTSYLVANIA CAMPAIGN Grant has ordered an attack on Lee's right flank today, but slow preparations and heavy rain give Lee time to oppose the attack and it is cancelled. Meanwhile, Sheridan's cavalry make contact with Butler's forces. Another element of Grant's master plan takes shape in Virginia's Shenandoah Valley; German-born General Franz Sigel (who often leads German-American troops, thus the slogan 'I fights mit Sigel') moves south toward the Confederate cavalry of General J D Imboden. Rebel reinforcements under Breckinridge are on the way.

WESTERN THEATER, ATLANTA CAMPAIGN There is heavy fighting all along the line as Sherman's men unsuccessfully try to crack Johnston's defenses around Resaca, Georgia. By the end of the day the lines have not significantly changed, and Johnston is confident enough of his defenses to stay where he is.

15 *MAY* 1864

EASTERN THEATER, SPOTSYLVANIA CAMPAIGN The only action today is a skirmish at Piney Branch Church. During the night the Federals entrench across from the Confederate right flank. Meanwhile, Sigel moves his army of 6500 men south down the Shenandoah Valley, one of the primary storehouses of Southern food supplies. Sigel runs into Imboden's cavalry, who delay his advance until the arrival of Confederate reinforcements under Breckinridge at New Market. By 11 o'clock in the morning Sigel's forces have been pushed back about a half mile. A series of costly but increasingly effective Southern assaults follows, and at 4 o'clock in the afternoon Sigel orders a general retreat. Of 5150 engaged, the Federals lose 93 killed, 482 wounded, and 256 missing, totaling 831 casualties; the Confederates lose approximately 42 killed, 522 wounded, and 256 missing, totaling 820 from about 5000 engaged.

Elsewhere, Butler has planned an attack on Drewry's Bluff today, but delays it to arrange his defensive measures, which include stringing wire entanglements between stumps in his front, this being among the first uses of these entanglements in war (they have been tried, with little success, by Burnside in Knoxville). There is not enough wire, however, to extend the obstacles as far as is needed.

WESTERN THEATER, ATLANTA CAMPAIGN A second day of sharp fighting round Resaca begins with a clash between the advancing Federal corps of General Hooker and advancing Confederates under General Hood. During a day of heavy but inconclusive fighting Sherman is unable to break through the Confederate defenses. However, Johnston learns that the Federals have crossed the Oostenaula River and are moving on his rear and accordingly he immediately orders another retreat. Southern forces pull back.

16 *MAY* 1864

EASTERN THEATER, BATTLE OF DREWRY'S

BLUFF In an early morning of thick fog with visibility about 15 feet, ten hastily-assembled brigades of Confederates under General Beauregard attack Butler's lines on the right; Federals under General K A Heckman repulse five charges before they are overwhelmed and Heckman captured along with 400 men. Other Union troops on the right become disorganized in the fog; but the fighting on the Federal left is inconclusive, the center holds, and wire entanglements are devastatingly effective in stopping advancing Confederates. Nonetheless, Butler at length gives up and orders a retreat in what is by now a heavy rainstorm. Beauregard has planned a pursuit but it does not take shape; thus is lost the opportunity to strike a serious blow at the enemy. By next morning the Federals will be safely back at Bermuda Hundred; there they will be, in Grant's phrase, 'bottled up' by Beauregard to the east and by the James and Appomattox rivers to the north and south. Thus, in two days, two major elements of Grant's master plan have failed miserably, the Red River campaign having previously done likewise; Grant himself has been stymied by Lee. Only Sherman in Georgia is fulfilling his assigned role. Furthermore, in Virginia Butler has lost over one-quarter of his 15,800 men engaged since 12 May, to Beauregard's 2506 of 18,025 engaged. Butler's bumbling exploits are to continue, but he is so influential in the North that Lincoln is afraid to relieve him until after the presidential election.

18 MAY 1864

EASTERN THEATER, SPOTSYLVANIA CAMPAIGN A new Federal attack is mounted at 4 o'clock in the morning on the strengthened breastworks that were at the neck of the Bloody Angle and are now the Confederate left (Lee's lines now stretch north-south). After brief fighting the attempt is abandoned, as is an ensuing effort by Burnside on the Federal left. Following this, Grant once more begins sidling to his left, trying to get around Lee's right flank.

Sheridan has begun a hazardous journey from near Richmond to rejoin the Army of the Potomac.

19 MAY 1864

EASTERN THEATER, SPOTSYLVANIA CAMPAIGN Trying to find if Grant is again moving to the Confederate right, Lee sends General Ewell to make contact at Harris's Farm. The armies meet and the Rebels are repulsed but reinforcements help Ewell to hold out until dark. In the Spotsylvania Campaign now drawing to a close, Federal casualties have been 17,500 out of 110,000 engaged; Grant's losses since the beginning of the Wilderness Campaign have been over 33,000. Confederate losses at Spotsylvania are uncertain.

WESTERN THEATER, ATLANTA CAMPAIGN Johnston again stops his army near Cassville, Georgia, with Sherman in pursuit. Deciding to strike at the Federals, Johnston orders General J B Hood, his best combat leader and worst enemy on his staff, to mount an assault on the Union center. But Hood, brilliant as a leader but blundering as a strategist, turns from his attack to face a supposed Federal threat on his right. He is mistaken about the threat, and his move spoils the timing of Johnston's plan. Finding the Union forces moving around both his flanks, Johnston again withdraws to the south.

TRANS-MISSISSIPPI, RED RIVER CAMPAIGN The failed Federal expedition comes to an end as troops cross the Atchafalaya River on a bridge made of steamboats. Elsewhere, Shelby's cavalry continue their raiding in Arkansas.

20 MAY 1864

EASTERN THEATER Grant sends Hancock's corps along the railroad toward Hanover Junction in Virginia, hoping to draw Lee's army into an offensive; the Federals with their greatly superior numbers could crush Lee before he entrenches. But once again Lee second-guesses his foe, and moves to entrench across Grant's path in Hanover Junction. The armies are again racing to the east and south, toward Richmond.

22 *MAY* 1864

EASTERN THEATER   In the morning Confederate General Ewell arrives ahead of Grant's forces at Hanover Junction and begins to entrench; Anderson arrives at noon. Grant is still moving the main body of his force.

WESTERN THEATER   Sherman again flanks Johnston's army, going around the Confederate left at Altoona and heading toward Dallas, Georgia.

23 *MAY* 1864

EASTERN THEATER   General A P Hill arrives early and adds his troops to the Confederate entrenchments on the south side of the North Anna River between Hanover Junction and the water. Lee arranges his army in a wedge, with the point on the river. In the afternoon Federals under Warren cross the stream to the north and are engaged by Hill, who advances slightly in severe but indecisive fighting. Meanwhile, Hancock's corps have moved southward to the north bank to confront the right side of the Confederate wedge opposite. Now the Union army is split in two, and Lee thus has a rare opportunity to deal Grant a serious blow. But on this day Lee is ill, delirious with fever, and confined to his tent. During the day the Confederates receive reinforcements led by Pickett, Hoke, and Breckinridge, the latter fresh from his defeat of Sigel near Richmond.

24 *MAY* 1864

EASTERN THEATER   The Battle of the North Anna River continues. Federal General Warren is reinforced on one side of the Confederate wedge while Hancock crosses the river toward the other side. Meanwhile, Burnside arrives on the north side of the river and begins to cross amid skirmishing at Ox Ford, the point of the Confederate wedge on the opposite bank.

Now the Union army is split into three parts, but Lee is still feverish and not able to direct his troops in pressing this advantage. Sheridan arrives back to the Army of the Potomac after his cavalry raid completely around Lee's army, during which he has not moved on Richmond but has nonetheless destroyed vital supplies, won four engagements, and killed Jeb Stuart.

WESTERN THEATER, ATLANTA CAMPAIGN   Realizing that Sherman is moving around him toward Dallas, Georgia, General Johnston orders his forces out of Altoona toward Dallas in order to remain in front of the Union army. Fighting breaks out at several nearby towns, with Southern cavalry under Wheeler harassing Federal supply wagons.

25 *MAY* 1864

EASTERN THEATER   The Battle of the North Anna River continues. Grant begins a series of fruitless attempts to find a vulnerable point in the Confederate lines.

WESTERN THEATER, ATLANTA CAMPAIGN   Johnston's army awaits Sherman's approach, Hood at New Hope Church on the road from Allatoona, Polk on his left, Hardee on his right. Federals under Hooker attack Hood's corps, but are turned back after two hours by murderous fire from sixteen cannon and 5000 Rebel muskets at short range. Union losses are heavy, and soldiers dub the area 'Hell Hole'.

26 *MAY* 1864

WASHINGTON   Major General J G Foster assumes command of the Federal Department of the South.

EASTERN THEATER   Failing to find a weakness in Lee's entrenchments, Grant and Meade late at night move the Army of the Potomac northward back across the river and for the fourth time begin sidling toward Lee's right, this time toward Hanovertown, 18 miles away. In the Shenandoah the new Federal commander of the Department of West Virginia, General David Hunter, heads toward Staunton with

16,000 men. Opposing this move is Breckinridge's replacement, General W E 'Grumble' Jones.

WESTERN THEATER, ATLANTA CAMPAIGN After a day of skirmishing along their line of advance, Sherman's men halt for the moment and begin entrenching in the New Hope-Dallas area.

27 MAY 1864

EASTERN THEATER Early in the day, Federals, led by Sheridan's cavalry, put two pontoon bridges across the Pamunkey River and occupied Hanovertown. Cavalry skirmishes erupt in several locations as the rest of the Army of the Potomac moves into Hanovertown during the day. To the south, Lee begins moving to head off the Federals.

WESTERN THEATER, ATLANTA CAMPAIGN Heavy fighting is seen around the New Hope-Dallas line as the opposing forces jockey for position. Sherman loses 1400 casualties in unsuccessful attempts to turn the Rebel right. Confederate losses are light. In the evening Johnston directs Hood to attack the end of the Federal left flank the next morning.

TRANS-MISSISSIPPI Confederate raider Jo Shelby, campaigning in Arkansas, is named commander of Confederate troops north of the Arkansas River.

28 MAY 1864

EASTERN THEATER Lee's Army of Northern Virginia hurries to get in front of Grant, moving toward Cold Harbor as the Federals cross the Pamunkey River near Hanovertown.

WESTERN THEATER, ATLANTA CAMPAIGN Hood, ordered to attack ground Sherman's left flank, reports to Johnston that the Union flank is guarded by entrenchments at right angles to the front. Johnston cancels the attack.

29 MAY 1864

EASTERN THEATER Having crossed the Pamunkey River, Grant and Meade's Army of the Potomac march southwest toward Richmond. Between them and Confederate capital stretch Lee's lines.

30 MAY 1864

EASTERN THEATER Grant's forces begin arriving at the north bank of the Totopotomoy River, facing Lee's line across the river and north of the Chickahominy. The Federals are now within ten miles of Richmond. Another day's skirmishing is seen in the area. Federals are reinforced by two corps under the contentious General W F 'Baldy' Smith.

WESTERN THEATER Confederate raider John Hunt Morgan, in action again after his escape from a Federal war prison in Ohio, begins attacking Sherman's distant supply lines in Kentucky.

31 MAY 1864

THE NORTH A group of Radical Republicans hostile to Lincoln's conduct of the war, emancipation, and reconstruction, meets in Cleveland, Ohio, to nominate their own presidential candidate, General John Charles Frémont.

EASTERN THEATER Grant, still trying to move around Lee's right, sends some of his forces south toward Cold Harbor. Lee moves again to cut him off. Skirmishes again mark the day's fighting.

WESTERN THEATER, ATLANTA CAMPAIGN The running battle between Sherman's forces and Johnston's Army of Tennessee has by now claimed about 9000 casualties on each side during May. Hostilities continue around the New Hope-Dallas area.

1 JUNE 1864

EASTERN THEATER, BATTLE OF COLD HARBOR Lee begins to shift forces to meet Grant's new threat, moving men out of Richmond north to the rivers near Cold Harbor. Before dawn Lee moves against Federal troops holding the important road junction of Cold Harbor, wishing to turn Grant's flank before he can attack the Confederate left. But two badly-managed

Southern attacks are repulsed, partly by Sheridan's cavalry using the new Spencer repeating rifles. Lee then orders reinforcements to his right flank, and three strong Federal advances against the right and center are turned back late in the day. Smith on the Federal side having been delayed in moving up by a mistake in orders. The attacks show that the Confederates have dug in with their usual efficiency and are able to direct a heavy fire all along their lines. Grant moves Hancock's corps southward to his left and orders an attack tomorrow morning.

WESTERN THEATER, ATLANTA CAMPAIGN The success of Sherman's advance toward Atlanta is absolutely dependent on his ever-lengthening supply line, and his careful planning and protection of that line are to mark the entire campaign. This day the vital connection between Chattanooga and the Federals' current position near Dallas, Georgia is secured by General George Stoneman's cavalry, who capture Allatoona Pass and its railroad line. Now Sherman will begin moving his troops away from the Dallas area northwestward to his lifeline along the railroad. At the same time, Sherman orders operations to protect the distant reaches of his supply line, particularly against the depredations of General Forrest, who is now gathering his forces in Tupelo, Mississippi. Sherman says, with his customary ferocity: 'That devil Forrest . . . must be hunted down and killed if it

Confederate lines near Atlanta.

costs ten thousand lives and bankrupts the Federal treasury.' To this end, Union General S D Sturgis is sent with 3000 cavalry, 4800 infantry, and 18 guns to deal with Forrest; Sturgis today leaves Memphis and heads toward Ripley, Mississippi. Meanwhile, Rebel raider John Hunt Morgan is active against Sherman's supply lines in Kentucky, today engaging in a skirmish near Pound Gap.

2 *JUNE* 1864

EASTERN THEATER, BATTLE OF COLD HARBOR Grant's general assault on Lee's lines, ordered for the early morning, is delayed by slow troop movements, fatigue, and supply problems. After a heavy rain begins in the afternoon, the attack is again delayed until tomorrow morning. Union soldiers see all too clearly what such a charge directly on strong fortifications will entail. Walking through the troops in the evening, General Horace Porter discovers an awesome sight: 'I noticed that many of the soldiers had taken off their coats and seemed to be engaged in sewing up rents in them. On closer examination it was found that the men were calmly writing their names and addresses on slips of paper and pinning them on the backs of their coats, so that their dead bodies might be recognized and their fate made known to their families at home.' After an abortive attack during the day, Lee's officers during the evening carefully lay out and strengthen their defenses for the expected attack. In the Shenandoah Valley, Sigel's replacement general David Hunter sees action against Confederates under W E Jones at Covington, Virginia. Hunter, ordered by Grant to do what Sigel failed to do and sweep the valley, is headed south for Staunton with 16,000 men, opposed by Jones's 8500 infantry and cavalry.

3 *JUNE* 1864

EASTERN THEATER, BATTLE OF COLD HARBOR Grant has determined to make a decisive blow on Lee's army, hammering his lines in a direct assault like the one that initially overran the Bloody Angle at Spotsylvania. The charge is to be led by the corps of Hancock, Wright and Smith, later to be reinforced by Warren and Burnside, on the center and right of Lee's lines under Anderson and Hill. The attack is intended to be pressed regardless of cost. It begins at 4.30 in the morning, countless thousands of Union soldiers rising from their entrenchments and marching straight toward the fortifications of the enemy. Then, 'there rang out suddenly on the summer air such a crash of artillery and musketry as is seldom heard in war.' The dead and wounded fall in waves like mown wheat. For a short time the Confederate breastworks are reached, but then a murderous countercharge sends the Federals back.

Within the space of a half hour 7000 Federal troops are killed and wounded, their bodies blanketing the ground before the enemy breastworks. Each of the three Union corps commanders complains to Meade that the other two have failed to protect his troops from enfilade fire; this is because the three corps have attacked on diverging lines toward the defenses, thus opening their flanks to fire. Incredibly, after the devastated troops have fallen back from the first attack, the order comes from Grant for a second general assault, this time by corps without reference to others, thus sacrificing unity of attack. This charge is mounted raggedly, with many troops holding back, and it is repulsed, leaving fresh heaps of dead and wounded. Finally Grant orders a third advance. This order is essentially ignored. In the evening Grant admits, 'I regret this assault more than any one I have ever ordered.' A later commentator puts it more directly: 'Cold Harbor represents a horrible failure of Federal generalship.' But the failure continues. A Union observer writes: 'The groans and moaning of the wounded, all our own, who were between the lines, were heartrending.' These wounded are simply to be abandoned. For three days Grant will make no effort to propose a truce to collect his wounded; to go out between the lines without a truce is suicidal, though some Con-

federates risk their lives to bring in nearby Union wounded. Not until 7 June will Union stretcher parties actually be sent out. By this time all but two men of those thousands have died, horribly, of wounds, thirst, hunger, and exposure, all in full sight of both lines. The reason for this callous abandonment is partly, perhaps, the tradition that says the first commander asking permission of the enemy to bring in wounded is the loser, and Grant will not admit to being the loser.

When Grant calls off the attack at noon, Federal killed and wounded for 3 June total around 7000, added to the 5000 casualties of 1 and 2 June. The day's Confederate losses are probably under 1500. Grant will observe in his memoirs: 'No advantage whatever was gained from the heavy loss we sustained.' A Northern observer notes that the Army of the Potomac 'has literally marched in blood and agony from the Rapidan to the James.' The men have marched, slept, and fought for one month in the same blood- and sweat-stiffened uniforms; the roads of their march are strewn with the carcasses of 6000 horses. Federal casualties in the month of incessant campaigning have been 50,000, 41 percent of their original strength; the South has lost 32,000, 46 percent of its strength, and these losses are irreplacable.

4 JUNE 1864

EASTERN THEATER   The armies of Grant and Lee lie quietly in their entrenchments, listening to the goans and entreaties of the Union wounded. Hunter's Federals, moving down the Shenandoah, skirmish at Port Republic and Harrisonburg, Virginia.

WESTERN THEATER, ATLANTA CAMPAIGN Realizing that Sherman is flanking him again, moving northeast toward the Atlanta-Chattanooga railroad, Johnston during the night moves the Army of Tennessee out of the New Hope-Dallas area toward his already-made lines in the mountains before Marietta. There are engagements at Big Shanty and Acworth, Georgia.

CHRONOLOGY

5 *JUNE* 1864

EASTERN THEATER   Confederate General W E Jones makes his stand against Hunter's advance toward Staunton, Virginia, turning 5000 men toward Hunter's main body. But the Federals drive Jones back to his defenses at Piedmont, where he is pounded by Union artillery. A series of attacks and counterattacks ensues, which finally sends the Confederates into a rout during which Jones is killed. Hunter loses 780 men to the South's 1600, of whom 1000 are taken prisoner. Tomorrow Hunter will enter Staunton unopposed.

7 *JUNE* 1864

THE NORTH   The National Union Convention—essentially the Republican Party but with some Democrats who supported the war—opens in Baltimore with Lincoln the unanimous candidate for President, but with some question about the Vice-Presidency and with the anticipated wrangles between Radical and mainstream Republicans.

EASTERN THEATER   The opposing armies still lie in their entrenchments at cold Harbor, Union men finally moving out to pick up their dead; only two of the wounded have survived since the battle of 3 June. Grant and his staff are despondent at their failure to overwhelm Lee; clearly, the direct-assault tactic will not work. Grant slowly accepts the inevitable next move—he must move his army south across the James to threaten Petersburg, the back door to Richmond. As a diversion for his coming move, Grant sends Sheridan's cavalry west to join Hunter at Charlottesville and operate against railroads from there to Hanover Junction. This will become known as Sheridan's Trevilian raid (so named after a town where some of the action occurred).

8 *JUNE* 1864

THE NORTH   By a large majority Lincoln is nominated for President by the National Union Convention in Baltimore. In a surprising move never quite explained—Lincoln claims he is neutral on the issue—Democrat Andrew Johnson of Tennessee is nominated for Vice-President over the incumbent Hannibal Hamlin. It is perhaps felt that a Southern Democrat who supports the war will be useful to the ticket. The party platform calls for reunification, pursuing the war to its end, no compromise with the South, and a constitutional amendment forbidding slavery.

WESTERN THEATER   Sherman's men gather around the Western and Atlantic railroad, ready to close in with Johnston before Marietta, Georgia. Sherman has increasingly to weaken his forces to protect his supply line, now including the railroad back to Chattanooga. In Kentucky, John Hunt Morgan captures a Federal garrison at Mount Sterling, and in the action his raiders help themselves to $18,000 from the local bank.

9 *JUNE* 1864

EASTERN THEATER   General Benjamin Butler makes yet another mismanaged attempt on Petersburg. Beauregard sends the Federals packing, despite having only 2500 defenders to Butler's 4500 troops.

WESTERN THEATER   Confederate raider Morgan and his men are routed from Mount Sterling, Kentucky.

10 *JUNE* 1864

THE CONFEDERACY   The Confederate Congress authorizes military service for all ages from 17 to 50.

EASTERN THEATER   A Union force of 8000 men under General S D Sturgis, sent by Sherman to take care of Forrest, meet their assigned foe at Brice's Crossroads in Mississippi. The Confederate leader has learned the preceeding evening of this advance, and beats the Federals to the crossroad. While his pickets hold the enemy, Forrest moves up his artillery and men, and when the Federals arrive in strength, tired from a forced march in fierce heat, they find themselves immediately under attack. Forrest pressures both Union flanks, which begin to give way late in the afternoon. Finally the Federals panic and run, leaving behind so much equipment that the Confederates have trouble getting around it to chase the fleeing enemy. Sturgis has been defeated by a force less than half as large as his own and has lost 227 killed, 394 wounded and 1623 captured, plus leaving 16 of his 18 guns and his entire supply train of 250 vehicles. Forrest reports losing 492 of 3500 engaged. It is one of 'that devil' Forrest's finest moments. At the end of the day the Federals are still running and Rebels still pursuing. Elsewhere, Morgan's increasingly riotous raiders burn a Federal depot and stables in Lexington, Kentucky. In Georgia, Sherman's men move toward Johnston's mountain positions northwest of Marietta.

11 JUNE 1864

EASTERN THEATER General Robert E Lee has dispatched his nephew, General Fitzhugh 'Fitz' Lee, and General Wade Hampton, Stuart's successor as cavalry commander, to stop Sheridan's depredations in Virginia, in fact a diversion from the planned movement of the Army of the Potomac on Petersburg. Hampton makes contact with Sheridan near Louisa. During the ensuing fight, Hampton is told that Federals are at his rear; these prove to be Custer's men, who have with their usual boldness struck between Hampton's and Fitz Lee's columns, capturing for the moment many Confederate horses and vehicles. Hampton turns to attack Custer with his own column, and after a confused battle Custer is fought back to Trevilian Station, by which time other Federals have driven Fitz Lee to Louisa. Elsewhere in Virginia, Hunter's men engage in depredations in and around Lexington, including burning the Virginia Military Institute. Robert E Lee dispatches General Jubal Early to deal with Hunter.
WESTERN THEATER Fighting off Forrest's men, Sturgis and his beaten Federals straggle back toward Memphis, where they will arrive on 13 June. Following this debacle, Sturgis will finish the war 'awaiting orders.'

NAVAL The CSS *Alabama*, most successful of Confederate seagoing raiders, sails into Cherbourg, France, for much-needed refitting.

12 JUNE 1864

EASTERN THEATER, PETERSBURG CAMPAIGN After several days of careful and secretive preparations, the four corps of the Federal Army of the Potomac pull quietly out of their positions at Cold Harbor and steal toward the James River on roads and bridges, several of which have been built within the week—including a massive pontoon bridge across the James, 2100 feet long, to be built in a half day on 14 June. By 16 June the entire army will have been moved to the south shore of the James. Meanwhile, Warren's corps stays behind to screen the movement on the left flank. In this brilliantly planned and executed maneuver, Grant seems for once to have outsmarted Lee, who does not discover the move for several days, thus leaving largely undefended the goal of Grant's march—Petersburg. At Trevilian Station Sheridan mounts a furious attack against Hampton's entrenchments, but the attack is thrown back with heavy losses. Sheridan decides at length that he will not try to join Hunter in the Valley as planned, but will move to rejoin Grant. After their repulse, Sheridan and his men begin moving back the way they came, having lost 1007 casualties of 8000 engaged (Confederate losses are uncertain but probably comparable).
WESTERN THEATER Confederate raider Morgan and his 1300 men, having the previous day taken Cynthiana, Kentucky, are met and defeated in that town by 1500 Federals under General Burbridge. The Confederates lose nearly half their party. Morgan and his remaining troops flee toward Abingdon, Virginia, where he arrives on 20 June. In Mississippi, Forrest continues his pursuit of Sturgis.

13 JUNE 1864

EASTERN THEATER, PETERSBURG CAM-

CHRONOLOGY

PAIGN Lee, realizing the Federals have moved but not yet certain of the import of the move, guesses wrongly that the enemy's object is Richmond. Lee therefore moves southward to cut off approaches to the capital; this will have no effect on Grant. The Army of the Potomac smoothly continues its massive movement.

14 JUNE 1864

EASTERN THEATER, PETERSBURG CAMPAIGN As the Army of the Potomac nears completion of its crossing of the James, Grant sends General W F 'Baldy' Smith's corps by water to Bermuda Hundred to join Butler in his 'bottle'. Grant goes along himself to plan an attack on Petersburg by Butler and Smith. Lee still does not perceive the import of Grant's move and thus has not reinforced Petersburg.

WESTERN THEATER, ATLANTA CAMPAIGN During a conference of Johnston's staff at their position on the summit of Pine Mountain near Marietta, Georgia, Federal Parrott guns send a few shells toward the summit from Sherman's new positions nearby. One of the shells hits General Leonidas Polk and kills him instantly.

NAVAL The USS *Kearsarge* moves toward Cherbourg, France, to blockade the raider CSS *Alabama*.

15 JUNE 1864

WASHINGTON The House votes 95 to 66 against a joint resolution abolishing slavery.

THE NORTH Notorious Copperhead Clement L Vallandigham returns to Dayton, Ohio, from Canada, to add his voice to the Democratic election efforts.

EASTERN THEATER, PETERSBURG CAMPAIGN Having urgently requested reinforcements from Lee, Beauregard's messenger is told by Lee that Beauregard is in error in thinking a large force of Federals are south of the James. Ironically, at that same moment Beauregard's force of some 5400 defending Petersburg is under assault by W F 'Baldy' Smith's whole corps of 16,000 men. Lee still does not understand

Grant's move, and Petersburg is thus in serious danger. But the Federals have had a day of mishaps: Smith's attack, scheduled for early morning with reinforcement from Hancock, is delayed until 7 o'clock in the evening by Smith's slowness; meanwhile, Hancock is being delayed by a combination of faulty maps, hazy orders from Grant, and an unnecessary stop for provisions. Nonetheless, Smith's attack in the evening makes good headway, not surprising since his force is three times the enemy's. When Hancock finally arrives, he suggests that both he and Smith use the moonlit night to press the attack on in to Petersburg. Success is in fact very likely. Then, making one of the great blunders of the war, 'Baldy' Smith decides against this. Instead, he asks Hancock to occupy the captured trenches while he withdraws. Hancock, though he is senior to Smith, agrees, thus perhaps prolonging the war by many months. During the night, Beauregard decides to abandon his position facing Butler in Bermuda Hundred and use the men to reinforce Petersburg.

WESTERN THEATER, ATLANTA CAMPAIGN Sherman's corps under Thomas, McPherson, and Schofield close in amid skirmishes on Johnston's positions near Marietta, Georgia.

16 JUNE 1864
EASTERN THEATER, PETERSBURG

Union trenches near Petersburg, Virginia.

CAMPAIGN Confederate commander Beauregard, having pulled in most of his Bermuda Hundred line, now has 14,000 men to defend Petersburg. By now the entire Union Army of the Potomac except for Wright's corps is across the James and at the door of Petersburg. Grant and Meade, arriving in the morning, direct the day's renewed assaults, which by late evening have with heavy losses captured several positions. Meanwhile, in the afternoon Federals overrun the remaining 1000 Confederates at Bermuda Hundred. Lee, still not aware of the threat to the city, sends replacements not to Petersburg but to Bermuda Hundred.

17 JUNE 1864

EASTERN THEATER, PETERSBURG CAMPAIGN Another series of Federal attacks on Petersburg make slow and costly headway, and late in the day Beauregard actually recaptures some positions. During the night the defenders pull back into a tighter and tougher position. Lee, perceiving at last the Federal threat, orders Hill and Anderson to Petersburg. Meade orders another attack for tomorrow.

18 JUNE 1864

EASTERN THEATER, PETERSBURG CAMPAIGN During the day a series of badly-coordinated assaults are launched against Petersburg as Confederate reinforcements begin to arrive from Lee. All the early Federal efforts meet with costly repulses. A major Union attack beginning at 2 o'clock in the afternoon makes some progress but is terribly costly—in 30 minutes one regiment loses 632 of 900 engaged, the highest casualties of any Union regiment in a single battle during the war. As the fighting ends with darkness, Grant gives up the idea of making an assault. In four days of storming the entrenchments, the North has lost 1688 killed, 8513 wounded, and 1185 captured and missing, a total of 11,386 casualties of 63,797 engaged; Confederates losses are unknown in the 41,499 engaged by the end of the day. The oppor-

tunity of taking Petersburg when it was weak has been lost; reinforcements have arrived along with Lee himself, and the city is now effectively impregnable. The only course hereafter is a siege, and Grant begins preparations to that effect. Grant has over 110,000 men to work with, to Beauregard's 50,000, and the North holds two rail lines and several roads. But poor Union leadership will mark the ensuing siege, and so will the continuing brilliance of Lee's defense. Meanwhile outside Lynchburg, Hunter is repulsed in an attack on Breckinridge and some of Early's corps. Finding Early is moving toward him in force, Hunter retreats, eventually to end up in Parkersburg and Martinsburg, Virginia. Having dispensed with Hunter, Early is now freed for other excursions.

19 JUNE 1864

NAVAL As crowds of observers watch from nearby cliffs and from a British Yacht, the CSS *Alabama* under Captian Raphael Semmes sallies out near Cherbourg, France, to meet the USS *Kearsarge* under Captain John A Winslow. A fierce battle ensues, the ships circling closer and closer while blazing away with their cannon. At length the *Alabama* is crippled and limps toward shore, striking its colors as it settles. The English yacht, the *Deerhound*, is given permission by Captain Winslow to pick up survivors as the *Alabama* goes down. While the men watch from the *Kearsarge*, the

The surrender of the Alabama *to the* Kearsarge.

yacht picks up a number of sailors, including Captain Semmes, and proceeds to steam rapidly out of reach; thus the defeated captain and some crew make a getaway to neutral England. The Confederates have 9 killed and 21 wounded to the Union ship's 3 wounded. This ends the high-seas career of the Southern commerce raider *Alabama*, which has taken 65 Federal merchant ships in the course of the war.

21 *JUNE* 1864

EASTERN THEATER, PETERSBURG CAMPAIGN   Wishing to extend his siege into a semicircle around Petersburg and cut Southern supply lines, Grant orders General Birney (who has replaced the wound-troubled Hancock) to seize the Weldon Railroad, and General Wright to cut the road to Lynchburg. Later in the day, Grant and the visiting President Lincoln tour the siege lines on horseback. Lincoln's visit to the area will conclude tomorrow after a talk with General Butler.

22 *JUNE* 1864

EASTERN THEATER, PETERSBURG CAMPAIGN   Pursuing their previous day's orders from Grant, Generals Birney and Wright move out on their separate operations around Petersburg. But both are met by Confederate divisions under A P Hill. Birney is attacked and driven back with 2962 casualties including 1600 prisoners, in an engagement on the Jerusalem Plank Road. Meanwhile, Wright's forces are blocked and Federal cavalry under Wilson are turned back amid heavy skirmishing after destroying some railroad track. Although these Union efforts to extend the siege lines have largely failed, Federal forces do next day gain a foothold on the Jerusalem Plank Road.

WESTERN THEATER, ATLANTA CAMPAIGN   Sherman's men have now closed in on Johnston's positions northwest of Marietta, Georgia. Today Confederate General Hood makes a determined but unsuccessful attack on the Federals near Zion Church.

23 *JUNE* 1864

EASTERN THEATER, PETERSBURG CAMPAIGN   Union cavalry briefly hold a section of the Weldon railroad near Petersburg, but are driven off. Federal cavalry under Wilson, moving against Confederate supply lines on the South Side Railroad, are in action at Nottoway Court House. Federal cavalry commander Sheridan moves toward Grant's army with a huge wagon train. In the Shenandoah, Confederate General Jubal Early moves north from Lynchburg while skirmishing with Hunter's retreating army.

WESTERN THEATER, ATLANTA CAMPAIGN   Two weeks of rain has kept action down between the armies of Sherman and Johnston near Marietta. As the rains end Sherman begins to gather his forces for a new effort. After his highly successful flanking maneuvers, Sherman has decided on a general assault on the strongly entrenched Confederates.

25 *JUNE* 1864

EASTERN THEATER, PETERSBURG CAMPAIGN   Based on an innovative plan by mining engineer Colonel Henry Pleasants, enthusiastically supported by Burnside and approved without enthusiasm by Grant, Federals begin digging a tunnel toward the Confederate earthworks at Petersburg. Eventually the mine is to be filled with powder and a crater blown in the Confederate fortifications. The 511-foot shaft will be completed on 23 July. Also today, after a skirmish with Confederate cavalry on 24 June, Sheridan's cavalry and wagon train are back from their Trevilian raid and nearing reunion with the Army of the Potomac.

27 *JUNE* 1864

WASHINGTON   Lincoln formally accepts the Union Party's nomination for President.

EASTERN THEATER, PETERSBURG CAMPAIGN   At Staunton, Virginia, Confederate General Jubal Early organizes his army of 10,000 into two corps. Early plans an invasion of the North.

WESTERN THEATER, ATLANTA CAMPAIGN
The day has arrived for Sherman's general assault on Johnston's positions at Kennesaw Mountain, near Marietta, Georgia. Sherman will describe the results in his memoirs: 'About 9 o'clock AM of the day appointed, the troops moved to the assault, and all along our lines for ten miles a furious fire of artillery and musketry was kept up. At all points the enemy met us with determined courage and in great force. . . . By 11:30 the assault was over, and had failed.' In three major uphill assaults into a hail of shot and shell, the Federal troops capture not one breastwork. A Southern soldier will recollect: 'A solid line of blue came up the hill. My pen is unable to describe the scene of carnage that ensued in the next two hours. Column after column of Federal soldiers were crowded upon that line. No sooner would a regiment mount our works than they were shot down or surrendered. Yet still they came . . . I am satisfied that every man in our regiment killed . . . fivescore men. All that was necessary was to load and shoot. In fact, I will ever think that the reason they did not capture our works was the impossibility of their living men to pass over the bodies of their dead.' Federal losses in the battle are 1999 killed and wounded and 52 missing, over 2000 casualties out of a total of 16,229 attackers; Confederates numbered some 17,733, their losses 270 killed and wounded and 172 missing.

30 JUNE 1864

WASHINGTON Radical Republican Secretary of the Treasury Salmon P Chase, after a number of wrangles with Lincoln, submits another in a series of resignations. This time, to Chase's apparent surprise, Lincoln accepts the resignation and begins looking for a new Secretary.

EASTERN THEATER, EARLY'S WASHINGTON RAID Putting in motion his projected invasion of the North, Confederate General Jubal Early moves his army to New Market, Virginia.

2 JULY 1864

EASTERN THEATER, EARLY'S WASHINGTON RAID Early's column heads north toward the Potomac, meeting little resistance as it moves into Winchester, Virginia.

WESTERN THEATER, ATLANTA CAMPAIGN
Realizing that, after his failed assault, Sherman is returning to his flanking tactics, Johnston pulls his army back south of Marietta, again to lines already prepared. In Charleston Harbor, South Carolina, Federal troops establish a beachhead on James Island.

3 JULY 1864

EASTERN THEATER, EARLY'S WASHINGTON RAID The Confederates meet forces under Franz Sigel and over two days drive them back near Harper's Ferry. Panic begins to spread among civilians north of the Potomac.

WESTERN THEATER In Charleston, two Union attacks on Confederate forts are turned back.

4 JULY 1864

WASHINGTON Receiving the Radically-inspired Wade-Davis bill just passed by the Senate, with its punitive plans for reconstruction, Lincoln pocket-vetoes the measure. In the storm of protest that follows, Lincoln will stand firmly by his more lenient policies, which he is now putting into effect in Louisiana and Arkansas.

WESTERN THEATER, ATLANTA CAMPAIGN
Finding Sherman about to get between his army and Atlanta, Johnston again pulls back, this time to the Chattahoochee River northwest of Atlanta.

5 JULY 1864

EASTERN THEATER, EARLY'S WASHINGTON RAID Avoiding Sigel's forces at Harper's Ferry, Early begins crossing the Potomac into Maryland at Shepherdstown. As consternation breaks out in Washington, Grant and Chief of Staff Halleck begin to take Early seriously, dispatching reinforcements on the morrow. Meanwhile,

militia are called up to defend Maryland.
WESTERN THEATER   Another Federal expedition against Confederate raider Forrest commences; Union troops leave LaGrange, Tennessee, under command of General A J Smith.

6 JULY 1864

EASTERN THEATER, EARLY'S WASHINGTON RAID   The Confederates finish crossing the Potomac and easily capture Hagerstown, Maryland, where $20,000 is demanded of the citizens, nominally in reparation for Hunter's raids in June.

7 JULY 1864

EASTERN THEATER, EARLY'S WASHINGTON RAID   Federal reinforcements arrive in Washington and Baltimore as Early's 'invading army' skirmishes in several places around Middletown.
WESTERN THEATER   In Charleston Harbor, Federals are driven from their beachhead on James Island. In ten days of fighting in the area, Union forces have lost 330 to the South's 163. Still another Federal bombardment begins on the rubble of Fort Sumter.

8 JULY 1864

WESTERN THEATER, ATLANTA CAMPAIGN Against the wishes of President Davis, Johnston responds to new Union flanking movements by ordering the Army of Tennessee back south of the Chattahoochee River, to the gates of Atlanta. Tomorrow Bragg will arrive, sent by Davis for consultation. Sherman is rapidly accumulating forces and supplies for the assault on Atlanta, and orders operations on Southern railroad lines between Columbus, Georgia, and Montgomery, Alabama; these are carried out by 22 July.

9 JULY 1864

EASTERN THEATER, EARLY'S WASHINGTON RAID   Arriving at the Monocacy River near Frederick, Early finds in his path a force of 6000 Federals under General Lew Wallace. A series of largely unplanned Confederate attacks eventually routs the hastily-assembled Union forces, many of whom are inexperienced and untrained. Confederate casualties are around 700 of 14,000 engaged; Union casualties are put at nearly 2000, most of them 'missing.' Rather than wasting forces in pursuit, Early presses on toward Washington, stopping to demand a $200,000 levy in Frederick. By now Washington is seriously worried: 'long guns sprouted with bayonets are going about in company with short clerks . . . and every body is tugging some sort of death-dealing tool.'

10 JULY 1864

WASHINGTON   Lincoln, seemingly unperturbed by Early's approach, tells a group in Baltimore: 'Let us be vigilant but keep cool. I hope neither Baltimore nor Washington will be sacked.'

11 JULY 1864

EASTERN THEATER, EARLY'S WASHINGTON RAID   By noon Early's army arrives at Silver Springs, Maryland, on the outskirts of Washington. Confederates spend the day reconnoitering for the proposed attack tomorrow. Skirmishing flares at Frederick and at Fort Stevens near Washington, where the President and his wife are sightseeing the battle; Lincoln at one point is under fire as he looks over the parapets. But Early begins to observe reinforcements moving into the capital from Grant's army—Wright arrives with a corps during the day. Many of the rest of the defenders are raw troops, however. Finally, during the night Early decides to give up the attack. Whether he could have actually taken the capital remains uncertain but some of his soldiers are sure he could have, and a correspondent inside the city observes: 'I have always wondered at Early's inaction. Washington was never more helpless. Our lines . . . could have been carried at any point.'

12 JULY 864

EASTERN THEATER, EARLY'S WASHINGTON RAID   Having decided to give up his assault on Washington, Early's men skirmish on the outskirts before pulling out at night. During action at Fort Stevens, Lincoln again stands up to watch, prompting an officer to shout, 'Get down, you fool!' Before their withdrawal, the Confederates burn the home of Postmaster General Montgomery Blair.

13 JULY 1864

EASTERN THEATER   Early's forces retreat toward the Potomac at Leesburg; in pursuit is a force of 15,000 under General Horatio Wright.

WESTERN THEATER   In their campaign to stop General Forrest and his raids on Sherman's all-important supply lines, Federals under A J Smith near their quarry at Tupelo, Mississippi. Forrest's men move up for an attack, and there are minor actions during the day.

14 JULY 1864

EASTERN THEATER   Early's forces safely cross the Potomac at Leesburg; Wright informs Washington that he does not advise pursuing the enemy into Virginia.

WESTERN THEATER   At Tupelo, Mississippi, Smith has established strong entrenchments on his front, and against these Forrest and General S D Lee throw a series of assaults that are turned back with heavy losses. The Confederates withdraw by noon while the Federals stay in their positions all day; an evening attempt by Forrest to envelop the enemy left is also unsuccessful. Of Smith's 14,000 men, there are 674 casualties to Forrest's 1347 of 9500 engaged. Plans are made to renew the battle tomorrow.

15 JULY 1864

WESTERN THEATER   A further southern assault on Smith's entrenchments is repulsed with little loss to either side. A worse problem is the heat, from which many soldiers are collapsing. Around noon a further Confederate advance reveals that Smith, worried about short supplies, is retreating. The Confederates follow amid skirmishing but are repulsed, Forrest being slightly wounded. While this action at Tupelo has been nominally a Federal victory, it has

been a defensive one when the point was to mount an offensive. Thus Forrest is still fully at large, though Smith does manage to protect the Nashville to Chattanooga railroad.

16 JULY 1864

EASTERN THEATER   Early and his men are moving with little immediate opposition back toward the Shenandoah Valley, where they will engage in a busy summer's raiding.

WESTERN THEATER, ATLANTA CAMPAIGN Johnston works on his fortification around Atlanta, planning to attack the enemy if opportunity presents. Sherman's army is moving across the Chattahoochee on pontoon bridges; McPherson is sent on a wide enveloping movement through Decatur, Georgia.

17 JULY 1864

EASTERN THEATER, ATLANTA CAMPAIGN A telegram arrives from President Davis relieving the cautious Johnston from command of the Army of Tennessee, and replacing him with General John Bell Hood.

19 JULY 1864

EASTERN THEATER   Federals catch up with Early's forces near Berryville and a sharp series of skirmishes ensues in the area. After a repulse at Berry's Ford and the news of Union troops threatening his supply trains, Early retreats toward Strasburg under heavy pursuit.

WESTERN THEATER, ATLANTA CAMPAIGN Sherman closes his forces on Atlanta, McPherson on one wing moving through Decatur to the east, Thomas on the other wing pushing across Peachtree Creek to the north, and Schofield advancing in the center. Sherman finds such feeble resistance that he wonders if the Confederates are evacuating. But Hood is readying his forces to fall on Thomas.

20 JULY 1864

EASTERN THEATER   Federals continue to harass Early's retreat on Strasburg, Virginia. There are many fierce, small-scale engagements. At Stephenson's Depot, near Winchester, a division of Confederates under S D Ramseur are defeated by Federal General W W Averell, who captures 250 men. But Early's main body is still intact.

WESTERN THEATER, ATLANTA CAMPAIGN Sherman's men are today introduced to what will be Hood's tactics for the remainder of the campaign. Federal General Thomas's Army of the Cumberland is resting in the afternoon after crossing Peachtree Creek, when Confederates under Hardee attack in force. The fighting is desperate and often hand-to-hand. Soon Thomas moves up cannon and as they begin firing he directs his resistance from the front, arranging a devastating enfilade fire. After two hours of frantic assault, the Confederates fall back with losses of 4796 from 20,000; Federal losses are about 1779 from the same number engaged. Hood has failed in his first test, and Thomas has preserved the reputation he gained as the 'Rock of Chickamauga.'

21 JULY 1864

EASTERN THEATER, ATLANTA CAMPAIGN Determined to press an offensive, Southern commander Hood sends Wheeler and Hardee toward McPherson's Army of the Tennessee; these Federals are in an exposed position near Decatur, from where they are moving to form Sherman's left wing around the south of Atlanta. Sherman's middle and right under Schofield and Thomas are already in position.

22 JULY 1864

WESTERN THEATER, BATTLE OF ATLANTA About noon McPherson and Sherman are conferring when firing is heard from the left; McPherson rides off to investigate the action. After a 15-mile march, Hardee has made his attack, which is intended to flank McPherson and get in the rear of the Union forces. A furious assault initially causes consternation in the Federals ranks, but McPherson arrives just as a successful

counterattack is mounted. Having seen this success, the general is riding to direct other positions when he is intercepted by Confederate skirmishers, who silently signal him to surrender. McPherson tips his hat to the enemy and bolts; he is shot from his horse and killed instantly. New charges by the Confederates then gain some ground, but by 3 o'clock in the afternoon these attacks are being halted. Realizing this, Hood orders General Cheatham to make another attack closer to the Federal center. This action makes some headway before being repulsed by a Federal counterattack. Meanwhile, Confederate cavalry under Wheeler are moving unsuccessfully against Federals in Decatur.

As evening falls, Hood's men have made no gains; failing for the second time to dislodge Sherman, they sink back to their entrenchments. Federal casualties for the day are 430 killed, 1559 wounded, 1733 missing, for 3722 casualties out of over 30,000 engaged. Sherman, now in effect besieging Atlanta, will next turn his attention to Hood's supply lines.

24 JULY 1864

EASTERN THEATER At Kernstown, Virginia, Jubal Early's army attacks a group of Federals under General George Crook. A rout ensues, and the Federals flee to Bunker Hill, West Virginia, with 1185 casualties to light losses for the Confederates. Early's cavalry will pursue Crook northward on the 25th, when the Federals will repulse their pursuers at Williamsport on the Potomac.

25 JULY 1864

EASTERN THEATER, PETERSBURG CAMPAIGN Grant attempts to tighten his hold on the city by sending forces against the railroads leading toward Richmond.

27 JULY 1864

EASTERN THEATER, PETERSBURG CAMPAIGN Work having been completed as of 23 July on the mine under the Confederate entrenchments, preparations are being made for its detonation on 30 July. The mine is being filled with 320 kegs of powder, and Burnside's black troops are engaged in special training for the assault, when they will run through the crater blasted into Southern positions. In the northern Shenandoah, Early's men destroy Union rail lines and prepare to recross the Potomac.

NAVAL The Union Navy under Admiral Farragut engages in reconnaissance preparatory to a long-planned attack on Mobile Bay, Alabama.

28 JULY 1864

EASTERN THEATER, ATLANTA CAMPAIGN Following up Stoneman's and McCook's raids around Atlanta, Sherman sends Howard and the Army of the Tennessee south of Atlanta to move against the vital railroads supplying the city from the South. Again the aggressive Hood takes the offensive, sending corps under General S D Lee against the Federals at Ezra Church. Howard digs in and repulses the enemy, and Hood's third sortie is turned back with losses of up to 5000. But Federals have been prevented from cutting the railroad.

29 JULY 1864

EASTERN THEATER Once more Early crosses the Potomac west of Williamsport and spreads consternation into Maryland and Pennsylvania. His men are engaged in fighting at Harper's Ferry, West Virginia, Hagerstown and Clear Spring, Maryland and Mercersburg, Pennsylvania.

30 JULY 1864

EASTERN THEATER, PETERSBURG MINE ASSAULT It is perhaps significant that two of the most incompetent Federal generals of the war, Butler and Burnside, are both attracted to novel methods of warfare. One of Butler's pet ideas, the wire entanglements used at his otherwise deplorable Drewry's Bluff action, has at least proved effective. Burnsides's mine, planned by

Colonel Pleasants to blow a crater into the enemy works through which an attack can be mounted, is in fact an innovative idea of possibly great consequence in the siege of Petersburg. Today after a month's work the detonation is scheduled and the troops are ready. However, the previous day Meade with Grant's approval has decided that the black troops of Ferrero's IX Corps, the only ones specially trained to pursue the mission, are not to lead the attack, since if it fails the Union will be accused of callously misusing its black soldiers (which, given the experimental nature of the operation, is very possibly the case). After this rebuff, Burnside is chagrined and proceeds with some indifference, drawing straws to select who will lead the assault (Ledlie, 1st Division, loses) and being a little hesitant about final preparations and instructions. The explosion is set for 3:30 this morning. At that moment every Federal eye strains toward the fortifications. Nothing happens. An investigation by two volunteers finds the fuse has gone out. They relight it. At 4:45 one of the largest explosions ever seen on the American continent sends flames, earth, cannon, bodies and parts of bodies a hundred feet into the air in the midst of a mushroom-shaped cloud. When all this has descended and settled, there is a crater 170 feet long, 60 to 80 feet wide, and 30 feet deep stretching well into the southern positions. At least 278 Confederates have been killed in the explosion or smothered in the debris. For the time being the defenders have fled the area as Union attackers descend into the hole. Finding themselves in a maze of trenches and pits, the men falter. Meanwhile, their commander, Ledlie, is cowering in a bombproof shelter behind his lines. Soon the Confederates collect themselves and in an exemplary manner begin to train their artillery into the hole; finding themselves somewhat sheltered from this fire, the ostensible attackers are even less disposed to pursue their assault. By the time 15,000 men have been herded into the crater, the enemy fire has become truly murderous and the Federal attackers are only interested in hiding. The Union army is now quite literally at the feet of the enemy. Finally, in desperation, the black troops originally slated to head the attack are ordered in; after dispatching them, their commander, Ferrero, joins Ledlie in the bombproof shelter. The black troops advance quickly and resolutely, followed by not one white soldier, and are cut to pieces on the other end. The whole inglorious affair ends with a confused melee of surviving Union soldiers rushing devil-take-the-hindmost back to their own lines. The North has lost 3748 casualties of 20,708 engaged, the Confederates about 1500 of 11,466.

Also on this day, Confederate cavalry from Early's forces ride into Chambersburg, Pennsylvania, and offer not to burn down the town if $500,000 in cash or $100,000 in gold can be raised, to help the raiders meet expenses and serve as more 'reparations' for Hunter's Federal raids in the Shenandoah. The sum is not obtainable, however, and the town is duly put to the torch. The Rebels move on west to McConnellsburg, pursued at some distance by Averell.

WESTERN THEATER, ATLANTA CAMPAIGN Sherman's raiders Stoneman and McCook, engaged in disrupting operations on Confederate supply lines around Atlanta, both run into trouble. Stoneman and 700 men are captured by the enemy on the outskirts of Macon; McCook has to fight his way out of a Confederate encirclement at Newman, and loses 500 men and many supplies.

1 *AUGUST* 1864

EASTERN THEATER, VALLEY CAMPAIGN Grant gives cavalry commander Philip H Sheridan the mission of clearing the enemy, especially Early, out of the Shenandoah Valley. Early's cavalry leader McCausland is now seriously threatened by Averell's pursuit.

3 *AUGUST* 1864

WESTERN THEATER, ATLANTA CAM-

PAIGN Sherman dispatches A J Smith for another crack at Forrest. Smith leaves today for Oxford, Mississippi, preparing for a movement on Columbus.

NAVAL Preparing for the naval move on Mobile Bay, Federal troops attack, but do not yet capture, Fort Gaines on Dauphin Island, one of the Confederate forts guarding the bay. Meanwhile, Federal Admiral Farragut's fleet of four monitors and 14 wooden ships is ready to move.

5 *AUGUST* 1864

WASHINGTON Furious at Lincoln's pocket-veto of their punitive reconstruction bill, Senator Benjamin Wade and Representative H W Davis issue what is called the Wade-Davis Manifesto, proclaiming 'their right and duty to check the encroachments of the Executive on the Authority of Congress.' At issue is whether Lincoln or the Congress will control reconstruction.

NAVAL, BATTLE OF MOBILE BAY At 6 o'clock in the morning, Admiral David Farragut's fleet begins to run past the three Confederate forts into the important Southern port of Mobile Bay head for the Confederate defending ships—the mighty ironclad ram *Tennessee* and three wooden gunboats under Admiral Franklin Buchanan. Soon the Federal ships come under the fire from Fort Morgan and the gunboats, and are also heading toward a treacherous maze of underwater mines (known as torpedos at this time). After 7 o'clock the Federal ironclad *Tecumseh* is sunk by a torpedo, and it is after this that the 63-year-old Farragut, standing high in the rigging of his flagship *Hartford*, is supposed to have exclaimed, 'Damn the torpedos, full speed ahead!' Whether or not this was said, the Union fleet does just that, led into the bay by the *Hartford* with little further damage from the forts or from torpedos. After repeatedly being rammed and shelled, the CSS *Tennessee* is disabled and surrenders, and the bay is secured. Federals have lost 145 killed (including 93 drowned in the *Tecumseh*), 170 wounded, and four captured. The Confederates lose few killed

18 AUGUST 1864

and wounded, but 270 men are taken (including Admiral Buchanan) and all ships sunk or captured. Besides removing a valuable port from the Confederacy, the action gives the Union army a staging area for planned operations against Mobile. Federal bombardment from the water will lead to the fall of Forts Gaines and Powell over the next few days; Fort Morgan will hold out until the end of the month.

7 *AUGUST* 1864

EASTERN THEATER   Part of Early's cavalry under McCausland are finally attacked in force by W W Averell at Moorefield, West Virginia. Federals capture 420 men and 400 horses.

9 *AUGUST* 1864

EASTERN THEATER, PETERSBURG CAMPAIGN   The siege remains quiet, and the defenders have already repaired the damage to their works caused by the Federal mine.

VALLEY CAMPAIGN   Sheridan prepares to move from Halltown and Harper's Ferry, West Virginia, to confront Early. Elsewhere, Rebel raider John S Mosby steps up his activities in the Federal-held part of Virginia.

WESTERN THEATER, ATLANTA CAMPAIGN   As the siege of Atlanta continues, opposing commanders Sherman and Hood probe, raid and search for ways in and out. On Mobile Bay Federal troops begin a siege of Fort Morgan, the last remaining Confederate works on the bay.

10 *AUGUST* 1864

EASTERN THEATER, ATLANTA CAMPAIGN   Confederate commander Hood dispatches much of his cavalry under Wheeler to raid Sherman's rail lines above the city. Wheeler will be active until 10 September in various locations but this action is in fact another blunder by Hood. Sherman already has the supplies he requires for the moment, and now the Confederate army is without needed cavalry.

12 *AUGUST* 1864

EASTERN THEATER, VALLEY CAMPAIGN   Sheridan moves toward Early, who is entrenched south of Winchester along Cedar Creek, where there is a small skirmish during the day. Small actions will go on until Sheridan withdraws on 14 August. It will be some weeks before the antagonists do much more than follow in one another's footsteps.

NAVAL   In a week of heavy raiding the Confederate cruiser *Tallahassee* takes six Union vessels off New York and seven off Sandy Hook, New Jersey.

15 *AUGUST* 1864

EASTERN THEATER, VALLEY CAMPAIGN   After further skirmishing with Early near Cedar Creek, Sheridan withdraws toward Winchester pending arrival of needed supplies.

WESTERN THEATER, ATLANTA CAMPAIGN   Wheeler's Confederate cavalry raid Sherman's supply lines on Tennessee railroads.

NAVAL   Confederate raider *Tallahassee* takes six more Federal ships off New England; four more will be captured on the 16th.

17 *AUGUST* 1864

EASTERN THEATER, VALLEY CAMPAIGN   Early's forces pursue the withdrawing Sheridan; a sharp action breaks out near Winchester, Virginia.

18 *AUGUST* 1864

WASHINGTON   Grant refuses a second Confederate request to exchange prisoners, thus cutting off Confederate reinforcements but also condemning to slow starvation many Federal prisoners in the South, who can scarcely be fed by their captors when the Confederate army is itself hungry.

EASTERN THEATER, PETERSBURG CAMPAIGN   In the first action since the mine disaster, Federals move to extend their lines around the city. A corps under Warren occupies a mile of the important Wel-

CHRONOLOGY

don railroad, fighting successfully at Globe Tavern, Yellow House and Blick's Station before being halted by the enemy in the evening.

WESTERN THEATER, ATLANTA CAMPAIGN Hoping to force the enemy out of Atlanta, Sherman sends two brigades under General Judson Kilpatrick to raid Hood's lines of communication south of the city. Strong Confederate resistance will interfere with this raid, and Kilpatrick returns to Decatur 23 August having had little success.

19 *AUGUST* 1864

EASTERN THEATER, PETERSBURG CAMPAIGN Warren's infantry is attacked by Confederates under A P Hill south of Petersburg, and the Federals with heavy losses are forced back to their position at Globe Tavern. However, the North still controls the important Weldon Railroad.

VALLEY CAMPAIGN Sheridan and Early continue skirmishing around Winchester.

21 *AUGUST* 1864

EASTERN THEATER, PETERSBURG CAMPAIGN In a final desperate attempt to dislodge Federals from the much-needed Weldon Railroad, A P Hill attacks Warren's forces south of Petersburg. The attack fails and the South has lost 1600 of the 14,000 in action around the railroad; Federal casualties are 4455 of 20,000.

VALLEY CAMPAIGN Early and R H Anderson have planned a dual attack on Sheridan today, but it fails to develop and the day sees minor skirmishing in several places around Charles Town. At night Sheridan withdraws to strong positions near Harper's Ferry.

WESTERN THEATER General Forrest makes another bold move, taking Memphis, Tennessee, for the day, and capturing several officers; Federal Generals Hurlbut and Washburn barely escape. Smith tries and fails to cut off Forrest's retreat, and then is called back. Forrest is now free to operate against Sherman's supply lines. Nearly two months of attempts against him

have largely resulted in Federal embarrassments such as this.

23 *AUGUST* 1864

NAVAL Fort Morgan falls, the last of the three Confederate forts on Mobile Bay. Now the Union controls one of the last two major ports that had been left for Southern blockade-running. Only Wilmington, North Carolina now remains.

25 *AUGUST* 1864

EASTERN THEATER, PETERSBURG CAMPAIGN After several days of destroying track along the Weldon Railroad, Hancock's Federals are assaulted at Ream's Station by a reinforced A P Hill, who drives them back from the railroad in heavy fighting. Federals lose 2742 men, mostly in captured and missing, and many armaments. Hill's men then withdraw to Petersburg, and the rail line remains broken.

VALLEY CAMPAIGN With Sheridan entrenched on the Potomac, Early leaves a force to hold him there and resumes his roaming in West Virginia, threatening a new invasion of Maryland and Pennsylvania.

NAVAL CSS *Talahassee* pulls into port at Wilmington, North Carolina, having captured 31 Union vessels in three weeks.

27 *AUGUST* 1864

WESTERN THEATER, ATLANTA CAMPAIGN The time has come to begin the final act of the Atlanta Campaign. Sherman pulls two corps out of his trenches on a wide circuit of the city. The Confederates think Sherman is retreating; the message 'the Yankees are gone' is telegraphed all over the South. But Sherman's men are moving to choke off Hood's last rail lines into the city, especially the Macon railroad at Jonesboro. Several previous expeditions have failed to accomplish this task but this effort will not fail.

29 *AUGUST* 1864

THE NORTH The Democratic National

Convention meets in Chicago, with the keynote address given by Copperhead activist Clement Vallandigham. Another speaker proclaims: 'Four years of misrule by a sectional, fanatical, and corrupt party have brought our country to the verge of ruin.'

EASTERN THEATER, VALLEY CAMPAIGN Sheridan is on the move again against Early, winning an engagement at Smithfield Crossing on the Opequon River.

TRANS-MISSISSIPPI A Confederate expedition prepares at Princeton, Arkansas, under General Sterling Price. Its object is to retake Missouri.

30 *AUGUST* 1864

THE NORTH As expected, the Democratic National Convention prepares to nominate General George B McClellan for President. The Peace Democrat- and Copperhead-dominated platform asserts that, 'justice, humanity, liberty, and the public welfare demand that immediate efforts be made for a cessation of hostilities.' The platform also assails Lincoln's 'usurpation of extraordinary and dangerous powers not granted by the Constitution' and says, 'the aim and object of the Democratic Party is to preserve the Federal Union and rights of the States unimpaired.'

WESTERN THEATER, ATLANTA CAMPAIGN Sherman's Generals Thomas and Howard cut one of Hood's two remaining rail lines, the Montgomery and Atlanta, in two places. Schofield is moving toward the second, the Macon and Weston Railroad. Still thinking that Wheeler's raids have forced Sherman to retreat for lack of supplies, Hood orders an attack on the Federals at Jonesboro.

31 *AUGUST* 1864

THE NORTH In the convention at Chicago General McClellan is nominated as the Democratic candidate for President.

WESTERN THEATER, ATLANTA CAMPAIGN Hood's attack on Howard's Army of the Tennessee near Jonesboro is turned back with heavy losses—1725 Southern casualties to Howard's 170. Meanwhile, Schofield cuts the Confederates' last railroad line at the town of Rough and Ready, Georgia. During the night Sherman orders General Slocum to try to enter the city on 1 September. In more ways than militarily, Atlanta is doomed:

1 *SEPTEMBER* 1864

EASTERN THEATER, VALLEY CAMPAIGN Elements of Sheridan's army clash with Jubal Early's Confederates at Opequon Creek.

WESTERN THEATER, ATLANTA CAMPAIGN General Hood and the Army of Tennessee evacuate Atlanta. Unable to carry off the munitions and stores, the Confederate rearguard blows up the much-needed supplies as they leave, sending billows of smoke and fire into the night air and shock waves reverberating to Union lines on the outskirts of the city. In Jonesboro, Union troops renew their counterattack against the enemy and, at the end of the day, Hardee withdraws his men to Lovejoy Station, where they rendezvous with the main body of the army leaving Atlanta.

2 *SEPTEMBER* 1864

THE CONFEDERACY Worried over the South's chronic shortage of manpower, General Lee suggests to Jefferson Davis that Confederate leaders replace white laborers in the army with black slaves to free a greater number of whites for combat service. Lee also argues that stringent new regulations governing exemptions and a more vigorous enlistment policy are necessary to offset the constant losses to battle and disease.

WESTERN THEATER, ATLANTA CAMPAIGN Led by General Henry Slocum's XX Corps, Federal troops begin to move into Atlanta in the morning. Sherman informs Lincoln of the successful completion of his four-week siege of the city with terse exultation: 'So Atlanta is ours, and fairly won.'

3 *SEPTEMBER* 1864

WASHINGTON President Lincoln, responding to the news from Sherman of the fall of Atlanta, and also in recognition of Admiral Farragut's victory at Mobile Bay in August, declares 5 September a national day of celebration.

EASTERN THEATER, VALLEY CAMPAIGN Answering Lee's request to return troops on loan from Richmond, Jubal Early sends General Richard H Anderson's corps toward the Confederate capital. At Berryville, though, they run into a part of Sheridan's army and, after some hard fighting, retreat to the shelter of the main body of Confederate troops at Winchester.

4 SEPTEMBER 1864

WESTERN THEATER   Union troops commanded by General A C Gillem surround the celebrated Confederate raider, John Hunt Morgan, while he and his men are bivouacked at Greeneville, Tennessee. Morgan, the commander of the Department of Southwest Virginia since his escape from an Ohio penitentiary last year, is less successful this time in eluding his captors and he is shot and killed as he tries to flee from the trap. One hundred Confederates are killed in the action and another 75 are taken prisoner.

NAVAL   A 60-day bombardment of Fort Sumter, at Charleston, South Carolina, ends.

5 SEPTEMBER 1864

EASTERN THEATER, VALLEY CAMPAIGN Though General Early yesterday moved his army south from its former position, Confederate troops continue to clash with the enemy along the Opequon Creek.

WESTERN THEATER   Following the procedure President Lincoln had outlined for the readmission of the state to the Union, those citizens of Louisiana who have taken the loyalty oath renouncing secession go to the polls and ratify a new constitution abolishing slavery in the state.

6 SEPTEMBER 1864

NAVAL   Federal ships again open fire on

Fort Sumter. This latest bombardment will continue for the next nine days.

7 SEPTEMBER 1864

EASTERN THEATER, VALLEY CAMPAIGN Sheridan's and Early's armies continue to skirmish near Winchester, Virginia.

WESTERN THEATER   General Sherman issues an order for the evacuation of all civilians from Atlanta. The order will provoke an angry exchange between the Union general and General Hood, as well as protests from the citizens of the town, but Sherman remains obdurate.

TRANS-MISSISSIPPI   Fighting occurs at Centralia, Missouri, between Federal soldiers and Confederates.

8 SEPTEMBER 1864

THE NORTH   General George B McClellan formally accepts the Democratic nomination for president. In his letter of acceptance, however, McClellan refuses to accept that part of the Democratic platform which labels the war a failure: 'I could not,' he writes, 'look in the face of my gallant comrades of the army and navy, who have survived so many bloody battles and tell them that their labor and sacrifice had been in vain.' Although he separates himself from the Copperhead faction of the party by this remark, McClellan makes it clear that his own ideas concerning the basis for peace between North and South are considerably different from those of the Republicans. In contrast to their demand for the unconditional surrender of the Confederacy and recognition of emancipation, the Democratic nominee insists only on reunion, and maintains that when 'any one State is willing to return to the Union, it should be received at once, with a full guarantee of all its constitutional rights.'

NAVAL   Following up last month's victory at Mobile Bay, Federals destroy over 50 Confederate furnaces at Salt House Point.

9 SEPTEMBER 1864

TRANS-MISSISSIPPI   Federals clash with

the enemy near Warrensburg, Missouri, and in Arkansas Confederates attack the *JD Perry* at Clarendon.

10 *SEPTEMBER* 1864

WESTERN THEATER Grant sends Sherman a telegram urging him to begin a new drive against the enemy as soon as possible. Although no definite decision has yet been made as to what Sherman's next move will be, both Union generals still see Hood's army as the primary target.

11 *SEPTEMBER* 1864

WESTERN THEATER Generals Sherman and Hood enter into a ten-day truce to allow for the removal of civilians from Atlanta. A citizens' committee in the occupied city draws up and presents a formal protest to Sherman against his policy of removal. The Union leader, however, will answer the petition with characteristic bluntness: 'You might as well appeal against the thunder-storm,' he will tell them, 'as against these terrible hardships of war.' In the next 10 days, 446 families will leave the city to take up residence either to the north or south.

12 *SEPTEMBER* 1864

EASTERN THEATER, VALLEY CAMPAIGN President Lincoln, anxious to break the stalemate between Sheridan and Early's army, suggests to Grant the possibility of 'quietly but suddenly' transferring troops to Sheridan to allow him to strike at the enemy.

13 *SEPTEMBER* 1864

EASTERN THEATER, VALLEY CAMPAIGN The two armies in the Valley continue to skirmish with one another with engagements today at Bunker Hill and at two fords on Opequon Creek.

14 *SEPTEMBER* 1864

EASTERN THEATER, VALLEY CAMPAIGN After one unsuccessful attempt already, General Richard H Anderson's corps

leaves Early's army to rejoin Lee at Petersburg. The loss of these troops substantially weakens the Confederate forces in the Valley.

16 *SEPTEMBER* 1864

EASTERN THEATER, SIEGE OF PETERSBURG South of the James River, General Wade Hampton and his force of Confederate cavalry engage a group of Federals herding cattle and, after defeating them, lead over 2400 head of beef back to the hungry army at Petersburg.

VALLEY CAMPAIGN Generals Grant and Sheridan meet at Charles Town, West Virginia, to discuss the military situation at Winchester. Sheridan, who is aware that some of Early's troops have recently left the area for Richmond, proposes offensive action against the Confederates. Grant approves the plans.

WESTERN THEATER With some 4500 men, General Nathan B Forrest leaves Verona, Mississippi to operate against Sherman's supply and communication lines. Until the beginning of November, Forrest will continue to harass Union outposts in northern Alabama and in Tennessee.

17 *SEPTEMBER* 1864

THE NORTH John C Frémont, who had been nominated as a candidate for president in the spring by a convention of Radical Republicans dissatisfied with Lincoln's handling of the war, announces his intention to withdraw from the race. Though he still feels that Lincoln's administration is a failure, he fears a Democratic victory would lead to either a recognition of the Confederacy or at the very least a re-establishment of slavery. To prevent this and to work for emancipation, he pledges his support to Lincoln.

EASTERN THEATER, VALLEY CAMPAIGN Though outnumbered by more than three to one, Jubal Early begins to move his troops northward in the direction of Sheridan's army in order to operate against the Baltimore and Ohio Railroad. In West

Virginia there is some fighting around Buckhanon.

18 SEPTEMBER 1864

EASTERN THEATER, VALLEY CAMPAIGN
After encountering enemy cavalry, Confederate troops in the Valley under General Early fall back slightly toward Winchester again. The 12,000 man force, however, is somewhat widely scattered and in poor defensive position. Informed of this, Union General Sheridan decides to attack the Confederates in the morning.

19 SEPTEMBER 1864

THE NORTH, THE LAKE ERIE CONSPIRACY Two Confederate agents put into action their plan to capture the US gunboat *Michigan* and then free Confederate prisoners being held at Johnson's Island on Lake Erie. Once freed, they hope to organize the men into an army which will operate in the area. Captain John Yates Beall of the Confederate Navy, accompanied by a band of men he had recruited across the border in Canada, commandeers the steamer *Philo Parsons* and the *Island Queen*, but the other agent, Charles H Cole, who had managed to plant himself on board the *Michigan*, is discovered and arrested before he can give the signal to his cohorts to board the ship. Beall scuttles the *Philo Parsons* and escapes but later will be captured and hanged as a spy.

EASTERN THEATER, VALLEY CAMPAIGN
Sheridan attacks the Confederates at Winchester: In the morning, bottlenecks develop as the Union troops try to cross the Opequon to engage the enemy and for a time it appears as though the outnumbered Southern army might successfully repulse the attack. As the day progresses, however, Sheridan is able to bring a larger number of his troops to bear against the Confederate breastworks. By the end of the day the Federals are forcing Early's troops into a full retreat. Union losses are 653 killed, 3719 wounded and 618 missing. The Southern army leaves 3000 of their wounded in Winchester as they flee the city

and suffer the loss of another 2000 taken prisoner during the day. News of the victory will be greeted with jubilation throughout the North but particularly by Republicans who see battle victories as indispensable if they are to win the political elections in November. Referring to the battle and its impact on the political climate of the North, Republican James Garfield will write that 'Phil Sheridan has made a speech in the Shenandoah Valley more powerful and valuable to the Union cause than all the stumpers of the Republic can make.'

TRANS-MISSISSIPPI General Sterling Price leads a cavalry force of 12,000 men into Missouri. Since the failure of the Federal Red River Expedition last April, Confederate authorities and General Edmund Kirby Smith had talked of launching a campaign to recover Missouri for the Confederacy. The South, however, will never be able to marshall a force necessary to implement such an ambitious plan, and Price's raid is to be the last offensive move by the South into Missouri. They cross into Missouri from Indian Territory. Just before entering the state, the Confederates capture a Federal supply train near Cabin Creek and then continue northward.

20 SEPTEMBER 1864

EASTERN THEATER, VALLEY CAMPAIGN
A Union cavalry force pursues Early's fleeing troops as they move southward after yesterday's defeat. The Union horsemen clash with the Southern rearguard at Middletown, Strasburg and Cedarville.

TRANS-MISSISSIPPI As Price's Confederate cavalry moves toward St Louis, fighting occurs with Federals at Keytesville and on the Little Black River, in Missouri.

21 SEPTEMBER 1864

EASTERN THEATER, VALLEY CAMPAIGN
General Early's troops dig in at Fishers Hill after halting their retreat from Winchester. Sheridan's army, following the Confederates, fortifies its own positions just north of Fishers Hill.

22 *SEPTEMBER* 1864

EASTERN THEATER, VALLEY CAMPAIGN
After following Early's fleeing army for two
days, Sheridan again throws his troops
against the enemy at Fishers Hill. The
battle develops into a complete rout and the
Southerners plunge into headlong retreat
further up the Valley. 'I do not think there
ever was an army so badly beaten,' Sheridan gloats in his message to Grant of the
battle. Despite the exaggeration, Fishers
Hill is both decisive and one-sided. Federal losses in the battle are only 528, while
the Confederates lose 1235 men as well as
12 artillery pieces. It will be almost a month
before Early's troops are again prepared to
fight.
TRANS-MISSISSIPPI There is skirmishing
at Patterson and Sikeston, Missouri.

23 *SEPTEMBER* 1864

EASTERN THEATER, VALLEY CAMPAIGN
Though Confederate cavalry battles Federals at Mount Jackson, Front Royal and
Woodstock, Sheridan's army does not
follow Early's troops up the Valley.
WESTERN THEATER General Nathan
Forrest and his cavalry force attack a
Federal garrison at Athens, Alabama.
Forrest's raid into northern Alabama is
part of a concerted Confederate effort to
harass Sherman's line of communications
to Atlanta.

24 *SEPTEMBER* 1864

EASTERN THEATER, VALLEY CAMPAIGN
Having defeated Early in two decisive
battles and forced his army to retreat up the
Valley, Sheridan begins to turn his attention to destroying the vast food resources of
the Shenandoah Valley. 'If the war is to last
another year,' Grant has written Sheridan,
'we want the Shenandoah Valley to remain
a barren waste.'

25 *SEPTEMBER* 1864

WESTERN THEATER, FRANKLIN AND

NASHVILLE CAMPAIGN Jefferson Davis
arrives in Palmetto, Georgia, where he
talks with General John B Hood about
campaign strategy against Sherman in
Atlanta. To the north, General Forrest
attacks Federal railroad lines, capturing
Sulfur Branch Trestle in northern Alabama. There is also fighting today at Johnsonville, Tennessee, and near Henderson,
Kentucky.
TRANS-MISSISSIPPI Price's men skirmish
with the enemy at Farmington and Huntsville, Missouri.

26 *SEPTEMBER* 1864

EASTERN THEATER, VALLEY CAMPAIGN
Elements of Sheridan's cavalry harass
Early's army near Port Republic, Virginia.
WESTERN THEATER Now in Tennessee,
Forrest assaults a Federal garrison near
Pulaski.

27 *SEPTEMBER* 1864

TRANS-MISSISSIPPI Sterling Price and
his cavalry force continue their advance
northward through Missouri. At Pilot
Knob, they attack a Federal garrison under
the command of Thomas Ewing Jr. The
Union forces, though badly outnumbered,
beat off the attack, inflicting some 1500
casualties, and then escape under cover of
darkness. Meanwhile, a small band of
Confederate guerrillas led by 'Bloody' Bill
Anderson ride into Centralia, Missouri,
looting and burning many of the town's
buildings. They then capture a train as it
pulls into the town and kill over 20 unarmed Federals on board. Later the band
ambushes a column of Union cavalry sent
out to intercept the raiders, killing another
100 enemy soldiers.

28 *SEPTEMBER* 1864

WESTERN THEATER There is scattered
fighting at Brownsville, Mississippi, and at
Wells Hills and Rheatown, Tennessee.

29 *SEPTEMBER* 1864

EASTERN THEATER, SIEGE OF PETERSBURG

Grant orders an attack on Forts Harrison and Gilmer, enemy fortifications in front of the Petersburg-Richmond lines. Troops under General George Stannard succeed in capturing Fort Harrison but the move against Fort Gilmore fails and that outpost remains in Confederate hands. Meanwhile, south of Petersburg, 16,000 Federal soldiers try to extend Union lines westward to capture Boydton Plank Road and the Southside Railroad, two important routes leading into that city.

VALLEY CAMPAIGN Elements of Sheridan's and Early's armies clash near Waynesborough.

TRANS-MISSISSIPPI Federals fight Price's advancing cavalry at Leasburg and Cuba, Missouri.

30 *SEPTEMBER* 1864

EASTERN THEATER, SIEGE OF PETERSBURG Confederate troops commanded by General Richard H Anderson try to retake Fort Harrison, lost to the Federals in yesterday's action. The assault fails. In the two days of fighting at the fort, Federal losses are 929 killed or wounded and 1756 missing. The Confederates lose a total of 2800, including 300 prisoners. Fighting also continues southwest of Petersburg, near Peebles' Farm, as a vigorous counterattack by Ambrose P Hill pushes back the advancing Federal columns.

1 *OCTOBER* 1864

EASTERN THEATER, SIEGE OF PETERSBURG Fighting continues around Peebles' Farm as Union troops try to extend their lines encircling Petersburg. In the Valley, meanwhile, General Sheridan prepares to move his army north to Cedar Creek from its present position in Harrisonburg. Also a Federal expedition into southwest Virginia and east Tennessee fights two small engagements at Clinch Mountain and Laurel Creek Gap, Tennessee.

WESTERN THEATER, FRANKLIN AND NASHVILLE CAMPAIGN General Hood moves his army around Atlanta to strike Sherman's railroad line, assaulting Union

troops at Salt Springs. In support of Hood's army General Forrest and his cavalry continue to hit at positions in Sherman's rear. Forrest and his men skirmish with Federal troops at Athens and Huntsville, Alabama, and also capture Union blockhouses at Carters Creek Station in Tennessee.

NAVAL The *Condor*, a British blockade runner, is grounded near Fort Fisher, North Carolina, as it is being chased by the USS *Niphon*. On board the *Condor* is Mrs Rose O'Neal, a Confederate spy, who to avoid capture tries to escape in a small boat with her secret dispatches and $2000 in gold. The boat capsizes in the heavy seas and Mrs O'Neal drowns.

2 *OCTOBER* 1864

THE CONFEDERACY President Davis gives General Pierre Gustave Toutant Beauregard command of the two armies in the west under Hood and Richard Taylor. Beauregard is to direct the overall strategy and coordinate the activities of the two armies but is not to interfere with field operations when visiting either of them.

EASTERN THEATER, SIEGE OF PETERSBURG Four days of fighting at Peebles' Farm comes to an end as the Confederates withdraw to their entrenchments. Between 30 September and the end of this day, Union forces have succeeded in extending their lines three miles westward.

VALLEY CAMPAIGN Skirmishing takes place between elements of Jubal Early's army and that of Sheridan at Mount Crawford and Bridgewater. In southwest Virginia, a Federal raid designed to destroy Confederate salt mines in the region is repulsed near Saltville. After the engagement, the Southern defenders put to death over 100 prisoners, most of whom are blacks. Although Lee will order a full investigation when he hears of the atrocity, only one man will be brought to justice, and he primarily for the murder of a white officer.

TRANS-MISSISSIPPI General Sterling Price, still moving northward through

Missouri, occupies the town of Washington.

3 OCTOBER 1864

EASTERN THEATER, VALLEY CAMPAIGN
Confederate cavalry hit at Sheridan's army near Harrisonburg.

WESTERN THEATER, FRANKLIN AND NASHVILLE CAMPAIGN The Army of Tennessee continues to disrupt Sherman's supply lines forcing him to send more troops from Atlanta to protect his trains. Meanwhile, General George Thomas, whom Sherman had directed to Nashville to protect that city from a possible attack by Hood's army, reaches the city and begins to prepare its defenses.

TRANS-MISSISSIPPI Sterling Price's men engage Federal troops at Hermann and Millers Station, to the west of St Louis. Though the citizens of that town had been considerably alarmed by the Confederate raid into Missouri, Price's foray has caused Union officials to deploy General A J Smith's corps, originally intended to reinforce Thomas in Tennessee, to St Louis to meet the new danger to the trans-Mississippi area.

4 OCTOBER 1864

WESTERN THEATER, FRANKLIN AND NASHVILLE CAMPAIGN There is more action between Confederate and Union forces in Georgia, with engagements at Acworth, Mom's Station and near Lost Mountain. General Sherman moves his headquarters to Kennesaw Mountain to place himself in a better position to strike against Hood's army.

TRANS-MISSISSIPPI Price, unwilling to strike directly at freshly reinforced St Louis begins to swing his troops to the west and away from the city. The raiders engage Federal forces at Richwoods, Missouri.

5 OCTOBER 1864

THE CONFEDERACY Jefferson Davis gives a speech in Augusta, Georgia. He attempts to rekindle the spirit of the people by assuring them that he has never been more confident that with determined and vigorous effort, the South can drive the enemy from its territory.

WESTERN THEATER, FRANKLIN AND NASHVILLE CAMPAIGN In an attack that will later gain much publicity, Confederate troops under General Samuel G French strike a Federal position at Allatoona, Georgia, hoping to destroy a railroad bridge there. General Sherman sends the commander at Allatoona a message telling him to hold his position ('General Sherman says hold fast. We are coming'), and though promised reinforcements never arrive, the Federals fight a heroic defense, beating off the enemy attack. Federal losses are 706, while the Confederates lose 799.

6 OCTOBER 1864

EASTERN THEATER, VALLEY CAMPAIGN
Though twice severely beaten last month, Confederates in the Valley still refuse to give up completely. Cavalry under Confederate General Thomas L Rosser hits General George Custer's cavalry at Brooks Gap, near Fishers Hill. Custer's troops succeed in beating off the attack.

WESTERN THEATER General Forrest continues to plague Union forces in Sherman's rear, fighting an engagement with Federals at Florence, Alabama.

7 OCTOBER 1864

EASTERN THEATER, SIEGE OF PETERSBURG
Confederate troops north of Richmond try to push back Federal troops and the two sides clash on the roads leading to Darbyville and New Market. The attack fails, though, as the Southerners are forced to retreat.

VALLEY CAMPAIGN Sheridan's cavalry continues its work destroying crops and rounding up livestock. Sheridan writes Grant that so far his men have burned 2000 barns filled with wheat, hay and farm implements, destroyed in excess of 70 flour mills, driven off 4000 head of livestock and killed over 3000 sheep to feed the army. When he is through, he adds, the area between Winchester and Staunton 'will have little in it for man or beast.'

CHRONOLOGY

WESTERN THEATER, FRANKLIN AND NASHVILLE CAMPAIGN Elements of Hood's and Sherman's armies collide at Dallas, Georgia, as the Confederate general tries to maneuver his troops toward Alabama.

NAVAL The USS *Wachusett* traps and then captures the CSS *Florida* at the Brazilian port of Bahia. The Brazilians protest and even fire at the US vessel, but it still makes off with its prize. To mollify the Brazilians, Secretary of State William H Seward will later condemn Union captain's action as unlawful.

8 OCTOBER 1864

EASTERN THEATER, VALLEY CAMPAIGN Union and Confederate cavalry skirmish at Tom's Brook and in the Luray Valley.

NAVAL The Confedeate *Shenandoah*, or *Sea King*, sails from London and on 19 October will be commissioned as a commerce destroyer.

9 OCTOBER 1864

EASTERN THEATER, VALLEY CAMPAIGN After suffering Confederate cavalry attacks for the past few days, Sheridan turns his cavalry divisions led by George Custer and Wesley Merritt against the enemy's horsemen. The Confederates flee up the Valley after an engagement in which they lose 300 prisoners and suffer another 57 casualties. There is also fighting in Fauquier County, Virginia, just to the east of the Valley.

TRANS-MISSISSIPPI Sterling Price and his men continue northwestward away from St Louis capturing the Missouri towns of Boonville, Russelville and California.

10 OCTOBER 1864

EASTERN THEATER, VALLEY CAMPAIGN Sheridan withdraws his army north to Cedar Creek. At the same time his VI Corps starts out toward Washington.

WESTERN THEATER, FRANKLIN AND NASHVILLE CAMPAIGN Hood's and Sherman's men skirmish near Rome, Georgia, as the Confederate army continues to move westward. Meanwhile, a Federal expedition tries to attack General Forrest at Eastport, Mississippi, by ferrying soldiers up the river with boats. The Confederates, however, disable the Union vessels, and the Northern troops are left stranded, able to do little more than make good their escape.

11 OCTOBER 1864

WESTERN THEATER, FRANKLIN AND NASHVILLE CAMPAIGN Sherman concentrates his troops at Rome, Georgia, after receiving word that Hood's army is just south of the city. Federal and Southern troops clash along the road between Atlanta and Flat Creek. Farther north, Confederate cavalry raid Fort Donelson, the site of a black recruiting station, but are driven off by Northern soldiers.

TRANS-MISSISSIPPI Sterling Price and his men continue to slash their way northwestward through Missouri, skirmishing with Federals at Boonville and at Brunswick.

12 OCTOBER 1864

WESTERN THEATER, FRANKLIN AND NASHVILLE CAMPAIGN Parts of Hood's and Sherman's armies clash at Reseca, La Fayette and on the Coosaville Road near Rome, Georgia, while farther north there is some fighting at Greeneville, Tennessee.

NAVAL Rear Admiral David D Porter assumes command of the North Atlantic Blockading Squadron relieving acting Rear Admiral Samuel P Lee. Porter, who was only a lieutenant at the outbreak of war, won renown for the role he played at New Orleans, and with Grant at Forts Henry and Donelson and at Vicksburg.

13 OCTOBER 1864

EASTERN THEATER, VALLEY CAMPAIGN Taking advantage of Sheridan's withdrawal to Cedar Creek, Jubal Early moves his army back to its old position at Fishers Hill. Fighting breaks out as the advancing Confederates probe enemy lines. Farther north, John S Mosby and his band of partisan rangers derail a passenger train near

Kearneyville. They rob two Federal paymasters on board of nearly $173,000 and then burn the train before making their escape.

WESTERN THEATER, FRANKLIN AND NASHVILLE CAMPAIGN Hood's troops seize control of the railroad north of Reseca, Georgia, leading to Tunnel Hill, and there are a number of isolated engagements along the rail line.

14 OCTOBER 1864

EASTERN THEATER, VALLEY CAMPAIGN Sporadic fighting continues between elements of Early's and Sheridan's armies as the two forces probe each other's lines at Cedar Creek.

TRANS-MISSISSIPPI Sterling Price calls on the people of Missouri to help him redeem the state. His men fight Federal soldiers near Glasgow. There is also an action at Danville, Missouri.

15 OCTOBER 1864

TRANS-MISSISSIPPI Shelby's 'Iron Brigade,' part of Price's cavalry, captures the town of Glasgow, Missouri, forcing the surrender of more than 400 Federals under the command of Colonel Chester Harding Jr. Shelby's men also occupy Sedalia after 700 defenders flee the town.

16 OCTOBER 1864

EASTERN THEATER, VALLEY CAMPAIGN General Philip Sheridan leaves his army at Cedar Creek for a conference with President Lincoln and General Grant on the military situation in the Valley.

WESTERN THEATER Elements of the two armies in northern Georgia continue to clash as the Confederates harass the Union supply lines.

TRANS-MISSISSIPPI In Missouri, Price and his men reach the town of Ridgely and occupy it as they continue to move northwestward along the Missouri River.

17 OCTOBER 1864

WESTERN THEATER General Beaure-

gard assumes command of the Confederate western armies east of the Mississippi. In northern Georgia General Hood and his army move toward Gadsden, Alabama, breaking off, for the most part, their attacks on Sherman's supply lines. The Confederate general hopes that by heading north and eventually into Tennessee, he will be able to force Sherman to do the same, thus freeing Georgia of the invading army.

TRANS-MISSISSIPPI Fighting continues with Federals both to the rear and in front of Price as his cavalry rides toward Lexington in northwest Missouri. Federal forces are now closing in on the Confederate raiders from three directions: General Samuel R Curtis, commander of the Department of Kansas, approaching from the west; Alfred Pleasonton and his cavalry pursuing from the rear; and General Alfred J Smith coming up from the south. The Confederate cavalry burns Smithville as it passes through the town and also occupies Carrolton during the day.

18 OCTOBER 1864

EASTERN THEATER, VALLEY CAMPAIGN General Jubal Early and his staff plan an all-out attack on the Federals at Cedar Creek to be launched in the morning.

19 OCTOBER 1864

THE NORTH A small group of Confederate raiders, led by Lieutenant Bennet H Young and composed mainly of escaped prisoners, crosses the Canadian border and descends upon the small Vermont town of St Albans. The men rob three local banks of over $200,000 but resistance by local citizens prevents them from carrying out their plans to burn the town. Eleven of the raiders escape back over the border where they will later be arrested and then released by Canadian officials after that government decides it lacks jurisdiction.

EASTERN THEATER, VALLEY CAMPAIGN Concealed by Three Top Mountain and early morning fog, the three divisions of Early's corps attack the left flank of the

Union army commanded by General George Crook. Completely surprised, the Federal flank falls back in disarray with one division forming a new line north of Middletown while the rest regroup to the west of the town. General Sheridan, on his way back from a conference in Washington, has spent last night in Winchester. He hears the sounds of battle and meets streams of stragglers retreating down the Valley Pike as he rides toward Cedar Creek. Turning his men around, he gallops on, arriving at the front about 10:30 in the morning. Meanwhile the Confederate charge slows to a stop as soldiers fall out of line to loot the enemy's camp. The Confederates fail to follow up their surprise attack and at four in the afternoon the Union forces counterattack, forcing them to flee in disorganized retreat. Although Union casualties are higher (5665 for the North compared to an estimated 2910 for the South), they decisively win the battle, not only forcing the enemy from the field but, it will later be seen, putting to an end the Confederates' last major threat in the Shenandoah Valley. Union generals on the field do a good job of preventing the early morning attack from developing into a complete rout but for most Northerners Sheridan's dramatic morning ride and inspirational arrival at the front will be seen as having saved the Union army from destruction. This romantic view of the battle later will be immortalized in T Buchanan Read's poem, 'Sheridan's Ride.' TRANS-MISSISSIPPI Shelby's brigade strikes Federal troops in front of the advancing Confederate cavalry at Lexington, Missouri, forcing the Northerners to fall back to the Little Blue River.

20 *OCTOBER* 1864

WASHINGTON President Lincoln formally establishes Thanksgiving as a national holiday.
EASTERN THEATER, VALLEY CAMPAIGN In the wake of General Early's defeat at Cedar Creek, elements of Sheridan's army strike at the Confederates as they retreat toward Fishers Hill.

21 *OCTOBER* 1864

TRANS-MISSISSIPPI There is more fighting between Federals and advancing Confederate troops under Sterling Price at the Little Blue River. The Union troops again fall back to the west.

22 *OCTOBER* 1864

WESTERN THEATER, FRANKLIN AND NASHVILLE CAMPAIGN General Hood's army is in Gadsden, Alabama, preparing to go to Guntersville and from there on to Tennessee. General Sherman's troops are in Gaylesville, Alabama, just west of Rome, Georgia. From this position, the Union general feels he can protect both Chattanooga and Atlanta from the Confederates.
TRANS-MISSISSIPPI Deciding that his best chances of survival lie in defeating the various enemy forces closing in on him before they can unite, General Price orders Shelby's troops to attack the Federals in front while John S Marmaduke holds off the enemy to the rear. After Shelby's men have completed their work, Price plans to turn his entire force around to meet Alfred Pleasonton's pursuing cavalry. Shelby hits the enemy and, finding an exposed flank, forces the Northerners under General Samuel Curtis to fall back to Brush Creek, near Westport, where they form a new line.

23 *OCTOBER* 1864

TRANS-MISSISSIPPI Following up its success of yesterday, Shelby's cavalry again strikes at General Curtis's troops, now near Westport, Missouri. The Federals check this assault, though, and launch a powerful counterattack. While this is going on, Pleasonton's Union cavalry breaks through General Marmaduke's rearguard defense, forcing the harried Southerners from the field. Pleasonton then closes in on Shelby's Confederates from the rear, who in turn are forced to retreat. The Battle of Westport, involving some 20,000 Federal troops and over 8000 Confederates, results in about 1500 casualties for each side and will mark the end of the last serious threat to Union control of Missouri.

24 OCTOBER 1864

TRANS-MISSISSIPPI Sterling Price retreats south along the border between Kansas and Missouri with a long train of plunder which his men have captured in their month-long raid through Missouri. After some delay, the Union cavalry pursues the fleeing Confederates.

25 OCTOBER 1864

WESTERN THEATER, FRANKLIN AND NASHVILLE CAMPAIGN Elements of Hood's army, still in northern Alabama, clash with Union troops near Round Mountain, at Turkeytown and on the Gadsden Road.

TRANS-MISSISSIPPI Federal cavalry catch up with Price's retreating columns at Marais des Cygnes, Kansas. In the fight that ensues, they capture two Confederate generals (including John Marmaduke), four colonels and 1000 men. The Southerners also lose ten pieces of artillery in the engagement. The two sides lose ten pieces of artillery in the engagement.

26 OCTOBER 1864

WESTERN THEATER, FRANKLIN AND NASHVILLE CAMPAIGN The Army of Tennessee arrives at Decatur, Alabama, which is held by Federal troops. Hood had originally hoped to launch his invasion of Tennessee from here but finds that General Forrest and his cavalry have been delayed. After some artillery fire against Federal positions at Decatur, Hood moves his army farther west.

TRANS-MISSISSIPPI Union troops ambush and kill the notorious 'Bloody' Bill Anderson near Richmond, Missouri. Anderson had once ridden with William Quantrill.

27 OCTOBER 1864

EASTERN THEATER, SIEGE OF PETERSBURG

General Grant orders an assault on enemy positions to gain control of the Boydton Road and Southside Railroad southwest of Petersburg. A strong defense under the leadership of General Ambrose P Hill, however, frustrates the Union drive. Unable to get necessary reinforcements, the Federals withdraw, leaving the transport lines still in the hands of the Confederates. The assault involves over 40,000 Federal troops and 20,000 Southerners, with the former suffering 1194 killed or wounded and 564 missing. Confederate casualties are not recorded.

NAVAL During the night, an expedition of 15 men led by Lieutenant William B Cushing ascends the Roanoke River in a steam craft and blows up the Confederate ram *Albemarle* by ramming through its protective log boom and then exploding a torpedo against the *Albemarle*'s hull. For planning and executing this bold scheme, Cushing (who manages to escape uninjured) will be promoted to the rank of Lieutenant Commander.

28 OCTOBER 1864

TRANS-MISSISSIPPI Troops under General Samuel Curtis again catch up with Price's fleeing troops and attack the Confederates at Newtonia, Missouri. The timely arrival of Federal reinforcements during the engagement again forces Price to withdraw.

29 OCTOBER 1864

WESTERN THEATER Cooperating with Abraham Buford, who had built a trap for Federal boats on the Tennessee River near Fort Heiman and Fort Henry, General Forrest and his men capture the steamer *Mazeppa*. Meanwhile, Hood, still waiting for Forrest to join his army so he can launch his invasion into Tennessee, continues to move his army westward.

30 OCTOBER 1864

WESTERN THEATER, FRANKLIN AND NASHVILLE CAMPAIGN The Army of

Tennessee moves into Tuscombia, Alabama. The Confederates also cross the Tennessee River and seize the town of Florence. Forrest, continuing to operate against Federal vessels, captures two transports and the gunboat *Undine* from the enemy. Meanwhile, Federal troops move from Chattanooga to Pulaski, Tennessee, as General George Thomas prepares to meet an invasion into Tennessee.

NAVAL The CSS *Olustee* runs the Federal blockade outside Wilmington, North Carolina, and begins to prey on enemy shipping.

31 *OCTOBER* 1864

THE NORTH Nevada enters the Union as the 36th state. Although Lincoln was considerably reassured by the elections held earlier in the month in Pennsylvania, Ohio and Indiana, he still believes the Presidential election will be very close. Nevada, which is felt to be safely Republican, can now contribute three electoral votes to the election because of its statehood.

NAVAL Seven Federal vessels under the command of William H Macomb capture Plymouth, North Carolina.

1 *NOVEMBER* 1864

WESTERN THEATER, FRANKLIN AND NASHVILLE CAMPAIGN General Alfred J Smith, who has been in Missouri to check Price's invasion, moves his men to Nashville, where they will reinforce General George Thomas. Thomas is preparing his defenses to meet a threatened attack by Hood's army. Meanwhile, General Forrest takes his makeshift navy of captured Federal vessels up-river to Reynoldsville Island, just south of Johnsonville, Tennessee, where he prepares another ambush for enemy boats.

2 *NOVEMBER* 1864

THE NORTH Secretary of State William H Seward warns the mayor of New York of rumors that Confederate agents in Canada are planning to set fire to New York City on election day.

WESTERN THEATER Federals recapture the *Venus* from Forrest just south of Johnsonville, Tennessee. The *Venus* is one of the boats that Forrest's men had taken at their 'trap' downstream a few days earlier.

3 *NOVEMBER* 1864

WESTERN THEATER The Federal IV Corps arrives in Pulaski, Tennessee. These troops had been sent by General Thomas to strengthen the detachment of troops already at the town against the threatened invasion by the Confederate Army of Tennessee.

4 *NOVEMBER* 1864

WESTERN THEATER Federal gunboats close in on Forrest's ambush station at Reynoldsburg Island, from the north and south, forcing the Confederates to burn the captured *Undine* to prevent its recapture. Forrest then moves his force to the outskirts of Johnsonville where they shell a Federal naval supply depot causing heavy damage.

6 *NOVEMBER* 1864

THE NORTH Colonel Benjamin Sweet and his men arrest close to 100 men in Chicago on charges of plotting against the US. Confederate agents and Copperhead sympathizers, according to the alleged plans, were to release prisoners being held at Camp Douglas on election day. The prisoners then would seize the polls, stuff the ballot boxes and burn the city of Chicago. Although the plot will never be entirely substantiated, many of those arrested are heavily armed, and at the home of one of the conspirators, a large cache of arms and ammunition is found.

TRANS-MISSISSIPPI Price's men, who have now retreated out of Missouri, fight Federal troops at Cane Hill, Arkansas. There is also fighting between Union soldiers and Indians in the Nebraska Territory.

8 *NOVEMBER* 1864

THE NORTH It is election day in the

North. President Lincoln is reelected to a second term over General George B McClellan. With Tennessee war-governor Andrew Johnson as his new running mate, Lincoln wins over 55 percent of the popular vote and carries every participating state except Delaware, Kentucky and New Jersey. His strongest support comes from the soldiers on active duty who give 'Old Abe' 119,754 out of slightly more than 154,000 votes. In the electoral college, Lincoln gets 212 votes to McClellan's 21.

9 NOVEMBER 1864

WESTERN THEATER   General Sherman in Kingston, Georgia, issues preliminary orders in preparation for a 'march to the sea.' Although Hood had hoped that by invading Tennessee he could draw Sherman northward, the Union general believes that Thomas's troops in and around Nashville will be able to handle the Army of Tennessee.

10 NOVEMBER 1864

WASHINGTON   President Lincoln addresses a crowd at the White House gathered to help him celebrate his recent victory at the polls. He tells the audience that he believes the results vindicate Americans' belief in democracy, and urges a united effort to save the country.
EASTERN THEATER, VALLEY CAMPAIGN Despite his recent defeat at Cedar Creek, Jubal Early moves his shattered army down the Valley toward Sheridan to continue harassing the Federals.
WESTERN THEATER, MARCH TO THE SEA Destroying all property which might be of use to the Confederates, Sherman's army leaves Kingston for Atlanta. He also gives orders for the destruction of railroad lines around Atlanta as well as those going north from Reseca, Georgia.

11 NOVEMBER 1864

WESTERN THEATER   Union troops in Rome, Georgia, destroy everything that might be of military use in that city and then move south to join the rest of the army at

Black troops at a picket station, Virginia.

Atlanta. Meanwhile, skirmishing continues between Federals and elements of Hood's army near Shoal Creek, Alabama; and in eastern Tennessee, there is fighting at Russellville.

13 NOVEMBER 1864

EASTERN THEATER, VALLEY CAMPAIGN Early moves his army back to New Market and part of his troops set off for Richmond and Petersburg to reinforce General Lee's troops.
TRANS-MISSISSIPPI   There is fighting between Indians and Federal soldiers near Fort Larned, Kansas, while in Missouri, Northern troops scour Pemiscot County in search of enemy guerrillas.

14 NOVEMBER 1864

WESTERN THEATER, MARCH TO THE SEA With Sherman's army now returned to Atlanta, soldiers continue their work tearing up railroad lines, burning bridges and destroying anything else of use to the enemy. Meanwhile, in Tennessee, General John M Schofield arrives in Pulaski to assume command of the forces in that city, the first line of defense against Hood.

15 NOVEMBER 1864

WESTERN THEATER, MARCH TO THE SEA

Confederate militia and Federals clash around Atlanta while other Northern soldiers complete the destruction of the city in preparation for the march to Savannah. In northern Alabama, Hood's army continues to skirmish with Federals near Shoal Creek on the Tennessee River.

16 *NOVEMBER* 1864

WESTERN THEATER, MARCH TO THE SEA About seven in the morning, General William T Sherman and his army leave Atlanta for Savannah carrying 20 days rations with them. By and large, however, the 62,000-man army is to live off the land, foraging liberally throughout the Georgia countryside. Sherman has also instructed his division commanders that they should take any livestock that they might deem necessary from the inhabitants and if they meet resistance 'should order and enforce a devastation more or less relentless.' To oppose them, the Confederates have about 13,000 men including 3000 state militia under the command of Geroge W Smith and a 10,000-man cavalry force led by Joseph Wheeler. These troops are concentrated around Lovejoy Station. Sherman's army marches out in two wings, the right heading down the Macon railroad toward Lovejoy Station while the left wing moves along the Georgia railroad toward Augusta. By deploying his troops along two diverging paths, Sherman hopes to deceive the enemy as to his true destination. As the right wing approaches Lovejoy Station, the Confederates there, except two cavalry brigades, move south toward Macon. The Union cavalry defeats the remaining troops, pursuing them to Beaver Creek Station where they capture 50 prisoners. In northern Alabama, Hood's army continues to battle Federal units at Shoal Creek as General Forrest and his cavalry finally arrive to reinforce the Army of Tennessee. Forrest's cavalry were intended to compensate for the loss of Wheeler's troops now harassing the Federals in Georgia. In eastern Tennessee, Breckenridge and his raiders skirmish with Federals at Straw-

berry Plains before he withdraws toward southwest Virginia.

17 *NOVEMBER* 1864

THE CONFEDERACY Jefferson Davis writes a letter to several Georgia state senators denouncing all plans involving individual states' negotiating for peace with the North.

WESTERN THEATER, MARCH TO THE SEA The two wings of Sherman's army continue to diverge, one going east and the other south. There is some fighting along the way at Towalega Bridge. Davis meanwhile orders General William J Hardee to assume command of all troops in Georgia. To the north, there is increased fighting in northern Alabama with clashes occurring at Maysville and at New Market.

18 *NOVEMBER* 1864

WESTERN THEATER, MARCH TO THE SEA At Macon, Georgia, President Davis orders Howell Cobb, commander of the Georgia reserves, to get out every man he can to oppose Sherman's army. He also tells him to employ black slaves to help obstruct roads in the path of the Federal army.

TRANS-MISSISSIPPI Even with Price driven from Missouri, Confederate bands and guerrilla units continue to harass Federal troops. Today there is fighting at Fayette between the two sides.

19 *NOVEMBER* 1864

TRANS-MISSISSIPPI Federal soldiers continue to battle Indians in the Nebraska Territory, today at Plum Creek Station.

NAVAL President Lincoln lifts the Federal blockade at Norfolk, Virginia, and at Fernandina and Pensacola, Florida. These ports are now under the control of Union forces.

20 *NOVEMBER* 1864

WESTERN THEATER, MARCH TO THE SEA Sherman's troops continue their progress, fighting enemy cavalry, home-guards and state militia at Clinton, Walnut Creek, East Macon and Griswoldsville, Georgia.

21 *NOVEMBER* 1864

WESTERN THEATER, FRANKLIN AND NASHVILLE CAMPAIGN Hood moves his Army of Tennessee out of Florence, Alabama, northward toward Tennessee. His force includes 30,000 infantry and 8000 cavalry. The Confederate general had originally hoped to launch his invasion from Decatur as long as three weeks ago but for a variety of reasons (including the belated arrival of General Forrest and his cavalry) he delayed. During this period General Thomas has had time to improve his defenses and strengthen his army in and around Nashville as well as to reinforce Federal outposts at Pulaski and Columbia, Tennessee. Now on the move, though, Hood plans to place his army between that of General Schofield in Pulaski and the remaining body of Federals to the north.
MARCH TO THE SEA General William J Hardee arrives in Macon to oversee the defenses of Georgia. From the disposition of the two wings of the enemy's army, he decides that Augusta or Savannah and not Macon must be the objective of the Northern army. He orders General Smith to move his troops eastward to oppose the advance of the Federal right wing. General Wheeler, meanwhile, is to continue to use his cavalry to strike at the enemy's rear columns.

22 *NOVEMBER* 1864

WESTERN THEATER, FRANKLIN AND NASHVILLE CAMPAIGN Hood's army moves northeastward toward Columbia, hoping to capture that city and cut off Union General Schofield's troops in Pulaski from the rest of the Federals to the north. Schofield, however, realizing what is afoot, begins to evacuate his troops northward to Columbia.
WESTERN THEATER, MARCH TO THE SEA In Millegeville, the Georgia state legislature issues a call for troops to check Sherman's invasion and then flees the state

capital just before Sherman's left wing, commanded by General Henry W Slocum, occupies the city. The Georgia state militia, meanwhile, attacks the Union right wing in a vain effort to halt its progress.

23 *NOVEMBER* 1864

WESTERN THEATER, FRANKLIN AND NASHVILLE CAMPAIGN Skirmishing breaks out at Fouche Springs, Henryville and Mount Pleasant, Tennessee, as Hood's army continues to march toward Columbia.
WESTERN THEATER, MARCH TO THE SEA In Georgia, the two wings of Sherman's army reunite in Millegeville, where there is more fighting between Federals and state militia. Fighting also takes place at Ball's Ferry and at a railroad bridge belonging to the Georgia Central over the Oconee River.

24 *NOVEMBER* 1864

WESTERN THEATER, FRANKLIN AND NASHVILLE CAMPAIGN The front column of General Schofield's troops under the command of General Jacob D Cox arrives in Columbia, Tennessee, just in time to help Federals already there drive off General Forrest's Confederate cavalry. By the end of the day, the rest of Schofield's men arrive and dig in south of the Duck River.

25 *NOVEMBER* 1864

THE NORTH Southern arsonists, acting under orders from agents in Canada, set fire to 10 hotels in New York City, including the Belmont, Metropolitan, Saint James and Astor House. Alarms also go off in two downtown theaters and a fire is set at Barnum's Museum. Strangely, none of the fires does serious damage and all are quickly extinguished. Later R C Kennedy will be arrested and executed for setting the blaze at Barnum's Museum.
WESTERN THEATER, MARCH TO THE SEA Cavalry under General Joseph Wheeler battle Federals outside Sanderson, Georgia before the Federals succeed in occu-

pying the town.

26 *NOVEMBER* 1864

WESTERN THEATER, FRANKLIN AND NASHVILLE CAMPAIGN Hood's Army of Tennessee arrives outside Columbia only to find Federal troops well-entrenched both south and north of the Duck River. MARCH TO THE SEA Fighting continues between Confederates and elements of Sherman's army at Sanderson, Georgia. TRANS-MISSISSIPPI The Nebraska Territory is again the scene of fighting between Federal soldiers and Indians, this time near Plum Creek Station and at Spring Creek.

27 *NOVEMBER* 1864

EASTERN THEATER, THE SIEGE OF PETERSBURG The steamer *Greyhound*, General Benjamin Butler's floating headquarters, blows up on the James River, apparently an act of Southern sabotage. In West Virginia, Federal soldiers skirmish with the enemy at Moorefield. WESTERN THEATER, FRANKLIN AND NASHVILLE CAMPAIGN Believing that Hood's army will attack from south of Columbia, General Schofield moves his troops north of the Duck River in the evening, burning the bridges behind him and digging in to prepare for the assault. MARCH TO THE SEA At Waynesboro, Georgia, Sherman's march is interrupted as the Confederate cavalry strike at the Union army.

28 *NOVEMBER* 1864

EASTERN THEATER, VALLEY CAMPAIGN Confederate General Thomas L Rosser leads his cavalry on a raid into Maryland where they destroy a bridge on the Baltimore and Ohio Railroad and then retreat back up the Valley into Virginia. WESTERN THEATER, FRANKLIN AND NASHVILLE CAMPAIGN With troops under Stephen D Lee staying at Columbia to create the impression that an attack will come from the south, General Hood moves the rest of his troops east of that city, plan-

ning to cross the Duck River north of the Federal army and cut off its retreat. During the afternoon Forrest's cavalry cross the river about 10 miles north of the Federals near Spring Hill driving the Union cavalry north toward Franklin. WESTERN THEATER, MARCH TO THE SEA Fighting in Georgia occurs along Sherman's advance at Buckhead Church and Buckhead Creek. There are also cavalry engagements at Davisborough and Waynesborough.

29 *NOVEMBER* 1864

WESTERN THEATER, FRANKLIN AND NASHVILLE CAMPAIGN Having been driven off to Franklin by enemy cavalry, General James H Wilson, Schofield's cavalry commander, sends back word to his commander at Columbia that the enemy has crossed at Spring Hill and the Federal army is in danger of being cut off to the north. Schofield still believes that he is to be attacked from the south but he does send some troops up to Spring Hill to investigate Wilson's report. Meanwhile, in the morning hours, Confederate infantry begin to cross over the Duck River north of the Federal Army, with more following in the afternoon. Reports of these activities come back to Schofield from his reconnaissance troops and around three o'clock in the afternoon the Union general starts his army north to Franklin. Although Confederate troops arrive at Spring Hill before him and Hood himself is on hand over an hour before dark, Schofield somehow manages to get his whole army past the enemy during the night. TRANS-MISSISSIPPI, SAND HILL MASSACRE Colorado militia under the command of Colonel John M Chivington descend upon the Cheyenne village at Sand Creek, Colorado Territory, without warning, killing almost one-third of its residents and torturing and mutilating many of their victims. A large proportion of the dead are women and children. For some time previous, there have been raids by Indians against gold miners and other settlers in the area. Although the Cheyenne, under the leadership of Chief Black Kettle, deny that they were involved in the raids and are under the protection of the Federal garrison at Fort Lyon, Chivington and his men decide to launch a reprisal on the settlement for the past attacks. The massacre will be later officially condemned by the Federal government.

30 *NOVEMBER* 1864

WESTERN THEATER, FRANKLIN AND NASHVILLE CAMPAIGN Escaping the trap the Confederates had planned for him, General Schofield arrives in Franklin with his 32,000 man force in the morning. The Union general deploys his troops in a long arc south and west of Franklin (nestled in a bend of the Harpeth River) while he works to get his supply train north of the river. The Confederates are slow to pursue the Federals but by 3:30 in the afternoon the Army of Tennessee has arrived south of the city and launches a full-scale assault over two miles of open field and against entrenched positions. Bloody hand-to-hand fighting develops as the Southerners several times reach the enemy lines only to be repulsed with heavy losses. While the infantry assaults are in progress, cavalry units from the two armies also fight each other both to the west and to the east of the city. On both flanks, however, the Confederates are utimately forced to withdraw. At nine o'clock at night Hood finally calls off his attacks and, during the night, Schofield withdraws his men across the river and toward Nashville. During the battle, 27,939 Union soldiers are engaged in fighting while the Confederates have 26,897 men in the field. Northern casualties are 2326, including 1104 missing, while the South loses 6252 men of whom 702 are missing.
WESTERN THEATER, MARCH TO THE SEA In Georgia, Sherman continues his march southeastward with a skirmish at Louisville. At Hilton Head, South Carolina, Federal troops launch an attack aimed at cutting the Charleston and Savannah Railroad. The Georgia militia, however, meets

these troops at Honeyhill and forces them to withdraw.

1 *DECEMBER* 1864

WESTERN THEATER, FRANKLIN AND NASHVILLE CAMPAIGN Schofield's army reaches Nashville where it joins the troops already there under the command of General George Thomas. Hood's army follows quickly on the Federal's heels and encamps southeast of the city.

2 *DECEMBER* 1864

WESTERN THEATER, FRANKLIN AND NASHVILLE CAMPAIGN Too weak to attack the strong Federal lines after its severe losses at Franklin, Hood's Army of Tennessee begins to fortify its own position southeast of Nashville. The Union lines, carefully prepared by Thomas during the last month, ring the Tennessee capital extending north on both sides to the Cumberland River. During the day, Confederate cavalry carry out raids against isolated positions on the Federal lines.

3 *DECEMBER* 1864

WESTERN THEATER, MARCH TO THE SEA The four corps of Sherman's army continue their march toward Savannah. They meet some resistance during the day from Southern soldiers at Thomas Station.

4 *DECEMBER* 1864

WESTERN THEATER, MARCH TO THE SEA Federal cavalry under General Hugh J Kilpatrick are struck by Confederate cavalry as they guard railroad wrecking crews near Waynesborough, Georgia. After some sharp fighting, the Federals finally force the enemy to retreat. More fighting breaks out at Statesborough, Lumpkin Station, along the Georgia Central Railroad, and on the Little Ogeechee River as the badly outnumbered Confederates continue to harass the enemy army. FRANKLIN AND NASHVILLE CAMPAIGN Around Nashville, Confederate cavalry strike at enemy outposts at Whites Station and Bell's Mills. During the next week Confederate horsemen will have little opposition in the area, as General George Thomas busies his cavalry in rounding up horses for several thousand soldiers without mounts.

5 DECEMBER 1864

WESTERN THEATER, FRANKLIN AND NASHVILLE CAMPAIGN General Hood sends Nathan B Forrest with his cavalry and a division of infantry to Murfreesboro where they are to operate against some 10,000 Federal troops garrisoned there under the command of General L H Rosseau.

6 DECEMBER 1864

WESTERN THEATER, FRANKLIN AND NASHVILLE CAMPAIGN General Grant, who has been urging Thomas to attack the Confederates as soon as possible ever since they arrived south of Nashville, now sends him a direct order to 'attack Hood at once.' Many of Thomas's cavalrymen, though, are still without mounts and he has been delaying until enough horses can be found. He warns Grant that an attack would be risky without cavalry. Confederates, meanwhile, launch a raid from Paris, Tennessee, to Hopkinsville, Kentucky.

7 DECEMBER 1864

WESTERN THEATER, FRANKLIN AND NASHVILLE CAMPAIGN In Murfreesboro, General L H Rosseau orders Robert L Milroy to make a reconnaissance in force against enemy troops commanded by General Forrest, who has been sent by Hood two days earlier to operate against Federals in the Murfreesboro area. Milroy defeats Forrest's men, forcing them from the field and capturing over 200 men and 14 guns.

8 DECEMBER 1864

EASTERN THEATER, SIEGE OF PETERSBURG Skirmishing takes place along Hatchers

Run, south of Petersburg, as Federal expeditions scout that area.

WESTERN THEATER, MARCH TO THE SEA In Georgia, Sherman's army, nearing Savannah, skirmishes at Ebenezer Creek and near Bryan Court House.

NAVAL General Benjamin Butler takes 6500 men down the James River to Fortress Monroe to join a naval expedition aimed at destroying Fort Fisher and closing the port of Wilmington.

9 DECEMBER 1864

EASTERN THEATER, SIEGE OF PETERSBURG More fighting takes place between Federal reconnaissance troops and the Confederates along Hatchers Run, south of Petersburg.

WESTERN THEATER, FRANKLIN AND NASHVILLE CAMPAIGN Grant issues an order replacing General George Thomas with John Schofield as commander of Union troops in Nashville. The general-in-chief suspends the order, however, when Thomas tells him that he had intended to attack on 10 December but a severe storm of freezing rain has forced him to alter his plans. To the south, fighting breaks out at the Ogeechee Canal, at Monteith Swamp and at Cuyler's Plantation.

10 DECEMBER 1864

EASTERN THEATER, SIEGE OF PETERSBURG Skirmishing occurs at Fort Holly, near Petersburg.

WESTERN THEATER, MARCH TO THE SEA General William T Sherman and his army of 60,000 men arrive south of Savannah. In and around the city there are 18,000 well-entrenched Confederates under the command of General William J Hardee. The Southerners have flooded the rice fields around Savannah so that there are only five narrow strips of land over which a Federal attack could be launched. Sherman, surveying the situation, rejects an assault and instead decides to besiege the city. His army, now stationary, must worry about providing itself with necessary supplies.

Although his men have adequate food, forage for horses is a daily concern. For this reason, Fort McAllister, located on the coast south of Savannah, is of vital importance. If the Federals can capture this fort, it will reopen contact with the US Navy and allow for the provisioning of Sherman's army. In Knoxville, a Federal expedition sets outs under the command of General George Stoneman aimed at destroying enemy salt and lead mines in southwest Virginia and eliminating enemy troops in the area.

NAVAL   Union troops capture and burn the Confederate steamer *Ida* on the Savannah River.

11 *DECEMBER* 1864

WESTERN THEATER, FRANKLIN AND NASHVILLE CAMPAIGN   Thomas is again bombarded by messages from Grant telling him to strike the enemy. He replies that he will do so as soon as weather permits.

WESTERN THEATER, MARCH TO THE SEA Along the coast of Georgia, Federal soldiers rebuild the King's Bridge, which the Confederates destroyed, in preparation for an attack on Fort McAllister.

12 *DECEMBER* 1864

WESTERN THEATER, FRANKLIN AND NASHVILLE CAMPAIGN   In Nashville, Thomas sends General Halleck a message telling him he will attack as soon as the ice on the ground melts sufficiently to allow troop movements. In eastern Tennessee, General George Stoneman and his cavalry force skirmish with the enemy at Big Creek, near Rogersville.

13 DECEMBER 1864

WESTERN THEATER, MARCH TO THE SEA Federal troops charge across a field strewn with mines and other obstacles and capture Fort McAllister from the 230 Confederates garrisoning the fort. The fall of Fort McAllister to Northern troops reopens communication and supply lines to Sherman's army. In Tennessee, meanwhile,

part of General Stoneman's force defeats Confederate troops commanded by General Basil W Duke at Kingsport.

FRANKLIN AND NASHVILLE CAMPAIGN Today also, Grant orders Major General John A Logan to proceed to Nashville to assume command of the army in that city. Grant himself leaves for Washington, intending to go on to Nashville to speed up operations there. While these proposed changes in the Union command are in the works, Confederates attack a railroad train near Murfreesboro.

NAVAL   A naval expedition designed to reduce Fort Fisher, sails from Fortress Monroe for the North Carolina port of Wilmington.

14 *DECEMBER* 1864

WESTERN THEATER, FRANKLIN AND NASHVILLE CAMPAIGN   General Thomas wires Washington that he plans to attack Hood's army on the 15th. To the east, Stoneman's Union raiders again encounter the enemy, this time at Bristol, Tennessee. After a fight they capture 300 Confederates.

NAVAL   US naval vessels begin a bombardment of Forts Rosedew and Beaulieu on the Vernon River. The action will continue for a week.

15 *DECEMBER* 1864

WESTERN THEATER, FRANKLIN AND NASHVILLE CAMPAIGN   Union troops at Nashville attack the Army of Tennessee.

The Battle of Nashville, 15 December 1864.

Using troops commanded by General James B Steedman to hit the enemy's right and divert Hood's attention in that direction, General Thomas throws the bulk of his army's strength at the Confederate left in an attempt to envelop it from the west. Outnumbered two to one, Hood's army also fights the battle without the aid of most of its cavalry (which is away at Murfreesboro). During the day, the Confederates gradually contract their lines as the Union assault pushes them from their original positions and to the south. The Federals gain considerable ground but by nightfall the enemy army, though bruised, is still intact. Thomas believes the enemy will withdraw, however, during the night. General Stoneman's raiders, meanwhile, again strike the enemy at Abingdon and Glade Springs, Virginia.

16 *DECEMBER* 1864

WESTERN THEATER, FRANKLIN AND NASHVILLE CAMPAIGN Morning finds the Confederate army still drawn up southeast of Nashville. After some initial probing, the Union army follows up its successes of yesterday by basically repeating the same battle plan. With Steedman's troops again holding the Confederate right, the bulk of the Northern army is thrown against the enemy's left. As Union soldiers finally succeed in turning the left flank, the Confederate center also collapses and Hood's shattered army flees in disorganized retreat. The right flank fights off the Federals with a desperate rearguard action as the Southern army plunges south toward Franklin. Close to 50,000 Federal troops see action in the two days of fighting while the Confederates have only slightly more than 23,000 in the field. Casualties are surprisingly light (387 killed, 2562 wounded and 112 missing for the Federals; probably not more than 1500 killed and wounded for the South). However, General Thomas reports capturing 4462 enemy soldiers. What is more, the battle effectively destroys the fighting capacity of the Confederacy's Army of Tennessee and it will be the last

major battle it will fight during the war.

WESTERN THEATER, MARCH TO THE SEA In Georgia, Sherman's troops skirmish at Hinesville. To the east, Stoneman's cavalry capture Wytheville, Virginia, during the day and also fight the enemy at Marion.

TRANS-MISSISSIPPI Fighting is reported during the day at Dudley Lake, in Arkansas.

17 *DECEMBER* 1864

WESTERN THEATER, FRANKLIN AND NASHVILLE CAMPAIGN In Tennessee, Union cavalry under General James H Wilson pursue the fleeing Army of Tennessee, skirmishing with its rearguard at Hollow Tree Gap, the West Harpeth River and at Franklin. The Confederates are still without most of their cavalry as Forrest's men have not yet rejoined the army. General James Chalmer's cavalry units, which were badly cut up at Nashville, are the only horsemen available to help fend off the Federals.

WESTERN THEATER, MARCH TO THE SEA In Savannah, General William J Hardee receives word from Jefferson Davis that Lee cannot spare troops from the trenches around Petersburg to reinforce him against Sherman. Sherman, meanwhile, sends the Confederate commander at Savannah a message demanding the surrender of his troops.

18 *DECEMBER* 1864

WASHINGTON President Lincoln issues a call for 300,000 additional troops to help put down the rebellion.

WESTERN THEATER, FRANKLIN AND NASHVILLE CAMPAIGN At Spring Hill, Federal cavalry again skirmish with Hood's retreating army.

WESTERN THEATER, MARCH TO THE SEA In Savannah, Hardee refuses Sherman's demand for a surrender of the Southern troops in the city.

NAVAL A fleet of ships commanded by Rear Admiral David Porter joins General Benjamin F Butler's force of 6500 men and together they sail toward Wilmington,

North Carolina, where they hope either to capture or destroy Fort Fisher and thus close the port to Confederate blockade runners.

19 *DECEMBER* 1864

EASTERN THEATER, VALLEY CAMPAIGN In response to Grant's orders, General Sheridan sends General Alfred Thomas A Torbert with 8000 men to operate against the Virginia Central Railroad. They will meet strong resistance from Southern troops along the line and will withdraw on 23 December. Although Early and Sheridan remain in the Shenandoah, their armies are considerably reduced as troops on both sides have been sent off to reinforce the armies in Petersburg.

20 *DECEMBER* 1864

WESTERN THEATER, FRANKLIN AND NASHVILLE CAMPAIGN In Tennessee, elements of General Thomas's army pursuing Hood's army pause to build a bridge over the rain-swollen Rutherford Creek and then continue on the trail of the Confederates. The two sides skirmish at Columbia.

WESTERN THEATER, MARCH TO THE SEA As the Federal left moves to encircle Savannah and cut off the Confederates' escape route, General Hardee moves his army out of the city northward toward South Carolina, where he hopes to be reinforced by troops in that state. The evacuating army leaves behind 250 heavy artillery guns which will be taken into Federal service. To the east, General Stoneman's expedition into southwest Virginia, reaches Saltville and destroys saltworks in and around the town.

21 *DECEMBER* 1864

WESTERN THEATER, MARCH TO THE SEA Federal troops occupy the city of Savannah. Tomorrow, Sherman will send Lincoln his memorable message: 'I beg to present you, as a Christmas gift, the city of Savannah.' In southwest Virginia, Stone-

Burning the Navy Yards at Savannah.

man and his cavalry, after accomplishing their mission to destroy enemy salt and lead mines and drive enemy troops from the region, begin to withdraw back toward east Tennessee.

23 *DECEMBER* 1864

WESTERN THEATER, FRANKLIN AND NASHVILLE CAMPAIGN Hood's army continues its retreat southward and Federal cavalry continue their pursuit. Both yesterday and today skirmishing occurs between the two sides in the vicinity of Columbus, Tennessee.

NAVAL After battling storm-tossed seas for several days, Rear Admiral Porter's fleet arrives off Wilmington. General Benjamin F Butler, commander of the landing force, has his men pack an old ship with over 200 tons of gunpowder and then explode it near Fort Fisher, hoping the fort will be destroyed in the blast. The plan fails, though, as the explosion does little but wake the fort's sleepy inhabitants.

24 *DECEMBER* 1864

WESTERN THEATER, FRANKLIN AND NASHVILLE CAMPAIGN There are slight skirmishes between Federals and Hood's retreating army near Lynnville and Richland Creek, Tennessee.

NAVAL The naval armada under Rear Admiral Porter begins its bombardment of Fort Fisher. By depriving the Confederates of this fortress, the Union command believes it can effectively shut the last major port available to Confederate blockade runners. During the day, troop transports also arrive. The plan is to storm and capture the fort after the naval bombardment has sufficiently weakened its defenses.

25 *DECEMBER* 1864

WESTERN THEATER, FRANKLIN AND NASHVILLE CAMPAIGN Federals skirmish with elements of the Army of Tennessee at Richland Creek, Devils Gap and White's Station, Tennessee. The Confederates finally reach the Tennessee River.
NAVAL With close to 60 ships bombarding the fort, Federal troops commanded by General Butler land north of Fort Fisher and move to within 75 yards of the fort, capturing Half Moon Battery as they advance. A strong fire from the 500 Confederates garrisoning the fortress checks the Union advance, though, and the Federals never renew the attack. Instead, after hearing that Confederate reinforcements (which General Lee had sent on 18 December) are within five miles of the fort, Butler decides an assault will be too costly and he withdraws his men. They will be transported back to Hampton Roads.

26 *DECEMBER* 1864

WASHINGTON President Lincoln sends a message to General Sherman congratulating him on his success in Savannah and also for Thomas's victory at Nashville. The President admits that he had been apprehensive about the march to the sea, but deferred to the general's judgement. For that reason, he explains, all the honor for the victory must go to Sherman himself.
WESTERN THEATER, FRANKLIN AND NASHVILLE CAMPAIGN Hood's army begins to cross the Tennessee River. There is some fighting at Sugar Creek. The retreat of the Confederates back over the Tennessee both symbolically and effectively brings to an end Hood's bold plan to take his army all the way to the Ohio River.

27 *DECEMBER* 1864

WESTERN THEATER, FRANKLIN AND NASHVILLE CAMPAIGN The Confederate Army of Tennessee finishes crossing the

Tennessee River and then marches toward Tupelo, Mississippi.

28 *DECEMBER* 1864

WASHINGTON President Lincoln, disappointed by the Federal failure at Fort Fisher, asks Grant for his comments on the ill-fated expedition. The general-in-chief, who has been calling for Butler's dismissal since summer, is very decided on whom he feels is responsible for the 'gross and culpable failure.'

30 *DECEMBER* 1864

WASHINGTON In a Cabinet meeting, President Lincoln suggests that Butler should be relieved of his command of the Army of the James. Butler's superiors have long felt that he is militarily inept, but Lincoln until now has hesitated to relieve this politically influential general. The expedition to Fort Fisher, however, is an embarrassment to the Administration and—some will later explain—in the wake of the recent election, Lincoln's position is less tenuous..
THE CONFEDERACY Francis P Blair, an aging but still powerful political figure from Maryland, writes to Jefferson Davis asking for a meeting with the Confederate leader in Richmond. Blair hints broadly that he is interested in exploring possible avenues for peace. This interview will lead directly to the Hampton Roads Conference next month between Lincoln and Confederate Vice President Alexander Stephens.

The Bombardment of Fort Fisher.

1865

1 JANUARY 1865

EASTERN THEATER, SIEGE OF PETERSBURG
A work crew under the direction of General Butler sets off a large charge of gunpowder on the James River designed to clear away the last remaining portion of a canal being constructed to allow Federal vessels to bypass a large bend in the river. The huge explosion fails to clear the ditch, however, and the ambitious project will remain uncompleted.

TRANS-MISSISSIPPI Union soldiers, trying to clear Arkansas of its troublesome and ubiquitous guerrilla bands, skirmish with the enemy at Bentonville.

3 JANUARY 1865

WESTERN THEATER, CAROLINAS CAMPAIGN General Sherman transfers a portion of his army north to Beaufort, South Carolina, in preparation for his campaign through the Carolinas. Skirmishing breaks out along the way at Hardeeville, South Carolina.

4 JANUARY 1865

NAVAL Union troops leave from Bermuda Hundred for a new assault on Fort Fisher. Although most of the 8000 soldiers on this latest expedition against the Confederate fortress at Wilmington, North Carolina, have also been on the unsuccessful mission in December, General Alfred H Terry rather than Butler is now commanding the men who are to launch the land assault against this important enemy position.

WESTERN THEATER Union troops operating against the Mobile & Ohio Railroad skirmish with the enemy at the Ponds, in Mississippi.

5 JANUARY 1865

WASHINGTON President Lincoln issues a pass through Union lines to James W Singleton. Singleton, like several others, hopes that through unofficial channels he may be able to instigate peace negotiations between the two governments and bring an end to the fighting. Although Lincoln doubts that a peace can be negotiated through the auspieces of the Confederate government consistent with the North's demand for reunion, he does not interfere with Singleton's mission and, to the extent of issuing the safe conduct pass, condones the unofficial peace-feeler.

6 JANUARY 1865

WASHINGTON In the House of Representatives, debate turns to the proposed Constitutional amendment abolishing slavery. Although passed by the Senate at the last session, it had failed to receive the necessary two-thirds vote in the House. The fall elections have increased the Union-Republican majority in the 39th Congress, but it is not scheduled to sit until December of 1865 and Republicans are anxious that the amendment pass before that time. They now set to work to convince enough Democrats to change their vote so that the amendment can be passed in the House and sent to the states for ratification.

THE CONFEDERACY Jefferson Davis writes a letter to Alexander Stephens, his continuous and outspoken vice president, criticizing him for actively working to undermine the people's confidence in their president. Stephens, a long-time critic of the Confederate chief executive and currently active in the Georgia peace movement, has accused Davis of secretly favoring the reelection of Lincoln over McClellan in the recent Northern presidential race.

TRANS-MISSISSIPPI Federal soldiers skirmish with the enemy at Huntsville, Arkansas.

7 JANUARY 1865

WASHINGTON The War Office issues an order relieving General Benjamin F Butler of commander of the Army of the James and of the Department of Virginia and North Carolina. Major General Edward

Ord is named to fill the vacated posts.

EASTERN THEATER, VALLEY CAMPAIGN More troops from General Philip Sheridan's dwindling army leave the Shenandoah Valley to reinforce the Union army besieging Petersburg.

TRANS-MISSISSIPPI Federal soldiers battle Indians in the Colorado Territory, at Julesburg and Valley Station.

NAVAL The Danish ironclad *Sphinx* sets sail from Copenhagen to Quiberon Bay, France. The Confederate government has already secretly bought the *Sphinx*, and it will become the CSS *Stonewall*.

8 *JANUARY* 1865

NAVAL The army forces of General Alfred Terry join up with a large naval fleet commanded by Rear Admiral Porter off the coast of Beaufort, North Carolina. This Federal expedition is aimed at seizing Fort Fisher.

9 *JANUARY* 1865

WASHINGTON Moses Odell, a Democratic representative from New York, comes out in favor of the proposed Constitutional amendment abolishing slavery. Odell will be one of the key Democrats whose vote will make its passage possible.

WESTERN THEATER, FRANKLIN AND NASHVILLE CAMPAIGN Hood's Army of Tennessee, after its long retreat from Nashville, arrives in Tupelo, Mississippi. In Tupelo, Confederate officials hope somehow to reassemble the broken army after its disastrous campaign into Tennessee. Davis also hopes to be able to transfer troops from Hood's army to reinforce Hardee's men opposing Sherman in the Carolinas.

CAROLINAS CAMPAIGN Secretary of War Edwin Stanton arrives in Savannah, Georgia, to confer with General Sherman on military matters. Stanton also plans to investigate charges made against Sherman of his alleged 'criminal' mistreatment of black freedmen.

10 *JANUARY* 1865

WASHINGTON Debate continues in the House of Representatives on the fate of the proposed Constitutional amendment abolishing slavery throughout the country. Fernando Wood of New York, arguing against the amendment, tells Congress that passage of the amendment would destroy any chances for securing peace with the South.

TRANS-MISSISSIPPI Federal soldiers battle Confederates near Glasgow, Missouri.

11 *JANUARY* 1865

EASTERN THEATER Riding in icy cold weather and deep snow, Confederate General Thomas L Rosser leads 300 men from his cavalry unit on a daring raid into West Virginia. The raiders attack unsuspecting Ohio troops stationed in Beverly, killing or wounding 25 Federals, and then retire with 583 prisoners.

12 *JANUARY* 1865

THE CONFEDERACY Francis P Blair, an important Maryland political figure, meets Jefferson Davis in Richmond to discuss possible avenues for peace between North and South. Blair's personal scheme calls for the two sides to join together to expel the French from Mexico. Such a course he feels would not only root out a dangerous incursion against the Monroe Doctrine, but would also help revive a feeling of brotherhood between North and South. Although the scheme does not meet the approval of either Davis or Lincoln, the Confederate president does promise to send a representative to discuss peace with Lincoln. This meeting will take place on 3 February.

WESTERN THEATER Davis sends a message to General Richard Taylor urging him to send troops from Tupelo, Mississippi, to reinforce Hardee in his operations against Sherman in the Carolinas. Meanwhile, in Savannah, Secretary of War Edwin Stanton calls a meeting of about 20 of 'the most intelligent of the Negroes' in that city to ask them how they feel blacks could best maintain their newly acquired freedom.

Their spokesman, Garrison Frazier, tells Stanton that blacks should be placed on land to farm until they can afford to buy it. He also tells Stanton that because of deepseated prejudice against them, he feels his people would be better off living by themselves rather than among whites. Because of charges concerning Sherman's alleged mistreatment of blacks, Stanton also asks the group what their attitude was toward Sherman. Instead of complaints, however, Frazier tells Stanton, 'We have confidence in General Sherman, and think that what concerns us could not be under better hands.'

13 JANUARY 1865

NAVAL   Just after midnight, Admiral Porter's fleet of 59 ships begins its bombardment of Fort Fisher. Having reinforced the fort since the last attack in December, the Confederates now have close to 2000 soldiers and 47 guns in and around the fort itself and another 6000 men at the northern end of the peninsula, commanded by General Braxton Bragg, to oppose any attempted landing by the enemy. In midafternoon, however, Union troops under the command of General Terry establish a beachhead north of Fort Fisher and during the night dig in opposite Bragg's force and prepare to fend off any attack from that quarter.

14 JANUARY 1865

WESTERN THEATER, CAROLINAS CAMPAIGN   Some troops under Sherman's command move from Beaufort to Pocotaligo, South Carolina. In Tupelo, Mississippi, General Pierre G T Beauregard assumes temporary command of the Army of Tennessee; this force will be turned over to General Richard Taylor on 23 January. NAVAL   General Terry's troops continue to prepare for their attack on Fort Fisher while they also work to secure their position against Bragg's Confederates. With Admiral Porter's fleet pounding away at the fort itself, Colonel William Lamb, commanding the Southern garrison there,

sends urgent appeals to Bragg to turn his men loose on the Federal landing expedition to the north of the fort.

15 JANUARY 1865

NAVAL   At eight in the morning, Admiral Porter's powerful armada opens up again on Fort Fisher, this time at point-blank range. Throughout the morning, the Federals pour a withering fire at the fort and its defenders. In midafternoon, Northern troops launch a twin attack against the fortress: one, composed of 2261 sailors and marines, strikes from the ocean side; the other, 3300 of General Terry's 8000-man landing force, assails the fort from the northwest. The remaining 4700, meanwhile, remain entrenched opposite General Bragg's Confederates to prevent them from interfering in the operation. The fort's defenders repel the assault from the sea but are unable to resist the land attack and at 10 in the evening are forced to surrender. Confederate casualties are about 500, while the combined Union losses are 1341. The Federals, however, take over 1900 prisoners, including General William H Whiting and Colonel William Lamb. Bragg will come under severe criticism from both these men for failing to attack the landing party during the operations.

16 JANUARY 1865

WASHINGTON   Back in Washington, Francis P Blair gives President Lincoln a detailed report on his recent discussion with Jefferson Davis over possibilities for peace between North and South. Later, Lincoln will turn down Blair's scheme for a combined effort to expel France from Mexico, but the Marylander's trip between Richmond and Washington does succeed in getting both sides to agree to meet with one another.

THE CONFEDERACY   In a move that is widely seen as a direct challenge to Davis's control over military matters, the Confederate Senate passes a resolution (by a vote of 14 to 2) advising the president to appoint

Lee as general-in-chief, to give Joseph Johnston his old command as commander of the Army of Tennessee and to make Beauregard overall commander in Florida, Georgia and South Carolina.

NAVAL   At Fort Fisher, two drunken sailors, looking for loot in the newly captured fortress, stumble into a magazine with their torches and explode 13,000 pounds of gunpowder. Twenty-five Federals die in the blast and another 66 are wounded. Some Confederates, captured in last night's battle, are also killed in the explosion. Meanwhile, Davis, learning of the loss of the fort, sends General Bragg a message urging him to retake the fort if at all possible.

WESTERN THEATER   To provide for the 10,000 black refugees that had followed his army through Georgia on its March to the Sea, General Sherman issues Special Field Order #15. The order sets aside all abandoned or confiscated land along the coast of Georgia, including the coastal islands, for the settlement of freedmen. Families are to be given 'possessory title' to not more than 40 acres until Congress regulates their title. Although Sherman will later insist that the order was intended as nothing more than a temporary war measure, and almost all of the land will eventually revert to its former owners, many blacks hope this order represents the determination of the government to make land available to the new freedmen.

19 JANUARY 1865

THE CONFEDERACY   After much prodding from Davis, General Robert E Lee agrees to accept the position of general-in-chief of all the armies of the Confederacy. Davis is anxious to head off mounting criticism of his control of the armies by acceding to Congress's 'advice' to appoint Lee as military commander of all Confederate forces.

WESTERN THEATER, CAROLINAS CAMPAIGN   General Sherman issues orders commanding the units of his army to begin their march into South Carolina. Heavy rains will delay the march until early February, but some troop movement commences.

20 JANUARY 1865

WESTERN THEATER, CAROLINAS CAMPAIGN   Sherman's army in the vicinity of Savannah continues preparations for its northward march.

TRANS-MISSISSIPPI   There is a fight near Fort Larned, Kansas, between Federal troops and Indians.

21 JANUARY 1865

WESTERN THEATER, CAROLINAS CAMPAIGN   General Sherman moves his headquarters out of Savannah toward Beaufort, South Carolina.

23 JANUARY 1865

THE CONFEDERACY   To help mollify elements in Congress critical of his handling of military matters, Davis signs into law a bill passed by Congress last week creating the position of general-in-chief. Both Congress and Davis are agreed that Lee is to fill the new post.

WESTERN THEATER   In Mississippi, General Richard Taylor assumes command of the Army of Tennessee. Because many of the troops formerly with this army have been transferred east to reinforce General Hardee in South Carolina, the Army of Tennessee now has fewer than 18,000 soldiers.

NAVAL   Eleven Southern ships set sail down the James River, hoping to attack the Federal squadron off the coast. Four of the ships, however, run aground and the Confederates are forced to abandon the project.

26 JANUARY 1865

WESTERN THEATER, CAROLINAS CAMPAIGN   Although Sherman intends to march his army to Goldsborough, North Carolina, he wants to deceive the enemy as to his real objective. To do so, he sends an expedition out toward Charleston to create the impression that his army will head in that direction. The troops skirmish with the enemy near Pocotaligo, South Carolina. Further west, there is also fighting near Paint Rock, Alabama.

27 JANUARY 1865

WESTERN THEATER Fighting breaks out between Union and Confederate troops in DeKalb County, Alabama.

28 JANUARY 1865

THE CONFEDERACY To represent the South in the upcoming peace talks with President Lincoln, Jefferson Davis appoints Vice President Alexander Stephens, Robert M T Hunter, president *pro tempore* of the Senate, and Assistant Secretary of War John A Campbell.
WESTERN THEATER, CAROLINAS CAMPAIGN There is skirmishing along the Combahee River in South Carolina between elements of Sherman's army and defending Confederates.

30 JANUARY 1865

WESTERN THEATER, CAROLINAS CAMPAIGN Reinforcements from the Army of Tennessee, from Tupelo, Mississippi, begin to arrive in Augusta, Georgia. Altogether some 4000 soldiers will arrive from Tupelo to help General Hardee defend the Carolinas against Sherman's army. Meanwhile, fighting breaks out between the two sides at Lawtonville, South Carolina, as elements of Sherman's army continue their activities in the lower part of the state. In Kentucky, there is fighting at Chaplintown, as Confederates harass Union troops in the state.

31 JANUARY 1865

WASHINGTON By a vote of 119 to 56, the House of Representatives passes the proposed Constitutional amendment abolishing slavery throughout the United States. The amendment will now go to the states. It must be ratified by three-fourths of them before it will become a part of the Constitu-

tion. A critical question is whether any of the states formerly or presently in rebellion should be included in ratification calculations. A number of Republicans believe that the rebellious states must first be accepted into the Union as new states, and until they are, should have no influence over the ratification process. This view, of course, improves the chances for adoption of the amendment. Today also, Lincoln gives Secretary of State William H Seward instructions concerning his upcoming conference with the Confederate peace commissioners. President Lincoln insists that recognition of Federal authority is a necessary precondition to peace, while Davis still clings to independence as the only basis of negotiations.

1 FEBRUARY 1865

THE NORTH Illinois ratifies the Thirteenth Amendment, becoming the first state to do so since its passage in the House of Representatives yesterday.
WESTERN THEATER, CAROLINAS CAMPAIGN After having been delayed for almost two weeks by heavy rains, Sherman's Union army sets out in earnest on its march through the Carolinas. By again dividing his army—his right wing making a feint toward Charleston while the left wing moves in the direction of Augusta—Sherman hopes to confound the enemy as to his true objective. As the army begins its march through South Carolina, many of the

Sherman's march through South Carolina.

soldiers seem determined to make the state, which they see as the heart and soul of secession and rebellion, suffer for its treason. Aside from the official work of destruction, the Federals also burn and destroy much private property. Although such destruction is against orders, Sherman seems to have anticipated South Carolina's fate in a letter he had written to General Halleck in December: 'The whole army is burning with an insatiable desire to wreak vengeance upon South Carolina,' he wrote: 'I almost tremble at her fate, but feel that she deserves all that seems in store for her.'

2 FEBRUARY 1865

WASHINGTON President Lincoln leaves the capital for Hampton Roads, Virginia where tomorrow he plans to meet with Confederate peace commissioners.

THE NORTH Rhode Island and Michigan become the second and third states to ratify the Thirteenth Amendment.

WESTERN THEATER, CAROLINAS CAMPAIGN Hindered by fallen trees and burned bridges, Union troops under General Sherman continue their march through South Carolina. To oppose them, the South has 22,500 soldiers brought in from various theaters of the war. About 12,500 of these are concentrated in and around Augusta, Georgia, and the remainder lie between Port Royal Sound and Charleston on the Carolina coast. With the two wings of the Federal army aimed in different directions, the Confederates are unaware that its true objective is Columbia.

3 FEBRUARY 1865

WASHINGTON President Lincoln and Secretary of State Seward meet with Stephens, Hunter and Campbell on board the *River Queen*, off Hampton Roads, to discuss possibilities for peace between North and South. The talks, which last about four hours, produce no positive results, however, as the Confederate agents want an armistice first and all talk of reunion postponed until later, while Lin-

coln insists on recognition of Federal authority as an essential first step toward peace. The President also informs the Southerners of the recent passage of the Thirteenth Amendment in Congress and expresses confidence that it will soon be ratified by the states.

THE NORTH Maryland, New York and West Virginia ratify the Thirteenth Amendment. To date, six states have done so.

WESTERN THEATER, CAROLINAS CAMPAIGN As Sherman's right wing continues to move in the direction of Charleston, Federal troops battle Confederates at Rivers' Bridge and at Dillingham's Cross Roads beside the Salkehatchie River.

4 FEBRUARY 1865

WASHINGTON President Lincoln returns to the White House after his unsuccessful peace mission to Hampton Roads, Virginia.

WESTERN THEATER, CAROLINAS CAMPAIGN Fighting occurs along Sherman's advance, at Angley's Post Office and Bufords Bridge.

5 FEBRUARY 1865

WASHINGTON President Lincoln presents a plan to his Cabinet pledging the Federal government to pay $400,000,000 to the slave states if they lay down their arms before 1 April. The Cabinet, though, is united in opposition to the scheme and the matter drops.

EASTERN THEATER, SIEGE OF PETERSBURG In another attempt to extend his lines westward, General Grant orders part of his army to move in the direction of Boydton Plank Road to stop Confederate wagon trains from using that road to supply Petersburg. This movement, which will continue for the next three days, will be the last major move by Grant to push his lines westward prior to the final assault.

6 FEBRUARY 1865

THE CONFEDERACY Davis also reports to

Congress on the meeting at Hampton Roads between Lincoln and the three Confederate peace commissioners. Lincoln, he says, insists upon unqualified submission as his terms for peace.

EASTERN THEATER, SIEGE OF PETERSBURG Heavy fighting occurs south of Petersburg, near Dabney Mills, as Confederate troops led by General John Pegram attack the positions Union troops had taken up on 5 February. Federals repel the attack and Pegram is killed in the assault.

WESTERN THEATER, CAROLINAS CAMPAIGN Fighting takes place at Fishburn's Plantation, on the Little Salkehatchie and near Barnwell as Confederates continue to operate against Sherman's advancing columns in South Carolina.

7 FEBRUARY 1865

THE NORTH Maine and Kansas both ratify the Thirteenth Amendment. In the Delaware legislature, however, it fails to receive enough votes for passage.

EASTERN THEATER, SIEGE OF PETERSBURG In the third day of action around Hatchers Run, south of Petersburg, Union troops fall back from the Boydton Plank Road after Confederate reinforcements arrive on the scene. In three days, the Union troops have succeeded in extending their lines to Hatchers Run at the Vaughan Road crossing. The movement costs the North 1512 casualties. Southern casualties during the action are unreported.

WESTERN THEATER, CAROLINAS CAMPAIGN Fighting swamps and swollen rivers, Sherman's troops continue their progress toward Columbia. Some fighting takes place during the day at Blackville, South Carolina.

8 FEBRUARY 1865

WESTERN THEATER, CAROLINAS CAMPAIGN At Williston on the Edisto River and along the banks of the South Edisto, Sherman's Union troops again battle Confederates. Sherman responds to a complaint from Confederate cavalry leader Joseph Wheeler that Union soldiers are

ruthlessly destroying private property along their path: 'I hope you will burn all cotton and save us the trouble,' Sherman tells Wheeler. 'All you don't burn I will. As to private houses occupied by peaceful families, my orders are not to molest or disturb them, and I think my orders are obeyed. Vacant houses being of no use to anybody, I care little about, I don't want them destroyed, but do not take much care to preserve them.'

9 FEBRUARY 1865

THE CONFEDERACY General Robert E Lee assumes the position of general-in-chief of the Confederate armies. He suggests a pardon be given all deserters who report back to their commands within 30 days. Davis approves the plan.

WESTERN THEATER, CAROLINAS CAMPAIGN General John M Schofield assumes his duties as commander of the Department of North Carolina and troops under his command arrive at Fort Fisher in preparation for an assault on Wilmington. Schofield's assignment is to move his troops westward, restoring communications, to provide Sherman's army with a shorter supply line than would be necessary if it were to continue to draw provisions from Savannah. Sherman's army, still marching northward, skirmishes with the enemy at Binnaker's Bridge on the South Edisto River and at Holman's Bridge, in South Carolina.

10 FEBRUARY 1865

WESTERN THEATER, CAROLINAS CAMPAIGN There is fighting around Charleston Harbor at James Island and at Johnson Station. Confederates in the city are still not sure whether Sherman's army intends to attack them and are forced to maintain defenses against both land and sea assault.

11 FEBRUARY 1865

EASTERN THEATER, SIEGE OF PETERSBURG Some fighting occurs near Williamsburg, Virginia.

WESTERN THEATER, CAROLINAS CAMPAIGN Sherman's army reaches the Augusta and Charleston Railroad, thus placing itself directly between Confederate forces in and around Augusta and those on the coast of South Carolina, near Charleston. Some action takes place at Aiken, Johnson's Station and around Orangeburg, South Carolina. In Charleston, General William J Hardee, who is now separated from potential reinforcements from the west, still believes the Federal army intends to strike at that city.

12 FEBRUARY 1865

WASHINGTON The electoral college meets and, by a vote of 212 to 21, Lincoln is declared elected as President. Although Tennessee and Louisiana had both voted in the November election, Vice President Hannibal Hamlin, presiding over the college, does not present the votes of these states.

WESTERN THEATER, CAROLINAS CAMPAIGN Sherman's army repulses Southern defenders at the Orangeburg Bridge on the North Edisto River and continues its northward march toward Columbia.

13 FEBRUARY 1865

INTERNATIONAL Lord John Russell complains to US commissioners of United States activities on the Great Lakes. Britain and Canada are particularly upset at the military buildup in that area. The Lincoln administration, however, believes it is necessary to counter raids by Confederate agents operating out of Canada. The Saint Albans raid of October 1864, in particular, has generated a good deal of animosity between the US and its northern neighbor. The raid not only originated in Canada but the Canadian government later released the perpetrators from jail for lack of jurisdiction.

14 FEBRUARY 1865

WESTERN THEATER, CAROLINAS CAMPAIGN Sherman's troops cross the Congaree River and then both wings turn toward Columbia, South Carolina. Meanwhile, Jefferson Davis urges General Hardee, who is still expecting the Union army to attack Charleston, to delay evacuating that city as long as possible. He does, however, leave the final decision to Hardee and Beauregard who, he admits, are better acquainted with the situation.

15 FEBRUARY 1865

WESTERN THEATER, CAROLINAS CAMPAIGN Fighting flares up along the Congaree Creek and Savannah Creek and also at Bates Ferry on the Congaree River as Confederates try to slow Sherman's march toward Columbia. There is also fighting during the day at Red Bank Creek and Two League Cross Roads, in South Carolina. In addition to the continuing attacks by Southern cavalry, the Union army must contend with deep swamps and rain-swollen waterways as well as the myriad man-made obstacles that the Confederates have thrown in their path.

16 FEBRUARY 1865

WESTERN THEATER, CAROLINAS CAMPAIGN Sherman's army arrives at the Congaree River, just south of Columbia, South Carolina. Both General Beauregard and Confederate cavalry leader Wade Hampton are in the city during the day, but are powerless to resist the Northern army. Beauregard tells Lee that there is nothing to be done to save the state capital and then in midafternoon leaves Columbia. To the east, in Charleston, General William J Hardee makes preparations to evacuate his troops from that city. With Sherman's army between him and potential reinforcements in Augusta, and with a formidable threat from the sea as well, Hardee's position is untenable.

17 FEBRUARY 1865

WESTERN THEATER, CAROLINAS CAMPAIGN In the morning, town officials of Columbia, South Carolina, ride out to surrender the city formally to the Union General William T Sherman and his army. As the remainder of the Southern cavalry flee the capital, the Northern trops occupy it and the officers and staff settle into a few of the fine mansions that grace the city. Some time during the night fires break out in a number of homes and, though many of the town's 20,000 residents futilely battle the flames, the wind-fanned blazes quickly spread to neighboring structures. By morning two-thirds of Columbia will lie smoldering in ashes. Sherman is quick to blame the fleeing enemy soldiers for the fires, but for residents of the town and for Southerners in general, the burning of Columbia will long stand as a symbol of the savage cruelty of Sherman's marauding army. Among the homes destroyed during the night is the magnificent mansion of General Wade Hampton, commander of the Southern cavalry opposing Sherman's march. Meanwhile, General Hardee evacuates Charleston, moving his troops northwestward to Cheraw, South Carolina. After the long siege Fort Sumter finally comes into Federal hands.

The ruins of Columbia, South Carolina.

and then begin to move westward hoping to outflank Confederate troops there. To the west, Confederates raid Fort Jones, Kentucky.

NAVAL After several days of refitting, the CSS *Shenandoah* leaves Melbourne, Australia.

18 *FEBRUARY* 1865

THE CONFEDERACY   In a letter to Mississippi Congressman Ethelbert Barksdale, General Lee endorses the idea of arming slaves to help the South win independence. The idea, which has gained considerable support in the Confederate Congress since its new session opened in November, was recently incorporated in a bill introduced by Barksdale in the Confederate House of Representatives. Lee tells Barksdale that he believes blacks would make efficient soldiers, but they should fight as free men.

WESTERN THEATER, CAROLINAS CAMPAIGN   General Sherman orders the destruction of all railroad depots, supply houses and industries in Columbia not already destroyed in yesterday's fire. Near Wilmington, North Carolina, Federal forces bombard Fort Anderson from the sea while troops under the command of General Jacob Cox land south of the city

19 *FEBRUARY* 1865

WESTERN THEATER, CAROLINAS CAMPAIGN   As Union troops try to outflank Confederate forces in Wilmington, North Carolina, by marching around the city from the south, fighting breaks out along the way, including one action at Town Creek. The Federal navy meanwhile, continues its bombardment of Fort Anderson, and during the night the Southern garrison evacuates that place. In Columbia, South Carolina, as Union soldiers finish their work of destroying everything of military use in that city, units of Sherman's army begin their march northward toward Goldsboro, North Carolina. In Alabama, Federals continue an expedition aimed at Selma and encounter enemy soldiers along the way.

20 *FEBRUARY* 1865

THE CONFEDERACY   The Confederate

House of Representatives passes a bill authorizing the use of slaves as soldiers. Since Jefferson Davis's November message to Congress calling for the increased use of slaves as laborers in the military, debate in the South has increasingly turned to suggestions of actually arming the blacks.

WESTERN THEATER, CAROLINAS CAMPAIGN General Jacob Cox's Union troops continue their flanking maneuver on the east bank of the Cape Fear River near Wilmington.

21 *FEBRUARY* 1865

THE CONFEDERACY The Confederate Senate votes to postpone consideration of the House bill authorizing the arming of slaves.

EASTERN THEATER, SIEGE OF PETERSBURG General Lee writes Secretary of War John Breckenridge that if it becomes necessary to abandon Richmond, he will move his army to Burkeville, Virginia, where it could stay in contact with Confederate troops in the Carolinas, and possibly join forces for a combined assault on either Grant's or Sherman's army.

WESTERN THEATER, CAROLINAS CAMPAIGN General Braxton Bragg orders the evacuation of Southern troops from Wilmington, North Carolina, the last major Confederate port. With enemy pressure from the sea, and Union General Jacob Cox's troops closing in from the west, the Confederates in the city begin destroying all supplies there which they cannot carry with them. Meanwhile, there is fighting at Eagle Island and Fort Strong as Federals keep up pressure on the enemy.

22 *FEBRUARY* 1865

WESTERN THEATER, CAROLINAS CAMPAIGN Union troops enter the city of Wilmington, which General Braxton Bragg's troops had evacuated last night. In their campaign against the city, the North lost 200 casualties. Further south, there is fighting at Cambden, South Carolina and again on the Wateree River as Sherman's army continues its march northward.

23 *FEBRUARY* 1865

WESTERN THEATER, CAROLINAS CAMPAIGN Fighting again erupts near Camden, South Carolina between elements of Sherman's army and Confederate troops.

24 *FEBRUARY* 1865

WESTERN THEATER, CAROLINAS CAMPAIGN As Union troops continue to wreak their vengeance on South Carolina as the birthplace of secession through unofficial acts of destruction, General Sherman complains to Confederate cavalry General Wade Hampton of the murder of Union foragers by Southern soldiers. Hampton will reply that while he is unaware of the specific episode to which Sherman refers, he has ordered his men to shoot on sight any Northerners caught burning people's homes. And, he will tell Sherman, 'This order shall remain in force so long as you disgrace the profession of arms by allowing your men to destroy private dwellings.' More fighting occurs between the two sides at Cambden, South Carolina.

26 *FEBRUARY* 1865

WESTERN THEATER, CAROLINAS CAMPAIGN Sherman's troops again encounter the enemy, today at Lynch Creek and Strouds Mill, South Carolina. The Federal XX Corps reaches Hanging Rock.

27 *FEBRUARY* 1865

EASTERN THEATER, VALLEY CAMPAIGN In response to Grant's orders, Sheridan sends a 10,000 man cavalry force under General Wesley Merritt to destroy the Virginia Central Railroad and James River Canal. They are then to take the city of Lynchburg, Virginia.

WESTERN THEATER, CAROLINAS CAMPAIGN There is fighting along Sherman's path at Mount Elon and Cloud's House, South Carolina. Southern troops also skirmish with Northerners at Spring Place, Georgia.

28 *FEBRUARY* 1865

WESTERN THEATER, CAROLINAS CAMPAIGN Rocky Mount and Cheraw, South Carolina, are the scene of fighting as Sherman's troops continue their march toward North Carolina.

1 *MARCH* 1865

EASTERN THEATER, VALLEY CAMPAIGN Union cavalry in the Shenandoah Valley engage the enemy at Mount Crawford.

2 *MARCH* 1865

EASTERN THEATER, SIEGE OF PETERSBURG Lee, as general-in-chief of the Confederate forces, sends a message through the lines to General Grant suggesting that the two of them hold a 'military convention' to try to reach 'a satisfactory adjustment of the present unhappy difficulties.' Lee's peace overture is the result of a conversation between General James Longstreet and General Edward Ord in which the latter reportedly said that the Union general-in-chief would respond favorably to such an invitation.

VALLEY CAMPAIGN At Waynesborough a Union cavalry force led by General George A Custer attacks the remnant of Jubal Early's Confederate army and completely routs it, breaking up and scattering the shattered enemy force. Although Early and his staff manage to escape, more than 1000 Southern soldiers are taken prisoner. The Federals herd their prisoners and over 200 wagons of supplies northward down the Shenandoah Valley with an escort and then head toward Charlottesville, Virginia. Meanwhile, Jubal Early and those of his command who had managed to escape capture, begin to make their way back to Richmond. The battle of Waynesborough marks the end of the last campaign in the Shenandoah Valley.

WESTERN THEATER, CAROLINAS CAMPAIGN The Federal XX Corps, one of the four corps of Sherman's army, reaches Chesterfield, South Carolina, after battling Southern troops at nearby Thompson Creek.

3 *MARCH* 1865

WASHINGTON Congress passes an act setting up the Bureau of Refugees, Freedmen, and Abandoned Lands. The Bureau, which will be known more commonly as the Freedmen's Bureau, is to have overall supervisory powers over those in the South dislocated by the war and in need of temporary assistance. A large part of its responsibility will be in aiding and providing work for the newly freed black population. After passing this important reconstruction bill, the 38th Congress adjourns.

EASTERN THEATER, Siege of PETERSBURG General Grant receives instructions from President Lincoln concerning Lee's peace overture of yesterday. The President directs his general-in-chief not to have any conference with Lee unless it is to accept the surrender of his troops 'or on some minor or purely military matter.' All political questions, Lincoln makes it clear, are to be settled by him personally. Tomorrow, Grant will relay the substance of this message to General Lee, thus completely laying to rest all talk of peace negotiations between the two commanding generals. To the west, Sheridan's troops, now riding east toward Petersburg, occupy the town of Charlottesville, Virginia.

WESTERN THEATER, CAROLINAS CAMPAIGN Sherman's troops enter Cheraw, South Carolina, while Confederate defenders fall back across the Pee Dee River. The Federal advance, however, is interrupted during the day by fighting at Thompson's Creek and Big Black Creek.

4 *MARCH* 1865

WASHINGTON President Lincoln is inaugurated for his second term of office, taking his oath from the newly appointed Chief Justice Salmon P Chase. Before taking the oath, Lincoln delivers an inaugural speech in which he tells the audience: 'Fondly do we hope—fervently to we pray—that this mighty scourge of war may speedily pass away. Yet, if God wills that it continue, until all the wealth piled by the bondman's two hundred and fifty years of unrequited toil shall be sunk, and until every drop of blood drawn with the lash, shall be paid by another drawn with the sword, as was said three thousand years ago, so still it must be said "the judgements of the Lord are true and righteous altogether." ' With an eye to the future, the President then gives the crowd his view of a proper peace: 'With malice toward none; with charity toward all; with firmness in the right, as God gives us to see the right, let us strive on to finish the work we are in; to bind up the nation's wounds . . . to do all which may achieve and cherish a just, and a lasting peace, among ourselves, and with all nations.'

7 *MARCH* 1865

WESTERN THEATER, CAROLINAS CAMPAIGN Federal troops commanded by General Jacob Cox work to repair railroad lines running from New Berne to Goldsborough, North Carolina. Cox and his immediate superior, General John M Schofield, plan to meet Sherman's army at Goldsborough; by restoring the rail lines to that city, they will provide a short supply line to Sherman's men from the North Carolina coast. Reinforcements arrive at Kinston, North Carolina today from the Confederate Army of Tennessee. General Braxton Bragg and Johnston hope to use these new men with those already under Bragg's command to launch an attack on Union General Cox's force moving westward.

8 *MARCH* 1865

EASTERN THEATER Sheridan's cavalry force, still moving eastward to join up with Grant in Petersburg, fights the enemy at Duguidsville, Virginia.

WESTERN THEATER, CAROLINAS CAMPAIGN Using the troops just arrived from the Army of Tennessee to supplement his own force, General Braxton Bragg attacks Federals under the command of General Jacob Cox just outside of Kinston, North Carolina. One brigade of new Federal recruits breaks under the Confederate

assault, but their battle-hardened comrades repulse the Southerners. Fighting will continue for the next two days as Bragg tries to destroy Cox's Federals before they can link up with Sherman's army moving north toward Goldsborough.

9 *MARCH* 1865

WASHINGTON Lincoln accepts the resignation of John P Usher as Secretary of Interior. It will take effect on 15 May.

THE NORTH Vermont ratifies the Thirteenth Amendment abolishing slavery in the United States.

WESTERN THEATER, CAROLINAS CAMPAIGN Confederate cavalry under the command of Generals Wade Hampton and Joseph Wheeler launch a surprise attack on General Judson Kilpatrick at Solemn Grove and Monroe's Cross Roads in the late evening. Many of the Federals are caught in their beds, and Kilpatrick only narrowly avoids that fate himself. The Union soldiers, however, rally and beat off the attackers. Fighting continues outside of Kinston, as Confederate General Bragg tries to defeat Union General Cox's troops before they can link up with Sherman's advancing army. Cox, however, is bolstered by reinforcements rushed to his aid from the east, while Bragg fails to receive additional troops that he had been promised. The Federals are able successfully to maintain their positions.

10 *MARCH* 1865

WESTERN THEATER, CAROLINAS CAMPAIGN Bragg withdraws his troops back to Kinston, North Carolina, after failing to defeat or turn back Federal troops advancing westward from New Berne. From Kinston, Bragg will move to Goldsborough where he plans to unite his forces with those of Joseph Johnston in preparation for an attack on part of Sherman's advancing columns. At Monroes's Cross Roads, South Carolina, General Judson Kilpatrick's men counterattack the enemy after being surprised in camp by them last night. The Federals defeat the Southern cavalry of Wade Hampton and drive them off.

11 MARCH 1865

EASTERN THEATER Sheridan's cavalry reaches Goochland Court House on its way to rejoin Grant in Petersburg.

WESTERN THEATER, CAROLINAS CAMPAIGN Sherman's army arrives at Fayetteville, North Carolina, where he plans to rest for a couple of days.

TRANS-MISSISSIPPI Fighting takes place today at the Little Blue River, in Missouri, as well as Washington, Arkansas.

12 MARCH 1865

WESTERN THEATER, CAROLINAS CAMPAIGN Soldiers in Sherman's army busy themselves in Fayetteville destroying all machinery, industries and transport facilities which might be of use to the Confederates. Sherman plans to remain in Fayetteville until 15 March and then head his army toward Goldsborough after making a feint toward Raleigh. He orders General Schofield, who is marching troops in from the east, to take them directly to Goldsborough. To the west, fighting takes place at Morganza Bend, Louisiana.

13 MARCH 1865

THE CONFEDERACY The Confederate Congress sends to Davis the bill calling for the arming of black slaves for use in the Southern armies. The law, as finally passed, leaves to the states the ultimate decision on whether the black soldiers should be freed, but it is the concensus that they will be liberated. Davis immediately signs the bill into law, but at the same time chastises Congress for its delay and calls for more legislation designed to close conscription loopholes.

14 MARCH 1865

EASTERN THEATER General Sheridan, still on his way to Petersburg with his cavalry, engages the enemy at the South Anna Bridge, in Virginia. In West Virginia, Federal expeditions near Moorefield and Phillipi comb those areas for bands of Confederates.

WESTERN THEATER, CAROLINAS CAM-PAIGN General Jacob Cox's troops reach Kinston, North Carolina, on their way to Goldsborough where they will join up with Sherman's army. Cox's men are repairing railroad lines along their path to provide Union troops in the state with a short supply line to the coast.

15 MARCH 1865

WESTERN THEATER, CAROLINAS CAMPAIGN As General Sherman moves his troops out of Fayetteville, fighting erupts along his advance at Smiths Mills and on the Black River. The Federal army moves northward in three columns, with the left wing commanded by General Henry Slocum making a feint toward Raleigh. The Confederate commander, Joseph Johnston, meanwhile, is trying to concentrate his troops north of Sherman's advance and hopes to defeat the segments of the Union army before they can unite.

16 MARCH 1865

WESTERN THEATER, CAROLINAS CAMPAIGN Union General Slocum's advancing column meets enemy troops blocking its path on a bridge near Averasborough, North Carolina. The Federals attack the Confederate troops, pushing them back but failing to completely sweep them out of the path. During the night, however, the Confederate commander, General Hardee, withdraws his troops to Bentonville where they rejoin the main body of Southern troops under Johnston. In the Battle of Averasborough, the Federals lose 682 men while Confederate casualties are near 865.

17 MARCH 1865

WESTERN THEATER, MOBILE CAMPAIGN Troops led by General Edward R Canby, commander of the Department of West Mississippi, begin their campaign to capture the city of Mobile, Alabama. Canby has some 45,000 men under his command, while the Confederate garrison defending the city numbers about 10,000. The Federals plan to approach the city from two directions, with one column advancing from Pensacola while the other winds its way up the east side of Mobile Bay from Mobile Point.

18 *MARCH* 1865

WESTERN THEATER, CAROLINAS CAMPAIGN As Sherman's left wing, commanded by General Henry Slocum, approaches the city of Bentonville it skirmishes with Wade Hampton's Confederate cavalry. Hampton is trying to slow the Union troops' advance long enough to give Johnston time to concentrate his force at Bentonville.

MOBILE CAMPAIGN Some 1700 Federal troops feint to the west side of Mobile Bay to create the impression that the attack will come from that direction. In fact, the main Union assault is to take place on the eastern side of the bay.

19 *MARCH* 1865

EASTERN THEATER After completing its mission to destroy the Virginia Central Railroad and the James Canal, Sheridan's Union cavalry arrives at White House on the Pamunkey River. Soon, Sheridan plans to join Grant's army south of Petersburg.

WESTERN THEATER, CAROLINAS CAMPAIGN As the left wing of Sherman's army, commanded by General Henry Slocum, marches toward Bentonville, it again fights Wade Hampton's cavalry, pushing the Confederates back as it advances. Joseph Johnston's 20,000 men then counterattack the Federals, forcing the latter to fall back and entrench. Slocum's men manage to repulse several more full-scale assaults before nightfall. Meanwhile, as word of the battle reaches the other two columns of Sherman's army on the right, they turn west to concentrate against the enemy. During the night, after failing to overwhelm the enemy, Johnston has his men fortify their positions opposite the Federals. To the east, General Schofield and his Union troops marching toward Goldsborough, North Carolina, from the coast, engage several enemy forces at the Neuse River Bridge and also near Cox's Bridge.

20 *MARCH* 1865

WESTERN THEATER, CAROLINAS CAMPAIGN With both Johnston's Confederates and Slocum's Union troops dug in at Bentonville, the rest of Sherman's army arrives and concentrates against the Southern force. Johnston had hoped that he could defeat Slocum's 30,000 before the remainder of the Northern troops could come to his support. Now his Confederates, numbering 20,000, face an enemy army of nearly 100,000. During the day, some skirmishing takes place, but neither side launches an all-out assault. To the west, General George Stoneman leads a cavalry force of 4000 Union soldiers from Jonesborough, in east Tennessee, toward North Carolina. Stoneman's raid, which is designed in part to destroy enemy transport lines, is also intended to aid Sherman's campaign.

21 *MARCH* 1865

WESTERN THEATER, CAROLINAS CAMPAIGN While some of his troops attack the enemy lines, Sherman sends another force around the rear of Johnston's army to capture Mill Creek bridge and cut off the Confederate's retreat. Johnston, however, detects the maneuver and blocks the Federals while at the same time holding off the frontal attacks. During the night, he withdraws his troops to Smithfield. Despite the disparate manpower of the two forces, those engaged during the day are fairly balanced, with about 16,127 Federals seeing action compared with 16,895 Confederates. In the three days of fighting, the Federals suffer 1646 casualties while Johnston loses 2606. Bentonville will be the last major attempt by the Confederates to check Sherman's advance.

22 *MARCH* 1865

WESTERN THEATER, RAID TO SELMA General James H Wilson leads a force of Union cavalry south from the Tennessee River toward Selma, Alabama. Selma is one of the last remaining manufacturing centers left to the Confederacy. By depriving the South of its munitions factories, Union officials believe they can significantly handicap the enemy war effort.

23 MARCH 1865

WASHINGTON President Lincoln leaves the national capital for City Point, Virginia, with his wife and son. In addition to a conference with Grant and Sherman, Lincoln hopes the trip will provide some time for rest and relaxation. Lincoln will stay close to the front lines until 8 April.

WESTERN THEATER, CAROLINAS CAMPAIGN Sherman's army reaches Goldsborough, North Carolina, joining Schofield's Union force which has come into the city from the coast. The Union march from Savannah to Goldsborough, some 425 miles, has been accomplished in 50 days and will give Sherman a reputation as one of the greatest Civil War generals.

24 MARCH 1865

WASHINGTON President Lincoln arrives at Fort Monroe to confer with Grant.

EASTERN THEATER, SIEGE OF PETERSBURG Confederates prepare to launch a full-scale attack on the Union right. Lee hopes that, by capturing Fort Steedman, he can cut the Federal supply line to City Point and perhaps force Grant to contract his lines.

NAVAL The CSS *Stonewall* leaves Ferrol, Spain, and encounters two Union frigates. The Northern wooden vessels refuse the *Stonewall*'s challenge to fight.

25 MARCH 1865

EASTERN THEATER, SIEGE OF PETERSBURG Confederate troops led by General John B Gordon launch a full-scale assault on Fort Steedman and nearby Federal lines. Union troops are caught completely by surprise and the Southern troops easily capture the Federal stronghold as well as the enemy entrenchments next to the fort. The initial success quickly evaporates as Northern troops counterattack later in the day and drive the Confederates out of all their newly acquired positions, including the fort itself. During the day the North suffers close to 1150 casualties, while the South loses nearly 4000, many of whom are taken prisoner.

WESTERN THEATER, MOBILE CAMPAIGN General Edward Canby's Union troops arrive outside of Spanish Fort, after marching along the east side of Mobile Bay. Spanish Fort is one of the important fortifications protecting the city of Mobile.

26 MARCH 1865

EASTERN THEATER, SIEGE OF PETERSBURG In the wake of the failure at Fort Steedman, Lee tells Davis that he doubts that it will be possible to prevent Grant's and Sherman's armies from joining up and it would be unwise for the Army of Northern Virginia to remain where it is until the two Union forces do connect. Meanwhile, Sheridan's Union cavalry arrives at the Petersburg front to reinforce Grant's army.

WESTERN THEATER, MOBILE CAMPAIGN Fighting takes place at Spanish Fort as Federals prepare to lay siege to that Southern fortification.

27 MARCH 1865

WASHINGTON At City Point, Virginia, Lincoln confers with Generals Grant and Sherman (who has come up from Goldsborough, North Carolina, for the talks) and Admiral David Porter. The discussions will continue through the 28th. It is at these talks, Sherman will later say, that Lincoln discusses the topic of reconstruction. According to Sherman, Lincoln tells him that as soon as Southerners lay down their arms, he is willing to grant them full citizenship rights. (The general will refer to this discussion of reconstruction to justify the peace agreement he makes with General Johnston in April.)

28 MARCH 1865

WESTERN THEATER, RAID TO SELMA Wilson's Union cavalry fight Confederates at Elyton, Alabama, as it continues to move toward Selma. In North Carolina, Stoneman's cavalry fights at Snow Hill and Boone after crossing into that state from east Tennessee.

29 *MARCH* 1865

EASTERN THEATER, APPOMATTOX CAMPAIGN   In what will develop into the final major campaign in the Civil War, Grant sends the newly arrived cavalry under Sheridan, together with some infantry units, to try to envelop the Confederate right flank to the southwest of Petersburg. If successful, Grant can not only cut the Southside Railroad, an important Confederate supply line, but also threaten the Southern escape route to the west. Anticipating such a move, Lee sends Generals George Pickett and Fitzhugh Lee to block any such Federal movements. The two sides clash at the crossing of Quaker and Boydton Roads and also on the Vaughan. The Federal advance, however, slows in the evening as rains hamper movement.
WESTERN THEATER   As Stoneman's cavalry continues its penetration of North Carolina from the west, it battles Confederates at Wilkesborough.

30 *MARCH* 1865

EASTERN THEATER, APPOMATTOX CAMPAIGN   Heavy rains interfere with Union plans to outflank the enemy on the right of the Confederate siege lines, but both sides continue to mass troops in the area. Fitzhugh Lee's Southern cavalry is successful during the day in repulsing an advance at Five Forks.
WESTERN THEATER, RAID TO SELMA   Wilson's expedition of Federal troops battles enemy cavalry from General Forrest's command at Montevallo, Alabama. Tomorrow, the Federals will destroy important iron and coal works near that town.

31 *MARCH* 1865

EASTERN THEATER, APPOMATTOX CAMPAIGN   As the rains end, Union troops

under the command of Generals Sheridan and Gouverneur Warren assault enemy positions around White Oaks Road and Dinwiddie Court House, southwest of Petersburg. Outnumbered nearly five to one in the area, Confederates succeed in repelling the Federal advance; but in the evening, feeling the Union force is too powerful, General Pickett moves his troops back to Five Forks. Although it is not yet absolutely determined, the fact is that this move is the beginning of the end for the Confederate forces, because their retreat from the defenses of Petersburg will soon force Lee to abandon the nearby capital of the Confederacy, Richmond, and this in turn will lead to the surrender at Appomattox Court House.

1 *APRIL* 1865

EASTERN THEATER, APPOMATTOX CAMPAIGN   Convinced that the loss of Five Forks would threaten the Confederate line of retreat, General Lee sends Pickett a message commanding him to hold that position 'at all costs'. Federal troops under the command of Generals Sheridan and Gouverneur Warren (whom Sheridan relieves during the day for allegedly moving too slowly) completely overpower and crush Pickett's troops, however, not only seizing the vital Southern position but isolating Pickett's command from the remainder of the Southern army. Southern troops engaged in the action are probably fewer than 10,000; the Federals, on the other hand, have about 53,000 men available, with about 27,000 of these seeing action during the day. Northern casualties are estimated at 1000 while almost half of the Confederate troops are captured.
WESTERN THEATER, CAROLINAS CAMPAIGN   Fighting occurs at Snow Hill, North Carolina, between elements of Sherman's army and Southern defenders.
MOBILE CAMPAIGN   General Edward Canby's operation against Mobile, Alabama, leads to fighting today at Blakely. The Union monitor *Rodolph*, one of the fleet supporting Canby's expedition, hits a tor-

pedo in Blakely River and sinks.

RAID TO SELMA   Wilson's Union cavalry force continues to move toward Selma, engaging enemy cavalry at several points between Randolph and Trion. General Forrest, who is directing the Southern resistance to Wilson's operations, is trying to delay the Federals long enough to allow reinforcements to arrive at Selma.

NAVAL   After several days of operations against Northern whaling vessels in the Pacific, the CSS *Shenandoah* arrives at a harbor in the Eastern Carolines.

2 *APRIL* 1865

THE CONFEDERACY   While attending church in Richmond, Jefferson Davis receives a message from General Lee telling him that he will have to evacuate the Confederate capital immediately because the Confederate troops are being forced to abandon the defense of Petersburg. Davis quietly leaves the church and in the evening he and several members of his cabinet board a special train bound for Danville, Virginia. Back in the capital, factories, warehouses and arsenals are destroyed and whole sections of the city gutted by flames as Confederate soldiers prepare to abandon the place to Federal troops.

EASTERN THEATER, APPOMATTOX CAMPAIGN   Learning from Confederate deserters that Lee has severely weakened his defense to reinforce his right flank at Five Forks, General Grant orders a full-scale assault on the Confederate siege lines. The Federals break through at several points but the most crucial success comes when General Horatio G Wright's VI Corps seizes Southern entrenchments around Fort Fisher and roll up the right flank. During the night Lee, who had already told Davis in the morning that the army would have to evacuate its position, leads his troops out of Petersburg and toward Amelia Court House. James Longstreet's and John B Gordon's troops hold Petersburg until the rest of the army can make its escape. During the day 63,299 Federals engage 18,579 Confederates, with the

former suffering 3361 casualties; Southern casualties are not recorded, but include among the dead General Ambrose P Hill.

WESTERN THEATER, MOBILE CAMPAIGN   Federals, already besieging Spanish Fort, now begin to lay siege to Fort Blakely. Both forts are important positions in the Confederate fortifications protecting Mobile.

RAID TO SELMA   After breaking through strong defensive fortifications held by 5000 Southerners under Forrest's command, Federal troops occupy the city of Selma, Alabama. Forrest and General Richard Taylor, both in the city, narrowly avoid capture but the Union troops bag some 2700 Confederate prisoners and a large store of enemy supplies.

3 *APRIL* 1865

THE CONFEDERACY   Jefferson Davis and members of his cabinet arrive in Danville, Virginia, after fleeing Richmond last night.

EASTERN THEATER   At 8:15 in the morning, Union General Godfrey Weitzel formally accepts the surrender of Richmond. After four years of repeated threats from the enemy, the Confederate capital has finally fallen to Federal troops. Richmond is not just important as the seat of government, however, but is a vital manufacturing center as well. The Tredeger Iron Works, located in Richmond, has been the South's most important munitions factory. To the south, Union troops have also occupied the city of Petersburg.

The burning of Richmond, 3 April 1865.

Fire-gutted Richmond.

WESTERN THEATER, RAID TO SELMA
Wilson's Union cavalry clash with elements of Forrest's command outside Tuscaloosa, Alabama. To the north, there is also fighting between Union and Confederate troops at Mount Pleasant, Tennessee.

4 *APRIL* 1865

WASHINGTON President Lincoln goes to Richmond and is cheered by crowds of Union soldiers and Richmond blacks as he tours that city after traveling up the James River from City Point, Virginia. Lincoln has been with Federal troops around Petersburg since 24 March and was on hand to witness Grant's final assault on Lee's defensive lines on 2 April.

THE CONFEDERACY From Danville, Virginia, Jefferson Davis issues a proclamation to the people of the South admitting the great loss the Confederacy has suffered in the fall of Richmond; he tells them that while the struggle is entering a new phase, they should not abandon the fight.

EASTERN THEATER, APPOMATTOX CAMPAIGN Lee's army clashes with pursuing Federals at Tabernacle Church and Amelia Court House. Hoped-for supplies do not arrive at the latter place and Lee is forced to feed his army off the surrounding countryside. Meanwhile, Sheridan's cavalry arrives at Jetersville, on the Danville Railroad, cutting off the possibility of further retreat by the enemy along that line. Lee's army is now effectively trapped between Meade's troops from the east and Sheridan's from the south and west.

5 *APRIL* 1865

WASHINGTON In Richmond, President Lincoln confers with Confederate Assistant Secretary of War John Campbell on the subject of peace. The President tells Campbell (who had been one of the three Confederate agents at the Hampton Roads Conference in February) that he will not back down on the abolition of slavery and to secure peace the South must first submit to the authority of the Federal government. In Washington, Secretary of State William H Seward is severely injured in a carriage accident. Seward will still be confined to bed over a week later when the President is assassinated.

EASTERN THEATER, APPOMATTOX CAMPAIGN Without supplies and with further retreat along the Danville Railroad blocked, Lee moves his army toward Farmville where he hopes to be able to feed his hungry forces. As the Army of Virginia moves westward, it skirmishes with Federals at Amelia Springs and Paine's Cross Roads.

6 *APRIL* 1865

EASTERN THEATER, APPOMATTOX CAMPAIGN As Lee's army approaches Farmville, it accidently diverges into two segments, each heading off in a different direction. The Federals, in pursuit of the fleeing Confederates, strike the divided enemy at Saylers Creek, completely overwhelming each of the two wings. In the battle, the Confederates lose almost one-third of their total strength as prisoners (close to 8000 are captured during the battle). Federal losses, meanwhile are about 1180.

WESTERN THEATER, RAID TO SELMA At Lanier's Mills, Sipsey Creek and King's Store, Alabama, Wilson's Union cavalry continues to battle elements of Forrest's command.

7 *APRIL* 1865

WASHINGTON Hearing through General Sheridan that Lee might surrender if pressed, President Lincoln tells Grant: 'Let the *thing* be pressed.'

EASTERN THEATER, APPOMATTOX CAMPAIGN Grant sends General Lee a message asking him to surrender his army to prevent 'any further effusion of blood.' Lee responds to the message by inquiring what would be the terms of such a surrender. Meanwhile, heavy fighting at Farmville delays the Confederate army's flight. Although the Federal assaults are repulsed, Sheridan's cavalry is allowed enough time to circle around to the south of the Army of Northern Virginia and place itself directly in the path of the Southern army's retreat.

INTERNATIONAL The US opens negotiations with Britain over claims resulting from damage inflicted by the CSS *Alabama*. Since the *Alabama* was built in Britain, the US government holds Britain accountable for such damage.

8 *APRIL* 1865

WASHINGTON President Lincoln, who has been in the Petersburg-Richmond area since the end of last month, returns to the capital.

EASTERN THEATER, APPOMATTOX CAMPAIGN General Grant writes Lee that his one condition of surrender is 'that the men and officers surrendered shall be disqualified from taking up arms against the Government of the United States until

McLean House, Appomattox Court House.

properly exchanged.' Although his staff is divided on the question, Lee turns down the idea of surrender for the time being and in the evening decides to try to break through Union troops blocking his path at Appomattox Court House.

WESTERN THEATER, MOBILE CAMPAIGN Following a heavy bombardment, Federals charge Spanish Fort, an important Confederate fortification protecting Mobile. After an initial repulse, the Union troops succeed in breaking through the Southern defenses. The Confederate garrison manages to avoid capture, however, by slipping out of the fort during the night.

9 *APRIL* 1865

EASTERN THEATER, APPOMATTOX CAMPAIGN In the early morning, the Confederate Army of Virginia launches an attack on Federal troops blocking their path to the south. The Confederates succeed in breaking through the Federal cavalry but are unable to penetrate the infantry units behind it. The Union infantry instead begins to advance against the Southerners while other Northern troops in the rear begin to push in Lee's rearguard. As the morning wears on, Lee realizes that further resistance is futile, so he orders that a white flag (actually, a towel is used) be carried through the Union lines with a request for a cease fire until he can work out terms of surrender with Grant. In the early afternoon, the two generals-in-chief meet at the home of a Wilbur

Lee and Grant at the surrender.

CHRONOLOGY

Union soldiers at Appomattox Court House.

McLean in Appomattox Court House. Lee agrees to turn over all munitions and supplies (sidearms excepted) to the Federal army and to send his soldiers home where they could not return to fight until 'properly exchanged' (that is, until a Union prisoner is exchanged for each, an eventuality both generals know will never take place). Grant writes down the terms of surrender in his own hand and, at Lee's request, adds: 'let all men who claim to own a horse or mule take the animals home with them to work their little farms.' After signing the surrender, Lee mounts his faithful old horse Traveller and rides back to his men, whom he then tells: 'Go to your homes and resume your occupations. Obey the laws and become as good citizens as you were soldiers.'

WESTERN THEATER, MOBILE CAMPAIGN Federal forces capture Fort Blakely, another important fortification guarding Mobile, Alabama.

10 *APRIL* 1865

WASHINGTON A brass band leads 3000 people to the White House as news of Lee's surrender sweeps through the city. Called on to make a speech, Lincoln tells the crowd that he will do so tomorrow. Lincoln then asks the band to play 'Dixie' remarking that it had always been a favorite of his, and although the South had claimed it as theirs, it now belongs to the Union.

THE CONFEDERACY Learning of Lee's

surrender at Appomattox, Davis and those members of his cabinet who had followed him to Danville set out for Greensborough, North Carolina, where they hope to be more secure from Federal cavalry.

EASTERN THEATER General Robert E Lee gives his formal farewell to the Army of Northern Virginia. Applauding their valor and courage, Lee tells his men that he feels the time has arrived when any more sacrifice by them could produce nothing that would compensate for the loss that would be suffered. He tells them to go home until properly exchanged and then bids them good-bye: 'With an increasing admiration of your constancy and devotion to your country, and a grateful remembrance of your kind and generous consideration of myself. I bid you an affectionate farewell.'

WESTERN THEATER, CAROLINAS CAMPAIGN General Sherman marches toward Raleigh, North Carolina, where most of Joseph Johnston's force of Confederates is located.

11 *APRIL* 1865

WASHINGTON Lincoln addresses a crowd gathered outside the White House on the subject of reconstruction. Although he defends the newly created state government in Louisiana, he admits that he would have preferred the vote to be given black soldiers as well as the 'most intelligent' of that race. He also tells his audience that reconstruction plans must remain flexible. This is to be Lincoln's last speech.

WESTERN THEATER, CAROLINAS CAMPAIGN Sherman's troops continue their march toward Raleigh, battling the enemy at Smithfield, Pikeville and Beulah, North Carolina.

MOBILE CAMPAIGN Confederates abandon Fort Hugar and Fort Tracy, the last remaining fortifications blocking Union troops from Mobile, Alabama. During the night, Confederates also pull out of Mobile itself.

12 *APRIL* 1865

EASTERN THEATER At Appomattox

Court House, a formal surrender ceremony takes place—although neither Lee nor Grant attend. General Joshua Chamberlain of Maine, who had distinguished himself in the last days of fighting, is accorded the honor of accepting the arms and flags of the Confederate Army of Northern Virginia. Chamberlain has his Union troops lining the roads; as the Confederate column, led by General John B Gordon, approaches, Chamberlain gives the command, 'Carry arms!' and the surprised Gordon orders the same, 'honor answering honor.' The Confederate units then fold and lay down their flags and stack their arms. For all practical purposes, the war is over.

WESTERN THEATER, CAROLINAS CAMPAIGN Sherman's troops battle Southern resistance in the outskirts of Raleigh, North Carolina. Meanwhile, General Stoneman and his Union cavalry, riding eastward through North Carolina, capture the city of Salisbury and take over 1700 enemy soldiers prisoner.

MOBILE CAMPAIGN Federal troops occupy the city of Mobile, Alabama. The campaign against Mobile has cost the Federals 1578 casualties and came at a time, Grant would later write, 'when its possession was of no importance.'

RAID TO SELMA Wilson's Union cavalry occupy Montgomery, Alabama, after skirmishing on Columbus Road.

13 *APRIL* 1865

WASHINGTON As part of a demobilization program, Lincoln halts the draft and reduces requisitions for war supplies.

WESTERN THEATER, CAROLINAS CAMPAIGN Sherman's army occupies Raleigh, the state capital of North Carolina, on its way to Greensborough, now the temporary seat of the Confederate government.

14 *APRIL* 1865

WASHINGTON After conferring with his Cabinet and General Grant during the day, Lincoln goes to the play, *Our American Cousin*, at Ford's Theater. He is accompanied by his wife and by Clara Harris, daughter of a Senator, and her fiancé, Major Henry Rathbone. About 10 that evening, John Wilkes Booth enters the President's box through the door in the rear. Booth is an actor in a family of famous actors, but where the other Booths sympathize with the North, John has long supported the Confederacy. Always an egomaniac and somewhat unstable, he has already failed at a plot to kidnap Lincoln. Now Booth walks up to the President and shoots him behind the ear; he stabs Rathbone and then hurls himself over the balcony onto the stage, breaking his left leg on impact and yelling (according to some) '*Sic semper tyrannus!*' ('Thus be it ever to tyrants!'). Booth then exits from a side door and rides off on a horse. The President is carried out of the theater to a house across the street where doctors examine him and pronounce his wound mortal.

Meanwhile, Lewis Payne (or Powell), an accomplice of Booth's, forces his way into the home of Secretary of State William Seward, still in bed recuperating from his carriage accident. Payne stabs Seward several times, but Seward's son and a male nurse fight off Payne who manages to escape. As news of the attacks on Lincoln and Seward reach the townspeople, Washington is seized by panic. (As it is, Booth's fellow conspirator who has been assigned to kill Vice President Johnson has lost his nerve.) Secretary of War Edwin

The assassination of Abraham Lincoln.

Stanton quickly declares martial law throughout the District and sets a dragnet to round up all suspects. Booth and another of his conspirators, David Herold, succeed in fleeing the city and during the night will reach the home of a Dr Samuel Mudd, who will set Booth's broken leg. (Later Mudd will be found guilty of aiding Booth but he will insist that he knew nothing of the events of this evening and was simply doing his duty as a doctor.)

WESTERN THEATER, CAROLINAS CAMPAIGN Sherman, marching with his army from Raleigh toward Durham Station, receives a message from Confederate commander Joseph Johnston requesting a temporary cessation of hostilities until a peace can be worked out. To the south, at Fort Sumter, South Carolina, during the day Federal officers and a number of distinguished guests hold a flag-raising ceremony at the fort where the war had begun four years before (and which had returned to Federal control only on 17 February). General Robert Anderson, who had surrendered the fort to the Confederates in 1861, is on hand to see the *Stars and Stripes* again raised over Fort Sumter.

NAVAL the CSS *Shenandoah* leaves the East Caroline Islands in the Pacific and heads toward the Kurile Islands.

15 *APRIL* 1865

WASHINGTON At 7:22 in the morning, with his son Robert, Senator Charles Sumner, Secretary Stanton, and others gathered at his bedside, President Lincoln dies. Andrew Johnson takes the oath at 11 that morning and assumes the office of President.

THE CONFEDERACY Jefferson Davis and members of his cabinet leave Greensborough, North Carolina on horseback, accompanied by a small bodyguard. Tomorrow they will arrive at Lexington.

EASTERN THEATER Some fighting takes place in West Virginia.

16 *APRIL* 1865

WASHINGTON John Wilkes Booth and David Herold arrive at Rich Hill, Maryland, southeast of Washington.

WESTERN THEATER, RAID TO SELMA Wilson's Union Cavalry moves eastward into Georgia, capturing the city of Columbus and West Point. Before crossing the border, the Northern cavalry skirmishes with the enemy at Crawford and Opelika, Alabama.

17 *APRIL* 1865

WASHINGTON Lincoln's body is brought to the East Room of the White House where it will lie in state until the funeral ceremony on 19 April. Southeast of the city, Booth and Herold arrive at Port Tobacco, on the banks of the Potomac, where they hope to find some means to cross the river into Virginia.

WESTERN THEATER, CAROLINAS CAMPAIGN Generals Sherman and Johnston meet at Durham Station to discuss peace. Unlike the talks between Grant and Lee, this conference looks beyond the surrender of Johnston's army to questions involving a peace settlement between North and South.

18 *APRIL* 1865

WESTERN THEATER, CAROLINAS CAMPAIGN Generals Sherman and Johnston meet again to discuss peace and sign a broad political peace agreement. It not only calls for the cessation of all hostilities, but also promises a general amnesty for all Southerners and pledges the Federal government to recognize all the state governments of the South as soon as their officials take an oath of allegiance. Both men realize that the agreement will have to receive approval from their governments, but Sherman apparently is unprepared for the severe criticism that he will be subjected to because of his part in the agreement.

19 *APRIL* 1865

WASHINGTON Funeral services are held for the dead President in the East Room of the White House. Afterwards a long and solemn funeral procession escorts the casket to the Capitol rotunda where the public will view it during the day.

THE CONFEDERACY Davis and his party arrive in Charlotte, North Carolina, where they will spend the next few days. Here, the Confederate president hears of Lincoln's assassination for the first time. General Wade Hampton writes Davis suggesting that the Confederacy continue its struggle from west of the Mississippi.

TRANS-MISSISSIPPI General John Pope writes to Confederate General Edmund Kirby Smith suggesting a surrender of all Southern troops west of the Mississippi on the same terms given General Lee.

20 *APRIL* 1865

THE CONFEDERACY Lee writes Jefferson Davis telling the Confederate president that he is opposed to the continuation of hostilities through guerrilla warfare and recommends an end to all fighting. For some time, Davis has believed that partisan warfare should be the second stage of Southern resistance to the North. Johnston is also opposed to such a course.

21 *APRIL* 1865

WASHINGTON The casket bearing the body of President Lincoln is taken from the Capitol rotunda and put on board a special funeral train bound for Springfield, Illinois.

EASTERN THEATER John S Mosby, the famed 'Gray Ghost,' disbands his troops. Most of the partisans then go in to the nearest Federal outpost and apply for parole.

22 *APRIL* 1865

WASHINGTON After several days of hiding out near Port Tobacco, Booth and Herold finally are able to cross the Potomac in a small fishing craft.

WESTERN THEATER Wilson's Federal cavalry is still active, taking the town of Talledega, Alabama, during the day.

23 *APRIL* 1865

WESTERN THEATER Stoneman's and Wilson's cavalry are still active, with Stoneman's troops fighting a skirmish near Henderson, North Carolina, while Wilson's men clash with Confederates at Munford's Station, Alabama.

24 *APRIL* 1865

WASHINGTON Federal troops under the direction of Secretary of War Stanton continue their search for Booth and any other persons connected with Lincoln's assassination or the attack on Seward. Meanwhile, Booth and Herold arrive at Port Conway, Virginia.

THE CONFEDERACY Unaware what response the Sherman-Johnston peace agreement has received in Washington, Davis sends Johnston his approval of the plan. Even after Lee's surrender, Davis had for a time held out hope that the struggle might continue, and as late as yesterday he had told his wife that he thought a return to the Union would bring oppression to the South.

WESTERN THEATER Grant arrives in Raleigh, North Carolina, where he informs Sherman that his peace agreement with Johnston has been rejected by President Johnson. Sherman is particularly stung by criticism that he exceeded his authority in agreeing to such terms as are included in the peace package. The Union generals immediately notify Johnston that the truce will end in 48 hours.

25 *APRIL* 1865

WASHINGTON Federal soldiers pursuing Booth and Herold trace the two fugitives to the farm of Richard H Garrett, south of the Rappahannock River in Virginia.

WESTERN THEATER Generals Johnston and Sherman agree to meet again to discuss peace.

26 *APRIL* 1865

WASHINGTON In the early morning, Federal soldiers following Booth and

Herold surround the Garrett barn and call out to the two fugitives to surrender. Herold comes out but Booth refuses. The soldiers then set fire to the barn and as it begins to burn a shot is fired. Booth falls mortally wounded. He is dragged from the barn and dies soon afterwards. (Whether the gunshot was fired by a soldier or self-inflicted will never be completely settled.) Booth's body is taken back to Washington for an autopsy and will be buried at Arsenal Penitentiary.

THE CONFEDERACY   Davis meets with his cabinet in Charlotte, North Carolina, and they agree to leave the state to try and get across the Mississippi.

WESTERN THEATER   General Johnston surrenders his army of nearly 30,000 men on terms virtually the same as those given Lee. Sherman, however, does agree that the Federal government will provide transport home to those soldiers who need it.

27 APRIL 1865

WESTERN THEATER   The *Sultana*, a steam-powered riverboat, catches fire and burns after one of its boilers explodes. On board are some 2031 passengers, mostly Federal soldiers recently released from Southern prisoner of war camps. At least 1238, and perhaps more, die in the mishap, the worst ever on the Mississippi.

28 APRIL 1865

THE NORTH   Lincoln's funeral train reaches Cleveland, Ohio, where over 50,000 citizens view the President's body.

29 APRIL 1865

THE CONFEDERACY   Davis and those members of his cabinet who are still traveling with him reach Yorksville, South Carolina.

30 APRIL 1865

WESTERN THEATER   Generals Edward Canby and Richard Taylor meet near Mobile, Alabama, and agree to a truce to arrange for the surrender of all Confederate troops in Alabama and Mississippi.

The armies of Taylor and Edmund Kirby Smith are the only large bodies of Southern troops which have still not surrendered.

1 MAY 1865

WASHINGTON   President Johnson orders the appointment of nine army officers as commissioners in the trial of those accused of conspiring to kill President Lincoln.

THE CONFEDERACY   Jefferson Davis and his party, still moving south, reach Cokesbury, South Carolina. Davis hopes to be able to get to the coast of Florida and from there go by boat to Texas.

2 MAY 1865

WASHINGTON   Accusing the Confederate government of complicity in the murder of Lincoln, President Andrew Johnson offers a $100,000 reward for the capture of Jefferson Davis.

THE CONFEDERACY   President Davis, a number of cabinet members, and their armed escort reach Abbeville, South Carolina. With the rejection of the first Sherman-Johnston peace agreement by President Johnson, the course that Davis and his advisers should pursue is extremely uncertain. That they are fugitives is sure. But whether they should surrender themselves to Federal authorities, seek refuge in a foreign country or try to maintain the struggle from west of the Mississippi is still unsettled. Davis seems to favor the last option but his cabinet advisers disagree.

3 MAY 1865

THE NORTH   Lincoln's funeral train reaches Springfield, Illinois, where tomorrow the President will be buried.

THE CONFEDERACY   Judah P Benjamin, Davis's Secretary of State, separates from the small band of fugitives fleeing toward Texas. Benjamin will eventually escape to Britain.

4 MAY 1865

WESTERN THEATER   Richard Taylor, commander of Confederate troops in Alabama, Mississippi and east Louisiana, surrenders to General Edward Canby at Citronelle, Alabama. Canby offers Taylor substantially the same terms as Grant gave Lee. In addition, though, Taylor is allowed to maintain the use of railways and transport ships to return his men to their homes. TRANS-MISSISSIPPI West of the Mississippi, Confederate forces are still officially at war. Today there is fighting near Lexington, Missouri.

5 *MAY* 1865

THE NORTH Connecticut ratifies the Thirteenth Amendment, abolishing slavery in the United States.

6 *MAY* 1865

WASHINGTON Secretary of War Edwin Stanton appoints the commissioners to conduct the trial of those accused of conspiring to assassinate Lincoln. Among those appointed are David Hunter, Lew Wallace (who will later write *Ben Hur*) and August Kautz. Joseph Holt, the Judge Advocate-General of the army, is to be the chief prosecutor.

8 *MAY* 1865

TRANS-MISSISSIPPI Federals clash with the enemy near Readsville, Missouri.

9 *MAY* 1865

THE CONFEDERACY Jefferson Davis, still moving southward with his small party of fugitives, joins forces with his wife at Dublin, Georgia. Meanwhile, Northern troops, who have been searching for the Confederate president, begin to close in on Davis and his fellow-travelers.
WESTERN THEATER General Nathan B Forrest disbands his troops.

10 *MAY* 1865

WASHINGTON President Johnson tells the people of the country that armed insurrection against the authority of the Federal government can be considered 'virtually at an end'.

THE CONFEDERACY President Davis, his wife, Postmaster-General Reagan, and Burton Harrison, the president's secretary, are captured by the 4th Michigan Cavalry near Irwinville, Georgia. The prisoners are escorted to Nashville, Tennessee, under heavy guard. From there, Davis will be sent to Richmond, Virginia.
WESTERN THEATER General Samuel Jones surrenders his command at Tallahassee, Florida. To the north, William Clarke Quantrill, the most notorious of all Confederate guerrillas, is mortally wounded near Taylorsville, Kentucky. He and a small group of followers have been looting in that state recently. (Included among those who rode with Quantrill during the war, are Frank and Jesse James and Cole Younger, among the most celebrated outlaws the West will produce.)

11 *MAY* 1865

TRANS-MISSISSIPPI General M Jeff Thompson, the famous Southern military leader of the Missouri-Arkansas region, surrenders the remnant of his command at Chalk Bluffs, Arkansas. Thompson is given the same terms that Grant gave Lee at Appomattox.
NAVAL The CSS *Stonewall* sails into Havana harbor.

12 *MAY* 1865

WASHINGTON President Johnson appoints General Oliver O Howard to head the Bureau of Refugees, Freedmen and Abandoned Lands. The Freedmen's Bureau will oversee the care of Southern refugees in the postwar period and also be charged with helping the newly freed blacks adjust to their freedom. Under the Bureau's supervision, too, are extensive tracts of land confiscated by the Federal government during the war. The eight defendants charged with conspiring to assassinate Lincoln plead not guilty today.
TRANS-MISSISSIPPI Federals under the command of Colonel Theodore H Barrett attack and capture the Southern camp at Palmitto Ranch, on the Rio Grande. Fear-

ing a counterattack, the Union troops abandon the ranch in the evening.

13 *MAY* 1865

TRANS-MISSISSIPPI The Confederate governors of Arkansas, Mississippi and Louisiana meet with Edmund Kirby Smith, overall commander in the trans-Mississippi area, and advise him to surrender under terms which they outline for him. Others in the western part of the Confederacy, including Jo Shelby, threaten to arrest Smith unless he continues the struggle against the North. In the second day of fighting at Palmito Ranch, in Texas, Northern troops return to the Southern encampment, again driving away enemy resistance. Later in the day, however, Confederates led by Colonel John S Ford launch an attack on the Federals there and force them to withdraw. The Battle of Palmitto Ranch is to be the last significant land battle of the war.

17 *MAY* 1865

WASHINGTON General Philip Sheridan is appointed commander of the district west of the Mississippi and south of the Arkansas River. Because of Sheridan's reputation for wholesale destruction, stemming from his campaign in the Shenandoah Valley, there is considerable Southern resistance to this appointment.

19 *MAY* 1865

NAVAL The CSS *Stonewall* surrenders to Federal officials in Havana harbor.

22 *MAY* 1865

WASHINGTON President Johnson declares that as of 1 July all Southern seaports except four in Texas will be opened for trade. Also effective that date, all restrictions on civilian trade east of the Mississippi will be lifted except on contraband of war.

THE CONFEDERACY Jefferson Davis arrives at Fort Monroe, Virginia where he is put in chains and locked in a cell. Al-

though Davis will never be brought to trial, many Northerners at this time, especially in the wake of Lincoln's assassination, are inclined to feel vindictive toward the Southern leader.

23 *MAY* 1865

WASHINGTON The nation's capital holds a grand review for the Army of the Potomac. As General George Meade's army marches past throngs of cheering Washingtonians, the flags in the city fly at full mast for the first time in four years.

THE NORTH The loyal government of Virginia (also known as the Pierpont Government) moves to Richmond, Virginia, the state capital. During the war, the pro-Union government of this state has been located in Federally-controlled northern Virginia.

24 *MAY* 1865

WASHINGTON Washington officially receives the North's other major army as the grand legions of William T Sherman march through the streets of the capital. Many are struck by the contrast between the polished Army of the Potomac and this more casual army from the west.

TRANS-MISSISSIPPI Federals continue to operate against guerrilla bands in the west, with some skirmishing near Rocheport, Missouri.

25 *MAY* 1865

WESTERN THEATER In Mobile, Alabama, close to 20 tons of gunpowder captured from the Confederacy explodes, destroying buildings and boats along the docks of the city. There are some 300 casualties resulting from the blast.

26 *MAY* 1865

TRANS-MISSISSIPPI General Simon B Buckner, as agent for General Edmund Kirby Smith, and General Peter J Osterhaus, a representative of General Edward Canby, meet to discuss the surrender of all Confederate troops west of the Mississippi.

The two agree on terms basically the same as those offered Lee at Appomattox. Smith will approve these terms on 2 June. Smith's force is the last major body of Southern troops to surrender. Some of these trans-Mississippi Confederates, most notably Jo Shelby and the remnants of his Iron Brigade, will refuse to accept defeat and instead will cross over the border to Mexico in the hopes of continuing the struggle.

27 MAY 1865

WASHINGTON With only a few exceptions, President Johnson orders the release of all persons held in prison by military authorities.

29 MAY 1865

WASHINGTON President Johnson issues a proclamation giving a general amnesty to those who have participated in the rebellion against Federal authority. Excepted from the provisions of the general amnesty are several special classes of Southerners, principally those who own more than $20,000 worth of property and those who held high rank in either the Confederate government or military; these must apply individually to the President for a pardon. (The President will be very liberal in granting these individual pardons.) An important implication of the executive action is that, once an oath is taken, all property rights, except those in slaves, will be fully restored. The large tracts of confiscated lands now held by the Federal government (much of it being farmed by black freedmen) will be turned over to the former owners.

The Aftermath of War

JUNE 1865

The military phase of the Civil War is now coming to an end as several Confederate units surrender. On 23 June, the last formal surrender of a large Confederate force occurs in Oklahoma Territory when the Cherokee leader Brigadier General Watie surrenders a battalion formed by Indians. The Confederate sea raider CSS *Shenandoah* continues to capture Union whalers in the Bering Sea. President Johnson is moving to impose the peace and union as quickly as he can. He declares released all Confederate prisoners of war, except for navy officers over the rank of lieutenant and army officers over the rank of captain, if they will take an oath of allegiance. He lifts trade restrictions throughout the United States, except for the contraband of war, and declares an end to the Federal blockade of the Southern states, in existence since April 1861. And in an effort to restore pro-union governments before Republicans in Congress can intervene, Johnson names provisional governors to six of the former Confederate states and restores to the Union the state of Tennessee since it has reorganized its own government. But bitter feelings are inevitably revived when on 30 June the eight alleged conspirators in the assassination of Lincoln are found guilty by the military commission. Four are to be imprisoned, and four are to be hanged.

JULY 1865

On 7 July, the four alleged conspirators are hanged at the Old Penitentiary in Washington, DC. There has been considerable public protest over the case of Mrs Mary Surratt, whose guilt seems to come down to little more than that she kept the boarding-house where Booth hatched his plot, but President Johnson refuses to intervene. The other convicted conspirators are imprisoned on an island off Key West, Florida. (Michael O'Laughlin dies of yellow fever in 1867; Dr Samuel Mudd is pardoned in 1868 because of his work in the epidemic; and Edward Spangler and Samuel Arnold are pardoned in 1869.) The execution and imprisonment of the assassination conspirators somewhat placates those seeking revenge but it by no means satisfies those determined to punish the Confederacy.

CHRONOLOGY

The hanging of the conspirators.

AUGUST 1865

Confederate General Jo Shelby, refusing to surrender to the Federal government, leads a force of about 1000 Confederate men to Mexico City where his offer to Emperor Maximilian to form a 'foreign legion' is turned down. However, Maximilian provides them with a large tract of land near Vera Cruz, and many of them settle there. The Confederate raider CSS *Shenandoah*, sailing from the Bering Sea toward San Francisco, is informed by a British ship that the war has ended. President Johnson proclaims that as of 1 September articles previously considered war contraband may be traded with the former Confederate states.

OCTOBER 1865

President Johnson paroles Vice President Alexander Stephens and four other high-ranking Confederate leaders who have been in prison since their government collapsed. Johnson also proclaims an end to martial law in Kentucky. At Morant Bay, Jamaica, a British colony, free blacks riot and kill 21 white and black people before British troops reassert command. When word of this incident reaches the United States, it feeds the fears of Southerners about the freed blacks.

NOVEMBER 1865

Mississippi adopts laws regulating labor service, vagrancy and such matters, the first of the post-war black codes by which the South moves to restrict the opportunities of blacks. The Confederate raider CSS *Shenandoah* surrenders to the British at Liverpool, England. Captain Henry Wirz, commander of the former Confederate prison at Andersonville, Georgia is hanged after being found guilty of charges of cruelty to Federal prisoners of war.

DECEMBER 1865

The United States Congress convenes and, under the control of Republicans, sets about undoing the conciliatory policies of President Johnson. It forms the Joint Committee on Reconstruction, and it rejects the senators and representatives elected by the former Confederate states. With 27 states having approved it, the Thirteenth Amendment to the Constitution—abolishing slavery—is formally put into effect.

FEBRUARY 1866

Congress passes legislation that broadens the powers of the Freedmen's Bureau,

The first black Senator and Representatives.

Cartoon promoting the Freedmen's Bureau.

including a provision that anyone accused of interfering with the civil rights of a freed person will be tried by a military court. President Johnson vetoes this as unconstitutional, but Congress will override his veto in July. Although this legislation is the Republicans' attempt to counter the efforts of President Johnson and use the Freedmen's Bureau for political purposes, the fact is that the former Confederate states are beginning to enact a series of discriminatory and restrictive black codes to keep the former slaves from participating in a free society.

APRIL 1866

President Johnson issues a proclamation stating that 'the insurrection which heretofore existed in [the Confederate states, except for Texas, since its government is not yet formed] is at an end and is henceforth to be so regarded.' Congress adopts a Civil Rights Act, previously vetoed by President Johnson on the grounds that it interfered with the rights of states, guaranteeing citizenship to all native-born individuals (except for untaxed Indians).

MAY 1866

Six ex-Confederate veterans in Pulaski, Tennessee begin an informal organization known as the Ku Klux Klan. Almost from the end of the fighting, several groups of Confederate men had begun to form vigilante groups they named 'The Pale Faces,' 'The White Brothers,' and such. These men were determined to oppose the attempts of freed blacks to claim their rights, and the Ku Klux Klan at first is only one of many such local groups.

JUNE 1866

Congress adopts the Fourteenth Amendment, which states that all laws governing citizenship extend to blacks. But another section prohibits former office-holders who engaged in 'insurrection or rebellion' from holding any office (unless Congress, by a vote of two-thirds of both houses, removes this restriction). Furthermore, no state can be restored to the Union without accepting this amendment. Although the extension of citizenship rights to the blacks will have a long-term benefit, the immediate goal and impact of this amendment is the Republicans' desire to prevent the return of the Democrats in the Southern states and to the national government.

AUGUST 1866

President Johnson, in a proclamation declaring the end of the insurrection of Texas, takes the occasion to conclude: 'I do further proclaim that the said insurrection is at an end and that peace, order, tranquillity, and civil authority now exist in and throughout the whole of the United States of America.' In effect, this marks the official end of the Civil War, but extremists on both sides of the political spectrum are

NOVEMBER 1866

In the Congressional elections, many

An anti-Freedmen's Bureau cartoon.

Andersonville Prison, 1865.

voters find themselves forced to choose between radical Republicans or compromised Democrats. President Johnson forced to support many Democratic candidates, and this allows the Republicans to intensify their efforts to portray him as sympathetic to the Southern cause. As a result of the elections, the radical Republicans strengthen their hold on their party and the national government. In Indianapolis, Indiana, Union veterans from ten states and the District of Columbia meet to form a national organization, the Grand Army of the Republic. Although nominally a nonpolitical organization, the GAR will become increasingly supportive of the Republican Party's policies, and the Republicans in return will enact legislation favorable to the Union veterans.

MARCH 1867

It is almost two years since the war ended on the battlefield, but a Republican-controlled Congress decides to punish the South by undoing the policies of President Johnson. Congress passes the first Reconstruction Act, which divides the South into five military districts to be headed by general officers. These military governors, furthermore, are to take their orders from the commander of the army, who at this time is General Grant, not from the President. The first assignment for these military governors is to register voters and supervise the election of conventions to draft new state constitutions. These conventions will soon draft constitutions that give the vote to blacks while disqualifying former Confederate leaders, and many white Southerners will thus begin to boycott the formal elections. Congress also passes the Tenure of Office Act, which requires the President to obtain the approval of the Senate for removing any official whose appointment originally required Senate approval. Johnson recognizes this as an infringement on the traditional balance of powers and vetoes it, but Congress overrides his veto.

APRIL–MAY 1867

The Supreme Court rules in two cases—*Georgia v. Stanton* and *Mississippi v. Johnson*—that it has no jurisdiction to stop enforcement of the Reconstruction Acts passed by Congress. This effectively leaves the former Confederate states under the rule of the Republican-controlled government.

MAY 1867

In Nashville, Tennessee, local Ku Klux Klans assemble to form an organization that they see as the 'invisible empire of the South'—the premise being that the newly freed blacks, 'carpetbaggers' and others are forming an 'empire' that must be fought. Former Confederate General Nathan Bedford Forrest accepts the post of Grand Wizard of the Empire, and the Democrats of Tennessee, quickly recognizing the Klan's potential, support it in the desire to gain backing in forthcoming elections. Jefferson Davis, after serving two years at Fort Monroe, is released on bail.

JULY 1867

Congress passes another supplement to the Reconstruction Act, this one assigning to the military governors the right to replace and select state officials.

AUGUST 1867

President Johnson has become increasingly bothered by his relationship with his

Secretary of War Edwin Stanton who, as a radical Republican, has been actively working against the President's policies. Johnson now calls for Stanton's resignation, but Stanton—citing the Tenure of Office Act—refuses to resign, so Johnson suspends him.

FEBRUARY 1868

President Johnson decides to make a test case on the constitutionality of the Tenure of Office Act and thus, having reinstated Stanton in January, dismisses him. This is what Johnson's enemies have been waiting for. On 24 February the House of Representatives votes to impeach President Johnson for 'high crimes and misdemeanors.' There are 11 articles in the impeachment resolution, but basically it comes down to one issue: the removal of Stanton. Secretary Stanton, with the support of the Senate, declares he will 'continue in possession until expelled by force,' assigns a guard to his office, and remains in the War Department building night and day.

MARCH-MAY 1868

On 5 March the Senate convenes as a court to hear the charges against President Johnson. Presiding is Chief Justice Salmon Chase: although a friend of many of the radical Republicans, he will preside over the trial with fairness and insistence on legal procedures. The prosecution is led by Representatives Benjamin Butler and Thaddeus Stevens, and they will attempt to ignore all legal restraints and to appeal to sheer partisan prejudice. (At one point Butler will wave a bloodied shirt that he alleges belonged to a Northerner beaten by Klansmen—this to prove the 'crime' of Johnson's reconstruction policies.) Johnson himself does not attend but he is ably defended by distinguished lawyers who demolish the prosecution's arguments.

MAY 1868

In the votes on the articles of impeachment,

Stevens and Bingham at the impeachment.

the Senate divides 35 to 19 for conviction —but a two-thirds majority is required, so President Johnson is acquitted by one vote. Johnson would have been convicted had not seven Republicans risked their political careers by voting to acquit. Secretary of War Stanton resigns, but the radical Republicans remain in control of their party and at their convention this month they gain the nomination for General Grant. Decoration Day is inaugurated, primarily through the efforts of former General John A Logan, for the purpose of decorating the graves of Civil War veterans. (Eventually this will become Memorial Day to honor all the war dead.)

JUNE 1868

Seven former Confederate states are re-admitted to the Union by Congress now that their governments are reorganized under the Reconstruction Acts.

JULY 1868

The Democratic Party, recognizing that Johnson is now a liability, nominates Horatio Seymour, Governor of New York, as its Presidential candidate. The Fourteenth Amendment, having been ratified by three-fourths of the states, comes into force.

273

CHRONOLOGY

AUGUST 1868

Thaddeus Stevens, the Representative from Pennsylvania who has been almost fanatical in his desire to reconstruct the South by his principles, dies. His passing takes some of the steam out of the radical Republicans' zeal to punish the Confederacy, but it by no means ends the excesses of the Reconstruction.

SEPTEMBER 1868

The legislature of Georgia expels its black members, so military government is reimposed. Increasing numbers of blacks are now being elected to state and local offices, but only in South Carolina will they gain a majority in either house and they never control a state government nor do they try to repeal laws such as those against mixed marriages or enact laws that punish white people. However, most Southerners greatly resent the presence of blacks in any position of authority, and they wait or work to remove them and their carpetbagger protectors.

NOVEMBER 1868

Ulysses S Grant wins the Presidential election.

DECEMBER 1868

President Johnson, even though a 'lame-duck' President, issues a proclamation that pardons all former Southerners except some 300 Confederate leaders, but Congress will proceed to enact laws that nullify much of the effect of this executive clemency.

JANUARY 1869

The Johnson-Clarendon Convention, an agreement settling various Anglo-American disputes, is concluded. But since the chief issue involves the damage done to Northerners' shipping by the *Alabama* and other Confederate ships that had been constructed or outfitted in Britain, the Senate will vote in April to reject ratification and press for better terms. General Forrest, having had second thoughts about the goals of the Ku Klux Klan, tries to disband the organization and resigns as Grand Wizard, but the local Klans continue.

FEBRUARY 1869

Congress proposes a Fifteenth Amendment to the Constitution. This one will guarantee the right to vote to every citizen, regardless of race or any previous condition of servitude.

MARCH 1869

Grant is inaugurated President and proceeds to establish an administration that is marked from the outset by ill-advised appointments to various high offices. Grant is a decent if naive man and allows those around him to go much their own way. In matters to do with the South, he has no sympathy for either the extreme anti-black element nor for the punitive approach of the radical Republicans, but the net effect of his moderation will be the reestablishment by white Southerners of their own rule and the denial of rights to the blacks.

JANUARY-MARCH 1870

Three more ex-Confederate states—Virginia, Mississippi and Texas—are restored to the Union after they have ratified the Fifteenth Amendment, which becomes the law of the land in February. Yet in practice blacks are increasingly being denied their right to vote. So, too, free public education for all children is now officially established throughout the South through the efforts of the Federal laws, but black children are forced into segregated schools.

MAY 1870

Congress passes a Ku Klux Klan Act, aimed specifically at the Klan's efforts to deny blacks their right to vote. Popularly known as a 'force bill,' it provides heavy penalties for anyone interfering with citizens exercising their right to vote under the Fifteenth Amendment.

Captured members of the Ku Klux Klan.

JULY 1870

Georgia, having ratified the Fifteenth Amendment, is readmitted to the Union, the last of the Confederate states to be so.

DECEMBER 1870

When the third session of the 41st Congress convenes, it is the first time since 1860 that representatives from all the states are present.

APRIL 1871

Congress passes another Ku Klux Klan Act, which declares that any acts by armed groups, including those like the Ku Klux Klan, may be treated as rebellion and put down by military force. The President is even empowered to suspend the writ of habeas corpus in enforcing the Fifteenth Amendment.

MAY 1871

Grant's Secretary of State, Hamilton Fish, secretly works out the Treaty of Washington with Canada and Britain. The dispute over the boundary line between Canada and the United States in the far west is to be decided by the Emperor of Germany and the issue of fishing privileges of Canadians and Americans is to be settled by a special commission. The most touchy issue, that of the claims resulting from the actions of the Confederate raiders such as the *Alabama*, is to be settled before a special tribunal which is to meet in Geneva, Switzerland. The tribunal meets first in December 1871, and in September 1872 it awards $15,500,000 to the United States for the depredations committed by these ships.

MAY 1872

The Grant administration is becoming increasingly tarnished and many Republicans are among the most disillusioned by Grant's lack of leadership. A group calling itself the Liberal Republicans holds a convention and nominates as their Presidential candidate Horace Greeley, editor of the New York *Tribune* and nationally known for his outspoken views on many public issues. In July Greeley also receives the nomination of the Democratic Party and in September he receives the nomination of the Liberal Colored Republicans. Congress adopts an Amnesty Act that removes restrictions from former Confederates and restores their political privileges such as holding public office.

JUNE 1872

President Grant is nominated for re-election by the Republican Party.

NOVEMBER 1872

Despite the scandals that are marking Grant's administration, and despite Greeley's hard campaigning, Grant wins easily. Greeley is so devastated by his political and personal setbacks that he goes insane and dies by the end of November. (His electoral votes will be divided among other candidates.)

APRIL 1873

The Supreme Court rules that the Fourteenth Amendment applies to barring states from interfering with the rights of blacks as citizens of the United States, not to protecting property rights. But this apparently idealistic ruling is actually a side issue of the cases under review, which involve slaughterhouses in Louisiana adversely affected by a monopoly created by the state legislature, and not everyone, in America's 'gilded age' will support the court's ruling.

NOVEMBER 1874

The Democrats gain a majority in the House of Representatives in the national elections, thus signaling the end of the grip held by the Radical Republicans. In the South, white Southerners are once again taking control of the political parties and governments. Even many blacks have become disillusioned by events and are voting for Democrats.

MARCH 1875

Congress adopts a Civil Rights Act that guarantees all citizens, regardless of race, equal enjoyment of public facilities such as transport, restaurants and hotels. It also declares that no one may be excluded from jury service on the basis of race. In the course of debating this bill, Representative Benjamin Butler, one of the last of the diehard radical Republicans, proposes an amendment that would compel the racial integration of all schools in the South, but President Grant has this amendment removed. And in 1883, the Supreme Court will find the entire act unconstitutional.

NOVEMBER 1875

Mississippi votes for its state legislature, and with most blacks and Republicans too intimidated to vote, the Democrats win a majority in both houses. There had been disorder in the state almost from the beginning of the term of Governor Adelbert Ames, a Northerner and Republican and a holdover from the Reconstruction days. Wanting to have Federal troops to stop the whites who were attacking blacks, Ames had appealed to President Grant. The Attorney General replied that 'the

whole public are tired of these annual autumnal outbreaks in the South,' but he refused to call out the troops. The Democratic legislature will take its revenge on Ames by threatening to impeach him in January 1876, but he resigns in March and leaves the state. A United States Senate committee will later investigate this episode and label it 'one of the darkest chapters in American history,' but the fact is that the nation at large has little interest in pursuing the subject.

JUNE 1876

The Republican Party nominates Rutherford B Hayes, Governor of Ohio, as its Presidential candidate. The Democratic Party nominates Samuel J Tilden, Governor of New York, as its Presidential candidate. The Democrats campaign on the issue of the need to reform the government after the years of Grant's administration. The Republicans campaign by reminding voters that those responsible for the Confederate rebellion were Democrats.

NOVEMBER 1876

Tilden wins the popular vote by a margin of 250,000 over Hayes, but there are disputes over the voting of Florida, Louisiana, South Carolina and Oregon so that neither candidate can claim a clear majority.

JANUARY–MARCH 1877

Since this presidential deadlock is not anticipated in the Constitution, Congress sets up an Electoral Commission of five Supreme Court Justices, five Senators, and five Representatives. The intention was to have seven Republicans, seven Democrats, and one Independent, but in the end there are eight Republicans. The voting over the disputed electoral votes is on strictly partisan grounds so that all are awarded by votes of eight to seven to Hayes. On 2 March Hayes is declared the winner and the next day President Grant allows him to take the oath of office privately so as to forestall any further challenge by the Democrats. On 5

March Hayes is inaugurated in the public ceremony. Only later will it come out that Republican leaders visited the disputed Southern states and got Democratic leaders to acquiesce in Hayes's election in return for which the Republicans promised that Hayes would withdraw the Federal garrison under the Reconstruction Acts and generally ignore the enforcement of the Fourteenth Amendment, which guaranteed the civil rights of the blacks. Hayes also agrees to appoint a Southerner to his cabinet.

APRIL 1877

President Hayes resolves a disputed election between two rivals for the governorship of South Carolina by awarding the office to the candidate of the 'redeemers,' the old guard of white Southerners, and withdrawing the Federal troops from the state. Then on 24 April Hayes removes the Federal troops from Louisiana, the last of the former Confederate states to be governed with Northern support. Reconstruction is over and the Civil War is ended.

The impeachment managers in the House.

The Palmetto Battery, Charleston, 1863.

II
WEAPONS OF THE
CIVIL WAR

WEAPONS

The American Civil War took place at a particularly interesting period in the history of weapon development. Until the early part of the 19th century there had been very little improvement in firearms since their first inception; it has been frequently observed that a soldier of the 15th century could have appeared during the Napoleonic wars and would not have found any weapon he was incapable of understanding or operating. But in the 1840s the percussion cap began to gain in popularity, thus making the flintlock obsolete, and then the sudden upsurge of interest in engineering, stimulated by the Industrial Revolution, began to make itself felt in the firearms world. It was as if inventors, having busied themselves with agricultural machinery, railroads and similar commercial matters, suddenly felt the need to try new fields. The Crimean War in Europe had been responsible for much of this; during the 'Long Peace' from Waterloo to the Crimea the engineering abilities and the manufacturing base of Europe and America had expanded, and the revelation, to engineers, that the science of war was still hampered by primitive weaponry was a considerable stimulus to them.

Thus the 1850s saw the beginning of a great deal of experimental work on artillery and firearms which was later to bear prolific fruit, but at the time the Civil War began, this fruit was scarcely out of the blossom stage and the new developments were largely what we would today call 'Production Prototypes'. As a result, the war was fought with possibly the most heterogenous collection of weapons seen in any war, from flintlocks on the one hand to breech-loading cartridge arms on the other.

The principal small arms were cap-and-ball percussion-fired pistols, rifles and muskets of various patterns, mostly deriving from 1840s and 1850s designs. A limited number of breech-loading small arms were to be found, but they were limited by the fact that the metallic cartridge was then in its infancy.

In the artillery field, the muzzle-load-ing black powder cannon reigned supreme, though small numbers of European breech-loaders were acquired by both sides. These, though, were in the earliest stages of development and their defects and shortcomings were all too obvious once they had been put to use. The principal problem with these early weapons was firstly that of sealing the breech against the unwanted escape of the gas produced by the explosion of the propelling charge, and secondly the problem of developing a suitable system of rotating the projectile as it passed up the gun's rifled barrel. Many and varied were the solutions propounded to these two questions, and indeed they were the anvil upon which the final designs of breech-loading artillery, as we know it today, were beaten out. But in the process, some Civil War gunners must have had a hard time of it, wrestling with ill-fitting Armstrong breech blocks or attempting to un-jam a Whitworth hexagonal shot firmly stuck in the gun bore.

One of the most significant facts in the matter of weapons provision for the opposing sides was the basic one of the location of most of America's manufacturing capacity; it was north of the Mason-Dixon line. This fundamental economic fact was overlooked by most people at the start of the war since, like all contestants in all wars, they were quite convinced that right would prevail and their side would win in a matter of weeks. It was not until the likely duration of the war began to become apparent that the disparity in production potential was appreciated. The South endeavored to make up for their lack of engineering plants by importing weapons from Europe, thus giving the chance of a lifetime to numbers of profiteers and swindlers, while the Union blockade made importation increasingly difficult. Nevertheless, sufficient reached the South to make a useful contribution to their armory and bring a wide variety of weapons into the war. In addition, a number of small companies were set up to try to provide the simpler weapons, such as pistols and muskets, and some of these firms produced quite creditable weapons in spite of the immense difficulties under which they operated.

On the Union side, procurement of weapons was easier because of the location of the major arms manufacturers, principally in New England, but as the war dragged on the established arms makers could not produce weapons fast enough and numerous other companies came into being. Some survived the war and continued in the business, others closed down as soon as the war was over; many fell between two stools and avidly accepted massive contracts and then failed to honor them, having little inkling of the difficulties of mass-production.

On the whole, then, the arming of the contestants in the Civil War became a matter of simple economics; but the various shifts and expedients led to an interesting and varied armory which has proved an interesting field of study for firearms historians.

PISTOLS & REVOLVERS

BY 1860 THE MANUFACTURE OF PISTOLS and revolvers in the United States had reached substantial proportions, though it was an industry with some peculiar aspects and unusual restraints. From 1836 to 1857, due to the possession of a shrewdly-drawn patent, Samuel Colt held a virtual monopoly over the manufacture of revolvers with mechanically-rotated cylinders. As soon as this patent had expired, Smith & Wesson stepped in with another 'master patent', this time covering the use of revolver cylinders with bored-through chambers, which gave them the monopoly of breech-loading cartridge-firing revolvers until 1869. Other aspiring revolver manufacturers, therefore, had either to devise some mechanism which evaded the patent restrictions, or pay a license fee to either Colt

or Smith & Wesson in order to utilize some patented feature of their designs. Neither patent, though, had validity outside the USA, which meant that European revolvers could be imported or even made in the USA under license. There were, of course, no patent problems with other types of pistol—single shot weapons, multiple-barrel pistols and 'pepperpot' revolvers could be freely made and were produced in some numbers. Add to this the existence of old flintlock pistols and it is probable that any pistol made prior to 1860 could be reasonably called a 'Civil War Weapon', since most soldiers managed to provide themselves with a handgun of some sort, as official issue or by private endeavor, though many of them were soon abandoned as excess baggage once it became clear that

Colt percussion Revolver, 'Dragoon' model.

there was little likelihood of their being called into use.

Although the Smith & Wesson company had begun marketing its cartridge revolvers in 1857, these weapons saw relatively little combat use except as last-ditch self-defense arms, principally because they were of too small a caliber to be practical military devices. The first Smith & Wesson 'Number One' revolver was chambered for the .22 rimfire cartridge which the manufacturers had developed alongside the revolver; it is the cartridge known today as the '.22 Short' and quite worthless as a combat cartridge since only an extremely accurate or very lucky shot shot in a vital organ would incapacitate an opponent. By contrast, the heavy lead ball from a .36 or .44 percussion revolver would put an opponent down even if it struck merely a glancing

Tip-up Smith and Wesson.

blow, and pin-point accuracy was not necessary. Smith & Wesson recognized this and later developed a heavier model in .32 rimfire caliber, but even this was only marginally combat-effective; it was not until the Civil War was over that the cartridge revolver was developed into calibers adequate for warfare.

Since the cartridge pistol was an unreliable quantity at that time—indeed it was regarded by most people as a novelty—the combatants relied almost entirely upon percussion pistols, the type broadly known today as 'cap-and-ball' guns, and undoubt-

Smith and Wesson 'Old Model No 2.'

edly the principal among these was the Colt revolver in its various manifestations. Samuel Colt had been in business for several years and had been making gradual improvements in his design. In 1851 he had produced the .36 caliber 'Navy' model, of which 215,000 had been made and sold; in 1855 came the 'Root side-hammer' model, somewhat out of the mainstream of Colt design and of which relatively few (less than 40,000) were made; these weapons were in wide circulation and thousands of them went to war with their owners. In 1860 came the .44 caliber 'Army' revolver, followed in 1861 by a slightly improved .36

Navy model and in 1862 by the short-barreled 'Police' model. These, particularly the Army and Navy models, were seized upon by the Union authorities and over

Colt .30 Police Model.

Short Barreled .36 Navy.

Short Barreled .44 Colt.

146,000 of both models were purchased by the Ordnance Department.

The Colt won its reputation because it was reliable; it was also versatile where ammunition was concerned since it could accommodate a variety of cartridge types. In this context, of course, 'cartridge' does not mean the familiar brass article of today, but a pre-packaged unit of black powder, wad and lead ball wrapped in paper, oiled silk or animal gut ready to be inserted into the front end of the revolver's chambers. Provided the caliber was the right one, one type was as good as another, and therefore the owner of a Colt rarely had supply problems. On the rare occasion when no prepared cartridges were available, the revolver could be loaded with loose powder and have the ball rammed down into the chamber and protected there by a smear of grease or fat. The only immutable demand was a supply of percussion caps; with the chambers loaded, a cap was placed on the nipple of each chamber and the pistol was ready for use. Most owners carried a second cylinder, fully loaded and capped, so that by knocking out the barrel-locking wedge and removing the barrel, the empty cylinder could be slipped off and the full one substituted; the barrel was replaced and wedged in position and the pistol was ready for use, a quicker proceeding than

.44 Remington New Army.

loading the individual chambers with powder and ball.

The next most popular revolver, and one which many experts consider to have been a better mechanical product, was the Remington. Like the Colt it was standardized into two models, the .44 caliber Army and the .36 caliber Navy. Over 125,000 of both models were bought by the Union, a

Top: *Remington 1863.* Bottom: *Adams, 1857.*

quantity limited only by the ability of the Remington factory to produce them.

But half a million Colt and Remington

revolvers, spread as they were over the war years, was far from sufficient to satisfy demand and replace losses, and the Ordnance Department turned to any other manufacturer who could produce a reliable weapon. The third largest producer of revolvers for the Union was the Starr Arms Company of Yonkers, New York, who supplied a total of 47,952 revolvers through the war years. Due to Colt's master patent covering the mechanical rotation of the cylinder, Starr's design used a double trigger mechanism which first unlocked and rotated the cylinder, then raised the hammer to fire the pistol. As with other makers, Starr settled on .36 Navy and .44 Army models, the latter appearing in 1863.

.42 Starr.

Eli Whitney of Massachusetts had been connected with Colt in the latter's early days, manufacturing some of the earliest Colt revolvers. He later went on to make his own designs, carefully avoiding Colt's patented features, but he seemed to

Top: *Imitation Colt.* Bottom: *Manhattan.*

have come to some accommodation with Colt since, in 1857, he was in communication with the Ordnance Department offering to supply 'repeating pistols like Colt's' at $12 each. Indeed, his pistols were so similar that one Ordnance Department inspector reported that they actually were old Colts, bought up cheaply from state militias and refurbished. But Whitney then improved the design, making his revolver a solid-frame model similar to the Remington, and over 11,000 of these were bought by the Union during the War years.

In addition to the makers of conventional revolvers there were, of course, innumerable inventors of aberrant weapons who canvassed the armies for orders. Few of them had any success, particularly in the North where the Union Army had fairly stringent inspection requirements, but the occasional oddity slipped through the net, largely by way of the state militia companies and similar organizations. One such weapon was the Walch revolver, which appeared in 12-shot .36 caliber 'Navy' or 10-shot .31 caliber 'Pocket' models. The cylinder of the Walch design had five or six exceptionally long chambers and was provided with two cap nipples, one of which fired directly into the rear of the chamber in the normal way, while the other 'piped' its flash to a point halfway down the chamber. Each chamber was loaded with two charges of powder and two balls (or two cartridges).

.44 Rogers and Spencer.

On pulling the trigger, the hammer fell first on the front cap, which flashed down the channel to the middle of the chamber and thus fired the forward cartridge or charge; the next pull on the trigger fired the rearmost cap and the rear charge

or cartridge, after which the cylinder was revolved to bring the next chamber in line. The Walch pistol seems to be one of the few 'superimposed-load' pistols which prospered; most designs of this type manage to fire both loads at once, to the detriment of the firer—and numbers were bought privately, though it was never afforded the accolade of a formal Army contract. There is a record of the 9th Regiment of Michigan Infantry being equipped with 10-shot Walch revolvers, and the opinions of the users were varied. One wrote a testimonial to the company averring that it was the most reliable pistol he had ever used, while another complained that it would not even kill a pig he had found during a foraging expedition.

Manhattan .36 'Navy' type.

A manufacturer who had been selling revolvers to the US Army and Navy for several years prior to the war was the Savage Revolving Firearms Company of Middletown, Connecticut. Under the name 'North & Savage' they had produced a revolver known widely as the 'Figure-of-Eight' due to the peculiar shape of the trigger, a double device which cranked the cylinder forward to make a gas-tight joint with the barrel before firing the cartridge. In 1861 the company was re-organized in order to produce an improved model which still used the figure-of-eight trigger but now enclosed it in a large guard. Great difficulties were encountered in obtaining and filling a military contract, but eventually some 11,000 Savage 'Navy Model' revolvers were bought by the Union.

In addition to contracting with these and other local manufacturers, the Union, like the Confederacy, had to go abroad for

North and Savage .36 caliber figure 8.

supplies in order to obtain the quantity of revolvers needed. Nearly 12,000 Lefaucheaux pinfire revolvers in .41 caliber were purchased from various makers in France. Numbers of Adams revolvers were also purchased in England, though few records survive to say precisely how many. The English Adams patent was licensed to the Massachusetts Arms Company of Chicopee Falls, and a number, estimated at perhaps 600 or more, were bought by the Union during the war. Several thousand were also made for the commercial market and many of these found their way to war in the hands of individual officers and soldiers. The Adams was the British service revolver of the period and was a particularly robust weapon. It was frequently claimed to be superior to the Colt in an emergency since it could be fired in the double-action mode, by simply pulling the trigger, instead of having to cock the hammer first, as with the Colt.

In the Confederacy the supply of revolvers was a constant problem. Cut off as they were from the main arms-producing areas, most of which were in New England at that period, they relied firstly upon whatever arms they could round up in the South, then upon foreign arms, and finally upon local manufacture. As early as January 1861 a purchasing agent for the

Virginia State Ordnance Department had bought 1,000 Deane & Adams revolvers in London, and in May a Captain Caleb Hulse, CSA, was in London making calls on gunmakers.

Probably the most famous of the foreign revolvers to be used by the Confederate forces was the Le Mat. Le Mat was a French-born American who at various times adopted the style of 'Doctor' or 'Colonel' as the mood took him; in 1856, living in New Orleans, he had patented a percussion revolver in which the arbor pin, around which the cylinder revolved, was in the form of a large-caliber barrel from which a charge of buckshot could be fired. This was, in effect, the close-range broadside to be loosed off in an emergency, in addition to the cartridges in the normal chambers. A number, possibly 300, were made in New Orleans in 1859-60, but on the outbreak of war Le Mat went to France to organize manufacture of the pistol for the CSA. The quality of the French-made pistols proved to be poor, and Le Mat placed further contracts in Belgium and England. Several thousand revolvers were eventually shipped to the Southern states, most of which were .40 caliber nine-shot weapons with an 18- or 20-gauge shot barrel. They appear to have been reliable and well-liked, and certainly the effect of the shot barrel at close quarters must have made them a fearsome weapon.

Le Mat revolver.

Le Mat revolver.

Locally made revolvers were almost always copies of the Colt 1851 or the Remington designs, because they were

Dance Brothers .36 Navy.

.42 caliber Le Mat (Paris)

readily available as patterns and because Confederate manufacturers were unconcerned about such minor matters as patent infringement. Not having access to major machinery in most cases, there were small differences from the originals in order to accommodate the design to the available means of manufacture, and this has led to a great deal of confusion. Numerous manufacturers patented, or claimed to have invented, or claimed to have the ability to make, revolvers, but the number of makers who actually managed to produce them in worthwhile numbers is relatively small. Of the several names which are known to gun collectors, the following are generally held to be the principal Confederate-manufactured pistols.

Leech & Rigdon of Columbus, Mississippi, and Greensboro, Georgia, was one of the most proficient makers. They made a copy of the 1851 Colt but with a 7½-inch 'Dragoon' style barrel. Possibly 50 were made in Columbus, after which the firm moved to Greensboro, receiving a contract from the CSA for their entire output. About 2500 were then made, after which the partners split up and each continued to make revolvers independently, Leech producing about 50 and Rigdon about 500 before the war ended.

Griswold & Gunnison, of Griswoldville, Georgia, was the Confederacy's most prolific manufacturer, producing over 3,500 .36 caliber Colt copies between July 1862 and November 1864. Another well-known maker was Dance Brothers of Columbia, Texas, who produced Colt copies in .36 and .44 caliber. Precise figures are not known, but the study of serial numbers indicates that about 500 of

each caliber were made.

Other makers included the Augusta Machine Works of Augusta, Georgia, about 100 Colt 1851 copies; the Columbus Firearms Company of Columbus, Georgia, who made about 100 copies of the Colt 1851 before the plant was closed by the Confederate Government and moved to Macon, Georgia; Spiller and Burr of Atlanta, Georgia, who made about 1,400 copies of the Whitney revolver before Sherman's advance closed the plant down; and Tucker, Sherrard & Co., of Lancaster, Texas who managed, in spite of several re-organizations and renamings, to produce about 500 of a 3,000 pistol order before the war ended.

Spiller and Burr, 1861.

In addition to these, numerous one-man 'cottage industries' turned out revolvers in small numbers—anything from 20 to 50—and the study of the various pistols turned out under the Confederacy is an involved one; it has not been made easier by the existence of numerous unmarked copies of Colt revolvers, some of which were undoubtedly made by small gunmakers in Europe in order to 'cash in' on the war, and, regrettably, by the numbers of fake 'Confederate pistols' which have appeared in subsequent years.

Rifles & Muskets

THE OUTBREAK OF THE CIVIL WAR found the contestants armed with a motley collection of flintlock and percussion muskets and rifles, the design of which had scarcely changed since the Revolution. The only major firearms innovation in the intervening years had been the invention of the percussion principle to replace the flintlock, but even so it was scarcely twenty years since the flintlock had been abandoned and vast numbers of them were still in existence. The percussion weapons were generally little more than the basic flintlock designs altered to the more modern form of ignition, and thus both weapons were operated in very similar fashion; a paper cartridge was torn open and the powder trickled into the muzzle of the gun, the wadded paper thrust in, and the lead ball rammed down on top. A cap was fitted to the nipple, or powder was sifted into the flintlock's pan, and the weapon was ready to fire.

Most of these weapons had started life as .69 caliber smoothbores, firing round balls, but in the 1850s the Minie Ball (a misnomer—it was not ball-shaped) appeared, and most muskets had been re-bored and rifled. The Minie bullet was a conical lead slug with a concave base containing a wooden cone. When the rifle was loaded, the ball could be rammed easily down the barrel since it was less in diameter than the bore of the weapon. But when fired, the explosion of the cartridge drove the cone into the bottom of the bullet and so expanded the bullet skirt into the rifling grooves. This sealed the propellant gas efficiently behind the bullet and made the bullet follow the twist of the rifling and

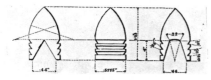

Balls for rifle-musket and pistol-carbine.

thus spin. The tight contact also scoured away fouling left by previous shots. The advantage of the Minie bullet thus lay in its improved accuracy, due to its spin and sealing, and the same factors gave it improved range.

Rifle with Maynard tape primer.

At the start of the war there were a variety of percussion rifles available to both North and South; of these the most important were the US models of 1855 and 1861. The model of 1855 Musket, and its shorter brother, the Model of 1855 Rifle, both used the Maynard Tape Primer, the invention of a Washington DC dentist. This used a roll of paper or linen tape of double thickness, with pellets of detonating compound spaced along it. This was coiled into a container near the weapon's lock and fed, by ratchet action, to the nipple of the gun whenever the hammer was cocked. This saved time and trouble in fitting a cap to the nipple, but the weapon still had to be muzzle loaded with powder and ball for each shot. The Model of 1861 did away with the Maynard priming and reverted to manual placement of the cap, but in other respects was similar.

US musket model 1855.

Other rifles and muskets in use included the Percussion Musket Model of 1841; this had started life as a smoothbore but had been later converted into a rifle. The 'Mississippi' rifle, or Model of 1841, was a .54 caliber weapon firing a round ball; it had received its name from being used to arm Jefferson Davis' Mississippi Volunteers during the Mexican War. The

287

only percussion weapons manufactured in the South were a number of .69 caliber muskets made in 1852 for the State of South Carolina at the Palmetto Armory in Columbia.

The mechanical revolution in firearms was having an effect on shoulder weapons, just as it was on other types, and breech-loading was waiting to take the stage by 1860; the war gave it the push it needed to bring it into the limelight. The most outstanding American breech-loading development of this period was the Sharps rifle, patented in 1848 by Christian Sharps of Philadelphia, though it was some years before he managed to bring it to a degree of perfection good enough to warrant manufacture. The Sharps relied upon a vertical sliding breech block actuated by a lever. The block was lowered and a paper cartridge inserted into the chamber; as the block was raised to close the breech, so the sharp edge of the block sliced the paper from the end of the cartridge, exposing the powder. On top of the block was a nipple for a percussion cap. Pulling the trigger dropped a hammer on to this cap and the resulting flash passed down a vent and struck the powder to fire the rifle. Over 80,000 of these rifles were bought by the Ordnance Department, mostly in the form of cavalry carbines, and many more were bought by state authorities or by soldiers at their own expense.

Maynard tape primer.

Sharps model 1855.

Another breech-loader used in great numbers was the American Arms Company's .52 caliber rifle designed by Gilbert Smith. This hinged at the breech, somewhat in the manner of a shotgun, and used a cartridge composed of a gutta-percha, rubber or metal case holding the powder and bullet and with a hole in its base to receive the flash from an externally-placed percussion cap. The Smith carbine was an efficient weapon, even though the method of closing the breech was somewhat less than perfect, and the Union government bought 30,062 carbines and over 13 million cartridges.

Maynard, the inventor of the tape priming system, had moved on and invented a complete breechloading rifle. This was very similar to Smith's design, a drop-barrel weapon using a special brass cartridge case with a hole to permit ignition from an external cap. One advantage of the Maynard design was that the case was of thick brass and could be re-loaded and refired several times.

General Ambrose E Burnside had retired from military service in 1853 and had set up a company to develop a breechloading rifle of his own design. As with the others it was a single shot weapon using a brass cartridge with a hole in the base, though in this case the brass was thin, deformed on firing and could not be re-used. Some 55,000 Burnside carbines were bought by the Union government during the war, while Burnside, of course, returned to duty.

After breech-loading, the next prospect in sight was the development of repeating weapons, and these also came to fruition in time for the Civil War. The first successful lever-action repeater was the Spencer of 1860 which used a tubular magazine set inside the shoulder stock. Operating the lever lifted one cartridge from the tube and fed it into the breech, after which an external hammer fell to fire it. In such a design as this a metallic cartridge was required, and the Spencer used a rimfire round of .52 caliber. The tubular magazine could be removed and replaced

depredations by raiders and by sales to various state militia units. The Henry rifle emerged from the war with a fine reputation and went on to become the famous Winchester; in commemoration of Henry's pioneering role, all Winchester rimfire cartridges to this day bear the letter 'H' impressed on their base.

Top: *US rifle, 1855.* Bottom: *Henry rifle.*

Action of the Spencer carbine.

by a full magazine of nine cartridges in a few seconds; not for nothing did one Confederate soldier immortalize the Spencer as 'That tarnation Yankee gun they loads on Sunday and shoots the rest of the week.'

According to legend, Spencer found innumerable bureaucratic obstacles in his way when he tried to interest the Army in his carbine but he eventually gained access to President Lincoln and gave him a personal demonstration, after which it was formally tested by the Army and Navy Departments and accepted for service. Over 60,000 carbines and 58 million cartridges were purchased by the Union forces during the war.

The other famous repeater which appeared in time for the war was the Henry lever-action carbine. This had a tubular magazine below the barrel which could be loaded by swinging it up on a pivot. It fired a .44 rimfire cartridge and operating the lever unlocked a toggle to open the breech and lift a cartridge up from the magazine, then closed the breech leaving an external hammer cocked. Unfortunately the Union Army was of the opinion that the Henry was too delicate, in comparison with the Spencer, and relatively few were bought. But this was more than compensated for by sales to civilians living in areas liable to

Machine Guns

THE DESIRE TO PROVIDE rapid-fire musketry from a single weapon was an old one and had been toyed with for centuries by a succession of inventors without much success. But the Civil War, like all wars, acted as a stimulant to inventors and, together with the improvements in mechanical engineering which had been achieved by that time, managed to produce some moderately serviceable weapons.

The oldest idea of all was that of the 'Battery Gun', a number of independent rifle barrels mounted on a wheeled carriage and discharged either in succession or as a volley. One such weapon made its appearance shortly before the outbreak of war, invented (or re-invented) by a Dr Joseph Requa and manufactured by William Billinghurst of Rochester, New York. Billinghurst was a well-respected gunsmith and he made a good job of the gun, which consisted of 24 rifle barrels on a wheeled carriage. In order to obviate the long delay while loading 24 rifles from the muzzle, Requa had designed a cartridge and made the weapon a breech-loader.

His cartridge was a brass tube containing powder and ball, with a hole pierced through the base. Twenty-five of these were fitted into a sheet-metal frame and dropped into the frame of the gun so that they were aligned with the rifle breeches. Two levers then thrust the cartridge carrier forward and mated it with the rifles, after which a single, centrally-located percussion cap was fired by a hammer. This ignited the nearest cartridges, and the flame from these communicated, via the holes in the cases, to the others, producing a ragged volley. The barrels were of .60 caliber and fired a 414-grain lead ball to good effect. Although there appears to have been no formal approval or procurement of the Billinghurst-Requa Volley Gun, several were bought by individual regiments, both in the Union and in the Confederacy. They were principally used for covering approach lines to which an advancing enemy would be confined by some obstacle and thus create a good target for the massed fire; one of the favorite applications was to defend bridges, and it was frequently referred to as the 'Covered Bridge Gun'.

Another volley gun of the period was the Vandenberg, a device which outwardly resembled a cannon. The 'barrel' however, was a tubular casing inside which were a large number of rifle barrels; models with anything from 85 to 120 barrels were built. The breech end of the casing was closed by a massive screw which also carried the requisite charges, each in a copper tube, and closing the screw forced the tubes into the breeches of the rifles to make a gas-tight seal. On firing a central cap the entire group of barrels was touched off and fired at one salvo, after which the breech had to be opened, the expended tubes removed and fresh ones loaded. As might be imagined, this a slow performance and the Vandenberg gun never appeared in any numbers.

The most practical of all these early weapons was the Ager Battery Gun, more popularly known as the 'Ager Coffee Mill' from its appearance. It was a single-barreled gun with a crank-operated breech mechanism, above which was a large brass hopper resembling the domestic coffee-grinder of the period. The gun used a cartridge prepared by filling a steel tube with

powder, forcing a ball into the front end, and then placing a percussion cap on a nipple at the rear end. Handfuls of these prepared cartridges were dropped into the hopper and the crank revolved, thereby forcing the tubes into the breech one at a time, firing them, and then extracting them to be picked up and re-loaded by the gun's crew.

The Ager gun worked, and for its day it worked very well. The difficulty was to convince the military mind of the period that it was a practical weapon. Ager claimed to be able to fire 100 shots a minute, provided the ammunition was prepared; military 'experts' derided this, saying that it was impossible to explode a pound or so of gunpowder inside the barrel every minute without overheating. They had a valid point, but they would have done better to solve the overheating problem instead of scorning Ager's gun. The question of its adoption was taken as far as President Lincoln, but he refused to commit himself, saying that he was not an ordnance expert; if the army wanted it, then they should say so and he would authorize it, but without their request he was not going to force it on them. As a result, poor Ager, with a war on his front step, sold no more than about 50 guns.

Nevertheless, it is a matter of record that the first machine gun ever used in combat was fired in the Civil War. This was the Williams Gun, invented by a Captain Williams of the Confederate Army who came from Covington, Kentucky. His gun was a single-barreled one-pounder of 1.57 inch caliber which was crank-operated. Turning the crank pulled back the breech block, whereupon the gunner's assistant dropped a paper cartridge and ball into the feedway. Further rotation of the crank forced the cartridge into the breech and fired it. The paper cartridge was entirely consumed, so that there was no extraction problem to be faced. The gun could fire up to 65 rounds a minute and was adopted by the Confederate Bureau of Ordnance in conditions of great secrecy on the outbreak of war. Several were manufactured, and a battery of them saw action at the Battle of Seven Pines on 3 May 1862. A number of guns, under the command of Capt Williams himself, were attached to Pickett's Brigade and saw action several times during the course of the war.

The most famous mechanical machine gun, one which became known and used throughout the world, was developed during the Civil War but, in fact, saw very little use in that conflict. This was the well-known Gatling Gun, invented by Dr Richard J Gatling. He was a doctor of medicine who never actually practiced in the profession, preferring to make his living as an inventor. He began designing his gun in 1851 and patented it in 1862. He demonstrated a prototype in that year and the Governor of Indiana was sufficiently enthusiastic about it to write to the Assistant Secretary of War and suggest that official tests be organized. With this encouragement, Gatling had six guns made by Miles, Greenwood & Company, of Cincinnati, but unfortunately the guns and all the drawings were destroyed in a fire. Gatling went back to his drawing board, made some improvements, and had another six guns made, this time by the McWhinney, Ridge Company, also of Cincinnati, with which he was able to stage a successful demonstration.

Gatling 5.

in from an overhead magazine; as the cluster rotated, so the cartridge would be loaded into a barrel chamber and the breech locked; as each individual barrel reached the lowest position it fired, after which, as it moved upwards, the empty case was extracted and the barrel was ready to receive another cartridge as it reached the top. By using this system, Gatling managed to achieve a useful rate of fire without overheating the barrel; if the gun were firing at 300 shots a minute, each individual barrel was only firing 50.

Plate from a Colt Gatling gun.

Gatling .50, 1865, on field carriage.

The 'definitive' Gatling was a six-barreled weapon, the six barrels being carried in a rotating cluster in front of the breech casing. As a side crank was turned, so the barrels revolved. At the topmost position of their rotation a cartridge was fed

Gatling had a good design and the gun was well made and effective; unfortunately he came from North Carolina and he was living in Cincinnati, and several people had the impression that his sympathies were with the Confederates. As a result his motives were suspect; some thought that his object was to obtain a military contract, fill his Cincinnati warehouse with guns, and then tip off his Southern friends to make a quick raid and steal them. Another viewpoint was that the whole gun was a dangerous fraud designed to blow up and

291

kill the Union crews. The only sale which Gatling made during the war was to General Ben Butler; Butler, a self-made soldier, was nobody's fool and knew a good weapon when he saw one. Despairing of getting official authority, Butler spent $12,000 of his own money on twelve Gatling guns and a supply of ammunition, and he put them to good use at the siege of Petersburg. But even this display did nothing to convince the Army, and it was not until the war was over that Gatling eventually received recognition and began to sell his gun in numbers.

Altogether, although the machine gun saw its first combat use in the Civil War, and although effective designs were available, military inertia prevented their general acceptance.

Artillery of the Civil War

THE ARTILLERY OF THE CIVIL WAR was, like the small arms, a remarkable mixture of types and styles and for the same reason; the science of artillery was just at the point where new techniques of manufacture and new theories of construction were jostling one another in the world's armies and market places.

The Crimean War in Europe had revealed the shortcomings of the traditional muzzle-loading artillery piece of cast bronze or cast iron. Soldiers had long ago learned to live with them, but the Crimean War had introduced the 'war correspondent' and, lacking any stirring battles to write about, they had written about the difficulties facing the armies, mentioning the problems of heaving massive artillery about in foul weather conditions. Numerous manufacturers had taken note of this and had attempted to bring artillery into the age of the Industrial Revolution; few armies had, as yet, made the plunge and moved from their old weapons to the newer designs, but the new designs were being

tested and, meanwhile, they were being offered to anyone willing to try them out. As a result, both sides in the Civil War found themselves acting as semi-official testbeds for various artillery theories.

Even so, the majority of the artillery engaged was of the traditional type. At the outbreak of war the standard field artillery battery would consist of four guns and two howitzers; a nominally 12-pounder battery would have two 24-pounder howitzers, while a nominally 6-pounder battery would have two 12-pounder howitzers. These weapons were smoothbores, dating from the 1840s, and usually of bronze. The 6-pounder had a caliber of 3.67 inches and was five feet long. On the usual type of wooden two-wheeled carriage it weighed about 1750 pounds and fired a six pound ball to about 1500 yards range. The accompanying 12-pounder howitzer was 4.62 inch caliber, shorter, weighed about 1700 lbs in action and fired a nine-pound shell to just over 1000 yards range.

The 12-pounder gun was the same caliber as the howitzer but was 6 feet 6 inches long, weighed 2900 pounds in action and fired a 12 pound ball to about 1700 yards, while the 24 pounder howitzer was 5.8 inch caliber, weighed 2500 pounds and fired an 18 pound shell to some 1400 yards.

US Napoleon.

Broadly speaking, the difference between gun and howitzer is that the gun fires on a flat trajectory while the howitzer fires up into the air so as to drop its projectile behind protecting walls or cover; moreover the howitzer normally has an adjustable propelling charge so that various trajectory options can be selected to suit the particular target. In the days of the Civil War, however, the distinction was rather a fine one, since neither guns nor howitzers had carriages which admitted of very much elevation. Where high trajectory fire was demanded, the 'mortar' was the chosen instrument; the principal feature of the howitzer was that it fired with a lower charge and propelled an explosive shell instead of a solid ball.

Other ammunition options available at this time were 'spherical case shot' better known by the name of its inventor Henry Shrapnel, canister shot and grape shot. All were anti-personnel weapons and the availability of three types was to allow a selection to be made according to the range. When enemy troops appeared at long range, spherical case was used; this was a round ball containing a very small charge of black powder and a filling of musket balls, operated by a burning time fuze. As the shell approached the target, the fuze ignited the black powder which split open the shell and released the musket balls, which flew onward with the forward velocity of the shell, so giving the effect of musket fire at ranges which no musket could achieve.

As the range shortened, canister shot would be brought into play; this took its name from its appearance, a thin-walled metal canister filled with musket balls but with no explosive or fuze. Fired from a smoothbore gun, the canister would disrupt in the bore, due to the pressure of the propelling charge, and was ejected from the muzzle in the manner of a shotgun charge. This was effective at ranges from about 100 to 400 yards.

When the enemy were at the gun's muzzle, grape-shot was used; this took its name from being a cloth bundle containing large lead shot, lashed around with cord, giving the appearance of a bunch of grapes. It, too, exited the gun like a shot charge but, with no canister to constrain it, spread immediately from the muzzle. Also, since the balls were heavier they had less range, and grape was useful up to about 200 yards from the gun. In an emergency, of course, grape could be extemporized by ramming a powder cartridge into the gun, following it by a wad, and then shovelling down any scrap iron which could be found—horseshoe nails, pieces of chain, even small rocks. The erratic flight of such a load made it, if anything, more dangerous than the regular grape shot.

Two technical innovations faced artillery in the 1860s; rifling and breech-loading. To most forward-looking artillerymen their utility was not in doubt, but the engineering aspects presented problems. There was, of course, a hard core of reactionary soldiers who would have nothing to do with either idea, but this was common in all countries and was perhaps best exemplified by the Prussian general who, on his death-bed, asked that the volley over his grave be fired by smoothbores and not by rifles. As younger officers assumed command during the Civil War, so the prospect of improved artillery was grasped and newer weapons began to appear.

In the 1860s the most advanced piece of artillery in existence was the English Armstrong rifled breech-loader, which had been adopted in 1860 by the Royal Navy and shortly afterwards by the British Army. This gun broke new ground in several directions; instead of being a solid cast piece it was built up from several tubes, shrunk one upon another, it was of wrought iron with a steel rifled liner to the barrel, and it loaded from the breech, using a heavy vertical wedge locked by an axial screw. The shell was coated with lead so as to bite into the rifling and spin, while the elongated shell allowed a greater weight of projectile for a given caliber. Armstrong guns were made in the Royal Arsenal for service use, but Armstrong also owned his own factory which was producing guns for export, and numbers of these were purchased by both sides in the war.

Armstrong's principal rival in England was Joseph Whitworth; he also owned a gun factory and actively promoted his own version of a rifled breech-loader. The notable feature was that his method of rifling was simply to make the inside of the bore hexagonal, twisting it so as to rotate the hexagonal projectile. The breech was closed by a screw cap, and the cartridge was contained in a tin cylinder which helped to seal the escape of gas at the breech end. A small number of Whitworth breech-loaders found their way to America and were used by both Union and Confederate forces, but while they were exceptionally accurate and long-ranging, the mechanical fit of the shell and barrel was a source of trouble and many guns went out of action at a critical moment due to a mis-loaded shot being stuck in the bore.

While breech-loading was attractive, it must be admitted that in the 1860s the mechanical problems of sealing the breech were still not adequately solved, and as a result the guns were not universally popular. On the other hand the advantages of rifling were appreciated, and therefore the idea of putting rifling into muzzle-loaders was widely adopted. This involved either rifling the existing smooth bore or boring the barrel out and inserting a new rifled liner; in practice the latter course proved best, producing a gun which was actually stronger than the original.

There was, though, a wide difference of opinion as to what form the rifling and, more important, the projectile, should take, which led to an interesting variety of weapons. The system which had seen widest adoption, in various countries, was that called the 'French' system, since it had been first adopted by the French Artillery. In this the gun had three or more broad rifling grooves, while the projectile had a matching number of rows of soft bronze or zinc studs standing proud of its surface and angled so as to match the twist of rifling. The shell was loaded by inserting the studs into the rifling grooves at the muzzle and then ramming it down on top of a cartridge and wad. When the charge exploded, the shell was driven up the bore and the studs rode in the grooves to impart spin. This system was used in the 12-pounder Blakely gun, among others. A similar system was to cast angled ribs on the shell body, coating them with lead to reduce friction. This system was used in a number of guns made

for the Union Army by Sawyer.

One advantage of rifling was the reduction of 'windage', the difference between the exterior width of the projectile and the interior width of the gun barrel. In smoothbores there had to be a clearance to allow the shot to be rammed, allowing for rust, poor machining of shot or bore, and powder fouling, and when the gun was fired a proportion of the propelling gases escaped past the shot to reduce power and impair accuracy. A rifled gun reduced windage to near-zero in the cases where studs or ribs were used, and if a tight-fitting wad was used behind the shell, windage was absent. Even so, there still had to be some clearance for muzzle-loading, and in another group of weapons this was automatically removed as the shell was fired. In these, a soft metal plate or collar was caused to expand under the pressure of the powder gases, so being forced into the rifling to both spin the shell and also seal off the windage space. The Parrott, Reed and some others used this system, attaching a saucer-shaped copper or brass disk to the base of the shell so that when rammed it was of smaller diameter than the shell but on firing it was driven flat and impressed into the rifling. Another idea was that advanced by Benjamin Hotchkiss, who was the Superintendent of the New York City Arsenal. He produced a shell which was in two parts, an iron forward section with a lead base stretching about halfway up the shell body. There was a gap behind the iron section so that on firing the lead was forced forward and expanded into the gun's rifling.

In spite of all these technically advanced weapons, though, the brunt of the artillery's war was taken by the smoothbores, and principally the 12-pounder 'Napoleon' Model of 1857. The Napoleon probably represents the zenith of the smoothbore, even though in appearance it was little changed from what had gone before. Its improved performance lay in more careful manufacture, more accuracy of the bore and the ammunition, screw elevating gear for more precision and a robust car-

TABLE OF FIRE. LIGHT 12-POUNDER GUN. MODEL 1857.

SHOT. Charge 2½ Pounds.		SPHERICAL CASE SHOT. Charge 2½ Pounds.			SHELL. Charge 2 Pounds.		
ELEVATION In Degrees	RANGE In Yards	ELEVATION In Degrees	TIME OF FLIGHT Seconds	RANGE In Yards	ELEVATION In Degrees	TIME OF FLIGHT In Seconds	RANGE In Yards
0°	323	0°50′	1″	300	0°	0″75	300
1°	620	1°	1″75	575	0°30	1″25	425
2°	875	1°30′	2″5	635	1°··	1″75	615
3°	1200	2°	3″	730	1°30′	2″25	700
4°	1325	3°	4″	960	2°	2″75	785
5°	1680	3°30′	4″75	1080	2°30′	3″5	925
		3°40′	5″	1135	3°	4″	1080
					3°45	5″	1300

Table of Fire for a 12-pounder.

Heavy artillery at Fort Richardson.

riage to give it stability when firing. Officially classed as a 'gun-howitzer', the Napoleon was lighter than previous 12-pounder guns by over 500 pounds, due to using a shorter, lighter barrel devoid of ornament, yet it fired the same cartridge and shot to the same range as the earlier guns. It could also fire shell—hence the 'howitzer' part of its title—and it emerged from the war with an extremely high reputation.

TABLE OF FIRE. 6 POUNDER GUN

SHOT Charge 1¼ Pounds		SPHERICAL CASE Charge 1¼ Pounds		
ELEVATION In Degrees	RANGE In Yards	ELEVATION In Degrees	TIME OF FLIGHT In Seconds	RANGE In Yards
0°	318	1°0′	2″	600
1°	674	1°45′	2″75	700
2°	867	2°0′	3″	800
3°	1138	2°45′	3″25	900
4°	1256	3°0′	3″75	1000
5°	1523	3°15′	4″	1100
		4°0′	5″	1200

Table of Fire for a 6-pounder.

SIEGE ARTILLERY

THE HEAVIER TYPES of ordnance which accompanied the field army were classed as Siege or Garrison artillery, depending upon whether their role was offensive or defensive. Most of the siege train weapons were elderly smoothbores which were still quite adequate for a leisurely approach to the beseiged place followed by an equally leisurely and sustained battering of the defences until something gave way. The principal factor in choosing the size of siege guns was the difficulty of getting them to the scene of the action by a team of horses.

The 24-pounder smoothbore was at the near-maximum weight, just over five tons and demanding a ten-horse team to shift it on a good surface. The 5700 pound barrel was carried on the usual type of wooden two-wheeled carriage, but for traveling the barrel was lifted back on to the trail and the trail itself was supported on a two-wheeled limber, so distributing the weight more equally between the four wheels of the assembly.

Numbers of these and other calibers of smoothbore were rifled, in an endeavor to improve their accuracy, and their worth was conclusively proved during the bombardment of Fort Pulaski in 1862 when the fire of rifled guns breached the southeast salient with comparative ease; the marks are still to be seen. But rifling these elderly guns frequently led to their destruction upon firing and in order to strengthen them numbers were 'hooped' or reinforced by having wrought iron bands shrunk over the chamber area, the point of greatest strain. As an expedient this was passable, but it did not entirely guarantee a long life to either the gun or its crew, and new designs were brought forward in which improved mechanical principles were adopted. The Blakely gun used a succession of hoops shrunk one upon another to reinforce the basic barrel, while the Parrott rifled gun used a thickened area around the chamber to provide extra strength. The most scientific, and successful, approach was by Major Rodman, who devised a method of casting guns by using a hollow central core through which cold water was passed while the metal cooled. This caused the outer layers of metal to act in compression on the inner,

WEAPONS

A Civil War cannon.

Civil War cannons.

so strengthening the gun as it was being made. Rodman guns were subsequently built in calibers up to 20 inches and proved to be adequately strong.

A 15" Rodman.

The most practical rifled siege gun proved to be the 30-pounder Parrott, used by Union troops. This was of 4.2 inch caliber and fired a 29-pound projectile to 2200 yards with immense destructive power.

Garrison artillery was almost entirely confined to use in seacoast defenses, and as with all such defenses the variety of weapons in use was considerable. Early works used 32-pounder and 42-pounder smoothbore guns for close-in defense, later supplemented by 8- 10- and 15-inch smoothbores designed to hold an attacking fleet at arms' length. With the adoption of rifled guns, a number of Parrott and Blakely designs were taken into coast artillery service, the largest of these being a 12.75 inch Blakely, the barrel of which weighed 27 tons. A few Armstrong breechloaders were also put to use in this area, but experience showed that they were not well suited to coast defense fire against ships

since their breech sealing was not sufficiently strong to stand the heavy charges needed to propel shot capable of penetrating ships. They were largely relegated to local defense tasks or protecting possible landing places by firing shrapnel or canister shot at short range.

The last group of artillery to see regular use were the mortars, short-barrelled high-angle pieces capable of overcoming defensive walls and protective obstacles. These always fired at 45° elevation, their range being varied by adjusting the charge of powder behind the shell. Mortars of 8 inch and 10 inch caliber were used by the field armies since they were light enough to be transported; mortars fired not from a carriage but from a 'bed', a simple frame of wood or iron set down upon layers of timbers, so that they had to be carried in carts or on specially strengthened wagons. Smaller, and extremely useful in trench warfare, was the 5.8 inch 'Coehorn' mortar, named for the famed Dutch fortress engineer who had designed it in the 17th century. This could be quickly emplaced by a group of men and fired a useful 17 pound bomb to about 1200 yards with good accuracy.

Heavy mortars of 10 inch and 13 inch caliber were used as seacoast defense weapons. The 13 inch fired a 220 pound bomb which could create immense damage to the upperworks and decks of a warship,

A cannon crew with their weapon.

A cannon crew.

but the time of flight of the bomb meant that the target could move a considerable distance between the firing of the mortar and the arrival of the bomb; moreover, fire control systems of the time were relatively primitive, and so the seacoast mortar was only of use against a ship which had anchored in order to bombard the land.

13-inch mortars each weighing 20,000 pounds.

Finally we should not overlook the 'lunatic fringe' of gun designers who appear in every war with improbable ideas. There was, for example, the steam gun designed by Ross Winans, a well-known locomotive builder; at least one of these

was built and went to the front, only to be captured by General Ben Butler. It relied upon a boiler to generate high pressure steam which was then tapped to propel a shot on its way. As might be imagined, the whole device was cumbersome and prone to mechanical disorders and was never used again.

An inventor called Pate devised a 're-volving cannon' and had two built in Petersburg, Virginia; his design was simply that of the hand revolver translated into artillery caliber, with the cylinder revolved by hand and firmly wedged to the barrel for each shot. The first gun exploded during its initial testing, killing three men; what happened to the other is in some doubt, but it survived to rest outside a Petersburg museum to this day.

Who invented the double cannon is not known, but, again, one survives in a museum to entertain us. The object in view was to discharge both barrels simultaneously, each having been loaded with a cannon ball. The two balls were linked by a long piece of chain, and the theory was that the two balls would travel at the same speed, side by side, carrying the chain stretched between them so as to scythe down anyone in their way. Unfortunately, no matter how carefully the thing is arranged, it is virtually impossible to make two guns fire identically; when the double gun was fired the two shot inevitably were unbalanced, whirled off to one side, broke the chain, and then set forth on their own unpredictable courses.

OTHER MUNITIONS

An alternative to artillery which had been explored in the past was the war rocket, and a few specimens of these managed to appear during the Civil War. The British Army had adopted Congreve's Rocket in 1805 and had used it with some success for many years, among the successes being the bombardment of Washington during the War of 1812. Numbers of Congreve rockets were bought by the Confederate Army and used on one or two occasions, but their performance tended to be erratic, particularly if the rocket struck the ground, or an obstacle, while still burning; it would then ricochet off on some totally new course, or even, on occasion, turn round and head back the way it had come. In appearance, Congreve's Rocket resembled the ordinary fireworks rocket used for entertainment, a cylindrical casing mounted on a long stabilizing stick. The body of the rocket contained a two-stage black-powder propelling charge, and the head carried a hollow shell filled with shrapnel or with some inflammable mixture, and when the rocket performed properly its effect was enormous. But since it performed properly only a percentage of the time, its use was eventually abandoned as being too speculative.

The Union Army adopted Hale's War Rocket, an American design which used three canted vents in the rear of the rocket to spin it and so stabilize its flight, instead of relying upon drag stabilization by means of a stick as had the Congreve rocket. Although Hale's design showed theoretical advantages, it fell down because of manufacturing defects, notably a tendency for the propulsive filling of black powder to crack in storage or transport and then flash through and explode instead of burning steadily. As a result it saw little use during the war.

Finally we should mention hand grenades; these, in the middle 19th century, were usually small iron balls filled with black powder and ignited by a length of burning fuze, and they were officially issued to be thrown into the ditch outside a fort to deter assaulting parties. The invention of the percussion cap made ignition somewhat easier (though very little safer) and the Civil War brought several primitive hand grenades into use, most of them locally manufactured to meet an urgent need. One of the few 'approved' designs was Ketcham's grenade, an oval powder-filled head with a finned tail which ensured that it flew straight and landed upon its fuse. This fuse consisted simply of a protruding plunger which, on striking the ground, was driven on to a percussion cap which then fired the black powder. The Union Army alone bought nearly 100,000 of these, and copies were adopted by the Confederate forces.

A Confederate battery before Bull Run.

III
NAVAL WARFARE IN
THE CIVIL WAR

Crew members cooking on the deck of the USS Monitor, *9 July 1862.*

NAVAL

It could have been said of the Federal Navy in the Civil War that it was expected to do nothing but ended up doing everything. Although that would be an exaggeration, it is fair to say that both belligerents started the War largely blind to the influence that sea power would have over the outcome. Early events only heightened the conviction that the War Between the States would be decided by land battles, but two years later this was clearly not the case.

At the outbreak of hostilities neither the Union nor the Confederacy had any particular naval strategy. This was partly a result of the neglect of the US Navy since 1815 but it must also be remembered that naval technology was in a state of flux, and no navy had any clear ideas of what warships to build. But the fact remains that out of 90 ships of all classes on the Navy List in 1861 only 41 were in commission and 50 per cent of those were officially regarded as obsolete. The best ships, the new steam frigates like the *Merrimack*, were as good as anything abroad, and indeed had caused some alarm in the Royal Navy when they appeared. The same could not be said, however, for such doughty veterans as the sailing frigates *Constitution* and *United States*, which were retained purely for sentimental reasons.

In one important respect, however, the United States Navy was as well equipped as any of its rivals. Thanks largely to Rear Admiral John A Dahlgren the design of naval guns had been pushed forward, and both rifled and smoothbore shell guns were standard by 1861. The standard rifled guns were designed by Captain Robert P Parrott, ranging from a 10-pounder (3-inch) up to the 150-pounder (10-inch). The Dahlgren guns differed in being smoothbores, firing a spherical shell, and the first, a 9-inch, was built in 1850, followed by an 11-inch in 1851. Unlike the Parrott guns the Dahlgrens had a distinctive 'soda bottle' shape; but both types served with distinction. The chief Confederate gun-designer, Commander John M Brooke, based his guns largely on Parrott's ideas.

'Teazer' gun on a Confederate gunboat.

Southern states produced the majority of the Navy's officers, and so it is not surprising that some 200 serving officers offered themselves to the fledgling Confederate States' Navy. But naval warfare is much more than an officer corps, and in other respects the balance was weighted heavily in favor of the North. Before the outbreak of war the shipping trade had been largely in the hands of Northerners, and so the Confederates lacked trained seamen to man the dozen revenue cutters and merchant ships that had been seized in Southern ports. The industrial situation was, of course, even more parlous, with virtually no heavy industry in the South.

What the Confederacy did have was energy, partly because it had recruited the cream of naval administrative talent. On 21 February 1861, only two weeks after the formation of the provisional government at Montgomery, President Davis put Stephen R Mallory in charge of the Confederate States' Navy. It was an obvious choice, for Mallory had been Chairman of the Senate Naval Affairs Committee for eight years and had played a major part in the modernization of the US Navy. His Federal opposite number, Navy Minister Gideon S Welles, had far less experience of naval administration, and certainly showed less inclination to back new ideas.

Union war ships made little or no attempt to prevent the surrender of Fort Sumter in April 1861, but when a few days later Jefferson Davis appealed to Southern shipowners to take out 'letters of marque', or in other words to turn themselves into privateers, President Lincoln retaliated by announcing a blockade of all Southern States. The thinking behind Davis' sudden switch to commerce-raiding was to involve European countries, particularly Great Britain, in the conflict. The main, possibly the only hope of the Confederacy, lay in getting the British to intervene to safeguard the cotton trade. Blockade-running would thus achieve a dual purpose, bringing in much-needed supplies and foreign exchange, and at the same time enmeshing Federal Navy ships in confrontations with the powerful Royal Navy.

The drawback was the lack of ships but Mallory set about equipping privately owned ships as privateers and purchasing warships abroad. On 18 May the first letter of marque was issued to the schooner *Savannah*, and within a short while she and other privateers were bringing Northern prizes into Charleston and New Orleans. The result was panic, and marine insurance premiums and freight rates soared, but however heartening these successes were to the Confederacy they brought little profit. The Northern blockade was soon too successful in sealing off Southern ports, so that the privateers had great difficulty in bringing their prizes into harbor. Nor could they sell them profitably abroad; intense diplomatic pressure from Washington ensured that European harbors were closed to Confederate prizes. By the end of 1861 it was clear that the great privateering venture had failed.

Although privateering fizzled out the Confederate Navy commissioned a number of highly successful 'auxiliary cruisers' for commerce-raiding. As early as 18 April 1861 Commander Raphael Semmes converted the requisitioned steamer *Habana*, lying in New Orleans. Two months later she was recommissioned as the CSS *Sumter*, armed with an 8-inch shell-gun and four 32-pounders. During the next nine months the *Sumter* seized 18 ships, and her career only came to an end when

Captain Semmes (foreground) on the Alabama.

she had to be laid up for repairs at Gibraltar. She was sold but continued to serve the Confederacy as the blockade-runner *Gibraltar*.

The success of the *Sumter* lay not so much in the paralysis of Northern commerce, for that had already been achieved by the privateers, but in the strain that she put on the blockade. Her depredations forced Gideon Welles to detach warships from the blockading squadrons, at a time when the Confederate Army's successes were making it even more imperative that the Federal Navy should stand firm. There were two theaters in which the Navy could bring pressure to bear on the Confederacy, the mighty Mississippi River and the Eastern Seaboard. The Mississippi divided the Confederacy into two halves, and if it could pass into Union control it would cut off the Southern states from the West. On the Eastern Seaboard, the Union armies were on the defensive before an apparently irresistible Confederate onslaught, and the Navy could at least redress the balance with the firepower of its guns.

Both these requirements dictated shallow-drafted warships, much as the peculiar conditions of the Crimean War had forced the British and French to build gunboats, armored batteries and mortar boats. The Federal Navy quickly adapted three wooden paddle-steamers as gunboats, protecting them against shellfire with a girdle of thick planking. These three

US gunboats of the Mississippi fleet.

gunboats were ready by early September, with seven more armored gunboats built to the design of the St Louis engineer James B Eads. This powerful river fleet was put under the command of Captain Andrew H Foote on 5 September.

Gideon Welles also deserves credit for tackling the blockade problem quickly and firmly. At first only three warships were available for blockade duty but hundreds of mercantile vessels were brought up and armed. They were a strange variety of screw- and paddle-steamers and their armament was usually an old 32-pounder smoothbore muzzle-loader or a 6.4-inch Parrott rifled gun but it was sufficient for the purpose. Speed was the main problem, for the Confederacy built a series of very fast blockade-runners, but the secret of blockade, as the Royal Navy had shown against Napoleon, was to have large numbers of ships on station.

Confederate blockade runner A D Vance.

There was another arrow in Mallory's quiver, the purchase of warships abroad, and at the beginning of May 1861 he dispatched Commander James D Bulloch to England to arrange the purchase of suitable

hulls. Bulloch was a shrewd man who achieved much, particularly by exploiting British sympathy towards the Southern cause. He ordered two ironclad rams from the Laird Brothers' yard in Birkenhead, and two more from Arman Fréres in Bordeaux, and all four were ostensibly ordered on behalf of the Egyptian Government, being given cover-names *El Toussan, El Monassir, Cheops* and *Sphinx*. Other ships were bought by Bulloch's agents, such as the Royal Navy gunvessel *Victor*, whose deckhands thought she was going to China but suddenly found themselves being sworn in as sailors aboard the CSS *Rappahannock* in mid-Channel.

The Alabama burns a prize.

By far the best-known and most successful of Bulloch's purchases was the *Alabama*, which was bought while still fitting-out as the SS *Enrica* in the Laird shipyard. Although not the most heavily-armed of the Confederate raiders, having only one 6.4-inch Blakely rifled muzzle-loader, a 68-pounder shell-gun and six 32-pounder smoothbores, she accounted for 65 prizes in a brilliant cruise under Raphael Semmes lasting from July 1862 to June 1864. She was finally brought to bay off Cherbourg by the steam sloop USS *Kearsarge*. The *Georgia* was sold in June 1864 because her iron hull was in bad condition, and the sister of the *Kearsarge*, the USS *Wachusett* captured the *Florida* off Bahia in Brazil, reducing the raider fleet to only four ships. Of these the *Sheneandoah* was the most successful, destroying much of the American whaling fleet, although the *Tallahassee* took as many prizes. Both of

The 11" *forward gun of the* Kearsarge.

these commerce-raiders survived, the *Shenandoah* ending her days interned by the British Government in November 1865 and the *Tallahassee* (now serving as the blockade-runner *Chameleon*) surrendering to Union forces after the end of hostilities.

The Alabama *in battle, 19 June 1864.*

The recent success of British and French ironclads against Russian forts was not lost on either the Confederate or the Union Navies, but the limited armor-making resources in the United States made ironclads an expensive luxury. Gideon Welles set up a committee on 3 August 1861 to look at plans for ironclads, and just over seven weeks later the building of three different prototypes was approved, to be called *Galena*, *New Ironsides* and *Monitor*. Although the first two have always been overshadowed by the third, they are nonetheless interesting examples of the very earliest seagoing armored ships.

The *New Ironsides* was the largest, a 4000-ton broadside ironclad armed with two 8-inch Parrott rifled guns, two 5.1-inch Dahlgren guns, 14 11-inch smooth-bores and two smaller guns, all protected by a sloped belt of 4½-inch iron. With only a single inefficient horizontal direct-acting steam engine she could not reach even her modest designed speed of 9½ knots; in addition she carried a barque rig to extend her meager endurance. She lived up to her quaint name (based on the nickname of the old wooden frigate *Constitution* in the War of 1812), surviving several bombardments without serious damage, and even a hit from a spar torpedo which blew a 40 foot hole in her side. After all that, her end was ignominious: her wooden hull caught fire and burned while lying in Philadelphia Navy Yard in 1866.

The *Galena* was much smaller, only 738 tons, and was basically a wooden steamer protected by 2½-inch iron plating and railroad iron on a backing of rubber. Unfortunately this novel form of protection did not keep out Confederate artillery shells when she went into action at Drewry's Bluff on 15th May, 1862. She was taken out of commission, stripped of her armor and returned to service as a wooden steamer—a unique reversal of the normal procedure. Being a comparatively small ship she could carry only a light armament, two 6.4-inch Parrott guns and four 9-inch smoothbores.

The third design, far and away the most original, was the brainchild of a Swedish engineer, John Ericsson. He avoided the conventional method of building an armored box around a battery of broadside guns, and conceived the idea of a raft of iron plating surmounted by a rotating armored 'cupola' or turret containing only two heavy guns. The armored raft would present a very small target, and as the low velocity shells of the day tended to skip across the water they were more likely to ricochet off the 1-inch deck than to penetrate it. But above all the armored raft used less weight than a casemate or battery, and so the ships would draw much less water, 10½ feet as against 15 feet by the *New Ironsides*, for example.

As might be expected, the *Monitor* was by no means perfect, and had Ericsson

The 172 foot long US Monitor.

been given a completely free hand by the Federal Navy she would have been a disaster. The original design submitted provided for a 6-inch side armor to the raft, and a 2-inch deck, and when calculations showed that the weight of this would sink the ship it had to be thinned to a 2-3-inch side and a 1-inch deck. When fully loaded her freeboard was only 14 inches, and although the waves constantly washing over the deck damped down the roll, she was in constant danger of being swamped by water coming down through the hatches and the twin funnels. Ventilation was appalling, and even with blowers working and hatches open a temperature of 178° F was recorded in the engine room (a mere 120° F was recorded in the messdecks on the same occasion).

The haste with which the *Monitor* design was accepted was caused by the receipt of disturbing news from the South. On 12 October, two weeks before the laying down of the USS *Monitor*, the Confederate ironclad ram *Manassas* had emerged from the mouth of the Mississippi and inflicted damage on two of the blockading squadron before returning upriver to safety. She had been converted from the small steamer *Enoch Train* and looked for all the world like a submarine surmounted by a tall funnel, having only 2½ feet of freeboard. Little more was heard of her until April the following year, when she was set on fire during the fighting around New Orleans and blew up.

Mallory was convinced that only armored ships could benefit the Confederacy, and his plans received a fillip when in April 1861 the Confederate Army overran the great naval arsenal at Norfolk, Virginia.

Something like panic had ensued and little was done to destroy the guns and ammunition, despite strenuous urging by Gideon Welles. The delighted Confederates discovered that they had acquired a thousand guns and two thousand barrels of gunpowder. But even more important was the discovery that the big dry dock was undamaged and that it could be used to repair the five-year old steam frigate *Merrimack*. She had been set on fire but had burned only to the waterline, and her engines and the major part of the hull were intact.

On 30 May the waterlogged hulk was pumped out and moved into the dry dock. Lieutenant John M Brooke is credited with the suggestion to rebuild her as an ironclad and his ideas were developed by the naval constructor John L Porter into a practicable design for a 'casemate ship' with a battery enclosed by sloping iron. Two 7-inch Brooke guns were positioned forward and aft, with three gunports to provide them with reasonable arcs of fire, and the broadside was made up of two 6.4-inch Brooke guns and six 9-inch smoothbores. The roof of the battery was protected by 20-inch pine logs surmounted by a layer of 4-inch oak planking to support 2-inch iron plates.

Seakeeping received as little attention as it did in the *Monitor*, for the forward and after end of the hull were awash at normal draft. She drew 22 feet of water, far too much for inshore operations, and her single-shaft machinery could only drive her at 5 knots. She was fitted with a giant ram, but was so difficult to maneuver that it is difficult to imagine an occasion on which she could have rammed anything but a stationary target. However, in spite of all these shortcomings she was commissioned on 17 February as the CSS *Virginia* under Captain Franklin S Buchanan. To posterity she would always be known by her original name, however, mainly because Northern newspapers were reluctant to lend any support to such secessionist ideas as renaming US Navy ships.

The role envisaged for the new ironclad was a vital one. The Union forces had already taken the initiative by seizing Port Royal, South Carolina at the end of October 1861, allowing gunboats to command the coastline between Savannah and Charleston. Early in February 1862 they repeated their success by capturing Roanoke Island, north of Hatteras Inlet, an important base for blockade-runners. This *coup de main* isolated Norfolk and tightened the stranglehold of the blockade. Major-General Robert E Lee complained that 'Wherever {the enemy's} fleet can be brought to opposition to his landing can be made except within range of our fixed batteries. We have nothing to oppose its heavy guns, which sweep over the low banks of this country with irresistible force.' The *Virginia/Merrimack*'s task would be to run the gauntlet of the Union artillary on the banks of the James River and then to drive off the blockading ships.

Fortunately for the Union, its industrial resources were equal to the task, and the building of the *Monitor* was remarkably fast. She was started at the Continental Iron Works shipyard at Greenpoint, New York on 25 October, 1861 and launched on 30 January 1862; a day later steam was raised in the boilers and on 19 February she was moved to Brooklyn Navy Yard to receive her armament. On 25 February, only four months after the keel was laid, she was formally commissioned and on 6 March she left for Hampton Roads.

Interior of the turret of the Monitor.

The rest is history, for on 8 March the *Merrimack* appeared in Hampton Roads,

being sighted by the frigate *Cumberland* at about 9 am. Buchanan had aimed to appear the previous day but had been delayed by bad weather. His crew was inexperienced but keen to get to grips with the Union ships, knowing how vulnerable the big wooden frigates would be to shellfire. He had little difficulty in destroying the sailing frigates *Cumberland* and *Congress* and withdrew only when darkness fell. It was a catastrophe for the Northern forces but salvation was at hand, for at 9 o'clock that evening the little *Monitor* dropped anchor in Hampton Roads.

The CSS Virginia *battling the* Monitor.

Next day the *Merrimack* reappeared, ready to finish off the demoralized remnants of the blockading fleet, and at first she hardly deigned to notice the little 'cheesebox on a raft' which moved up to protect the *Minnesota*. The two ironclads traded blows without doing serious damage to one another, for the *Merrimack* had no armor-piercing shot on board and the *Monitor* had most peremptory orders not to exceed 15 pounds of powder for each gun. Even when the *Merrimack* went aground for a short while the *Monitor*'s 11-inch shells could not penetrate the casemate armor, and eventually the *Merrimack* pulled herself clear and turned back to the safety of Norfolk. Her parting shot did the first serious damage to the *Monitor*, for a shell burst outside the pilothouse, blinding Captain Worden. In fact the *Merrimack* had suffered damage herself when her ram bow had been wrenched off during her collision with the *Cumberland* the previous day, and she was leaking.

Each side had plans to turn the tables the following day but nothing further happened. The *Monitor*, the only Union ironclad in existance, was too precious to risk in battle, but as long as she was present the *Merrimack* could not repeat the success of 8 March. Finally the Confederates were forced to abandon Norfolk in May 1862, and their magnificent achievement, the CSS *Virginia* had to be burned because her enormous draft prevented her from being taken upriver to Richmond.

The Battle of Hampton Roads was by no means the turning point in ship design that it is sometimes claimed, for in Britain the decision had already been taken to build turret-armed ironclads but it did confirm publicly that the day of the sailing warship was over, and that the turret-ship was tactically superior to the broadside ironclad. A new class of improved *Monitors* was ordered, the ten *Passaic* class, and shortly afterwards another nine *Canonicus* class of slightly enlarged design. These were all similar to the *Monitor* in layout, with a single turret amidships but they were given proper funnels and pilothouses. Many of the vices of the prototype were eliminated but monitors remained unsuited for anything more than river and coastal operations. The *Monitor* herself foundered in heavy seas off Cape Hatteras in December 1862 and the *Weehawken* was lost from progressive flooding through hatches and the forward hawsepipe.

There was an understandable desire to produce much bigger ironclads and the Union Navy even tried the expedient of converting a sister of the *Merrimack*, the frigate *Roanoke*, to a three-turret monitor in 1862-63. She was a dismal failure, largely because the enormous weight of three twin turrets was too much for her wooden hull and because her 22-foot draft ruled out inshore operations. An attempt to build a large casemate ship, the *Dunderberg*, was also a failure, because too much green timber was used in her hull.

The new monitors would not be ready until the fall of 1862 at the earliest, but in the meantime the Union Navy was winning fresh laurels on the Mississippi. Early attempts to force a way past the forts at the junction of the Ohio and the Mississippi were beaten off, but eventually the ironclad

The CSS Virginia.

gunboats succeeded in getting through, and control of the upper Mississippi passed into Union hands. An attempt by the Confederates' River Defense Fleet to drive off the Union gunboats and mortar schooners on 10 May failed, although one gunboat was rammed and another ran aground. On 6 June the Union warships took their revenge at Memphis, where they totally destroyed the River Defense Fleet and caused the capitulation of the city.

The last major port still in the hands of the Confederacy was now New Orleans, and it was essential that the Union forces regain control of it as it was frequently used by blockade-runners. But the mission was daunting, for New Orleans was well protected by fortifications. Fort St Philip and Fort Jackson commanded the channel through the Mississippi Delta, and both had to be neutralized before the city could be attacked. In charge of the operation was Captain David Farragut, who proposed to use the 13-inch mortars of his bomb-schooners as the spearhead of the attack on the forts. In all there would be 17 ships mounting a total of 154 guns.

Against this force the Confederates mustered the ironclad ram *Manassas* already mentioned, and the new paddle-and-screw ironclad *Louisiana*, armed with 20 guns, and six gunboats. But they were powerless against Farragut's bold attack, and after a brisk gun-duel lasting some two hours, the Union ships broke through. His flagship, the screw sloop *Hartford*, ran aground but managed to refloat herself. In this action the *Manassas* was blown up, and other Confederate warships were sunk. New Orleans fell the next day, and although Forts Jackson and St Philip held out another three days, they had been outflanked and the way to Vicksburg was now open. The *Louisiana* was set on fire and abandoned, and the Confederacy had frittered away more of its scarce resources.

Farragut's attempt to take Vicksburg was foiled by the falling water-level in the river, but he put another rebel ironclad out of action. CSS *Arkansas* got through to besieged Vicksburg in mid-July, greatly heartening the defenders, but when she was used to support an attack on Farragut at Baton Rouge on 24-25 July she was put out of action by Union gunfire, and had to be destroyed by her crew. Although progress was much slower than had been expected, Farragut's ships were wearing down the Confederacy just as the Navy intended. The adroit use of seapower in support of land operations had won important gains, but it was all in vain, because the South was about to win the first part of a series of brilliant land victories which almost wiped out the previous Union successes.

The brilliant leadership of Robert E Lee and 'Stonewall' Jackson exploited muddled Union tactics, and between June and September 1862 Lee and the Army of Northern Virginia carried the war from the gates of its own capital, Richmond, to the gates of the enemy's capital, Washington. The results are described elsewhere in this volume, but the effect on the North's naval strategy was nearly disastrous as the fruits of Hampton Roads and the Mississippi campaign were all lost. Fortunately, sea power is a long-term weapon, and the victories won on the Mississippi ultimately proved their worth. Nor had the Union lost the diplomatic battle, for although the British Government was skeptical about the North's chances of bringing the South to its knees, a policy of neutrality was reaffirmed. Even more important, on 11 November 1862 Britain turned down a French proposal for Britain, France and Russia to negotiate an armistice. This

armistice would have resulted in the blockade being lifted for six months, just what the South would have needed to renew the sinews of war and sell its cotton crop.

British neutrality was absolutely crucial to the North's naval strategy, and President Lincoln wisely restrained his hotheaded subordinates from turning minor irritations into excuses for war. Although to the average Englishman the dashing Confederacy seemed far more romantic than the stolid and apparently incompetent Union, there were deeper forces at work on British official opinion. For one thing, King Cotton was not sufficient to take the British to war, as Britain's cotton mills could import cotton from elsewhere, including the North itself. Another point was that a series of bad harvests in Europe had boosted exports of grain and beef from the Union, but above all Charles F Adams in London and Lord Lyons in Washington were diplomats in the true meaning of the word, who intended to keep their countries at peace. Recognition as an independent nation continued to be denied to the Confederate States, and that left them at a considerable disadvantage under the laws governing blockade. And, inevitably, once the tide of Confederate victories turned, the British had less reason to expect a Union defeat; after the Battle of Antietam there was no more talk in London of mediation.

The struggle to cut the Confederacy in two continued in 1863 as Grant struggled to take Vicksburg, and the gunboats and mortar schooners were fully occupied in the endless attempts to find a way to take the city. When the Union forces finally invested the fortress in May they provided a heavy bombardment and made a material contribution to the surrender on 6 July. It had been an unconventional campaign by any standards, with literally scores of minor actions against enemy sharpshooters, attended by the constant risk of running aground or setting off a mine.

By the beginning of 1863 the first of the new fleet of monitors were ready, and they joined Rear-Admiral Samuel F

DuPont's attack on Charleston. Eight of them, the *Passaic, Weehawken, Catskill, Montauk, Patapsco, Nantucket, Nahant* and *Keokuk* followed the flagship *New Ironside* into the harbor, between Fort Moultrie and Fort Sumter. There were many underwater obstacles and some of the 'infernal machines' or moored mines which the Confederates had developed, and the monitors had very little room to maneuver. The gunfire from the first was more accurate than the Union forces had estimated, and the *Keokuk* was hit no fewer than 90 times. She sank the next day, and as several monitors had been badly knocked about, Du Pont called off the attack. Doubts about the old admiral's pessimism led to his relief on 4 June by Rear Admiral Foote, who had led the first attack on the Mississippi forts with such elán, but Foote died on 26 June, and command passed to the ordnance expert John A Dahlgren.

It was appropriate that Dahlgren should see his magnificent new 15-inch smoothbores in action when the attack re-opened on 10 July, but in spite of carrying on the bombardment sporadically until December and firing about 8000 11-inch and 15-inch shells, the ironclads were unable to subdue Charleston without adequate numbers of troops to support them. The bombardment did, however, settle any lingering doubts about the monitors' ability to take punishment, for apart from the *Keokuk* they sustained nearly 900 hits without suffering serious damage.

The Confederates holding Charleston were not content to sit back and wait for the Union ships to wear them down, and the fertile brains which had devised workable mines or 'moored torpedoes' now turned to building submarines to break the blockade. It was not that the South had a monopoly of genius, for the Union Navy had looked at a submarine called the *Alligator* in June 1862, but it had been rejected because it would take too long to develop and test. For the Confederacy, however, all measures had to be tried, for time was running out, and early in 1863 an engineer named Stoney started work on a 'sub-marine torpedo boat' christened *David* (in the hope that she would slay the Federal Goliath). She was in fact not a real submersible, but rather a steam-driven torpedo boat which could be ballasted down until only the funnel and conning tower were above water. On a dark night she could approach unseen and ram her 14-foot 'spar torpedo', a canister filled with about 11 pounds of gunpowder, against the side of a ship. Clearly this was likely to be a one-way trip but there was no lack of volunteers for the task.

The tedium of blockade duty meant that ships frequently lay at anchor offshore, and the night of 15 October 1863 the first attack by a 'David' was made against the *New Ironsides*, lying off Charleston. The tiny boat rammed her spar torpedo against the ironclad's side and it detonated, but it did not cause sufficient damage to sink the ship. Lieutenant William T Glassell was washed overboard from the 'David's' conning tower and was later rescued, but his tiny command made her escape in the confusion.

Other attacks were made by 'Davids', but without success, but further south at Mobile, Alabama three designers were working on a more sophisticated design of submersible. Known as the *H L Hunley* from her chief sponsor, Horace L Hunley, she was propelled by a crank coupled directly to the propeller, and turned by eight men. She was about twice as long as a 'David' and, unlike them, could submerge fully by flooding ballast tanks. Like the 'Davids' her only means of attack was the spar torpedo, which meant virtually certain destruction for the attacker.

Initial trials proved satisfactory and the tiny submarine was moved to Charleston on 7 August 1863. There she ran into severe problems, and she sank several times. After 13 men had died, including Hunley himself, General Beauregard ordered that she was only to be used semi-submerged on the surface, much like the 'Davids'. On the night of 17 February 1864 she finally slipped out of Charleston, under the command of Lieutenant George E

Dixon, a young Army volunteer, with the intention of attacking one of the block-aders. Her chosen target was the wooden screw sloop *Housatonic*, lying at anchor, and she managed to get close enough to fire a volley of musketry at the *Housatonic* when challenged by lookouts. The sloop was now doomed, and seconds later an enormous explosion blew a hole in her side; she rolled over two minutes later and sank, the first warship in the world sunk by a submarine. The little *Hunley* was swamped by the blast, and years later, when divers examined the wreck of the *Housatonic* they found her tiny assailant a few yards away, with nine skeletons still on board.

The North also turned its attention to submarines but the government-sponsored *Intelligent Whale* was not a success. The conditions of the war at sea gave little opportunity for such methods of attack to the Union forces, and so there was little incentive to pursue such ideas. In contrast the building of monitors and gunboats proceeded rapidly, and by the end of 1863 11 had been commissioned, and a year later another 14 had been delivered. They grew bigger, and after the *Passaic* and *Canonicus* class were ordered, orders were placed for a series of double-turret monitors, the *Onondaga*, and the *Miantonomoh* and *Kalamazoo* classes. Experience on the Western rivers showed that shallow draft was needed, and this led to a series of small monitors, the *Milwaukee* and *Casco* classes, which were only a qualified success.

The USS Monadnock *(1864-1874)*.

On the high seas the Confederate commerce-raiders continued their depredations but the Union Navy tightened its hold on the blockade to such an extent that eventually it captured or sank a total of 295 steamers, 44 large sailing ships and 683 schooners. The freight carried by these ships was worth $24.5 million, and a further $7 million of freight was lost to the Confederacy in wrecks. The strain on the Confederacy's economy grew worse as the months passed, and although there were sufficient weapons and ammunition for the Confederate Army right up to the end, every other commodity, from uniforms down to necessities of life, became unobtainable.

The last significant naval action of the war was the Battle of Mobile in August 1864, when a combined force of 18 warships and 2400 troops attacked the two forts guarding Mobile Bay in order to deny the harbor to blockade-runners. The two opponents were Farragut on the Union side and Buchanan, former captain of the *Merrimack*, on the Confederate side. Buchanan had laid a number of 'moored torpedoes' as well as fixed obstacles in the 500-yard wide channel between Fort Gaines and Fort Morgan. In addition he had the latest ironclad, CSS *Tennessee* protected by a 5-6-inch casemate and armed with two 7-inch and four 6.4-inch Brooke rifled muzzle-loaders. In general conception she differed little from the original *Merrimack*, and like her was slow and clumsy.

Early in the morning of 5th August Farragut's ships steamed in two columns towards the harbor entrance, led by the flagship *Hartford*. At about 6:30 AM. the four monitors opened fire and shortly afterwards the *Tennessee* appeared, heading for the Union squadron with three gunboats in company. The line of monitors altered course and then disaster struck as a mine exploded under the *Tecumseh*. The monitor heeled over rapidly, sinking with the loss of nearly all hands. It was a moment of crisis, but Farragut rose to the occasion with a signal which has become part of naval folklore. 'Damn the torpedoes! Full speed ahead!' Although the rest of the squadron actually heard mines rumbling along their bottom-plating, the gamble paid off, and no more exploded.

The fight which followed was a fierce one, the fiercest of all the Civil War naval

The surrender of the USS Tennessee.

engagements, but in the end the Union squadron wore down their opponents. Even the *Tennessee* was overwhelmed; the 15-inch guns of the monitors were able to inflict so much damage on her that she was finally forced to surrender. It took another 16 days before the forts capitulated, and even then Mobile itself had not fallen, but another bolt-hole for blockade-runners had been closed.

It would taken another nine months before the war ended and much bloody fighting on land, but the US Navy had achieved all that was asked of it. With comparatively primitive resources it had created a revolutionary type of warship and had built up a large and efficient fleet in only four years, come close to achieving miracles, but in the long run the struggle was hopeless. The South could never have been made to surrender by sea power alone, but without it the Northern cause could not have triumphed either.

The attack on the gunboats at Galveston, Texas by the Confederates, 1 January 1863.

IV
BIOGRAPHIES

Abraham Lincoln.

BIOGRAPHIES

ADAMS, Charles Francis
1807-1886

ADAMS SERVED as the United States ambassador to Great Britain throughout the war, and his efforts there have been compared in importance to many military victories. Son and grandson of two former Presidents, Adams had shown some interest in a political career—having even run for Vice President in 1848—but by background and temperament he was never that comfortable with the rough-and-ready ways of the young American democracy. As a moderate Republican opposed to slavery, however, Adams was needed by Lincoln, who put him in exactly the right post (even though Adams did not report being too impressed after their first and only meeting in April 1861). Adams had spent much of his youth in Europe, including two years in an English school, and his more cosmopolitan manner (he was as comfortable speaking French as English) allowed him to get on well with the British leaders. Adams' primary goal was to make sure that England in particular, and Europe in general, did not give formal recognition to the Confederacy and certainly did not provide aid. This was no easy task, as there was considerable support among many British, especially among the influential, for the South's position—not for slavery as such but for the rights of a group of states to conduct their affairs as they saw fit. By his cautious, reasonable and sophisticated diplomacy, Adams managed to get Great Britain to observe the naval blockade that the Union had set up around the Southern ports. Meanwhile, Confederate agents in Britain were buying, building and outfitting ships, and Adams was frustrated in his early efforts to stop this. But by late 1862 he felt confident enough to lay down an ultimatum: either stop providing ships to the Confederacy or the North would engage in open warfare against British interests. The British government thereupon effectively stopped the activities of the Confederate agents. And to the extent that Adams helped to move Britain around to supporting the Union cause, he also helped to keep the rest of Europe in at least a neutral role. After the war ended, Adams stayed on in England till the fall of 1868 and began the negotiations over Britain's reimbursing the US for losses inflicted on Northern commerce by the Confederate ships that had come out of England. Returning to the US, Adams then played a crucial role in the treaty and arbitration that settled these so-called *Alabama* claims.

ASHBY, Turner
1828-1862

ASHBY WAS A CONFEDERATE GENERAL whose death in combat seemed to typify the doomed gallantry of the South's military efforts. He was from an old Virginia family. His grandfather had fought in the Revolution and father had fought in the War of 1812. Turner was opposed to secession in principle, but as a planter and grain dealer, he defended the practice of slavery. He personally organized a troop of mounted volunteers to ride to Harper's Ferry when he heard of John Brown's raid, but he arrived too late to take action. When Virginia seceded, Ashby immediately organized another troop of horsemen that, incorporated into the 7th Virginia Cavalry, he led in the early operations in the Upper Potomac. In the spring of 1862, Ashby helped cover Jackson's retreat to Swift Run Gap, but by late May he was pursuing the retreating federal forces under General Banks. On 27 May Ashby was commissioned a brigadier general, by which time he was commanding a cavalry brigade that was fighting rearguard actions to protect Jackson's army as it retreated from the Shenandoah Valley. On 6 June, Ashby was killed by Federal troops.

BAKER, Edward Dickinson
1811-1861

BAKER WAS ONE OF THE MOST PROMINENT of the early Union casualties in the war. His death seemed all the more heroic because he had refused to exploit his friendship with Lincoln and avoid active duty. As a young lawyer in Springfield, Illinois, Baker had known both Stephen Douglas and Abraham Lincoln. In 1844, Baker bested Lincoln in a contest for the Whig Party's nomination for Representative. Baker moved on to the West coast and was elected Senator from Oregon in 1860, and returning to the East in a time of crisis, he soon found himself becoming one of Lincoln's personal advisors. Baker became a captain and commanded a regiment but was able to retain his Senate seat, and in August 1861 he gained some notoriety by speaking before the Senate while in his uniform. He refused the rank of brigadier general, and while leading his brigade into action at Ball's Bluff on 22 October 1861 he was killed in action.

BARTON, Clara

1821-1912

ONE OF SEVERAL POSITIVE INSTITUTIONS that came out of the Civil War was the American branch of the Red Cross, and this is most directly attributed to Clara Barton. Born in rural Massachusetts, Barton had been a school teacher and then was working as a clerk in the US Patent Office when the war began. She volunteered to help care for the wounded soldiers and soon recognized the need not only for medical nursing but also for supplies and support for morale. Going to Union camps and even to battlefields, Barton became known among the troops as 'the angel of the battlefields'. By 1864 she was officially appointed the 'lady in charge' of the hospitals of the Federal army of the James. Lincoln asked her to lead the search for the many missing Union men, and in 1865 she went to Andersonville, the site of the Confederate prison in Georgia, to identify and mark the graves of the thousands of Union dead. When the war ended, Barton turned to lecturing on her experiences, and finding herself in Europe during the Franco-German war in 1870, she worked at the front with the International Red Cross. Growing out of an organization started in 1863, the Red Cross impressed Clara

Barton as the instrument to achieve her goals, and on returning to the US she worked to establish the American National Red Cross. It was 1881 before she obtained formal recognition from the President and she was to serve as its head until 1904. During these years she was influential in extending the organization's activities beyond the casualties of wars to those suffering in floods, famines, fires and other disasters.

BATES, Edward

1793-1869

BATES WAS THE ATTORNEY GENERAL in Lincoln's cabinet who, as a moderate devoted to the rule of law, found himself at odds with the more radical Republicans. Bates had been raised in the Quaker tradition, and this seems to have influenced many of his later actions. He settled in Missouri and by 1816 he had started his career in law. When he moved into politics, he made his views known gradually in speeches and articles, speaking against any repeal of the Missouri Compromise or the admission of a pro-slavery Kansas. By 1860 he had become a Republican of sufficient reputation that he was a serious challenge to the nomination of Lincoln. His reward for stepping aside was to have a choice of any cabinet position except that of State (which Seward claimed), and Bates chose to be Attorney General. (Bates, however, holds claim to another distinction: the first man from west of the Mississippi to serve in any US cabinet.) Bates soon fell out with Lincoln, not as so many did—over the conduct of the war itself nor over the issue of slavery—but over what Bates saw as the encroachment of the military on the constitutional rights of all citizens. Bates also found that strongwilled and influential cabinet members such as Seward, Stanton and Chase were all too ready to usurp some of his powers. Bates resigned in November 1864 and returned to Missouri, and there he found himself once again in conflict with fellow Republicans, this time the radicals with their strong positions against the

BIOGRAPHIES

South. Bates tried to convince people throughout the North after the war that the radicals' vehemence would backfire, but his health failed and he died just as the radicals were beginning to impose their version of reconstruction.

BEAUREGARD, Pierre Gustave Toulant

1818-1893

ONE OF THE MOST IMPORTANT of the Confederate generals, Beauregard experienced the frustrations that must inevitably bedevil a good soldier in a lost cause. As his name suggests, Beauregard came from a prosperous old Creole family in Louisiana. He graduated from West Point, and after distinguished service in the Mexican War and many years with the Corps of Engineers', Beauregard was appointed Superintendent of West Point in January 1861. Within five days he was removed for saying that he would serve with the South if it seceded. He soon had his chance and was appointed the first brigadier general in the Confederate army (and designed its battle flag). He commanded the Southern troops that took over Fort Sumter and thus became the Confederacy's first hero, and as a commander of the line at the First Bull Run he also gained the Confederacy its first victory on the battlefield. After taking over when General Albert Johnston was killed at Shiloh, Beauregard lost the battle at Corinth; accused of imposing an overly elaborate strategy, he was relieved of his command by Jefferson Davis. Assigned to what was considered a 'safe post' at Charleston, South Carolina, he performed valiantly in holding it against constant Federal attacks. In April 1864 Beauregard again enjoyed a field victory when he helped defeat the Federal troops at Petersburg, but he was then assigned to an essentially administrative post as commander of the Confederate's army of the West. Beauregard's failure to gain more authority was undoubtedly due to his open opposition to Davis's conduct of the war, but he was not alone among the Confederate officers whose careers were marred by intraservice conflicts. After the war, he rejected offers from the Romanians and Egyptians to command their armies. He returned to Louisiana and was active in railroads and public works. Beauregard showed considerable talent as a writer in his work on military theory and his history of the battles of the Civil War.

BENJAMIN, Judah Philip

1811-1884

BENJAMIN, WHO HELD SEVERAL CABINET posts under Jefferson Davis, was one of the more complex and capable figures to emerge in the Confederacy. Born to Jewish parents in the British West Indies, Benjamin was raised in the US Carolinas. As a young man he settled in New Orleans where he became a highly regarded lawyer and a wealthy sugar planter. He was elected to the US senate in 1852 and then in 1858. As the South moved toward secession in December 1860, he gave a stirring defense of its position before the Senate, and then resigned in February 1861 when Louisiana seceded. He was chosen as the first attorney general of the Confederacy but in September he was appointed Secretary of War. Benjamin probably did as well as anyone could at a time when the South had more ambitions than supplies, but after the loss of Roanoke Island with some 2,500 prisoners, Benjamin came under such criticism that Davis transferred him in March 1862 to be Secretary of State. In this post, he took a broader view than many of the other Confederate leaders, even urging Davis to emancipate the slaves so that Britain and France might support the South. Benjamin was disliked and criticized by many Confederate leaders but Davis considered him one of his most respected and loyal friends. Benjamin stayed with Davis until the final collapse, and then made his way via Florida and the West Indies to England. There he made a notable career as a lawyer and an author on legal subjects. He was buried in Paris, where his wife had chosen to live.

BOYD, Belle

1843-1900

ONLY ONE OF SEVERAL WOMEN who worked as spies behind the lines in the war, Belle Boyd was perhaps the most colorful and certainly the most publicized. Born in Virginia, Belle had some education but was only 17 when the war broke out. Her area was soon overrun by Union and Confederate troops in the first Shenandoah Valley campaign. Belle sided with the Confederacy, so she would talk to and observe the Union forces and then pass on information to the Confederate army. She was twice arrested by the Federal troops, but each time was released. After the second time, in the spring of 1864, she sailed to England—allegedly carrying letters from Jefferson Davis to Confederate agents in Europe. A Union officer who had been one of her captors followed her to England and they were married that August. He died in 1866 so Belle took up a career as an actress. Her success in England led her to return to the US in 1867, and she continued to tour until her death. She had earlier (1865) published her own 'true story,' *Belle Boyd In Camp and Prison*, but there is little surviving evidence for some of her tales. For instance, once a Union general occupied her aunt's house and held his war council in the dining room while Belle lay in a closet overhead and listened with her ear to a hole; she then got on a horse and rode 15 miles to pass on the plans to the Confederate troops. She also claimed to have been made a captain and honorary aide-de-camp to General Stonewall Jackson. But allowing for exaggeration, a bad habit that most spies indulge in, Belle Boyd did some spying in the course of her fabulous life.

BRADY, Mathew

1823-1895

BRADY IS THE PHOTOGRAPHER whose pictures of the Civil War have endured to form an indelible image for posterity. With little formal education, Brady began to study painting in New York. There he was intro-duced to Samuel F B Morse, the artist who was also experimenting with the new medium of photography. Brady learned from Morse, and then opened his own portrait studio in New York City in 1842. Soon Brady had more customers than he could handle; he began to win prizes, and by 1850 he was publishing a *Gallery of Illustrious Americans* with great success. By 1860, he had another studio in Washington, DC and among his subjects was the new President, Abraham Lincoln. When war broke out, Brady convinced Lincoln that he could photograph the camps and battles and he was quickly authorized to accompany the Federal troops. He and his assistants spent much of the next four years taking over 3500 photographs of every conceivable subject connected with the war—portraits of military and civilian figures, camp life and many battle scenes. Photographing the battles often involved considerable risk for Brady and his crew, and there were constant problems with the awkward wet-plate process and gear they used. When the war ended, Brady was left with a priceless encyclopedic collection—but his private business had so suffered that he was financially ruined. In 1875 the government purchased a set of 2000 of his photographs, but Brady never regained his former prestige or prosperity. Much of his work had been dispersed among private collectors by the time Brady died, and it was 1954 before the Library of Congress purchased the best of these collections for the nation's archives.

BRAGG, Braxton

1817-1876

BRAGG, ALTHOUGH CONSIDERED ONE OF the leading generals for the South, ended up antagonizing his fellow Confederate leaders almost as often as he defeated the Union forces. A West Point graduate who had fought in the Florida Indian wars and the Mexican War, Bragg had retired to run a sugar plantation in Louisiana. When the war started, he volunteered to serve in the Confederate army and was at once assigned to command the forces in Florida and then transferred to the coastal defenses of the South. In the Confederate victory at Shiloh, Bragg commanded the II Corps, and after the death of General Albert Johnston he was promoted to full general and assigned to command the Army of Tennessee. Bragg planned the Kentucky campaign in the fall of 1862, and after his initial success at Munfordville he suffered defeat at Perryville. In September 1863 he was victorious at Chickamauga in the tactical sense but he failed to follow through and the Confederate forces had about 26 percent of their forces killed or wounded. And in the subsequent Chattanooga campaign, Bragg's inability to take advantage of his superiority led to another costly loss and retreat. The now discredited Bragg was reassigned to Richmond as 'military adviser' to President Davis with whom he was personally friendly. Bragg helped to plan the final defensive strategy of the Confederacy in the East, but by this time it was too late. Bragg withdrew with Davis and was captured with him in Georgia in May 1865. After the war, Bragg worked as a civil engineer and as a railroad executive. Whether Bragg might have been a more successful general with a winning army is questionable, as he seemed unable to deal with either his superiors or subordinates, he was often ill and always irritable and he seemed unable to move decisively and aggressively in the field.

BRECKENRIDGE, John Cabell

1821-1875

BRECKENRIDGE HOLDS THE DISTINCTION of being the Confederate general and statesman who had previously attained the highest office in the federal service—the Vice-Presidency of the United States. From an old Kentucky family (his grandfather had sponsored the Kentucky Resolutions of 1798-79), Breckenridge practiced law and then served as a US Representative. His solid abilities and oratorical skills won him the Vice-Presidency in 1856 on the victorious Democratic ticket with James Buchanan. Personally a moderate, he could do little as Vice-President to avert the imminent crisis, but when the Southern Democrats broke away from the party in 1860, he became their presidential candidate, thus splitting the vote away from Douglas and giving the election to Lincoln. He returned to Washington as a Senator and worked to avert war, but even though he did not defend slavery, he drew the line at interference by the Federal government in the operations of states. He stayed on until September 1861, but then went back to Kentucky where he helped to organize a provisional Confederate government (and so was expelled from the US Senate in December). In November he accepted an appointment as brigadier general in the Confederate army and saw action at Bowling Green, Shiloh, Vicksburg, Baton Rouge, Chickamauga and Missionary Ridge, but when his line broke at the last-named battle, he was removed from command. He participated in one more Confederate victory, at New Market, until in the closing months of the Confederacy he was called to Richmond to serve as the Secretary of War. He fled with Davis, and then, fearing arrest, he escaped to Cuba. He then traveled in Europe and Canada until 1868 when he took advantage of the presidential pardon and returned to Kentucky. He practiced law and worked at developing railroads but was prevented by law from holding any political office. Just as his family was one of many with close relatives on both sides in the conflict, Breckenridge was one of many individuals whose life and loyalty were split by the Civil War.

BROWN, John

1800-1859

OF THE SEVERAL almost mythical figures to emerge from the era of the Civil War, the abolitionist John Brown is certainly among the most controversial. From an old New England family with a tradition of opposing slavery, Brown was writing as early as 1834 of his intention to devote his life to abolish slavery. Although he worked at various jobs —the wool business, surveying, postmaster—this was his real concern. In 1855, he deliberately moved to Kansas with his five sons in order to bring that territory into the Union as a free state. Possessing the physical courage to back up his moral views, he soon emerged as a leader of the anti-slavery settlers, and in 1856 he led an attack that killed five pro-slavery men in retaliation for raids and murders by their side. What distinguished Brown, however, was his insistence that he was acting as an instrument of God. With a national reputation, he then conceived of a plan for establishing a stronghold in the Appalachian Mountains where escaped slaves and freed blacks could take refuge—and then possibly come out to lead an armed uprising throughout the South. It was all rather vague, but Brown did get several of the most reputable abolitionists to endorse his general goals. He rented a farm near Harper's Ferry, Virginia (now West Virginia), and from this base he launched an attack, with 21 men on 16 October, 1859. He seized the town and the US Armory there, but the local militia kept them under seige until a troop of US Marines, led by Robert E Lee, assaulted the engine house where Brown and his followers were making their last stand. Ten of them were killed, and the wounded Brown was captured. Tried and convicted of treason, Brown was hanged in Charlestown on 2 December. But if his raid failed, Brown's eloquent defense during the trial convinced many Northerners that the abolition of slavery was a noble cause that required drastic, possibly violent action. At the same time, Brown's raid convinced the South that Northerners were planning just such action, and so Brown's last prediction that 'much bloodshed' would follow proved to be right. Although his violent tactics were not approved by many (and were discreetly disowned by the prominent abolitionists who had encouraged him), Brown became something of a martyr, and he inspired the words to a marching song, 'John Brown's Body Lies A'mouldering in Its Grave', that

was the unofficial anthem of the Union troops.

BUCHANAN, James
1791-1868

BUCHANAN WAS ONE of many politicians who spent years trying to straddle the issues dividing the North and South, and then had the misfortune to become President of the United States when such an approach was impossible. A lawyer by training, Buchanan had become a Jacksonian Democrat in 1824, by which time he had already made a public statement that would characterize the dilemma he confronted decades later: he denounced slavery as a moral and political evil, but then admitted that if the slaves were to rise up in revolt, he would aid his fellow whites. As a Representative and then a Senator from his native state of Pennsylvania, Buchanan was a solid party man. He served as President Polk's Secretary of State and handled the negotiations over Texas and Oregon that balanced the demands of the pro- and anti-slavery forces. Then, as ambassador to England in 1854, he met with the American ambassadors to Spain and France in Ostend, Belgium where they issued a 'manifesto' claiming that the US had the right to take Cuba from Spain rather than allow it to become 'Africanized'. Such a claim (officially disowned) was recognized by Northerners as an expression of pro-slavery sentiments, but it made Buchanan acceptable to Southerners and he got the Democratic nomination for President in 1856. He ran and won on a platform of non-interference, but during the next years he made it clear that he supported the pro-slavery forces—fully endorsing the Dred Scott Decision, trying to admit Kansas with its pro-slavery Lecompton Constitution—and the Union disintegrated around him. When the Democratic Party split in its conventions of 1860, Buchanan tried to appear to be supporting Douglas but his words and actions actually brought him closer to Breckenridge. And when Lincoln won, Buchanan passed his four months as a truly 'lame duck' President—still claiming to be against secession yet unable to take decisive action against secessionists, wanting to preserve the Union but unable to reinforce Fort Sumter. Finally, in January 1861 he sent a ship to supply the fort, but he was still trying to avoid the hard decisions by advocating a national referendum on whether the President should call out the militia. All this was too little too late, and when he turned over the government to Lincoln in March, war was inevitable. Retiring to his estate in Pennsylvania, Buchanan at least publicly supported Lincoln. And in his favor it may be observed that had he been able to act more decisively, it most certainly would have brought on a war that much sooner, and Buchanan, not Lincoln, would have been the war President.

BUCKNER, Simon Bolivar

1823-1914

A CONFEDERATE GENERAL, Buckner was one of the lucky few for whom the Civil War seemed but an interval in his long life. Kentucky born and a West Point graduate, he had given many years of service to the military and then to his state before the war broke out. Personally opposed to slavery and secession, he worked to keep Kentucky neutral, but when the Federal troops moved in, he offered his services to the Confederacy. By September 1861 he was in command of the Confederate army in Kentucky; by February, having been left to surrender Fort Donelson, he was taken prisoner, not to be exchanged until August. Thereafter he participated in numerous battles—at Munfordville, Perryville, Chickamauga—and by late 1864 he was a corps commander in the Trans-Mississippi Department and saw little more action. After Lee surrendered, Buckner quickly surrendered—he had little liking for Jefferson Davis. Buckner had many years ahead of him, serving for some 20 years as the editor of the Louisville *Courier*, as governor of Kentucky and even running for Vice-President of the USA in 1890 on the ticket of the gold-standard Democrats. Buckner has the unique distinction of being the only man who served as a pallbearer at the funeral of US Grant (an old friend from West Point) and also having a son who became a general in World War II.

BUELL, Don Carlos

1818-1898

BUELL WAS A UNION GENERAL who saw his professional career ruined during the Civil War but more by political than military causes. A West Point graduate, he was serving in the Adjutant General's Department when the war broke out; he was quickly made a brigadier general and helped to organize the Army of the Potomac. By November 1861 he was given command of the Army of Ohio, and he led this in its campaign to free eastern Tennessee from the Confederate forces. In April 1862 he led his units up the Tennessee River on the first day of the Confederate attack on Shiloh, and by ferrying his troops across the river he forced the Confederate troops to retreat. In June 1862, Buell was assigned to lead four divisions to Chattanooga, but he spent so much time repairing the railroad enroute that General Bragg got his Confederate troops there first. In October, Buell led his army to Louisville and then challenged Bragg at Perryville. In the heavy fighting, neither side gained a clear victory, but Bragg managed to get his forces away because Buell failed to pursue them aggressively. The Federal government then removed Buell from command and a military commission was convened to investigate his failure. Buell argued that he had not pursued because he lacked the means to supply his troops—but it was pointed out that Bragg managed to do just that even while retreating. The commission reported the facts in April 1863 without making any recommendation, but Buell was not assigned any further command, so he resigned from the army in June 1864, returned to Kentucky after the war and engaged in mining. Buell has since been considered to have been a victim of politically motivated officials: a non-political man himself, he was a friend of General McClellan and so was perceived to be opposed to Lincoln, for McClellan set himself up as the rallying point for many disaffected Northerners. And if Buell was hardly a military genius, the Union lost a solid general when he was eased out of service.

BURNSIDE, Ambrose Everett

1824-1881

BURNSIDE WAS A UNION GENERAL whose Civil War service took him from the heights of command to a literal trench of disaster. A West Point graduate from Indiana, Burnside invented a breech-loading rifle and left the army in 1853 to try to manufacture it in Rhode Island. The army, however, failed to place orders, and Burnside lost his company to creditors. Meanwhile he had become active in the Rhode Island militia, and when the war broke out he led a regiment to Washington, one of the first volunteer units to rally around the capital. After leading his brigade at the first battle of Bull Run, Burnside took command of a division from New England; setting out on January 1862, Burnside led them through a series of operations that seized numerous Confederate harbor forts, ships and prisoners. Commissioned a major general, his reputation high among both his fellow officers and the public, Burnside was asked by Lincoln to command the Army of the Potomac, but he declined on the grounds that he lacked the experience. After the Antietam campaign, in which Burnside was fairly successful, Lincoln—desperate for good generals—simply assigned him to that command. Burnside still expressed doubts about his abilities, but he worked out a plan to take Richmond, the Confederate capital. There was disagreement with Lincoln and his top commander, General Halleck, and Burnside was delayed in crossing the Rappahannock, so that Lee was able to get his forces (under Jackson and Longstreet) onto the heights of Fredericksburg; when the Federal

troops did come to cross, they were confronted by the well-positioned Confederate force and had to retreat back across the river with terrific casualties. Burnside assumed responsibility and in an extraordinary letter to Lincoln he wrote: 'It is my belief that I ought to retire to private life.' Lincoln kept him on, so Burnside decided in January 1863 to attempt another crossing. When other generals in his command opposed his plan, Burnside wrote an order transferring them and demanded that Lincoln either approve the order or fire him. Lincoln fired Burnside. But in March, Burnside was reassigned to command the Department of Ohio. Discovering that the Union army's operations were being compromised by Confederate sympathizers, he issued a General Order concluding that 'the habit of declaring sympathies for the enemy will no longer be tolerated.' It was this controversial order that led to the arrest of the leading Copperhead, Vallandigham and to Burnside's suppression of the *Chicago Times*, both actions raising protests from Northerners who felt the military were intruding too far into civilians' rights. Burnside took to the field again, and in September 1863, by capturing and holding Knoxville, he aided Grant to win at Chattanooga. By 1864, Burnside was in charge of IX Corps and was assigned a principal role in the assault on Petersburg, an important communications center south of Richmond. A tunnel over 500 feet long was dug underground to the Confederate defenses, and then long underground galleries were filled with powder; when this was ignited by a fuse on 30 July, a tremendous explosion killed many Confederate soldiers. But partly due to Burnside's errors, the subsequent attack by the Federal troops led to their being slaughtered in the crater made by the explosion. Grant later called it 'a stupendous failure', and a court of inquiry found Burnside among those most responsible. He went on leave and never again returned to active duty. After the war, Burnside's reputation recovered sufficiently for him to be elected governor of Rhode Island and then a US Senator. And except for students of the Civil War, he is now best known for having lent his name to the distinctive side whiskers he wore—'burnsides' having been turned into 'sideburns'.

BUTLER, Benjamin Franklin

1818-1893

BUTLER WAS A UNION POLITICIAN and general who frequently confused his two roles, and in so doing became perhaps the most controversial, even scandalous, figure of the era. Settling in Boston he prospered at his law career and in his investments and turned to politics, soon becoming prominent in the Democratic Party. At the Democratic convention in 1860, he opposed Stephen Douglas and then joined the Southern secessionists in nominating Breckenridge. As with so much of what he did, Butler seems to have been motivated more by his own egotism than by any ideology. In any case, when Fort Sumter was fired on, Butler immediately activated his rank as brigadier general in the Massachusetts militia and led his regiment to Washington. After helping to secure the capital, Butler occupied Baltimore and then participated in a series of field operations that were militarily successful and also managed to keep the spotlight on Butler. In May 1862 he commanded the land forces that entered New Orleans and was then appointed the military governor of that exceptional city. He proceeded to run affairs like some independent baron— seizing bullion that Southerners had handed over to the French consul (and thus bringing protests from many foreign governments), hanging a man who had taken down the Union flag. But his most notorious doing was his *Order No. 28*, in which he declared that when any woman of New Orleans showed contempt for Union soldiers, she was to be treated as a common prostitute. This again aroused international protest, and when Butler was also suspected of corruption, he was removed from New Orleans in December 1862. He spent most of the rest of the war in com-

mand positions in Virginia and North Carolina, but saw little more battle action. In November 1864 he was assigned to New York City when it was feared that there might be riots, but nothing actually happened. In December, Butler was given one more command by Grant, to take Fort Fisher and close the port of Wilmington, North Carolina, but the expedition failed and Grant relieved Butler from any further command. But Butler was not removed from controversy. He had by this time joined the Republican Party and was elected to the House of Representatives in 1866. He went with the most radical wing and took one of the leading roles in impeaching Johnson; when Thaddeus Stevens died, he tried to take over his role in advocating a most punitive approach to Reconstruction. With his wealth and confident manner, Butler cut quite a figure in Washington society; in 1873 he bought the famous yacht *America* (and was later charged with using public money to recondition it). He lost his Congressional seat in 1875, but after several attempts he attained his ambition of becoming governor of Massachusetts. Defeated after one term, he ran for President on the National (Greenback) Party but received few votes. Of such an extravagant person little can be said except that he defied ordinary rules and judgments.

CAMERON, Simon

1799-1889

CAMERON, typical of the freewheeling politician of the day, got to be Secretary of War in Lincoln's cabinet, but so mismanaged affairs that in less than a year he was removed. Pennsylvania born, Cameron did not follow the usual route from law to politics but was a printer and editor who, through his political contacts, moved into construction, banking and other commercial enterprises. He became active in Pennsylvania politics in the Democratic Party, becoming Senator in 1845, but when he was shunned by party regulars and lost that seat, he shifted to the Republican Party and regained it in 1857. He went to the Republican convention of 1860 as a favorite-son candidate and his supporters got Lincoln's managers to promise him a cabinet post in return for Pennsylvania delegates' votes. Lincoln then appointed Cameron Secretary of War, but now the wheeling and dealing that had brought him to the top in business and politics became inappropriate. Although Cameron seems not to have sought profit for himself, he staffed the department with personal and political appointments whose mismanagement soon came under attack. Trying to gain support, Cameron openly called for the freeing and arming of slaves, but this ran counter to Lincoln's policy so Cameron was effectively 'kicked upstairs', becoming ambassador to Russia in January 1862. But even though the Senate censured his mismanagement of the War Department, this didn't stop Cameron from returning to the US in 1863 and running for the Senate. He lost that time, but succeeded in 1867, and for the next 10 years he remained the dominant figure in Pennsylvania politics. And when he failed to get President Hayes to appoint his son James to be Secretary of War, Cameron got the Pennsylvania legislature to agree to appoint his son to his Senate seat when he resigned. With no particular talents as an orator or statesman, with no identifiable policies or goals, with no memorable bills or attainments, Cameron survived through his masterful, if blatant, politicking.

CARROLL, Anna Ella

1815-1893

ONE OF THE MORE CURIOUS footnote-characters of the era, Carroll was a publicist at the fringes of Washington politics who achieved both less than she claimed and more than many people realize. From the old and distinguished Carroll family of Maryland, Carroll was extremely close to her father, a political force in Maryland until the rising sentiments of the states – righters pushed his type of Jacksonian Democrat and Nationalist aside. When his

personal finances also collapsed, Anna Ella opened a boarding school to help out, but between 1837 and 1852, little is known of her activities; possibly she felt humiliated by her father's political, financial, and social reverses. But during the 1850s, Carroll emerged as an advocate of the newly formed American, or Know Nothing, Party, lecturing and writing in support of its stand against Catholics and other 'foreign elements' in American society. This led to her traveling from Baltimore along the East coast, and when the war broke out she settled in Washington, where she set herself up as a hostess and spokesperson supporting the Union. She wrote pamphlets in which she argued that secession should be treated as merely a series of individual acts of rebellion, so that states would be taken back once the fighting ended (although she also argued that the federal government had no right to free the slaves). She managed to get the Assistant Secretary of War Thomas Scott to agree to promote her pamphlets, but when she demanded $50,000 for them, Lincoln —whom she personally approached for payment—called her claim 'outrageous' and she settled for $750. Whether her arguments had any influence is doubtful, but the fact is that this was the approach to the seceding states that Lincoln and others advocated. After the war ended, Carroll claimed to have been an adviser to the government on various matters, but her most publicized claim was that she had devised the strategy by which General Grant moved up the Tennessee River to capture Forts Donelson and Henry. In 1870 she petitioned Congress for payment for her contribution to the war, and she continued to resubmit her claim for the next 14 years. Although several important and even informed people supported at least parts of her claim, she never received formal recognition or payment. And although she evidently had been involved in some discussion of this strategy with a river pilot on one of her trips to St Louis and then submitted her proposal, the Tennessee River strategy had been discussed in

BIOGRAPHIES

Washington well before this. But if Carroll were something of a crank, she also could write vividly and cogently about issues that concerned American society.

CHASE, Salmon Portland
1808-1873

CHASE WAS THE SECRETARY of the treasury in Lincoln's cabinet who behaved almost treacherously yet who was appointed Chief Justice by a President who was quite able to outmaneuver such men. A lawyer from Ohio, Chase was originally a Democrat yet he had taken an early and outspoken stand against slavery, not only in public speeches and writing but working as a lawyer to aid fugitive slaves. Going to the Senate in 1849 as a Democrat, his opposition to slavery and to compromise with the South drove him into the new Republican Party. He made a serious bid at the 1860 Republican convention for the presidential nomination, but by then he was so associated with the strong anti-slavery wing that he lost out to the more moderate Lincoln. Chase got himself appointed Secretary of the Treasury in March 1861 and inherited the most difficult task of finding money, not only for the general budget, but also for the increasingly expensive demands of the war. This was at a time, moreover, when there was no income tax and the war was far from popular throughout the North. Chase, with the aid of private financiers, succeeded fairly well, although he finally had to accept 'greenbacks', Federal paper money backed by little more than the government's word. But beyond his formal duties at the Treasury, Chase was a member of that inner circle of Republicans who felt their own power base was stronger than that of Lincoln's, so did not hesitate to oppose him. Chase was a hard-driving, ambitious, self-righteous man who found Lincoln too casual in his general approach to problems and particularly in his actions against slavery. Even the Emancipation Proclamation did not satisfy Chase, and in December 1862 he attempted to lead other radical Republicans in what would have been a

virtual coup against Lincoln. The President defused the crisis by simply inviting Chase and the other schemers to express themselves in a cabinet meeting. But by early 1864 the anti-Lincoln movement had gathered even more steam, and although Chase did not necessarily take the lead, he did nothing to stop the move to replace Lincoln by his candidacy in 1864. This failed, but when Chase offered to resign over another relatively minor issue in the summer of 1864, Lincoln accepted his resignation. Then, in a gesture somewhere between magnanimity and manipulation, Lincoln appointed Chase to be Chief Justice of the Supreme Court after Roger Taney died in October 1864. It was an amazing turnabout, for Taney was a Southerner who had openly supported the South's positions in such decisions as that on Dred Scott, while Chase—however unprincipled in his behavior to Lincoln—was sincerely dedicated to the rights of blacks. As Chief Justice, Chase openly encouraged blacks when he could and supported the Reconstruction Acts as much as possible, but he tried to take a fair and judicial stand. And when President Johnson was impeached, Chase presided over his trial before the Senate in a manner that confounded his radical Republican friends. Accused of being overly supportive of Johnson, Chase insisted that, although he disapproved of impeachment, he had conducted the trial in an impartial spirit. Disowned by the Republicans, he was adopted by the Democrats and his name was even put forward as a possible presidential candidate in 1868. Nothing came of this, so Chase served as Chief Justice till his death. Chase was a sincerely idealistic and religious man, and although often difficult—and hardly admirable in his dealings with Lincoln—it could never be said that he acted out of petty motives.

CHESNUT, Mary Boykin Miller
1823-1886

KNOWN IN HER DAY as the wife of her prominent Confederate husband, Mary

Chesnut is now admired as one of the most insightful witnesses of the Civil War era. Mary's father had risen from a farmer to become governor of South Carolina and a Senator, so she had been given a good education. Undoubtedly influenced by her father's conservative views on states' rights, she could also express sympathy for the lives of black slaves and American Indians. At 17 she married James Chesnut, a lawyer of high social standing and son of one of the great landowners of South Carolina. He served in the Senate from 1859-60, during which year Mary got a glimpse of Washington society, but when South Carolina seceded she and her husband went back to their home state. It was at this time that she began to give more attention to a daily journal she had been keeping for some years. Through her husband's roles in the Confederacy, first as a delegate to the provisional Congress and then as a general, Mary got to know the South's leaders at first hand and was often at the edge of major events in Richmond, where she chose to live and maintain a social life even during the dark days of the war, claiming it was either 'distraction or death'. Although she was hard on the North, she could be equally hard on her South, and she occasionally took issue with slavery. Especially interesting to later generations were her deft portraits of the Confederacy's leaders such as Stonewall Jackson—'a one-idea man {with} no sympathy with human infirmity'—or Varina Davis, wife of the President—'as witty as {Jefferson} is wise'. When the war ended, Mary returned to South Carolina to support her husband in his career, but she also worked on the original manuscript version of her diary, and by 1876 she had revised and copied its 400,000 words. On her death in 1886, it was left to a young friend, and when a first edition was published in 1903 it contained only about one-half the original. Not until 1981 was a fuller and more scholarly edition published, and although it is recognized that Mary Chesnut revised her original words to some extent, her diary is regarded as one of the best sources for the talk, feelings and life of the Confederacy.

COBB, Howell
1815-1868

COBB WAS ONE OF MANY Southern politicians who had personally opposed secession but ended up fighting with the Confederate army. From a wealthy Georgia plantation family, Cobb was a lawyer who became a US Representative and then was elected Speaker of the House in 1849. Buchanan appointed Cobb Secretary of the Treasury in 1857, but Cobb supported the Southern walkout from the 1860 convention and when Lincoln won the election, Cobb resigned from the cabinet in December. Returning to Georgia, Cobb now became a leader in the secession, serving as chairman of the provisional Confederate Congress. In July 1861 he accepted a commission as colonel in the Confederate army and proceeded to perform a variety of military duties, eventually participating in the battles at Shiloh and Antietam. In 1864 he was credited with the Confederate victory at Macon. But as an experienced politician, Cobb spent much of his time working to resolve the many differences among the Confederate leaders themselves, both military and civilian. After the war, Cobb practiced law in Macon and ran his plantation.

COOKE, Jay
1821-1905

COOKE WAS THE PRIVATE FINANCIER who took it upon himself to help the Federal treasury raise the money needed to pay for the war. Ohio born, Cooke eventually settled in Philadelphia; in 1861, after some experience in banking, Cooke formed a partnership of his own, Jay Cooke & Company. Through a brother who knew Salmon P Chase, Lincoln's new Secretary of the Treasury, Cooke made direct contact with Chase, who increasingly turned to Cooke for help as the government's financial problems mounted. At first Cooke gave only advice, but after the Union's loss at the first battle of Bull Run in July 1861, Cooke personally went around to the bankers of Philadelphia and collected $2 million on the security of treasury notes. A few days later, Chase and Cooke went to New York and together they got bankers there to subscribe $50 million for the same bonds. Cooke now turned his Philadelphia office into the chief agency for promoting these bonds, and opened an office in Washington to handle still more government work. By January 1864 Cooke had convinced Americans to subscribe another $500 million in loans. After Chase resigned in June 1864, Cooke continued to serve as 'fiscal agent' for the Treasury Department and succeeded in selling still more government securities than the government itself could. Cooke's reputation obviously gained from such achievements, and after the war he converted his large operation into a general banking house with branches in New York City and London. His next success came in raising millions of dollars to support a railroad from the Great Lakes across the northern route to the Pacific. When his speculations left him overextended, his office in New York closed in September 1873, and the general panic that ensued led to a financial crisis with worldwide repercussions. But the American public remembered his contributions during the war and he was not drummed out of society. He eventually regained much of his wealth.

CUSHING, Caleb

1800-1879

CUSHING WAS AN EXTREMELY intelligent lawyer and politician from Massachusetts whose devotion to preserving the Union led him to support the South's stand on states' rights. Cushing came from an old Massachusetts family and was a precocious youth, being admitted to the bar at 21. When he first ran for the House of Representatives in 1826, he was defeated, mainly due to the opposition of William Lloyd Garrison, the fiery abolitionist. A man of essentially conservative-legal cast, Cushing was strongly opposed to slavery, but at the same time he hated extremists and loved the Union. He resolved the apparent contradictions by adopting the position that the North had no constitutional right to abolish slavery. But there was still time to avoid making a choice, and Cushing managed to get himself elected to the House in 1834. After eight years, his associations with the Democrats led to his defeat. But Cushing was a man of great energy and talent, and he continued in government service—negotiating an important treaty with China, equipping and leading a regiment in the Mexican War, holding state offices, serving as Franklin Pierce's Attorney General. As the years passed, Cushing found himself increasingly aligned with the Southern view of events: in 1858 he introduced Jefferson Davis at a public meeting in Boston, and he denounced John Brown's raid. When the Democrats convened in April 1860, Cushing turned up as chairman, and he sincerely worked for compromise between the North and South. When this failed, Cushing left with the Southerners. So it was that this New England Brahmin ended up presiding over the convention in Baltimore that nominated Breckenridge and essentially prefigured the Civil War. But even though Cushing blamed the secession on the extreme abolitionists, once the war began he sided with the federal Union. By this time, however, Cushing was so compromised that Lincoln turned down his offer to serve in the military. Yet Cushing was such a skilled diplomat and sound lawyer that Lincoln turned to him for advice throughout the war. And before the war had ended, Cushing was among the relatively few who supported Lincoln's emergency measures and he switched to the Republican Party and openly endorsed Lincoln for a second term. After the war, Cushing stayed on in Virginia and served in the administrations of Johnson and Grant. Grant appointed him Chief Justice of the Supreme Court in 1873, but Cushing was too controversial and he finally stepped aside. It was an appropriate conclusion for this man, one of the most versatile and intelligent in public life in this era yet a man who never quite found a proper role for his talents.

CUSTER, George Armstrong
1839-1876

ANOTHER OF THE LEGENDARY FIGURES to emerge from the Civil War, Custer first came to prominence as a dashing young cavalry officer in the war and then entered the history books with his fateful stand at Little Big Horn. A descendant of a Hessian mercenary who had stayed on in the US after fighting for the British in the Revolution, from his boyhood, Custer wanted to be a soldier. He went to West Point, where he showed little patience for coursework or discipline and graduated last in his class of 1861. A few days after graduation, Custer was officer of the guard and failed to stop a fight between two cadets; judged guilty by a court martial, the proceedings were simply set aside and he was ordered to duty, for the war now required every able-bodied officer. Custer fought at the first battle of Bull Run and soon became an aide to General McClellan; when McClellan was pushed out of his top position, Custer temporarily lost favor, too. Soon his abilities as a cavalry officer were recognized, and he fought successfully at Gettysburgh and in the Virginia campaigns. His personal style made him one of the best known Union officers, and his great moment came in April 1865 when he relentlessly pursued Lee's army in its retreat from Richmond. The Confederate truce flag (a towel) was actually brought to Custer, and as indication of his reputation, Grant later presented Custer and his wife the small table on which he had written the terms of surrender. Honorary promotions had brought Custer up to major general, but after the war he went to his real rank of captain. He spent the next decade, mostly based at Fort Riley in Kansas, fighting in the campaigns against the Indians, and it was in one of these that Custer and 265 of his men were killed on 26 June, 1876. With his long hair,

stagey uniform and often bravura manner, Custer was a colorful and controversial figure, but his service in the Civil War was beyond reproach.

DAVIS, Jefferson
1808-1889

DAVIS WAS THE PRESIDENT of the Confederate States, and in his public and private life he seemed to embody many of the elements that both made and unmade the Confederacy. Born in Kentucky, Davis was taken as a child to Mississippi where his father was a modest farmer. Although a Baptist, Davis studied for two years at a Catholic seminary back in Kentucky, and went on to West Point in 1824. (Robert E Lee was at the Academy at this time.) After graduation, Davis served as an officer in remote posts in Wisconsin and Illinois. He saw a little action in the Black Hawk Indian War of 1832 (as did Abraham Lincoln) but had no occasion to become an experienced combat soldier: this became an issue in the Civil War, when he often set himself up as a strategist and tactician against his own generals. The commandant of one of his posts was Colonel Zachary Taylor, whose daughter Sarah Davis married against her father's wishes and only after he resigned from the army. Sarah died within three months of malaria, and for the next decade Davis immersed himself in running a plantation in Mississippi. It was during this period that he came to identify with the whole Southern plantation mentality—the social system it valued (including slaves), the pride in one's State and a feeling that the South must be allowed to choose its own way. Encouraged by an older brother, Joseph, a man of some wealth and influence, Davis was elected to the House of Representatives in 1845. That year, too, he married Varina Howell, a beautiful, vivacious and accomplished daughter of one of the local upperclass families. Davis was in Washington only a few months before he resigned his seat to go fight in the war in Mexico, where he participated in enough combat to confirm his own image of himself as a military man. In 1847 he returned to Washington as a Senator, and during the next three years he gained a minor national reputation by his stands on various issues; in particular, he defended the right to hold slaves and advocated extending at least that right into the new territories. President Franklin Pierce appointed Davis his Secretary of War in 1853, and during his term Davis took an expansionist approach to foreign affairs, one that he saw as consonant with the Southern desire to extend slavery. Davis then returned to the Senate where he became an even more ardent defender of the South's position on slavery. Yet Davis was opposed to secession and continued right through the Democratic conventions of 1860 to urge some type of compromise. With the election of Lincoln, however, and his declaration that he was absolutely opposed to any more slave territories or states, Davis saw no alternative but to go along with his own state and the South, and he formally withdrew from the Senate on 21 January 1861. Not unexpectedly in view of his past, his ambition was to command the armies for the South, but he was soon asked to become the Confederacy's provisional president—mainly because the delegates could not agree on any other candidate—and was inaugurated on 18 February and named regular president the next year. From the outset, Davis confronted a tremendous challenge. For one thing, the Confederate states were not only unprepared for a war, they lacked the resources for largescale military enterprises and the blockade soon cut off prospects of earning money or buying supplies abroad. But aside from lacking material resources, the Confederate states could never agree on how many of their rights they should be expected to give over to their central government in Richmond—for example, the right to conscript troops, the power to tax, the suspension of civil laws. Davis saw himself as leading a truly united South but he was constantly opposed by confirmed states-righters: Davis was in the position of making the same demands as Lincoln, who was meeting similar resistance in the North, but what made Davis's situation so ironic is that he was trying to establish authority over states that had left the Union to avoid that very demand. Davis faced many other problems. One was his own hot temper, and another was his ill health. His wife once referred to him as 'a mere mass of throbbing nerves', and almost everything that transpired during his presidency simply aggravated his personal condition. He was constantly quarreling with most of the other Confederate leaders, military and civilian, and those he chose as his most loyal friends—such as Judah Benjamin—were often unpopular with many Southerners. The notable exception was Robert E Lee, whom Davis trusted thoroughly. But Davis was constantly quarreling with other Confederate generals, in part because of his insistence on telling them how to fight the war. Another of his moves that created opposition was his proposal that the Confederate government purchase 40,000 slaves and put them into the military; when no longer needed, they would be declared free. In other words, Jefferson Davis was proposing to emancipate slaves. It was not out of philanthropy, to be sure; the South was desperately short of men, and Davis also hoped to gain the support of the British and other European nations by such a gesture. But it never got much support from the Confederate leaders, and in any case a few thousand more men could not have turned the war around. In retrospect it seemed that the Confederate cause was doomed from the outset. But even as military resistance was collapsing during the winter of 1864-5, Davis persisted in claiming that he could still set conditions for a peace. As late as February 1865 he was saying in Richmond that 'we may well believe that before another summer solstice falls upon us it will be the enemy who will be asking us for conferences'. By 3 April Davis and his government were fleeing from the capital. Captured by a Federal cavalry unit on 10 May near Irwinville, Georgia, Davis was at first kept in irons at Fort Monroe, Virginia. But he was soon given better treatment and was eventually provided with comfortable quarters that his wife shared with him. In the end, although charged with treason, he was never tried but simply released on bond on 13 May 1867. His home, health, and fortune gone, he spent some time traveling in Europe and eventually regained some equilibrium. He settled with his family at Beauvoir, an estate on the Gulf of Mexico, and there wrote his account of the Confederacy. Davis refused to request a pardon from the Federal government, so he could not take up the seat in the Senate that Mississippi wanted to vote him. It was typical of the honor that his fellow Southerners would extend to Davis, and typical of his own sense of honor that he had to decline it.

DAVIS, Varina Howell
1826-1906

AS WIFE OF JEFFERSON DAVIS, Varina Davis played a crucial role in supporting an often difficult man through the very difficult years of the Civil War. Raised in a Mississippi plantation 'aristocracy' family, Varina Howell spent two years at a girls school in Philadelphia and was a bright, high-spirited young woman when she became the second wife of Jefferson Davis in 1845. During his several posts in Washington— as Senator, Secretary of War and again as Senator—she gained a reputation as one of the capital's more brilliant hostesses, known for her own wit and spirit as well as for the distinguished guests she assembled. When her husband was elected President of the Confederate States, Varina Davis settled in Richmond and assumed the most demanding of roles: playing the 'first lady' of a new nation yet sustaining the leader of a losing cause. She came in for some of the same criticism that attended Mary Todd Lincoln: because of her ancestry—in Varina's case, from the North; in Mary's case, from the South—she was suspected of not being in fully sympathy with her side; and because she was an intelligent, strong-willed person, she was accused of being overly influential in her husband's decisions. In fact, Jefferson Davis was moody,

often ill, and obviously under great strain, and Varina probably kept him functioning. She stayed by his side until they were captured, and she eventually convinced the authorities to let her share his imprisonment with him. Their last years till Jefferson's death in 1889 were spent at Beauvoir, a Mississippi plantation. In 1890 she published her own account of her husband's role in the Confederacy. Then, donating the plantation as a home for Confederate veterans, she moved with a daughter to New York City, where she continued to write for various magazines. At her death she was buried by her husband's side in Richmond after a military rite extended by a grateful South.

DIX, Dorothea Lynde
1802-1887

DIX WAS THE SUPERINTENDENT of Women Nurses for the Union side in the Civil War, but this was but one of a long series of tasks undertaken by one of America's most notable social reformers. Working as a teacher in Boston in 1841, she had occasion to visit a jail and was shocked to see the crude conditions. In particular she was dismayed at the practice of that day of putting insane people alongside the criminals, for both populations suffered from this. She set about inspecting other such institutions in Massachusetts, and in 1843 she submitted an impassioned plea to the state legislature to reform the hospitals for the insane. She then began to travel in various states (she had inherited money) and persuaded them to provide proper facilities for the insane. By drawing on her personal investigations, then appealing to the public through the press and by petitioning Congress, she became recognized throughout the US and even in Europe. Within hours of the firing on Fort Sumter, she volunteered her services to the surgeon general and in June 1861 the Secretary of War appointed her Superintendent of Women Nurses. As the war proceeded, along with getting the work of nursing accomplished under the most difficult conditions, she also had to fight to retain her independent control over the women nurses. After the war, Dix took up her crusade to provide more humane treatment for institutionalized people and extended her efforts to Europe. An independent, reserved, often sick person, Dix worked unceasingly in an area where few of either sex then ventured.

DOUGLAS, Stephen Arnold
1813-1861

THE LIFE OF STEPHEN DOUGLAS was one of frustrating ironies: a major politician from Illinois who happened to be overshadowed by a truly great politician from Illinois, a shaper of presidential affairs who never got to be more than Senator, a definer of the Civil War who died just as it was beginning. Born in Vermont, Douglas moved westward as a young man and settled in Illinois, where by 21 he was licensed to practice law and by 28 he was a judge. Through his talents and energies, he rose in the Democratic Party in his adopted state, and by 1847 he was elected to the US Senate. An expansionist by temperament and thus supporting the acquisition of territories by the Mexican War, he also worked to reach compromises between the North and South. Thus, without defending slavery as such, he asked that the South, and any new territories or states, be allowed to choose to maintain slaves if the white made him popular with the strong Southern wing of his party, and in 1852 he was nominated for presidential candidate. He lost, but he remained in the Senate to play a major role in the disputes that marked the 1850s, constantly trying to keep the issue of slavery from upsetting all other issues. One of his best known attempts to satisfy all sides was his approach to the Kansas-Nebraska Bill of 1854, where Douglas espoused the doctrine of 'popular sovereignty', the concept that the residents of each state or territory should be allowed to vote for or against slavery. But he ended up antagonizing both parties—the newly formed Republicans, because they had organized expressly to protest slavery, and

his fellow Democrats, because they saw no reason to put slavery to the vote over and over again. And when he ran for Senator in 1858 against a little-known fellow Springfield lawyer, Abraham Lincoln, Douglas continued to try to straddle the issue in the famous series of debates. Douglas won the Senate seat but his own prominence and arguments ended up making Lincoln into a national figure. So it was that when Douglas emerged after 58 ballots—and two conventions—as his party's candidate for President in 1860, he found himself again competing against Abraham Lincoln. Douglas campaigned vigorously and sincerely; he was, in fact, the only one of the four major candidates who traveled throughout the nation to appeal to all sides. And he did something even more extraordinary: as he sensed that Lincoln was probably going to win, Douglas actually began to ask the electorate to accept the coming results and work to preserve the Union. After his loss—and it was due more to the split within his own party than to any overwhelming popular support for Lincoln —Douglas continued to work for compromise. At the inauguration, in a gesture of support, Douglas held Lincoln's hat during the address, and Douglas and his wife, who were at the top of Washington society, were among the first to call on the Lincolns. After the firing on Fort Sumter, Douglas went to the White House and publicly endorsed Lincoln's call for volunteers. He then went out to the Northwest Territory to try to rally support for Lincoln, and it was on this trip that he contracted typhoid fever. He died on 3 June 1861, his final words asking his sons to support the Constitution, and the Civil War the 'Little Giant' had tried so hard to avert raged on. An honorable man, Douglas had failed to see that there was no longer any compromising with the force of human history.

DOUGLASS, Frederick
1817-1895

DOUGLASS, THE FORMER SLAVE who became the most famous black American of the era, did not so much contribute to the Civil War as embody its issues in his life and person. He was born about 1817 on a Maryland plantation, the son of a black woman, Harriet Bailey, and an unknown white man. (Douglass later adopted his own surname from the hero of Scott's *Lady of the Lake*.) Reared as a field hand and houseboy, Douglass eventually became literate, thanks to the wife of his master, and as his consciousness and contacts broadened, he became determined to escape. He was successful on his second attempt and made his way to Massachusetts in 1838. He found work as a laborer in New Bedford (where white workers refused to work alongside him), and after giving a spontaneous speech at a meeting of the Anti-Slavery Society he was employed in 1841 by that organization to lecture for the abolitionist cause. Through his lectures and the publication of his autobiography, Douglass became so prominent in the mid-1840s that he feared he would be seized as a fugitive slave, so he went off to England. There he lectured and raised enough money so that on returning to the US in 1847 he could buy his own freedom. He founded an abolitionist newspaper, the *North Star*, and because he came to accept that wiping out slavery was probably going to require resorting to violence, he fell out with one of his early supporters, William Lloyd Garrison, who called Douglass a 'traitor' for deviating from the approach of moral persuasion. Douglass was one of several leading abolitionists who supported John Brown, but he drew the line at accompanying him on his raid. When the war broke out, Douglass was one of many prominent individuals who saw it as pure and simply a crusade to abolish slavery, but he could never persuade Lincoln to define his goals that decisively. Douglass did persuade Lincoln to use blacks as soldiers, however, and personally recruited many. When the war ended, Douglass naturally supported those who wanted to extend the full panoply of civil rights to the blacks, but he himself was not a radical nor did he quarrel with the basic US political or economic system. He accepted several government appointments, including the ambassadorship to Haiti in 1889, and added to his reputation and influence through his autobiographical writings. Douglass was limited by forces beyond his influence, but he served as an inspiration to later generations of blacks, and in his advocacy of passive resistance yet violence in retaliation against violence, Douglass anticipated the modern civil rights movement.

DUPONT, Samuel Francis
1803-1865

ONE OF THE TRUE MAKERS of the American navy, DuPont was a Union admiral who began the war with the greatest acclaim but went on to see his career ruined by one unfortunate naval action. Born into the distinguished French-immigrant family, young Samuel passed up a presidential appointment to West Point to go to sea as a midshipman in 1817. In the ensuing decades, he saw service in various parts of the world, rose in rank and reputation, and in his years at shore duty played a major role in shaping the new navy. He helped to establish the Naval Academy at Annapolis, he revised the rules and regulations of the navy and he encouraged the use of 'the new element', steam. After a tour through the Pacific to China, he returned to be assigned in December 1860 to command the Philadelphia Navy Yard, and this was the post he held when the war broke out. He was recalled to Washington to prepare plans for blockading the South's coast and ports, and in September 1861 he was given command of the South Atlantic blockading squadron, the most crucial command in the navy at that point. By November he had led a successful attack, coordinated with land forces led by General Sherman, that forced the surrender of Port Royal, South Carolina, selected by DuPont as the best home port for his squadron. As the North had become discouraged by its losses in land battles, this success made DuPont a hero, and he

BIOGRAPHIES

continued to seize ships, forts and islands along the South Atlantic coast. After setting up 14 blockading stations, Confederate ships could only elude the Union fleet from one port, Charleston, South Carolina, and after the battle between the ironclads, *Monitor* and *Virginia* (formerly *Merrimac*) in March 1862, it was decided to send a Union fleet, led by an ironclad, to take Charleston. DuPont was assigned to command the action, even though he was less convinced than some that an ironclad ship was so unstoppable. He led his fleet against Fort Sumter and the Confederate ships on 7 April 1863, and met disaster: five ships were put out of action, the Union casualties numbered 50 and his own ironclad flagship sank the next day. It came as a double blow to the North, convinced that DuPont was invincible. Lincoln ordered DuPont to simply hold his fleet off Charleston, and DuPont—sensitive to the implied lack of confidence—replied that he would gladly resign if the government felt there was an officer who could do better. When Washington sent an officer to relieve him in July, DuPont lowered his flag of command, thereby essentially ending his active naval career. By this time, too, DuPont had become involved in a dispute with the Secretary of the Navy over the blame for the Charleston loss. (Later historians would assign blame to both the Navy Department's plan and DuPont's tactics.) DuPont retired to his home in Delaware, and after serving on one more naval board in March 1865, his health failed and he died that year.

EARLY, Jubal Anderson
1816-1894

ONE OF THE MORE AGGRESSIVE of the Confederate generals, Early—'Old Jubal', or 'Jubilee' as he was known—participated in a mixture of victories and defeats but was finally doomed to fighting for a lost cause. Virginia born, a West Point graduate, a veteran of the Florida Indian wars, Early resigned from the army in 1839 to practice law. When Virginia's secession convention met, he opposed leaving the Union, but once it had voted, he volunteered for the Confederate army. He commanded a brigade at their victory at First Bull Run, and then went on to fight in most of the major battles and campaigns: Second Bull Run, Sharpsburg, Fredericksburg, Gettysburg, the Wilderness Campaign. He was wounded at Williamsburg. In the summer of 1864, he was sent to the Shenandoah Valley to divert the Federal force from Lee's army; he won at Lynchburg, moved east and won at Monocacy; then he moved so close to the defenses of Washington in July that he caused panic in the capital. Reinforced Federal troops drove Early back into Virginia, but his raid was one of the last moments of glory for the fading Confederacy. Thereafter, Early was outgeneraled by Sheridan in the Shenandoah Valley, and after his defeat at Waynesboro in March 1865, Lee removed him from command. By this time, the war was almost over, but when the end came, Early was among the few who declined to accept that and surrender. He went to Mexico and then on to Canada, but in 1869 he returned to Virginia and took up the practice of law. He wrote his memoirs and became president of the Southern Historical Society. Everything about Early—his appearance, manner, wit, behavior—tended to put off many of his fellow Southerners as well as his troops, but no one denied he was a loyal and solid soldier.

EDMONDS, Sarah Emma Evelyn
1841-1898

AS MANY AS 400 WOMEN, it has been estimated, may have served in the Union army disguised as men, but Sarah Edmonds was the only one to have achieved the fame that allowed her to enroll as a veteran in the Grand Army of the Republic. Born in New Brunswick, Canada, Edmonds ran away from home as an adolescent girl to escape her 'tyrannical father'. Dressed as a young man, she got a job selling Bibles for a Connecticut firm. When the war broke out, she was in Michigan, and she joined a volunteer company as 'Frank Thompson': no physical examination was required and she was, in any case, experienced in 'passing'. She went to Virginia in June 1861 and participated in several battles, including First Bull Run, as a hospital orderly, mail carrier and aide to a colonel. At least twice she went behind Confederate lines as a spy—once she went 'disguised' as a woman. Meanwhile, some of her comrades had discovered her secret—one even confided it in his diary—and in April 1863 she deserted. She claimed later that it was because an illness would have required her to be examined by a doctor, but other evidence suggests she had fallen in love with a fellow soldier. She went to Oberlin, Ohio and taking up the dress and life of a woman became a nurse in a hospital. There she wrote a fictionalized account of her war experiences, published in 1865 as *Nurse and Spy in the Union Army*, in which she claimed to have been a female nurse. By 1867, she was married, and over the years she confided her secret to only a few people, until in 1882 she decided to apply for a veteran's pension. She got her old army comrades to write affidavits supporting her petition to Congress, which authorized a pension. Eventually she was enrolled in the Grand Army of the Republic and was buried among veterans in a Houston, Texas cemetery.

ELLSWORTH, Elmer Ephraim
1837-1861

ELLSWORTH WAS REGARDED as the first Union hero of the Civil War, his death made all the more poignant because of his friendship with Lincoln. A New York State youth, he lacked the education to get into West Point as he had hoped, so he turned to studying law and ended up practicing in Chicago. Still interested in the military, he took command of a volunteer company and turned them into a drill unit known as the US Zouave Cadets. With their exotic uniforms (based on the original Zouaves, the Moslem units in the French army in

Algeria) and elaborate drill, the company toured widely. In 1860, Ellsworth entered the law office of Abraham Lincoln in Springfield and worked on his presidential campaign. Ellsworth then went to Washington and proposed that he be appointed head of a militia bureau, but when the fighting broke out he went to New York and recruited a volunteer regiment that he uniformed and drilled as he had his earlier Zouave unit. He brought the regiment to Washington, and on 24 May 1861 he was with the Union troops that took Alexandria, Virginia. Seeing a Confederate flag flying over a hotel, he went up to the roof and tore it down; as he descended the stairs, the hotel proprietor shot him. Because of his youth and because he was well known for his Zouave units, his death caused widespread sorrow in the North. His body lay in state in the White House before being taken to his home town for burial, one of the first of many promising young men who would die on both sides.

ERICSSON, John
1803-1889

ERICSSON WAS THE INVENTOR of several of the major advances in nautical engineering, and it was essentially his ship, the *Monitor*, that revolutionized naval warfare. Born in Sweden, where his father was a mine owner and inspector, Ericsson grew up interested in mine machinery, and by the age of 13 he was a cadet in a corps of mechanical engineers working on canals. By 17 he was in the Swedish army, and soon concentrated on improving the steam engine. In 1826 he went to London to continue his own work on inventions or improvements for steam boilers, power transmission and related engineering projects. His most important work was the development of the screw propeller for steam vessels; coupled with the placement of the engine below the water line, this not only produced a more efficient and powerful power system (compared to the paddle wheel then in use) but also meant that the engines could be protected against shellfire. Approached as early as 1837 by representatives of the US Navy, Ericsson came to the US in 1839 and worked to introduce the propeller on American ships. The first steam frigate of the US Navy was his design, the USS *Princeton* of 1844, but at its trials one of its large guns exploded and killed several people, including the Secretaries of the Navy and State. Even though it was not Ericsson's fault, this disaster so tarnished his name and work that he found it hard to get support. Then, early in 1861, the Federal side learned of the Confederacy's intention of converting the *Merrimack* to an ironclad. Ericsson proposed that the Union construct an ironclad of his design; the keel was laid in October 1861, and the *Monitor* was launched in January 1862—only 100 working days thanks to Ericsson's sound design. The showdown between the *Monitor* and the *Merrimac* (renamed the *Virginia*) on 9 March ended in a draw but it was nevertheless a turning point in naval warfare and in the Civil War. The North saw it as a much-needed victory, and Ericsson was accorded many honors including the formal thanks of Congress. With his reputation restored, he set about building a fleet of *Monitor*-type ships that greatly aided the Union. After the war, Ericsson got other nations to order ships from him (although many just copied his design) and continued working on torpedoes, naval ordnance, and other problems in engineering and science, including solar energy. A wealthy man, he cared little for anything except his work, and even there he cared little for the practical results once his designs had taken form. Ericsson's remains were returned to Sweden in 1890, and he has been internationally recognized as having provided the frame for all modern ships.

EVERETT, Edward

1794-1865

EVERETT WAS AN EXTRAORDINARY FIGURE in his day, a minister, orator and politician, but he would go down in history for a forgotten speech: it was Everett who gave the other address at Gettysburg. Everett had succeeded at everything he undertook—as a brilliant college student, as a Unitarian minister, as a Harvard professor and as a public orator. In 1824 he was elected to the US House of Representatives, where during ten years he took a generally restrained position on slavery. He then served in a variety of positions—governor of Massachusetts, ambassador to England, president of Harvard, Secretary of State—before being elected to the US Senate in 1853. In the debate over the Kansas-Nebraska issue, Everett seemed less than committed to the anti-slavery cause, so after 15 months he resigned his Senate seat when he came to feel that he no longer represented his constituency. But Everett accepted that his real problem was his willingness to compromise in the interest of preserving the Union at a time when the nation had moved too far to compromise. He continued to participate in public affairs, and in 1860 he accepted the nomination for Vice-President on the Constitutional-Union Party, formed to rally all moderate pro-union forces by softening the issue of slavery, but he and the presidential candidate, John Bell, were totally rejected. When the war broke out, Everett—now 67—threw his support behind the federal government and traveled all over the North, lecturing to rally people behind the war. On 19 November 1863 he gave the long oration at the dedication of a national cemetery at Gettysburg, after which Lincoln gave his brief address. By this time, Everett had adopted a strong position against slavery, and he urged the reelection of Lincoln in 1864. But he could not forget his old ideals, and his last public speech was one which urged, now that the war was ending, that Southerners be treated with generosity and compassion.

FARRAGUT, David

1801-1870

PERHAPS THE BEST KNOWN naval figure from the Civil War, Farragut was one of the relatively few military men who emerged with their professional and personal reputations greatly enlarged. Farragut came from one naval family and was essentially adopted by another American naval hero, David Porter. (Farragut even changed his given name to honor Porter.) As a youth, Farragut sailed under Porter, who in the War of 1812 made the 12-year-old Farragut 'master' of a seized ship; in a fierce battle that followed, Farragut was taken prisoner, but was eventually released. In the decades that Farragut spent in the US Navy, a generally unexciting period, he saw some action against pirates in the Caribbean, but arrived off Mexico too late to participate in the war there. In the winter of 1860-61, Farragut was at the Norfolk Navy Yard; he had been in the navy almost 50 years, but despite this he did not have that high a reputation among his fellow officers, for he was something of an independent, undiplomatic type. When Virginia seceded in April 1861, Farragut simply left and went to New York to await his orders; when they came in September 1861, it was to serve on a naval board in selecting officers for retirement. Meanwhile, the Federal government had decided that New Orleans had to be taken so as to have clear passage up and down the Mississippi. In January 1862 Farragut—now 60 years old—got himself appointed to command the squadron assigned to 'reduce the defenses which guard the approaches to New Orleans, when you will appear off that city and take possession of it under the guns of your squadron'. It was easy enough to write such a plan in Washington, another thing to carry it through. Farragut sailed from Hampton Roads on 2 February, and after assembling his fleet off the mouth of the Mississippi, he began the attack in April. Failing to silence the guns of the two forts guarding the approaches, he defied his orders and had his fleet make a run past their guns. He lost three ships and came close to disaster, but he then proceeded to defeat the Confederate fleet guarding New Orleans and took that now defenseless city. Farragut suddenly emerged from obscurity to become the most admired officer in the US Navy; Lincoln approved a Congressional resolution giving thanks to Farragut and his men, and he was promoted to rear admiral. His next mission, an attempt against Vicksburg up the river, failed, and he suffered some losses in assisting the blockade around New Orleans, but after helping to take Port Hudson, a strong point guarding the Mississippi, he sailed to New York and more acclaim. Finally, in January 1864, he got the assignment he had been waiting for: to capture the Confederate defenses around Mobile Bay. On 5 August, Farragut began the assault against the two defending forts with his four ironclads and 14 wooden ships. When one of his ships, The *Tecumseh*, hit by a moored mine and sank, his fleet became confused and hesitated. 'Torpedoes ahead!' Farragut was warned; Farragut was high up on the main rigging of his flagship and called out, 'Damn the torpedoes!' His fleet got by the forts, dispersed the Confederate ships, and took the bay. The North became ecstatic. A new rank of vice admiral was created for Farragut; wealthy citizens of New York City gave him a purse of $50,000. His health failing somewhat, Farragut drew one more assignment, on the James River, but it was not that serious. After the war, Farragut made a goodwill tour to Europe where he was received with great admiration. It was while visiting the Portsmouth Navy Yard, in New Hampshire, that Farragut had a heart attack and died. President Grant himself came to New York for the funeral procession. Farragut's success came from his aggressive approach to any engagement: he accepted that there would be losses, but refused to consider the possibility of defeat. His basic strategy and tactic was expressed in the order he gave to his officers before the assault on Port Hudson: 'The best protection against the enemy's fire is well-directed fire from our own guns.'

FLOYD, *John Buchanan*

1806-1863

FLOYD WAS A VIRGINIAN whose reputation

suffered from two instances of leaving his post—first, a President's cabinet, and then a Confederate fort. A lawyer by profession, Floyd served in the Virginia legislature before three terms (1849-52) as his state's governor. As a States' Rights Democrat, he was appointed Secretary of War by newly elected President James Buchanan in 1857, and he was among those who supported Buchanan in his dilatory tactics in dealing with the emerging crisis in the Union. After the election of Lincoln left many Southerners convinced that secession was inevitable, Floyd resigned from the cabinet in December 1860. But there were solid grounds for believing that he would have had to resign under any circumstances, as he was implicated in a scandal involving the sale of Indian lands and he appeared to have transferred federal armaments to arsenals in the South when he realized they were going to be taken over by Southerners. Floyd then accepted a commission as brigadier general in the Confederate army, and he saw action in western Virginia. He was then assigned to command Fort Donelson in Tennessee, but under seige and attack from Grant's forces, Floyd left another officer in charge and escaped with about 3,000 of his troops before the fort surrendered. Floyd's excuse was that as a former Federal official he might have been executed as a traitor, but President Davis removed him from his high command. His own Virginia assembly, however, voted to make him a major general—typical of the internal divisiveness within the Confederacy. Floyd died in 1863.

FOOTE, Andrew Hull
1806-1863

FOOTE, ONE OF THE SUCCESSFUL Union admirals, was distinguished by the religious zeal he brought to the pursuit of his enemies, whether liquor, slave traders or the Confederate forces. After his appointment as a midshipman in 1822, Foote had a long career in the US Navy, one that took him literally around the world on various assignments. From his early years in command, his strong religious bent showed when he formed a temperance society on his ship and eliminated the daily grog ration—an old tradition in navies. (By 1862, due primarily to Foote's persistence, the liquor ration was eliminated on all US Navy ships.) During his service off the African coast in 1849-51, Foote applied the same idealistic zeal to pursue the slave traders, and on returning to the US his speeches and writings helped to arouse Americans against this traffic. When the war started, Foote was in charge of the Brooklyn Navy Yard, but he was given command of the naval operations on the upper Mississippi. In February 1862 he led his flotilla in bold attacks to support the capture of Forts Henry and Donelson; wounded in the latter action, he was on crutches when he led another successful assault on another Confederate fort on the Mississippi, Island No 10, a month later. When his wound didn't heal, he was given shore duty as chief of the bureau of equipment and recruiting. A year later, anxious to get back to sea duty, he persuaded his old school friend, Secretary of the Navy Welles, to give him command of the squadron off Charleston, but he died on 26 June 1863 before he could take over. Foote was not regarded as an especially brilliant officer, but he was conceded to be a hard worker with impeccable standards. He was best characterized by a sermon he himself preached after his victory at Fort Henry, when he chose as his text, 'Ye believe in God; believe also in me'.

FORREST, Nathan Bedford
1821-1877

REGARDED AS ONE OF THE MOST brilliant generals on either side, Forrest had a storybook life that took him from the lowest level of society to the heights of Confederate leadership. With little formal education, and having to assume responsibility to his family while still in his teens when his father died, Forrest worked as a blacksmith and farmer in Mississippi. As he prospered, he became a planter and dealt in horses and slaves, and in 1851 he moved to Memphis, Tennessee and entered the real estate business. When the war broke out, he soon had recruited and equipped a cavalry battalion at his own expense. In February 1862 Forrest was with the forces under siege at Fort Donelson, and when it was decided to surrender to the force under Grant, Forest led his cavalry and some infantrymen out through Union lines. He went on to participate in several battles as a cavalry commander, but was most famous for his dashing raids in Tennessee during July 1862 and in December 1862-January 1863, when he destroyed bridges and railroads, captured many prisoners and stores and generally disrupted the federal forces and plans. He had been seriously wounded at Shiloh in April 1862, and in June 1863 he was shot by a disgruntled subordinate—whom he promptly killed. After the Chickamauga campaign in August-September 1863, Forrest quarreled with his superior, General Bragg, but President Davis resolved the dispute by promoting Forrest to major general and assigning him an independent command in northern Mississippi and western Tennessee. In April 1864 Forrest was involved in the most controversial action in his career. He was in charge of the Confederate troops that had surrounded Fort Pillow, Tennessee, and the Federal commander had refused Forrest's request to surrender. Forrest's troops then moved into the fort with little resistance–losing only 14 dead and 86 wounded. But the Federal casualties were 231 killed and 100 seriously wounded—and most of the dead were blacks. The North charged that Forrest had allowed his men to kill the Federal troops as they were surrendering, while Southerners contended that the losses were incurred because they refused to surrender. (Although not all historians agree, the more scholarly studies conclude that it was a massacre.) Forrest went on to one of his major victories, at Brice's Cross Roads in Mississippi, where, against a force over twice the size of his troops, he

drove the Federal troops into a confused retreat and captured large amounts of their equipment. Forrest's last action came at Selma, Alabama where he was defeated in April 1865, but by then the war was virtually lost anyway, and he surrendered in May. His personal fortune gone, he took up a plantation in Tennessee and in the 1870s went to work as a railroad executive. He became involved in another controversy when he accepted the title of Grand Wizard of the newly organized Ku Klux Klan in May 1867; in January 1869 he resigned and disbanded the organization because he realized it was engaged in activities he did not approve of (and he would always insist that he had in fact never really joined the KKK). Undeniably a dynamic personality and aggressive leader, Forrest characterized himself by saying that success came from 'getting there fustest with the mostest'.

FRÉMONT, *John Charles*
1813-1890

FRÉMONT WAS AN EXTRAORDINARY PERSON for any era, but his service as a Union general was only one episode—and an unsettling one at that—in his own personal epic. Son of a French immigrant who had run off with an American woman, Frémont was born in Georgia and became an officer in the US Topographical Corps. This launched a career that saw him conducting several major surveys of the great unknown territories in the West, revealing to Americans the geographic features and potential resources of the Rockies, the Oregon Trail, California and other regions. Frémont was given to making daring, even foolhardy, expeditions, and the vivid reports he would then write helped to make him something of a national hero. By revealing the possibilities for routes, settlements, railroads, forts, farms, mines and such, Frémont also appealed to the expansionist spirit of the 1830s and 1840s, and Frémont was personally committed to the idea of 'manifest destiny', the sense that North American settlers had a right to all these lands. Thus, when Frémont found himself in California in the 1840s, he openly encouraged the Americans there to provoke a war with Mexico; and when war broke out, Frémont rushed about, essentially taking California away from Mexico. Then, in a quarrel with General Kearney over their authority, Frémont was courtmartialed in 1847-78 and found guilty of mutiny. President Polk remitted the penalty, but Frémont resigned from the army and led a disastrous expedition of his own to California (losing 11 men in its winter passage). Property that Frémont had earlier acquired in California turned out to have gold, and Frémont soon became rich. He served for a year as a Senator from California and then in 1856 was given the new Republican Party's first nomination for the presidency. Frémont showed no talent for politics, however (and the Democrats made much of the fact that he was illegitimate while falsely claiming he was Catholic), and he lost to Buchanan. Frémont returned to California to look after his mining interests, and when thhe war began he was in Europe raising money for his ventures. He rushed to England and all on his own purchased arms for the Union, then returned to the US; he was made a major general in charge of the Department of the West annd took up his post in St Louis in July 1861. Frémont quickly organized the Union's forces and positions, yet was unfairly blamed for some of the early defeats in his department. In August 1861 he issued a proclamation declaring the property of disloyal Missourians confiscated and their slaves emancipated. Lincoln forced this to be modified and removed Frémont from command, but the radical antislavery Republicans in Congress in turn got Lincoln indirectly censured, and forced him to give Frémont a new command, that of the mountainous region of western Virginia. But lacking sufficient troops and real support from Washington, Frémont was defeated by Stonewall Jackson; when Frémont was then placed under the command of an old adversary, General Pope, he refused to serve and so was re-

lieved in June 1862. By this time, Frémont had become something of a rallying figure for the radical Republicans who supported him against Lincoln in the summer of 1864, but Frémont had the good sense to withdraw that September. He returned to California to try to rescue his failing property, but losing this he got involved in railroads; his reputation was tarnished when in 1873 he was found guilty of swindles, and he declared bankruptcy. It was a sad climax to a once glorious career, and its anticlimax came in 1890 when, feeling sorry for the poor old man, the army restored him to the rank of major general—but Frémont died before he could enjoy the pension.

GARFIELD, James
1831-1881

GARFIELD WAS ONE OF SEVERAL Union generals who went on to become President of the United States. He was also the last of the American Presidents to have been raised in a log cabin. Growing up in some hardship, Garfield worked his way through college, became the principal of an institute in Ohio, and was elected in 1859 to his state senate. When the war broke out, Garfield used his position in the community and his oratorical skills to encourage enlistments and support for the Union cause. By the summer of 1861 he had organized a regiment of volunteers (many of them his own students)—trained literally 'by the book', since Garfield had no military experience. Soon after his regiment was assigned to the command of General Buell in Kentucky, Garfield was ordered to lead a brigade against a Confederate force commanded by an experienced West Point officer. Garfield won his first battle, at Middle Creek, in January 1862, and was promoted to brigadier general. In April he fought at Shiloh, but when his health failed he was assigned to Washington. Early in 1863 he was back in the field, and as chief of staff to General Rosecrans, Garfield emerged from the Chickamauga campaign in September 1863 with a solid reputation for both his strategic sense and personal courage. Garfield then resigned in December to take a seat in the House of Representatives (and it was rumored that Lincoln gladly accepted his resignation because it was easier to find major generals than supportive Republicans). Garfield was elected to Congress for eight more terms, and although he identified with the antislavery wing of the Republicans, he was basically a hardworking, intelligent parliamentarian who served as a moderating influence. He went to the Republican convention in 1880 as manager of a fellow Ohioan's candidacy, but in the ensuing stalemate Garfield was nominated for President. Taking office in March 1881, he was shot that July by Charles Guiteau, a disappointed office-seeker, and died in September.

GARRISON, William Lloyd
1805-1879

ONE OF THE MOST RADICAL of the abolitionists who helped to force the nation toward war, Garrison himself took an apparently contradictory position on the Civil War—welcoming the secession of the South and warning against the use of military force to effect emancipation. Yet no one who knew Garrison well would be surprised at anything he said or did. From Massachusetts, with little formal education, he began as a printer and moved up to becoming a newspaper editor. As early as 1829 he had published a book in which he advocated emancipating all slaves, and in 1831 he started his own newspaper, *The Liberator*, vowing to continue it until this was accomplished. Garrison used his paper to advance his attacks on slavery and his uncompromising views and manner often led him to fall out with even his fellow abolitionists—particularly over his somewhat idiosyncratic argument that moral persuasion, not the political vote or military force, was the way to eliminate slavery. Garrison was a leader in founding the American Anti-Slavery Society in 1832, and as a delegate in 1840 to the international anti-slavery convention in

London, he refused to take his seat when the women delegates from the US were refused their seats. Garrison never shirked extreme gestures, but his high point came on the Fourth of July in 1854 when he publicly burned a copy of the US constitution, denouncing it as 'an agreement with Hell'. Despite his initial opposition to the war, Garrison eventually came to accept the significance of Lincoln's Emancipation Proclamation, and in 1863 he actually worked to reconcile the differing abolitionists at a meeting of the Anti-Slavery Society. In April 1865 Garrison attended the official ceremony raising the Union flag over Fort Sumter; defiant as ever, he declared that slavery 'is not only a crime but the sum of all criminality'. The previous January, Garrison had proposed dissolving the Anti-Slavery Society on the grounds that its main goal was achieved; he was rejected, but he ceased publication of his paper at the end of the year once the Thirteenth Amendment was ratified. He continued to crusade for various causes— against alcohol and prostitution, for the rights of women and Indians—and was given honors and gifts of money by his admirers. Never much of an administrator, always a difficult person, he may not have done anything very tangible or practical to aid the blacks, but Garrison had the courage to take up the torch for a cause when few others dared to.

GOLDSBOROUGH, Louis Malesherbes
1805-1877

GOLDSBOROUGH WAS A HIGHLY professional and successful Union naval officer who retired from active sea duty in the early stages of the war because he felt he lacked proper support. Son of a chief clerk in the Navy Department, Goldsborough went to sea as a midshipman in 1816. He saw varied service, rose in rank, and after a period as a civilian, returned to the navy, saw action in the Mexican War and served as superintendent of the Naval Academy from 1853-7. He was commanding a squadron off Brazil when the war broke out, and it was October 1861 before he was to enter action as the commander of the North Atlantic Blockading Squadron. It was this fleet that, coordinated with the land forces of General Burnside, attacked the coast of North Carolina, captured Roanoke Island and destroyed many Confederate ships, and Congress gave Goldsborough a vote of thanks for this important victory. He then went on to the James River, where he commanded a flotilla and kept close watch on the Confederate ironclad, the *Virginia* (formerly the *Merrimack*); when the Confederates had to destroy it (because it could not move up the river), Goldsborough advanced his flotilla in an effort to take Richmond. His efforts failed, and Goldsborough became convinced that only land forces could take that city, but he found himself being criticized by his fellow navy officers as well as by the press. Evidently not as thick-skinned as many in the military, who spent much of the war under attack from their own side, Goldsborough asked to be relieved of command in September 1862. He spent most of the rest of the war at administrative duties in Washington, until in 1865 he took command of a squadron assigned to hunt down the last of the Confederate raiders. Goldsborough retired from the navy in 1873.

GRANT, Ulysses Simpson

1822-1885

GRANT BECAME THE COMMANDER of the Union Army and went on to become the President of the United States, but behind that public success was a man for whom the Civil War proved to be the only truly satisfying experience in his life. Born in Ohio to a restrained, religious woman and a father who achieved some success with a leather tannery, Grant went to school until he was 17, but he also worked hard on his family farm. Appointed to West Point, he arrived there to discover that he was incorrectly listed as Ulysses Simpson, whereas his baptismal name was Hiram Ulysses, so he

accepted this new name for the rest of his life. Grant had an undistinguished record at West Point, although he excelled at horse riding, and on graduation in 1843 he was assigned to the infantry (the best students going to the engineers). After service in the South, he went off to the war in Mexico and fought in most of the major battles under General Zachary Taylor. (Later Grant must have reflected over how this unsophisticated professional soldier became President.) Despite some honors in the war, Grant remained unenthusiastic about a military career as he was assigned to posts, first in Mississippi and then to a lonely outpost on the Pacific coast; this latter assignment appears to have led to his drinking heavily, and on being reprimanded by his commanding officer, he resigned from the army in 1854. Unemployed and with little money, married and with one child, he settled in St Louis, and during the next six years he took up and failed at various careers—farming, real estate, custom house clerk—until in 1860 his two brothers took him on as a clerk in their leather store in Galena, Illinois. That was Grant's frustrating life up to the firing on Fort Sumter. He quickly answered Lincoln's call for volunteers, but had trouble getting anyone with authority to assign him a true command. But in June 1861 he was made colonel of a regiment of Illinois volunteers; by September he was promoted to brigadier general and assigned to command a district with headquarters in Cairo, Illinois. Grant's first action came that November, when he led an attack on a Confederate camp at Belmont, Kentucky; it almost ended in disaster when his troops broke ranks to loot the camp and the Confederates regrouped, but Grant got his men back to their boats. In February 1862 Grant led a daring and successful campaign against the crucial Forts Henry and Donelson in western Tennessee; it was during his masterful assault on the latter that he issued his famous ultimatum: 'No terms except an unconditional and immediate surrender can be accepted'. The whole North celebrated one of its first major victories and Lincoln promoted Grant to major general. Grant then fought in the Shiloh campaign in April, and although he was not really responsible for the Federal strategy and the Union troops did force the Confederates to retreat, Grant had in fact been caught off guard and only avoided disaster through sheer numerical superiority. The Union took such heavy casualties that Grant was greatly criticized, but Lincoln stood by him: 'I can't spare this man—he fights'. And Grant redeemed himself, both as a strategist and tactician, with his daring assault and capture of Vicksburg in July 1863, which led to the opening of the Mississippi to all Federal traffic and dividing the Confederacy in two. Grant's public reputation was high once more, and after his success in November in driving the Confederate forces off Missionary Ridge and Lookout Mountain outside Chattanooga, Grant was a national hero. Congress voted official thanks and a gold medal and he was promoted to lieutenant general. More important, Lincoln sent for him, and finding Grant was a man he could work with, he made him General in Chief of the Armies of the United States.

In addition to getting a fighting soldier, the Union Army for the first time had a man with a unified and coordinated plan for all its forces. His basic strategy was to make three simultaneous movements against the Confederate's major elements: Meade would take the Army of the Potomac against Lee, Butler would lead the Army of the James against Lee's support and Richmond and Sherman would take the Army of the Tennessee against General Johnston's force and to Atlanta. It was 4 May 1864 before the three armies moved to carry out Grant's plan. The Civil War had been underway for over three years. Unlike most commanders in his position, Grant chose not to stay in the comparative security and comfort of the capital but went off into the field with the Army of the Potomac. The fact was that Grant was never more comfortable than running operations from the field and

among his fellow soldiers. He maintained communications with the other two major armies and personally directed many of the actions of the Army of the Potomac. Nor were they all that successful. Spotsylvania, Cold Harbor, the whole Wilderness Campaign had taken a fearful toll on the Union forces; the siege of Petersburg that dragged on from June 1864 to April 1865 succeeded less through any superior plan of Grant's and more because the Confederates simply ran out of supplies. And Grant's famous line, 'I propose to fight it out on this line if it takes all summer', lost its aura of grand heroism when it turned out that Grant's determination resulted in simply calling up more and more troops to replace the thousands of casualties. But his overall strategy finally succeeded, and when Grant accepted the surrender of Lee at Appomattox Court House on 9 April 1865, he showed he could be sensitive and generous to a defeated enemy. With the end of the war, Grant's reputation was at its zenith. In 1866 Congress voted to reactivate the rank of full general—last held by George Washington—but even this honor was partly contaminated by those radical Republicans determined to overrule President Johnson. Grant personally felt that the South was ready for a more moderate policy of reconciliation, but as commander of the army he had to enforce the more punitive Reconstruction Acts. And when Grant fell out with Johnson, he inevitably became the candidate of the Republicans in 1868, and just as inevitably swept the election. Never having shown much interest in politics, and with the military man's traditional distrust of politicians, Grant ended up finding his eight years in the White House spoiled by just that— politics and politicians. The scandals never touched Grant personally in the sense that he profited from or condoned them, but he was held responsible for allowing his administration to get out of control. And after a triumphal world tour and many public honors, Grant saw his years in retirement turn as frustrating and financially ruinous as his years before the war. Clearly Grant had never been better employed than when he was in the field, on his horse or in his tent, leading his troops.

GREELEY, Horace

1811-1872

GREELEY WAS THE NOTED EDITOR, abolitionist, and politician, one of several extraordinary 19th-century Americans for whom the Civil War seemed but a way-station in their personal odysseys. Greeley was born in New Hampshire and raised on a farm (and to the end of his life he never quite lost the appearance and manner of a hayseed). Although he read widely on his own, his formal schooling stopped at 14, when he went to work for a Vermont newspaper. Starting as a typesetter, he worked up to become a printer and then a journalist; by 1841 he founded a newspaper in New York City, the *Tribune*, that within five years was considered one of the best in the US. In its combination of stimulating ideas and balanced opinion, Greeley's paper set a new standard in American journalism, and it soon became a major influence in shaping public opinion. And Greeley did not hesitate to expound his own quite progressive views in his paper—particularly his opposition to slavery. Greeley became one of the first to join the new Republican Party, and although he initially opposed the nomination of Lincoln, he ended up supporting him; after the election, Greeley took the position that even the end of the Union was preferable to any compromise with the extension of slavery. Once the war was underway, Greeley became so zealous in his hatred of slavery that in 1862 he wrote an editorial that denounced Lincoln's 'mistaken deference to Rebel slavery'. By 1864, Greeley joined other Republicans in an attempt to deny the nomination to Lincoln, but by September his *Tribune* announced its support for the inevitable. And in yet another seeming turnabout, Greeley began to argue that Lincoln should negotiate a peace with the Confederacy—even trying to negotiate on his own—and that both sides should declare an armistice for a year, during which time they could restock for the next bout! After the war, Greeley displayed similar inconsistencies, as when he attacked President Johnson for not dealing hard enough with the South, yet going out of his way to sign the bond that allowed Jefferson Davis to be paroled (a gesture that cost Greeley half the subscribers to his *Tribune*). Disillusioned with Grant, he joined with others to form the Liberal Republicans and got himself their nomination for the presidency—something he had been angling for over many years—and then went off and got the Democratic nomination. Although he campaigned vigorously and sincerely, he had by this time so confused people that the opposition could attack him as everything from a national traitor to a country bumpkin. He was thoroughly defeated by Grant; his wife had died a few days before the election; he was denied the editorship on his former paper; a broken man, he became insane and died on 29 November.

HALLECK, Henry Wager

1815-1872

HALLECK WAS A UNION GENERAL who brought a solid variety of experience, skills and intellect to his high command, but 'Old Brains', as he was known by his troops, failed to bring them to bear in an aggressive fashion and thus was moved aside to make room for Grant. Yet it should have been no real surprise that a man of Halleck's background and temperament ended up as a stickler for administrative detail and tactical caution. After graduation from West Point, for example, he had visited France and its fortifications, and then wrote a book *Elements of Military Art and Science* (1846) that gained him considerable reputation. He did fight in the Mexican War, but seeing little opportunity in a military career, he resigned in 1854 and turned to the practice of law in California, where he also became involved in mining, railroads and various business enterprises.

When the war began, Halleck was appointed a major general, his first command being to succeed Frémont in Missouri. The two generals could hardly have been more opposite: Where Frémont was outspoken in his support of the anti-slavery movement but a poor administrator, Halleck excelled at ridding the military district of inefficiency, waste and graft but was regarded by many in the North as being less than fully committed to ridding the country of slavery. Meanwhile, the successes of his field generals—Grant, Foote, Pope—reflected well on Halleck so that in March 1862 he was assigned a larger command, the Department of Mississippi. His only real field action came when he gained a victory at Corinth in April 1862, but his forces greatly outnumbered those of the Confederate army and even at that he did not pursue Beauregard. Lincoln, however, needed any victor he could find, and that July he called Halleck to Washington and appointed him 'general-in-chief' and his personal military adviser. But Halleck's blunt ways soon antagonized everyone, both in civilian and military circles. In particular, he bombarded his field generals with details and advice, yet failed to provide them with any overall strategy or plans; and he constantly held to the conservative approach while criticizing his subordinates for not grasping victories. Gradually Lincoln became disillusioned with Halleck, and when Grant was brought to Washington in March 1864, Halleck was demoted to 'chief of staff'. But solid professional that he was, Halleck remained in this administrative post, for which he was, in fact, better suited. After the surrender at Appomatox, Halleck was sent to command the Division of the James, and he had one more run-in with a fellow Union general, this time countermanding Sherman's attempt to arrange a truce with Confederate forces. Halleck stayed on in the army until his death, but although he had done a decent job in the sphere he was suited for, he never attained much of a reputation among his peers or affection among the public.

HAMPTON, Wade
1818-1902

HAMPTON WAS A MEMBER of the rich plantation aristocracy of South Carolina who became a thrice-wounded general in the Confederate army. As a man who took an active role in running his large cotton plantations, Hampton had a somewhat ambivalent view of slavery. He was not opposed to it on principle but on the ground that it was economically inefficient. This led him to oppose the reopening of slave trade from abroad, and initially he was also against secession as the answer to the South's problems. But when South Carolina seceded, he threw his support to the Confederacy and quickly ordered his cotton to be sold in Europe to raise funds for arms. Then, with troops he equipped at his own expense, he fought at First Bull Run, where he was wounded; promoted to brigadier general in May 1862, he helped to defend Richmond and was wounded again at Seven Pines.

Hampton was then transferred to the cavalry of the Army of Northern Virginia and fought in the eastern campaigns till the end of the war, receiving his third wound at Gettysburg. In the final resistance after Appomatox, Hampton fought with General Johnston's units and was among those advocating that the Confederacy continue its struggle in the West. After the war, Hampton supported the moderate policies of President Johnson but soon found himself opposing the reconstruction policies of the radical Republicans. By 1876 he was elected governor of South Carolina and he went on to become a Senator.

HARDEE, William Joseph
1815-1873

ONE OF THE MORE SUCCESSFUL if less glamorous Confederate generals, Hardee had the distinction of having 'written the book' used by the infantry on both sides. From an old Georgia plantation family, Hardee graduated from West Point and fought in the Mexican and Indian wars. In

BIOGRAPHIES

1855 he published a manual, *Rifle and Light Infantry Tactics*, which was so highly regarded that both Union and Confederate used it during the war. When that war broke out, Hardee resigned from the army and accepted the rank of colonel in the Confederate Army. He was a successful commander at Shiloh, Perryville and Stones River, and in November 1863 it was Hardee's solid tactics that saved the Confederate force at Missionary Ridge. Although offered the command of the Army of Tennessee, Hardee chose to serve under General Joseph Johnston. Hardee did his best to stop Sherman's advance through Georgia, but eventually he was forced to retreat and he lost many men. Hardee then fought hard before evacuating Savannah, and he continued to resist Sherman as the Union forces made their way up into the Carolinas. Hardee himself was captured in North Carolina in the final phase of the war.

HARRISON, Benjamin
1833-1901

HARRISON WAS ONE OF SEVERAL Union generals who went on to become President of the United States, but he might well have made it by another route. From an old Virginia family, his great grandfather had signed the Declaration of Independence and his grandfather had been President of the United States. Harrison was a native of Ohio, became a lawyer, and settled in Indianapolis in 1854 just as the Republican Party was organizing around the issue of slavery. Harrison joined this party and held various local and state offices. By 1862 he had helped to organize a regiment of Indiana volunteers and was named its colonel; because he lacked professional military training, he and his unit were assigned to guard railroads; it was frustrating duty, month after month, and Harrison did not make it any more appealing by his strict discipline. In 1864 his command was attached to Sherman's forces as they made their way to Atlanta, and he won the praise of his superiors. But after the city fell,

Harrison was assigned to Indiana to help repress the influence of the Copperheads in the election campaign of 1864, so he was not present for Sherman's march to the sea. Harrison rejoined his unit in the final campaign into the Carolinas. After the war, Harrison returned to practice law in Indiana and rose high in the Republican Party, becoming President in 1888 by defeating Grover Cleveland.

HAY, John Milton
1838-1905

HAY WAS THE YOUNG MAN who served as the assistant private secretary to Lincoln during his presidency, became his confidant and eventual biographer, and went on to be a notable Secretary of State. Hay grew up in Illinois and after college in the East he drifted into reading law in the office of an uncle in Springfield, Illinois. Next door was the office of another lawyer, Abraham Lincoln, and young Hay soon became friendly with the older man. Hay also became friendly with an editor in that city, John Nicolay. When Lincoln was elected President, he asked Nicolay to become his private secretary, and Nicolay had no trouble getting Lincoln to accept Hay as his assistant. So it was that this 23-year-old found himself at the very center of the war. His duties were varied and often ill-defined; he was sometimes little more than a messenger, but he also dealt with many of Lincoln's visitors and he wrote many letters; he had to deal with Mary Todd Lincoln, too; and working long hours with Lincoln and under great strain, Hay became more than an official secretary. Hay was a true admirer of Lincoln, but he had his affectionate nicknames for the President—'The Ancient' or 'The Tycoon'. Hay was also privileged to see many sides of Lincoln, off-guard and close-up, but Hay would later write of the man's genuinely magnanimous spirit. By 1864, Hay got himself appointed major in the army and assigned to the White House as a military aide, where he displayed considerable ability at balancing the demands made by the military and the politicians. In March 1865, Hay was named secretary to the American legation in Paris, and this gave him his first taste of foreign service; by 1898 he was being appointed Secretary of State under President McKinley, and later historians would rank him among the best in that office. Before this, however, he and John Nicolay had collaborated in a 10-volume biography and study of Abraham Lincoln, and despite all that has since been learned and said about Lincoln, the Hay-Nicolay work's firsthand knowledge makes it indispensable to later generations.

HAYES, Rutherford Birchard
1822-1893

HAYES SERVED IN THE CIVIL WAR with enough distinction to emerge as a major general, earn a seat in the House of Representatives, and go on to become the President of the United States. A native of Ohio where he practiced law, Hayes traveled in Texas and the South in 1848 and seemed to have accepted the institution of slavery rather naively. As he enlarged his intellectual horizons, he began to oppose the extension of slavery if not its existence in the South, and he eventually joined the Republican Party and participated in local politics. In the 1860 election campaign, he made several speeches in support of Lincoln, but his personal hope was that some compromise would be negotiated. Once the war came, however, Hayes declared: 'I would prefer to go into it if I knew I . . . was to be killed . . . than to live through and after it without taking any part.' It was a sentiment that led many men on both sides to glory—and death. By June 1861 Hayes had accepted a post as major in a Ohio regiment and was assigned to western Virginia. During the ensuing months he served in a variety of situations: a judge advocate, fighting with Jackson in the Shenandoah Valley; being wounded in 1862 at the battle of South Mountain, Maryland; fighting with Sheridan in the 1864 Shenandoah Valley campaign. In 1864 he was nominated for the House of

Representatives from his district in Ohio; he refused to leave his military post to campaign, but he was elected; it was December 1865 before he took his seat in the House. Hayes had little sympathy for the radical Republicans' approach to reconstruction, and when he went on to become the governor of Ohio from 1868-72, he gained a national reputation as a solid, balanced administrator. In 1876 he got the Republican Party's presidential nomination and after the famous disputed election, he received 185 electoral votes to Tilden's 184; that was announced on 2 March 1877, and the very next day Hayes was administered the oath of office in a private ceremony in the White House. The price of at least some of those disputed votes was Hayes' agreement to remove the last Federal troops from the South, and when he did so on April 20, the Reconstruction Period effectively came to an end.

HIGGINSON, Thomas Wentworth
1823-1911

HIGGINSON WAS A MINISTER from Massachusetts who served in the Civil War as the commanding officer of the first regiment of blacks in the Union army. From an old Boston family, Higginson became a Unitarian minister, but he soon found even that liberal denomination too restrictive, so in 1852 he moved on to Worcester to preach at a 'Free Church'. For some years before this he had been calling himself a 'disunion abolitionist', indicating his desire to dissolve the Union based on a constitution that condoned slavery, and now he not only preached against slavery but began to take an active role in rescuing fugitive slaves. In 1856 Higginson journeyed to the Kansas Territory to support the antislavery forces there; he met John Brown and would later lend his support to Brown's vague plans to provoke a rebellion of blacks—although when the raid at Harper's Ferry resulted in violence, Higginson and several other abolitionists disclaimed any responsibility. When the war itself began,

BIOGRAPHIES

Higginson left his pulpit and helped to raise and train a regiment of volunteers from Massachusetts, but just as he was ready to take this unit to the front he was offered the command of the first regiment of blacks. They were mainly volunteers from South Carolina, and Higginson became their colonel in November 1862. During the 18 months he led them, they did not participate in any major battles but they did take part in various raids and skirmishes. Higginson was wounded in May 1864 and had to resign from the army. In 1870 he published his *Army Life in a Black Regiment*, one of the more unusual and revealing books to come out of the Civil War.

HILL, Ambrose Powell

1825-1865

HILL WAS A CONFEDERATE GENERAL, one of those most valued by Lee but whose mixture of victories and defeats ended with his own death in the final phase of the war. A native of Virginia and a graduate of West Point, Hill saw action in the Mexican War and in the Seminole Indian wars. In March 1861 he resigned from the US Army and entered the Confederate army as a colonel of the 13th Virginia Volunteers. He participated in the First Bull Run, and in 1862 he was regarded as one of the heroes of the Peninsular Campaign in Virginia. Promoted to major general in May 1862, he led a division (known as 'Hill's Light Division' because of its ability to march fast) through battles at Cedar Mountain, Second Bull Run, Antietam and Fredericksburg. By this time he was attached to Stonewall Jackson's command, and when Jackson was killed at Chancellorsville in May 1863, Hill assumed command and then was wounded. Now in command of the III Corps, Hill led it through the battle at Gettysburg and then at Bristoe Station, Virginia, in October 1863, where Hill's troops suffered heavy losses. Hill went on to fight in the Wilderness Campaign in May 1864 and then participated in the defense of Petersburg against the many months of Union attacks;

it was in the final assault, on 2 April 1865 that Hill was killed while attempting to get to his troops. Often away from his post because of illness, Hill was considered a genial man in his personal affairs but less than consistent in his military command; his death in action made such distinctions superfluous.

HILL, Daniel Harvey

1821-1889

HILL WAS A CONFEDERATE GENERAL whose relatively successful career in the field ended because of a quarrel with his superior. A West Point graduate, Hill served in the Mexican War and then resigned from the army to teach mathematics in a college. At the outbreak of the war he was the superintendant of the North Carolina Military Institute, but when the war broke out he joined the Confederate army and led his North Carolina troops into the first land battle of the war at Big Bethel, Virginia on 10 June 1861. He fought at Williamsburg in May 1862—by which time he had been promoted to major general—and went on to fight in the Seven Days' Battles of the Peninsular Campaign. After the last of these, at Malvern Hill on 1 July 1862, he criticized Robert Toombs, in charge of a Georgia brigade, for losing control of his men; the fiery Toombs challenged Hill to a duel but they never found the occasion to fight it. Hill fought at Antietam and then in the Chickamauga Campaign in August-September 1863; after the latter, he criticized the decisions of his commander, General Bragg, but Jefferson Davis withheld confirmation of Hill's promotion to lieutenant general and removed him from field command. He spent the remaining months of the war in a minor position in North Carolina. After the war, Hill worked as an editor, writer and college administrator.

HOOD, John Bell

1831-1878

HOOD WAS ONE OF THE MORE AGGRESSIVE

344

Confederate generals, famed for fighting the later battles while strapped to his saddle because of his loss of a leg. A West Point graduate, Hood fought in the Indian wars on the frontier where he took his first wound. In April 1861 he resigned his commission to join the Confederate army. His first action came as a cavalry commander at Yorktown in April-May 1862, and he went on to lead a brigade from Texas at Gaines' Mill, Second Bull Run and Antietam. After this he was promoted to major general and assigned a division, which he led at Fredericksburg and Gettysburg; he performed heroically at the latter and was so badly wounded that he lost the use of his left arm. But within two months he was back fighting at Chickamauga, and this time he lost his right leg. Again, he would not retire from action but, strapped to his saddle, he led his men against Sherman in his march on Atlanta. He led the attempted counter-offensive against Sherman, but it was a disaster for the Confederates and Hood asked to be relieved of command. In so doing he gave up the temporary rank of full general. He fought with Beauregard in Tennessee, and after an attempt to join Kirby Smith in the Trans-Mississippi Department at the end of the war, Hood surrendered in May 1865. After the war he worked as a businessman in New Orleans, and he was financially ruined by a yellow fever epidemic in 1878 that then killed him, his wife and a child the next year. With no talent for strategy or staff work, Hood was a superb combat soldier.

HOOKER, Joseph
1814-1879

HOOKER WAS ONE OF THE LEADING Union generals, and like several generals on both sides he ended up defeated more by rivalries on his own side than by the enemy's forces. Massachusetts born, a graduate of West Point, Hooker saw considerable action in the Mexican War but afterwards, like many ambitious young officers, he saw little chance of a career in a peacetime army so he resigned in 1853.

Hooker settled in the West, working as a farmer and a superintendant of military roads; in 1859-61, while serving as a colonel in the California militia, he had a quarrel with Henry Halleck, another former army officer and then a lawyer there —a quarrel with later repercussions. When the war broke out, Hooker was named a brigadier general of the volunteers defending Washington in August-October 1861. He then led a division in the Peninsular Campaign, and in May 1862 at Williamsburg he had his horse shot from under him and fell in the mud but he continued to lead his troops bravely. A news dispatch of this incident called him 'Fighting Joe Hooker', a name he could never get rid of, as much as he personally disliked it. He continued to show his courage in succeeding campaigns, and at Antietam in September 1862 he was so badly wounded that he had to be carried off the field. That November-December at Fredericksburg, Hooker was one of those serving under Burnside who led the disastrous Union attack, but after Lincoln accepted Burnside's resignation Hooker was named to succeed him as commander of the Army of the Potomac. The letter from Lincoln appointing Hooker (26 January 1863) was remarkable for its blunt, even steely, analysis and sly irony: 'I have heard . . . of your recently saying that both the Army and the government needed a dictator', wrote Lincoln. 'Only those generals who gain success can set up dictators. What I now ask of you is military success, and I will risk the dictatorship.' Hooker reorganized the army and then set forth to confront Lee at Chancellorsville in April-May 1863; through a lack of aggressiveness and a temporary loss of command due to a concussion, Hooker was outmaneuvered by Lee, who had only half as many men as did Hooker. This did not stop Hooker from issuing a general order congratulating his troops on their victory. And he did pursue Lee and drive him up to Gettysburg, but just before the battle, Hooker felt that his old adversary from California, Halleck—by now general in chief of the Union army—was working

BIOGRAPHIES

against him, so on 28 June 1863 he resigned his command. Hooker continued to fight in other campaigns, including the seige of Atlanta, but when he once again felt that he was being denied authority by rival generals he resigned his command in 28 July 1864. This ended Hooker's field duties; he served out the war in administrative posts and remained in the army until 1868.

JACKSON, Thomas Jonathan
1824-1863

JACKSON WAS THE CONFEDERATE GENERAL who lost his life at the mid-point of the war but who, as 'Stonewall' Jackson survived as one of the most admired American soldiers. Born in Virginia (a part now in West Virginia), orphaned as a child and raised by an uncle, Jackson went to West Point with considerable disadvantage in his education, but by studying hard (and never speaking to a woman during his years there, he claimed) he graduated 17th in his 1846 class of 59 cadets. He was immediately sent off to fight in the Mexican War, where he fought with such distinction that within 18 months he was made a major. On returning to the United States, he was assigned to various posts until in 1852 he resigned his commission to become a professor of military tactics and natural philosophy at Virginia Military Institute. Jackson was hardly a popular teacher, his main reputation being that of a stern taskmaster, nor did he show much interest in public life—although in 1859 he happened to command the VMI cadets sent to attend the hanging of John Brown. By 1861 the 36-year-old Jackson seemed to have settled into a life largely focused on such personal pleasures as his travels and his membership in the Presbyterian Church. When the war broke out, Jackson was ordered to take some of his cadets to Richmond, but he was not immediately regarded as a Confederate commander. But he was sent to Harper's Ferry to train infantry, and by June the rapidly expanding army promoted him to brigadier general. He then took his well-

trained units to the first battle at Bull Run, and they held off such a crucial Union assault that a fellow general, Bernard Bee, was reported as saying, 'There is Jackson standing like a stone wall'. Bee intended this to describe the whole unit, but the name 'Stonewall' became attached to Jackson where it has stayed ever since. In October 1861, Jackson was promoted to major general and given command of the Army of the Shenandoah Valley, but his early months were most frustrating. Starting in March 1862, Jackson began a march up the Valley; the campaign of the next three months was to become a model for students of military strategy and tactics. Greatly outnumbered, Jackson deployed his troops with such intelligence and speed that he was able to keep the major Union forces in northern and western Virginia from attacking Richmond. Jackson absorbed heavy losses at Kernstown on 23 March, but he struck back at Front Royal on 23 May and at Port Royal on 9 June. By this time Lee had assumed command of the Army of Northern Virginia, and the two old friends spent the next two months in a disappointing collaboration of plans and executions, with Jackson almost physically exhausted from the long marches. But at the very end of August 1862, Jackson led some 20,000 men over 50 miles in two days and then played a crucial role in defeating General Pope at Second Bull Run. (It was this kind of fast marching that gained Jackson's infantry units the name of 'foot cavalry'.) Now advancing into Union territory in Maryland, Jackson distinguished himself at Sharpsburg in September and at Fredericksburg in December. By this time Jackson had been promoted to lieutenant general, and after the winter suspension, he moved out in late April to join Lee in confronting the Union forces under Hooker coming along the Rappahannock. On 1 May the Confederates were forced back toward Chancellorsville, and the next day Jackson led his men in a brilliant and daring march around to the rear of the Union troops. Jackson struck before sunset and forced the enemy to retreat, but as he was returning to his own lines in the twilight he was mistakenly shot by a Confederate soldier; his left arm was amputated to save him, but he died of pneumonia on 10 May 1863. Jackson's reputation and achievements had by this time become a mainstay of the Confederate struggle: 'I know not how to replace him', wrote Lee. Yet Jackson never got on well with his superior or subordinate officers, and although his troops respected him, he was almost a martinet in the discipline and demands he imposed. These were the men who actually carried out the strategy and tactics that would gain Jackson a place in military history—the emphasis on speed, surprise, deception, pursuit, all the while maneuvering to avoid confronting any large force, attempting rather to engage only small elements. Jackson seemed to have little interest in military glory; he was a devout Presbyterian, a man given to prayer in private and little small talk in public. His closest subordinate actually believed he was insane, but posterity has simply judged him to have been a great general.

JOHNSON, Andrew
1808-1875

JOHNSON'S EXTRAORDINARY CAREER from uneducated tailor to the only President of the United States ever impeached is generally familiar, but less known is the difficult circumstances he found himself in during the Civil War. Fatherless at the age of three, poor, apprenticed to a tailor, Johnson was largely self-educated with the aid of his wife. As his tailor shop in Tennessee prospered, he ran for the office of local alderman in 1828, and from that point on Johnson rose higher in public office—the House of Representatives, two terms as governor of Tennessee and finally the Senate in 1857. A Jacksonian Democrat, Johnson represented the new working and middle classes as opposed to the older landed gentry, but he was hardly that radical; in fact, although he came from eastern Tennessee, where there were few slaves, he had no liking for the abolitionists,

and in February 1860 he supported his fellow Senator, Jefferson Davis in his resolutions supporting the rights of citizens to take slaves into any states or territory. His basic moderation, however, led him to support compromise among his fellow Democrats, and after Lincoln's victory in November 1860 Johnson spoke out for support of the Union. When the war broke out, Johnson had become something of a symbol—to the North, of a Southerner of principled loyalty; to the South, of a traitor. Always trying to walk the difficult 'borderline', in July 1860 Johnson introduced a resolution in the Senate that would declare the war was to be fought only to defend and maintain the Union. In March 1862 Johnson was appointed by President Lincoln to be the military governor of Tennessee, a most trying post since his state was roughly split between the pro-Northerners and pro-Southerners. Johnson was by now hated by many in his state, and a smoother politician might have kept a much lower profile, but he refused to avoid the challenge and spent all his energies in trying to convert Tennessee from a microcosm of the larger Civil War into a precursor of the postwar reconstruction. As the war raged about him, Johnson actually restored civil government to the state and gained enough reputation so that in 1864 he was asked to run as Vice-President with Lincoln as the National Union Party's attempt to provide a coalition government. The ticket won, but virtually exhausted by the strains of governing Tennessee and by the campaign, Johnson unfortunately fortified himself for the inauguration ceremony with a bit too much liquor—an episode that would often be held against him. But this was nothing compared to what lay ahead. Within six weeks Johnson was being sworn in as President of the United States, and he immediately found himself caught between the extreme forces generated by the many years of divisiveness and hostilities. His first actions were basically little more than carrying through the plans of Lincoln—extending amnesty as widely and quickly as possible, turning the former Confederate states back to their own civilian governments, generally trying to return a united nation back to normality. But as soon as Congress convened in December 1865, Johnson came under attack from the radical Republicans. Some of their strong feelings was politically motivated: they could not accept a Southern Democrat as the chief executive at this point in history. But some of it was a longstanding and principled dedication to obtaining full rights for the former slaves, and there is no denying that Johnson seemed more interested in normality than in forcing the South to reform. In the end, the confrontation came over a secondary issue, the Tenure Act of 1867, which denied the President the right to fire his appointments. Again, Johnson might have avoided the challenge, but he went ahead and fired Secretary of War Stanton; the eleven articles of impeachment were presented to the Senate in February 1868; the trial dragged on from 13 March to the first vote on 16 May, when the lack of only one vote saved Johnson. With less than a year to serve, Johnson was essentially powerless, although he continued to extend grants of amnesty. Both parties naturally passed over him in their conventions, and he returned to Tennessee as a somewhat ambivalent figure. As dogged as ever, he ran twice for public office before winning the third time and taking his seat back in the Senate of the United States in March 1875. Some national voices were already beginning to appreciate his strengths, but he died that very July, long before he was fully vindicated. Later historians would agree that Johnson had his limitations and had made many errors, but he had always behaved with honor and courage in a situation that might have broken a less remarkable man.

Johnston resigned from the US Army in 1834 and went to Texas; when he was appointed the brigadier general to command the army of the Republic of Texas in 1837, a jealous Felix Huston challenged him to a duel and wounded him; Johnston recovered and went on to become the secretary of war for the Republic, 1838-40. He then returned to Kentucky, and when the Mexican War began he accepted a commission in the US Army; he remained in that service until April 1861, when he resigned to join the Confederate army. His first command was that of the Western Department, and his first act was to take control of Bowling Green, Kentucky, and to start training troops. Then came a series of defeats—at Mill Spring, Forts Henry and Donelson, Nashville—but when Jefferson Davis was urged to replace Johnston, he replied, 'If Johnston is not a general, I have none'. By March 1862 Johnston had regrouped his forces at Corinth, Mississippi while the Union troops, superior in number, were concentrated around Shiloh Church near Pittsburg Landing on the Tennessee River. Johnston boldly moved out on 3 April and caught the federal units by surprise on 6 April; the Confederate troops struck so suddenly and aggressively that the Union troops were routed and almost pushed back to the river. But Johnston himself was mortally wounded (and in the next day's fighting the Union forces recovered and forced the Confederates back to Corinth). His death came as a great blow to the Confederacy, and he was temporarily buried in New Orleans; in 1867 his body was taken to Texas, and when General Sheridan forbade any military honors to Johnston, his admirers in Texas cities simply walked in silence behind the body.

JOHNSTON, Albert Sidney
1803-1862

A GREATLY RESPECTED CONFEDERATE general, Johnston was killed in action at the moment of his one true victory. A native of Kentucky and a West Point Graduate,

JOHNSTON, Joseph Eggleston
1807-1891

UNLIKE THE OTHER CONFEDERATE general named Johnston, Joseph Johnston fought through the entire war to final defeat, and perhaps because of this he never quite gained the respect or popularity accorded the former. Virginia born and a West Point graduate, Joseph Johnston saw considerable action and was wounded in wars with the Indians and in Mexico. In June 1860 he was named Quartermaster General of the US Army, but he resigned in April 1861 and helped organize the volunteers in Virginia. He was appointed a brigadier general in the Confederate army in May 1861, and that July he was the commander of the Confederate troops that won the first major battle of the war, at Bull Run. (Johnston moved his own unit there by railroad, the first time in history that this had been done.) Appointed to command the Department of the Potomac and promoted to full general, Johnston was wounded at the battle of Seven Pines in May 1862 and temporarily relieved from duty. That November he was assigned to command the Department of the West, but Jefferson Davis would not support Johnston's strategy and the Confederate forces suffered a series of defeats—at Stones River, Vicksburg, Chickamauga and Chattanooga—and Johnston's standing with the leaders of the Confederacy declined. Transferred to command the Army of Tennessee, Johnston did his best to stop Sherman's march toward Atlanta that began in early May 1864, but he was not considered aggressive enough and was replaced by General Hood on 17 July. Reassigned to command the Army of Tennessee in February 1865, he led it through the final resistance in the Carolinas but surrendered to Sherman on 26 April—in defiance of Davis's order to move south and continue the fighting. After the war Johnston worked in insurance and railroads and served as a federal railroad commissioner in 1885-91. He died from pneumonia contracted, ironically, from standing hatless in the rain at the funeral of the man who had cost him his command, General Sherman.

KEARNEY, Philip

1814-1862

KEARNEY WAS A UNION GENERAL whose lifelong romantic obsession with war culminated in his death in action. Born into a wealthy and socially prominent New York family, Kearney's ambition was to go to West Point but his family would not allow this, so he read law. When his grandfather died in 1836 and left him independently wealthy, Kearney secured a commission in a US Army cavalry unit and spent two years with it on the western frontier. He then went to France to study their army's cavalry tactics, and even served with them in Algiers in 1840. Returning to the United States, he served as an aide to superior officers, and when the war with Mexico began he recruited a cavalry unit that he outfitted with dapple-gray horses and trained to gallop in unison. He then took the unit to Mexico where, leading a charge, he had his left arm so shattered that it had to be amputated. This did not stop Kearney from leading an expedition against Indians in California, but in 1851 he retired from the army and devoted himself to his estate in New Jersey. Once again restless for action, he went to France in 1859 and rode into combat with the French cavalry in their battles against the Italians (for which he was awarded the Cross of the Legion of Honor). When the Civil War broke out in America, Kearney rushed back to Washington and got himself appointed brigadier general in command of a New Jersey brigade. He had all the men of his unit wear a piece of scarlet cloth that became known as the 'Kearney patch' and instilled in them the sense of being an elite unit: 'You must ever be in the front', he told them. In the early months in Virginia he led his men in at least 12 major engagements. Then in September 1862, while reconnoitering a new position near Chantilly, Kearney unknowingly crossed into Confederate territory and was killed. Lee had known Kearney and sent his sword, horse and saddle to his widow; eventually Kearney's body was buried at the National Cemetery in Arlington, Virginia where New Jersey erected an equestrian statue. A man of undeniable confidence and courage, Kearney inspired respect in his fellow

BIOGRAPHIES

officers and enthusiasm in his troops, but his view of war as high adventure was also undeniably that of a man of class.

LEE, Robert Edward
1807-1870

LEE IS ONE OF SEVERAL individuals who emerged from the Civil War to become almost mythical figures, yet this is hardly explained by his military achievements in the field nor by his official position as commander-in-chief of the Confederate armies. In fact, military historians can fault many of his strategic and tactical decisions, and he did not even attain the supreme command until the final weeks of the war. The strength and appeal of Robert E Lee clearly lie elsewhere. Lee was the son of 'Lighthorse Harry' Lee, a famous cavalry officer in the American Revolution and a governor of Virginia; but his father's financial losses and then his death when Robert was only 11 meant that he was raised in genteel poverty. Good at his studies but a normal active boy, Lee went on to West Point where he compiled an excellent scholastic and military record, graduating second in his class of 1829. His high standing earned him service in the Engineers Corps, and the next 17 years saw him assuming the routine posts and duties of an army engineer officer in various states of the Union. Then came the war in Mexico in 1846, and Lee distinguished himself by his commitment and competence in the combat assignments of an engineer. His next assignment in the States was in 1848 when he took charge of the construction of Fort Carroll in Baltimore harbor. Then in 1852 he was made superintendant of West Point, but he soon chafed at the life there and got himself transferred in 1855 to the 2nd Cavalry Division, with which he spent some time in Texas. He happened to be in Washington at the time when John Brown carried out his raid at Harper's Ferry, and Lee was assigned to lead the Federal troops that put down this 'rebellion'.

By this time the North and South were moving rapidly toward a major confrontation, and although Lee had little sympathy for the arguments justifying either slavery or states' rights, he realized that his first loyalty was to his home state. As the southern states began to secede in the first weeks of 1861, Lee was recalled to Washington in the hope of keeping such a highly respected officer on the Union side; in April he was offered the command of the US Army in the field, but Lee declined; realizing he could no longer avoid the hard decision, when Virginia voted to secede, Lee resigned his commission. He still hoped he might not have to fight against the Union he so respected, but the Confederacy could not allow such a man to sit on the sidelines, and by June Jefferson Davis had appointed him a general and his personal military adviser. For the next year, Lee had to combine this rather ambiguous assignment with his military duties; he halted the Federal advance from western Virginia and helped organize the defenses of the Atlantic coast, but he had no great success in the field. It was in June 1862 that Lee was named to command the Army of Northern Virginia —his first true field command. He was 55 years old. Taking over the command from the wounded General Johnston, Lee inherited a crisis, as the Union troops under General McClellan were besieging Richmond. Lee moved quickly and decisively, and during the ensuing months, collaborating with Stonewall Jackson, Lee directed a campaign that, although by no means a total triumph for the Confederates, ended by forcing McClellan to withdraw. Beyond advancing Lee's abilities as a strategist and field general, this campaign raised the morale of his troops. Lee's next test came that August when he confronted the army under General Pope, and it was principally Lee's strategy and tactics— aided of course by such capable commanders as Jackson and Longstreet—that gained the Confederates their victory at Second Bull Run. Lee then moved his force into Maryland, but although the two weeks cost the Federals some 27,000 casualties, it also cost the outnumbered

Confederates some 13,000—many of them on 'the bloodiest single day of the war', September 17, at Sharpsburg. Lee had to withdraw back to Virginia. His next engagement came in November at Fredericksburg, where he repulsed the Federal assaults under Burnside—again with great losses on both sides. After the winter moratorium, Lee's next confrontation came in May 1863 at Chancellorsville; through his combination of speed and daring, Lee defeated the Union force led by Hooker—but at great cost to the Confederacy, for Stonewall Jackson died of a wound in this battle. In reorganizing the Confederate army in Virginia after the loss of Jackson, Lee made one of his most serious errors in judgment: he placed too many inexperienced officers over too many unfamiliar units. Then Lee decided to invade the North by driving up the Shenandoah Valley and on through Maryland into Pennsylvania, where in a three-day battle, 1-3 July 1863, the Confederate forces were turned back at Gettysburg with casualties of some 28,000. Although there were many factors outside Lee's control, he had to assume responsibility for the defeat —as he did, characteristically offering to resign his command. This was rejected, but Lee could do little else through 1863 as his troops lacked provisions and supplies—almost starving over the winter. In May 1864 Lee confronted Grant in the Wilderness Campaign; sparring and feinting throughout the month, inflicting terrific casualties on the Union forces, Lee beat Grant to a standstill. Then began the campaign at Petersburg, the communications center south of Richmond. Starting in June 1864, it dragged on month after month as Lee's units were worn down—by casualties, malnutrition, exhaustion, desertion— while the Confederate forces elsewhere were also in retreat. When Lee in February 1865 was named general-in-chief of all Confederate armies, it was virtually an empty title and command. As the Federal forces closed in on him, Lee was forced to evacuate Petersburg and Richmond on 2-3 April; from that point he was on the run

from superior forces until he had to surrender on 9 April at Appomatox Court House. Up to this point, Lee would have been known as a superb commander in a lost war, but from the time he rode up to Appomattox on his horse, Traveller, the mythical Lee began. Grant contributed greatly by his generous terms and sensitive treatment, but Lee inspired and vindicated such idealism. He was paroled home and officially indicted for treason but he was never brought to trial; when he applied for a pardon in June 1865, he urged his troops and all Southerners to accept the outcome and get on with rebuilding their homeland. Genuinely interested in educating the young, he accepted the presidency of the small, destitute Washington College (later renamed Washington and Lee University); he avoided the details of politics and tried to channel the affection and idolatry of the South into a less personal dedication to the Union. His reputation as a master of strategy and tactics would survive even various criticisms—one of which was that he was too considerate of other generals' failings. A man of great faith, dignity, patience, a true gentleman, Lee was one of the few heroes who owes his greatness · his actions in defeat.

LEE, Samuel Phillips
1812-1897

LEE WAS FROM AN OLD Virginian family as was his distant relative Robert E Lee, but chose a naval career and then served on the Union side in the war. After joining the Navy in 1825, Lee served in waters around the world; in 1851 he commanded the *Dolphin* on an oceanographic research voyage throughout the Atlantic that provided much valuable data. In 1861 Lee was taking a US Navy ship around the Cape of Good Hope when he heard that the Civil War had started; on his own authority he brought his ship back and it was assigned to the blockade of Charleston. In 1862 Lee commanded one of the three gunboats that Farragut sent to run past the forts protecting New Orleans and then to engage the

Confederate fleet. Lee also participated in the naval action at Vicksburg. In September 1862 Lee was made acting rear admiral and assigned to command the North Atlantic Blockading Squadron operating off Virginia and North Carolina. He was successful at this, in part because he intercepted ships that got through the primary blockade by stationing another cordon of ships out at sea. But because Secretary of the Navy Welles did not consider Lee to be aggressive enough, he was sent in 1864 to command the Mississippi Squadron, where Lee in fact performed perfectly well in supporting the campaign of General Thomas against the troops under General Hood along the Cumberland and Tennessee rivers. Lee remained in the Navy until his retirement in 1873, never gaining the reputation of the Confederate Lees but deserving recognition as a competent professional.

LINCOLN, Abraham
1809-1865

FAR MORE THAN THE MAN who happened to be President of the United States during its traumatic Civil War, Abraham Lincoln seemed destined by his personal life and public experiences to be the chief personage in a drama that would make him a mythical hero. The mythmaking began with his youth, and most of the stories were true: the barely literate father, the log cabin home, the stepmother who encouraged his bookish side, a total of only about one year in school, work in the village store, reading law on his own. But in addition to the rough-frontier Lincoln there was the upwardly mobile Lincoln. In 1834 he was elected to the Illinois legislature; by 1836 he was a licensed attorney; by 1837 he settled in Springfield, the state capital; in 1842 he married Mary Todd, who came from a relatively higher class; and in 1847 he went to Washington to serve in the House of Representatives. Up to that time, Lincoln had not found it necessary to take that strong a stand on slavery; if he was

definitely not pro-slavery he was also not really pro-abolitionist. But he voted for the Wilmot Proviso, which stated that slavery could not be introduced into territory acquired in the Mexican War, and he proposed prohibiting slavery in Washington, DC. Such stands contributed to his loss of his seat after one term, and Lincoln returned to Springfield and at first devoted himself to his private law practice. But his reputation grew, in part due to his public speeches: in place of the elaborate rhetorical style of oratory admired by many, Lincoln took a more straightforward, down-to-earth, analytical approach. As the issue of slavery continued to divide the nation's political life during the 1850s, Lincoln shifted from his Whig Party to the new Republican Party, and as early as 1856 he was receiving some votes for the party's nomination for Vice-President. Then came the Illinois Republicans' nomination for the Senate in 1858 and the legendary series of debates with Stephen A Douglas. In the course of these, Lincoln indicated he was opposed to extending slavery into any more territories, but he did not really endorse the abolitionist position. He lost that election, but he gained a national reputation. Yet even when he was nominated by the Republicans as their presidential candidate, it was as a compromise on the third ballot. During the campaign he remained in Springfield and avoided provocative statements, but it became increasingly clear to the nation at large: if Lincoln won, the South would secede. And even before Lincoln became president, the Southern states began to do just that. Lincoln did his best not to exacerbate the situation during those months, and even in his inaugural address he tried to assure the South that he was not intent on doing away with slavery in those states where it already existed. But it was too late, and when Lincoln gave the order to provision and defend the besieged Fort Sumter, it seemed almost academic which side fired first. Congress would not even meet until July, so Lincoln fought the war during its opening months with his own executive orders.

From the beginning, he probably exceeded his constitutional authority—expanding the army, committing monies—and as the war proceeded he found that Congress was often an outright obstacle to his pursuit of the enemy, so he continued to bypass Congress. His own cabinet was also a source of trouble, with various members constantly scheming against him; Lincoln ended up manipulating and maneuvering these supposedly sophisticated men, but it was an unfortunate drain on his energies. The problems of the home front, in fact, often seemed as demanding as those of the battlefields. It was true that he suspended the writ of habeas corpus in order to detain thousands of individuals without any solid charges, and he allowed some publications to be suppressed. But it was also true that Lincoln tolerated verbal criticism and acts of protest that went far beyond the accepted politics of the day. Meanwhile Lincoln was under constant fire from the two extremes in the North: the Abolitionists, who attacked him for not pursuing the issue of slavery singlemindedly enough, and the Copperheads, who attacked him for pursuing the war in the first place. Even many more moderate Northerners failed to appreciate that Lincoln was trying to fight a war that would gain victory for the North yet not humiliate or devastate the South. Lincoln never lost sight of the true goal of the war: to restore the United States of America. To achieve that goal, of course, required employing a military force in a situation that would have defeated most men. The armed forces simply were not organized for a war of such ambitious extent in time and space. The system of conscripting individuals was never properly worked out. There was incredible confusion among competing military commands. Many of the generals gained their positions through political or social standing and lacked experience and competence for command. Many of the professionals seemed less interested in prosecuting the war than in advancing their own careers over rival officers. Lincoln had to cajole and flatter them, and often accepted their

insults and insubordination. He spent the early years of the war seeking generals who could employ aggressive tactics in the field and develop strategies to conclude the war: It was March 1864, after all, before Grant was brought to Washington and given overall command. Lincoln himself took an active role in military affairs: he outlined strategies and tactics for campaigns, prepared specific orders, concerned himself over logistics of supply, followed day-to-day movements with maps, even chased his generals to their tents in the field to make his points. All this while he had to retain their loyalty—and persuade the homefront to supply still more youths for the dreadful casualty figures. Even those figures fail to account for the extent and depth of the dissatisfaction with Lincoln among so many segments of his society. He was accused of being a dictator, and he almost was denied the nomination for a second term. That would have saved his life, but even though his plans for reconciliation and reconstruction did not get carried out, Lincoln provided an ideal for Americans to strive for. He was not without his flaws and limitations, but it would be hard to imagine a real human being who could have managed the presidency better during such a war. For a civil war like this was by definition a time of irreconcilable stresses and strains, and it was Abraham Lincoln, with his great spirit to match his height, who worked through the storm like a lightning rod for a nation's passions and frustrations.

LINCOLN, Mary Todd
1818-1882

A SOMETIMES TROUBLING and troubled person, Mary Todd Lincoln was called upon to perform a most difficult task: to be the wife of Abraham Lincoln during their nation's Civil War. And although she had been raised in Lexington, Kentucky, in a family of some social standing and had received a good education for a young woman of her day, there was no real preparation for the life that lay ahead. In

1839 she settled in Springfield, Illinois to live with her sister, a daughter-in-law of the governor of that state. Because of this family's status and also because of her own attainments, Mary Todd soon became one of the more eligible young women in a circle that included many people prominent in politics. Among these was Abraham Lincoln, who since locating in Springfield in 1837 had become a promising lawyer and politician. The courtship of Mary Todd and Abraham Lincoln was to inspire many tales, but there seems no denying that it was an on-again, off-again relationship, he being a rather moody man and she being no less temperamental. But they were finally married on 4 November 1842, and during the next decade they would have four sons, only one of whom, Robert, would survive into full manhood. Although Lincoln went to Washington for a term in the House of Representatives in 1847-49, their only true home for the first 20 years of their marriage was in Springfield. Again, many stories were told of their difficulties, the recurrent theme being that Mary felt herself superior to her husband's rather plain style, but Lincoln's own words gave the impression of a man who had affection for her and joy in their family. All of these domestic concerns were suddenly pushed aside when in 1860 Lincoln—a man who had not even been able to win the office of Senator—found himself elected President of a nation on the brink of a civil war. As the war dragged on, month after month, Mary came under considerable criticism—in part because of her Southern ties (four brothers and three brothers-in-law served in the Confederate army), in part because she tried to maintain certain social activities during those grim times. Yet when she tried to participate in her husband's concerns she was accused of meddling. And it could not have been easy to be the wife of a president who responded to charges of acting like a dictator by turning the other cheek. The shooting of her husband before her very eyes was only the most drastic of the personal shocks she had to endure. One of her sons died during the war, and a

third died in 1871; often appearing to be a disturbed person, in 1875 she was declared insane and was confined, but the next year she was released as sane. Her last years were spent in travel and then in residence at the home of her sister in Springfield. There were contemporary accounts of her extreme and erratic behavior, but there were also accounts of her many sympathetic ways, and if she occasionally caused turbulence in her husband's life, she deserves gratitude for helping to keep him on even keel and steady course throughout many years.

LOGAN, John Alexander
1826-1886

LOGAN WAS A VOLUNTEER who rose to become a Union general, only to be relieved of command, but he never let that stop him from devoting his political career to the cause of the veterans. A native of Illinois, he had interrupted his law studies to serve in the Mexican War. After starting his law practice and holding local offices, he went to the House of Representatives in 1859, where, as a Democrat who supported Douglas in the 1860 election, he found himself accused of being sympathetic to the Southern cause. Logan denied this, and as the Southern states began to secede he clearly supported the Union in his speeches and even went off to fight in the first battle at Bull Run. After that he returned to Illinois to organize a regiment and as its colonel he led it through various engagements—at Belmont, Fort Donelson, Vicksburg—where he was twice wounded and had his horse shot from under him. Logan then commanded the XV Corps in the campaign against Atlanta, and in July 1864 he was promoted to head the Army of Tennessee. But five days later, Logan was removed from this command because General Sherman believed that Logan had shown 'a species of contempt' for the detailed work required of such a commander. Logan always felt that it was because he was a volunteer, not a West

Point professional, that he lost this post. But when he resigned from the Army, he swallowed his personal disappointment and helped organize the Union veterans into the Grand Army of the Republic, serving as its president three times. Returning to Congress in 1866 and then to the Senate in 1871, he remained a spokesman for veterans' rights. His most enduring contribution was his work in establishing Memorial Day, first observed on 30 May 1868, to honor Civil War veterans but eventually to honor veterans of all wars.

LONGSTREET, James

1821-1904

LONGSTREET WAS A PROFESSIONAL soldier who served as a Confederate general, only to see his reputation spoiled by his role at Gettysburg. Born in South Carolina (to a mother related by marriage to Ulysses S Grant), Longstreet went to West Point and then saw service in garrison and frontier posts; he was in combat and wounded in the Mexican War, and then went on to various assignments, serving in the Paymaster Department when the Civil War began. In June 1861 he resigned from the US Army and accepted a position as brigadier general in the Confederate army. Longstreet served under General Beauregard at First Bull Run, and made a fair showing in the Peninsular Campaign of 1862 (although he was charged with some errors that led to a loss at Seven Pines). At the battle of Fredericksburg he inflicted heavy losses on the Federal troops, and by October 1862 he was promoted to lieutenant general. Then in July 1863, at the battle of Gettysburg, Longstreet commanded the right wing; he delayed his attack on the second day, and then on the third day he failed to show urgency in organizing the action that became known as 'Pickett's Charge'. It would be some time before the full significance of the events at Gettysburg could be recognized, and then Longstreet would find himself receiving much of the blame for the Confederates' defeat. But Lee did not blame Longstreet, who went

on to fight in several more campaigns; in the Wilderness Campaign in May 1864 he was wounded (accidentally by his own men), but he rejoined Lee that autumn and fought alongside Lee to the end. Known as Lee's 'Old Work Horse', Longstreet was present at the surrender at Appomattox. After the war he engaged in various business enterprises and held several Federal appointments. Longstreet's major failing would seem to have been his cautious nature that led him to delay in combat.

LOWE, Thaddeus

1832-1913

LOWE WAS A SCIENTIFIC investigator who was probably the first to use an aircraft for military purposes when he employed his gear and expertise for the Union army. By 1856 Lowe had expressed interest in using hot air balloons to investigate his theories about air currents at high altitudes; in 1858 he made his first ascent in such a balloon, and he continued to make voyages, eventually getting some support from the Smithsonian Institution. Then, on 20 April 1861, with the Civil War already underway, Lowe chose to make a flight from Cincinnati, Ohio and after traveling over 900 miles he came down near the border of North and South Carolina; he was arrested as a Union spy and was being threatened by a mob when he was saved by a man who was able to confirm that he had seen Lowe making a previous ascent for his scientific investigations. After this adventure, though, Lowe went to Washington to try to convince the authorities of the value of balloons for military observation, and to prove his case he made an ascent in June 1861 during which he sent President Lincoln a telegraph message—the first time in history for such a feat. Convinced, Lincoln and Secretary of War Cameron appointed Lowe chief of the aeronautics corps of the Federal army; Lowe supervised the construction of a small fleet of balloons that were used to make observations from First Bull Run through Gettysburg, and although they did not make a crucial difference, they pointed to future possibilities. Lowe was also the first to take photographs from a balloon. After the war, Lowe turned to other interests, such as making artificial ice and improving the production of gas and coke. He also built an inclined railway to a peak in California—since named Mount Lowe—where he built an observatory.

MAGRUDER, John Bankhead

1810-1871

MAGRUDER WAS A CONFEDERATE GENERAL who tended to seek the spotlight and ended up being blamed for a crucial defeat and thus losing the support of Lee. A Virginian and a West Point graduate, Magruder served in the Seminole Indian and Mexican Wars, and if he was soon known for being 'restless and hot-tempered', he was also credited for not avoiding action. In the years of relative peace after the Mexican War, he came to be known also as 'Prince John' because of the elaborate social life he maintained. As early as March 1861 he had cast his lot with the Confederate cause, and by May he was leading troops in the Virginia Peninsula; in June, he helped defeat the Federal force at Big Bethel, the Civil War's first actual battle on land—although Magruder exaggerated its significance. His next major campaign culminated in the Seven Days' Battles of June-July 1862, but for some reason he failed to act quickly and decisively and the Federal forces were able to remain on the offensive; on the last day's battle, at Malvern Hill, Magruder mistakenly led his division down a road away from the battle, and this contributed to the major defeat suffered by the Confederates. In the reports that followed, Lee was highly critical of Magruder, and although Magruder naturally defended his actions, his relationship with Lee was compromised. Magruder transferred in October 1862 to command the District of Texas, where he initiated some action that was by then peripheral to the outcome of the war. And when the war ended, Magruder was one of a few Confederate generals who declined to ask for parole; instead, he went to Mexico and served as a general under Emperor Maximilian; after the latter's death in 1867, Magruder returned to the US and, never one to avoid the public, lectured on his adventures.

MALLORY, Stephen Russell

c. 1813-1873

MALLORY HELD THE MOST FRUSTRATING position of Secretary of the Navy for the Confederacy, and was the only such official to remain throughout the entire war. Born in Trinidad, West Indies to parents who moved to Florida in 1820, Mallory made a career in Florida that included time as a customs inspector and a county judge. In 1851 he was sent to the US Senate from Florida, and his 10 years there included service on the Naval Affairs Committee. Although he was not for secession, when Florida seceded he resigned from the Senate, and by 4 March 1861 he was being named by Jefferson Davis to be Secretary of the Navy. It was a thankless assignment as there was really no such institution and few resources to establish one. About one-sixth of the officer corps of the US Navy defected to the South, as did hundreds of individual sailors, but the Confederacy could never hope to match the manpower of the Federal fleet. It also lacked ships; even when the Union was forced to abandon the Norfolk Navy Yard in April 1861 with its 11 ships, the Confederacy could never catch up to the Union fleet; the South did not have the means to manufacture marine engines or shafts; the blockade soon cut the South off from imports. Mallory did his best, going to England himself in 1862 to help develop a new cruiser that was built there and then sent forth to attack Federal shipping. He understood such new technologies as ironclads, submarines and mines, although he usually had to compete with those in the Confederate War Department for limited facilities, labor, materièl and money. The only way his job was easier than many other Confederates was that Jefferson Davis left Mallory alone. Mallory repaid this consideration by staying with Davis to the moment when they were taken prisoner in May. Mallory was released from prison in March 1866 and practiced law in Florida until his death.

MAURY, Matthew Fontaine
1806-1873

MAURY WOULD ENJOY a reputation as one of the world's great navigators, oceanographers and marine inventors, but what would be less remembered was that he was a loyal Southerner who served in the Confederate Navy. Born in Virginia and raised in Tennessee, Maury became a midshipman in the US Navy in 1825, commanded his first vessel by 1831, and wrote the first edition of his famous text on navigation in 1834. In 1839 an accident left him lame and hindered much further sea duty, but he had time to write on the need for reform in the Navy—and proposed founding a naval academy—and a book titled, *A Scheme for Rebuilding Southern Commerce.* By 1843 he was in charge of the Navy's Depot of Charts and Instruments, and he soon took over the Naval Observatory. Turning his talents to scientific work, in 1849 he got the Navy to send out a fleet of ships to carry out deep-sea soundings; from the masses of data reported, Maury constructed charts indicating currents, surface winds and other climatic factors. In 1855 he wrote his epochal work, *Physical Geography of the Sea and its Meteorology,* and went on to become responsible for getting international cooperation in the reporting of weather. President Buchanan promoted him to commander in 1858, the same year that he planned the route for the first Atlantic cable. With the war underway in April 1861, Maury resigned from the US Navy and went to Richmond where he was appointed commander in the Confederate navy and placed in charge of harbor and river defenses. Then in 1862 he went to England where he helped to purchase and

outfit ships for the Confederacy and also conducted investigations in the use of torpedoes. He was in England when the war ended, and he then went to Mexico where he joined the cabinet of Emperor Maximilian and made some efforts to establish a 'new Virginia' of Southern expatriates. He went back to England in 1866 to instruct British naval students in the uses of torpedoes, and in 1868 returned to Virginia where he spent his remaining years as professor of meteorology at the Virginia Military Institute.

McCLELLAN, George Brinton
1826-1885

McCLELLAN WAS LINCOLN'S FIRST choice as general-in-chief of the Union armies, but after Lincoln removed him for failing to be aggressive enough, McClellan became an outspoken critic of Lincoln's policies. Born in Pennsylvania, a graduate of West Point, a hero of the Mexican War, McClellan gained a reputation for bringing intelligence and thoroughness to all he undertook. He resigned from the army in 1857 to become a railroad executive, and it was as vice-president of the Illinois Central that he came to know one of its lawyers, Abraham Lincoln. When the war broke out, McClellan was made a major general and soon given command of the Department of Ohio; his success in keeping Kentucky and western Virginia for the Union brought him to Washington in July 1861 as commander of the Division of the Potomac. He soon improved the organization, discipline and morale of the troops, and in November 1861, when the aged Winfield Scott retired as general-in-chief of the army, McClellan was given this top position. But the very qualities that had gained McClellan high marks over the years—his thoughtful approach, his detailed preparation, his careful deployment —proved to be unsuited to the prosecution of the war in the field. Lincoln soon became impatient with McClellan's inability to take the offensive and then began to disagree with McClellan's basic strategy;

BIOGRAPHIES

by January 1862, Lincoln himself was issuing War Orders that were not very subtle attempts to force McClellan to get moving. In March, Lincoln removed McClellan from his top command and reassigned him to head the Army of the Potomac in the field.

As might have been anticipated, McClellan continued to conduct his operations in the same conservative manner—never really confronting the enemy but playing a kind of cat-and-mouse game, continually rationalizing his lack of aggressiveness by referring to his lack of troops, the poor weather or the need for more engineering support. In July McClellan's forces defeated Lee's at Malvern Hill, but even then McClellan was unable to pursue the enemy. And at Antietam that September, McClellan first delayed in engaging the Confederates at Sharpsburg and then, when they were weakened by casualties, he failed to maintain the offensive. A few weeks later Lincoln was writing McClellan: 'Are you not overcautious when you assume that you cannot do what the enemy is constantly doing?' In November, McClellan was told to give up the command of the Army of the Potomac to General Burnside. McClellan was assigned to Trenton, New Jersey and would not see any further action in the field, but he was not unsurprisingly highly sensitive about the direction his career had taken. He actually issued his own report in defense of his actions, and he also let himself become a magnet for the many highranking officials who were becoming dissatisfied with Lincoln's handling of the war. In 1864, while still in the Army, McClellan accepted the Democratic Party's nomination for President and ran on a platform that called for an immediate end to the fighting—a position, in fact, that McClellan himself did not really endorse. In any event, he was thoroughly defeated in the election, after which he displayed his fundamental decency by going abroad as a sort of voluntary exile for the next three years to avoid stirring up controversy. He returned to the US in 1867 and later served as governor of New Jersey. McClellan had been a fine commander in many ways; he was simply not suited temperamentally to action in the field.

McCULLOCH, Ben
1811-1862

MCCULLOCH HAD LED a colorful life as a soldier in the American West, only to lose his life while fighting for the Confederate Army. Born in Tennessee, McCulloch was a neighbor and friend of Davy Crockett, and after Crockett's death at the Alamo, he went to fight against the Mexicans. He then settled in Texas in 1838 and became a land surveyor; he participated in raids against Indians and soon became a renowned Texas Ranger. In the Mexican War, McCulloch led a cavalry unit in various daring actions, so that by the end of the war he was something of a national hero. In 1849 he went off to California in the 'gold rush', but by 1852 he had returned to Texas where he held several Federal appointments. As the nation was choosing sides in the civil war, McCulloch volunteered in February 1861 to command the Texas troops that took the surrender of the US Army garrison at San Antonio. He was then commissioned a brigadier general in the Confederate army and commanded the Confederate troops in their victory at Wilson's Creek in August 1861. In March 1862, he was reconnoitering the Union lines at Elkhorn Tavern when he was killed by Union sharpshooters.

McDOWELL, Irvin
1818-1885

MCDOWELL WAS ANOTHER of several Union generals who were fine administrative officers but ineffectual in the field and thus saw their careers tainted by the war. Ohio born and a West Point graduate, McDowell had a career typical of an army officer of his time, including service in the Mexican War. By the time the Civil War broke out, he was well regarded by members of the new Republican administration, so in May 1861 he was given the most crucial command, that of the Army of the Potomac and the Department of Northeastern Virginia. As a very meticulous administrator, McDowell knew that the Union troops were not that ready for battle when they met the Confederates at First Bull Run, so he accepted the loss, but the government and public in the North were not so detached and McDowell was replaced in his top command by General McClellan and demoted to head a division. In the ensuing months, McDowell was shifted from one command to another; by the Second Bull Run campaign in August 1862 he was in command of the III Corps, Army of Virginia, and although the Union forces were generally beaten, McDowell was particularly singled out for his failures and was removed from command. Although he demanded an official inquiry and was eventually exonerated, he was never given another field command. He retired from the army in 1882, and spent his last years in San Francisco. Totally dedicated, with no interest in political or popular considerations, McDowell simply lacked the inspirational and decisive qualities required of a leader at a certain point in history.

MEADE, George Gordon
1815-1872

ONE OF THE MOST VALUABLE if less spectacular of the Union generals, Meade came through in two very difficult situations—as commander of the Federal forces at Gettysburg and as Grant's immediate subordinate in the field. A West Point graduate, Meade saw little future in a peacetime army, so resigned in 1836 to become an engineer for a railroad and to work on a survey of the northeast boundary of the US. He rejoined the Army in 1842, working as a military engineer, on lighthouse construction, and on field surveys, but he also saw some action in the Mexican and Seminole Indian wars. When the Civil War began, Meade was named a brigadier general assigned to command a brigade of Pennsylvania volunteers; he assisted in the construction of the defenses of Washington and was then assigned to McDowell's Army of the Potomac. By June 1862 Meade was in the Peninsular Campaign, and for the next year he participated in many of the major engagements of the war—Mechanicsville, Second Bull Run, South Mountain, Antietam and Chancellorsville —taking a serious wound at Glendale and rising and rank and responsibility. By June 1863 Meade was appointed commander of the Army of the Potomac, a position he himself did not especially want—among other reasons because he realized he was about to take over a strategy for troops already in place. And it was thus that Meade found himself only two days later in command of the Union Army that confronted the Confederate troops at Gettysburg. Meade would be criticized for not taking more initiative both in the course of the three days of battle and then in pursuit of the Confederates, but the fact was that this battle proved to be a turning point in the war. Meade retained his command of the Army of the Potomac, but this soon left him in the awkward situation of finding General Grant, the general-in-chief of all Federal troops, accompanying him in the field. Meade was notorious for his short temper, and it would have been trying for any general to find himself in this position, but Meade's total dedication to duty and the Union took him through from the Wilderness Campaign to Appomattox. Meade remained in the army after the war and took on another difficult assignment as commander of one of the military districts responsible for administering the reconstruction laws. After a brief retirement, Meade died of illness aggravated by his wound in battle.

MEMMINGER, Christopher
1803-1888

MEMMINGER ASSUMED THE THANKLESS position of Secretary of the Treasury for the Confederacy and resigned when the government's finances—and his own reputation—began to crumble. Born in Germany, Memminger was brought to South Carolina as an infant where he was left an orphan at the age of four; at 11 he was adopted by a man who later became governor of South Carolina. Memminger himself became a lawyer and assumed the social standing and views of his adoptive family: he believed that slavery was justifiable, although he opposed secession as a solution to the issues—even writing a satirical booklet attacking the more ardent secessionists. Memminger was elected to his state's legislature, where he gained a reputation for his sound grasp of finances. By December 1860, when secession was imminent, he went over to that side and served as chairman of the committee that drafted the provisional constitution of the Confederate government. Davis then appointed him Secretary of the Treasury, a most challenging job considering the precarious state of the Confederacy's finances. As a fiscal conservative, Memminger hoped to finance the war by bonds, but he soon had to issue more treasury notes; his efforts to raise money by taxes and other schemes failed and the Confederate currency depreciated. The blockade cut off revenue from cotton sales, the main hope of the South's economy, and prices rose. Meanwhile, the Confederate congress showed little inclination to support any strong measures, and by the middle of 1864 the government's credit had essentially collapsed. In July 1864, Memminger resigned and retired to South Carolina; after the presidential pardon of 1867 he took up his law practice and worked to establish public schools in his state for blacks as well as whites. Under the circumstances it would have been hard for anyone to have done much better: Memminger's failures were part of a larger pattern of failures of the Confederate government to gain the full support of the South.

MITCHEL, Ormsby MacKnight
1809-1862

MITCHEL WENT INTO the Civil War as America's leading astronomer, assumed a command in the Union army, and then died of disease, cutting off what would most certainly have been an even more productive life as a scientist. Born in Kentucky, Mitchel went to West Point where he excelled in mathematics; after graduation he was assigned to the academy to instruct this subject, but he resigned from the Army in 1832 to take up the practice of law. He soon discovered he preferred teaching, and by 1836 he was a professor of mathematics, philosophy and astronomy at Cincinnati College. Although largely self-taught, Mitchel soon mastered the known astronomy of his day; beyond that, he was so enthusiastic and eloquent at conveying the wonders of the universe that his public lectures attracted overflowing crowds. By 1845 he was gaining support for erecting an astronomical observatory outside Cincinnati with the second largest telescope in the world (and the largest in the Western Hemisphere). Between 1846-48 he also published the first magazine devoted to popularizing astronomy, and in 1859 he moved on to head the Dudley Observatory in Albany, New York. When the Civil War started, Mitchel loyally accepted an appointment as brigadier general in command of the Department of Ohio. In April 1862 he led his troops so quickly and unexpectedly from Shelbyville, Tennessee to Huntsville, Alabama that he took the latter city without a shot being fired. He received official thanks and a promotion to major general, but he had such poor relations with his immediate superior, General Buell, that he tried to resign that summer. Instead he was asked to take on a command in the South but before he could undertake any campaign he contracted yellow fever and died in Beaufort, North Carolina.

MORGAN, John Hunt
1825-1864

MORGAN WAS THE CONFEDERATE CAVALRY officer whose unit was celebrated for the endurance, speed, daring and success of their raids. Largely raised in Kentucky, Morgan went to college there and then volunteered to fight in the Mexican War; on returning to Kentucky in 1847 he became a merchant and the proprietor of a hemp and woolen mill. He took an active part in civic and political affairs and in 1857 founded the Lexington Rifles, a militia troop. As the citizens of Kentucky found themselves choosing sides when the war broke out, Morgan went with the Confederacy and by late 1861 he was a captain of a squadron assigned to scouting under the command of General Buckner. Then in April 1862 he was made a colonel in the 2nd Kentucky Cavalry, and by July he had led this unit on the first of his raids. During the ensuing months he made a series of raids in Kentucky, Mississippi, Tennessee, Indiana and Ohio, culminating in the December raid at Hartsville, Tennessee where he took 1700 federal prisoners. In June 1863 he led 2000 men on a 1100-mile ride in Ohio and they were so exhausted that they were defeated and Morgan himself was captured; after being imprisoned in the Ohio Penitentiary for four months, Morgan escaped and got back to the Confederate lines. He continued his raids in Kentucky and Tennessee, which were marked as before by the swiftness with which he struck, the destruction of property, the taking of prisoners and supplies, and the general disruption of Northerners' morale. In September 1864, while making a surprise raid at Greenville, Tennessee, Morgan was killed by Union troops.

MOSBY, John Singleton

1833-1916

MOSBY, famed as the Confederate leader of a troop of irregulars who harassed Union forces, was himself something of an 'irregular'. While attending the University of Virginia, for instance, he shot another student who provoked him; then, while in jail, he started reading law with his defense counsel so that on release he took up the practice of law. At the outbreak of the war, Mosby quickly enlisted as a private in the Virginia cavalry and fought at First Bull Run, but by February 1862 he was commissioned a lieutenant and assigned to the command of J E B Stuart. Mosby made numerous scouting missions for Stuart in the Peninsular Campaign, at Second Bull Run and at Antietam. Then in January 1863 he got permission to organize his own troop, known officially as Partisan Rangers but soon famous as 'Mosby's Irregulars'. Operating in counties of Virginia and Maryland around Washington, DC, Mosby's unit used hit-and-run tactics with such effectiveness that the area where they moved about at will became known as 'Mosby's Confederacy'. Their dashing, daring ways inspired many stories, such as the one that Mosby once captured a Union general asleep in his bed, after pulling down the covers and slapping him on the behind. Beyond such stories, though, Mosby's unit did divert a disproportionate amount of Grant's strength and thus prolonged the war. After Lee's surrender, Mosby simply disbanded his men and never formally surrendered. He resumed his law practice, but then lived up to his reputation for irregularity by joining the Republican Party, then so hated in the South, and actually campaigning for Ulysses S Grant for President. Mosby was later given Federal appointments as US consul in Hong Kong and in the Department of Justice—an appropriate climax to a career that began in jail.

NICOLAY, John George

1832-1901

NICOLAY WAS THE EDITOR who became President Lincoln's private secretary and then went on to collaborate on his biography. Nicolay was born in Germany and his family emigrated to the USA in 1838, eventually settling in Illinois. Both parents died when he was relatively young, so Nicolay was forced to support himself by working as a printer on a newspaper; by 1854 he became the editor of a paper in a small town in Illinois. It was in this position that he came to know the young John Hay, who in turn came to know Lincoln when he took up law practice in Springfield. Nicolay, who had educated himself by his reading, joined the new Republican Party and also got to know Lincoln. When Lincoln was elected President, he invited Nicolay to become his private secretary, and Nicolay then invited Hay to be his assistant. In Washington, Nicolay lived in the White House and soon became much more than a formal secretary—more like a confidential assistant. He and Hay were probably as close to Lincoln as any men during the trying years of the war, and it was a tribute to Lincoln's genuine greatness that they ended up with such regard for the man. After Lincoln's death, Nicolay accepted various government posts but his main efforts went into his 15-year collaboration with John Hay on a 10-volume biography of Lincoln, the last volume appearing in 1890. Although considered to be lacking in the detachment required by modern scholarship, this work provides a starting point for all subsequent studies of Lincoln. Nicolay spent his last years on writing other works on Lincoln and history.

PEMBERTON, John Clifford
1814-1881

PEMBERTON WAS A NORTHERNER who chose to join the Confederate army and then, after surrendering Vicksburg to Grant, found himself distrusted by Southerners. From an old Philadelphia family, a graduate of West Point, Pemberton had married a Virginian; but beyond that he had expressed strong support for states' rights and so when the South broke away in 1861 he sided with the Confederacy. He was assigned to supervise the defenses of the South Atlantic coast, but he was constantly under suspicion because of his background. In late 1862 he was promoted to lieutenant general and given command of the Department of Mississippi, which included Vicksburg and Port Hudson; Pemberton's main task was to hold these so as to assure that the Confederacy could control the Mississippi River traffic. But

Pemberton was given conflicting orders and in the end he found himself and his main unit caught under siege by Grant at Vicksburg; his forces and the civilians in the besieged city were soon weakened by illness, wounds and malnutrition, and Pemberton surrendered on 4 July 1863. (At the time he was criticized for surrendering on that date, but he claimed he agreed to it in hopes of getting better terms.) Pemberton himself was held prisoner by the Union until May 1864; on his return, the Confederates never quite forgave him and he was not assigned any major command. After the war, Pemberton retired to a farm outside Philadelphia.

PERRY, Benjamin Franklin
1805-1886

PERRY WAS A SOUTH CAROLINIAN who strongly opposed secession but in the end stayed with his state in the Confederacy. Perhaps because his father was from Massachusetts and his mother from Virginia, Perry felt strongly about the need to maintain the Union, and when he became a newspaper editor in South Carolina he took every occasion he could to speak out against the doctrine of nullification that many people in his state in particular were espousing. Between 1832 and 1852, he attended various conventions in his state and there, too, opposed secession—although he defended slavery—and he went to the Democratic convention of 1860 at Charleston still opposing secession. In the end, though, when South Carolina voted to secede, Perry went with it, but only after stating: 'You are all now going to the devil and I will go with you. Honor and patriotism require me to stand by my State, right or wrong.' Undoubtedly these were the sentiments of many in the Confederacy. During the war years Perry held only minor posts in the government, so that President Johnson was able to appoint him provisional governor of South Carolina in 1865. This appointment brought criticism from many Northerners, but Perry was in fact able to bring his state back into the Union relatively gracefully. He was elected to the US Senate but was denied his seat so he spent the rest of his years working to solidify his state's links to the Union he had always revered.

PHILLIPS, Wendell
1811-1883

ONE OF THE LEADING abolitionists, Phillips had no need to preserve a Union based on a Constitution that accommodated slavery, but he was won over by Lincoln's gradualist approach. Phillips came from an old New England family, secure in its wealth and social standing, and although he took up the law he was not that enthusiastic about such a career. It was at a meeting in 1837 at Faneuil Hall in Boston—called to protest the murder of Elijah Lovejoy, an abolitionist editor in Illinois—that Phillips found his true vocation. He spoke out so eloquently that he immediately found himself in a position of leadership. And because he was independently well-off, he was free to devote himself to traveling and lecturing against slavery, and along with William Lloyd Garrison, Phillips became one of the best known and most radical of the abolitionists. (Phillips' family felt he was far too extreme in his views, but his invalid wife supported him.) Like Garrison, Phillips was even ready to condemn the US Constitution for its acceptance of slavery, and at a public meeting in Boston in 1842 he said, 'My curse be on the Constitution of these United States!' Phillips was against all compromises such as that of 1850 and was ready to dissolve the Union to be rid of slavery. When the Civil War finally came, he felt that Lincoln was far too cautious, but when Lincoln issued his Emancipation Proclamation in 1862, Phillips was able to extend his support to this approach. When the war ended, Phillips took over as president of the American Anti-Slavery Society and spent his remaining years working for many progressive causes—including women suffrage, penal reform, and prohibition. He once ran for governor of Massachusetts on the platform of the Labor Reform Party calling for 'the overthrow of the whole profit-making system', and many of his contemporaries came to think that his radical positions resulted from some mental failings. But later generations would recognize his type—the patrician who devoted his life to those less fortunate.

PICKETT, George Edward
1825-1875

PICKETT WAS THE CONFEDERATE GENERAL whose association with the fatal charge at Gettysburg—an action he had little responsibility for—totally obscured his controversial and disappointing career during the war. From a Virginia planter family, a graduate of West Point, Pickett fought in the Mexican War and on the western frontier; inevitably for a man of his background, he resigned from the US Army when the Civil War began and volunteered for the Confederate army. As colonel of a Virginia unit known as the Game Cock Brigade, Pickett served under Longstreet at Williamsburg and in the Seven Days' battles, where he was wounded at Gaines's Mill. By October 1862 he was promoted to major general and his division held the center at Fredericksburg that December. But his footnote in history was earned on the third day of the battle at Gettysburg. Pickett had arrived with his fresh division after the first two days of fighting; against the advice of General Longstreet, Lee decided to make a major attack on the center of the Union lines; Longstreet had to go along with Lee and so he ordered Pickett to direct the formation of the Confederate troops that were to make the assault; when the charge was made, it was not Pickett's plan nor did his troops make up the largest part of the Confederate force, yet after the disastrous assault, it was his name that became attached to it. Pickett never truly recovered from this episode, although he continued in command positions to the end of the war. He was defeated at Five Forks on 1 April 1865 and then again at Sayler's Creek on 5 April; within four days Pickett

BIOGRAPHIES

was surrendering at Appomattox. Because he had executed—after courts martial—some 'turncoat' Confederate soldiers, Pickett was declared a war criminal by the Federal Congress, so he fled to Canada, returning only after Grant had declared an amnesty. Pickett returned to his home in Virginia, but he refused Grant's offer to appoint him a US marshal just as he refused an offer from Egypt to make him a general in its army. Clearly disturbed by what he felt was the blame that unfairly settled on his name, Pickett spent his final years as a modest insurance salesman.

PIERPONT, Francis
1814-1899
PIERPONT WAS THE VIRGINIAN who not only served as the pro-Union governor of Virginia during and after the Civil War but also played a crucial role in creating the new state of West Virginia. Born in Virginia but taken by his father to an area near Morgantown (later to be part of West Virginia), Pierpont became a lawyer; a staunch pro-Union and anti-slavery man, he supported Lincoln in the 1860 election. When Virginia voted to secede in 1861, Pierpont organized a convention that met in Wheeling in June; it elected him governor of Virginia on the grounds that all the secessionist officials had given up their claim to their offices. Pierpont then organized the pro-Union legislators from the western part of the State to form a 'rump' legislature that adopted a new constitution in April 1862 and declared a new state, West Virginia. Their representatives were accepted in the Federal Congress at once, and in 1863 West Virginia was admitted to the Union. Meantime, Pierpont had been named governor of the 'restored' state of Virginia, those counties that had come under Federal control. He made Alexandria his capital; when the Confederacy collapsed in April 1865 he moved to Richmond and became the governor of all Virginia. Pierpont through all this had actually done his best to ease things for all Virginians during those difficult times, and he

was not fully appreciated until the Reconstruction laws replaced him with a military governor in 1868. He went to West Virginia to take up his law practice.

PIKE, Albert
1809-1891
PIKE WAS AN UNUSUAL MAN, a Confederate general who got involved in a personal feud with other Confederate officials and ended up resigning from the army. Born in Massachusetts, with a fine traditional education and an interest in writing poetry, Pike set off for the West in 1831 and after various adventures settled in Arkansas as a teacher. A series of articles he wrote for a Little Rock newspaper led to a position as editor and by 1835 he was the owner-editor of a paper. In 1837 Pike took up the practice of law and soon became one of the best lawyers in the region. When the Mexican War began, he recruited a troop of cavalry and personally led them into action. Through all this, Pike had identified himself as a Whig among a largely Democratic society, and he was opposed to both slavery and secession in principle (although he had publicly supported a provision in the Arkansas constitution of 1836 that allowed slavery on the grounds that because Arkansas had been settled by slaveholders it simply had to be recognized as a fact of life). When the Civil War began and Arkansas went with the Confederacy, Pike stayed with his adopted state and by the fall of 1861 he was being commissioned a brigadier general and assigned to command the Indian Territory, the region west of Arkansas and north of Texas where Indians were still most active. Pike approached his assignment with the same thoroughness he brought to everything and was soon recruiting Indians to fight for the Confederacy. But when their performance in their first battle under Pike—at Pea Ridge (Elkhorn Tavern), Arkansas 7-8 March 1862—came under criticism, and Pike found that he did not have total command of the Indian Territory, Pike wrote and circulated a letter to President Jeffer-

son Davis in which he set forth his complaints. Davis reprimanded him for airing his quarrel in public, so Pike resigned, meanwhile continuing to argue his position with other Confederate officials and even involving the Indian tribal leaders. Finally his superior, General Thomas Hindman, had him arrested in November 1862, but the Confederate authorities then accepted his resignation, and he went back to Arkansas; he spent the rest of the war there and in Texas. When the war ended Pike realized he was out of favor with Southerners as well as Northerners, and he also feared he would be charged for inciting Indians, so in 1865 he fled to Canada. After President Johnson's pardon in 1867, Pike returned to Memphis and practiced law. In addition to his careers as editor, lawyer and general, Pike was active in the Masonic movement in America and even had some reputation as a poet. What was typical, though, was that a man of Pike's abilities was frustrated by the internal maneuvering of the Confederacy.

PILLOW, Gideon Johnson
1806-1878

PILLOW WAS A TENNESSEE POLITICIAN who became a Confederate general and then was involved in a surrender that cost him his military career. Pillow had become wealthy as a lawyer and planter and was active in Democratic Party politics. A moderate in most issues that were dividing the South and North, he worked to avoid secession but when the war broke out he helped to mobilize Tennessee troops for the Confederacy. By November 1861 he was a brigadier general and helped to drive Grant's forces away from Belmont, Missouri. By February 1862 Pillow was, second in command, under General Floyd, at Fort Donelson, Tennessee, by then under attack from the same General Grant. Pillow believed the fort could be defended but Floyd felt it should be abandoned so he turned the command over to Pillow; in the end, Pillow turned the command over to General Buckner and fled with Floyd.

Buckner was thus left to surrender the fort with its garrison. In the inquiry that followed, both Floyd and Pillow were reprimanded and removed from their important commands; Floyd went back to Virginia to serve and Pillow remained with the Confederate Army but never got another major position. After the war he returned to his law practice in Tennessee.

PINKERTON, Allan
1819-1884

PINKERTON WAS ALREADY a well-known private detective when the war began, and after helping to set up a Secret Service branch for the Union army, he went on to become virtually synonymous with detective work. Born in Scotland, the son of a police sergeant, Pinkerton emigrated to the USA in 1842, going on to Illinois where he set up as a barrelmaker. One day he was on an uninhabited island on a nearby river to cut wood when he accidentally came across a meeting of counterfeiters; he went back to town and organized a posse to capture them, and this led to his appointment as deputy sheriff in 1846. Pinkerton had by this time declared himself an abolitionist and let his workshop be used as a 'station' on the underground railroad for fugitive slaves. He then moved on to become the first detective of the Chicago police force in 1850, but as the railroads turned to him increasingly for help in robberies, he resigned in 1851 to set up his private detective agency. His reputation grew during the decade, so it was natural for a major eastern railroad to turn to him in January 1861 when it was threatened by Southern sympathizers; while his agents were working on this case in Baltimore they learned of a plot to assassinate Lincoln on his journey into Washington for the inauguration; Pinkerton advised Lincoln's staff and together they worked out the plan that brought Lincoln into the city in secret during the night of 22-23 February. Impressed by this, Lincoln asked Pinkerton that April to consider establishing a secret service for the Federal Army; his first commission

BIOGRAPHIES

came from General McClellan, then in the Ohio Department, and when McClellan was made general-in-chief that July he brought Pinkerton along with him. Pinkerton operated out of Washington, directing counter-espionage activities, but he also liked to go into the field himself, assuming the name of Major E J Allen so as to get an unbiased view of affairs. Then in November 1862 McClellan was removed from his top post, so Pinkerton resigned, turning to work as an investigator of claims against the government. When the war ended, Pinkerton returned to his private detective work, establishing branches in Philadelphia and New York and branching into protective work; much of his success was undoubtedly due to his network of criminal contacts. He also wrote 18 volumes of detective narratives drawn from his agency's work, and these enjoyed the popularity of novels in their day, making Pinkerton a household name for many generations.

POLK, *Leonidas Lafayette*
1806-1864

POLK WAS A CONFEDERATE GENERAL, exceptional in that he had been a minister, and in a sense he owed his death to his friendship with Jefferson Davis. From a prosperous and prominent North Carolina family, Polk went to West Point but six months after graduation he resigned to study for the ministry. Ordained an Episcopal priest in 1830, he held various church posts in the South and Southwest, operated plantations on occasion, and was active in founding the University of the South in Sewanee, Tennessee. At the start of the Civil War, Polk left the Protestant Episcopal Church because of its Northern links and volunteered for the Confederate Army; as a close friend of Jefferson Davis's from their West Point days, Polk was appointed major general in June 1861. Davis named him commander of Department No 2, which included much of the West but was in fact more a symbolic position than an actual military command. Still, Polk took a hand in supervising the construction

of fortifications, and in November 1861 he commanded troops at Belmont, Missouri; later he led his troops into action at Shiloh, Perryville, Corinth, Murfreesboro and Chickamauga. Although he had shown his personal courage on occasion, he was not that highly regarded by his fellow soldiers (who complained that he carried himself like a bishop), but Jefferson Davis continued to think highly of him. Polk meanwhile had a falling out with General Braxton Bragg, who removed him from command and even threatened a court martial. But Davis intervened and kept him in his post, and so it was that Polk was killed while on reconnaissance in Georgia in June 1864.

POPE, *John*
1822-1892

POPE WAS A UNION GENERAL whose war record seemed relatively successful until he antagonized many of his fellow Union officers and ended up embroiled in a quarrel with one that cost them both their careers. Born in Kentucky, a West Point graduate, Pope had the career typical of a professional officer of his generation, including combat in the Mexican War; when the Civil War broke out, his first assignment was to recruit troops in Chicago but he was soon appointed a brigadier general and assigned to General Frémont's command in Missouri. By February 1862 he was promoted to command the Army of the Mississippi, and he led his troops in several bold actions that helped to open the Mississippi River to the Federal forces and traffic. Promoted to major general, Pope was assigned to command his unit along with Grant and Buell in the attack on Corinth, Mississippi; successful in this, he was named to command the Army of Virginia in June 1862. The dashing soldier type in appearance and manner, Pope started off on the wrong foot with his new command by issuing a rather pretentious address: 'Let us understand each other. I have come to you from the West, where we have always seen the backs of our enemies

... I hear constantly of "taking strong positions and holding them", of "lines of retreat", and of "bases of supplies". Let us discard such ideas.' Unfortunately Pope's first major confrontation came at Second Bull Run in August, where Lee and Jackson combined at their brilliant best to rout the Union forces. It was true that many of the Union officers resented Pope's command but after he was relieved of command he reacted by claiming that the loss at Bull Run was due to outright disobedience by subordinates. In particular, Pope singled out General Fitz-John Porter; Porter was tried, found at fault, and dismissed from the Army; eventually Porter was reinstated but the dispute between him and Pope lasted throughout the rest of their lives and did nothing to make Pope more popular with his fellow professionals. Pope had no more field commands after Bull Run but stayed on in the army until retiring in 1886, a victim, to some extent, of the intraservice rivalries that so disrupted both sides, yet also a man who seemed to invite trouble. It was Pope who inspired one of the best-known jokes of the war: when he announced that his headquarters would be 'in the saddle', wits claimed that 'Pope had his headquarters where his hindquarters should have been'.

PORTER, David Dixon

1813-1891

PORTER WAS AN ADMIRAL in the Union Navy who participated in several of the same actions as the better-known Farragut and emerged from the Civil War as one of the most successful commanders in any branch or on either side. Porter was the son of a renowned naval commodore and in place of formal schooling sailed as a youth with his father; at 13 he was a midshipman in the Mexican Navy, which his father then commanded, and was once captured by the Spanish. In 1829 he became a midshipman in the US Navy and for the next 20 years he saw service typical of a navy officer of that era, including oceanographic survey work and some action in the Mexican War. In 1849, convinced there was no more action to be seen in the Navy, Porter resigned to captain merchant and mail ships, but in 1855 he rejoined the Navy (and commanded the ship that brought camels to the American Southwest to use as pack animals). Porter happened to be in Washington in April 1861, when after what for most men would have been a full lifetime in the Navy, he was presented with his new challenge and career. His first assignment was to participate in blockade duty off southern ports—Pensacola, Florida, Mobile and at the southwest pass of the Mississippi River—after which he was sent to the West Indies to search for the Confederate raider, the *Sumter*. Porter helped to plan the Federal attack on New Orleans, but Farragut outranked him and so commanded the actual movement in April 1862; Porter commanded the mortar flotilla that eventually forced the surrender of two forts guarding the approach. Two months later Porter performed the same supporting action when Farragut took his fleet up to Vicksburg. As a result of these successes, Porter was named to command the crucial Mississippi Squadron—thereby jumping over the heads of 80 other officers. Porter took over his new command in October 1862 and in the next seven months his fleet performed invaluable service in keeping open the upper Mississippi and its tributaries and, in May 1863, in supporting Grant's assault on Vicksburg. Both Grant and Sherman credited Porter with significant contributions and in July 1863 he was promoted to rear admiral. That August he took charge of the lower Mississippi to New Orleans, and he displayed his administrative abilities by organizing a naval command that included 3000 miles of river, over 80 ships and a major navy yard. Porter personally commanded the naval force that accompanied the Union army in its Red River expedition, and when that failed on land he led the difficult retreat. Porter was then transferred to the North Atlantic Blockading Squadron and after an initial unsuccessful effort he captured Fort Fisher, the chief defense still controlled by the Confederacy, and the city it guarded, Wilmington, North Carolina. For this he received the official thanks of Congress for the third time—the only naval commander so honored—and he ended the war with service on the James River. After the war, in August 1865, Porter realized a long-held desire to be superintendent of the US Naval Academy, and in his four years there, and subsequently as an adviser to the Secretary of the Navy, Porter did much to place his imprint on the future navy (not without antagonizing many other officers). When Farragut died, Porter became the ranking admiral of the US Navy in August 1870. In his later years Porter also wrote several books, both histories of his experiences and fiction that was highly regarded in its day. But something about Porter's manner prevented his extraordinary accomplishments from gaining him a place among his nation's popular heroes.

PORTER, Fitz-John

1822-1901

PORTER WAS A UNION GENERAL who found his career ruined by the battle of Second Bull Run and then spent 23 years working to clear his name. Born into the famous Navy family of Porters (Admiral David Porter was his cousin), Fitz-John Porter chose to go to West Point; he fought and was wounded in the Mexican War and then taught at West Point before serving on the frontier. By late 1860 he was assigned to the army headquarters in the East to supervise various preparations for the war that seemed imminent. In May 1861 he was promoted to brigadier general and he fought in the Shenandoah Valley and Peninsular campaigns, and it was Porter's troops who held Malvern Hill in the final bloody encounter of the Seven Days' Battles in July 1862. But at the end of August, Porter failed to cut Jackson's force off from Longstreet's and thus allowed the Confederates to emerge from Second Bull Run, if not with a decisive victory at least a stronger position than they might have had the Union army exploited its advantages.

General Pope chose to blame the Union army's failure on Porter, charging Porter with willfully disobeying his orders; Porter was removed from his command and courtmartialed; he contended that his orders were too vague and in any case came too late for him to have executed with any chance of success, but he was found guilty in January 1863 and forced out of the Army. It is not hard to imagine what this meant to a man of Porter's background, and he spent the next 23 years trying to clear his record; in a series of decisions, he eventually got his rank back and then was formally reinstated so that he could honorably retire, and the final investigation board decided that he had indeed shown better judgment in ignoring his orders.

PORTER, Horace

1837-1921

PORTER WAS A UNION OFFICER whose close working relationship with Grant survived the war and led to a valuable account of the Civil War. Graduating from West Point on the eve of the Civil War in 1860, Porter's first active duty in the war was to command the artillery used in capturing Fort Pulaski, which guarded the harbor of Savannah, Georgia. That was in April 1862. That July Porter was appointed ordnance officer of the Army of the Potomac, and in January 1863 he was reassigned to that same post with the Army of the Cumberland. At Chickamauga in September 1863, Porter served with great courage in covering the Union Army's retreat (an action for which he was awarded the Congressional Medal of Honor 39 years later). From November 1863 until April 1864 he served with the War Department in Washington and he was then appointed aide-de-camp to Grant, who had only just taken over as chief of the armies of the Union. Porter held this crucial post through the end of the war, an especially demanding one since Grant preferred to command all the armies while operating in the field with the Army of the Potomac. Porter was with Grant at the surrender of Lee at Appomattox, and then stayed on with him, first as a member of his military staff and then, when Grant became President, as his military adviser. Porter resigned from the army in 1872 and went to work for the railroads; prominent in civic affairs in New York, he was active in erecting the Grant Memorial Tomb. But his finest memorial to Grant was his volume, *Campaigning with Grant* (1897), in which Porter's first-hand experiences provide an indispensable view of the way Grant conducted the war.

PRICE, Sterling
1809-1867

PRICE WAS A CONFEDERATE GENERAL, one of many for whom the Civil War proved to be as frustrating on the field of battle as it was disruptive of his private life. Born in Virginia, Price moved to Missouri where he was elected to the House of Representatives from that state and then, in 1853-57, its governor. Missouri was divided over the issues that were splitting the North and South, and in 1861 Price himself presided over the Missouri convention that rejected secession; but when the pro-Unionists of Missouri took to a show of force for their side, Price's Southern loyalties took over and he went over to command the troops favoring secession. He then led these troops in the Confederate victories at Wilson's Creek in August 1861 and at Lexington in September 1861, but after withdrawing to Arkansas he shared in the Confederate defeat at Pea Ridge in March 1862. Promoted to major general, he was assigned to the Mississippi Department and was driven off from Corinth; he went back to Arkansas and in September 1863 he had to abandon Little Rock to the federal troops. Price engaged in several more battles, most of which saw his troops beaten as part of the general collapse of the Confederate resistance. Price fled to Mexico but returned in 1867.

QUANTRILL, William Clarke,
1837-1865

QUANTRILL WAS THE BEST KNOWN of the 'bushwhackers', a word originally applied to American backwoodsmen but during the Civil War limited to Confederate guerrilla fighters who were not above making a personal profit from their raids. Born in Ohio, Quantrill seems to have started out as a schoolteacher but went on to become a gambler and thief after emigrating to the Kansas Territory in 1857. In the conflicts between the free-state and pro-slavery elements in Kansas and Missouri, Quantrill seemed to side with the former, but when the Civil War broke out he began to fight for the Confederate side. After he led a raid that captured Independence, Missouri in August 1862, Quantrill was commissioned a captain in the Confederate Army. His unit continued fighting in the Kansas-Missouri area, and then in August 1863 Quantrill—by now a Colonel—led them on a famous raid on Lawrence, Kansas, the headquarters for the free-state guerrillas. About 150 pro-Union males were killed and Quantrill's men sacked and burned Lawrence; among those with Quantrill were Cole Younger and Frank James (and, some claimed, his brother, Jesse), who became notorious outlaws after the war. After General Sterling Price led a daring raid into Missouri in September-October 1864, he was forced to retreat back to his Confederate lines. Quantrill correctly saw this as the beginning of the end for the Confederacy, so he set off for Washington with the intention of assassinating Lincoln; Booth beat him to it, and on 10 May 1865 Quantrill was shot by Federal troops in Kentucky. He died 20 days later and was said to have left his money to a girlfriend who used it to start a brothel in St Louis, an appropriate memorial to this somewhat colorful yet shady character.

RAWLINS, John A.
1831-1869

RAWLINS WAS A LAWYER in Galena, Illinois who was invited by Ulysses Grant to become his aide-de-camp and went on to become what General Grant later described as 'the most nearly indispensable' of all his officers. A native of Galena, Rawlins only met Grant when the latter came there in the months before the war to work in his brothers' leather store. Rawlins helped to organize the Illinois volunteers, and Grant, as a professional soldier, was impressed enough to invite Rawlins to become his aide when he was appointed brigadier general in August 1861. Although he lacked any training or experience in the military, Rawlins had all the qualities that Grant needed as a staff assistant—the ability to analyze, to administer and to work hard. Rawlins soon was serving as more than just a mere aide and was providing advice that appears to have influenced Grant in some of his major decisions. And as Grant rose in rank and command, Rawlins moved up with him, becoming Chief of Staff of the US Army and ending the war as a major general. Meanwhile, Rawlins had begun to suffer from the tuberculosis that had killed his wife, and in the hope that it might alleviate his respiratory problems, Rawlins was assigned to make a trip across the West in 1867. (A town in Wyoming was named after him.) In 1869 newly elected President Grant named Rawlins his Secretary of War, but Rawlins died within five months.

REAGAN, John Henninger
1818-1905

REAGAN WAS THE POSTMASTER GENERAL of the Confederacy and one of Jefferson Davis's most loyal assistants, but when the war ended he performed a notable act of encouraging loyalty to the Union. Born in Tennessee, Reagan went to Texas in 1839 and at first worked as a frontier scout, Indian fighter and surveyor; by 1844 he had acquired a small farm and was reading law; by 1846 he was a probate judge and in 1847 he was elected to the Texas legislature. In 1857 Reagan went to Washington for the first of his two terms as a Representative, but as a Democrat and secessionist he became a delegate to the Texas secession convention and resigned from

the US Congress when the Civil War broke out. Reagan helped to write the constitution for the Confederacy, and then Davis appointed him Postmaster General in March 1861. Reagan did his best to make the Confederate postal service function well and hoped to make it self-supporting, but despite his administrative abilities he never had enough resources. As Davis's administration and aides began to crumble, Reagan remained loyal, advising Davis on surrender negotiations and staying at his side until his capture in May 1865. Reagan was imprisoned in Fort Warren in Boston Harbor, and from there he wrote a public letter to his fellow Texans, urging them to set aside any bitterness from the war and to rejoin the Union in the proper spirit. Reagan was released in October and returned to Texas to practice law, later serving as a US Representative and Senator.

RHETT, Robert Barnwell
1800-1876

RHETT WAS ONE OF THE RELATIVELY few Southerners who had actively sought secession, but when the Confederacy was established he found himself one of its critics. A native of South Carolina, Rhett was admitted to his state's bar in 1824 and his law practice prospered so that he bought a plantation and became active in Democratic politics. Between 1837-49, he served in the US House of Representatives, and in 1850-52 he was in the US Senate. Always a staunch pro-slavery and states' rights man, by the 1840s he was organizing a secession movement in his state; he went as a delegate to the Nashville convention of 1850, which seriously considered secession. Meanwhile, he had acquired a newspaper, the *Charleston Mercury*, and serving as its editor he used this as a forum to promote his ideas. Although he advocated invoking the procedure of nullification to effect secession, he made it clear that outright rebellion might have to be considered. After Lincoln's election, Rhett went to the South Carolina convention in December 1860 and helped to draft the secession ordinance. When the Confederacy was established in the spring of 1861, Rhett served in its provisional Congress and was influential in drafting its constitution. He was an obvious candidate for the presidency, but by this time his views were considered too extreme and the more moderate Jefferson Davis was chosen. Then Rhett ran for the Confederate House and was also defeated, so he remained in South Carolina, using his newspaper as the platform for his attacks on the Davis administration. As the defeat of the Confederacy became more imminent, Rhett continued to oppose any compromises or efforts to rejoin the Union. After the war, Rhett went to the Democratic national convention in 1868, but his political views had been discredited. Once so influential that South Carolina was known as 'Rhettsylvania', he moved to Louisiana where he died in 1876.

ROSECRANS, William Starkie

1819-1898

ROSECRANS WAS A UNION GENERAL who, like so many others, enjoyed considerable success in the field (and later in the history books) but who fell out with his superiors and thus was lost to the Union effort. Born in Ohio, a graduate of West Point, Rosecrans served in various army assignments until he resigned in 1854 to work as a civil engineer and then with an oil company. When the war broke out, Rosecrans rejoined the army and became aide-de-camp to General McClellan, the commander of the troops in Ohio, and enjoyed some of the acclaim resulting from McClellan's victory at Rich Mountain in western Virginia in July 1861. Rosecrans was rewarded by given command of the Department of Western Virginia, and by that autumn he had expelled the Confederate forces and helped to form the pro-Union state of West Virginia. In June 1862, Rosecrans succeeded General Pope as commander of the Army of the Mississippi and took an active part along with Grant in the attack on Corinth. In October 1862 Rosecrans was

given command of the Army of the Cumberland, and in December 1862-January 1863 he helped to force General Bragg back after the heavy fighting at Stones River, Tennessee. In the ensuing months, Rosecrans became involved in a quarrel with his superiors in Washington over whether he was pursuing the enemy aggressively enough; Rosecrans refused to be rushed, but when he did finally take on Bragg at Chickamauga in September 1863 his Federal forces were soundly defeated. Rosecrans was relieved of his command and then, after several months, given what was essentially an administrative command, the Department of the Missouri, where he served out the war. But Rosecrans was one of only 15 US Army officers voted the formal thanks of Congress, in recognition of his success at Stones River, and after resigning from the army in 1867 he served in 1868-69 as the US Ambassador to Mexico. Later students of the Civil War would regard Rosecrans as one of the best strategists on either side.

RUFFIN, Edmund

1794-1865

RUFFIN WAS ONE OF THE MOST INTELLECTUAL and prominent Southerners to support secession, showing his support by his lifelong work in agriculture and finally by taking his own life rather than accepting the Federal victory. Born in Virginia to a prosperous planter family, Ruffin served in the War of 1812, after which he turned to farming. Over the years he became much more than a gentleman farmer, turning his own farms in Virginia into models for the whole South. During the 1820s and 1830s he also edited a periodical, the *Farmers' Register,* which encouraged the South to strengthen its agricultural base by promoting such new methods as the use of marl for fertilizer. By the mid-1850s, Ruffin was dedicating himself to the movement for secession, using his writing talents in newspaper and periodical articles. He joined the South Carolina militia unit that set itself up opposite Fort Sumter on Cum-

BIOGRAPHIES

mings Point in Charleston Harbor; because of the honor in which Ruffin was held by Southerners, he was said to have been allowed to fire the first shot from this battery. Because of his age, Ruffin did not take an active part in the military operations during the war. And when the Confederacy was finally defeated, he shot himself.

SCHURZ, Carl

1829-1906

SCHURZ WAS A GERMAN-BORN politician and editor whose reputation was to grow from his role in the reform movement in American politics but who also took an active part in the Civil War. Schurz had to flee Germany after becoming involved in the revolutionary movement in 1848-49 and he arrived in the United States in 1852. Settling in Wisconsin, he joined the newly formed Republican Party; he campaigned for Lincoln in the latter's senatorial race against Douglas in 1858, and then he campaigned for Lincoln in his successful presidential race in 1860. Lincoln named Schurz as Ambassador to Spain in 1861, but as the war dragged on Schurz became impatient so he resigned that post and took a commission in 1862 as a brigadier general of the volunteers. He fought in various battles—Chancellorsville, Gettysburg, Chattanooga—and was with General Sherman in the final campaign through the Carolinas in 1865. After the war, Schurz became an influential newspaper editor and a US Senator; he rejected the reconstruction policies of the radical Republicans and helped to form the Liberal Republican party of 1872. Later he served President Hayes as Secretary of the Interior, and through his writings, speaking and general integrity, exercised considerable influence on responsible and reformist political life in the United States.

SCOTT, Dred

ca 1795-1858

SCOTT WAS THE BLACK SLAVE whose suit for freedom led to a landmark decision by the United States Supreme Court, a decision that served to widen the gap that eventually resulted in the Civil War. Born to slaves in Virginia, Scott belonged at one point to the Blow family in St Louis; the Blows sold him in 1833 to an army surgeon, John Emerson, who a year later took Scott from the slave state of Missouri to reside with him in Illinois, a free state; after three years there, Emerson took Scott to live in Wisconsin, a free territory; after two years there, Emerson took Scott back to Missouri. Emerson died shortly thereafter, and Scott was left with his family (he had married a slave, Harriet, purchased by Emerson, and they had two children) to Emerson's widow. Unable to provide enough for his family, Scott turned on occasion to the wealthy sons of the Blows, his original owners, and in 1846, Henry Blow initiated a legal suit to gain freedom for the Scotts on the grounds that Dred Scott had essentially gained his freedom by residence in free territory. Scott himself was illiterate and could only make a mark on the petition; he won the case in the lower court but the Missouri Supreme Court reversed this decision. During the years that Scott's case was in the courts, he was placed into custody of a sheriff who hired him out for a monthly wage. In 1852, the case was moved into the Federal court system; by this time, he had been transferred by a fictitious sale to Mrs. Emerson's brother, John Sandford, the executor of Dr Emerson's estate, so by the time the case got to the Supreme Court it was called *Scott v Sanford* (somehow the *d* was dropped from the name). Scott remained in St Louis during all these years, becoming a local celebrity. In 1857, Chief Justice Roger Taney handed down the majority decision that Scott was still a slave. However, by another fictitious sale one of the Blow brothers bought Scott from the Emerson family (Mrs Emerson meanwhile having married a strong anti-slavery congressman from Massachusetts), and in May 1857 Taylor Blow freed Scott. By this time he was not physically fit for much work, and he lived only another 16 months, working as a porter at a hotel in St Louis.

Although Scott was something of an agent for others' designs, it is a tribute to the suffering, both physical and psychic, of all slaves that his name survived as one of those who made a difference to America's history.

SCOTT, Thomas Alexander

1823-1881

SCOTT WAS A RAILROAD EXECUTIVE whose personal career and Pennsylvania railroad both aided the Union effort and in turn profited from the war. Pennsylvania born, Scott had risen to become vice-president of the Pennsylvania Railroad by 1860. When President-elect Lincoln came through Harrisburg in March 1861, enroute to Washington, it was Scott who helped Lincoln to take an alternate and unpublicized route to the capital to avoid the threatened attempt on his life. When the war broke out, Secretary of War Simon Cameron asked Scott to help run a railroad to transport Union troops and supplies; Scott went to Washington (taking with him one of his prize young telegraph operators, Andrew Carnegie), and by August 1861 Scott was made assistant secretary of war in charge of all Federal railroads and transport lines. Although Scott did not retain that particular post throughout the entire war, he did continue to provide advice and organization to the government's railroads. Inevitably his former Pennsylvania Railroad expanded during these years, too, and when the war ended Scott returned to that line and was responsible for making it into one of the greatest of all American railroads.

SCOTT, Winfield

1786-1866

SCOTT HAPPENED to be the general-in-chief of the Army when the Civil War broke out, but even though he was by then too old to play a direct role in the fighting, his long career in military and public service had involved many of the elements that had led up to the war. Descended from an old Virginia family, Scott emerged from the War of 1812 as a genuine national hero,

having been wounded, had two horses shot from under him and at one point been taken prisoner by the British. During the next 35 years, Scott dedicated himself to improving the Army, fighting in various campaigns against the American Indians and taking a crucial role in a diplomatic incident with Canada. By 1841, Scott was being named general-in-chief of the Army in what must have seemed the climax to the most distinguished military career since George Washington's. Then came the Mexican War, and once again Scott emerged as a national hero, responsible for both the strategy and many of the field actions that led to victory. It was one of the ironies of Scott's life, however, that the same man who was so successful in defeating his enemies in battle and so successful in his diplomatic dealings with Indians and Canadians, could be so undiplomatic and unsuccessful in his relations with American Army officers. Having already been subjected to two courtmartials, Scott found himself in 1848 facing a court of inquiry; he threatened to retire, but ended up being promoted to lieutenant general and holding onto his command as well as his reputation with the American public. In 1852 Scott was nominated by the Whig Party as their presidential candidate, but his blunt-soldier ways failed to win many votes away from Franklin Pierce. Scott went back to being the general-in-chief and by 1860, at the age of 74, he was near the end of his long career. After the election of Lincoln, however, Scott saw clearly that war was imminent, and he urged President Buchanan to reinforce the Federal forts in the South over the winter of 1860-61. Buchanan continued to stall, but Scott himself took steps to recruit and train the army for defending Washington. So it was that when the hostilities actually began, the Union found itself with a 75-year-old general in chief of its army. The new generals such as McClellan soon made it clear that they could not take orders from Scott, and he chose to retire in October 1861, with full honors extended by Lincoln and his cabinet. He survived the war, and in

1865 presented to his former subaltern, Ulysses Grant, a gift inscribed, 'from the oldest to the greatest general'. In fact, 'Fuss and Feathers', as Scott was called (because of his stress on protocol and uniform), earned the gratitude of his nation for much more than mere seniority.

SEMMES, Raphael

1809-1877

SEMMES WAS THE CONFEDERACY'S most successful naval commander, whose two ships took a tremendous toll of Federal shipping and then had an impact on negotiations after the war. Born in Maryland, Semmes first enlisted in the US Navy in 1826 but during the years up to the Civil War he alternated between service in the Navy and his private law career. In March 1861, Semmes accepted a commission in the Confederate Navy; his first contribution was secretly to purchase valuable naval supplies in the North. Then he was given command of the cruiser *Sumter*, and avoiding the blockade at New Orleans he set off on a six-month cruise that captured 18 Federal ships and generally disrupted shipping to the North. When the *Sumter* was trapped by a blockade in Gibraltar, Semmes himself went to England and assumed command of a new ship built there, the *Alabama*. Setting out from the Azores in September 1862, Semmes commanded the *Alabama* as it cruised thousands of miles throughout the Atlantic, sinking, burning or capturing 65 Federal ships until it was sunk by the *USS Kearsarge* in June 1864 off the French coast. Semmes was rescued by an English ship and got back to the Confederacy, where he remained. In December 1865 the Federal government arrested Semmes and he was imprisoned until April 1866; no full explanation was given for singling him out.

SEWARD, William

1801-1872

AS SECRETARY OF STATE in Lincoln's cabinet, Seward behaved in many ways that would be considered intolerable but his long career in public service would generally be judged as based on high principles. New York born, a lawyer by profession, a Whig in politics, Seward rose through New York State politics to become a two-term governor from 1838-1842. Although he had not taken much of a position on the issue of slavery up to then, he did refuse as governor to extradite three sailors to Virginia where they had aided slaves to escape. And after returning to private life, two of his most famous law cases involved defending blacks, so that when he was elected to the US Senate in 1848 Seward had become identified with strong anti-slavery views. In the Senate's debate over Clay's proposed compromise of 1850, Seward predicted that unless slavery were eliminated voluntarily, it would lead to civil war; in this same speech, he referred to acting under 'a higher law than the Constitution'—a phrase that would haunt Seward for many years because it could be used by believers in many causes. During the next decade, Seward remained outspoken in his views against slavery, moving over to join the new Republican Party and arriving at that party's 1860 convention as one of the leading candidates for president. But his outspoken views cost him the nomination, so he threw his support to Lincoln and was appointed in return to be Secretary of State. Seward considered himself, and was regarded by many prominent Republicans, as the real leader of his party, and in the weeks before Lincoln's inauguration he acted almost as though he, Seward, would be running the country, going so far as to write a notorious memo advocating that Lincoln start a war with European countries as a means of uniting the country (and then closing the memo with a not very subtle hint that Lincoln essentially give the true powers of government to himself!). Seward even went behind Lincoln's back and negotiated with Confederate agents and confused the reinforcement of Fort Sumter, but Lincoln simply outsmarted Seward and let him remain as Secretary of State. And in the matters that did fall within his department, Seward proved himself to be most able, diplomatic and resilient—whether limiting the British aid to the Confederacy or containing the French interference in Mexico. Although personally uncertain about the Emancipation Proclamation, Seward gave it his official support, and he ended up becoming one of Lincoln's valued counselors; it was Seward, indeed, who was attacked by the Booth conspiracy that killed Lincoln—he was stabbed in his bed at his home. Quickly recovering, Seward stayed in his post through President Johnson's troubled administration, even supporting Johnson's conciliatory policies toward the South. He was attacked for this position, just as his purchase of Alaska in 1867 was scoffed at as 'Seward's Folly', but history was to vindicate him on both counts. Considering the realistic need to leaven high principles with practical politics, and allowing for Seward's insensitive actions at the outset of his secretaryship, historians would conclude that Seward was an independent and honorable leader.

SHELBY, Joseph Orville

1830-1897

SHELBY WAS ONE OF THE MORE 'dashing' of the Confederate cavalry generals, and he extended his dedication to the cause by trying to prolong the Confederacy in Mexico. Born in Kentucky to a wealthy and prominent family of planters and manufacturers, Shelby moved to Missouri in 1849; during the next decade he became one of the wealthiest landowners in Missouri, and in the border troubles between this state and Kansas he supported the pro-slavery faction. When the Civil War broke out, Shelby naturally joined the Confederate side, organizing his own cavalry company and accepting a commission as captain. He participated in all the early battles west of the Mississippi—Elkhorn and Prairie Grove, Arkansas, Newtonia and Cane Hill, Missouri, Corinth, Mississippi—and in January 1863 joined Quantrill's

Irregulars in a raid on Springfield, Missouri. In July 1863 he led an attack on Helena, Arkansas, but was wounded in this poorly directed action. By December 1863 he was promoted to brigadier general, and during 1864 he continued to make his daring raids while participating in the campaigns in Arkansas and Missouri. As the war was ending and the various Confederate units surrendered, 'Jo' Shelby refused to do so, and led about 600 former Confederates into Mexico, where in return for land to establish a Confederate 'colony', he offered to provide some military support for the Emperor Maximilian. When Maximilian was executed in 1867, Shelby returned to Missouri and took up his life as a planter. President Cleveland appointed him a Federal marshal in 1893, a sort of 'official pardon' for this rather romantic soldier—a cavalry man who could quote Walter Scott and wear a black plume on his hat.

SHERIDAN, Philip Henry

1831-1888

UNTIL MAY 1862, Philip Sheridan's youth and experience would have failed to signal that he was going to emerge from the Civil War as one of the most successful Union generals—even to become one of the most respected military men of all times. Born in New York, Sheridan graduated from West Point—but only after a year's suspension because he had assaulted another cadet with his bayonet and fists. Sheridan saw some service in Texas and the Northwest, but when the Civil War started he was still only a lieutenant; his first assignments were merely administrative, and at one point he was threatened with a courtmartial. Finally, in May 1862, after having been reduced to purchasing horses for the Union army, Sheridan was made a colonel and given command of the 2nd Michigan Cavalry Regiment. Then followed a series of victories—at Booneville, Mississippi, at Perryville, Kentucky, at Stones River, Winchester, and Chickamauga, Tennessee; and in the Chattanooga campaign, at

Missionary Ridge, in November 1863, in which Sheridan's bold tactics and disciplined command virtually sealed the Federal victory. Grant was the first to appreciate a former misfit who had found his vocation in battle and in April 1864 he gave Sheridan command of the cavalry of the Army of the Potomac. Sheridan was soon taking the cavalry through a series of engagements—in the battle of the Wilderness, at Spotsylvania, in a raid on Richmond—that if not always complete victories at least demonstrated aggressive leadership and tactics that kept the enemy offguard. So over the objections of many who felt Sheridan to be too young (33), Grant gave him command in August 1864 of the Army of the Shenandoah, and Sheridan moved quickly through a series of victories at Winchester, Cedar Creek, and Waynesboro. At Cedar Creek, Sheridan's army had in fact been caught by surprise while Sheridan himself was about 20 miles away, but he made a famous rise on his horse Rienzi and arrived in time to rally his troops to victory. (The ride was immortalized in a poem by Thomas Buchanan Read, while Rienzi was later stuffed and stands in the Smithsonian Institution in Washington.) Sheridan continued his aggressive tactics right to the end, making a raid into northern Virginia in February-March 1865, defeating General Pickett at Five Forks on 1 April, and then cutting off Lee's way out of Appomattox and thus forcing his surrender. In these closing weeks of the war, Sheridan had been promoted to major general and voted the thanks of Congress, and immediately after the end of the fighting he was assigned to lead a large force of Federal troops along the Mexican border as a sign to Maximilian and the French that the United States would no longer tolerate their machinations. In 1867 Sheridan was made a military governor of the district that included Louisiana and Texas, but he enforced the Reconstruction Acts so strictly that President Johnson had him transferred to the Department of the Missouri. President Grant promoted his old comrade in arms to lieutenant general in 1869, and by

1884 he was succeeding General Sherman as commander-in-chief of the US Army. In 1888, he was promoted to full general, saw his memoirs published, and died—young (only 57) and small in stature (only 5 feet 5 inches), but regarded as one of the most brilliant tacticians, aggressive fighters and respected commanders in any nation's roster of military heroes.

SHERMAN, William Tecumseh
1820-1891

AS A UNION GENERAL, Sherman came to be regarded as one of the most successful military heroes by the North, but the South would always consider him as the archenemy because of his famous march to Atlanta and the sea. Born in Ohio, Sherman was originally named after the Shawnee chief and 'William' was added by the religious couple who reared him after his father died. He graduated from West Point and eventually fought in the Mexican War, but resigned from the army in 1853 to work as a banker and lawyer; soon tiring of this life, he became a superintendant of a military school in Louisiana in 1859. When the Civil War broke out, Sherman—despite his years of service in the South—rejected a commission in the Confederate army and in May 1861 accepted an appointment as a colonel of the infantry in the Federal Army. His first engagements were in the First Bull Run campaign of July 1861, a major defeat for the Federal forces, but that August Sherman was promoted to brigadier general and assigned to Kentucky, where he worked with volunteers to hold the state for the Union side. By October 1861 he was made commander of the Department of the Cumberland, but he soon became involved in quarrels with his superiors in Washington and with the press. Accused of being unstable, practically removed from command, Sherman at one point considered suicide, but he regained his balance and in March 1862 he was given a new chance as commander of the 5th Division, Army of the Tennessee. In the battle at Shiloh in April, Sherman was wounded and lost three horses, and the press tried to blame the Federal force's defeat on him, but Generals Grant and Halleck commended him for his bold actions. In July 1862 Sherman was given command of the District of Memphis, and along with General Grant he fought in the long series of engagements aimed at taking Vicksburg, the last of the Confederate strongholds on the Mississippi. It was Sherman's amphibious assault that led to its capitulation in July 1863, and finally, after so many years of failures and frustrations, Sherman had a conclusive victory. He was promoted to brigadier general, named to succeed Grant as commander of the Department of the Tennessee, and then took part in the successful campaigns to relieve Chattanooga and Knoxville. When Grant went to the East to command the entire Union army, Sherman in March 1864 succeeded him as commander of the Military Division of the Mississippi. As part of Grant's grand strategy, Sherman was soon assigned to move east from Chattanooga to capture Atlanta. He spent the first few weeks building up supplies, but by early May 1864 Sherman was ready to move. He proceeded in a series of maneuvers against the Confederate forces led by General Joseph Johnston; it was slow going, involving no dramatic battles but a constant wearing down of the enemy, but by 1 September, the Confederate troops (by now under General Hood) had to evacuate Atlanta. Sherman moved in, ordered the removal of civilians so that he could use it as a base for his operations in the area, and then—after giving orders on 15 November to burn anything in the city that might aid the military—he set out with an army of some 62,000 men to clear a zone from Atlanta to the Atlantic—the idea being to cut off the supply lines of the Confederacy. For the next month, Sherman and his army were virtually isolated from Washington and Grant as his force made its way to the sea; Sherman gave orders that there should be no destruction of private property nor violence against noncombatants, but there were undoubt-

edly individual acts that violated his orders, and although Sherman saw his march as a necessity in the grand strategy, the South would never quite accept this. In any case, Sherman took over Savannah, Georgia on 21 December 1864, and then in February 1865 he set forth on another march, this time northward through the Carolinas; the city of Columbia, South Carolina was half destroyed by a fire on 17 February, but it seems that this was not caused by Sherman's Federal troops. After Lee's surrender at Appomattox, Sherman negotiated a surrender with General Joseph Johnston, but by adding terms of a political nature to the merely military capitulation, Sherman came under attack from his superiors and the Republican administration. He felt he was simply extending the conciliatory hand that Lincoln would have had he lived, and when he attended the review of the Federal army in Washington, Sherman refused to shake hands with Secretary of War Stanton. Sherman went on to accept various assignments in the postwar years, succeeding Grant as commander in chief of the US Army in 1869, retiring from active duty in 1883. Although it was Sherman who said (in an 1880 speech) that 'war . . . is all hell', he himself was not the ravaging firebrand that his controversial marches made him seem to be. What he was was a brilliant and determined general, and a more serious charge might be that he anticipated 20th-century ideas by his recognition of the need to conduct total war, even against the civilian economy, in his dedication to total victory.

SICKLES, *Daniel Edgar*

1825-1914

SICKLES WAS A UNION GENERAL whose military attainments almost seem secondary to an extraordinary life that included a murder, an amputation and a great city park. Born in New York City, Sickles became a lawyer and after service in the state legislature and a diplomatic post in London, he went to the US Senate in 1857. In 1859, Sickles shot and killed the son of

Francis Scott Key for carrying on an affair with his wife; in the trial, his defense invoked the concept of 'temporary insanity'—one of the earliest uses of this—and later he accepted his wife back. When the Civil War began, Sickles volunteered to serve, raising a brigade in New York and then commanding it through the Peninsular Campaign of March-August 1862. In November 1862, now a major general, he was given command of the III Corps, and in April-May 1863 he led this through the Chancellorsville campaign, helping to stop the Confederate advance by his strong attack on General Jackson. At Gettysburg, in July 1863, Sickles advanced his unit beyond his assigned position and occupied high ground that became known as 'Sickles' salient'; in the bloody fighting that followed, his unit stopped the Confederate advance but he lost about half his men and was himself so seriously wounded in his right leg that it had to be amputated in the field. After the battle of Gettysburg, Sickles was criticized by some for his unauthorized initiative that proved so costly, but little could be done to punish a volunteer who had given his leg for a victory. He recovered to serve as the military governor of the Carolinas after the war, but President Johnson found him overly zealous and dismissed him from that post in 1867. After retiring from the Army in 1869, Sickles lived a long and often controversial life, but ironically this rather belligerent and troublesome man was also one of those most responsible for purchasing the land that would become New York City's oasis of tranquillity, Central Park, and also for making the battlefield at Gettysburg into a national monument.

SIGEL, Franz

1824-1902

THE GERMAN-BORN Sigel became a Union general, and if he did not play a very important role on the battlefield, the very fact that he supported the Union served as an inspiration to some. After becoming involved in the revolutionary movement of the late 1840s in Germany, Sigel had to flee, emigrating to the United States in 1852, where he became a teacher. When the Civil War broke out, he was director of a school in St Louis, and he quickly worked to organize a regiment that helped to keep the city and its Federal arsenal for the Union. Throughout 1861 he continued to fight to keep Missouri within the Federal camp; he played a crucial part in the Union victory at Pea Ridge, Arkansas and as a major general he served in Virginia under General Pope and fought at Second Battle Run in June-September 1862. After a major loss at New Market in the Shenandoah Valley in May 1864, he was removed from the front lines to Harper's Ferry. That July he helped to delay General Early's thrust toward Washington, but by this time his superiors had decided he simply didn't move decisively enough so he was relieved of any field command. He stayed in the army till May 1865 and then went on to make a career as an editor and politician, but he would be most honored as an intelligent foreigner devoted to the cause of liberty who had cast his lot with the Union cause.

SLIDELL, John

1793-1871

SLIDELL, one of a small number of Northerners who sided with the South, served as the Confederacy's Ambassador to France, a position that involved him in several international incidents. Born in New York City, Slidell traveled in Europe after graduating from Columbia College and then became a lawyer; a duel forced him to leave the city, however, and by 1823 he had settled in New Orleans. There he practiced law, engaged in land speculation, and soon became an influential politician in Louisiana; in 1843 he was elected to the US House of Representatives; in 1845, President Polk sent him on a special mission to Mexico (and its failure led to the war against Mexico); by 1853, Slidell was a US Senator from Louisiana. As a Democrat and supporter of states' rights, Slidell remained in the Senate until 1861, when he resigned with Louisiana's vote to secede. With his diplomatic experience, Slidell was a natural choice to represent the Confederacy abroad, and he was soon appointed a commissioner, or agent, to represent the Confederacy in France. In November 1861, he and James Mason, the Confederacy's agent to Britain, were enroute to Europe on a British mail ship, the *Trent*; Captain Charles Wilkes of the USS *San Jacinto* stopped the ship off Cuba and removed the two agents; when news reached England, it led to an outburst of condemnation of the United States government; diplomatic maneuyerings freed Slidell and Mason from the prison at Fort Warren in Boston harbor in January 1862, and the two men resumed their trip. In the end, Slidell had little success, at least in his mission to get the French government to formally recognize the Confederacy; he did negotiate a loan from the Paris banking house of Erlanger, with bonds supported by cotton, and this made millions of dollars for the Confederacy (with the bonds eventually becoming worthless). Slidell also became involved in Napoleon III's adventure in Mexico with the Emperor Maximilian, but that, too, collapsed without ever really aiding the South. When the Civil War ended, Slidell remained in France, leaving with the fall of the Second Empire in 1870 and going to England, where he died the next year.

SMITH, Edmund Kirby

1824-1893

SMITH WAS A NOTABLE Confederate general, most closely associated with his command of the Trans-Mississippi Department that became known as 'Kirby Smithdom'. Born in Florida to parents from New England, Smith went on to West Point and was soon fighting in the Mexican War; from 1849-52 he taught mathematics at West Point, and then he took other assignments, including fighting the Indians in Texas. Smith was opposed to secession, but when Florida eventually voted to secede, Smith resigned from the US Army in March 1861 and accepted a commission as colonel in the Confederate army. Appointed chief of staff to General Joseph Johnston that May, he helped organize the Army of the Shenandoah; by June, Smith was a brigadier general; in July he participated in the Confederate victory at First Bull Run but he was wounded (and later married the young woman who made him a shirt while recovering). Promoted to major general in October 1861, Smith assumed command of the Department of East Tennessee, and then went through the Kentucky campaign with General Bragg. Smith became so frustrated with Bragg's lack of aggressiveness, however, that he asked to be transferred, and in February 1863 Smith was assigned to command the Trans-Mississippi Department. He had both civil and military responsibilities for this large area, and the dissension and disobedience among many of the civilians often forced Smith to serve more as an autocrat than a general; this plus the district's increasing isolation from the Confederate government in the East led to its becoming known as 'Kirby Smithdom'. (Kirby was simply his middle name, but to distinguish himself from other Smiths he began to sign his name as 'Kirby Smith'.) His most important military victory was against General Banks in the Red River campaign in Louisiana in the spring of 1864. When Kirby Smith approved the agreement with the Federal Army on June 2, 1865, he was the last Confederate general to surrender a major Confederate military force, his Trans-Mississippi Department. Smith himself fled to Mexico and Cuba, but before the year was over he had returned to Florida. From 1870-75 he served as president of the University of Nashville, and from 1875 till his death he was a professor of mathematics at the University of the South.

STANTON, Edwin McMasters

1814-1869

A DEMOCRAT and a critic of Lincoln,

Stanton served as Secretary of War through most of Lincoln's administration and ended up as one of Lincoln's crucial supporters. Stanton was born in Ohio, read law, and by 1847 had established his practice in Pittsburgh; as he grew in reputation and wealth with a practice mainly in civil and constitutional law (once he had a joint client with another lawyer, Abraham Lincoln), he moved in 1856 to Washington. Stanton then gained something of a national reputation as a special counsel for the United States government in its fight against fraudulent land claims in California, and President Buchanan named him Attorney General when he reorganized his cabinet in December 1860. Up to that time, Stanton had taken little active part in politics, but although a Democrat opposed to the extension of slavery, he accepted the Dred Scott decision. In the Democratic Party's split in 1860, Stanton supported Breckinridge in the belief that only he could preserve the Union, and it was this same motive that led him to rally behind Buchanan. When Lincoln took over, Stanton went back to private life and was soon criticizing the 'imbecility of this administration'. But he was also acting as an unofficial adviser to Simon Cameron, the Secretary of War, and aided Cameron in preparing a report that recommended arming the slaves; when Lincoln dismissed Cameron—in part because he disapproved of this proposal—Stanton was named to succeed him in January 1862. It was a most extraordinary situation: Stanton, a Democrat in a Republican administration, a critic now within its innermost circle, a lawyer with no military experience, as the Secretary of War. But Stanton was an honest, efficient, capable man, and he moved quickly to reorganize the War Department; he did his best to get rid of the fraud and patronage in the contracts, and he established better communications with the generals, the governors and the Congressional Committee on the Conduct of the War. Stanton showed another side when he joined with others in the administration in removing General McClellan from com-

mand of the Union armies—for Stanton had been a personal friend of McClellan. Stanton also moved decisively to provide the army with the men, equipment and supplies that were constantly being requested. At the same time, his somewhat arrogant personality and meddling ways antagonized almost everyone else trying to win the war; even the usually understated Grant said Stanton 'cared nothing for the feelings of others'. Stanton had begun with little enthusiasm for Lincoln's abilities as a leader, but he came over the years to appreciate and admire the President. After Lincoln's assassination, Stanton pursued the alleged conspirators with professional zeal. President Johnson asked Stanton to remain in his post, and this then began the least admirable chapter in Stanton's career. Professing support of Johnson in cabinet meetings, Stanton actually supported the radical Republicans in their efforts to impose far more punitive measures on the South. When Johnson finally dismissed Stanton from his post in February 1868, in defiance of the Tenure of Office Act, this precipitated the impeachment of President Johnson; Stanton literally camped in his office during the weeks until the first vote on 26 May, and when he realized that Johnson was winning, Stanton resigned and left his office. In declining health, Stanton never regained his former standing in his public or private career, and although Grant appointed him to the Supreme Court in 1869, Stanton died before he could take his seat. By his behavior to President Johnson, Stanton forfeited the standing in his country's history that he might have gained from his contributions to winning the war.

STEPHENS, *Alexander Hamilton*
1812-1883

STEPHENS WAS A GEORGIA POLITICIAN opposed to secession whose personal 'war' of principles led him to become Vice-President of the Confederate States and then to oppose President Jefferson Davis. Born in Georgia in a poor family, Stephens went to college with the aid of a benefactor and went on to become a lawyer. As his career prospered, he had time to devote to public life, and after serving in the Georgia legislature he was elected to the US House of Representatives from 1843-59. His clear intelligence and ability as an orator soon saw him emerge as one of the leaders of his Whig Party; a strong unionist, he nevertheless could argue on behalf of states' rights and slavery. By 1860, he had come to accept that the nation was dividing along other lines, so he gave his support to the Democrat, Stephen Douglas. After Lincoln's victory, Stephens called for a convention of all Southern states in hopes of preventing secession; he went to Georgia's own convention in January 1861 to argue on behalf of the Union, but he ended by signing the Ordinance of Secession. In February he went to Montgomery and took the lead in writing a moderate constitution for the new Confederacy—and then found himself elected Vice-President of the provisional Confederate government. Stephens had arrived at this point by his sincere desire to be a moderating influence; now his own dedication to states rights led him into opposition to President Davis's desire to impose some centralized authority over the Confederate states. Stephens increasingly defied Davis, whether in the Confederate Senate or back in his home state of Georgia. And in February 1865, Stephens was one of three Confederate leaders who met with Lincoln and Seward on a ship in Hampton Roads in a last-minute attempt to negotiate a peace settlement. Arrested as the war was ending, he was imprisoned in Boston Harbor for some six months; returning to Georgia, he was elected to the US Senate in 1866 but the radical Republicans were by this time refusing to seat all such former Confederates. Stephens bought a newspaper in Atlanta in 1871 and used it as a platform for his outspoken attacks on the Reconstruction policies, but from 1873-82 he was serving in the US House of Representa-

tives, and in 1882-83 he was rewarded by his fellow Georgians by being elected their governor. Stephens wrote a bestseller of his day, *A Constitutional View of the Late War Between the States* (1868-70), a title that reveals much about Stephens' lifelong efforts to take a high-principled approach to events that nevertheless involved him in open conflict.

STEVENS, Thaddeus
1792-1868

ONE OF THE TRULY phenomenal figures in American political life, Stevens was so strongly opposed to slavery that he ended up hectoring Lincoln, practically ruining Andrew Johnson and antagonizing virtually everyone who might have joined his struggle for social justice. Born in Vermont, his father died while he was still a child, and Stevens grew up working hard and disliking anyone or anything associated with wealth or class. He did get to college, though, and after teaching in Pennsylvania he was admitted to that state's bar in 1816. Since his county bordered Maryland, Stevens became increasingly aware of the wrongs of slavery, and he would often defend fugitive slaves without any fee. As his law practice prospered, he also in 1826 entered the iron business. He entered politics as an anti-Mason because he was opposed to all such 'secret orders' in American society, and after going to the Pennsylvania legislature in 1833 he became increasingly outspoken in defense of his progressive views; at a state convention in 1837, for instance, he refused to sign the new constitution adopted because it did not extend the right to vote to blacks. In 1848 he went to Washington as a Representative; he was soon denouncing slavery as 'a curse, a shame, and a crime', but his intemperate language was soon offending Northerners as well as Southerners. He switched to the new Republican Party, and, although not originally for Lincoln, he did support him in the election of 1860; reelected also, Stevens returned to Congress so strongly opposed to compromise as well as to secession that some of his colleagues had to surround him on the floor of the House to protect him from those he attacked. Although he felt he deserved to be in the cabinet, he had to settle for chairmanship of the House Ways and Means Committee, but this gave Stevens great power over all bills, including appropriations, affecting the conduct of the war. Stevens did support Lincoln in financial matters, but he constantly attacked the President for his efforts to pursue a moderate course; as the war dragged on, Stevens became more extreme than ever, demanding that the Confederates be 'utterly annihilated', even proposing that the old state lines in the South be redrawn and that the South be recolonized. All this might have been confined to rhetoric were it not that Stevens chose to apply this extremist view literally to the reconstruction of the South. Even while Lincoln lived, Stevens opposed any efforts to deal leniently with the former Confederacy; and with Johnson in office, Stevens felt absolutely compelled to force his views on the South. Stevens took the lead in the House in passing the radical Reconstruction Acts—imposing both military rule and suffrage for the blacks—but not content with such successes he took the lead in the movement to impeach President Johnson. By the time of the trial itself, the aging Stevens was in poor health so he did not take that active a part, and within three months of Johnson's acquittal, Stevens was dead. But even in death, Stevens got in the last word: he had himself buried in a remote cemetery in Pennsylvania because he found other cemeteries off limits to blacks. Stevens was a gifted, even brilliant, man, and he was sincere in his dedication to equality and justice for all, but he took such a fanatical course that, partly in reaction to his approach, others condemned blacks to many more years of second class citizenship.

STOWE, Harriet Beecher
1811-1896

AS THE AUTHOR OF *Uncle Tom's Cabin*,

Stowe helped to dramatize and personalize some of the issues that were to erupt in the Civil War. Born to the remarkable Beecher family in Connecticut, Harriet's father was a minister of strong Calvinist views, while her mother—who 'never spoke in company . . . without blushing'—died when Harriet was only four. The family had black servants, and it was the washerwoman, Candace, who was one of the young girl's special influences. Another was an uncle, Samuel Foote, a seafaring man who would visit and provide somewhat more sophisticated glimpses of the world. But Harriet read Byron, played the piano and early came to question her father's strict religion; she was also extremely close to her brother Henry, a man of broad interests. In 1832, the father took his family to Cincinnati, where he was to head a new theological seminary, and in 1836 Harriet married Calvin Stowe, a professor of Biblical literature at this school. She had tried a little writing before this, and her husband encouraged her to continue, but she devoted herself during the next 14 years to raising their six children. The seminary, meanwhile, was a center of the anti-slavery movement in that area; once, too, Harriet visited a plantation in nearby Kentucky and caught a glimpse of the life of the slaves. In 1850 she went with her husband to Maine where he took on a position at Bowdoin College, and now she gave in to the urgings of her family to write something about the slavery issue that was so bothering many of her circle. The result was *Uncle Tom's Cabin, or Life Among the Lowly,* which began to appear as a serial in the *National Era*, an abolitionist periodical, in Washington, DC on 5 June 1851. By the time the last installment had appeared on 1 April 1852, a Boston publisher had brought the completed novel out in two volumes; within a week, 10,000 copies were sold, and within a year, 300,000; it was also published in England where 1,500,000 copies were soon sold. Adapted for the stage, it became one of the most popular plays of all time, yet Stowe did not profit at all from these dramatic versions (and many other editions were soon 'pirated'). Literary critics pointed out that the book lacked the esthetic values of important works, and the South condemned it for what it insisted were distortions, but the fact remained that Harriet Beecher Stowe had written the first American novel to portray blacks as serious protagonists. She was treated as a celebrity in the North, in England and on the Continent, and her second anti-slavery novel, *Dred, A Tale of the Great Dismal Swamp* (1856), was widely read. After the Civil War, she continued to publish, but she never matched the success of *Uncle Tom's Cabin*. Then again, very few books could match that work's impact on history.

STUART, James Ewell Brown
1833-1864

'JEB' STUART, more than just the most successful of the Confederate cavalry commanders, more than a general noted for his daring rides and raids, was one of the romantic legends created by the Civil War. Born in Virginia (his father was a prosperous lawyer), Stuart attended West Point and then served with cavalry units in the West. He had come to know John Brown, the abolitionist, during their time in Kansas and when Brown seized the arsenal at Harper's Ferry in 1859, Stuart volunteered to serve as aide to Robert E Lee in the attack on Brown. By 1861, Stuart was a promising captain, but he inevitably resigned from the US Army and joined the Confederate army, becoming a lieutenant colonel of the 1st Virginia Cavalry (although his father-in-law was a Union general). Stuart led his unit through the First Bull Run campaign and was promoted to brigadier general in September 1861. In the Peninsular Campaign in June 1862, Lee wanted to know more about the Federal Army led by General McClellan; Stuart took 1200 cavalry troops into enemy territory and for three days made a complete circuit of the Union force, capturing prisoners, arms, horses and equipment and helping to set up the Confederate victory at

Gaines's Mill. Promoted to major general in July, Stuart was given command of all the cavalry in the Confederate Army of Northern Virginia and led them through Second Bull Run, Sharpsburg and Fredericksburg, making another daring raid at Catlett's Station (and capturing many of the personal belongings of General Pope) and a second ride around McClellan's army at Chambersburg. After Stonewall Jackson was killed at Chancellorsville in May 1863, Stuart temporarily assumed command of II Corps. In the Gettysburg campaign, Stuart fought a major cavalry engagement at Brandy Station, Virginia in June, and suffered one of his worst defeats. Then, with unclear instructions from Lee, he took another of his long rides, setting forth on a raid on June 24 across the Army of the Potomac's supply route; although successful enough, this meant that Stuart arrived at the battlefield at Gettysburg too late to be of any use to the Confederate force. Stuart went on to fight in the Wilderness and at Spotsylvania; and then at the battle at Yellow Tavern, Virginia on 11 May 1864, he was mortally wounded after he had emptied his pistol while firing at the Union cavalry, dying the next day. It was a great blow to the hopes of the Confederacy because even though Jeb Stuart had more than a touch of exhibitionism (he was called 'Beauty' by his West Point classmates), his courage and professionalism, coupled with his sense of humor and style, provided the Confederacy with an ideal that would long survive.

SUMNER, Charles
1811-1874

SUMNER WAS THE SENATOR from Massachusetts whose lifelong habit of supporting good causes with his wicked tongue often led to unwanted results—the most celebrated being his physical beating in the Senate. Sumner's father was a Massachusetts lawyer and sheriff who held advanced views such as educating black children in schools with whites and intermarriage between the races. Sumner became a lawyer in Boston but spent much of his time lecturing and editing, and it was an oration he delivered on Independence Day in 1845—in which he denounced wars of any kind—that gained him his first public notoriety; he became so outspoken in his campaign against the Mexican War that he was virtually treated as an outcast by many, but in the end he was able to maneuver himself into one of the Senatorial seats from Massachusetts in 1851. By this time Clay's compromises of 1850 had been accepted, but Sumner insisted on opening up the divisive issue of fugitive slaves by speaking for hours against appropriating money to enforce the law. Southern Senators even considered expelling him, but worse was to come. In December 1855, during the debate on Kansas, Sumner used typically intemperate language, at one point characterizing Senator Andrew Butler of South Carolina as a 'Don Quixote who had chosen a mistress . . . though polluted in the sight of the world is chaste in his sight—I mean the harlot, slavery'. Two weeks later, Sumner was seated at his desk in the Senate when he was attacked by Representative Preston Brooks, a relative of Butler, who beat Sumner with a cane; it was 1858 before Sumner could take up his Senate seat—to which the Massachusetts legislature had unanimously elected him—and by this time Sumner had become a symbol of the bitter and violent fate confronting the North and South. After Lincoln was elected in November 1860, Sumner simply ignored the petitions signed by thousands of his Massachusetts constituents who wanted him to support the movement toward compromise, and as the war proceeded he remained as unyielding as ever in his demands for eliminating slavery. As chairman of the Senate committee on foreign relations, however, he urged a more conciliatory approach to the Confederacy in order to retain the support of foreign powers. And although he seemed to have great personal respect for Lincoln, Sumner worked against Lincoln's plans for a lenient approach to the South. After the assassination, Sumner then joined Thaddeus Stevens of the House of Representatives both in pushing through the strict Reconstruction acts and in attacking President Johnson. In 1872 he provoked yet another controversy when he introduced a bill forcing the Federal Army to stop listing the names of the battles each unit had fought—to help wipe out the bad memories of the Civil War, Sumner claimed; even the Massachusetts legislature felt he had gone too far this time and in 1874 it passed a bill denouncing him. Sumner has been compared to one of the old Hebrew prophets in his uncompromising zeal and fiery rhetoric, and for all his unsympathetic ways, he was sincerely devoted to equality for everyone.

TANEY, Roger
1777-1864

As Chief Justice of the Supreme Court, Taney issued several decisions that served to widen the gap between North and South, but it was his Dred Scott decision that proved most divisive. Born in Maryland to a prosperous, slave-owning planter family, Taney was admitted to his state's bar in 1799 and by 1827 was Maryland's attorney general. A Democrat and supporter of Andrew Jackson, Taney was made attorney general of the United States by President Jackson in 1831, and in 1836, when the great John Marshall died, Jackson appointed Taney to succeed him as Chief Justice. In the ensuing years, as the North and South maneuvered their way toward open hostilities, Taney handed down numerous decisions that bore on the issues, particularly those involving economics and slavery. In the area of economics, for instance, in such matters as the regulation of banks, business and transportation, Taney usually came down on the side of local control, states' rights, *laissez-faire* capitalism—essentially supporting, that is, the Southern position that they should be allowed to run their plantation economy as they saw fit. And in his position on interstate traffic of commerce, Taney found it acceptable to include slaves within this category and then to deny that the Federal government had any special right to regulate the slave trade. One of his most important decisions, for instance, came in 1851, in *Strader v. Graham,* where Taney ruled that the status of a slave was governed by each state's laws, so that if a slave voluntarily returned to a slave state after living in a free state that individual could again be treated as a slave. This, of course, anticipated his decision in the most famous of his cases, that of Dred Scott. When the case first came to the Supreme Court it was assumed that the justices would avoid any of the broader issues and rule on strict legal-procedural grounds; soon, though, the justices were taking sides along sectional issues, and Taney took the lead in asserting the most Southern position. In his decision of 1857 (and all nine of the justices chose to issue opinions), Taney not only ruled that Dred Scott himself was still a slave but that no black person descended from a slave could be a citizen and that the Missouri Compromise, or for that matter any Congressional prohibition of slavery, violated the Constitution. Taney's decisions provoked a bitter national debate; several Northern states actually voted to repudiate it, and when South Carolina came to declare for secession in 1860 it was able to refer to this repudiation as precedence; the decision also led to the split within the Democratic Party in 1860, and thus contributed to Lincoln's victory. Once the war began, Lincoln essentially ignored Taney and the Supreme Court and proceeded to run the government as he saw fit. As early as May 1861, for instance, Taney ruled that the Federal government had no right to suspend the right of habeas corpus in pursuit of those favoring the Confederate cause, but Lincoln asserted that the Constitution gave him that right in cases where rebellion affected public safety—and then went on ignoring Taney. But Taney had been forced to administer the oath of office to Lincoln in March 1861, and when Taney died in October 1864, President Lincoln attended his funeral. Later students of the Supreme Court would claim Taney as one of the more important justices, and undoubtedly the North and South were on their collision course independent of his decisions, but there is no denying that Taney forced certain issues to the breaking point.

THOMAS, George Henry
1816-1870

THOMAS WAS A UNION GENERAL whose meticulous ways did little to make him a popular hero but who came to be regarded as one of the most effective of all the commanders in the war. Born in Virginia, a graduate of West Point, a veteran of the war in Mexico and campaigns against the Indians, Thomas might have been expected to follow his comrade Robert E Lee into the Confederate army, but he stayed with the Federal Army and as a colonel, and then a brigadier general, he took an active role in organizing and training troops throughout the early months of the war. Thomas commanded a division at Shiloh (April 1862) and then was made General Halleck's assistant in the campaign against Corinth, April-June 1862. After the battle at Perryville, October 1862, General Buell led the Federal forces back to Louisville, and Thomas was then ordered to take over from Buell; Thomas refused on the grounds that Buell had already set the strategy; then, when General Rosecrans replaced Buell, Thomas protested that Rosecrans did not have seniority; when Lincoln antedated Rosecrans' commission, Thomas went along with this like a good soldier. Thomas next major battle was in September 1863 at Chickamauga; when the Confederate forces routed the main Federal units under Rosecrans and they retreated to Chattanooga, Thomas held the line until nightfall and thus kept the Confederates under Bragg from gaining full victory; for this action Thomas came to be known as 'The Rock of Chickamauga'. Promoted to replace Rosecrans, Thomas now led a Union force trapped under siege in Chattanooga; when Grant told him to hold on, Thomas replied that 'we will hold the town till we starve'—which was what his troops were close to doing. But the Federal forces got supplies through and in November 1863 Thomas and other Union generals were able to drive Bragg away. In May 1864 Sherman began his march on Atlanta, and it was Thomas's Army of the Cumberland that comprised over half the total force, saw some of the worst action and were the first to enter Atlanta. When Sherman then set off on his march to the sea, Thomas was sent to confront General Hood to the west; after some delay (which prompted Grant to try to dismiss Thomas), Thomas soundly defeated the Confederates outside Nashville in December 1864. Thomas was promoted to major general and voted the thanks of Congress for this victory. When the war ended, Thomas remained in command of the Army and Department of the Cumberland in Tennessee till 1869; President Johnson tried to promote him to full general but Thomas, with his typical demand for protocol, declined on the grounds that it was a politically motivated move. Typically, too, when he was urged by some to run for President in 1868, he refused to challenge his comrade and superior, General Grant; Thomas stayed on active duty, dying in his command at the Military Division of the Pacific. 'The fate of an army may depend on a buckle', Thomas is reputed to have once reprimanded a sloppy officer, and it was this insistence on detail and propriety that characterized 'Slow Trot', as he was sometimes called, and probably kept him from ever becoming a widely admired military hero.

TOOMBS, Robert Augustus
1810-1885

TOOMBS WAS ONE of the 'founding fathers' of the Confederacy and served as both its Secretary of State and as a general, yet his outspoken independent ways led him to fall out with other Confederate leaders and left him a frustrated man. Born to a family of the Georgia planter aristocracy, Toombs studied law and became a successful lawyer and planter in Georgia; rising in state politics, he was then elected to serve in the US House of Representatives from 1845-53. A Whig and a spokesman for the Southern point of view, he nevertheless negotiated Georgia's support for the Compromise of 1850. Elected to the US Senate in 1852, he switched to the Democratic Party in 1856; he joined in the walkout of the Democratic convention of 1860 and supported Breckinridge, but over the winter of 1860-61 he did try to support the efforts at compromise. He finally decided that there was no more chance of negotiating a peaceful compromise, so he turned to advocating secession, resigning from the Senate in February 1861. He attended the Georgia secession convention and went on to the convention at Montgomery with some hope of becoming the president of the Confederate states; when he lost to Davis, Toombs accepted the position of Secretary of State in the provisional government. He took an active role in drawing up the Confederacy's constitution, but Toombs soon became frustrated with Davis and in July 1861 he resigned. He accepted a commission as brigadier general of the Georgia militia and was soon leading a brigade in Virginia, then through the Peninsular campaign (March-July 1862). After the last of the Seven Days' battles, Malvern Hill (July 1862), Toombs was admonished by his superior, General Daniel Hill; Toombs, always impatient with what he considered the over-caution of such professional soldiers, challenged Hill to a duel, but they never found the occasion to fight it. Toombs went on to fight and be wounded at Antietam in September 1862; he expected to be promoted as a result of this action, and when this was not forthcoming Toombs resigned from the Confederate army in March 1863. He returned to Georgia and when Sherman made his march on Atlanta from May-August 1864, Toombs did serve as inspector general of the Georgia militia, but by this time he was constantly quarreling with other Confederate leaders, both civilian and military. When the war ended,

Toombs feared arrest and fled to Cuba, and then on to London; he returned to Georgia in 1867 but because he refused to ask for formal pardon he was never again to regain any standing as a politician. He took up his law practice, regained his personal fortune, and fought the 'carpetbaggers' and reconstruction policies, but when his wife became insane and he became blind, he turned to drink and died an embittered man.

TUBMAN, Harriet

c 1821-1913

TUBMAN WAS AN EXTRAORDINARY person in any era, for born a slave she had escaped to freedom and then spent many years, at great personal risk, helping other slaves to escape from the South. Born to two slaves in Maryland, she was first named Araminta, only later assuming the name 'Harriet'. She worked as a field hand and was forced by her master to marry a fellow slave, John Tubman. In 1849 she made her way to the North and she soon became active in the so-called underground railroad, the network of individuals—white and black, free and slave, committed abolitionists and the merely sympathetic—who worked from about 1840 to 1861 to help slaves escape from the South. Harriet Tubman made repeated trips back to the South and led other slaves North—sometimes 'encouraging' them with a loaded revolver, it was said; in 1857 she was able to get her own parents up to New York; altogether she was credited with leading at least 300 blacks to freedom. Illiterate but possessed of great natural skills in planning, she came to know many of the prominent abolitionists. When the war broke out, she volunteered to go back to the South and served as a nurse, cook and laundress to the Union troops in South Carolina; she also was said to have gone behind Confederate lines as a spy on occasion. After the war, she returned to Auburn, New York where she worked to help children and the elderly, using the profits from her autobiography for her causes. Harriet Tubman's actions helped to sharpen the conflict between the North and South, but her own life became a vindication of the need to end slavery.

VALLANDIGHAM, Clement Laird

1820-1871

AN INTELLIGENT, talented, and sincere man, Vallandigham became a leader of the so-called Copperheads—those Northerners opposed to the war—and came to be regarded as virtually a traitor to the Union. Born in Ohio, Vallandigham left his college in Pennsylvania before graduating because of a bitter argument with its president over constitutional law—thus prefiguring his life in opposition. He was eventually admitted to the Ohio bar and he combined that with a career in journalism and politics. He was personally opposed to slavery, but he was against the Federal government's 'interference' in this or in any issue that he felt was the 'right' of a state. He attacked the new Republican Party, and as a Democrat got elected to the US House of Representatives in 1858. He denounced extremism and sectionalism on all sides, and in the 1860 Democratic Party split he supported Stephen Douglas, claiming that if only the 'extremists' such as Lincoln would step aside the South could negotiate a compromise. Once the war itself was underway, Vallandigham began to use his considerable talents as a lawyer and strict constitutionalist to oppose all measures needed to carry on the war, thereby gaining the enmity of even his home state, Ohio, which supported Lincoln. Beyond that, Vallandigham believed he should have the right to say anything he pleased at a time when many people saw any criticism as close to treason. His eloquence found some support among those confused by the frustrations of a war, but he lost his seat in the House in 1862. Before leaving in 1863, however, Vallandigham made a speech calling for peace negotiations, and from that point on he was marked as the leader of all the disaffected elements in the North, particularly those

BIOGRAPHIES

Democrats who came to be known as 'Copperheads.' General Burnside was by then in command of the District of Ohio and he issued an order in the spring of 1863 declaring that any sympathy for the South would be considered treasonable; Vallandigham would not stop, even calling for resistance to conscription, so on 5 May 1863 Burnside had him arrested. Tried immediately by a military commission, he was sentenced to prison for the duration of the war; Lincoln commuted this, however, and had him sent behind the Confederate lines. Vallandigham eventually surfaced in Canada, and he even ran for governor of Ohio that fall. In June 1864 Vallandigham reappeared in Ohio, traveling about in open defiance and referring to 'King Lincoln', but by now the government chose to ignore him. As the war was drawing to an end, his message lost its appeal, and he himself expressed regret at the assassination of Lincoln because he foresaw that the more radical Republicans would be far more unsympathetic. After the war, he failed to obtain elective office again; he came to realize that the old issues were dead and tried to form a new political party around more contemporary concerns, but he was perceived as too controversial. In an end somehow fitting a sincere man who became his own worst enemy, Vallandigham shot himself while demonstrating how an alleged murder victim had been shot.

VANDORN, Earl

1820-1863

VAN DORN WAS A CONFEDERATE GENERAL whose reputation was marred by a cloud over his professional career and a tragedy in his personal life. Van Dorn was born in Mississippi (to a mother who was a niece of the wife of Andrew Jackson) and went on to West Point; after graduation, he served in the Mexican War and in various wars against the American Indians, rising to the rank of major by 1860. In January 1861 Van Dorn resigned and became a brigadier general in the Mississippi units of the Confederacy. Transferred to the Confed-

erate army, he moved through several commands—in New Orleans, in Texas (where he captured the *Star of the West*, the Federal ship that had tried to relieve Fort Sumter in January 1861) and then as commanding general of the 1st Division of the Confederate Army of the Potomac. In January 1862 Van Dorn assumed command of the Trans-Mississippi Department; in March 1862, at Pea Ridge, Arkansas, Van Dorn directed his troops from an ambulance, but the result was a costly loss for the Confederate army. By October 1862, Van Dorn was in command of the District of Mississippi, and his poorly prepared attack contributed to the disastrous defeat of the Confederate troops at Corinth; he was courtmartialed for his role, and although he was not found guilty he was to remain under suspicion by some of his fellow officers. Transferred to a cavalry command, he somewhat regained his reputation by defeating Grant at Holly Springs, Mississippi in December 1862. In March 1863 his cavalry troops routed a Federal brigade at Spring Hill, Tennessee, but that May he was killed by a physician there who claimed Van Dorn had become involved with his wife. Van Dorn's friends insisted the doctor had shot him for political motives, but the fact was that Van Dorn was yet another victim of the civil strife.

WALLACE, LEWIS

1827-1905

ONE OF THE MORE UNUSUAL individuals to be caught up in the Civil War, Wallace was an urbane man—later to be a best-selling author—who through sheer intelligence and energy turned out to be a successful general for the Union side. Born in Indiana (of which his father later became governor), Wallace resisted formal schooling but he read a great deal and eventually studied law on his own. When the United States went to war against Mexico, Wallace volunteered and saw some service in Mexico. During the 1850s he held political offices in his state but he was equally at home with literature and the arts. When the

Civil War began, Wallace was adjutant general of Indiana and he helped to raise the state's volunteers for the Federal cause. Then accepting the rank of colonel, he led his regiment through several actions. Promoted to brigadier general, he participated in the capture of Fort Donelson in February 1862; promoted again to major general, he led a division at Shiloh. After several administrative assignments, Wallace went back into the field in March 1864, and that July he turned back the raid led by General Jubal Early at Monocacy and thus saved the city of Washington from possible disaster. But for all his successes in the field and his popularity with his troops, Wallace never got on with his superior, General Halleck, who had twice dismissed Wallace (who was restored each time, once by Lincoln and then by Grant). When the war ended, Wallace sat on the courtmartials of the alleged assassin conspirators against Lincoln and of the commander of the Confederate prison at Andersonville, Henry Wirz. Wallace then resigned from the army in November 1865 and spent two years in Mexico helping to raise an army for the liberals there; when Maximilian was shot, Wallace returned to Indiana and took up the practice of law. Through all his highly adventurous years, Wallace remained most interested in literature, and by 1873 he was publishing his first work, *The Fair God*, a fictional account of the Spanish conquest of Mexico. Wallace went on to serve as the appointed governor of New Mexico (1878-81) and ambassador to Turkey (1881-85), but continued writing various works of fiction and non-fiction. The best known was *Ben Hur; A Tale of the Christ* (1880), which sold millions of copies throughout the world and was later made into major films. Greatly admired in his lifetime, Wallace was chosen by his state to be its representative in the sculpture gallery in the capitol.

WELD, *Theodore Dwight*

1803-1895

WELD WAS ONE OF THE MOST INFLUENTIAL abolitionists of the Civil War era but he was so intent on avoiding personal publicity that he never became as well known as some of his contemporaries. Born in Connecticut, Weld moved to upstate New York as a young man and there joined the revivalist movement of Charles Finney. He began to study for the ministry and first made his reputation speaking out for temperance, but by 1830 Weld had taken up the cause of abolition of slavery. He was affiliated with the leaders of the American Anti-Slavery Society, and when he went west to help organize a new seminary in Cincinnati, he came to influence Harriet and Henry Beecher, children of the seminary's president. By 1834, Weld's anti-slavery activities had become so pervasive at the school that he was dismissed, but most of the students left with him and became agents for the anti-slavery movement. Many of his 'converts', such as Edwin Stanton, would play important roles in public life. Weld himself married one of his agents, Angelina Grimké, a South Carolinian who with her sister had early embraced abolitionism. Weld gave so many speeches that he injured his voice, but that only led him to writing a steady stream of articles and pamphlets. From 1836-40 he was based in New York City where he edited the anti-slavery paper, the *Emancipator*, but he thereafter centered his activities in Washington where he took the lead in the campaign to introduce anti-slavery petitions in Congress. His society's periodical, the *National Era* would publish Harriet Beecher Stowe's *Uncle Tom's Cabin* and she was the first to acknowledge that she had drawn a great deal from one of Weld's books, *American Slavery As It Is* (1839). In 1844 he withdrew from his public activities on behalf of abolitionism to run his own school in New Jersey, but during the Civil War he was persuaded to speak out for the Union and for Republican candidates. Because he avoided holding all offices, spoke mainly in smaller towns, and refused to publish any of his writings under his own name, Weld long went unrecognized by people who knew of such Abolitionists as

BIOGRAPHIES

William Lloyd Garrison or Wendell Phillips, but all the leaders of the anti-slavery movement knew of Weld's crucial role.

WELLES, Gideon
1802-1878

WELLES SERVED AS the Secretary of the Navy throughout Lincoln's administration and emerged not only as an extremely capable administrator but as one of the more moderate individuals in an era often characterized by extremists. Born to an old Connecticut family, Welles read law but by 1826 he had become part owner and editor of the *Hartford Times*. That same year he was elected to his state's legislature, serving there till 1835. A Jeffersonian in his emphasis on individual freedoms and states' rights, he became an early supporter of Andrew Jackson and then was a personal adviser to President Jackson. Although he failed in his first tries at national office, he built up a reputation among a wide circle of influential Americans through his writings and travels. In 1856 he left the Democratic Party to help organize the new Republican Party, all the while promoting a more moderate view as the nation moved toward confrontation. After Lincoln was elected in 1860, he knew his cabinet had to include at least one New England Republican, so Welles was appointed Secretary of the Navy, and if Welles had had no experience as a naval man, there was little navy to run. The few ships were spread all over the world; the Confederate states seized two of the most important navy yards; many officers and men left the Union Navy to serve in the Confederate Navy. Welles did an extraordinary job in building up the Federal Navy in a relatively short time; he was accused of being extravagant, but the costs came to seem insignificant once the results were considered; and if there were some scandals, Welles at least took steps to put a stop to them. He offended politicians who wanted navy installations in their districts, no matter what, and he was not afraid to rebuke or dismiss naval officers when he felt they had been delinquent. He took a direct part in shaping naval strategy and tactics, and if Welles cannot be credited with specific Union victories he at least deserved credit for the general success of the Federal Navy. He also kept up with the new developments in naval technology, particularly in encouraging the new ironclads of Ericsson.

Meanwhile, Welles did not get on all that well with some of his fellow cabinet officers such as Seward and Stanton, and he would sometimes make policy beyond his naval concerns; as early as July 1861, for instance, he was ordering Union naval officers to protect runaway slaves and by that September he was allowing former slaves to enlist in the Navy. As a Jeffersonian, he was also against Lincoln's suspension of habeas corpus, the arrest of the Copperhead Vallandigham and the suppression of newspapers critical of the government. The same moderation that led him to support Lincoln's announced plans for reconstruction led Welles to support President Johnson even through the impeachment crisis and in opposition to many of his former Republican colleagues. Welles stayed through Johnson's administration as the Secretary of the Navy, working for the modernization of the Navy, and after retiring he wrote many articles on his experiences with the government and navy during the war. Religious, reasonable, reserved, Welles remains one of the sturdiest examples of public servants in American history.

WHEELER, Joseph
1836-1906

WHEELER WAS THE SENIOR cavalry commander of the Confederate army and fought in an almost incredible number of battles—yet he was only 28 years old when the Civil War ended. Born in Georgia, Wheeler spent much of his youth in Connecticut and went on to West Point, graduating only in 1859. He saw some service on the frontier but by April 1861 he was resigning his commission to join the

WHITMAN, WALT

Confederate Army. His first major campaign was at Shiloh in April 1862; that October, at Perryville, Kentucky Wheeler's bold action at the head of only 1,200 men virtually immobilized 20,000 Federal troops. Wheeler was promoted to brigadier general and assigned to a cavalry command, which he led in the Confederate victory at Stones River, Tennessee in January 1863, after which he was promoted to major general. He went on to fight in an amazing succession of battles—127 altogether—was wounded three times and had 16 horses shot from under him; promoted to lieutenant general in February 1864, he ended up being captured near Atlanta in May 1865 as the war was ending, the ranking cavalry commander of the Confederate army. A long life still lay ahead for 'Fightin' Joe', as he was known, and after many years as a merchant, lawyer and US Representative, he reenlisted in the Spanish-American War and took a cavalry division to Cuba and the Philippines. Although he never showed great skill in independent actions, Wheeler was a superb cavalryman in a supporting role.

WHITMAN, Walt
1819-1892

WHITMAN, universally recognized as one of America's major poets, saw his life involved in the Civil War as few poets have ever been involved with any war. Ironically, too, Whitman was born—on Long Island, New York—to a Quaker family. By the age of 13, Whitman was a printer's assistant in Brooklyn, and as he progressed up to printer and then editor, he also took an active role in Democratic Party politics and wrote short stories and a novel. Editor of the Brooklyn Daily Eagle beginning in 1846, a Democratic Party paper, he spoke out so strongly against the party's position on slavery that he was fired in January 1848. He went to New Orleans for three months, then returned to Brooklyn and a career in journalism, but he also was writing the poems that he published at his own expense in 1855 as Leaves of Grass.

Although the public did not know what to make of these quite novel poems, some perceptive critics recognized him as a true poet; a second, slightly enlarged edition appeared in 1856 and a third and still larger edition appeared in 1860, both receiving much the same mixture of popular rejection and critical recognition. When the Civil War began, Whitman was writing for New York newspapers, but he began to visit the Broadway Hospital as a volunteer aide to the sick and wounded from the war, and he also began to write poems influenced by the war. On hearing that his brother had been wounded, Whitman rushed to Virginia; the brother recovered, but Walt (as he called himself from 1855) had seen enough of the horrors of the war to decide he would do something. He stayed in Washington, and earning some money by copying documents for an army paymaster, he devoted as much time as possible to nursing the wounded, both Northerners and Southerners. Using his own money, Whitman brought gifts such as fruit, candy, and stationery; he wrote letters for those who couldn't; and at times he assisted in changing dressings and even in operations. He was able to add to his income by writing for newspapers, but he tried to get a clerk's job in the government; he finally got such a position with the Department of the Interior in March 1865, but he was dismissed that very June for his scandalous poems and opinions. During his years in Washington, Whitman had never met Lincoln, but he had seen the President around town occasionally. (The story that Lincoln had read Leaves of Grass has never been proved.) After Lincoln's death, Whitman wrote 'When lilacs last in the dooryard bloom'd', and added this to a collection of war poems, Drum Taps, then at the printer; a second poem about Lincoln, 'O Captain! my Captain!' appeared in a sequel to this volume. In 1873 he suffered a stroke that left him partially paralyzed, and he lived out his final years in Camden, New Jersey. His poetry never attained its earlier peaks, but he lived on the earnings from his revisions of Leaves of Grass, several other books, occasional articles—and a lecture he would give, 'The Death of Abraham Lincoln'. He had by this time attracted numerous disciples and was visited by all the literary lights of the day—especially those from England, where his reputation had always stood higher than in America. Eventually, however, 'the good gray poet' as he was called, came to be honored by his countrymen, in part for his serving as a witness to their terrible Civil War.

WIRZ, Henry
1822-1865

WIRZ WAS THE CONFEDERATE OFFICER who had commanded the infamous Andersonville Prison, where many Union prisoners died, and was executed for his role there. Wirz was born in Switzerland and emigrated to the United States in 1849, taking up the practice of medicine in Louisiana. When the Civil War broke out, he enlisted as a private and saw early service as a clerk in Libby Prison, near Richmond, Virginia. In the Peninsular Campaign, Wirz was seriously wounded at Seven Pines in May 1862; promoted to captain, he was then sent to Europe as a Confederate dispatch bearer and purchasing agent. In January 1864 he returned and was assigned to head the newly formed military prison in Georgia that came to be known as Andersonville (although its formal name was Camp Sumter). A log stockade enclosing some 17 acres (later 26 acres), Andersonville quickly grew to take in some 33,000 Federal prisoners—all enlisted men—by the summer of 1864. Although they were given the basic rations of the Confederate troops, there was such overcrowding and poor sanitation that the diet plus exposure to the elements soon led to diseases spreading. There would eventually be some 13,000 identified graves there, but it was estimated that many others died. As General Sherman drew near in September 1864, the Confederates transferred the healthy prisoners to Charleston. Wirz was taken prisoner later, and then charged with committing specific crimes, even conspiring to kill prisoners, and in November 1865, after being found guilty by a special courtmartial, he was executed. He was, in fact, the only individual executed after the war for any crime committed during the war.

WISE, Henry Alexander
1806-1876

WISE SERVED AS A GENERAL in the Confederate army, but it was as governor of Virginia that he laid his claim to history. Born in Virginia, he practiced law there and served as a US Representative from that state between 1833-44; although he held to some of the traditional views of the South as regards states' rights and such, Wise did indicate some doubts about slavery and the slave trade. Between 1856-60, Wise was governor of Virginia, and he was well aware that the Virginians living along the northern and western borders tended to be nonslaveholders. Thus, when John Brown made his raid at Harper's Ferry in 1859, located in that very region, it was Wise as governor who urged that Brown be given capital punishment as an example to any waverers in that part of his state. When the war broke out, Wise took a commission as brigadier general in June 1861 and led the forces that tried to hold western Virginia to the Confederate cause. He failed at this, and then went on to fight to hold Roanoke Island, North Carolina in February 1862; again he was defeated, losing his own son in the battle as well as some 2000 prisoners. But Wise returned to fight in the final defense of Richmond and Petersburg and in the retreat that finally led to his surrendering at Appomattox (where he was met by his brother-in-law, the Union general George Meade). After the war, Wise practiced law in Richmond, and remained one of the relatively few old Southerners who refused to request pardon from the Federal government.

YANCEY, William Lowndes
1814-1863

YANCEY WAS A SOUTHERN POLITICIAN, an arch-secessionist who had worked all his life to split the Union on the principle of states' rights and thus ended up opposed to the government of Jefferson Davis. Yancey was born in Georgia, but when he was only three his father died, and his mother remarried a New England preacher who took the family north, where Yancey attended various schools, including Williams College. He went down to South Carolina and was admitted to the bar there; he also became a planter and a newspaper editor. By 1837, he had mismanaged his financial affairs and he had also killed his wife's uncle in a quarrel, so Yancey left and settled in Alabama. Again he took up planting and journalism, and by 1841 he was serving in that state's legislature, moving on to the US House of Representatives in 1844-45. During the next 15 years, Yancey took every possible step to force the issue of secession to the fore. By 1860 he was in a position to lead the Alabama delegation to the Democratic Party convention and then to be among the leaders in the walkout that produced Breckinridge as a candidate. Inevitably he introduced the ordinance to dissolve the Union at Alabama's convention in January 1861, and in February he was among those determined to dissolve the Union. He failed to get elected to the provisional Congress, however, so Jefferson Davis sent him to England and France to seek diplomatic recognition for the Confederacy. Unsuccessful at this mission, Yancey returned in 1862; meanwhile, he had been elected to the Confederate Senate, but because he was such an absolute proponent of states' rights, he ended up as a constant critic of the centralized government that Jefferson Davis felt was necessary to pursue the war. Long in poor health, Yancey died while in office, only 49 years old but disillusioned at seeing what his life's goals had brought about.

General James E B Stuart, CSA.

INDEX

INDEX

INDEX

INDEX

ACKNOWLEDGMENTS
The publisher would like to thank the following people who have helped in the preparation of this book: Thomas G Aylesworth, who edited it; Chris Simon, who designed it; Gisele Knight, who prepared the index.

PICTURE CREDITS
Chicago Historical Society: 89 (second from top), 138, 141 (below), 158, 159 (below), 185, 260, 261 (left), 297 (below, left), 300, 303 (below), 393
Cincinnati Art Museum: 43
Courtesy Commander Charles Moran: 309
Ian Hogg: 281, 282, 283, 284, 285, 286, 287, 288, 289, 291, 292, 295 (left top and bottom), 296 (below left)
Library of Congress: 9, 10-11, 14, 15, 16, 33, 38, 39, 40, 41, 44, 45, 46, 51, 52, 57, 60, 72 (bottom), 82, 83, 84, 86, 88, 90 (bottom), 94, 101, 113, 114 (left), 121, 140, 142, 151, 157 (above), 162, 166, 167, 177, 178, 184, 199, 206, 210, 270, 271, 272, 273, 275, 277, 295 (above right), 296 (above left and right), 297 (top left and right), 298, 302 (top left), 303 (top), 306, 310 (bottom), 311
National Archives: 80, 117, 159 (above)
Richard Natkiel: 18 (above), 19 (below), 21 (above), 24 (above), 30
Official Navy photograph: 6-7, 68, 72 (top and center), 89 (top and bottom), 102, 104, 241, 302 (right and bottom left), 304, 305 (left), 310 (top)
Peabody Museum of Salem: 27 (below)
US Army: 24 (below), 25, 28 (below), 29, 32
US Army photograph: 7, 18 (below), 157 (below)
US Naval Historical Center photograph: 21 (Below), 27 (above), 114 (right), 125, 211, 247, 299, 301, 305 (right)
Virginia State Library: 89 (second from bottom)